E. H Delmar

Delmar's new, Revised and Complete Classified Trades Directory

And Mercantile Manual of Mexico, Central America, and the West India Islands

E. H Delmar

Delmar's new, Revised and Complete Classified Trades Directory
And Mercantile Manual of Mexico, Central America, and the West India Islands

ISBN/EAN: 9783744729642

Printed in Europe, USA, Canada, Australia, Japan

Cover: Foto ©Suzi / pixelio.de

More available books at **www.hansebooks.com**

THE ONLY WORK OF THE KIND PUBLISHED.

DELMAR'S

New, Revised and Complete Classified

TRADES DIRECTORY

AND

MERCANTILE MANUAL

OF

MEXICO,

CENTRAL AMERICA AND THE WEST INDIA ISLANDS,

GIVING THE NAMES AND ADDRESSES OF ALL THE

Leading Merchants, Dealers, Planters, Mine Owners, Professional Men
and others in the Principal Cities and Towns of

MEXICO,

Costa Rica, Guatemala, Colombia, Honduras, Nicaragua, San Salvador,
Cuba, Jamaica, Porto Rico, Santa Croix, St. Thomas,
Antigua, St. Lucia, St. Vincent, Trinidad,
New Providence and Demerara.

OFFICIALLY ENDORSED BY THE GOVERNMENTS OF THE COUNTRIES NAMED.

COMPILED AND EDITED BY

E. H. DELMAR,

*Author of " Delmar's Business Directory of Central and South America," "How to Secure
Trade with Spanish-America," "A Winter in the Tropics," etc.*

COPYRIGHT, 1889, BY BELFORD, CLARKE & CO.

PRICE - - - $12.00.

CHICAGO AND NEW YORK:
BELFORD, CLARKE & CO.,
PUBLISHERS.
1889-90.

CAUTION.

Soon after the publication of my last South American Directory, in 1887, some rascally and unprincipled speculators procured copies of the same, from which they prepared MSS. and type-written lists of names, boldly stolen from my work — which these scamps elaborately padded with many bogus names to swell the lists — and palmed off these alleged lists of foreign addresses as ORIGINAL, charging the foolish purchasers for a small list four or five times the price charged for my entire work.

I hereby notify these pirates and frauds, that, if this thing is again attempted, I will prosecute them to the fullest extent of the law. And I caution the public, in this country and Europe, to refrain from purchasing these stolen lists of addresses.

E. H. DELMAR.

☞ To find anything and everything, always **CONSULT THE INDEX PAGES.**

PREFACE.

The object of this work is to present to the mercantile community a thoroughly practical, comprehensive, instructive and useful Commercial Guide and Classified Business Directory of the countries named. I have endeavored to present a work which will afford the greatest amount of useful information in the briefest and most direct manner possible.

In compiling this work for business men, I decided to eschew all unnecessary historical and political statistics and other useless twaddle, of little or no interest to the business community, confining myself solely to such statistical and general information as will prove useful to business men seeking or desiring trade relations with the countries named in this work.

Besides a practical commercial guide book, this work presents a full, complete and strictly reliable, recently compiled Classified Business Directory of Mexico, Central America and the West Indies, giving the names and addresses of all merchants, dealers, planters, mine owners, professional men, and others who are buyers of and dealers in American and English goods.

I also point out, from my own long experience in those countries, the best and most practical methods of trading with the natives — how to secure their patronage, and how to trade with safety and profit.

In a work of this magnitude and complex character, especially when treating of foreign countries, there may be found a few unimportant errors, and, possibly, omissions; but, as a whole, this work is PERFECTLY RELIABLE and TRUSTWORTHY, and our patrons may rest assured that the names herein contained are *bona fide*—live, active merchants, dealers and professional men.

This work is compiled and revised up to January, 1889.

In offering this Business Directory to the public, I do not represent it as containing every insignificant town, village and hamlet in the countries named, nor does it contain the names of every little shopkeeper, barber, milliner, boarding-house, cigar-shop, tavern or bar-room, or any trades or professions that are in no way interested in or of interest to our manufacturers and merchants. I have endeavored to include all the leading wholesale and retail merchants and dealers, and all professional men who deal in or who require American or English manufactures and products.

I present an interesting, plain business talk on the value and importance of Mexico and the West Indies as a profitable and ready market for the sale of American, English and Canadian products and manufactures, showing how you can work off your surplus stock to advantage in the above-named markets; fully and clearly explaining the customs, character and wants of the people of Mexico, Central America, Cuba, Porto Rico and the other West India Islands, their manner of doing business, and how American merchants and manufacturers can successfully compete with Europeans for the valuable trade of the above countries.

If the patrons of this work will devote an occasional leisure hour to a careful perusal and examination of the contents, they will find many items that are not only instructive but of considerable business importance, the study of which will well repay the time and trouble of investigation.

E. H. DELMAR.

CHICAGO, April, 1889.

INDEX
TO
GENERAL CONTENTS.

	PAGE.
A Brief Introduction	9
A Business Tour through Mexico and Cuba	11
About Passports	260
About Samples of Merchandise	259
Advantages in Mailing Circulars, etc.	257
American Goods Suitable for the Markets of Mexico, Cuba and West Indies	35
American Trade with Cuba	263
Along the Line of Mexican Central Railway	14
Allegations of Lawlessness in Cuba	18
Antigua, Trades Directory	210
Arrival at Havana	21
Attractions for American Tourists	19
British West Indies Customs Tariff	485
Business Hints and Pointers	37
Business Opportunities in Cuba	258
Caution	2
Commercial Travelers in Cuba	17
Commercial Data	272
Costa Rica, Trades Directory	119
Cuba, Trades Directory	150
Custom House, Havana	21
Cuban Custom House Tariff	451
Drummers' Samples	260
Demerara, Trades Directory	212
Exports to British Honduras	284
Exports to British West Indies	289
Exports to Central America	281
Exports to Cuba	285
Exports to Danish West Indies	300
Exports to Dutch West Indies	302
Exports to French West Indies	298
Exports to Hayti	294
Exports to Mexico	275
Exports to Puerto Rico	292
Exports to San Domingo	296
Exports to United States of Colombia	301
Explanatory Notes	7
Foreign Weights and Measures	271
French West Indies, Customs Tariff	490

(5)

Index to General Contents.

	PAGE.
Getting Ready for the Trip	20
Gold and Silver Coin, Imports and Exports	306
Guatemala, Trades Directory	121
Havana and its Attractions	17
Hotels, in Spanish America	21
Horse Cars and Stages, Havana	23
How to Sell Goods	257
Honduras, Trades Directory	127
Imports from British Honduras	283
Imports from British West Indies	288
Imports from Cuba	285
Imports from Danish West Indies	299
Imports from Dutch West Indies	301
Imports from French West Indies	297
Imports from Central America	280
Imports from Hayti	293
Imports from Puerto Rico	271
Imports from San Domingo	295
Imports from United States of Colombia	303
Jamaica, Trades Directory	217
Mexico, Trades Directory	41
Mexican Cigar Industry	263
Mexican Money	273
Mexican Tariff	315
Mexican Weights and Measures	317
Mexican Maritime and Frontier Custom Houses	318
Nassau, Trades Directory	222
Nicaragua, Trades Directory	130
Packing and Shipping Goods	261
Pointers on Cuban Railway Travel	33
Political Outlook for Cuba	34
Preface	3
Puerto Rico, Trades Directory	224
Republics of Central America	265
Selling Goods in Spanish America	260
Sending Out Commercial Travelers	258
Speaking the Spanish Language	39
Steamship Lines from the United States to the Countries named in this Directory	254
Supplementary Mexican Tariff	435
San Salvador, Trades Directory	147
Santa Cruz, Trades Directory	234
St. Thomas, Trades Directory	236
Santo Domingo, Trades Directory	235
St. Lucia, Trades Directory	237
St. Vincent, Trades Directory	239
Steamship Connections in Cuba	37
The West India Islands	269
Traveling in Cuba	38
Trinidad, Trades Directory	240
United States of Colombia, Trades Directory	135
Values and Classification of Imports from and Exports to the Countries named in this Work	309

EXPLANATORY NOTES

FOR THE GUIDANCE OF

THOSE USING THIS DIRECTORY AND MANUAL.

SPANISH-AMERICAN MERCHANTS.

With comparatively few exceptions, the wholesale and "jobbing" merchants marked ("general"), the importers and the "warehousemen" in almost all the Central and South American countries, are *buyers* and *dealers* in every description of foreign merchandise and manufactures, from pins to machinery, powder, fire-arms, toys, lumber, provisions, beer, pianos, organs, medicines, hardware, carriages; also wines, flour, groceries, dry goods, novelties, oils, varnishes, paints, hats, boots and shoes, etc. As a rule, wholesale houses do not handle watches and jewelry, that line of goods being confined to the retailer. The commission merchant also imports and deals in general merchandise, but usually on consignment or commission.

HOW TO ADDRESS LETTERS.

In addressing Spanish letters, the following rules should be observed: Place before the name, if in the singular, Sr. Don; if in the plural, Sres. The *y Ca.*, means *& Co.* The words at the end of some firm names: *e Hijo* or *Hijos. Hermano* or *Hermanos*, *Sobrino* or *Sobrinos*, *Viuda de*, mean, respectively, Son or Sons, Brother or Brothers, Nephew or Nephews, and *Widow of.*

Before the Portuguese names (Brazil only), place Sñr. for the singular, and Sñrs. for the plural, the *Don* is not used. The words *Irmao* or *Irmaos*, *Filho* or *Filhos*, *Sobrinho* or *Sobrinhos* and *Viuva*, mean also: Brother or Brothers, Son or Sons, Nephew or Nephews, and *Widow of.*

PREPARING CIRCULARS AND PRICE-LISTS.

It is of great importance to manufacturers and merchants that the circulars and price-lists they send abroad should be short and to the point, and in the language of the countries to which they are addressed; otherwise they will waste time and money, since it is obvious that a merchant receiving a circular in a language he does not understand will take but little notice of it.

POSTAL RATES.

The rate of postage to Cuba, Mexico, Central and South America is five cents per half ounce, sealed letters, and one cent for two ounces or less printed matter (opened), all of which must be prepaid by stamps.

COMMERCIAL RATINGS.

We do not undertake to give the rating or responsibility of any firm named in this Directory. In dealing with parties in foreign countries, of whom you know nothing, the usual, and likewise the safest, way is to politely request your correspondent to send you a reliable New York, Boston or London acceptance, at sixty or ninety days, the usual time asked. This is customary, and no respectable firm in Central or South America, Cuba or Mexico will refuse this reasonable request.

In most instances, after you have mailed your circulars, catalogues and price-lists to the merchants in the countries named, these merchants will send their orders for your goods *through* some commission house in New York, Boston or London, and, in that case, you look to the merchant *here* for the payment of your bill.

EXAMINE THIS WORK CAREFULLY.

Examine *well* each column of names under appropriate headings, before jumping at the conclusion that the name you are seeking is not in this Directory. In compiling and arranging the names and addresses from the original MSS., we found it difficult to classify the various names in strict alphabetical order. But the name of every merchant, now in business, will be found here all the same.

In order to be better understood by Americans and Englishmen addressing names from this work, the addresses in this Directory are, as a rule, arranged with tho "given" name first and surname following, as "John Smith," instead of "Smith, John," as is usual with our Directories. Write the addresses just as they are here printed. Following the names are the street addresses.

THE VARIOUS DEPARTMENTS OF THIS WORK.

Recollect that this work is divided into three separate and comparatively distinct departments, combined in one volume, namely: A MERCANTILE MANUAL or GUIDE; A CLASSIFIED BUSINESS OR TRADES DIRECTORY, and the CUSTOM HOUSE TARIFFS AND REGULATIONS for the countries named. To find what you want, always consult the Index pages for each Department.

A BRIEF INTRODUCTION.

The eminent success and universal popularity attained for the last edition of my "CLASSIFIED BUSINESS DIRECTORY OF MEXICO, CENTRAL AND SOUTH AMERICA, CUBA AND PORTO RICO," published in New York in May, 1887, and which was highly indorsed by the press and public, and by the accredited ministers of all the countries represented in the work, induced me to prepare a new, revised and greatly enlarged CLASSIFIED BUSINESS DIRECTORY AND MERCANTILE MANUAL OF MEXICO, CENTRAL AMERICA AND THE WEST INDIA ISLANDS for 1889-90.

This new work is most thorough and complete in all its details, embracing every city and town in all the countries named, besides furnishing the CUSTOMS TARIFF and the shipping laws and regulations of each and every country mentioned in the work, together with valuable information and instructions for shippers and commercial travelers, and other interesting commercial data of importance to merchants, manufacturers and others trading directly or indirectly with those countries.

HOW THESE ADDRESSES WERE PROCURED.

The author of "DELMAR'S BUSINESS DIRECTORY AND MERCANTILE MANUAL OF MEXICO, CENTRAL AMERICA AND THE WEST INDIES," spent the past fourteen months (from September, 1887), and nearly $6,000 in money; traveling the countries named, and, in most instances, personally supervised the canvass of these addresses. In each town visited, he employed a number of local agents to go from house to house, procure the names, and then classify them under their different business headings, paying these agents from four to five dollars each per day for their services.

☞ The United States Consuls at the various cities and towns contained in this Directory were empowered to supervise the work of the local agents who were employed in canvassing for the names in this work, and these Consuls guarantee the genuineness and perfect reliability of the names and addresses as published.

SOME OF ITS COMMERCIAL ADVANTAGES.

Among the many important, useful and valuable commercial features of this work are:

FIRSTLY—A reliable classified BUSINESS OR TRADES DIRECTORY, enabling merchants, manufacturers and others to mail circulars, price-lists, samples, etc., direct to the merchants and consumers in the countries named.

SECONDLY—A thoroughly comprehensive and instructive COMMERCIAL MANUAL OR GUIDE BOOK, giving every desired information relating to the class of goods most desirable and salable in the markets of the countries named; how to trade successfully with the natives; how commercial travelers or agents should conduct themselves and their business while traveling; how to pack and ship goods, and how to make your business and your goods favorably known.

THIRDLY—The complete CUSTOMS TARIFF and regulations of every country named.

FOURTHLY—Shipping directions and routes to all the countries mentioned.

☞ Every merchant and manufacturer having, contemplating, or desiring business relations with the people of the countries to which attention has been called, and every commercial traveler or agent who contemplates visiting any of those countries will save many a dollar and avoid many vexatious annoyances, and perhaps loss, by purchasing a copy of this important and indispensable commercial work.

It may here be mentioned that DELMAR'S commercial works are not untried experiments, but ESTABLISHED FACTS. They have been before the public in all parts of the United States and Europe for the past five years, and have received the cordial approval and indorsement of the United States Government and of the governments of all the countries represented in the work, by their resident ministers in the United States, besides the approval of merchants, manufacturers and shippers everywhere.

☞ CONSULT THE INDEX PAGES.

A BUSINESS TOUR

THROUGH

MEXICO AND CUBA.

MEXICAN CENTRAL

RAILWAY.

EL PASO ROUTE.

The only STANDARD GAUGE RAILWAY from the United States to Chihuahua, Santa Rosalia, Jimenez, Lerdo, Fresnillo, Zacatecas, San Luis Potosi, Aguas Calientes, Encarnacion, Lagos, Leon, Silao, Guanajuato, Irapuato, La Barca, Guadalajara, Celaya, Queretaro and City of Mexico.

The only line running **PULLMAN PALACE DRAWING-ROOM SLEEPING-CARS** from the Rio Grande River to City of Mexico.

This road — constructed with steel rails, iron bridges and stone culverts, and located along the high table lands of Mexico, and at no point less than 3,700 feet above sea level — is equipped with first-class rolling stock and motive power, and offers to shippers and passengers the safest, pleasantest and most expeditious route to all principal cities in the Republic of Mexico.

By this route, carload shipments of freight from the United States may be forwarded in same car from initial point of shipment to destination, thereby avoiding risk of loss and damage occasioned by transferring from one car to another.

For the purpose of facilitating the importation of goods into Mexico, and reducing the cost of such service to a minimum, this Company has established an **IMPORTING AGENCY AT EL PASO, TEXAS**, in charge of T. J. Woodside, Customs Agent, who will cheerfully furnish all information relative to duties, custom house formalities and brokerage charges. All goods consigned in his care will receive quickest possible dispatch through the Custom House, and prompt forwarding to destination.

For further information, rates, maps, time-cards, etc., apply to or address

M. H. KING, Genl. Western Agt.,
    236 So. Clark St., Chicago, Ill.

        G. W. KEELER, Genl. Eastern Agt.,
            261 Broadway, New York.

G. W. HIBBARD.   A. C. MICHAELIS,
  Asst. Genl. Frt. and Pass. Agt.,   Genl. Frt. and Pass. Agt.,
      CITY OF MEXICO, MEX.

A TOUR THROUGH MEXICO AND CUBA.

MEXICO.

A WONDERFUL AND INTERESTING COUNTRY FOR THE TOURIST AND TRAVELER.

To those American and English tourists and travelers who have never visited Mexico, the famed "land of the Montezumas," we would say go, and "stand not upon the order of going."

To all intelligent people, especially those who appreciate the value and advantages of foreign travel, who admire the grand, the beautiful and the picturesque in nature, we earnestly and conscientiously recommend an early visit to Mexico.

In that grand, famous and historical country, now so conveniently near and accessible to Americans, the tourist will find no end of pleasant and agreeable surprises. A mild, uniform and healthy climate, the grandest and most superb scenery, elegant cities, quaint and picturesque towns and a quaint and picturesque people. Rean Campbell, in his bold, dashing, gossipy style of writing, thus describes a recent trip to Mexico:

It has always seemed a far-away country, and so it was, when the tedious monotony of a long sea voyage must be endured before one could even reach the boundaries of Mexico; but now, when one may step into a palace car at New York, Chicago or St. Louis, and get out of it at the City of Mexico, it does not seem such a foreign land, but more of a next-door neighbor, especially to the American traveler, who is used to stretches of long-distance travels in his own country.

Another thing which reduces the distance is the constant change of scene that obtains on the all-rail journey that is denied the ocean voyage of other days; for, after St. Louis, there is something new in almost every mile, the routes leading through a comparatively new and most picturesque country, either along the high bluffs of the Mississippi, through Arkansas and Texas, or the Indian Territory to El Paso, the gateway to Mexico.

I have said that one might travel from New York to Mexico in a single car. This on special excursions. On regular every-day trains from almost any important city the tourist need leave the cars but twice, at St. Louis and El Paso, the cars running between those cities without change, and from the latter to the City of Mexico.

For a journey to Mexico, no other preparations need be made than would be for any part of this country. Passports are not required. As to money, United States gold and currency are worth a premium in Mexico, and American bankers there will exchange it for the coin and currency of the country. Letters of credit and bills of exchange on New York, Chicago and St. Louis, are readily cashed. At Paso del Norte the Mexican customs officers examine baggage (have your keys ready). The officers are extremely courteous, and the ordinary contents of a traveler's trunk are passed under rules that are fair and liberal.

It is not possible on a continuous journey to see all the country between El Paso and the City of Mexico by daylight, but stop-over privileges are allowed on first-class through tickets, and stops may be made anywhere on the line.

Baggage must be rechecked at El Paso. One hundred and fifty pounds are allowed on each ticket from points in the United States; on local tickets in Mexico only thirty-three pounds are carried free. Other passenger regulations are about the same as in this country.

A day can be most pleasantly passed at El Paso and Paso del Norte; but the first place of importance on the line is Chihuahua, the capital of the State of the same name, a city of 20,000 people, where there are very many attractions to induce the first request for a stop-over check.

A branch of the Mexican mint has long been established here, and considerable capital has been acquired in mines and mining. The building occupied by the mint was formerly a church, and from its tower, where he had been confined, the patriot Hidalgo was taken to execution July 30, 1811, on the spot now marked by a simple monument of white stone. The cathedral, so famous for architectural beauty, was built with the proceeds of a special tax on the product of the Santa Eulalia silver mine, situated about fifteen miles south of the city. There is a handsome plaza and an aqueduct of some 220 years' standing. Leaving Chihuahua, the train winds around the beautiful "El Coronel" mountain, and runs through the valleys of the Concha and San Pedro, reaching, a little before noon, Santa Rosalia, famous for its sanitary hot springs, and pronounced by foreigners who have visited it to be, as to the quality of its waters, probably the finest health resort in America.

Fresnillo, once a great mining town, contains now 20,000 people. Its overflowed mines are waiting the magic touch of capital to bring to light their hoard of untouched silver, and reawaken the old busy life.

Zacatecas, a city of 75,000 souls, capital of the State of Zacatecas, is reached by a sharp rise through the mountains, and is of great commercial importance. All around it lie piles of rich slag, openings into hills, square inclosures, tall chimneys indicating its ancient and present industry, which is silver mining. The coinage of the mint here located is exceeded only by that of the City of Mexico. Zacatecas is a point of great interest to the tourist. It is situated about half way between Paso del Norte and the City of Mexico, and is wedged so closely into its narrow valley that it has foamed over the edges and crept up the hillside in terraced clusters of adobe. Its cathedral is a marvel of stone carving, and its people are of the true and ancient Mexican type. The road now descends rapidly through the hills to the broad, cultivated valleys of the State of Aguas Calientes.

Aguas Calientes (Hot Waters), a city containing 40,000 inhabitants, and justly reputed one of the most attractive places of the Republic, takes its name from the hot springs in which the region abounds. Its luxurious baths, clean streets and beautiful buildings combine to make it interesting for the tourist who spends a few days here.

Silao is situated in the midst of a beautiful and highly cultivated valley, and contains large flouring mills. This is the supper station, going south, and the junction point of the branch line to

Guanajuato — a city among mountains, a fortified place set upon the side of heights so steep that the houses seem to be fastened to the rock rather than resting upon it, and a misstep on the dizzy uppermost level of the narrow, steep streets, would precipitate the unlucky one into the midst of some plaza three or four hundred feet below. A lovely, bewildering spot, full of lanes and archways, and winding, twisted market places with a crowd of picturesque people selling every oddity under the sun and a screen of matting, with a crossing and interlacing of narrow paved ways which give at every ten steps the effect of a kaleidoscope, with a vista of infinite beauty and novelty at each turning.

The upper balconies of the many really beautiful houses are gay with bright awnings and marvelous flowers; the old Church of the Jesuit is magnificent in fine arches of soft pink stone and wonderful carvings fine as strips of lace work ; the overhanging hills topple against the deep blue sky; and through a hundred different arches some vision of softly frescoed, slender-pillared inner courts, bright with blossoms and fresh with greenery, flashes out, no matter how swiftly one passes. And into this ravishing spot we are whirled without any more warning than the corners of a few sharp mountain spurs could give us.

Queretaro, the next point of interest, has a population of 40,000, and is the capital of the State of Queretaro. On a hill north of the city are three crosses, marking the spot where Maximilian, Miramon and Mejia were shot, June 19, 1867. It is a fine city, located in a fertile valley, and contains much of interest to the traveler.

San Juan del Rio has a population of 18,000 people, active and enterprising. As the train climbs the low mountains to the south, we have a lovely view of the valley, the distant mountains and the great haciendas scattered along the plains. Upward, through the broken and picturesque country, across the broad plain of Cazadero, and over the summit at Marquez, the train goes down into the Tula Valley, amid timber and foliage, and evidences of approach to the tropics. The towns through which we now pass are full of interest to the student of antiquity, and contain many relics of Toltec civilization.

Through the celebrated Tajo de Nochistongo, the great Spanish drainage cut, dating back to the seventeenth century, we enter the Valley of Mexico, than which nothing in the world can be more lovely, and on through fertile fields to the capital and largest city of the Republic.

The City of Mexico is justly entitled, by reason of its population, intelligence, culture, beautiful location, healthful and even climate, historical, political and commercial pre-eminence, to its reputation as one of the celebrated cities of the world. It is well lighted, supplied with pure water, has a police force uniformly polite, attentive and efficient; abundance of public carriages at reasonable rates, under careful city regulations; fine hotels, conducted on the European plan; restaurants, cafés, gardens, baths, theaters, public library, museums, art galleries, fine houses and public buildings. Its colleges and schools are large and thoroughly organized. The National Palace, the City Hall, the great Cathedral, and many of the churches are grand in proportions and architectural and artistic effects. The suburbs are attractive and easily reached. In about twelve hours one can reach the eternal snows of the summit of Popocatepetl, or the tropical heat and fruits of the " tierra caliente."

At the further end of the Paseo rises the hill and Castle of Chapultepec, surrounded by a forest of cypress, which is not surpassed for magnificence on this continent.

The grand old trees, most of which must date back over twenty centuries, rise in somber majesty above those of ordinary growth, like a race of giants among pigmies, and the dim aisles beneath their lower branches are made still more beautiful by the almost intangible softness of draperies of gray moss festooned and swaying from limb to limb.

Through this wood, shadowy as twilight even at midday, the carriage road winds and mounts to the summit.

Standing on the terrace, whence rises the grand old castle, one looks across the Valley of Mexico. Surely, of all beautiful outlooks in this beautiful world, the most wondrous is this!

With the remembrance strong upon me of other scenes in other lands which have inspiration and delight, with the memory of the Yosemite in its blended aspect of mystery and majesty, still foremost in thought, this heavenly landscape loses nothing. Even the glamour which ever surrounds the past fades before the reality. From this beautiful spot one looks across a valley fair as a dream of paradise, with soft green fields and waving hedges and avenues of lofty trees outlining gray country roads that fade into azure distance. A faint line of pale blue mountains, purple sometimes with deep shadow, rest like brooding and watchful spirits around the dim horizon; and farthest of all, beautiful with that sublime sense of remoteness and awfulness which belongs only to them, the solemn presence of Popocetapetl and Ixtaccihuatl rise like radiant clouds against the serene heaven above. Everything we had before known of mountain scenery becomes secondary in the imagination compared with these wonderful heights! The great serenity of the plain, the softly changing greens which cover its entire extent, and the undulating, exquisite line of hills, like the frame of some rich jewel, is something unspeakable when contrasted with the grand, solitary state of these twin monarchs who dominate them all. If no more of loveliness than this view can give were added to one's inner life, the journey to Mexico would be fully requited.

ALONG THE LINE OF THE MEXICAN CENTRAL RAILROAD.

EL PASO, TEXAS, one of the most enterprising and interesting cities of the Southwest, with new and comfortable hotels, is the connecting point of the Mexican Central with the railways of the United States, passengers and baggage being transferred directly from car to car at the Union Station. Starting southward, the train crosses the Rio Grande River and enters the Republic of Mexico at PASO DEL NORTE, a long, narrow town extending along the river, with a population of 6,000, and stops for supper at the company's station, a fine structure, built of adobe, around an open court, with ample verandas, upon which open the offices, waiting-rooms and restaurant. Here the Mexican customs officers will examine baggage. Passengers must have their keys ready, and those who have only the ordinary effects of a traveler need fear no annoyance on either side of the river, as the rules are fair and liberal, and the officers are gentlemen desiring only to do their duty with courtesy, celerity and propriety. The special checks given for baggage at El Paso, Texas, must be surrendered at Paso Del Norte, and the baggage rechecked to its destination on this road.

A day could be pleasantly spent here in seeing the old church, with its parchment records antedating the settlement of the United States, and the fertile farm and vineyards along the river. The train passes through the country south of the Rio Grande in the night, along valleys walled by low mountain ranges, through the rich pastures of San José, Galego, Encinillas and Sauz, arriving for breakfast at the flourishing city of Chihuahua, capital of the State of the same name, finely located upon the Chubiscar

River, near its junction with the Sacramento, a well-built and cleanly city of about 20,000 people, with the good order and thorough police organization characteristic of all Mexican cities.

Its cathedral, so famous for its architectural beauty, was built with the proceeds of a special tax on the product of the Santa Eulalia silver mine, about fifteen miles south of the city.

The government mint was formerly a church, and from its tower, where he had been confined, the patriot Hildago was taken to execution, July 30, 1811, on the spot now marked by a simple monument of white stone. The city is amply supplied with pure water by the great Spanish aqueduct, and in the plaza, in the center of the city, is a handsome fountain. South of the plaza is a beautiful alameda and drive shaded by gigantic cottonwood trees. Leaving Chihuahua, the train winds around the noble " El Coronel " mountain, and runs through the valleys of the Concho, San Pedro and Florida, and the towns of SANTA ROSALIA, near which are some of the finest hot springs in the world, and Jimenez, fifty miles west of which is the great mining district of Parral. Dinner is served at Jimenez. The famous " Laguna Country " is reached by night, and supper is taken at LERDO, a few kilometers from the city of Villa Lerdo, a prosperous town of 10,000 inhabitants, and the emporium of the Laguna cotton district, which now yields 30,000 bales a year, all of which goes south for consumption. The soil and climate are so favorable that the plants need renewal only every fourth or fifth year, and, with improved machinery and presses, greater areas would be brought under culture, and the ratio of production largely increased. Durango, capital of the State of that name, lies 150 miles west. It may be reached by stage from Lerdo and also from Fresnillo. It is a handsome city of 35,000 inhabitants, and located in a great silver and iron district.

Leaving FRESNILLO, once a great mining town, having now 20,000 people, about ten kilometers to the west, waiting with its overflowed mines for the magic touch of capital to expose their hoard of untouched silver and reawaken the old busy life, the train reaches

ZACATECAS by a sharp rise through the mountains which surround it, a city of 75,000 souls, the capital of the State, and of great commercial importance, its interests being mainly those of a mining and distributing center. The coinage of its mint is exceeded only by that of the City of Mexico. Its cathedral is a marvel of stone carving. Located high up on the uneven valley between the mountains, its streets are narrow and tortuous, but full of life and animation. From the railway station street cars run to all parts of the city. The road now descends rapidly through the hills to the broad, cultivated valleys of the State of Aguascalientes. Here great quantities of corn, wheat, barley, and wool are raised, and the horses are famed for size, style and beauty. The train stops for dinner at the capital, also called Aguascalientes, a city of 30,000 people. Its clean streets, fine buildings, hot springs, luxurious baths, salubrious and delightful climate throughout the year, and the fine country around it, conspire to make this one of the most delightful places in Mexico. Among its thriving industries is the manufacture of fine woolens, serapes, etc.

At Encarnacion, the train crosses the largest bridge on the line, 150 feet above the stream, and soon arrives at Lagos, a well-built manufacturing city of 40,000 inhabitants.

GUADALAJARA lies 150 miles west, with a population of 100,000; a great commercial city located in the midst of a fertile country and celebrated for its educational and charitable institutions. The city of San Luis Potosi, the bright and enterprising capital of the State of the same name, with its 50,000 population, lies 200 miles to the east. The Pacific branch of the Mexican Central will pass through Guadalajara, and its Tampico branch through San Luis Potosi. Both branches are in active construction. At present both points are reached by first-class stage lines from Lagos.

LEON, a city of 100,000 people, is largely engaged in the manufacture of leather, cotton and woolen goods, saddlery, hats, cloth, boots, shoes and cutlery, and is surrounded by cultivated valleys. It has a fine theater and public buildings, and is an important center of trade.

SILAO, the supper station going south, is a pretty city of 30,000 people. It has large flouring mills, and is the junction point of the branch line to

GUANAJUATO, the capital of the State, a city of 75,000 inhabitants, mainly devoted to mining interests, twenty-four kilometers east of Silao. There is great charm in the novelty and picturesqueness of its scenery, architecture and bustling life. The "patio" process for extracting silver may be seen daily. Guanajuato resembles Zacatecas, but is 1,500 feet lower. From Silao, the line runs through a magnificent agricultural country, and, in the midst of the great grain and stock haciendas, the train reaches, successively, the thriving towns of IRAPUATO AND SALAMANCA, having each over 20,000 population, mostly interested in farming, with some growing manufacturing industries.

CELAYA, population 30,000, has extensive cotton and woolen mills and bleacheries. A short distance below Celaya, the line is crossed by the "National" (narrow gauge) Railway, and connection is made for Morelia and other points on that line. QUERETARO, population 35,000, capital of the State of the same name, is a fine city, located in a charming valley. Three crosses mark the spot on the small hill north of the city where the Archduke Maximilian and Generals Miramon and Mejia were shot, June 19, 1867. South of Queretaro, the train runs under the massive aqueduct which supplies the city with water.

Passing Hercules, where there are extensive cotton mills, supplied with modern machinery and power, turning out yearly great quantities of cloth, we enter the valley of SAN JUAN DEL RIO. The city of that name has a population of 18,000, active and enterprising. As the train climbs the low mountains to the south, we have a lovely view of the valley, of the distant mountains, and the great haciendas scattered along the plains at their feet. Upward through the broken and picturesque country, across the broad plain of Cazadero, and over the summit at Marquez, the train goes down into the tropics. Tula is full of interest for the student of antiquity, and has many relics of the Toltec civilization. It is a growing city of about 10,000 inhabitants.

On through the celebrated

TAJO DE NOCHISTONGO, the great Spanish drainage cut, dating back to the seventeenth century, and we enter the Valley of Mexico. Passing over the hill of Barrientos, and across the broad, fertile fields and the numerous irrigating canals, we reach the end of our trip at the CITY OF MEXICO, the capital, and the largest and most important city of the Republic. It is justly entitled, by reason of its population, intelligence, culture, beautiful location, healthful and even climate, historical, political and commercial pre-eminence, to its reputation as one of the celebrated cities of the world. It is well lighted, supplied with pure water, has a police force uniformly polite, attentive and efficient, abundance of public carriages at reasonable rates under careful city regulations, fine hotels conducted on the European plan, restaurants, cafés, gardens, baths, theaters, public library, museum, gallery, fine houses and public buildings. Its colleges and schools are large and thoroughly organized. The National Palace, the City Hall, the great Cathedral, and many of the churches are grand in their proportions and architectural and artistic effects.

The suburbs are attractive and easily reached. In about twelve hours one can reach the eternal snow of the summit of Popocatepetl, or the tropical heat and fruits of the "tierra caliente."

THE COMMERCIAL TRAVELER AND TOURIST IN CUBA.

HAVANA

AND ITS MANY ATTRACTIONS AS A CHARMING WINTER RESORT AND BUSINESS PLACE.

Thousands of Americans, anxious to escape the rigors and penalties of the severe, inclement and health-trying Northern and Western winters, make annual pilgrimages to the sunny clime of Florida, there to breathe the "fragrant aroma of the orange groves, and inhale the health-laden odor of the pine woods"—while taking in a sufficient quantity of miasma and malaria with which to inoculate the entire system for years to come. These tourists would do well to take in the island of Cuba while in the vicinity, and compare its attractions as a delightful and charming winter resort with those of Florida. A short run over to Havana will surprise the average tourist, and delight the invalid. They will be enchanted with its many attractions, and especially pleased with its balmy and healthy winter climate, where malaria, coughs, colds and bronchial affections are unknown, and which, if carried with you, disappear in a day or two as if by magic.

Florida, now the Mecca of the American winter tourist and pleasure seeker, may be a very delightful and attractive winter resort to some; but, with all the alleged manifold attractions of that much-advertised land of flowers (?), the tourist is liable to soon tire and weary of the never-changing monotony of sand-hills, swamps, pine trees, "'gators," orange groves, and visionary Utopian Edens, which exist mainly in the fertile brain of the Florida land speculators and hotel proprietors.

Comparatively few of the tourists, invalids and pleasure seekers visiting Florida ever consider the interesting fact, that, within the short distance of 100 miles, or twelve hours' pleasant steaming from Tampa, there lies, almost at our very doors, one of the richest, most beautiful and most interesting lands on the face of the globe.

CUBA, "THE PEARL OF THE ANTILLES," is famed as the first abiding place of Columbus; famed for its beautiful women and its gallant gentlemen; famed for its glorious, health-invigorating winter climate, is incomparable natural resources and wealth, its great commercial importance, its immense manufactures of cigars, sugar and tobacco; its ancient churches, convents, colleges and institutions of learning; its large, elegant and attractive theaters and bull rings; its beautiful shops, stocked with the richest goods and wares; its magnificent private residences, many of them veritable princely palaces; its extensive and grandly equipped sugar and tobacco plantations, and its cultivated, refined and most hospitable inhabitants.

ALLEGATIONS OF LAWLESSNESS GREATLY EXAGGERATED.

This rich and beautiful island, which has suffered so severely from a prolonged and most disastrous civil war, is trying, by every effort, to recover its commercial prosperity. The merchant and the planter, measurably aided by the government, are striving in the most commendable manner to regain lost ground, and, by putting forward great energy and effort, repair the injuries and losses incurred by the late civil war. While the inhabitants of the island are engaged in these praiseworthy efforts, it is both unjust and cruel that citizens of the United States, and more especially certain portions of the American press, should adopt a course calculated not only to retard the improvement of affairs, but to injure American shipping and commercial interests engaged in Cuban trade, by promulgating untruthful sensational reports regarding the social and political condition of the island. During the past winter, certain American papers published absurdly sensational stories regarding the political and sanitary condition of Cuba — tales of brigandage, murder, assassination and pestilence. These have originated in the imagination of the writers, and never occurred in fact. Among the many injurious results produced by these publications, was the preventing of hundreds of Americans from visiting the island — not more than ten per cent. of the usual number of tourists visiting Havana the past winter. But a still greater loss was that inflicted on the commercial prosperity of the island and on American merchants, shippers and ship-owners having business relations with the natives. As an instance of the disastrous effects produced by the reports referred to, the following letter from the general manager of the Plant system of railway and steamships to Havana speaks for itself:

TAMPA AND HAVANA STEAMSHIP LINE,
TAMPA, Fla., February 23, 1888.

Messrs. Lawton Bros., Agents, Havana, Cuba.

GENTLEMEN — I herewith inclose extracts from New York *Telegram* and other papers of recent date. Articles, evidently from the same hand, are appearing in different newspapers, very much to the injury of our business. Can you put us in a position to contradict tthe whole or any part of these statements? At all events, please let me know just how far they are true ; also, as to the real danger tourists would incur from exposure to small-pox, as this is being made a great deal of to keep people from going to Havana this season.

Very truly yours,
H. S. HAINES,
General Manager.

In order to dissipate the bad impression which these sensational newspaper articles conveyed, the writer called upon the American consul-general at Havana, and urged him to officially deny them. But, while fully alive to the injurious character of these reports, and while personally acknowledging them to be false and misleading, he declined to take official action in the premises, on the ground that the rules and regulations of the service forbade public action without the sanction of the State Department at Washington. Failing to obtain a proper public denial from this source, and urged by many prominent American and Cuban merchants to endeavor to secure an authoritative statement from some source such as would carry conviction to the minds of the American and English public interested in Cuban affairs, the writer sought the British consul-general, Mr. DeCapel Crowe, and from him obtained the following interesting statement, in the form of an interview:

" Mr. Crowe said it was neither his duty nor inclination to make official statements with respect to the sensational articles which had lately appeared in American papers on crime in Cuba. His reports were reserved for his own government; but, in the general interest and information of his own countrymen desirous of visiting the island, he had no objection to giving an opinion on the present state of Havana and other seaports in the island. It was not true, as reported, that a reign of terror, in any form, existed in the city of Havana, and that 'robbery, brigandage and murder are openly and daily perpetrated in the streets of the capital,' or other cities. Such sensational statements not only do great injury to trade generally, but prevent many of our countrymen from coming here to enjoy the splendid and healthy winter climate. A considerable amount of crime does exist in the towns, the result of a long civil war, the emancipation of 300,000 slaves and the commercial decadence consequent upon the late civil war. From these, among other causes, a defective prison system and the poverty and mode of life of the lower classes, there is doubtless a considerable percentage of crime; but from such crimes as murder, arson, or indecency, as mentioned by the American press articles, the cities of Cuba are singularly free.

"It is not to be expected that a heterogeneous urban population of blacks, Chinese and poor creoles in the tropics should behave with quite the same propriety of manner as better educated natives of colder climates; but, apart from untidiness, there is nothing to offend the eye of the most fastidious foreigner — nor need the fear of the 'terrible reign of terror,' depicted by the journals in question, prevent any sensible person (not especially in search of adventures) from coming here as heretofore. From the end of November to April he will be less exposed to disease, and not more exposed to the dangers of the streets, than he would be in many parts of New York or London; moreover, he will enjoy an unequaled climate, with an immunity from all lung diseases. What the private life of the individual or that of the native may be, how the natives are treated or governed by the Spanish authorities, is no concern of ours; but we may reasonably expect a certain amount of public decorum, and in this respect Havana compares favorably with many larger capitals. Travelers coming here, content to mind their own business, can, with ordinary precaution, lead a very healthy, pleasant and secure life during the four or five months indicated.

"It is not necessary to speak here of the interior portions of the island. Brigandage, sequestration and other crimes occasionally occur, but people of a nervous temperament need not go there. If they will keep to the lines of railways and to the towns, they will run but small risks. Both in town and country, tourists will find the inhabitants friendly and willing to serve them, and even a small share of politeness and interest on their part will meet with a ready return. In the capital (Havana) there are good hotels and most of the conveniences of cultivated life. I can really see no serious reason why travelers should keep away."

ATTRACTIONS FOR THE AMERICAN TOURIST.

To many people Cuba has been only the scene of filibustering expeditions, of a protracted and sanguinary civil war, waged between the natives, under the banner of "Cuba Libre," and their Spanish oppressors, perhaps as a scene for a romantic novel, the memory of a geographical lesson, or the place from whence good cigars come. To the average American traveler and tourist, Cuba, which is only "across the road" from Florida, might be 5,000 miles away, for it seems to many a far-off land, a land that comparatively few Americans ever get to, but, when once visited, always to be remembered with pleasure and profit.

One of the most interestingly graphic descriptions of a winter tour in Cuba is given by the "Pointer," which we here reproduce.

HOW TO GET THERE.—The points of departure of the direct lines from the United States to Cuba are New York, New Orleans and Tampa, respectively, as to length of sea voyage, the cost of travel from interior points being about the same, except those places nearer the place of debarkation; hence it is impossible to name a rate here. The steamer rate from New York to Havana and return is $90, from New Orleans $60, from Tampa $30, from Punta Gorda $30, from Cedar Key $40, which includes meals and state-room berth.

From New York the direct steamers sail due south, and after forty-eight hours' sail, come to summer weather, transition from winter being gradual and altogether pleasant, and the voyage being less conducive to sea-sickness than many others that are shorter. The ships are staunch and reliable, with excellent accommodations for passengers, cozy state-rooms and an ample *menu* which includes the delicacies of American and Cuban markets. The ships' officers and attendants are courteous and attentive to travelers. The route is down the coast of the United States, passing the Bahama Islands, coming to Cuba at Havana.

From New Orleans the ships sail down the Mississippi, passing the sugar, cotton and rice fields of lower Louisiana, out through the jetties at the mouth of the great river, crossing the Gulf of Mexico to Cedar Key or Punta Gorda and Key West, and, after a sail over a summer sea, comes to Havana. These lines are the oldest in the trade from any southern port, and tourists always profit by the long experience of the officers and agents.

From Tampa a new and most excellent service has been established, operating a schedule with frequent trips over the shortest route, touching at Key West on going and returning, landing at Havana after a sail of twenty-four hours. The ships are newly built, of iron and steel, with every modern improvement for safety and comfort, with appointments of cabin and excellence of cuisine that is not surpassed on any steamer afloat.

To all these ports passengers may proceed in through palace cars, and, as the passenger agents delight to say, with only one change to Havana from almost any prominent city in the United States.

GETTING READY.

When a journey to foreign ports is to be made, a passport must be thought of. But when the destination is Cuba, that state paper is wholly unnecessary. So says the Queen Regent of Spain in a royal decree promulgated July 30, 1887, and the only protective document needed is the certificate of a notary public that the bearer is an American citizen, and he may have the freedom of the island, to go where he listeth, and depart on the homeward journey when he will, with no one to question or require *vised* papers.

MONEY is a passport most anywhere, and a most valuable and convenient one everywhere, and in Cuba, as other places, is essential, though not more so than elsewhere, the hotel and traveling expenses not being above the average tariff.

It is not necessary to buy Spanish gold or Cuban paper before starting, because the bankers on the island will pay the highest prices for greenbacks, American gold, or New York exchange, and the tourist may suit his pleasure or convenience as to what shape his funds are in, and, after arrival at destination, can deposit his home money in an American banker's vaults, and draw the Cuban currency or Spanish gold, as it is needed for daily use. A letter of credit from reliable bankers in the United States will also be honored by American bankers in Cuba.

Hotel bills and railway fares are payable in Spanish gold, or its equivalent in Cuban paper; purchases in stores or shops are charged in gold or paper, the information being announced with the price. Cab fares, tickets to theaters and places of amusement, are priced in paper; also cigars and liquid refreshments have a paper value.

The paper currency is very much depreciated; one American dollar will usually buy two and a half in Cuban paper — our dollars and cents translate to *pesos y centavos* in Cuban; in Spanish gold (oro Español) an *onza* is worth $17; half *onza*, $8.50; a *centen*, $5.30; a *doblon*, $4.25; an *escudo*, $2.12, of American money.

Postage to the United States is five cents *(cinco centavos)* per ounce or fraction of an ounce. Cablegrams to New York, fifty cents per word, with a corresponding tariff to other cities.

The tourist will find it to his interest to call on an American banker soon after arrival, and post himself financially as to rates of exchange, etc. The bankers will be found to be most courteous and obliging, and ready to assist their compatriots at all times.

THE ARRIVAL AT HAVANA.

A ship not sailing under the Spanish flag, cannot enter the port of Havana between sunset and sunrise, a custom long enforced by the government, which, if it was intended for the tourist's pleasure, could not have suited him better, because the ships' schedules are so arranged that arrival is made at sunrise, and when she sails up under the guns of Morro Castle, with the brightening daylight tinging the eastern sky and showing the frowning walls of Morro and Cabaña, and, behind them the distant hills through whose crowning palm trees the earliest sunshine is streaming, the picture is wonderfully beautiful, and a look to the starboard shows the city just awakening, and ready to give you the warmest welcome.

At the entrance of the harbor on the east side is Morro Castle, just back of which, on the same side, is Cabaña Castle; on the other side, opposite Morro, is La Punta, the forts constituting the defense of the city from attacks by sea. Sailing past these forts, the ship comes to an anchor in mid-stream; no foreign vessel ever goes to a pier at Havana.

The "doctor's boat" comes alongside just after the ship has entered the harbor, and, by the time anchorage is made opposite the Custom House, the health and port officers have examined the papers, and given permission for the passengers to disembark.

In the meantime there have come out to meet the ship what seem to be a hundred country wagons, afloat with their wheels under the water — these are the boats that are to take the passengers ashore — boats with bowed awnings, for all the world like a country wagon down in Tennessee. These are propelled by oars or sail (I mean the boats, not the Tennessee wagons), and the fare to the Custom House is twenty-five cents. There have come out, also to meet the tourists, agents of the various hotels, agents polite and attentive without being obtrusive, speaking English and Spanish, and, unless one is posted or speaks the language, it is well to select your hotel and turn your baggage over to him, as some of the hotels have their own boats and carts for transfer of baggage. The rowing to shore is but the work of a few moments, and the novel ride winds up at the stone steps of the

CUSTOM HOUSE.

Here all baggage must be examined by the customs officers, who are most liberal and courteous gentlemen — you declare your baggage, that there is nothing but your personal effects and no dutiable articles, a hasty look to carry out the law, the thing is done, and you may proceed to your hotel — there are no delays, except when there is a crowd of tourists, then, if desired, keys may be left with the hotel agents, and the travelers go on to

THE HOTELS.

The tourist, especially he who has listened to the yarns of the old-time travelers, will be most agreeably surprised when he discovers the many excellences that pervade the best hotels in Cuba, in parlor, dining-room and bed-chamber. All of the old objectionable customs and arrangements have been done away with, and very many innovations introduced that brings them very near the modern standard of the American hotel.

There is a register, of course, and you are expected to write more of your personal history than usually appears on the register of your native land. The book is ruled in columns, and each has its heading; the first is *Fecha de Entrada*, date of arrival; the next is *Nombres*, names; then the *Naturalidad*, or nationality; next *Residencia*, residence; then the one that ladies, at least, should not be required to fill out, the one which shows *Edad*, age of the guest; the next is also peculiar, it is *Estado*, the state of arrival, married or single, I suppose, as the average is sober. Then follows the *Profesion* column, to show your profession; after that is the one showing *Procedencia*, whence you went; then *Fecha de Salida* tells date of departure, and the last column is *Numero de Orden*, giving the number of guests.

These columns are not now imperatively used, but in the days of wars, revolutions and insurrections, when they wanted to know all about everybody, they were required to be filled out, but the war taxes remain the same, and a revenue stamp must be placed on the register opposite each name.

Bell-boys are plenty, and very properly do not wait in the office, but on the floor where they attend; so, when you ring, he does not have to tramp up four flights to find out what is wanted, tramp down, and then back to your room. The Cuban bell-boy waits near the annunciator on each floor; ring your bell, and he is at your door in a moment, and *not* with a pitcher of ice-water — they don't drink ice-water in Cuba — at least Cubans don't; an earthen jar, very porous, so that the water does not get too warm, is placed in each room, and kept filled with fresh water, so that only Americans call for ice-water, and that is brought in a glass, as it is not supposed that anybody wants much ice-water.

An early morning ring from the average room means coffee, in Spanish café, but from the American occupied room it may mean "cocktail," for which there is no Spanish word, and the American one is adopted and understood, and, I may say, well made. Coffee is served at any hour desired, in your room or in the dining-room; breakfast from nine till noon; dinner from five to eight p. m.; and in the dining-room is where the most grateful surprises await the tourist. The *menu* is ample, and the dishes nicely prepared. There are many familiar ones, and some mysterious, but I was never disappointed in one, and soon was not afraid or suspicious. The vegetables and fruit were fresh and crisp — no hot-house forcings or stale importations, but just in from the gardens. The fish were superb, being taken direct from the water to the frying-pan, it being against the law to sell a dead fish. They must be taken alive, and kept in floating coops till sold. The meats were sweet and well prepared, the poultry young and tender. This was my experience wherever I stopped. Ice is an expensive luxury in Cuba, and all productions must be consumed at once, nothing can be kept in the market. Eggs must be new-laid always, or no sale. Milkmen don't drive wagons, and can only water their stock in the way provided by nature — give it to the cows to drink — and when he sells milk, he drives his herd around town and milks at the door of his customer, and the out-put is immediately boiled.

The rates at Cuban hotels are about the same as at the same class houses in America, and are conducted on both plans, American and European; but it is best to understand the terms when you register—which is a good rule in this country as well. The figures are from $3 to $5 per day, wines extra. The price includes room, coffee and fruit in the morning, breakfast and dinner. Families and parties can have suits with private parlors and dining-rooms. English-speaking chambermaids are in attendance on the ladies' apartments, and all toilet arrangements are complete on each floor.

Every hotel has its corps of interpreters, who are courteous and obliging, and will attend parties to theaters and on sight-seeing tours—these gentlemen are on the hotel staff, but it is customary to remunerate their service—it must be left to the guest's appreciation of the service to say what the amount will be—but I will say that in most cases the money is well earned.

Now that the tourist is comfortably bestowed in one of the excellent hotels of Havana, he must see the city—nobody walks, it must be done IN A CAB. There are thousands of them, easily found night or day in any part of the city; each cab is a four-wheeled Victoria, equipped with one horse and one driver, and generally speaking, all in good condition, capable of making good time, and at a rate of fare that is astonishingly low—the fare to any point east of Belascoain avenue is only 40 cents, in paper, for one or two persons, equal to 16 cents in United States money; for three persons the fare is 50 cents; beyond the avenue the fare increases to 50 and 60 cents.

If there are several places to visit, the cab had best be secured by the hour, at $1.35 for two or $1.85 for three persons per hour—if so engaged, say "*per hora*" when you get in, and tell the driver where to go.

How?

Oh, you don't speak the language? Just call the name of the place, it is not necessary to fatigue yourself by translating the phrase "drive to;" the driver will understand the situation. If you get in and say "*Correo*," he will "drive to" the post-office, or *La Punta*, the point opposite Morro at the terminus of the "*Prado*;" the *Catedral*, *La Merced*, *San Augustin*, if you are going to church; or "*Plaza de Toros*" if your taste carries you to the bull fights the cab will—or if to the theater say "*Tacon*," *Irijoa* (ery-ho-a) or *Albisu*. To the railways, "*Ferro Carril de la Bahia*," "*Ferro Carril de la Habana*," or "*Ferro Carril del Oeste*." If to any particular street call the name of it, and look out for the number of the desired address. If you get muddled beyond the hope of extrication, and your vocabulary is exhausted, call the name of your hotel, go back, get the interpreter to speak for you, and start out again.

The best way to call a cab in Havana is to whistle for it (if you can), and, when you have attracted the driver's attention, motion with your hand for him to go away, and he will drive right up. (This reminds me they do many things upside down in Cuba: the key-holes in the doors are made that way.)

In driving through the streets, it is easy to become confused; but, if you will remember that the streets are so narrow that a city ordinance requires to drive down certain streets and up others—so, if your driver does not go down the one desired, don't be alarmed, he will go down the one next to it, and come up the other.

At the end of the trip, or the time the cab was taken for, pay the driver, or he will wait at the door and count time on you, an imported trick from the United States.

These cabs of the Victoria pattern are an innovation in Havana on account of the narrow streets; they were introduced some time ago to supplant the unwieldy, long-shafted and hard-to-turn-round *volante*—an easy-riding vehicle, propelled by one horse in shafts, and another buckled alongside to carry the driver, or rather, postillion, as he rides the other horse, but both horses travel so far ahead of the volante that very few of them could get into any one part of town at a time, and, in case of a block, must have gone to the country to turn round. The increase of business down town drove the volante from Havana, but they might be used to great profit and pleasure in the parks and drives, and it is a wonder some enterprising liveryman does not re-introduce them. Every American would take a ride in a volante just to talk about it at home. Volantes are used now only at Matanzas for excursions to the Yumuri Valley and the caves of Bella Mar.

Besides cabs and volantes, there are other and cheaper methods of locomotion in Cuban cities. I refer to the inevitable and irrepressible

HORSE CARS AND STAGES.

The fares are ten, twenty and thirty cents in paper, according to the distance traveled. One line at Havana leads out Charles III. avenue to the botanical gardens, base ball grounds, and the *plaza de toros* (bull-ring), another to Cerro, one along the shore in front of the city, another to the famous Henry Clay cigar factory. Cars start from Plaza San Juan de Dios every fifteen minutes from 6 a. m. to 10:30 p. m.

The stages have a uniform fare of twenty cents in paper, which is higher in proportion than the cabs, being about eight cents in American money. Starting from the Plaza de Armas and the Castillo del Principe, they run to Jesus del Monte and the Cemetery.

There are no "bob-tail" cars; you are not to be trusted to "put the exact fare in the box." A uniformed conductor punches in presence of the passenger.

There is another way to see the city which involves still less outlay of capital — that means of going which was in fashion in the days of Adam. The walks about Havana are attractive, but they must not be long walks, and are most pleasant in the evening. Walking in Havana is not popular at best; the sidewalks are not built that way, many of them are scarcely three feet wide, and some in the business district are less than two, while in the new city there are some that will compare favorably with other cities. It is said that the curbs in the old portion were originally laid only to prevent wheels from defacing the walls of the buildings.

In the Campo de Marte, on the Prado, in Central Park, are excellent promenades. On certain evenings of the week fashionable Havanese drive to Central Park, stop opposite the statue of Isabella, and listen to the music of the military band, and promenade up and down the plaza. Here you may see la Cubana in all her dark-eyed beauty, with snowy laces and mantillas falling gracefully over head and shoulders. The carriage stops at the curb, in an instant it is surrounded with cavaliers, dark and black mustached. La Señorita enjoys the homage so gallantly paid; the duenna, I think, often pays strict attention to the music, to give the girl a chance; but, if she left the carriage, the duenna went also, perhaps with watchful eye, and ear only half turned to the music. The Central Park is one of the places to walk in the evening when the band plays; but, if you want to sit and rest, chairs are twenty cents each. Another walk in the morning, is along the Prado from the statue of India to La Punta, all the way under the laurels that shade the street.

From any of the hotels one may also walk to the theaters. Havana has elegant places of amusement that would ornament a greater city. The Tacon is the third largest theater in the world, La Scala, at Milan, and the theater at Seville, in Spain, only being larger. The Tacon is the home of opera in Havana. There are five tiers of boxes, one above the other, extending all around the house. These boxes seat six people, and are patronized by the élite — always in full dress. Behind the boxes is a wide passage-way, through which one may pass from one box to another, or serves as a promenade between the acts — and between the acts the lobbies are filled with promenaders, with visitors and with lookers-on through the Venetian blinds into the boxes occupied by some especially brilliant party — and it is said that boastful belles brag on the size of the crowd that assembled behind the box and watched the beauties within.

The Albisu is the theater of the Casino — the swell club of the city. Every Cuban city has its Casino club, noted for its balls and entertainments.

The Irijoa (e-ry-hoa) is called the summer theater because it is arranged with Venetian blinds from the roof to the foundation, instead of solid walls, and by a simple turning of the slats admits the breezes that nearly always blow in Cuba; this theater is surrounded by a garden into which the audience empties itself to drink *penales*, eat ices, or smoke between the acts, and are recalled to the auditorium by a bell like unto that on a locomotive.

Managers of Cuban theaters are particular as to music, it must be good; the orchestras may be mixed as to race of the performers, but their performances are satisfactory; often in third-class theaters one hears as good or better music than in the best American theaters.

Each performance at a place of amusement has its president, appointed by the municipal government; his duties are to settle differences between the audience and the performers and to preserve order. A Cuban audience is critical, insists on the granting of encores when demanded, and goes behind the scenes between the acts; this is their prerogative. It is told of a prestidigitateur, who advertised the decapitation act, but whose wires and paraphernalia were so disarranged by his visitors behind the scenes that he could not illusively cut off his own head, and was disposed to cut that part of the programme, as he could not carry it out actually without physical discomfort to himself; the audience insisted; the president decided for the audience; the illusionist was in despair, but did not lose his head; he went to work, repaired his traps, and did the trick amid the applause of his audience.

At every theater, or other place of amusement, a box decorated with the coat of arms and colors of Spain is reserved for the Captain-General, and remains vacant unless he attends or sends a representative. Seats are also reserved for the press, and names of the papers are pasted on the seats.

The prices of admission are about the same as American theaters; the price at the Tacon is $5 and $6 in paper; at other performances $3 to $4 is the figure. Some theaters sell a seat for a single act for a dollar; and at most theaters the general entrance is only $1 to $1.50, but does not include a seat. Seat coupons are collected by the ushers prior to the opening of the last act. Speculators sell almost the entire house on the sidewalk, though reserved seats may be bought beforehand. It is best not to pay a speculator the first price asked, as he always tacks it on, and will reduce the price before he will miss a sale.

After the opera is over the audience vacates the theater with a rush, and, coming out, unanimously holds a handkerchief over the nostrils to prevent them breathing the night air; some get into carriages and are whirled home; but many gentlemen and ladies frequent the cafés and enjoy ices, coffee, and other refreshments.

The gala days for theaters and other amusements are Sundays and church feast days; then are they all filled to overflowing, to standing room only, as are the cock and bull fights. These take place on Sundays only, and both are popular sports in Cuba. The cock fights are of minor importance compared to the other. They take place in a pit very much like the wheat and stock pits in a Chicago or New York exchange, and the calls of the betters are about as intelligible in one as the other. Around a ring twelve feet in diameter are arranged seats like unto a circus — here sit the lookers-on. The owners of the birds and the betters are everywhere, in the ring and out of it, on the seats and under them. On a balance suspended from the roof are hung bags, each containing a chicken — they must balance exactly — which is the only fair part of the fight. They are taken out of the bags, and with long, keen knives fastened to their spurs they are placed in front of each other — it is not a question of courage or endurance, but as to which gets the first strike — one fowl is always killed, and often both, and it takes only a minute to settle the difficulty — the dead cock is removed, and two fresh birds introduced with the same result all day long.

At the Plaza de Toros, or Bull Ring, the programme is pretty much the same, only on a larger scale. Bull fighting is to Cuba and Spain what base ball is to the United States, and the "bloods" of that country become amateurs at that sport as they do at ball in this — and also, as in this country, the stars and the company are imported; also the bulls.

In the season of 1886-7 Mazzantini came from Spain with his *banderilleros* and *picadores*, and brought eighty thoroughbred bulls. Bulls are bred in Spain for their fighting qualities, as race-horses are in Kentucky for their speed, and the great *matador* was paid $40,000 for thirteen performances.

About the first thing an American thinks of on landing is where to get a cigar, and nine times out of ten his first smoke in Cuba rivals in bitterness the first of his life. A good cigar to the Cuban would seem vile to the smoker from the United States, and those on sale at the stands are not intended for other than Cubans. Ninety-nine per cent. of Cubans smoke, but none chew tobacco—I mean ninety-nine per cent. of the men. Cigarettes are charged to the ladies, but the act of smoking never came under my observation, though they do not object to smoke. The men smoke everywhere and at all times and under all circumstances.

Cigars are made for all nations, and a different cigar for each nation; hence do not buy a cigar till you know where to get one made for this country, or you will lose faith in the reputation of Cuba's chief product. Different nations require different sizes as well as qualities—Europeans using the largest, and Americans the smallest cigars. The eight-hundred-dollar-gold-wrapped *Soberanos* of the Henry Clay factory is twice the size of any American cigar, and would cost $1.50 each—not much sale here—these go to the nobility of England, while the dainty little *Bouquets* or *Perfectos* come to America. There are stands where you can buy cigars you will like, and for half the money they cost at home; but it is best to go to the factory and buy a supply for two or three days' smoking; any of the factories will sell a single box, and the proprietors will be found to be most courteous gentlemen; and, when one finds what elegant cigars can be sold for very much less than home prices, one becomes a free trader at once, no matter how much of a protectionist before. The laws of the United States do not allow the traveler to bring a single cigar past the custom house; if the officer passes a few dozens, it is purest courtesy; the fallacy of "49" or "99" being admitted free of duty has no foundation in the statute, and, when an American smokes a cigar in Cuba, it is with a peculiar satisfaction at the thought that he is beating the government out of the duty, and I believe all smokers are free traders after one trip to Havana; and to make a returned tourist vote against the tariff, it will be only necessary to puff the fragrant blue smoke in his nostrils.

All smokers in Cuba do not smoke cigars, nor is the pipe seldom ever seen; very many indulge in cigarettes. But they are not the rank, dudish thing of America. The Cuban cigarette is made of the same fragrant tobacco that has made the island famous the world over. Cigarettes are made by hand and by machinery, with paper wrappers and tobacco. One factory has a single machine that turns out a hundred thousand cigarettes every day—"La Honradez," of Havana—and the output is nearly half a million every day. I can't describe the wonderful machine, the invention of a Virginian. The tobacco is thrown into a hopper, passes through a tube onto a ribbon of paper a mile or two long, like the paper of a telegraph ticker; the paper, with the coil of tobacco resting on it, passes into another tube, and is curled up and pasted around the tobacco, is cut off at proper lengths, and drops into a basket "just as easy." It all seemed simple enough, as I saw two small boys stand by, shovel in the tobacco, turn on the bands, and make the wheels go round.

In riding about the city, the churches must not be forgotten. The Cathedral is the principal one, but not the oldest. San Augustin was formerly a monastery, and was built in 1608, and the Nunnery of Santa Clara in 1644, while the Cathedral was not commenced till 1656 and completed in 1724. One of the numerous tombs of Columbus is in the Cathedral; here the ashes of the great discoverer lie beneath a bust of himself, the tablet bearing an inscription in Spanish, which, being translated, means

> O, remains and image of the great Columbus,
> A thousand Ages endure preserved in this Urn,
> And in the remembrance of our nation.

The fashionable church of Havana, "La Merced," built in 1746, is attended by the élite of the city, and is a place of special interest to tourists; the decorations are superb, and there are some fine paintings. High mass may be heard at the Cathedral and any of the churches on Sundays and feast days at from 8 to 9 a. m.; they are always open, and visitors cordially welcome.

The others are Santa Catalina on O'Reilly street, where repose the bodies of the martyrs Celestino and Lucida, brought from Rome as relics. The Nunnery of Santa Clara and the Monastery of Belen are places of interest.

There are no pews or seats in Cuban churches. The people kneel on the floors while the prayers are said, there being no long, tedious sermons to listen to. Some worshipers bring a small cushion to kneel on, or a small camp-stool.

It is permitted to visit the different forts and fortifications; the principal one is MORRO CASTLE, and the next Cabaña. Visitors are admitted only by permit from the military authorities, which is easily obtained through the hotel agents, or the American Consul can put you in the way to get the necessary papers. Drive to the Muelle de Caballeria and take a boat (at a cost of 25 cents each) to the east side of the bay, less than a mile, present your papers to the very civil military gentleman in charge, who will courteously send a soldier with you, and you will be glad you came. The bay you have just crossed is smooth and calm as a mill-pond, but just at the base of the castle's north walls the sea is as wild as the mid-Atlantic. The tower of Morro Castle is a lighthouse, showing a flash-light of exceeding brilliancy fifteen leagues to seaward. The view from the ramparts is a magnificent one. To the west the city of Havana lies spread out, to the southeast the palm-covered hills extend away to the mountains, to the north the boundless ocean lies, the waves washing in and out way out to where they meet the skies. Morro Castle is connected with the other forts on the same hill by a tunnel under ground.

All the forts and castles may be visited, and there is no word of particular advice to give except to bear the necessary papers, and while in the forts avoid making notes, as the act might be misconstrued.

There is one thing that must not be forgotten; a visit to the markets. They are all attractive; the best time to go is early morning. The Tacon is the leading market, and there is none finer anywhere; the Colon has been recently completed, and the Christina is the oldest. Step into a cab and drive to either, dismiss the cab, for an hour or so may be most pleasantly spent; there is everything for sale in the Havana markets, fish, flesh and fowl, dry goods, hats, boots and shoes; chickens are cut up and sold in pieces; if a whole one is not wanted, you can buy a drumstick or wing—anything from a piano to a banana; there are fresh vegetables in December as we see them in New York in July, and every variety of tropical fruit at surprisingly low prices, and there are some fruits that many Americans never heard of. There is a special market for fish, which should by all means be visited: the fish are kept in coops, so to call them sunk in the bay, and it is a good market regulation that no dealer is allowed to sell a dead fish; he (the fish) must be "alive and kicking" when the sale is made; ice is too high for use in the fish market. By all means include the markets in your tour of the city, so you can tell at home of seeing green peas, beans, green corn and lettuce in the open market in January; that you saw wagon loads of pine-apples offered at five cents a piece, and oranges, with the leaves yet green on the stems, for a cent. The markets are good places to get cheap souvenirs to take home with you.

In driving about the city, one will not be impressed by the exterior of the Cuban residences. There are several palaces in Havana, belonging to Spanish noblemen, which, if you are fortunate enough to obtain the entrée, will prove a most interesting feature of your visit. The average Cuban residence does not make much display on its exterior, and many are not particular as to who their neighbors are, or where the location. The line is drawn between their homes and the world by the street wall, and whatever may be outside that wall has nothing to do with the inside; outside may be a dirty, squalid street; a peep through an archway will show a court, white and clean, with marble floors and stairs, playing fountains, growing plants and flowers. Cane and willow furniture is used exclusively; there are no carpets, only rugs laid on marble tiles; the chairs in the parlor are arranged in a hollow square; there is no getting off in a corner, or tête-à-têtes in quiet nooks. The entrance is through a wide, high archway, which closes both by iron gratings and heavy doors; an attendant sits in this archway at all times, combining the services of guard and porter. The bright interior, amounting many times to even luxuriousness, sets one to wondering as to the inmates and how they appear at home. This is hard to know, but one day I did—I called by mistake at the wrong door; the old colored servant could not be made to understand, and went back and forth to some one inside, and, finally, that some one had to come and direct me where to go; there came from the innermost recesses of that court to the grating door, a woman in the white, airy costume of the land, a perfect vision of beauty, tall, and shaped like a Venus, with a fortune of raven black hair, eyes that sparkled when she spoke, with a voice of exquisite loveliness. If I could I would have insisted that I was then at the house I was hunting for; but I had to go, and after that, in my dreams I was a Spanish cavalier and serenaded beneath her casement—but I only do this in dreams. The lady's direction was correct, and I found a man, but had time to glance quickly at a Cuban residence.

The family carriage and coupé is kept in the archway that leads from the street, but the horses in the rear of the court. In the center of the court was a playing fountain with rich flowers blooming under its sprinkling waters; all around this court were wide galleries whence came the song of birds, and onto these galleries opened the family rooms—marble floors everywhere. The grand saloon parlor walls were hung with rich paintings, on the marble tiles were Oriental rugs, in the center a large one, about which the light fancy-wood chairs were placed in a hollow square. There was every evidence of luxurious ease within, but outside, the low walls might be taken for such as inclose a warehouse or cotton yard. But when one comes to the suburbs of Havana, then does the ideal tropic home come to view in all its luxurious loveliness. The Captain-General has a summer residence in the surburbs, where he resides from May to December, and the drive there is especially fine. While you are inspecting these villas, drive to Vedado, the Cerro and Tulipan, the fashionable residence districts, and, after these, extend the ride to the beautiful city of the dead. The cemetery is usually the last place you drive to, but I will bring it in here as one of pleasure, seeing there is to be no procession. The entrance to the cemetery and the chapel within the gates, are the most exquisite pieces of architecture of the kind to be found anywhere, and the whole cemetery is filled with tombs, monuments and statues that would adorn a Greenwood or a Spring Grove. The grounds are located on the hills west of the city, and besides the local beauty of the place command a fine view of the island and the sea.

When one has seen Havana, it is not all of Cuba by any means. The tourist, in justice to his own pleasure, must do Cuba by rail. First the suburban railways; a "dummy" train leaves from the sea front near La Punta, and runs along the shore to the suburbs, and extends to the cemetery.

The Marianao Railway extends west from Havana fifteen miles to Marianao (*Marry-ah-now*), a pretty little city of over 5,000 people, where there is a fine beach and excellent bathing, and near which are the famous Toledo sugar plantations, that may be visited by securing a permit from the manager in Havana.

The suburbs of Tulipan, Cerro, Ceiba, Buena Vista and Quemados, are all reached by the Marianao Railway.

La Prueba Railway and a branch of the Bahia Railway lead to the city of Guanabacoa, six miles east of Havana, cross by ferry to Regla, thence trains run half-hourly. Guanabacoa is one of the oldest towns in Cuba, and has a population of

42,000. One of the places of interest to visit is the garden "Las Delicias," a private garden, planted for the amusement and pleasure of its owner — strangers are always welcome. Cut flowers and plants may be bought, and there are all kinds known to the tropics. On the commutation trains between Havana and Guanabacoa you may buy a brass check instead of a ticket, drop it in a box, pass through a turn-style and get on board. There are no conductors.

The station of the Bahia Railway in Havana is at the Muelle de Luz, from whence passengers cross in ferry-boats, not unlike those in New York, to Regla, where there is a nice station, from which trains leave for eastern points in Cuba, and the ride is a most attractive one. The full name of the road is "Ferrocarril de la Bahia de la Habaña," meaning literally the "Railway of the Bay of Havana," and my notes say good track, good cars and fast time; and, if I remember right, a seat on the left-hand side is the best, but on both sides there is much to see. The road runs through a rich valley, with rolling hills covered with palms and cocoa trees on each side, rising to high mountains, that lift up in fantastic shapes like old Polonius' clouds in Hamlet, like a camel, or backed like a weasel, or like a whale — or like the old man of the mountains in the Catskills, all blue in the distance sometimes, and sometimes near at hand. Near the road are the low, thatched houses of the country people, built of palm logs, thatched with palm leaves, and weather-boarded with palm bark, with here and there the white house of the planter's home, or that of his manager.

The train makes fast time, and comes to the stations in rapid succession, stopping at each one, and, before it starts, a Chinaman stands on the platform and rings a dinner-bell, which is the Cuban for "all aboard." This same Chinaman acts as train-boy, and passes through the cars offering guava jelly and native cheese spread on plantain leaves, but no morning papers or yellow-back novels.

When the whistle sounds for Matanzas, a seat on the left will show the best view of the city, and, on the high hill beyond, the church of Montserrat, which overlooks the valley of the Yumuri, which, with the caves of Bella Mar, form the chief attractions.

The railway station at Matanzas is a fine building, and a much nicer station than is usually found in towns of the same size in America; by the way, you will read the signs in Cuba, and may not know what they mean. "*Boletines*" is over the ticket office, "*Equipages*" over the baggage-room, "*Señoras*" is over the door to the ladies' room, and "*Señores*" over that for gentlemen. Tickets are shown on entering the stations at Havana, punched by the conductor, and taken up by the gateman at Matanzas.

Matanzas is eighty-five miles from Havana, located on the bay at the junction of the San Juan and Yumuri Rivers, a city of the pure Cuban type, with narrow streets opening into plazas, low buildings, luxuriant trees and gardens, and good hotels withal. One goes to Matanzas to see the caves and the valley of the Yumuri. The journey may be made from Havana, and return to that city in a day, allowing time to visit the valley and the caves. A longer stay is desirable, but the average American is in a hurry, and this story is written to suit him. Consult the schedules of the railways without relying on this, for schedules change sometimes, even in Cuba.

Interpreters of the various hotels meet the trains on arrival at Matanzas, and will secure the volantas while you are at breakfast or securing rooms. The volanta is the easiest riding vehicle in the world; it rests on two wheels, the body of the volanta suspended on leather throughbraces, like a stage coach; long shafts of elastic wood connect with the horse; another horse, ridden by the driver, is attached outside the shafts. With this rig a ride over the hills of Cuba is the event of a lifetime. The horses start off at a full trot, and keep it up all the way, up hill and down. Leaving the hotel, the route is through the city, past the Plaza, the Palace, and the Casino, then through long, narrow streets of low houses to the hills outside the city, where a long, white road leads to the highest, on the top of which is the Church of Montserrat overlooking the beautiful valley, than which there is no more lovely view in all my world of travels; it is worth all the journey to Cuba to go and look at it; one does not drive through the valley, but to the hills that hedge it in, and enjoys the enchantment that distance lends.

The church stands on the top of the hill; and but for the stone walls that surround it one might fall and roll down the steep sides hundreds of feet; far below the little Yumuri river runs, no bigger than a brook; the white road winds about through the palms and up the hills on the other side; looking from the east wall, the city of Matanzas is in the near distance, the bay beyond, and further on the hills where the caves are.

The Church of Montserrat enjoys the fame of many miracles, and the grateful pilgrims who have sojourned here, and been cured, are numbered in legion; you may purchase a charm or relic at Montserrat that may have a talismanic effect on your future fortunes. The church is not an imposing structure; it is of a greenish hue, built of stone, surmounted by a cross; in front, under the trees, are four statues, with the inscriptions: Ledida, Taragona, Barcelona and Gerona. Inside are glass cases, containing relics and offerings made by pilgrims. On the walls are curious pictures; one depicts the wreck of a passenger train, the cars rolling down an embankment, reminding the traveler of the uncertainties of life, even on the best regulated railways.

This is one of the places it is hard to get away from; but, if we go back to Havana this afternoon, we must hurry on to the Caves of Bella Mar. The route is back through the city again, but by different streets. Passing over a bridge across the St. John, the road comes to the sea-shore, skirting the bay, and passing some beautiful suburban residences and the local summer resorts — then climbs the hills, about three miles, to where the caves are. I do not know whether the boundaries of the infernal regions come nearer the earth's surface at any one place; but, if they do, it must be near Bella Mar, and the caves may be a disused side entrance; the weather in the caves is of that summer nature to make one ask questions. Ladies, remove your wraps; leave them at the entrance. Gentlemen, the ladies will excuse you; take off your coats, and, unless your collar is celluloid, or you have an extra one, divest yourself of that too — because it's warm enough for you down-stairs — but, withal, a wonderful underground journey.

Guides with torches precede you down a flight of stairs. Thence on for a mile or so it is easy walking, through lofty chambers, dazzling in their decorations, ceilings hung with glittering stalactites, varying in size from my lady's finger to tons in weight, and like diamonds reflecting from their crystals a thousand hues. These are in fantastic shapes; some from their resemblances have acquired names — there is a "Mantle of Columbus;" a "Guardian Spirit;" and a piano composed of a series of small stalactites of different lengths, which, on being struck, give forth a melodious chord. There is a "Monkey Salon," suggesting a convention of frozen monkeys, evidently not frozen in the cave, though. There is a pool of water called the "Baño de la Inglesa," from the fact that an English lady tourist once bathed in its waters. The caves have never been fully explored; there are other chambers — at a point on the route is an opening, where a stone being thrown can be heard bounding from side to side till the sound is lost in the distance; and the guides say they never have gone as far as it is possible through the different openings. It is a mammoth cave that will compare with Kentucky's or Virginia's Luray.

Now, those who wish may return to Havana, and those who wish proceed to Cardenas, the very youngest city in Cuba, and its growth is something wonderful, there being now nearly 25,000 inhabitants. The city is located on a fine bay, is backed by a most fertile country, and contains a sugar refinery and other manufacturing interests., The train which leaves Regla (opposite Havana) in the morning, arrives at Cardenas about noon, a fast train over a good road, and passing through a country totally unlike any other I ever saw; a country of rolling hills with fertile sugar valleys in between; high mountains, not in long, continuous ranges, but sharp, abrupt peaks, whose sides appear almost perpendicular. Cardenas is the first city in Cuba to erect a statue to Columbus; this is, perhaps, because the ashes gave out; so many cities could not have ashes, and so Cardenas must have a statue. The journey by rail may be continued on through middle Cuba to Santo Domingo, Sagua, Santa Clara and to Cienfuegos, either of which cities may be reached by a twelve-hours daylight ride, that will show the American tourist more newness than he can get in any twelve in his own country. Starting from Havana on morning trains of either the Bahia or Havana Railroads, arrival can be made at either of the places before nightfall.

The railway system of Cuba extends over the central portion of the island, traversing the fertile interior, touching the northern coast at Havana, Matanzas, Cardenas and Concha, and the southern shore at Batabano and Cienfuegos.

La Linea de la Compania de Caminos de Hierro de la Habana is a long name, meaning the Havana Railway.

The road starts from *Villa Nueva* station, Havana, runs eastward to Matanzas and Union, connecting there with other lines for interior and coast cities. It is a fine railway, and well equipped. Tourists who have not time for further rail journeys, should go over one line to Matanzas and return by the other. This company has a line west from Havana to Guanajay, and southward to Batabano and the south coast, crossing the island at one of the narrowest parts, being only thirty-one miles. The run from Havana is made in one hour and twenty minutes; pretty good time, considering the ten stops and the slow entrance to Havana, where it is required that a man on horseback must ride between the rails in front of the engine from the limits to Villa Nueva, the city station. Batabano is the port where the steamships sail for Santiago de Cuba, The Isle of Pines, Vuelta-Abajo and other ports on the south coast on regular days, which change sometimes, and the sailing dates will not be written down.

The Isle of Pines is about seventy-five miles from Batabano, and requires about eight hours' sail. Trains leave Havana in the morning, arriving at Batabano an hour and a half later, arriving per steamer at the Isle of Pines in the afternoon. The island is noted principally for its fine woods — mahogany, redwood, ebony, rosewood and other valuable timbers; pines, of course, hence its name. It is truly the most tropical place within easy American reach; all tropical birds, animals and reptiles abound in the forests. There are mineral springs on the island which enjoy a local reputation for their curative qualities. From the Isle of Pines also comes a valuable marble in various colors. Altogether a most interesting tour to make.

Santiago de Cuba is the chief city of eastern Cuba, and is the capital of the State of Santiago de Cuba, and, of course, the residence of the civil governor and the church functionaries, located on the south shore on one of the finest bays, in the midst of a fine coffee and sugar region, for which it is the shipping point. Near Santiago are also the celebrated iron ore beds and copper mines, most favorably known for their excellent qualities; ores which are shipped to the United States and other parts of the world. The metal deposits are pronounced very rich, and are attracting the attention of our capitalists. The mines are worked now by native companies, but not to their fullest capacity nor to the best advantage.

As yet, Santiago de Cuba cannot be reached by rail from Havana; the tourist for that point must sail from Batabano, Cienfuegos or from Havana and around the island.

The line running west from Havana is called the Ferrocarril del Oeste. Trains leave Cristina station, Havana, in the morning, and, returning in the evening, give the hurrying American time to make the tour in a day, and travel through the famous tobacco regions. It is a curious fact that all the finest tobacco in the world should be grown in so small a country as Cuba, but still more curious that it should be confined to so small a portion of that country — and it is well worth while to make the little trip necessary, to see where grows the weed the fragrance of whose blue smoke is the delight and talk and solace of two hemispheres.

Morning trains from Havana connect at Paso Real with stages and volantas for the mineral springs and baths of San Diego de los Baños, noted for wonderful cures of rheumatism, paralysis and diseases of the blood. The resort is called the Cuban Saratoga, and is largely patronized by wealthy natives both for health and pleasure; there are ample hotel accommodations. The stage or volanta ride is only nine miles from Paso Real on the main line of the West Railroad.

The scenery along the line is lovely in the extreme, and the added attractions of the tobacco regions give another subject to talk on at home — you can tell them you saw where the cigars grow.

After "doing" the capital and near-by cities the tourist should recollect that Havana, with its 300,000 inhabitants, is not the whole island of Cuba, which is nearly 750 miles in length, and contains a population of 1,600,000 souls. Besides a number of small towns and villages, there are fourteen cities with populations exceeding 20,000 each.

The manners and customs of the Cubans are in many cases peculiar, but always pleasing. They have maintained a good name for courtesies and kindness to strangers. If you admire anything that belongs to a Cuban, he says it is at your service; if you call at his house, he says, in his words of welcome, "this house is yours;" but it would hardly be proper to ask him to make out the deeds till you call again.

Cuban ladies possess a beauty above the average pretty woman, and are modest withal. They do not go out alone or receive gentlemen unless in the presence of a duenña or older member of the family. 'Tis well; for it always seemed to me that those great black eyes and long lashes, drooping on pretty cheeks with such lips as theirs, could do a world of mischief, and, if left alone and untrammeled, break up whole families. Their costumes are most bewitching, all light and airy. They wear no hats or bonnets, but, instead, the lace mantilla, hanging in graceful folds from their inky hair — a black mantilla for the street, and a white one for the theater — bless 'em for that one fact alone — no hats at the theater. The milliner's is an undiscovered art in Cuba, and she would starve to death if she depended on the patronage of the ladies there.

I have often wondered how a Cuban lover ever got a chance to say his pretty talks and tell his sweetheart what was his opinion of her; but, when I went to a ball and saw the "*Danza*," I ceased to wonder. In the maneuvers of that slow and peculiar dance he has the best chance in the world, a man can dance the *Danza* with but one woman at a time, and the *Danza* is danced by the hour. I think its duration is only measured by the endurance of the musicians. The *Danza* is not a polka, nor a schottische; more of a waltz, with the time and steps divided by about eight; it is hardly even a dance, but a slow walk around, and, though not fatiguing, with frequent stoppages, I think not to rest, but to talk. The positions of the dancers are the same as in a waltz, and give ample opportunity for extended embraces to slow music, and here it is that I have figured it out that the Cuban lover has his opportunity.

The fêtes and balls are largely attended, and the people seem to devote their energies to complete enjoyment, and they last till sunshine dims the gaslight. The people go to church early in the morning, but the balance of the day is devoted to pleasure.

The ladies go shopping on wheels, and do not, as a general thing, get out of the carriage at the stores, the goods being brought out for their inspection, and, if satisfactory, the goods are taken home, and, I suppose, the bill sent to Papa.

Business men take coffee at home in the morning, breakfast down town about our lunch time, and dine at home after business hours; it sounds queer to go into an office at noon and be told the party inquired for has gone to breakfast.

On account of the climate, I suppose, nobody seems in a hurry in Cuba, and many people look tired; I saw a cart backed up to a front door, it was loaded with brick, a negro piled up four bricks in the end of the cart, and waited for a Chinaman to carry them in, and thus after a while unloaded his cart. I suppose some man in the back yard (like Paddy's man at the top of the scaffold, where he carried bricks) did all the work. The average costume of the laborers is a knit shirt and a pair of overalls, whether it's December or May.

Everything goes in and out the front door of an Havana house. Marketing goes in and garbage goes out. Horses and carriages use the same entrance the guests do.

Horses carry instead of draw their burdens. If you see green objects coming down the street, don't imagine that "Burnham wood has come to Dunsinane." There are little horses under those piles of green fodder.

I saw tandem teams of eight horses and donkeys to one two-wheeled cart. Mules and horses wear heavy woolen head-dresses of tassels as protection against the sun, and oxen wear their yokes on the back of their heads just aft the horn, and some of them do business as switch engines in the depot yards.

People get "broke" in Cuba just as they do here at home, perhaps more so, as the government undertakes to do the pawnbroker's business; so, if you have anything to put up, the Queen of Spain will act as your uncle, or, more properly, your aunt. Money would seem hard to get in Cuba, and also that many people desire to get it, as it is common to see armed soldiers in the entry and the corridors of the bank — but perhaps they are only there to look after the cashiers; that would be a good idea in some American banks, and likely reduce the tide of travel to Canada.

POINTERS ON CUBAN RAILWAY TRAVEL.

The different railways publish folders or time cards in Spanish, but it is easy to understand them — the names of stations of course are the same in English, so are time figures; then it is only necessary to know that mañana means morning, and *tarde*, afternoon; *tarifa* is the tariff, and *precios* the price of tickets, both terms being used; *hora* is the hour, and *minutos* the minutes; *trenes* means the trains and *linea* the line; now take the folder and read it, the lesson is easy.

There are first, second and third class cars with a different rate of fare for each car, for instance, the first-class fare from Havana to Matanzas is $4.25; second, $3, and third, $1.75.

Tickets must be purchased before entering the cars. Conductors punch the tickets, but do not take them up; the agent at the destination does that.

On all the main lines, there are good accommodations, the track is good, and the trains make fast time. The following are some rules in force:

The sale of tickets will be closed five minutes before departure of trains.

Tickets only good for date stamped on.

Babies free.

Children to seven years old will pay half-fare, employés to decide the age. A child without a ticket will pay full fare.

Passengers must show their tickets as many times as so exacted by the conductor.

Passengers without tickets will pay one-third additional for first tract, and the total afterward, from point of departure.

If trains do not arrive on time, passengers can desist from their trip, price of tickets being refunded.

Employés of the train can eject passengers without tickets, unwilling to pay their fare, or behaving improperly, and, in case of resistance, to be delivered to the authorities.

Passengers losing a ticket must pay its price till justification of loss.

THE POLITICAL OUTLOOK FOR CUBA.

The political situation improved apace since the advent of the Liberal party in Spain to power, under the leadership of Sagasta. The autonomic aspirations of the natives are, however, far from realization. The right of assembly, a free press, religious toleration, civil registration and marriages, and complete emancipation from priest rule on the question of burying grounds, are no longer a myth but realities. A civil Governor-General is likely soon to be appointed to supersede Marin, whose usefulness has terminated. Native civil judges have also been recently appointed to preside over the courts where trials by juries are to be had, though on a more restricted scale than in Anglo-Saxon countries. The war issue of currency, amounting to ten millions, is to be canceled from the proceeds of a loan negotiated for the purpose in Madrid by the government. The electric light for streets and parks will soon be in operation, under the management of the Spanish Gas Light Company. The unfinished Vento Aqueduct is under way, and, when finished, will endow the city with an excellent and unlimited water supply.

AMERICAN GOODS SUITABLE FOR MEXICAN AND WEST INDIA MARKETS.

The inexperienced American who desires to open trade with South and Central America is naturally anxious to know what are the most desirable and suitable goods, of our manufacture, for those markets. For the benefit of such inquirers we have prepared the following list of articles, which, among some few others, will almost always find a ready sale in the above countries:

Agricultural implements and tools.
Alcohol.
Apples.
Brushes — toilet, clothes and horse.
Biscuits and crackers.
Baby carriages.
Boots and shoes, mainly for ladies and misses.
Billiard tables.
Brads and tacks.
Bells, for churches and plantations.
Butter, in earthen pots and tins.
Beef, salt and smoked.
Clocks, all styles and grades.
Carriages, buggies, victorias, phaetons.
Cutlery, all kinds.
Chairs and rockers.
Canned goods, oysters and meats in particular.
Corrugated iron.
Cotton goods.
    " prints.
    " sheeting.
    " shirtings.
Chemicals, general.
    " photographic.
Crackers and biscuit.
Drugs, prepared, ground and fluid extracts.
Druggists' glassware.
Drills, for mining and blasting.
Dental instruments and supplies.
Electric apparatus and supplies.
Fire-proof and burglar safes.
Fire extinguishers.
    " engines, hand and steam.
Flour.
Farinaceous preparations.
Furniture, every description.
    " school.
Fish, salted.
    " smoked.
Gas fixtures.
Gas-making machines.

Guns and pistols.
Gunpowder.
Hay, in bales.
Harness.
Horses, stylish, for family carriages.
Horse cars.
Hams, bacon, tongues.
Ink, printing.
" writing.
Iron ships and boats.
Jewelry, cheap grades.
Knitting machines.
Kerosene oil, in cans.
" lamps.
Leather and morocco.
Lumber, every description of pine.
Lard, in earthen jars and cans.
Locomotive engines.
Machinery, all descriptions.
" and lubricating oils.
Nails, all kinds.
Oysters, canned.
Patent medicines.
Pianos and organs.
Pails, wooden and paper.
Paints, dry and mixed.
Paper, for printing.
" writing and wrapping.
" bags.
Printing presses.
Potatoes.
Pork, salted.
Provisions, general.
Railway cars and supplies.
Sewing machines.
Saws, straight and circular.
Scales, weights and measures.
Saddlery hardware.
Starch.
Stoves, cooking, oil and coal.
Shooks and headings.
Steam pumps.
Surgical instruments.
Soap, family.
Tobacco, plug, chewing and smoking.
Tools, hand and machine, all kinds.
Tubs and pails, wooden and paper.
Type and printers' material.
Wagons, for farming and mining.
Windmills.
Washing machines and wringers.
Woodenware and brooms.
Watches, gold and silver.

BUSINESS HINTS AND POINTERS FOR COMMERCIAL TRAVELERS VISITING CUBA.

STEAMER LINES FROM THE UNITED STATES.

PLANT STEAMSHIP LINE from Tampa, Fla., tri-weekly, connecting with through express trains from New York and all important cities.

WARD'S LINE from New York, weekly, direct to Havana.

SPANISH TRANS-ATLANTIC LINE, New York to Havana, every week.

MORGAN'S LINE from New Orleans to Punta Gorda, Cedar Key, Key West and Havana, every two weeks.

STEAMSHIP CONNECTIONS IN CUBA.

TRANS-ATLANTIC LINES.

TRANS-ATLANTIC CO.—Lopez Line—Leave Havana 5th and 25th of each month for Cadiz and Barcelona; 15th, for Corurna, Santander and Havre—San Juan, P. R., being a port of call. Agent, M. Calvo, 28 Officios street.

FRENCH MAIL S. S. CO.—Leave Havana 15th each month for St. Nazaire; calling at San Juan, P. R., and St. Thomas. Agents, Bridat & Co., 23 St. Ignacio street.

ROYAL MAIL—English—Leave Havana every four weeks for Jamaica, connecting with steamers for Southampton; calling at San Juan, P. R., and St. Thomas. Agent, G. R. Ruthven, 16 Officios street.

HAVANA, PUERTO RICO AND ST. THOMAS.

HERRERA LINE—Leave Havana 10th, 20th, 30th each month for St. Thomas; calling at Santiago de Cuba, San Domingo, Ponce, Mayaguez, Aquadilla and San Juan. Steamer on the 10th goes via Porto Plata, and, returning, calls at Port Au Prince. Agents, Ramon de Herrera, 26 Pedro street.

HAVANA, PUERTO RICO, VENEZUELA AND PANAMA.

TRANS-ATLANTIC CO.—Formerly Lopez Line—Leave Havana the latter part of each month; calling at Nuevitas, Gibara, Santiago de Cuba, Mayaguez, San Juan, Ponce, La Guaira (Caracas), Porto Cabello, Savanilla and Cartagena. Agents, M. Calvo & Co., 28 Officios street.

HAVANA, SANTIAGO DE CUBA AND PANAMA.

TRANS-ATLANTIC CO.—Formerly Lopez Line—Leaves Havana 19th each month for Santiago de Cuba, Cartagena and Colon; returning via Savanilla, Porto Cabello, La Guaira (Caracas) and Santiago de Cuba. Agents, M. Calvo & Co., 28 Officios street.

HAVANA AND VERA CRUZ.

TRANS-ATLANTIC CO.—Lopez Line—Leave Havana 10th, 20th and 30th each month for Vera Cruz; calling at Progreso. Agents, M. Calvo & Co., 28 Officios street.

FRENCH MAIL S. S. CO.—Leave Havana 6th of each month for Vera Cruz. Agents, BRIDAT & Co., 3 Amargura street.
ROYAL MAIL—English—Leave Havana monthly for Vera Cruz. Agent, G. R. RUTHVEN, 16 Officios street.

HAVANA AND JAMAICA.

ROYAL MAIL—English—Leave Havana for Kingston every fourth week from January 25th. Agent G. R. RUTHVEN, 16 Officios street.

HAVANA AND CUBAN PORTS.

COASTWISE LINES—Leave Havana every few days for Cardenas, Sagua, Caibarien, Nuevitas, Port Padre, Gibara, Mayari, Baracoa, Guantanamo and Santiago de Cuba; also every Saturday for Bahia Honda, San Gayetano and Malas Aguas.

BATABANO AND SOUTH SIDE PORTS.

COASTWISE LINES—Leave Batabano Sundays for Cienfuegos, Trinidad, Tunas, Jacaro, Sta. Cruz, Manzanillo and Santiago de Cuba; Wednesday, for Cienfuegos, Trinidad and Tunas; Thursdays, for Colon, Punta de Cartas and Bailenny Cortes; Saturdays, for Colona and Colon.
STEAMER—Leaves Batabano for the Isle of Pines every Sunday.

SANTIAGO DE CUBA AND ST. THOMAS.

FRENCH S. S. LINE—Leaves Santiago de Cuba first of every month for St. Thomas and the French Islands; calling at Jacmel, San Domingo and San Juan, P. R.
SANTIAGO DE CUBA AND GUANTANAMO, semi-weekly, on Sunday and Thursday.

Passengers traveling in Cuba are only allowed, free, a hat-box, valise or satchel 24 inches long, by 12 wide and 9 high. All other baggage to go in the baggage-car paying freight.
Traveling on the platforms strictly prohibited.
No animals allowed on the first-class car, except fighting cocks in their baskets.
In other cars, muzzled dogs and six chickens are tolerated, paying freight.
Fire-arms to go in the baggage-room.
No colored persons allowed in the first-class cars.
No packages allowed containing fish or ice in such a state as to annoy passengers.
The delivery of baggage will be made upon presentation of the check by order of numbers.
$50 will be paid for a trunk lost, $20 for a valise or satchel, and hat-boxes $4.
The fractions of money will be charged as wholes by the company.

TRAVELING IN CUBA.

THE CUSTOM HOUSE OFFICIALS are very liberal and courteous gentlemen, far more so than the average American custom house inspector. You declare your baggage—which is opened on long forms or counters, instead of on the floor, as is customary here—state, orally, that there is nothing but your personal effects, and nothing dutiable, a hasty look at contents of baggage, to carry out the law, no mauling and spilling of your effects, the thing is done, and you may go on your way rejoicing. There are no delays at the Custom House examining office, the officers being always on hand to examine and pass passengers' baggage as expeditiously as possible.
HOTELS—There are several excellent and commodious hotels in Havana, the lead-

ing hotels being the Grand Hotel *Telegrafo*, the Grand Hotel *Pasaje*, and the Grand Hotel *Inglaterra*, with three excellent second-rate houses, known respectively as the *Perla de Cuba*, the *Saratoga* and the *Mascotte*. At the three leading houses the very best accommodations, with modern improvements, and unusually excellent fare, can be obtained at reasonable prices, the rate per day, including meals and attendance, being from $3 to $5, gold, according to size and location of room.

The attendance at the Havana hotels is very prompt, and generally excellent. Chambermaids are never seen, that is, by the male guests, men being employed for that service. Of course, there are female servants who attend on the lady guests of the house. The Cuban bell-boy is quite an institution. He is usually very bright, always prompt and very useful. The bell-boy does not wait in the office, but is located on the floor which he attends. When you ring he does not have to tramp up four flights to find what you want, tramp down and then back again to your room.

Coffee, with biscuit and fruit, is served, in your room or in the dining-room, from early morning until breakfast, which is on from nine until twelve o'clock. Dinner is served from five to eight o'clock. Only two regular meals per day. The dining-rooms of the best hotels are spacious, elegantly fitted up and very invitingly located on the ground floor, open to the street, and surrounded with tropical plants and flowers.

The bed-rooms of the Cuban hotel are a novelty. The floors are tiled, with soft rugs in front of the bed, dresser and toilet stands. The bedsteads are usually of brass or iron, highly ornamented. Hair mattresses, or in fact upholstered mattresses of any kind, are the exception, not the rule. The beds are furnished with close-woven wire mattresses or springs, over which a comforter is laid, and with snowy sheets, coverlet and long bolster instead of pillow, your bed is made. Everything is kept clean, nice and orderly at all times.

As a rule, the waiters and servants in the best Cuban hotels, unlike those in our country, do not expect, and are not continually on the *qui vive* for "tips;" and it is just as well not to create by encouraging the desire. The Cuban hotel waiter (the majority of whom, by the way, speak English and French as well as their native tongue) is content to serve you well, and await your pleasure in compensating him when you take your departure. At the close of your sojourn at the hotel, if you feel disposed to compensate your waiter or your bell-boy (who is also your chambermaid and general servant), you need not tax your generosity beyond the sum of one dollar to each, which amount is considered a liberal "tip."

SPEAKING SPANISH.

The commercial traveler who visits any Spanish-American country and cannot converse freely in the language of the country labors under the greatest disadvantage. He may employ an interpreter, but the interpreter will prove of but little or no practical assistance, as it is impossible for one to expatiate to advantage on the merits and quality of one's goods and wares, unless the salesman is able to do it himself directly to the buyer.

If you cannot speak the language you will perhaps get along quite as well, if not better, without the services of an interpreter, trusting to chance that your customer speaks English, which many of them do, and especially will this be found the case among the larger dealers and more prominent merchants.

Make it a point to ask more for your goods than you expect to receive, as the best merchants are sure to barter with you and beat you down, even if you were to offer your goods at bottom prices at the start. The same rule holds good in buying of them; they never expect you to pay the price they ask.

DELMAR'S

CLASSIFIED

TRADES DIRECTORY

OF

MEXICO,

CENTRAL AMERICA AND WEST INDIES.

1889-90.

INDEX

TO

DELMAR'S TRADES DIRECTORY.

REPUBLIC OF MEXICO.   PAGE.

Acapulco	60
Aguas Calientes	60
Campeche	62
Carmen	65
City of Mexico	45
Chilpanzingo	60
Chihuahua	62
Colima	64
Chiapas	65
Cordoba	66
Cuernavaca	66
Coahuila	67
Ciudad Guerrero	68
Durango	68
Guaymas	69
Guadalajara	70
Guanajuato	73
Hermosillo	76
Irapuato	76
Jimenez	77
Jalapa	77
Leon	78
Matamoros	80
Merida	80
Morelia	83
Monterey	84
Mazatlan	86
Oaxaca	87
Orizaba	87
Paso del Norte	90

	PAGE.
Pachuca	90
Puebla	93
Queretaro	98
Salamanca	99
Saltillo	100
San Juan Bautista	101
Salvatierra	102
San Luis Potosi	103
Toluca	106
Vera Cruz	107
Valle de Santiago	111
Villa Lerdo	111
Zacatecas	113

COSTA RICA.

San José	119
Alajuela	121

GUATEMALA.

Guatemala	121
Quezaltenango	126

HONDURAS.

Amapala	128
Comayagua	127
Tegucigalpa	127
Trujillo	128
Yuscaran	128

NICARAGUA.

Chinandega	132
Grenada	133
Leon	130
Managua	130
Rivas	130

UNITED STATES OF COLOMBIA.

Bogotá	135
Cartagena	141
Medellin	142
Panama	144
Socorro	146

SAN SALVADOR.

City of San Salvador	147
San Miguel	148
Santana	149

	PAGE
ISLAND OF CUBA.	150
Cardenas	163
Cienfuegos	166
Gibara	168
Guanabacoa	169
Guantanamo	171
Havana	150
Manzanillo	172
Matanzas	173
Neuvitas	176
Pinar del Rio	177
Puerto Principe	178
Sagua la Grande	180
San Juan de los Remedios	181
Santa Clara	182
Santiago de Cuba	184
Planters and Plantations of Cuba	186
ANTIGUA	210
DEMERARA	212
JAMAICA	217
NEW PROVIDENCE	222
PORTO RICO	224
Aguadilla	227
Arecibo	228
Guyama	229
Mayaguez	230
Ponce	231
San Juan	224
SANTA CROIX	234
SANTO DOMINGO	235
ST. THOMAS	236
ST. LUCIA	237
ST. VINCENT	239
TRINIDAD	240

The population of the following cities in the Republic of Mexico should read :

City	Population	City	Population
City of Mexico,	300,000	Mazatlan,	35,000
Durango,	20,000	Salamanca,	12,000
Hermosillo,	20,000	Salvatierra,	12,000
Leon,	100,000	Zacatecas,	75,000

"Metamoros" should read *Matamoros*.

TRADES DIRECTORY.

REPUBLIC OF MEXICO.

CITY OF MEXICO.
Population, 255,000.

Agricultural Implements.
(See also Hardware and Tools.)
Carlos Becerer, 2 Balvanera
Roberto Boker y Ca., 4 Pte. Espiritu Santo
Bowes, Scott, Read, Campbell & Co., 13 San Augustin
Charreton Hermanos, 24 Revillagigedo
Alberto Malo y Ca., 6 Puente Santa Ana
Rapp Sommer y Ca., 4 Palma
José Maria del Rio, 6 Palma
A. Guthiel, 13 Palma
Hoffmann Hermanot, 10 Donceles
Leffmann y hijos, 12 Palma
S. Lhose, 12 San Augustin
Wexel y Degress, 5 Plateros
E. Badoin y Ca., Delicias
Hulvershorn y Ca., 1 and 2 Monterilla
Alijandro Jacot, 4 Plateros
José Maria del Rio, 6 Palma
D. Ulrick y Ca., 22 Juan Manuel
J. Arce, 1 San Francisco
F. Adams (successor of), 45 de Mayo
Guillermo Dorn y Ca., 5 de Mayo
German Garth, 19 Tlapoleros, T. 324
Guillermo Lhose y Ca. (successors de), 9 Palma
N. Y. Plow Co., Plaza de Guardiola
Charreton Hnos, 24 Revillagigedo
Juan White, 4 Revillagigedo

Ales and Beer.
(See also Groceries and Provisions.)
Roberto Blackmore, Exacordada
Bernardo Bolgard, 5 Segunda Fila Seca
Carlos Frendenhagen, 12 Rinconada de S. Diego
Felix Barrey, Callejon de Aranda
Elias Durand, 4 Alconedo
Federico Herroys, Plazuela de la Candelarita
Vicente Landin, 20a de Guerreso
Dreher y Ca.
F. Herzog

Arms and Ammunition.
Alfredo Boche, 1½ Espiritu Santo
C. Carrion, 1 S. Bernardo
M. Mendiola y Ca., S. José el Real
C. Morel, 11 Refugio
Fernando Pagliri, 9 Zuleta
D. Sanchez, 10 Balvanera
Urbarrena y Quintana, St. Clara
Wexel y De Gress, 5 Plateros

Arms, Etc.—*continued.*
Patricio Aizpuru, 16 S. Agustin
Ramon Alva, 26 Alvarado
Joaquin Alvarado, 4 Avenida Juarez
Modesto Alvarez
Antonio Andrade, 26 Arcos de Belen
José Anzoutegai, 3 Empedradillo
Manuel Aranzubia, 26 Acequia
Joaquin Arena, S S. Lorenzo
Alejandro Argandar, 13 Cadena

Army Contractors.
For Arms, Ammunition, Clothing, Shoes, Etc., for Federal Army and National Guard, Etc.

T. L. Garcia, 15 Pte. San Francisco
Juan Llamedo, 15 San Agustin
Ignacio Pombo, 7 San Felipe Neri

Architects, Etc.
Juan Agea, 23 Acequia
Ramon Agea, 23 Acequia
Luis Anzonera, 6 Aguila
Manuel Alvarez, 22 Chavarria
Angel Angeuano, 4 Santa Ines
Juan Bustillo, 7 San Francisco
Manuel Gargollo, 10 San Andres
Refugio Gonzalez, 2 Primera San Roman
Ignacio Dosamantes, 2 San Cosme
Manuel Fernandez, 3 Cordobanes
Francisco Garay, 11 Independencia
Juan Cardona, 5 Alfaro
Manuel Conto, 11 Primero Sto. Domingo
Manuel Calderon, 20 San Felipe Jesus
José Collado, 15 San Agustin
Emilio Dondé, 6 y 7 Canoa
Enrique Grifos, 1 San Juan de Dios
Eusebio de la Hidalga, 12 Mariscala
Ignacio de la Hidalga, 12 Puente Mariscala
Ventura Heredia, 11 Primera San Ramon
Ramon Ibarrola, Colonia Arquitectos
J. M. Iglesias, En Puebla
Manuel Llera, 2 Humbolt
Vicente Manero, 6 Perpetua
Eluterio Mendez, 3 Nuevo Mexico
Miguel O. Gorman, 15 Tadre Lecuona
Manuel Patino, 20 Guleta
Francisco Paredes, 1 Santa Clara
Manuel Rincon, Guerrero
José Rego, 5 Estampa de la Merced
Francisco Somera, 9 Santa Clara

(45)

Architects, Etc.—continued.

Mariano Soto, 6 2a Indio Triste
Toriga Torres, 6 2a India Triste
Mariano Tellez, 8 Violeta
Apolnio Tellez, 15 Arcos San Agustin
Francisco Vera, 7 Escalerillas
Estanislao Velazco, Secretaria de Fomento

Banks.

Banco de Londres Mexico y Sud America
Banco Nacional de Mexico
Banco Hipotecario Mexicano
Banco de Empleados (Official Clerk's Bank)
Monté de Piedad (Loaner's Bank)

Bankers.

Barron, Forbes y Ca., 9 la S. Francisco
Bermejillo y Ca., 10 Capulhinas
E. Benecke y Ca. (Successor), 7 Capuchinas
P. Martin
Benfiel y Brecker, 2 Iturbide
Struk Bone y Ca., 10 San Agustin
J. R. Cardena y Ca. (Successor), 1-2 Betlemitas
Viuda de Escalante, 1 2a San Francisco
Escandon hnos., 11 Capuchinas

Bedsteads, Iron and Brass.

Leonardo Fortuny, 22 Tacuba
F. Gandry, 6 Gante
Luis Linet, 14 Spiritu Santo
Mata Antonio Lopez, 11 Ortega
Eutimio Zapata, 4 Pte. del Correo Mayor
Manzaneda y Inestrillas, 8 2a de la Monterilla

Billiards.

P. Bermejillo, Hotel Agustin
G. Boyrie, 3 Independencia
Juan Buclon, 1 Independencia
Manuel A. Gonzalez, 13 San Francisco
Iglesias y Ca., San Francisco
C. Recamier, Hotel San Cárlos
Schesneau y Ca., 14 Coliseo Viejo
Zivy y Ca., Hotel de Iturbide
S. Clemente, 3 Tacuba
George Delahaye, Independencia
Heclion Clare, Coliseo Viejo
Velez y Velazco, 20 Escalerfllas
Ambrosio Sanchez, Gante 7 S. Fco.
Uhink hnos y Zahn, 9 San Francisco

Blacksmiths, Etc.

Lorenzo Aguilar, 16 San Andrés
Gregorio Aguirre, 1 Canoa
Geronimo Alguisira, Misericordia
Manuel Avilla, 15 Vizcainas
Juan Baez, 13 Espl. de S. Andres
Felipe Balderrama, 3 Ratas
Manuel Blancas, 2 Alconedo
Juan Bonilla, 30 Pte. Quebrado
José Claire. 4 Guatimotzin
Juan Claire, 11 Guatimotzin
Julian Calzada, 8 S. Juan de Dios
Claudio Codean, 25 Lopez
Filomena Diaz, 27 Aguila
Julian Dieguez, 6 Arco de S. Augustin
Mateo Flores, S. Lorenzo
Cornelio Fonte, 6 Pte. de Gallos
Manuel Garcia, 1 Cerra da de Jesus
Simon Garcia, 12 Nuevo Méjico
Francisco Garrido, D. Amargura.

Pédro Gaudry, 7 Gante
Angel Gonzalez, 13 Montialegre
Luciano Guzman, 4 Alconedo
Pedro Hernandez, Puerta Falso de St. Domingo
Antonio Jimenez, 3 de S. Pablo
Martin Jimenez, 4 Correo Mayor
Pedro Leprince, 6 Nuevo Méjico
A. Lopez, Mata, 29 Ortega
Lorenzo Martinez, 8 del Degollado
Pascual Mondoza, 3 Estampa de San Andrés
J. M. Mercado, 8 Carzuela
Luis Morales, 5 Cerrado de Jesus
Desiderio Naranjo, 14 Cocheras
M. Ogamachea, 4 Parque del Conde
Florentino Oliver, 6 Chiquihuiteras
Miguel Ordonez, 6 Quemada
Francisco Pozo, 22 S. Lorenzo
Sucesor de Richaud, Zuleta
Vicinte Rodriguez, 2 Providencia
José Maria Romero, 8 Estanco de Mujeres
Viuda de Rossemberg, 13 S. Francisco
Roque Ruiz, 2 Perpétua
M. G. Salgado, 5 Mina
Francisco Sanchez, 4 Comonfort
Joaquin Silva, frente la Academia
Ventura Solis, 13 de S. Pablo
Prospero Torrejoh, 25 Zaragoza
Domingo Vargas, 3½ Estampa de Balvanera
Espiridion Vasquez, 6 Puesto Nuevo
J. M. Vergara, de Amargura
Manuel Zuñiga, 22 Misericordia

Booksellers and Stationers.

Vincente Martinez, 4 Monterilla
Gregorio Palacio, Cinco de Mayo
José Ramirez, 3 Espiritu Santo
Ricardo Saenz, 3 Plateros
C. Sanchez, 7 Pte. del Espiritu Santo
Fedrico Vaugier, 9 S. Francisco
A. Bernard, 9 Tacuba
Guillermo Dorn, Cinco de Mayo
Mariono Galvez, 11 1a Sto. Domingo
Kauser y Martin, 7 Espiritu Santo
Fredrico Ludert, Profesa
J. Ortega, 11 Santo Domingo
Treuber Hermanos, 14 Cadena
Francisco Abadiano, 17 Escalerillas
Aguilar y Ortiz, 6 Primera Sto. Domingo
Andrade, Viuda de, 4 Portal de Agustinos
Andrade y Soriano, 10 Joya
Ballesca y Ca., Callejon de Amor de Dios
N. Budin, 2 Segunda S. Francisco
Juan Buxo y Ca., 4 Portal del Aguila de Oro
M. Cambeses y Ca., 8 Tacuba
Ramon Cuero, 3 Seminario
Nabor Chavez, Portal del Aguila de Oro
Dublau y Ca., 3 Segunda Plateros
L. Duarta, 8 San José el Real
Jesus Herrara, Portal de Agustinos
J. F. Jens, 22 San José Real
E. Murguia, 18 y 19 Flamencos
Rafael Ortega y Vasquez, 11 Primera Sto. Domingo
Valdes y Cueva, 3 San José el Real
Vicente Villada, 8 Primera Reloj
Juan Canals, 3 Portal de Agustinos
Carlos Buret, 14 Cinco de Mayo
Carlos Tamborrel, 9 San Ildefonso
Francisco de Leon Diaz, 18 San José el Real
Juan de la Parres Fuente 11 Chiguis
Adrian de Garay, 6 Pepetua

Booksellers, Etc.—continued.

H. P. Hamilton, 1 Vegara
Antonio R. Urrea, 6 Cinesde Mayo
Carlos Vincourt, 5 Espiritu Santo
F. P. Hoeck, 13 San Francisco
Joaquin Nicolau, 5 Espiritu Santo
E. Portu, Cincode Mayo
José Rioy Revira, 14 Puente Quebrado

Bookbinders.

Antonio Arroyo, S½ Perpétua
Jesus Calvillo, Esclavo
Andrés Castillo, 16 S. José el Real
Alejandro Freire, 8 Moneda
Mariano Galvez, 16 S. Lorenzo
M. Guerra, 4 Cinco de Mayo, 4
Celso Jara, 15 Zuleta
Jesus Machuca, 21 Medinas
Filomeno Mata, S. Andrés
Parres y Ca., Independencia
José Rodriguez, 7 Cordobanes
Ricardo Sainz, 4 Plateros
Miguel Torner, 6 S. Lorenzo
C. Vargas Machuca, 3 Reloj
Leon F. de Diaz, 10 Callejon Santa Clara
Alejandro Marcué, 18 Tiburcio

Boot and Shoe Dealers, Retail.

Andrés Acevedo, 10 Coliseo
Jorge Araujo, 7 Reloj
A. Arellano, 10 Seminario
Pablo Carrillo, 11 Ortega
R. Castellanos, Victora E.
Gabriel Chacon, 11 Coliseo
F. Davalos, 11 Seminario
Agustin Delgado, 1 S. Juan
Felipe Flores, 7 S. Francisco
Jesus Gonzalez, 18 Sta. Clara
Salvador Guardarrama, 8 Vegara
A. Hurtado, 6 Portacoeli
Jesus Leite, 8 Monterilla
Diego Leon, 10 Seminario
Alejandro Mendez, 16 Vergara
Jesus Nuñez, 4 S. Juan de Dios
Pedro Ordoñez, 17 Vergara
M. Pascual, 3 Espiritu Santo
Santa A. Pietra, 10 S. Hipolito
Luis Portron, 16 Refugio
J. Buenrostro, 7 Segunda Reloj
Sabino Nuñez, Damas y Ortega
Pichardo y Ca., 19 Santa Clara
Santa Maria y Ca., 1 Primera Indio Triste
M. Segura, 19 Aguila
Sevilla y Villagran, Segunda Reloj y Monte Alegre
Canuto Sigales, 7 Vergara
Sobrinho y Garcia, Vergara y Cinco de Mayo
Francisco Trejo, 6 Segunda S. Francisco
Miguel Valencia, 2 Hospital Real
Ignacio Valle, 3 Estampa Jesus
R. Borga, 2 Primera Indio Triste
Manuel Briseño, 24 Ortega
Isidero Castillo, 12 Coliseo Viejo
Ildefonso Espinosa, 8 Coliseo
Juan Lopez, 15 Ortega
Guadalupe Montroy, 14 Coliseo
Marcos Peña flor, 7½ Correo Mayor
M. Hormigo, letra F Vergara
Juan Alfaro, 1 del Reloj
Lorenzo Almazan, Puente de Monzon
Prisciliano Alvide, 3 Mayor Corre de Pte.

José M. Anaya, 7 de la Pilaseca
Junan Arévalo, 24 Lorenzo San de
Guadalupe Balderrama, 11 Neri Felipe San
Vicente Barranco, 1 Santo Domingo
Josefa Becherel, 7 de Mesones
Vincente Belmont, 1 Balvanera
Emili G. Benitez, 10 Viejo Coliseo
Antonie Bermeo, 12 San Francisco
Abrahana Bermudes 18½ Clara Santa
Ramos Angel Bernal, 11½ Vergara
José de la Luz Bernal 4 San Ramon
Alberto Bucardo y Ca., 14 Viejo Coliseo
Felicitas Carmona, 6 Rebeldes
Epitacio Cardenas, 9 Puentede Monzon
Ignacio Cardoso 2 de la Granada
Rafael Casillas, 8 Joya
Teófilo Celada, 8 Del Reloj
Enrique Cervantes, 4 Portacoeli de Bajos
Gabriel Chacon y Ca., 15 Vergara
Juan M. Dávalos, 1 Coliseo
Francisco Davó, 21 Tacuba
Jacinto Daza, Sur al, A Venero
Santos Delgado, 13 Portacoeli
Policarpo Diaz, A 3 de San Ramon
Jesus Diaz, 13 Refugio
Fortino C. Diosdado, 11 A Jose de Gracia
Juan J. Dominguez, 6 San Francisco
Elugio Espinosa, 4 Parque del Conde
Sabino Estevez, 7 Indio Triste
Rita A. de Fernandez, 7 Arcade San Agustin
Elugio Figuero, 4 Alegria
Dionisio Gallegos, 4 Portal de Agustinos
Francisco Garcia, 26 Tacuba
German Gonzalez, 8 Cerea de San Domingo
M. Gonzalez, 15 Maurique
Amalia Gonzalez, 33 Ortega
Juan Gonzalez, 5 Indio Triste
Catalina Gonzalez, 3 Santa Catilina
J. Goroztinga, 14 San Hipolito
E. Iturriaga, 6 del Reloj
Ignacio Izunza, 7 Sapo
Braulio Zaramillo, Amagura al Norte
Hilario Juarez, 6 Calle Verda
José Langot, 16 Coliseo Viejo
Larrea y Gonzalez, 9 Vergard
José Maria Lopez, 11 San Lorenzo
Luis Lopez, 4 San Felipe Feri
Gregorio Lopez, 8 Correo Mayar
Ignacio Lopez, 7 Santa Teresa
Francisco Llamas, 2 Mariscala
Adolfo Martinez, 7 Parque del Conde
Concepcion Martinez, 10 Puente Quebrado
Mayorga Justo, 1 Calle de las Bonitas
Luis Mejia, 2 Puente de la Leña
Higin Mendoza, 4 de Mesones
Hilario Molina, 10 Sepulcros Santo Domingo
Angel Montano, 9 Jesus Nazareno
Lazaro de Oca Montes, 15½ San Juan
Antonia de Oca Montes, 8 del Rastro
Lucas Morales, 2 Bajos de San Agustin
Ana Maria Moreno, 3 San Juan
Abraham Muñoz, 3½ Sapo
Juana Nava, 12 Alfaro
Augustina Naval, 4 del Factor
Agapita Nunez, 3 Bajos de Portacoeli
Jacobo Ocampo, Guerrero
Guadalupe Olguin, 16 Balvanera
Manuel de J. Ortiz, 14 Parque del Conde
Teodosio Ortiz, 1 Parque del Conde, al Sur
Refugio Hernandez y Pardinas, Quesadas
Petra Perea, 5 de Mesones
Juan Perez, 5 Bajos de Portacoeli

Boot and Shoes, Retail—*continued.*

Suarez y Perez, 5 Vergara
Felix de la Portilla, 13 Calle Ancha
Agustin Portocarrero, 6 la Damas fior Ortega
Eusebio Ramirez, 9 San Felipe Neri
Ramirez L, 4 Jesus Nazareno
Manuel Raso, 7 Balvanera
Cirilo Rellat, 1 de las Damas
Apholonio Reyes, 2 de San Francisco
Domingo Rincon, 4 Estampa de Balvanera
Felipe Rivera, 8 Acequia
Rodriguez E., 8 Arco de San Agustin
Casimiro Rojas, 18 Parque del Conde
Concepcion Romanos, 6 Jesus Nazareno
Soledad Rosas, 3 Bajos de Portacoeli
Manuel Ruiz, 11 San Pedro y San Peblo
L. S. Santamaria, y Ca., 16 José el Real
Marciano Sarmiento, 4 del Indio Triste
G. Segura, 10½ Sepulcros de Santo Domingo
Julio Siegel, 24½ Medinas
Santos Sigales, 24 de Mesones
Albino Somera, 2 Portillo de San Diego
Masia Soto, 5 del Reloj
Masia Refugio Suarez, 21 Santa Clara
Luis G. Tafua, 19 Chavania
Francisco Tapia, 11 y 12 Mercado de Santa Catarina
Encarnacion Tellez, 17 Vereno
Luciano Tinoco, 15 Cuadrante S. Miguel
Antonio Torres, 3 Talavera
Anselmo Troncoso, 1 Nuevo Mexico
Tomasa Uribe, 4 del Reloj
Angel Urosa, 2 Puerta Falsa de la Merced
Maria de Jesus Torres, 15 Coranzon de Jesus
Pedro Vargas, 4 de la Pilareca
José Victoria, 9 Puente de Peredo
Torres y Villaseca, 2 de San Francisco

Brickmakers.

Apolonio Castaneda, 14 S. Ramon
Pablo Gutierrez, Chilpa
J. M. Herrerias, 5 Pte. de Santo Tomas
J. M. Morales, Colonia de Buenavista
Bonifacio Olvera, B. de los Reyes
Vidal Rivero, Barrio de Santiago
Jacinto Silva, Chilpa
Manuel Vivar, Barrio de Santiago
Francisco Zuñiga, 6½ Sto. Tomas
Vicente Gutierrez, Calzada del Campo Florido
Jesus Patino, Colonia Arquitectos
E. Salgado, Tlaltelolco
Atilano Vargas, Callejon Vivero
Francisco Zuñiga, 6½ Puente Sto. Tomas

Brokers and Manufacturers' Agents.

Pedro Arriaga, No. 11 Sta. Ines.
Ignacio Beltran, 4 Estampa S. Lorenzo
Miguel Beltran, 2 Sto. Domingo
Sebastian Berra, 15 Chiquis
V. Cosio, 1 Moscas
Pedro Diaz, 14 Doncelas
J. M. Echeverria, Hotel de San Carlos
Ignacio Esquivel, 5 Ratas
Manuel Gil, 9 Puerto Nuevo
Vicente Guillen, 10 Montealegre
Angel Islas, 16 Zuleta
Gregorio Lauda, 1 Agustinos
Miguel Laso, 2 S. Agustin
Manuel Miranda, 6 de Sta. Clara
Julian Montiel, 22 Mesones
J. Amberg, 16 Capuchinas

Francisco Perez, de Cara
Juan Perez de Leon, 1 Palacio
Manuel Armijo, 16 Cocheras
Francisco de P. Azpe, 6 Sta. Isabel
Simon Baeza, 13 Escalerillas
Felipe Bala, 10 Zapateros
José Julian Baron, 712 San Lorenzo
David Bache, 8 de Tezontlale
Jesus Benavides, 8 Calle Nueva
Rafael Benavides, 7 Apartado
Octaviano M. Betancourt, 13 Escalerillas
Ignacio Boisso, 10 de Toribio
Juan Borbolla, 14 Tacuba
Antonio Bravo, 10 Nuevo Méjico
José Breier, 5 Tiburcio
Manuel Bulnes, 21 Medinas
José Maria Calero, 4 Cazuela
Manuel Campos, 9 Jesus
Rafael Cancino, 2 Angel
Narciso Carreno, 6 Capuchinas
Longinos Cesar, 21 Hospicio de San Nicolas
Manuel Cordoba, 6 del Carmen
Pablo Cordoba, 11 Ortega
Alberto Crombe, 2 Esclavo
Luciano Cueto, 2 Angel
Alberto Chastanier, 17 Don Juan Manuel
Mariano Duran, 25 Medinas
Adolfo Durruty, 6 Seminario
Domingo Durruty, 9 Capuchinas
Pascual Eguia, 4 R. de Jesus
Vicente Enciso, 6 Capuchinas
Tomas Enriquez, 11 S. Andrés
Vortino España, 17 D. Juan Manuel
Manuel Espejel, 2 de la Condesa
Ramon Fajardo, 4 de Santiaguito
Alberto Fribolin, 20 D. Juan Manuel
Luis Friesch, 5 Coliseo Viejo
Emilio Froger, 6 S. Agustin
Farciso de la Fuente, 20 S. Cosme
Salvador de la Fuente, 11 Capuchinas
Crescencio Galvan, 17 Moras
Manuel Galligo, 20 Mesones
Joaquin Gamboa, 5 Buenavista
Antonio Garcia, 9 S. Lorenzo
Estanislao Garcia, 20 Don Juan Manuel
Amado Garduno, 26 Donceles
Desiderio Gariel, 1 Monterilla
Antonio Gonzalez, 13 Dolores
Joaquin Gonzalez Cardenas, 11 Alfaro
Juan Goyhenne, 12 S. Agustin
Gustavo Guichenne, 4 Ocampo
Valeriano Gutierrez, 3 D. Juan Manuel
José Maria Haro, 7 Portal de las Flores
Tomas Herrera, 5 San Felipe de Jesus
Ignacio Hinojosa, 6 S. Miguel
Hurtado, 5 de Tezontale
Manuel Ibarrola, 4 Angel
Alfredo Labadie, Via de S. Cosmo
José de la Lama, 23 D. Juan Manuel
Avelino Lamadrid, 10 Rosales
Daniel Lazo, S. Bernardo
Enrique Ledoyhen, 20 Alcarceria
Vicente Martinez, Segunda de Monterilla
Isidor Maciel, 20 Aguia
José Mangino, 4 Monterilla
Manuel Martinez, 5 Seminario
José Maria Mendez, Real de Santa Ana
José Mendoza, 12 Manzanares
Juan N. Monterubio, 10 Corazon de Jesus
José Maria Montes, 2 Reloj
Casto de la Mora, 3 D. Juan Manuel
Antonio Muller, 4 S José el Real

Brokers, Etc.—continued.

José Maria Najera, Balvanera
Juan Munar de la Torre, 11 Balvanura
Fernando Noriega, 8 Ruemada
Joaquin Ortiz de la Huerta, 4 San Francisco
Manuel Orvananos, 2 bajo de Portacoeli
Gregorio Palacio, 3 S. Agustin
Placido Pastor, 15 Venero
Enrique Pena, 9 Reloj
Ignacio R. Piquero, 7 Regina
Enrique Pomier, Espiritu Santo
Narciso de la Puente, 20 S. Cosme
José Maria Revelo, 11 Ansinas
José Maria Rico, 16 Chavarria
Paulino Richaud Monterilla
Herman Rosler, 5 Cadena
Francisco Reriz Torres, 2 Cocheras
José Maria Salas, 3 de Sta. Sues
Florencio Saldana, 10 Estanco de Mujures
Agustin Salguero, 9 Balvanera
Telesforo Sanroman, 17 S. Bernardo
Jueto Santamarina, 9 S. Agustin
Agustin Santiago, 13 Don Juan Manuel
Juan N. Sevella, 4 Plateros
Leon Stein, 3 Angel
Francisco Vega, 20 Don Juan Manuel
Francisco de P. Suarez, 4 Tarasquillo
Cayetano Tellez, 4 Aduana Vieja
Rodolfo de la Torre, 21 Don Juan Manuel
C. Vazquez, 9 Don Juan Manuel
José Maria Veraza, 7 Tacuba
Ignacio Napiain, 3 Cadena
Ricardo Perez, 2 de la Santisima
Martiniano Pino, 19 Santa Clara
Cárlos Pina, Colonia de Colon
José Ruheda, 8 de Tierra
Ricardo Sandova, Escalerillas
Ignacio Solares, 13 Lopez
Leandro Teija Senade, 4 S. Lorenzo
Antonio Trigueros, 8 Veronica
Maximino Zozaya, 16 Donceles
Guadalupe Romero, 11 Victoria
Santamaria y Ca, 1 Indio Triste
M. Segura, 19 Aguila
L. Sevilla y Villegran, Reloj
Canuto Sigales, 7 Vergata
Sobriny Garcia, Vergara y 5a de Mayo
Dolores Soria, 4 Factor
Francisco Trejo, 6 S Francisco
Miguel Valencia, 2 Hospital Real
Ignacio Valle, 3 Estampa de Jesus
Isauro Arsinas, Ausente
Guerra y Joaquin Valle, 6 1a de la Merced
Mariano Naveda, en Toluca
Maximo Zozava, 16 Donceles

Brokers, Financial, Stock and Exchange.

José Auyano, 5 Aduana Vieja
Baron Forbes y Ca., 9 S. Francisco
Delgado y Camacho, 274 Pte. de Curtidoris
Juan Dueñas 19 3a del Cinco de Maye
M. Gutierrez, 9 Puente de S. Pedro
Leon Salazar y Mont, 9 Empedrillo
E. Peredo y Ca., 15 Don Juan Manuel
J. Pinzon, 5 Inditas
V. Rivero, 1 A. Manuel Gonzalez
Domingo Sanches, 16 Tiburcio
Francisco F. Sanchez, 418 Escalerillas
Beneke y Ca. (successors of), 7 Capuchinas
Cardeña y Ca. (successors), 12 Betlemitas
J. Escalante de Contreras, 16 Puente del Cirevo

J. P. Dueñas, 5 Victoria
Francisco y Manuel Diaz, 1 Plq. de Palacio.
Antonio Escandon, 4 Estampa de Jesus
Angela Garduño, 1 Pl. de San Pablo
Guadalupe Garduño, 3 las Moseas
José Gargollo, 5 la Independencia
Bruno Guerrero, 11 Parque del Conde
Manuel Gutierrez, 9 San Pablo
Carlos Hagenbeck, 5 Codena
Bernado Hönig, 7 San Andres
E. Humana, 6 Puesto Nuevo
Manuel Ibañez, 2 Capuchinas.
F. G. Jaurigui, 14 Escalerillas
Dolores Lopez, 2 Arcade San Agustin
Ciriaco Llorente, 10½ Callejon de S. Innes
P. Mortin y Ca., 21 Cadena
Luis Migoni, 3 las Damas
Monroy y Morales, 6 Escalerillas
Pedro Mutio, 8 Corazon de Jesus
Guadalupe Olvera, 11 Maravillas
Huerta R. de la Ortiz, 22 Tiburcio
Agustin Pacheco, 3 Cuevas
José C. Pinzon, 5 Inditas
Agustin Portocarrero, 1 Porteria Regina
F. M. de Prida, 5 S. Agustin
M. Ramirez, 17 la Merced
Rapp, Sommer y Ca., 1 Ocampo
F. P. del Rio, 9 Zuleta
Vidal Rivero, 1 Avineda Manuel Gonzalez
A. Roldan, 9 Seminario
M. de la Rosa, 4 del Factor
Enrique M. Rubio, 16 San Augustin
R. M. Salgado, 5 Portalde Sto. Domingo.
Nicolas Serrano, 4 Cerradade S. Teresa
Ignacio Sevilla, 5 Ortega
H. Scherer y Ca., 8 Don Juan Manuel
Nicholas de Teresa, 4 Lerdo
Francisco Torres, 5 Canoa
José Uribe, 4 Callejon del Espiritu Santo
Paula Vargas, 9 Quemada
Jesus P. Vega, 6 Santa Teresa
H. D. Watermeyer, 18 Cadena
Rosa Yera, 3 San Pedro
Maria Zenteno, 2 Golosas

Brokers—General Merchandise.

Who sell by sample only, for merchants, manufacturers and others.

Alcantara y Carrasco, 1a de Santa Catarina, 2
Demeterio Baremque, 8 Arcode S. Agustin
Benitez, Landa y Ca, 7 Tiburcio
Luis Borel, 2 Lerdo
Agustin Bornemann, 11 Don Juan Miguel
German Bossier, 4 Angel
Cabusut y Derbesy, 6 Cincode Mayo
Fedrico Caine, 10 Refugio
Castello, Gutierrez y Ca., 16 Cadena
F. Coblentz, 11 Palma
Diego Corral, 2 San Agustin
José Christen y Ca., 7 Pte. del Espiritu Santo
Edmundo Dalhaus, 13 Palma
Darqué y Pérez, 2 Tiburcio
S. Diego Dunbar, 9 Don Juan Manuel
M. During, 13 Refugio
Eugenio Frey, 8 Zuleta
Luis Frisch y Ca., 11, 2d de Plateros
José Maria Gaston, 7 Gaute
Gonzalez Hermanos, 22 San Felipe Neri
Moriz Horner, 2 Angel
Vicente Ibarra, 10 San Bernado
Martin de Irigoyen, 8 San Agustin
Mestas y Garcia, 2 Don Juan Manuel

Brokers—*continued.*

Prida, Navarro y Ca., 5 San Agustin
Federico Ritter y Ca., 9 Capuchinas
Gil Rico, 15 Cadena
José F. Riva, 11 Mariscala
Rafael Salcido, 13 San Francisco
Francisco Sanchez de Tagle, 6 Seminario
Rudolfo Schwarzer, 7 P. del Espiritu Santo
G. M. Stankiewicz, 10 Alfaro
Simon Thomka, 4 de Mesones
Rodolfo de la Torre, 21 Don Juan Manuel
Trueba Hermanos, 14 Cabena
Juan Ulibarri, 3 San Agustin
Francisco del Valle, 16 San Agustin
Willkomen, Sittig y Ca., 17 San Bernardo.

Carriage and Wagon Dealers.

Roberto Boker y Ca., 8 Betlemitas
Masseron y Seres, 27 Sapo
Felipe Nava, 2 Pte. San Pablo
Agustin Olaez, 9 la Magnolia
José G. Ortego, Alconedo
M. Pascal
Andres Vent
Avineda Balderes
Gabriel Martinez Suarez, 2 de San Pedro
Juan Ramirez, 3 Rebeldes
Joaquin Ceasar, Chiquihuiteras
E. Decastraque, 27 Sapo
Valentin Elcoro, 4 Comonfor
J. Maza, 5 Amargura
J. Moricard, 1 Rinconada de Santa Ana
Victor E. Orozco, 4 Real de Santa Ana
Hugo Wilson, Tercera del Sapo
Tomas Wilson, y Ca., Ex-convento de San Diego
Adolfo Risser, 13 1a de San Francisco
Wexel y De Gress, 5 1a de Plateros

China, Crockery and Glassware.

Miguel Albear, 19 Escalerillas
Aguirre y Hermanos, Cinco de Mayo
J. M. Del Rio, 6 Palma
Guillermo Dorn y Ca., Cinco de Mayo
M. Espejel, 5 Portal de Agustinos
José Gomez de la Vega, 10a Santo Domingo
E. Hillebrand y Ca., 4 Plateros y Epemdradillos
Tomas del Pino, 5 Portal de Agustinos
Rigal Lubet y Ca. (successor), Portal de Agustinos
Nestor Gutierrez, 10 Portillo San Diego
Mariano Aranjo, 14 Soledad de Santa Cruz
Alberto Caisseiller, 15 Refugio
Camilo Avalos, 2 Plazuela Zaragosa
Mariano Olea, 11 Santo Domingo
Carmen Bravo, 13 la Merced
Antonis Derflinger, 11 Tacuba
Rufo y Ca., 14 San Francisco
Juan M. Dupont, 2 Bajos de Portacoeli
Miguel Zimenez, 28 la Merced
Francisco Mendez, 11 Bajos de Portacoeli
Agustin Ocampo, 3 La Cadena
Antonio M. Priani, Santo Domingo
J. Sarraille, 18 Callejon de Santa Clara
M. del Rio Uriarte, 3 Encarnacion

Chocolate Factories.

T. Aranguren, 5 Bajos San Agustin
S. Fernandez, 22 Tacuba
Ignacio K. Ferrer, 19 Tacuba
Franco y Ca., 4 Moras

Juan Gavito, 19 Tacuba
Francisco Iturria, 10 Acequia
C. Maurique, 6 Pelaseca
P. Manquia y hijos, 8 la Merced
Alonzo Noriega, 7 la Merced
F. Rafals y C., San Lorenzo

Coal, Wood and Fuel Dealers.

Ignacio Capetillo, 5 Primera del Reloj
A. Guerrero y Ca., 16 Cuanhtemotzin
Feliz Ortega, 1 Puente Pipis
F. Sequeiro, 4 y 11 Matadero
Frejo y Zormoza, 16 Cuantemozin
Julian Arechavala, 2 P. San Lorenzo
J. M. Hernandez, 8 S. Barbara
Ignacio Mora de Arroyo, 5 Escobillera
Remejio Noriega
Diego Ortiz, Plaza San Lazaro
José Rodriguez, 10 Matadero
José A. Roldan, Pl. San Lazaro
José Ramos Sanchez, Pl. San Lazaro

Commission Merchants, Importing and General.

Julio Albert y Ca., 4 Monterilla
Benneke y Ca., 7 Capuchinas
Bermejillo Bros., 10 Capuchinas
Ebrard y Ca., San Bernado
Fourcade y Goupil, 8 Plateros
G. Gathz, 19 Tlapaleros
Guerin y Ca., 11 Monterilla
Lavie y Ca., 3 Ocampo
Levy y Martin, Monterilla
Martinez y Ca., 2 Angel
Roves y Ca., 1 Capuchinas
Ignacio Noriega, 5 Angel
Pedro Pelaez, 16 Cadena
Richaud Aubert, y Ca., 12 Empedradillo
Juan N. Sevilla, 3 Plateros
Schultze y Ca., 19 Monterilla
The Seeger & Guernsey Co., 5 Calle de San Agustin
Suinaga Bros., 20 Cadena
Nicolas Teresa, 4 Lerdo
Uhink y Ca., 22 Don Juan Manuel
Watermeyer y Ca., 2 Angel
Watson, Phillips y Ca., 10 Don Juan Manuel
Santiago Lohse, 4 D. Juan Manuel
Guillermo Lohse y Ca., Sucesor de 9 Palma
J. Ollivier y Ca., 5 y 6 Séptima Monterilla
Portilla y Hijos, 13 Capuchinas
Ignacio Aguirre y Hermanos, Cinco de Mayo
Abascal y Perez, Corres Mayor
Vicente Alonzo, 4 San Bernado
Basagoite y Posada, Plateros y Alcaicera
Maximo Cabrera, 7 Puente de la Leña
C. Duverdon, 2 Puente del Espiritu Santo
Genin (Viuda) 3 Plateros
Larco Hermanos, 1 Coliseo
Mancina Hermanos, 9 Independencia
Alonso Noriego, 7 Puente de Jesus Maria
Brehm y Ca., 7 Don Juan Manuel
Max. Chauvet y Ca., 19 San Bernado
Robert Boker y Ca., 4 Puente Espiritu Santo
Balloneau, Casson y Ca., 1 Lerdo
Pablo Bonnerue, 9 Refugio
T. Castañeda, 12 Palma
A. Cambaluzier, 5 Plateros
Eugenio Delarue, 1 Plateros
Diehl y Ca., 1 Flamencos
Elcoro Lopez y Ca., 24 Cadena
Lohse y Ca., 9 Palma

Commission Merchants—continued.

José Azcona, 16 Escalerillas
Max A. Phillipp y Ca., Empedrillo
Marcial Pezana, 19 Refugio
Ponton Hermanos, 3 Rejas de Balvanera
Ramon Ponton, 1 Portacoeli
Agustin Rovalo, 3 Reloj
Trueba y Calleja, Estampa de Jesus
José Guerra Torriello, 2 Jesus Nazareno
Isadoro de la Torre Hermanos, 8 Reloj
Ambrosio Sanchez, 1 San Francisco Santo, Muñuzuri y Ca., Santo Domingo
Rafael Salcido, 13 San Francisco
Rapp, Sommer y Ca., 4 Palma
José Maria del Rio, 6 Palma
Martinez y Ca., 2 Angel
F. P. de Portilla Hijos, 13 Capuchinas
Feliciano Rodriguez, 10 Puente de Palacio
M. del Rio Uriarte, 10 Empradillo
Uhink y Ca., 22 Don Juan Manuel
Uhink Hermanos y Zahn, 9 San Francisco
Schultze y Ca., 9 Monterilla
Signoret, Honorat y Ca., 8 Monterilla
Tron y Ca., 1 Portal de las Flores
V. Viadero, 4 San Agustin
Watson, Phillips y Ca., 10 Don Juan Manuel
Simon Weil y Ca., 1 Plateros
Francisco Zepedia, 7 San Francisco
Shemidt y Baujeau, 23 Don Juan Manuel
M. Gutierrez, 3 Don Juan Manuel
Daniel Levy, 2 Cinco de Mayo
Simon Thomka, 8 San José el Real
Formento y Ca., 20 Coliseo Viejo
Salvador de la Fuente, 11 Capuchinas
Antonia G. Guerra, 14 Capuchinas
Adolfo Torre, 24 D. Juan Manuel

Coppersmiths.

Finamori y Amelio, 16 Arco S. Agustin
Julio Nevé, 11 San Juan de Letran

Corn Mills.

Alberto Bracho, Parados
Estanislao Caballero, Puento Solano
Manual Caballero de los Olivos, 3 Beas
Cárlos Ditner, 2½ 2a Delicias
Felix Garibay, Magueyitos O.

Cotton and Woolen Mills.

José M. Carballeda, 13 de Belen
Agustin Villegas y Ca, 10 San Cipriano
Joaquin Lara, Garrapata
Arena y Hermanos, Pl. de Madrid
R. Nariega, San Antonio
Suinaga, Hnos, 2 Callejon de Busque
J. Viadero, Puente de Jamaica

Dentists.

Benito Acuna, 20 Refugio
Tijera y Blessel, 13 Refugio
Emigdio Carillo, S. Francisco
Ricardo Crombe, 12 Plateras
Mariano y Ignacio Chacon, 13 Refugie
Hassel, 1 Puente San Francisco
Antonio Roque, 11 Santa Clara
José Soriano, 50 de Mayo
W. H. Keller, 7 Espiritu Santo
R. Aristi, 13 1a San Francisco
F. Landecho, 1 Segunda de San Francisco
R. Rico, 9 Empedradillo
R. Sevilla, 13 1a de San Francisco

Drugs, Chemicals, Etc., Wholesale.

Miguel Bachiller, 2 Espiritu Santo
Enrique Biester, 13 Refugio
Alfonso A. Brito, 4 Empedradillo
Henry B. Carman, 1 Puente San Francisco
Carmona y Aparicio, 5 Cerea Sto. Domingo
Agustin Chorne, 24 Meesones
Serafina C. Daumy, Hotel Colon
J. Falero, 22 San José el Real
Ignacio Gallardo, 22 San Lorenzo
Justo Z. Gudiño, 1 Balvanera
Pedro Hinojosa, 69 Moctezuma
Miguel E. Leiter, Puente del Espiritu Santo
Z. M. Perez, 5 Profesa
Joseph Spyer, 3 Palma
Luis Tejera, 13 Cadena
Andrea y Soriano, 10 Joya
Bennet y Ca. (successor of), 1 Cordobanes
José E. Bustillos (estate of), 8 Tacuba
Drogueria Universal, 1 Puente Espiritu Santo
Farine y Sanders, Lerdo y Refugio
C. Felix y Ca., 4 Profesa
Uhelein y Ca. (successors of), 3 Coleseo
A. Vargas y Ca., 2 Espiritu Santo

Druggists, Retail.

José Abeleira, 8 Pte. de Jesus
Evaristo Bustillos, 7 Tacuba
Juan Bustillos, Tacubaya
José Maria Carmona, 4 Segunda de Sto. Domingo
A. Silva Cervantes, 9 Leon
Agustin Franco, Botica de Santa Ana
J. B. Gaona, 6 R. de la Concepcion
Isidoro Gomez Tagle, S. Hipolito
Julian Gonzalez, 3 Homeopata, Cinco de Mayo
Agustin Guerrero, S. Gosme
M. Iriarte, Sto. Domingo
Francisco Kasca, Espiritu Santo.
José Laso de la Vega, 12 Reloj
Francisco Lelo, 1 Reloj
Francisco Llamas, 1 Coliseo
Crescencio Marin y Ca., 17 S. Hipolito
F. Oca de Montes, Niño Perdido
Ricardo Navarrete, Hospital de Jesus
Joaquin Aguilar, 30 San Cosme
E. Aguilera y Ca., 23 Necatitlan
Baez Hermanos, 13 Guerrero
Beguerisse y Ca., 16 Puente San Francisco.
Francisco Bernal, 4 Moriscala
Antonio Bermudez, 13 Aduana Vieja
Bermudez y Ca., 7 Santa Catarina.
Felipe F. Oropeza, 10 Avenida de Lerdo
Cárlos Patino, de Villamil
Francisco Patino, 7½ Andrés
Severiano Perez, 7 Rio de S. Cosmo
Franciso Rio de la Loza, Segunda de Vanegas
Isaac Rio de la Loza, Hospital Real
Maximino Rio de la Loza, 4 Primera de Sta. Catarina
Manuel Sanchez, Portacoeli
Salvador Tricio, 6 Damas
Manuel Urbina, 1 S. Juan
Bernardo del C. Urueta, 5 S. Francisco
José Maria del Rio, 6 Palma
Agustin Coronado, 1 Olmedo
A. D. Gonzalez, Toribio
Francisco J. Boez, Primera de Guerrero
Francisco Bernal, 6a de Guerrero
Cárlos Margain, esquina del Apartado
Jesus Gonzalez, 3a Cinco de Mayo

Druggists, Retail—continued.

Juan de I. Cañas, 13 Verdeja
Enrique C. Corral, 11 Juarez
Carlos Cortes, 17 Soto
Roman Diaz, 9 Don Toribio
Agusto Ducland, 8 Amaqura
M. Flores y Ca., Plaza Juan José Baz
Agustin Frias, 4 Avineda de la Paz
Ignacio Gonzalez, 10 San Juan
Joaquin M. Gomez, 8 Talevera
Francisco B. Gordilla, 5 Alhondiga
Antonio Guerrero, 9 Manzanares
Florintino Guerrero, Puente San Pedro.
Miguel Guerrero, 56 Guerrero
Herrera y Ca., 6 Factor
Vicente Licea, 19 San Felipe Neri
Benjamin Liz, Mexico y Dolores
Clara Lefort, 5 Nino Perdido
Agustin Martinez, 3 Soledad Santa Cruz
A. A. Mayer, 25 San Lorenzo
A. Mena, 37 Magnolia
Jesus Mercado, 4 Puento de Alvaredo
Jesus Oñate, 5 Rejasde Balvanera
Lorenzo A. Ortega, Zapateros
Guillermo Portilla, 10 Espiritu Santo
Rafael Rio de la Loza, 4 Santa Catarina
Manuel A. Salazar, 7 del Rastro
Carlos J. Silva, 7 Quemada
Manuel Torres, 1 de Mina
P. Verdugo, 2 Moneda
Maximo Villagran, 17 San Hipolito
Juan G. Zubieta, 2 Sapo

Dry Goods (Importers).

Vicente Algara y Ca., 6 y 7 Flamencos
Coria Alvarez, 2 Flamencos
Manuel Bauche, Segunda Monterilla
Telesforo Castillon, 14½ San Bernardo
A. Coria, 1 Portacoeli
Simon Coronado, 20 y 21 Flamencos
A. del Castillo, 10 Puente Palacio
Manuel Gonzalez, 14 San Bernardo
L. Espinoza Hurtado, Puente Palacio
Monterde y Hermanos, 2¼ San Bernardo
Anastasio Olveria, 16 y 17 Flamencos
Luis Ortega, 5 San Bernardo
Trinidad Quintana, 25 Niño Perdido
Feliciano Rodriguez, 10 Puente Palacio
A. Rullo, 13 y 15 Mercado
Cerefino Torres, 6 Flamencos
José Velasco, 4 y 5 Flamencos
Angel Villar, 8 San Bernardo
Zaldivar Hermano, 879 Flamencos
Felipe Zaldivar, 7 San Bernardo

Electrotypers.

Pedro Cordoba, 6 del Espiritu Santo
Filomeno Mata, 7 Betlemitas
Muguia Bustamante, 8 Merced
Pedro Llagostera, 7 Nuevo Méjico

Electric Light Co.

Samuel Knight, Prest., 5 Providencia

Fireworks, Dealers.

Valentin Guardiola, 3 Cuevas
Maximo Pereira, 8 Rosales
Valentina Guardiola, 3 Callejon de Cuevas
E. Mata, 5 Peralvillo
Maximo Pereyda, 44 Magnolia
Dario Torres, 7 del Topacio

Fire Insurance Agencies.

A. Levy y Martin, 3 Ocompo, agents for "La Confiance"
Robert Boker y Ca., 4 Puente del Espiritu Santo, agents for "North British" and "Mercantile" of London
E. Benecke, 7 Capuchinas, agent German Ins. Co. of Stettin
H. Scherer y Ca., 8 Don Juan Manuel., agents "London Assurance Co."

Flour and Corn Mills.

Benfield, Breker y Ca., S. Cárlos
Charreton Hermanos, 24 Revillagigedo
Fortino Aguslar, Calxada del Campo
Sixto Arroyo, Soto y Magnolia
José Maria Echenique, 25 Arcos de Belem
S. Fernandez, 27 S. Cosme
Alberto A. Bracho, 12 Estanco de Hombres
J. M. Caballero, 3 Callejon de Beas
Gervasio Clotas, Puente de Salano
Carlos Dettmer, 3 Delicias
José Maria Garibay, 32 Puente del Zacate
Joaquin Lara, 3 Calle de Munoz
M. Sanchez, 1 Pueblita
Casto Villademoros, 4 Espalda Misericordia

Flour, Grain and Seed Merchants.

Charreton Hermanos, 24 Revillagigedo
Bernardo Monasterio, 11 Merced
Alberto A. Bracho, 2 San José el Real
Vicente de P. Castro, 9 Callejon de la Olla
J. Ceballos, 7 Migueles
Enrique Diffonty, 9 Gante
G. Galnares, 13 Alhondiga
Juan Llamedo, Ex. Convento
Miguel Pacheco, 3 Puente de Molena

Foundries.

Bandoin y Ca., 2 Delicias
J. Brandi, 19 Ortega
Luis Dantan, 17 Zuleta
Finanmore y Ca., Arcos de San Agustin
Antonio Fusco, 34 Ortega
Neveu Hermanos, 64 S. Juan de Letran
J. M. Pascuali, 1 Ortega

Furniture and Cabinet Ware.

Victor Aldama, 1 Independencia
Lazaro Urrutia, 24 Donceles
Carlos L. Velasco, 23 Sta. Clara
José Barrera, 10 Vergara
B. Benac, 1 S. Francisco
Eusebio Delgado, Cinco de Mayo
Pedro Fontaine y Ca., 12 Sta. Clara
José M. Garnica, 5, 6 y 9 Canoa
Francisco Arteaga, 4 Canoa
Cornelio Carrillo, 21 San José el Real
Juan J. Chavarri, Santo Domingo
Jesus M. Garrido, 29 Donceles
Juan Herrera, 13 Canoa
Eduendo M. Kuhn, 6 Angel
Adrian Lara, 9 Canoa
Miguel Martinez, 25 Medinas
Porfiria Mondragon, 10 Canoa
Antonio Olvera, 5 Canoa
Quintana Hermanos, 7 Coliseo Viego
Faustino Reynoso, 5 Puente Correo Mayor
Lorenzo Rico, 12 Canoa
C. Blas Rodriguez, 28 Donceles
Enrique Sanchez, 5 Canoa

WILL SOON BE PUBLISHED.

DELMAR'S
HOTEL AND RAILWAY DIRECTORY,

AND

GENERAL COMMERCIAL GUIDE BOOK

OF THE

UNITED STATES.

Designed for European Circulation, and as a Useful, Practical and Reliable Guide for Merchants, Commercial Travelers, Tourists, Emigrants, and Others Visiting or Contemplating a Visit to the United States for Business, Pleasure, or as Actual Settlers.

PRICE, $1.00.

The object of this interesting and useful work — which is arranged upon an entirely different, more practical, more comprehensive and useful plan than the average traveler's "Guides" or "Hand-Books" — is:

FIRST — To acquaint the traveling public with all Hotels, of the first and second class, in all parts of the United States and Canada, with their terms, etc.

SECONDLY — Giving a synopsis of all Railway and Steamer Lines, with distances from point to point, fares, and other information of value and interest to travelers.

THIRDLY — Pointing out the true advantages and disadvantages of various portions of the United States as places for residence, pleasure, travel, sight-seeing, or in which to settle, whether as merchant, skilled mechanic, farmer, clerk or laborer.

FOURTHLY — Pointing out the snares, swindling schemes and other pit-falls into which strangers are liable to fall.

COMPILED AND EDITED BY
E. H. DELMAR,

Author of "Delmar's Business Directory of Central and South America," "How to Secure Trade with Spanish-America," "Delmar's Trades Directory and Mercantile Manual of Mexico, Cuba and the West Indies," "A Winter in the Tropics," etc.

CHICAGO:
1889-90.

PRICE BAKING POWDER CO.

NEW YORK.   CHICAGO.   ST. LOUIS.

La calidad tan superior de esta famoso LEVADURA sí ha probado en milliones de familias y por mas de viente cinco años. Es usada por el gobierno de los Estados Unidos, y está endorsada por los profesores de to los las gran les universidades, estando la mas fuerte, mas pura y mas saludable.

SE VENDE SOLAMENTE EN LATONES.

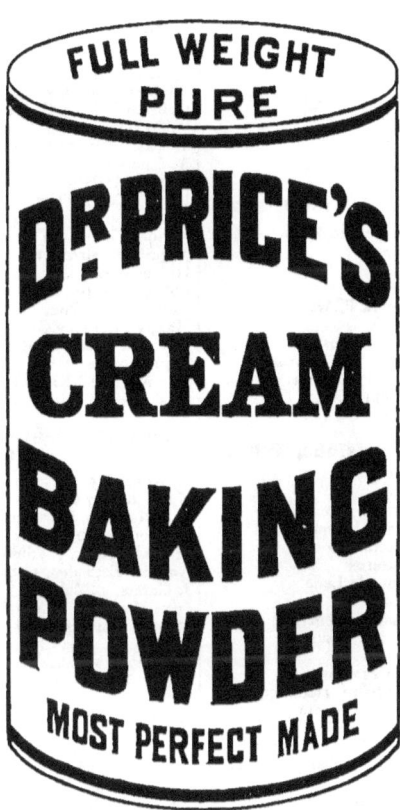

POR MAYOR.
¼ libra, 4 de 6 doc en caja
6 onzas, 4 " 6 " " "
¼ lebra, 4 " 6 " " "
¾ " 2,4 " 6 " " "
1 " 2,4 " 6 " " "
2½ " 1 " " "
4 " 1 " " "
5 " " ½ " 1 " " "

WHOLESALE PRICE LIST.
¼ lb. 4 or 6 doz. - $1.40
6 oz. 4 or 6 doz. - 2.00
½ lb. 4 or 6 doz. - 2.60
¾ lb. 2, 4 or 6 doz - 3.90
1 lb. 2, 4 or 6 doz. 5.00
2½ lb. 1 doz. - 12.00
4 lb. ½ or 1 doz. 18.25
5 lb. ½ or 1 doz. 22.75

PRECIOS, CORRIENTE.
En Neuva York, Chicago ó St. Louis.
$1.40 doc.
2.00 "
2.60 "
3.90 "
5.00 "
12.00 "
18.25 "
22.75 "

These prices are deliverable f. o. b. in New York, Chicago or St. Louis.

Trade Discounts made known on application.

PRICE BAKING POWDER CO.

NEW YORK.   CHICAGO.   ST. LOUIS.

The superior excellence of this unequaled Baking Powder has been proven in millions of homes for more than a quarter of a century. It is used by the United States Government, and indorsed by the heads of the great Universities as the Strongest, Purest and Most Healthful. Dr. Price's Cream Baking Powder does not contain Ammonia, Lime or Alum. **Sold only in Cans**.

Furniture, Etc.—continued.

Ines Villaverde, 27 Donceles
Placedo Zendejas, 22 Donceles

Gas Fixtures, Lamps, Etc.

Aguirre Hermanos, 10 y 11 Pte. del Correo Mayor
Juan A. Bennet Sucesores, la Santo Domingo y Cordobanes
Roberto Boker, Purente Espiritu Santo y Cadena
Felipe Cejudo, 10 Esclavo
J. M. Del Rio, 6 Palma
Guillermo Dorn, Cinco Mayo
Elcoso Lopez y Ca., 1 Cadena y Angel
J. J. Finlay y Ca., Mina
Agustin Gutheir, 4 Palma
German Garthz, 19 Tlapaleros
Izquierdo y Garibay, 4 Cinco Mayo
Martin Leffman y Hijos, 12 y 13 Palma
Lhose y Ca.. Sucesores, 9 Palma
A. Philip Max, Cinco, Mayo
Eduardo Roa, 10 Vergara
Valdes y Rufo, 10 y 12 Cinco Mayo.

Glass Dealers, Plate and Mirror.

Ignacio Aguirre, 10 y 11 Correo Mayor
Luis G. Arnaldo, 6 Profesa
G. Dorn y Ca., Santa Clara
Miguel Jiminez. 28 Merced
Hillebrand y Ca., 1 Primera Plateros
José Azcona, 12 Escalerilla
Alfonso Dabat, 3 Portal de Agustinos
Agustin Martinez, 45 y 46 Plaza Mercado
Martinez y Ca., Portals de Portacoeli
J. Serreille, 7 Callejon Santa Clara
N. Wissel, 6 San Agustin

Groceries and Provisions, Wholesale.

Torre Hermanos, 8 Reloj
Chink Hermanos y Zahn
Chink y Ca., 22 Don Juan Manuel
Vicente Alonzo, 4 San Bernardo
Basagaiti y Posada, 2 Plateros
Maximo Cabrera, 7 Puente de Leña
Larco Hermanos, 1 Coliseo
Mancina Hermanos, 9 Independencia
Trueba y Calleji, Estampa de Jesus
Ranon Ponton, 1 Portacoeli
Ambrosio Sanchez, 1 San Francisco
Santo, Muñuzuri y Ca., 1 Santo Domingo
Abascal y Perez, Rejos de Balconera
Mendoza M. Cortina, 1 Tiburcio
H. Deverdun, 2 Puente del Espiritu Santo
Gomez y Hermano, Tacuba y San José el Real
Lavie y Ca., 7 Juan Manvel
Remigio Noriega, Cinco de Mayo
Ignacio Noriega, 5 Angel
Ponto y Hermano, 3 Rigas de Balvanera
Agustin Rovalo, 9 Puente de Jesus
José Guerra Torriclo, 2 Jesus Nazareno
Viuda Genin, 3 Segunda Plateros
Francisco Zepeda, 7 2a S. Francisco
Formento y Ca. (sucesor), 20 Coliseo Viejo

Hardware and Tools.

Roberto Baker y Ca, 4 Espiritu Santo
H. Cuats Nueva Cinco de Mayo
Bizet Hermanos, 7 Angel
M. Candil, 20 Tlapaleros
José M. Del Rio, 6 Palma
F. Delarrue, 1 Segunda Plateros
G. Dorn, Cinco Mayo y Santa Clara
Elcoro Lopez y Ca., Cadenay Angel
A. Gutheil y Ca., 4 Palma
German Gahrtz, 17 Tlapaleros
Izquierdo y Garibay, 173 Plaza Mercado
M. Leffman y Hijos, 12 y 13 Palma
Lhose y Ca., Sucesor de, 9, 10 y 11 Palma
S. Lohse y Ca., 4 Don Juan Manuel
M. Mendiola y Ca., San José el Real
Marcial Pezana, 19 Refugio
Pascual Soto, 4 Primera Factor
Fogno y Ca, 9 Espiritu Santo
Kaiser y Martin, 7 Espiritu Santo

Hardware, Tools and Notions, Wholesale.

Ignacio Aguirre y Hermanos San José el Real
Billoneau Cassou y Ca., 1 Lerdo
Roberto Boker y Ca., 4 Puente Espiritu Santo
Pahlo Bonnerue, 9 Refugio
T. Casteñeda, 12 Palma
A. Cambaluzier, 5 Plateros
Eugenio Delarue, 1 Plateros
Deihl y Ca., 1 Flamencos
Elcoro, Lopez y Ca, 24 Cadena
German Gahrtz, 19 Refugio
Miguil Gutierrez, 11 Puente de Palacio
Hulvershorn y Ca, 1 Monterilla
Lohse y Ca. (successors of) 9, Palma
Santiago C. Lohse, 4 Don Juan Manuel
Max A Phillipp y Ca., Empadrallo
Marcial Pezaña, 19 Refugio
Rapp, Sommer y Ca, 4 Palma
José Maria del Rio, 6 Palma
M. del Rio y Uriarte, 10 Empedradrillo

House Furnishing Goods and Tinware.

H. Aburto, 5 Zuleta
N. Aschart, 7 Canoa
J. Ballesteros, 2 Donceles
Gil Bonilla, 10 Chiquis
M. de la Torre, 7 Tiburcio
Antonio Escanden, 14 San Ramon
J. Garcia, 15 Zuleta
Juan Martinez, 10 Moras
Manuel Pinto, 2 Angel
V. Sanchez, 6 San Ramon
Victoriano Vazquez

Hotels.

Hotel de Bilbao
" de la Bella Union
" Comonfort
" Contabro
" Colon
" Café Ingles
" del Comercio
" Espiritu Santo
" Las Estrella
" Español
" Gillow
" Humbolt
" del Havre
" del Jardin
" de Oriente
" San Agustin
" del Seminario
" del Turco
" Americano
" de Europa
" de Vergara

Hotels—continued.

Hotel del Refugio
" Continental
" de la Gran Sociedad
" del Bazar
" Iturbide
" de San Càrlos
" Grandiola
" Nacional
" Central
" La Universal

Horse and Mule Dealers.

Domingo Martinez, 2 Tenexpa
Antonio Quintanilla, 6 Don Juan Manuel
Juan C. Ramirez, 3½ Revillagigedo
Zubieta y Murua, 4 Escondida

Ice Manufacturers and Dealers.

Aguirre, Ignacio, Hermanos, 10 y 11 Correo Mayor
Juan Gonzalez, 1 Puente del Padre
Harrsch y Goettig, 18 Refugio
A. Fulcheri, 18 Refugio
Carlota Mayen, 22 Santa Clara
Juan Minetti, 1 Portal Mercaderes
Marcos Montero, 4 Tacuba
Antonio Amarini, 2a Plateros
Augustin Raso, 1 Indio Triste
Josefa Sanchez, 6 Monrique

Importers.

(See Commission and General Merchants.)

Instruments, Surgical and Dental.

Andrade y Soriano, 10 Joya
E. Bustillos Sucesores, 7 y 8 Tacuba
Calpini, 12 2a de S. Francisco
Carlos Felix, 4 Profesa
Jorge Henning y Ca., 3 Cinco de Mayo
Càrlos Joransson, 3a S. Francisco
Julio Labadie, 5 Profesa
Leiter Sucesores, S. José el Real
Philipp A. Max, Emperadillo
Maximo Rio de la Loza, 20 y 21 Merced

Iron Merchants.

Charreton Hermanos, 10 Cadena
Elcoro Lopez y Ca., Cadena
Juan Petherie, 8 Ortega
Alfredo Bourlou, 3 2a de la Providencia
A. Gutheil, 4 Palma
M. Leffman y Hijos, 12 y 13 Palma
G. Lhose y Ca., Sucesores, 9, 10 y 11 Palma
S. Lehose, 4 D. Juan Manuel
J. M. Del Rio, 6 Palma
Bizet Hermanos, 7 Angel
Spaulding, Cadenas
Togno y Ca., 9 Pte. Espiritu Santo

Jewelry, Watches and Silverware.

Adolfo Ducommun, 4 Plateros
Tomas A. Hernandez, 6 San Francisco
Alejandro Jacot, 4 Plateros
German Lane, 12 S. Francisco
Francisco Vasquez, 8 S. Francisco
Bernardo Villareal, 5 Plateros
Lagyarrigue y Ca., Empedradillo Plateros
Muiron y Ca., 11 Plateros
M. Shaffer, 11 Plateros

Schrieber y Ca., 3 S. Francisco
E. Sommer, 11 Plateros
Gabriel Zivy y Ca., 7 Plateros
Jesus Velarde, 24 S. Felipe Neri
Luis Zapffe, 10 Vergara
Diener y Rothacker, 14 Plateros
Agustin Diener, 11 Plateros
Ricardo Klein, 2 Plateros
Luis Lagarrigue, 4 Empedradillo
J. Llopp, 1 Plateros
José Santibanez, Empedradillo
Van Rooten y De Broé, 1 Espiritu Santo
A. White, 3 Espiritu Santo

Lamps, Fixtures, Etc.

(See Gas, Etc.)

Life Insurance Agencies.

Montes de Oca y Crocker, Vegara y Cincodi Mayo—" The Equitable," New York
Thomas Horncastle, 15 Refugio
" The Mutual," New York
John Davis, 11 Calle Gante
" New York Life "
Ricardo K. Allen, 1 Puente de San Francisco, " Bankers and Merchants' of U. S."

Lithographers.

Maximo Fernandez, 23 S. José el Real
Hesiquio Iriate, 23 Sta. Clara
M. Moreau, 6 Tarasquillo
Murguia y Hijos, 50 Puente Quebrado
Gregorio Palacio, 11 S. Salvador el Seco
Salazar y Ca., 3 Del Raton
Secretaria de Guerra, Palacio Nacional
J. L. Revuelta, 27 Balen

Looking Glasses.

Francisco Arce, 3 S. Francisco
Hillebrand y Ca., 1 Plateros
Pellandini, 10 S. Francisco

Lumber Merchants.

José Arrasti, 4 Escobillera
Anastasio Baez, 5 Recabado
Manuel Cobos, 1 San Lazar
Pedro Estanol, 60 Magnolia
M. Fabre, Plaz. San Lazaro
José Franco, de Mina
Manuel Guerrero, Pl. San Lazaro
G. Guerrero, 4 Matadero
Trinadad Hidalgo, Mina
Adolfo J. Jimenez, 6 Juan Carbonero
Nicolas de Meca, Estanco de Majeres
Diego Galindez, M. de S. Lazaro
Antonio Huerta, 20 Matadero
Manuel Guerrero, 16 Guatimozin
Palacios y Ca., 3 Providencia
Francisco Romero, 2 Chaneve.
Enrique Sanchez, de Villamil
Isidro Valle, 1 Necatitlan
M. Villar, 14 Mosqueta
Luis Monterde, Salto al Agua
Ponca y Aranzabel
Francisco Romero
Juan de la Sancha
M. Trejo
Isidro del Valle

Machinists and Machinery.

S. Adorno

LÁMINAS DE METAL PERFORADAS.

para

Molinos de aceite, de semillas, de Algodon. Molinos de Arroz, Refinerías de Azúcar, Alambigues. Molinos para Fosfatos y Abonos.

Planchas y Cilindros de acero y Hierro para pasar Mineral, Carbon, Piedra, Fosfatos, etc.

Separadoras, Descascaradoras de maiz y todas clases de maquinária para limpiar, grano. Tambien para haciendas de beneficio y concentracion.

Obras de agua y gas. Molinos de Papel, Lana, Harina y Aceite. Percoladores Coladores, Ventiladores, etc.

Cribas Giratórias, Recondas y Exágonas. Cribas ó surejados para minas de placer.

Cribas para laterias de pilones de todas clases y dimensiones.

Cribas mineras para todas clases de minerales.

Lata y Laton de todas tamaños.

Hierro, acero, cobre, laton y zinc perforados a cualquier tamaño y de cualquier espresura que se requieran.

PRESUPUESTOS Y MUESTRAS AL PEDIRLOS.

The Harrington & King Perforating Co.

OFICINA PRINCIPAL Y FÁBRICAS,

224 & 226 CALLE UNION (NORTE),

CHICAGO, ILL., E. U. de A.

Machinists, Etc.—continued.

Cárlos Blakesley Laubley
N. Campa
Pedro Cordova, 6 del Espiritu Santo
Charreton Hermanos, 24 Revillagigedo
G. Gahrtz, 19 Tlapaleros
Leffman y Hijos, 12 Palma
Santiago Lhose, 9 Palma
J. White, 4 Revillagigedo
Boudain y Ca., Delicias
Roberto Baker, 4 Puerta Espiritu Santo
J. M. Del Rio, 6 Palma
Dorn y Ca., Calle Santa Clara
Elcoro Lopez y Ca., Cadena y Angel
Agustin Guthal, 13 Palma
Hoffman y Hermano, 10 Donceles
M. Ibarrola, 4 Angeles
G. Lhose y Ca., 9, 10 y 11 Palma
Acuña Claudio de la Sanz, 25 Arco de Belen
Vanduin y Ca., 2 Segunda de las Delicias
Wexel y De Gress, Sucesores

Merchants, General.

(See Commission and Wholesale Merchants, General.)

Mining Companies and Promoters of Mining Enterprises.

Compania del Real del Monte, 11 S. Bernado
Compania de San Rafael, 1 Encarnacion
George D. Barron, 6 Cinco de Mayo
J. Campero Vega, 3 San Agustin
Celso Acevedo, 12 S. Lorenzo
Trinidad Acuña, 14 Real
Blas Balcarcel, 6 Cerca de Sto. Domingo
Agustin Barroso, Ministerio de Fomento
A. Castillo, 19 Donceles
Pedro Espejo, Zacatecas
Luis Espinosa, Zumpango
Francisco Guheni, Guanajuato
Ignacio Haro, Méjico
T. L. Laguerennu, Tacubaya
Pedro Lopez, S. Luis Potosi
Jesus Manzona, Pachuca
Cárlos Medina, 13 Arsinas
Francisco Morales, Méjico
Francisco Palacis, Tabasco
Santiago Ramirez, 15 Buenavista
Manuel Rivera, S. Cosme
Sebastian Segura, Méjico
Manuel Urquiza, Méjico
Francisco Zarate, Zacatecas
Juan Barquera, Mextitlan
Gilberto Crespo, Ministerio de Fomento
Mariano Leon
Luis Pozo
Mariano Barcena, 2 Santa Ines
Eduardo Garay, 9 Donceles
Tito Rosas, 13 Chavarria

Musical Instruments, Pianos, Etc.

José I. Espinoza, 2 San Ramon
Cipriana Granados, 22 la Merced
Manuel Hidalgo, 8 San Ramon
Tomas Hernandez, 7 del Reloj
Jesus Oñati, 9 San Ramon
J. B. Sanchez, 10 Canoa
Romulo Solano, Puente de Jesus
Beizet y Hnos., 4 Cadena
José Fernandez, 27 Ortega
H. Nagel y Ca., Sucesors, 5 Palma
Wagner y Levien, 15 Coliseo Viejo

Newspapers.

(See Publishers and Printers.)

Opticians.

Calpini, Sucesor, 12 2a S. Francisco
Julio Favre, 4 2a de Plateros
N. Jhoranson, 3a S. Francisco y Callejon del Espiritu Santo
Cipriano Trujillo, 8 Portal de Mercaderes
A. Whitte, Espiritu Santo

Outfitters, General (Retail).

Dealers in Dry and Fancy Goods, Cheap Jewelry and Ornaments, Pictures, Furniture, Hardware, House Furnishing Goods, etc., etc.

Cayetano de Abiega, 3 Santa Calarm
Antonio Maria Aburto, 13 Donceles
José Aguirre, 7 Soledad de Santa Cruz
Altuna Hernanos, 9 Vegara
Victor Aldama, 3 Calegio de Niñas
Ramon Alonso, 1-2a de Vanegas
Altuna Hermans, 1 San Hipolito
Luis Arenal, 6 Bajos de San Agustin
Fernando Ayllon, 31 Ortega
Manuel Barcena, 2 Plaza de Madrid
Ramona Barsurto, 12 Don Taribio
Angela Becerril, 2 Consuelo
Esteban A. Becerrie, 1 de la Pilascea
José Mirin Berruecos, 7 Conaa
Luis Bose, 1 de San Ramon
Santos Bastillos, 7 Plazuela de Madrid
R. Butron, 10 Santa Clara
Rosa de J. Camba, 27 Merced
Rafael Campillo, 3 Pte. de Misericordia
Federico Ceballos, Estampa de Jesus
Angela S. Contreras, 9 Canas
Federicio Cortes, 3 Calle Real de Santa Ana
Juana B. Chavarria, C. Cando
S. Dozal, 3 Santa Catarina
Vicente Espinosa, Plazuela de Carbonero
Gregoris Fernandez, 3 Puente de Leña
Felipe Flores, 7 San Francisco
Alonzo Garcia, 6 de la Magnolia
Francisco Garriko, Portal de Santo Domingo
Juana Gayoso, 10 Venero
Vicente Goña, 4 Alfaro
Manuel Guterrez, 1 la Merced
Julian Gutierrez, 2 Colosio Viejo
José Guzman, 14 la Regina
Hermosa Hermanos, 3 Santisema
Angel Junco, 18 Camarones
Braulio Junco y Ca., 38 Niño Perdido
Eduardo Larque, 19 Santa Clara
José Lezameta, 7 Puente de Tezonttale
Porfirio Llanas, 22 Merced
Francisco Llop, 7 Santa Clara
Vicente Manilla, 16 Jesus Nazareno
Mateo Mejia, 2d de San Juan
G. Milla, 15 Avenida Ledro
Manuel Moyeda y Ca., 6 Santo Domingo
Juan R. Ortiz, 1 Bajos de Portacoeli
Manuel G. Perez, Puente de Jesus
José Perez, 12 Victoria
Joaquin Poo, 3 Olmedo
Manuel Pumariega, 1 la Merced
G. Ramirez, 14 Aveneda Lerdo
Antonio Rivera, 1 Ste. Domingo
Nicasio Rodrigo, 6 Pte. Santo Domingo
Antonio Rodrigez, 21 Mercado de Merced
Rafall Taenz, 7 Esclavo
Vicente Sordo, 5 Planzulade Carbonero

Outfitters, General—continued.

Juan Pablo Soto, 3 Santa Catarina
José del Torno, 4 de la Merced
José Uribe, 8 Santo Domingo
Juan Urrutia, 8 Aducina Vieja
Amado Varela, 2 Merced
Domingo Verdeja, 3 Hospital Real
Pedro Via y Sobrino, 1 Factor
Alejandro Villegas, 12 Medinas
José Zalboro, 12 Nahnattato
José B. Zapata, 18 Santa Clara
Francisco Zarala, 6 Portal Santo Domingo
G. Zyas y Ca., 14 Coloseo Viejo
Antonio Zepeda, 1 Manzanares

Paints, Oils and Varnishes.

(See also Druggists, Wholesale.)

Timoteo Ayala, 8½ Cerca de Santo Domingo
Pedro Balling, 9½ Santa Isabel
José del Barca, Hotel Vergara
Benito Castro, 7 Gachupines
José Maria Carmona, 7 Espalda San Lorenzo.
Felix Flores, 9 Misericordia
Regino Garcia, Colonias de Tepito
Francisco Guadarrama, 9 E. S. Lorenzo
Vicente Hernandez, Callejon Ratones
J. B. Hernandez, 3 E. San Juan de Dios
J. M. Mondragon, Colonias de Tepito
Angel Morales, 15 Medinas
Andres Padilla, 3 Pte. Crámen
Luis Rosas, Tlapaleria
Jesus Vanegas, 9 Misericordia
J. M. Villegas, 2 Espalda S. Juan de Dios
Eutimio Zazaya, 8 2a San Lorenzo
Lorenzo Zazaya, 8 S. Lorenzo
Nicanor Arce, 4 Pte. S. Tomas
Mariana Green, 1 Calvario
R. Velasco, 15 Puente de Cuevo

Paper Warehouses.

Guillermo Dorn, 5 de Mayo
Kauser y Martin, 7 Pte. del Espiritu Santo
Remirez y Ca., 3 Espiritu Santo
Trueba Hnos, 14 Cadena

Paper Boxes, Manufacturers.

Amado Barroso, 5 Cinco de Mayo
Rafel Paez, 6 Cinco de Mayo
Valdes y Cueva, Providencia
Carlos Gonzalez, 8 Sta. Teresa

Paper and Paper Hangings.

Luis Arnaldo, Segunda San Francisco
J. M. Del Rio, 6 Palma
E. Delarrue, 1 Segunda Plateros
Cárlos Felix, 4 Segunda San Francisco
Julio Labadie, 5 Segunda San Francisco
Lehman y Hijos, 12 Palma
Tellez y Bauche, 13 Refugio
Federico Vaugier, 7 Segunda S. Francisco
Vanden Stein Wingaert, Plazuela del Espiritu Santo
Wirlanti, Cinco de Mayo
A. Bernard, 6 Tacuba
Pedro Cordova, Cinco de Mayo
Federico Ludert, Profesa

Perfumery and Toilet Articles.

(See, also, "Outfitters, General.")

Luis Arnaldo, 5 Profesa
Jesus Acosta, 15 Coliseo Viejo
Benet, Sucesor, Cordobanes
Cuats y Ca., 10 y 12 Cinco Mayo
P. Claverie, 1 Coliseo Viejo
J. M. Del Rio, 6 Palma
Cárlos Felix, 4 Profesa
Julio Labadie, 5 Profesa
Leffman y Hijos, Palma
P. Saint-Marc, Calle S. Clara
Tellez y Ca., Primera de Plateros

Photographers.

Jesus Alvarez, 8½ Correo Mayor
Antonio Calderon y Ca., 4 San Francisco
Cruces y Campa, 4 Empedradillo
Agustin Campa Figuerea, 5 Plateros
Gove y Nortt, 7 Espiritu Santo
Luis Manero, 16 de Francisco
Francisco Iglesias, 3 Sto. Domingo
N. Mayo, 7 Vergara
Guadalupe Suarez, 3 Chiconautla
Valleto Hermanos, 4 S. Francisco
Luis Werazа, 15 Balvanera
Ameira Yanez, 11 S. Francisco
Guerra y Ca., 11 S. Francisco
Valleto Hermanos, 4 la S. Francisco
Luis Veraza, 15 Balvanera
Yanez Ameneyra, 11 2a S. Francisco
Gomez, Flores y Pacheco, 7½ Pte. del Correo Mayor

Physicians and Surgeons.

Francisco Buenrostro, Tlalpam
Camilo Calderon, 5 Trompete
Ignacio Capetillo, 5 Reloj
Manuel Carmona, 21 S. H. de S. Nicolas
Trinidad Carmon, 4 Indio Triste
Angel Carpio, 5 Pte. de Leguizaneo
Francisco Cerda, 27 Quebrado
Crescencio Colin, 11 S. Felipe Neri
Juan Collantes, 6 Montealegre
Miguel Cordero y Gomez, 44 Santa Clara
Pablo Cordoba y Valois, 13 Tiburcio
Agustin Coronado, 7 S. Felipe de Jesus
José de la Cueva, 11 S. Hipolito
Francisco Chacon, 13 Sto. Domingo
Ignacio Chavez, 5 Tercera del Rastro
Genaro Alcorta, 3 Aguila
Manuel Alfaro, 5 Damas
Fernando Altamarino, 4 Aduana Vieja
Minuel Alvarado, 10½ Canoa
Jesus Aranjo, 11 Olmedo
Mánuel Aveleyra, 7 Alfaro
José Maria Bandear, 1 Factor
Miguel Barbachano, 11 S. José el Real
José Barragan, Hospital de Jesus
Ernesto Below, 14 S. Francisco
L. de Bellina, 18 Tacuba
Ignacio Berrueco, 11 S. Ramon
Francisco Bla-guez, 2 S. Diego
Francisco Buenrostro, 10 Mesones
Pedro Diaz de Bonilla, 4 Sta. Catarina
Manuel Dominguez, 10 Chavarria
Ricardo Egea, 5 Monterilla
Alberto Escobar, 3 S. Agustin
Maximiliano Galan, 10 Refugio
José Galindo, 19 Sta. Catarina
José Gama, Patoni
J. A. Gamboa, 3 Dolores
L. Francisco Garcia, 7 S. Juan
Angel Gavino, 5 S. Pedro y S. Pablo
Amado Gazano, 1 Sexta del Reloj
Antonio Gomez, 21 S. Hipolito

Physicians and Surgeons—*continued.*

Joaquin Gomez, 12 Manzanares
Regino Gonzales, 6 Escondida
Manuel Gordillo, Hospital Militar
Juan N. Govantes, 2 S. José de Real
Marcelino Guerrero, 19 10 Puerto Nuevo
Angel Gutierrez, 21 P. Alvarado
Manuel Gutierrez, 10 Primera de Mesones
Joaquin Huici, 11½ P. de San Diego
Francisco Hurtado, Maternidid
Francisco Iberri, 23 Cocheras
Ramon Icaza, 10 Correo Mayor
Ricardo Jubera, 3 Rosales
Francisco Larrea, 8 Toza
Rafael Lavista, 1 Pte. de S. Francisco
Francisco Leal, 1 Pte. Zacata
José Leal, 9 Pte. Gallegos
Jesus Lemus, 4 S. Lorenzo
Vicente Licea, 6 Sta. Catarina
Eduardo Licéga, 4 Andrés
José Lobato, 13 Sta. Catarina
L. Lucio, 25 Aguila
José Marie Lugo, 4 Leon
Ramon Macias, 7½ Correo Mayor
Fernando Malanco, 1 S. Ramon
Ignacio Maldonado, 12 Reloj
Miguel Martel, 7 Jesus
Anastasio Martinez, 7 Santisima
Ignacio Martinez, 17 Pte. Quebrado
Demetrio Méjia, 15 Rebeldes
Vicente Morales, 11 Nuévo Méjico
Miguel Muñoz, 2 Puente de Santo Domingo
Tomas Noriega, 3 Hospital de Jesus
Tobias Nuñez, S. Factor
Jesus Onate, 7 Nahunartato
Francisco Ortega, 3 Medinas
Lazaro Ortega, 6 Pl. de San Domingo
Manuel Ortega, 7 Cordobanes
Domingo Orvananos, 3 Tercera del Nastro
Ramon Pacheco, 2 Quinta de la Magnolia
Porfirio Parra, 4 Parque del Conde
Cárlos Patiño, Pl. de Villamil
Ramon Peña, Hotel de S. Cárlos
Manuel Perez, S. Cosme
Manuel Poza, 4 Pte. de Jesus
Ismael Prieto, 1 Violeta
Andres Quijano, 12 S. Felipe de Jesus
José Ramirez, 3 y 4 Pl. de la Concepcion
Juan José Ramirez Arellano, 2 Moneda
Nicolas Ramirez y Arellano, 2 Moneda
Roman Ramirez, 3 y 4 Pl. de la Concepcion
Pedro Rangel, 8 Salto del Agua
Agustin Reyes, 13 D. Juan Manuel
Joaquin Rivero, 1 Damas
Juan Rodriguez, 9 Jesus
Sotero Romero, 10 Quesada
Alfonso Ruiz, 14 S. Pedro y San Pablo
Nicolas San Juan, 30 Ortega
Adolfo Schmidtein, 3 Ocampo
Gil Servin, 8 Parque del Conde
Manuel Soriano, 13 Portal del Tejada
Manuel Suarez, 92 Moras
Cristoforo Tamayo, 15½ Pl. de Buenavista
Antonio Velarde, 5 Alhondiga
Antonio Velasco, 21 S. Miguel
Joaquin Vertiz, 2 Sta. Clara
Jesus Viellagran, 18 Sta. Teresa
Augustin Villalobos, 4 Damas
Miguel Wilson, 4 Caleras
Esteban Calderon, 13 Amargura
Fernando Escobar, Primera Damas
Juan Fenelon, 7 Tatuba

Francisco Galvan, Hotel San Augustin
Miguel Hurtado, 6 Calle de 51
Ignacio Magaña, Hospital Jesus
Joaquin Martinez, Fabrica S. Fernando
Rafael Miranda, 3 Callejon Groso
V. Poli, 12 S. Juan Letran
Silvino Reguelme, 6 2a Damas
Federico Semeleder, S. Esclavo
Antonio Teraazas, 4 Eitanco Mujeres
Alejandro Uriba, 2 Cadena
Eduardo Vargas, 11 2a Sta. Catarina
Pomposo Verdugo, 6 Bayos S. Agustin
Ricardo Vertis, 10 Cordobanes
Miguel Wilson, 4 Caleras
J. S. Zubieta, 2 Sapo
Carlos Aguilera, 59 Magnolia
A. Aizpuro, 18 San Agustin
Francisco Alvarez, 8 del Reloj
Ponciano Arriaga, 7 Puente de Santa Ana
Winter A. Barredo, 11 Santa Isabel
Francisco Bernaldez, 3 Alliondiga
Juan Siller y Cabello, 8 del Reloj
Waldemaro G. Canton, 6 Rejas Concepcion
Enrique Carrera, 7 San Ildefonso
Lucas Castro, 15 Arco de San Agustin
José M. Contreras, Moneda Ex Arzobispado
Agustin Chacon, 2 de las Damao
Aparicio Lovenzo Chavez, 5 Academia
Barriga Jesus Diaz, 13 Cocheras
Carlos Echagaray, 3 Espiritu Santo
Ortigosa Fernandez, 11½ Santa Isabel
Nicolas A. Franco, 7 Real de Santa Ana
J. P. Gayou, 7 Calle de Santa Teresa
Alberto Gomez, 23 Aguila
Romero Alberto Gomez, 14 Jesus
Abel F. Gonzalez, 8 Machincuepa
J. Gustine, 6 Corpus Christi
Alfonso Helguera, 3 Tiburcio
Eduardo Hickman, 30 Puente de Alvarado
Manuel S. Izaquirre, 19 Don Toribio
Ferreol Labadie, 5 Profesa
José M. Leal, 10 Costado de la Sta. Veracruz
José Huenta Lopez, 2 Merced Estampa
Fernando Lopez, 17½ Corazon de Jesus
Rafael Lopez, 9 Triste del Indio
Mucio Maicot, de Mina
José Mangino, 9 Pilaseca
A. Mantienyo, 9 Ex-Seminario, vivienda
Francisco Mendoza, 3 Perpetua
Matilde Montoya, 18 Medinas
Vincente J. Morales, 5¼ Nuevo Mexico
Vincente Moycelo, 17 San Hipolito
Marcelo Ihucel, 3 Ratas
José Cayllet y Neira, 14 Cosme
E. Nicolin, 10 Vergara
Luis Ocampo, 4 de Sta. Catarina
José Olvera, 8 de Vanegas
Gregorio Orive, 1 de San Juan
Lorenzo M. Ortega, 4 Zapateros
Cristobal Ortega, 3 Medinas
A. W. Parsons 4 Puente de San Francisco
Pomposo Patino, 14 Jesus Nazareno
Manuel Bibbins Perez, 12 Juleta
Francisco Pulido, 2 Regina
Plotino Rodakanaty, 10 Callejon de la Santa Vera Cruz
Manuel Roman, 10 Chapitel de Monserrate
Alejandro Ross, 17 Don Toribio
Enrique Rubalcaba, 10 de Santa Catarina
Perado J. y Segura, 18 Santa Teresa
Guillermo Lenisson, 4 de la Montevilla
Gabriel Silva, 13 de Guerrero

Physicians and Surgeons—continued.

Jesus Tojonar, 17 Ortega
Luis Alcala Troconis, 11 Chickonantla
Jesus Valenzuela, 1 de Mecatitlan
J. L. Vallejo, 6 Lopez
Vaquie, 4 Gaute
Legorreta O. Vazquey, 8 de Santo Domingo
Manuel Villada, 24 Aguila
Miguel Wilson, 4 Caleras
Ruperto Zamora, 2 Chiconantla
Juan G. Gubieta, 2½ Safco

Physicians, Homeopathic.

Francisco A. Aguilar, 3 La Cadena
Jesus Aranalde, 3 Ciegos
Juan N. Arriaga, 10 Buena Muerte
Panfilo Carrauza, 7 Corpus Christi
Antonio Caroillo, 6 Delicias
Rafel U. Castro, 3 Puente del Cuevo
Enrique C. Corral, 11 Benito Juarez
Antonio Dromundo, 11 San Lorenzo
Esteban Frias, 19 Hospicio de San Nicolas
Pablo H. Fuentes, 5 Nenero
Julian Gonzalez, 17 Cinco de Mayo
Juaquin Gonzalez, 1 Cinco de Mayo
Manuel M. Legarreta, 21 Buena Muerte
José Moran, 5 Factor
Antonio N. Muñoz, Ex-Leminario
Salvador B. Perez, 8 Machincuepa
Teodoro Quintana, Avinida de la Paz
Benito Quintana, 40 San Cosme
Miguel Ramirez, 6 Colon
Manuel D. Ruiz, 2 Puente del Fierro
Antonio Blanco y Salas, 6 Neuvo Mexico
Ambrosio J. Vazquez 14 Alfaro

Pianos and Organs, Dealers in.

Bizet Hermanos, 24 Cadena
Sucesores de Nagel, 5 Palma
Sanchez Barquera y Hijo, 10 Canoa
Emilio Sittner, 6 Seminario
Leandro Urquiola, 7 Joya
A. Wagner y Levien, 44 Zuleta
Cárlos Wisseman, 23 Donceles
Emilio Wisseman, 6 Seminario
Adolfo Lednatz, 5 Palma
J. Guzman, 9 Chiquita Regina

Plumbers and Gas-Fitters.

Iglesias y Nalazi, 19 Zuleta
Antonio Lari, 1 Segunda de las Delicias
Guillermo Mora, 1 Nuevo Mejico
Paterson y Henderson, 6 Primera de lá-Providencia

Printers and Publishers.

J. M. Ortiz Aguilar, 3 1 Sta. Catalina de Sena
José Barbedillo, 15 Montealeagre
Isidor Berthier, 5½ S. Juan de Latran
Ignacio Cumplido, 2 Rebeldes
Francisco Diaz de Leon, 3 Lerdo
Dublan y Ca., S. Cosme
Escalante y Riesgo, 1 S. Juan de Letran
Gonzalo Esteva, 6 S. Juan de Letran
Gonzalez, Cerrada de Jesus
J. Guerra y Valle, 29 Merced
J. F. Jens, 22 S. José el Real
Lopez, 11 Escalerillas
Filomeno Máta, 8 Betlemitas
Epifanio Orozco, 19 Escalerillas
Ireno Paz, 2 Independencia

José Vicente Villada, 8 Reloj
Petra Zuniga, 16 S. José el Real
Barbier, 328 Apartado
Fernandez, 12 Zuleta
Pedro J. Garcia, 7 Escalerillas
Lara y Bustos, 3 Pte. S. Domingo
Francisco Lugo, Ex-Convento Santa Brigida
Enrique G. Fernandez, I2 Zuleta
Galindo, Martinez y Ca., Pte. San Domingo
E. Haegeli, 4 Rastro
F. P. Hoeck, 8 Gante
Parres y Ca., 21 Independencia
J. Abadiano, 17 Escalerillas
Juan B. Acosta, 20 Escalerillas
V. Agueros, 20 Mesones
Berrueco Hermanos, 20 San Felipe Neri
John W. Butler, 5 Gante
Juan Canosa, 3 Tacuba
José Correa, 12 San Lorenzo
Eduardo Dublan, 3 San Cosme
F. Dufuez, 6 Coliseo
Imprenta del Gobierno Federal (Government Printers)
Imprenta de *El Combate*, 20 Cinco de Mayo
J. Largaza, 12 Venero
Jesus A. Laguna, 2 Puente del Santisimo
Mariano Lara, 3 Callejon del Raton
Leal y Vega, 23 Mesones
Alfonso E. Lopez, 21 Escalerillas
Juan R. Mata, 11 Escalerillas
A. Mena, 37 Magnolia
José Moreno, 18 Providencia
Department of Interior, printing office
Carlos Paz, 8 Factor
Juan de Dios Peza, 4 Plazuela de Regina
Antonio C. Ramirez, 2 San Juan de Dioz
Daniel R. Salazar, A. Escondida
José G. Sanchez, 4 Chavaria
Wm. H. Sloan, 10 Santa Isabel
David C. Smith, 10 Vergara
Miguel Tornel, Espalda de la Concepcion
Francisco Villagrau, 9 San Bernado
Atanasio Villanueva, 11 Arsinas
Antonio Venagas y Arroyo, 10 Encarnacion
Guillermo Peterson, 11 Alvarado
Miguel Tornel, 6 Segunda San Lorenzo
R. Velasco, 5 E. de Balverna
G. Veraza, 6½ Canoa
Pedro Zubieta y Ca., San José el Real

Printing Materials, Dealers in.

P. Cordova, 5 de Mayo
P. Llagostera, 7 Nuevo Méjico
Guillermo Lhose, 9, 10 y 11 Palma
Santiago Lhose, 4 Don Juan Manuel
Filomena Mata, Esquina de San Andrés
Munguia y Bustamente, 8 de la Merced
J. S. Ponce de Leon, Cuarta Reloj

Public Libraries.

National Library
Library of the 5th of May
Library of School of Jurisprudence
Library of School of Engineers
Library of Geographical Society

Saddlery and Harness.

Mariano Aguilar, 19 S. Bernardo
G. Arroyo, 9 Vergara
Juan A. Balleteros, Medinas y Esclavo
Manuel Castro, 9 Balvanera
D. Lozano, 7 Tiburcio

Saddlery and Harness—*continued.*

Miguel Martinez, 49 San Fernando
Francisco Ruiz, 8 Cerca Santo Domingo
Reynaud y Salles, 6 Jesus Nazareth
Eduardo Ruiz, 10 Gante
Vasquez, 16 Escalerillas
Amedo Zepeda, 17 Capuchina

Saw Mill.

Leon Buhatt, Iturbide

Scientific Instruments.

Andrade y Soriano, 10 Joya
Evaristo Bustillos, 7 y 8 Tabuca
N. Calpini, 12 2a San Francisco
Cárlos Felix, 4 Profesa
Jorge Herming, 3 Cinco Mayo
Carlos Joransson, San Francisco
C. Leiter Sucesores, 16 Nueva Cinco Mayo
Philips, Max, Empedradillo
Taussaint y Ca., San José el Real
Maximino, Rio de la Loza, 20 y 21 Merced

Sewing Machine Agents.

Francisco Adam, Sucesor, 4 la Cinco de Mayo
Roberto Boker y Ca., 4 Espiritu Santo
Alejandro Jacot, 4 Primera Plateros
Lhose y Ca., Sucesores, 8 Refugio
Uhink y Ca., 22 Don Juan Manuel
Julius Bacmeister, 4 Espiritu Santo
J. L. Kehoe, 15 Escalerillas
Oscar R. Graham, 6 Vergara
Rapp, Sommer y Ca., 10 Refugio

Ship Chandlery.

J. Enriquez, 15 Don Juan Manuel
Vicente Lozano, 21 Don Juan Manuel
Theodosio Villagra, Santa Catalina

Telegraph Companies.

De Jalisco, Oficinas 8 Monterill
Del Comercio, Oficinas 10 Refugio
Del Ferro-carril de Morelos, Oficinas 14 S. Agustin
Del Ferro-carril de Toluca, Oficinas 12 Cadena
Del Ferro-carril de Vera Cruz, Oficinas 11 Guardiola
Del Gobierno federal, Oficinas 5 Del Espiritu Santo

Telephone Companies.

Del Centro Telefonico Oficinas generales, 2 Tacuba
L. G. Wiley, 1 Balderas
Cable Submarino, Oficinas en Méjico

Undertakers.

Ascorbe y Ca., 7 Gante
J. Carmona y Ca., 6 San José el Real
Gayosso y Ca., de Mayo
G. Moctezuma, Encarnacion
M. Trevino, Santa Clara.

Veterinary Surgeons.

Manuel G. Aragon, 4 Corazon de Jesus
Romulo Escobosa, Rastro de Cuidad
Emilio Fernandez, 7½ Victoria
Miguel Garcia, 7 Calzada del Penctenciaria
José L. Gomez, 11 Estampa de San Andres
Manuel Granados, 10 San Miguel
José E. Mota, 4 Empedradillo
Emilio Navarro, 1 Pachito
Manuel Peñuñuri, 8 Rivera
Enrique Santoys, 3 del Rastro
Agustin Torres, 14 Balvanera
Luis Villaseñor, Rivera de San Cosme

ACAPULCO,

STATE OF GUERRERO.

Population, 4,000.

Principal Merchants.
Alzuyeta Hermanos y Ca.
P. Arumela y Ca.
R. Pimental
Antonio Pintos
Ignacio Gonzales
Angel Oribe
Tinto Hernandez

Druggists.
Roberto S. Posada
Antonio Butron

Plantations.
La Providencia
La Sabana
El Potrero
Egido Viejo
Dos Arroyos
San Marcos
Egido Nuevo

There are in this district four steam cotton presses and one steam oil mill.

CHILPANZINGO,

STATE OF GUERRERO.

Population, 7,000.

Druggists.
Alberto Rodriguez
Miguel Parra
Juan Cruz Manjarrez

Principal Merchants.
Tomas Rodriguez
Alberto Rodriguez
Gabriel F. de Celis

Rafael A. Campos
A. Reyes y Hermano
Jose M. Cabañas
Castulo Salazar.
J. M. Villamar
Manuel Patino

Physicians.
Alberto Morales
Juan Cruz Manjarrez

AGUAS CALIENTES,

Population, 40,000.

Agricultural Implements.
(See also Hardware and Tools.)

Aguila Hermando
Martin I. Pilon

Ales and Beer Dealers.
Eugenio Craumont
Refugio Reyes
Bazin de Viuda

Banks and Bankers.
Aguilar Hermanos, Agentes del Banco Nacional
J. Rufujio Guinchard

Billiards.
Vicente Berber
Luis Maguin
Wasson y Ca.

Books and Stationery.
Aguilar Hermanos
Cleto Dávilla

Boots and Shoes.
Cruz Alvarez
Mariano Nunez
Monico Parga
Manuel Trejo
Pedro Cornou
Reyes Duson
Simon Jiminez
Francisco Masson

Carriage and Wagon Dealers.
Chaves Hnos
Pedro Santiago
Antonio Navarro

Commission Merchants, General.

Aguila Hermano
Refugio Guinchard
Eugenio Graumont
Emeterio Palacio
Elizondo Valera y Ca.
Viuda de Chavez y Hijos
Vicenne Berber

China, Glassware, Oils, Etc.

Andrés Bernal
Margarito Castañeda
Francisco Espino
Bonifacio Iturbide
Emeterio Palacio
Cárlos Sagredo
Pedro Valdés
Valera Elizondo y Ca.

Druggists and Chemists.

Luis de la Rosa
Alcibiades Gonzalez
Juan Marin
Miguel Sandoval
Cleto M. Dávila
Cárlos Sagredo
Valera Elizondo Ca.

Dry Goods, Wholesale.

Pedro Corpu
Reyes Duron

Engineers, Civil and Mechanical.

Mariano Dávalos
Locadio de Luna
Tomas Ugarte Medina
Perez Maldonado

Flour Merchants.

Manuel Anteago
Quirino Diaza
Francisco Rosa Flores
Francisco Sandoval

Flour Mill.

José Bolado

Hardware, Cutlery and Tools.

Andrés Bernal
Margarita Castañeda
Francisco Espino
Espino Hijo
Esperidion Gonzalez
Florentino Herrera
Emetrio Palacio
Esteban Perez
Pedro Valdés
Nicanor Ventura
Vicente Berber
Refugio Guinchard

House-furnishing Goods and Tinware.

Florencia Aguilar
Eduardo de la Cruz
Atanasio Hernandez

Iron Merchants.

Vicente Berber
Refugio Guinchard

Jewelry, Watches and Silverware.

Ricardo Romo
Victor Robles
Juan Sancedo
Bonifacio Iturbide
Cárlos Sagredo
Ricardo Von Faber

Lithographers.

Nestor Davalos
Trinidad Pedrosa

Lumber Merchants.

Manuel Azco

Machinery Depots.

Philon R. Martin

Merchants, General.

Vicente Berber
Eugenio Gramont
Refugio Guinchard

Merchants, Dry Goods.

Hermanos Aguilar
Leantand y Barbaroux
Cleto Marja Davila
Leon Diaz
Jesus Gonzalez
Severino Martinez
Manuel Martinez
Martin Pilon
Antonio Puga
Guillermo Puga
Elizondo Valera y Ca.

Mining Engineers.

Leocadio de Luna
Thomas Medina Ugarte
Jesus Perez Maldonado

Perfumers, Etc.

Cleto Davila, Primera Reloz
Cárlos Sagredo, Primera Relox
Elizondo Valera y Ca., Portal Allende

Photographers.

Antonio Chavez

Physicians.

Luis Maguin
José Astey
Isidro Calera
Refugio Gamarena
Leon de Diaz
Mariano Dávalos
Rodsigo Gasibay
Satusmino Gonzalez
Portugal Gomez
Carlos Lopez
Francisco Maldonado
Janacio Masin
Francisco Macias
Francisco Muñoz

Printers.

Salvador Correa
Arnulfo Chavez
Paul Fesniza
Alcibrades Gonzales
Trinidad Pedsoza
Epigmenio Pasgo
Eduardo Ortega
Aldana Carios Sanchez
Raul Ferniza

Provisions and Groceries.

Vincent Berber.
Santiago Enriquez
Ciprian Enriquez
Antonio Roman
Florentino Torres
Leonardo Torres

E. Gonzalez
Refugio J. Guinchard
Eugenio Gramont

Pianos and Organs.

Cipriano Avila
Angel Garcia
Rafael Garcia

Sewing Machine Agents.

Elizondo y Ca.
Chavez y Ca.
Felipe Parra
M. Valera

Wall Papers.

(See Stationers.)

CAMPECHE,

STATE OF CAMPECHE.

Population, 15,000.

Arms and Ammunition.

Zaldivar y Castillo

Dentists.

J. M. Arjona
Juan Porez

Druggists.

Manuel Espinola
Manuel Lanz
Agustin Leon
Pedro Lavalle
Olivier Lopez
Pedro Ortega
Pedro Reyes

Merchants, General.

E. Barron
F. Berron Berron
Berron Hermanos
Juan de Dios Bujia

Castellot, Guttierrez y Ca.
José Castellot
Costillo y Zaldivar
Manuel Diaz Campos
Estrada McGregor y Ca.
Francisco Otero Ferren
José Ferren
Ferren y José Fur
Francisco Superano Ferren
José Hilario Lavalle
Pedro Ortega
José Zuloaga Regil y Ca.

Physicians.

Joaquin Benglio
Domingo Duret
Angel A. Gurdiano
Patricio Nueva
José Rosario Hernandez
Juan Perez
Antonio Velazco

CHIHUAHUA,

STATE OF CHIHUAHUA.

Population, 20,000.

Agricultural Implements and Hardware.

José Lerma
Ramon Amendari
Luis Fandoe, Sucesors
Ketelsen y Dejetao
Felix F. Taseira
Juan Serraga

J. M. Brittinghaus
H. O. Reinhardti
Narciso Balderran
Lynch y Ca

Architects and Builders.

Enrique Esperon
Pedro y Yrigoyen

Bankers.
F. Macmanus y Ca.

Billiards.
Casino, Calle del Progreso
R. Fernandez, Callejucia
H. Harlow, Plaza Principal
Reisura y Ca., Calle de la Libertad
José M., Calle de Ojinaga

Bookbinders.
Donato Miramontes
Manuel Altamirano
Domingo Puchi
Rembez y Bezaury
Enrique Norwald

Boots and Shoes.
Dario Coriche
Policarpo Ortegon
José Martinez
J. J. Molina
J. Williams
Matias Vidal
Mariano Zeldivar
J. A. Larrang
José Perchoz

China and Glassware.
Ernique Creel
Eduardo Rutiaga
Mathias Vidal

Carriages.
Juan Lerma
Lynch y Ca.

Commission Merchants.
Trinidad Castro
Francisco Ruiz
Anastasio Vega

Druggists, Retail.
Urbano Burmudez
Francisco Indico
L. Emilio Lafon
Evaristo Ordaz

Dry Goods, Wholesale.
J. Genaro Chaves
Felix F. Maceira
Pedro Minagoren
Hermanos Navarro
Anastacio Vega
Arrelano, Serrano y Ca.
Trinidad Castro

Furniture Dealers.
George H. Anthony
Ketelsen y Dejetao
Lynch y Ca.
Enrique Norwald
Rembez y Bezamy

Flour Mills.
Paschal y Marshal
Juan Manuel Azunzolo
Enrique Esperon
Celso Gonzalez
Manuel Herrera

Gas Fixtures.
Hooper y Ca.

Hotels.
Chihuahua
Estados Unidos
American House
Hidalgo
Maceira
Nacional
San Juan
Europeo

Jewelers and Watchmakers.
Antonio Alguin
Enrique Hogland
C. Zalvaza
Hermanos Chacon
Serrlano Arellano y Ca.
Zabalza y Pina
N. Gautier

Machinists and Machinery.
Enrique Esperon
Manuel Garneros
Rafael Jaurrieta
Manuel Marino
Angel Persa
Ignacio L. Roig
Primitivo Saaenz
Juan B. Solis

Mine Owners and Mining Engineers.
Manuel Gameros
Rafael Jaurrieta
Manuel Marino
Angel Persa
Juan B. Solis
Enrique Esperon
Ignacio L. Roig
Primitivo Saaenz

Merchants, General.
Manuel M. Altamirano
Arellano Serrano y Ca.
Ramon Armendario
Juan M. Azumolo
R. S. Aldana
Bembez y Berauri
Felix Bessauri
Enrique C. Creel
Genaro J. Chaves
Ketelsen y Dejetao
Luis Fandoa
Hooper y Ca.
M. Lorenzo
Carlos Loya
F. Macmanus y Hijos
Pedro Miñagoren
Silvino Muñoz
Hermanos Nevarro
Norwald y Ca
Hermanos Partida
Puig y Domingo
Francisco Kuiz
Miguel Salas
José Maria Sanhez
B. Schusster
Juan Terraza

Machinists, General—*continued.*

Anastasio Vega
Antonio Azrinzulo
Gonzalez Treviño Hermanos
Domingo Leguinázaval
Felix F. Maceyra
Gustavo Maye
Benigno Navarro
J. Stalfordt
Refugio Tejeda
Guillermo Venmehren

Photographers.

Victor Moreda
B. Velardi
Addis y Hijo

Physicians.

Francisco Echeverria
Canuto Elias
Antonio Lafon
Miguel Marquez
Daniel Muñoz
Jesus Muñoz
Luis Muñoz
Francisco Paschal
Andrés Romero
Ignacio Torres
C. L. Robertson
M. B. War

J. B. Lowe
F. Rubio

Pianos and Organs.

Gregorio Inostrosa
José Perchez

Printers.

Del Comercio
Del Gobierno
Del Progreso
El Obrero
Viuda de Carmona y Hijos
La Mariposa
José de la Luz Navarro
Abraham Eriberto Perez
José Dolorez Solis
Gomez Del Campo

Paints and Varnishes.

Anastasio Vargas
Adalberto Irigoyen
José Vargas
Jesus Carrasco

Sewing Machines.

Ketelsen y Dejetao
Enrique Norwald
M. Adler

COLIMA,

STATE OF COLIMA.

Population, 30,000.

Ales and Beer Dealers.

(See Groceries and Provisions.)

Bankers and Importing Merchants.

José M. Alcarez
Guizar y Ca.
Oethling y Ca.
Flor y Rofani

Billiard Halls.

Portal de Medellin
Alonso Francisco

Druggists.

Francisco C. Cuera
Ignacio Fuentes
Agustin Morril
Crescencio Orozco
Cosmo Suarez
Agustin Moni

Dentists.

José M. Garcia
Rafael Ponce de Leon

Groceries and Provisions (Wholesale and Retail).

Gregorio Alvarez
Antonio de la Calleja

E. Diaz
Flor y Rofani
Esteban Garcia
S. Gomez
Dolores Guizar y Ca.
Keve, Vanderlinden y Ca.
Alejandro Oetling y Ca.
Oetling Hermanos y Ca.
Jorge Oldenbourg
Alberto de la Plaza
Francisco de la Plaza
Manuel Rodriguez
Francisco Vargas

Hardware, etc.

Manuel Rodriguez
Smith y Madrid
Agustin Eschacht

Merchants, General.

J. Ma. H. Alcaráz
Enrique Almeyer
Gregorio Alvarez
Rios Antonio Alvarez
Miguel Barreto
Antonio de la Calleja
Alberto de la Plaza
Enrique de la Plaza
Francisco de la Plaza
Epifanio Diaz
C. Flor

Merchants, General—*continued.*

Aristeo Gomez
Salomé Gomez
Dolores Guisard
Kebe, Vanderlinden y Ca.
Cenobio Madrid
Alejandro Oetling y Ca.
Oetling Hermanos y Ca.
J. Oldenbourg
Antonio E. Orosco
Francisco Perez
Riensch, Held y Ca.
Manuel Rodriguez
José Maria Romero
Agustin Schacht

Physicians.

Salvador Abad
Pedro Altamirano
F. de P. Arriola
Francisco J. Cuera
G. Hurtado
José E. Murillo
V. Megia
Crescencio Orozco
J. E. Palacios
Isadoro Revera
Gregorio Vazquez

Printers.

La del Estado
I. Fuentes

CARMEN,
STATE OF CAMPECHE.
Population, 6,500.

Agents and Attorneys.

Eduado L. Castillo
Anastasio Arand
Luis P. Choza
Rudolfo Navarette

Druggists.

A. Ibarra
Manuel Lagunera

Civil and Mining Engineers.

Alejandro Marcin
Juaquin Musel
Luis Choza

Principal General Merchants.

Burgos Hermanos
Benito Aniza
B. F. Colarelo y Ca.
Felipe Ferrer

José Otero Ferrer
Quirino Hernandez
Manjarrez Hermanos
Domingo, Perez y Field
Juan Luis Ropeto
Juan Slovero
Antonio Martinez
Nieves y Ca.
Francisco Pallas
Esteban Paullaada
Juaquin Quintana
Policarpo Saens
Willms y Ca.
Antonio Zaldivar
José Poveda Escribano

Physicians.

Tomas Cano y Aznar
Francisco B. Campos
Herculano Menesis

Carmen has a large steam mill for extracting and grinding dye stuffs, one flour mill, one do. coffee, one do. cocoa, and two iron foundries.

CHIAPAS,
STATE OF COAHUILA.
Population, 10,500.

Business Agents and Attorneys.

Ignacio Armendares
Juan Balboa
Lauro Cartas
Francisco Castellanos.
Miguel Castillo
Lucio Dominguez

Druggists.

Chanona Domingo
J. C. Gonzalez

General Merchants.

Agusto Lazos
Vincente Farrera
Benedicto Ramos
Wenceslao Parriagua
Romualdo Flores
Narciso Guirao
Refugio Solorzano

Physicians.

P. Flores
José C. Gonzales
Bernado Martinez

CARDOBA,
STATE OF VERA CRUZ.
Population, 15,000.

Booksellers.
Antonio Ortega
Albino Leal

Chemists and Druggists.
Daniel Limon
Francisco Arenas
Carlos Rois

Billiard Halls.
El Casino
Vicente Sarmiento
Dionisio Mantilla
Pedro Diaz
Aspra y Noriega

Coffee Warehouses.
Manuel Abascal
José Gomez Dias
Rafael Aragon Benito
Carlos Fagoaga
Luis Lopez
Cirilo Mingo
Manuel Mateos
Victor Yzquerdo

Clothing and Tailoring.
Rafael Aragon
Raymondo Carretero
Camilo Lopez
Basilio Iraola
Antonia Ortiga
Lauro Bonilla
Antonio Leal

Chocolate Factories.
Manuel Labogné
Mariano Valdez

General Stores, Retail.
Tranquilino Calima
Moises Tapia
Bauper y Ca.

Noriega Aspray
Lucas Cordova
Pedro Costafreda
Pedro Diaz
Rufino de la Torre
José Camacho Fernandez
José Diaz Fernandez
Enrique Galan
Ramon Garay
Rafael Hernandez
Herrero y Ca.
Junque y Isidro
Anselmo Lopez
Francisco Jimenez
Moral y Portilla
Francisco Natali
Victor Louistalot
Gregorio Lopez
Antonio Rodriguez
Ramon Rodriguez
Francisco Cordova Quevedo
Mariano R. Valdez
Ramon Tavares

Hardware and Housefurnishing.
Manuel Abascal
Calleja y Ca.
José Tresgallo
José Maria Salamanca
Cortes Hermanos
Guadaloupe Herzandez
Rafael Vargas

Hotels.
Juan Barral
Faustino Moral
S. Vargas

Physicians.
Enrique Herrera
Cuthberto Peña
José F. Elguera
Alfredo Russell
Ramon R. Rodriguez

There is a railway and a telegraph station in this town. Coffee and all kinds of tropical fruits flourish and abound in this vicinity.

CUERNAVACA,
STATE OF MORELOS.
Population, 8,000.

Druggists.
"La Merced"
"La Providencia"
Botica de Argandar
Botica de Miguel Cruz y Cano

Clothing, Hats, Shoes, Etc.
Manuel Fiz
Honorato Teissier y Ca.
Ramon Hernandez

ESTABLECIDOS EN 1863.

Chas. Kastner & Co.,
MAQUINASTAS, FUNDIDORES
Y SURTIDORES DE MOLINOS.

Suministramos planos y contratamos para Fabricas completas de Cerveceria, Alambiques, Almidon, Glucosa y Vinagre.

MOLINOS DE HARINA, ELEVADORES DE GRANO. DEPOSITOS DE MALTA.

Segun los métodos mejorados y mas recientes. Estamos preparados a guarantizar resultados. Vendemos a precios bajos, máquinas de vapor, calderas, bombas de aire y de vapor, valvulas y ajustes. Tuberia, Tubos, de goma y Correas de Poleas, de las que tenemos surtidos completos en nustra sucursal en VILLA LERDO, MÉXICO, donde nuestro agente el Sr. Ernesto Fuchs, tendrá gusto en cotizar precios, etc.

OFICINA Y FABRICAS:
303-311 SOUTH CANAL STREET,
CHICAGO, ILLS., E. U. DE A.

Taladros de Punta de Diamante de Bullock
PARA
Explotar y Desarrolla
YACIMIENTOS DE MINERALES y CARBON.

Agujeros perforados a cualquier ángulo y a cualquier profundidad requerida, sacando un ÁNIMA CILÍNDRICA DEMOSTRANDO EL CARÁCTER EXACTO DE TODO EL ESTRATO PENETRADO.

Construimos 15 Tamaños y Estilos de Taladros desde máquinas para fuerza de Sangre hasta las máquinas mas grandes para sondar pozos.

Tambien construimos LOS MALACATES DE BANDA DE FRICCION DE LANE. Y TAMBORES desde 2 piés, hasta 30 piés de Diámetro.

MÁQUINAS DE VAPOR "CORLISS" DE BULLOCK.

Desde 50 hasta 2,000 caballos.

PÍDASE CIRCULARES Y PRECIOS,

M. C. BULLOCK MANFG. CO.,
138 JACKSON STREET, - - CHICAGO, ILL., E. U. de A.

EL LABORATORIO MAS GRANDE Y MAS VIEJO DE SU CLASE EN EL MUNDO.

Frederick Stearns & Co.,

FARMACÉUTICOS FABRICANTES.

Establecidos en 1855.

DETROIT, MICH., E. U. de A.

NUEVA YORK, WINDSOR, ONT., y SAN FRANCISCO, CAL.

Ofrecemos al Comercio SURTIDOS COMPLETOS de los siguientes productos de nuestra manufactura. EXTRACTOS LÍQUIDOS (ENSAYADOS), oficial y no oficial.
EXTRACTOS SÓLIDOS (ENSAYADOS), Blandos, en polvos y sacarificados (extractos).
PÍLDORAS Y GRÁNULOS, cubiertas con azucar, gelatina y Perla. Gránulos coloreados.
MEDICAMENTOS SEGUROS—Líquidos, alcalíticulos, alcalímetricos, alcalizados.
ELÍXIRS, Vinos, Tinturas *(ensayadas)*, Soluciones, Ungüentos, Ceratos.
CÁPSULAS, Rellenas duras, Blandas y vacias. Confecciones, oleatos.
DROGAS EN POLVOS, Ensayadas y Garantizadas. Extractos y Preparaciones de Cebada.
SIROPES, Medicinales y médicos. Preparaciones de aceite de hígado de Bacalao.
CONCENTRACIONES (Resinosas), Oleoresinas, Cordiales concentrados (conveniencias).
PREPARACIONES GRANULARES FERMENTOSAS, Calas.
PASTILLAS, Hechas, a mano y Comprimidas. Lápizes é Inhaladores de Menthol.
PASTILLAS Y PÍLDORAS COMPRIMIDAS. Píldoras Hipodérmicas. Pastillas de Frutas.
PEPSINA, Pura, Cascara, Azucarada, Lactinada, Sacarino puro.
SAXOLINE, Simple, Perfumada, Medicinal, sus preparaciones y combinaciones.
PARCHES en Rollos, Porozos, Tafetan, Ingles de Cirujano. Preparaciones narcóticas.
SAZONADORES—Extractos concentrados, Jugos de Frutas, Sabores para Agua de Soda, etc.
PERFUMES—Para pañuelos, Aguas para el tocador, Polvos para el cutis, etc.
Etc., Etc., Etc., Etc., Etc.
Pídase nuestro Catálogo Farmacéutico, 100 páginas, 1,000 ilustraciones.

LAS MEDICINAS NO SECRETAS.

Fueron *originadas* por nosotros hace mas de trece años, y son simplemente recetas preparadas para usos caseros, farmacéuticamente preparadas sin secreto ni fraude. Reemplazan enteramente los medicamentos falsos y privilegiados, con provecho al vendedor y satisfaccion al consumidor. NUESTRO CATÁLOGO ILUSTRADO No. 84 trata ámpliamente sobre el plan, precios y condiciones. Libre al pedirlo. "THE NEW IDEA," un periódico mensual de la Verdadera Farmácia, como opuesta al secreto y Falsedad en la Farmácia. Precio 50 centavos anuales. Cópias de muestras libres.
NUESTRA ESPECIALIDAD es la preparacion y envase de fórmulas particulares, las que podemos hacer mejor, mas baratas y con mas elegancia que el mismo vendedor Pídanse precios.

General Stores, Retail.

"La Niña," Vinda de F. Azcarate
"El Pabellon Mexicana," Aramburo Hermando.
"El Vapor," Juan Pagaza
"La Poblana," Luis Rios Bustamente
"La Luz del Dia," Francisco Sobrino
"La Geratimoe," Jose Barquin
"El Trumfo," Agustin Muñoz
"Panaderia del Cazador," Felipe del Sol

Physicians.

José C. Marquez
Gustavo O'Farrell
Victor Blay
Miguel Cruz y Cano

Theatre.

"Porfirio Diaz," seating capacity, 1,200

COAHUILA,

STATE OF COAHUILA.

Population, 6,000.

Business Agents and Attorneys.

Pedro Radriquez
Tomas Berlanger
Antonio G. Carrillo
Santos Davila
Manuel Flores
Bruno Garcia
Miguel C. Gomez
Patricio Gonzalez
José Maria Muzquiz
Treviño Fernandez

Pianos, Music and Sewing Machines.

Francisco Villanueva
F. Francesconi
Maricino Grande

Machinery and Agricultural Implements.

Estorg y Hayer
Mazo y Hermano
Guillermo Purcell
Bernado Sato

Insurance Agent.

David Zamora

Banks.

Banco Comercial

General Merchants.

Bernado Sota
Guillermo Purcell
Marcelino Garza
Eusebio Calzada
Mariano Grande
Rumulo Garza
José Negrete
Damaso Rodriquez
Pulido Ramos

Druggists.

Carillo y Garcia Fuentes
Mauricio C. Barreda

S. De la Fuente
José Figureo
Hilario Hernandez
M. Warremosch

Clothing, Shoes, Hats, etc., Retail.

Antonio Aguirre
Mazo Hermanos
Florencio Llaguna
José M. Huici
Donato Volpe
José Maria Ramos
Benito Goriba
Acencio Molina.

Physicians.

José Maria Barreda
Anastasio Carrillo
R. H. L. Bebbee
Ramon Davila
José I. Figueroa
Dionisio Fuente
Jesus M. Gill
Jesus Fuestes
Mauricio Garcia
Santiago Smith
Matias Porth

Dry Goods, etc., Retail.

Hayer y Estorg
H. Hernandez
Dolores Maria Rios
Carlos Martinez
Siber Perez
Juan Sandrez

Ales, Beer, etc.

Haussen y Ca.
Perez y Hermano

Printers.

Severo Fernandez
Gonzalez Fuentes
Simon Pena
Mariano Cardenas

CIUDAD GUERRERO,

STATE OF TAMAULIPAS.

Population, 10,000.

Boots and Shoes, Retail.

Tomas Mejid
Manuel Siller
Agustin Vergard

Clothing and Tailoring.

Vicente Ruiz
Francisco Sanchez

Chemists and Druggists.

Martin Gonzalez
Antonio M. Fernandez
Carlos Winslow

Commission Merchants.

Crescencio Soltero
Lorenzo Yañez
Manuel Ramirez

Dry Goods, Hosiery, Etc.

(Retail.)

José Ruiloba
Volpe Hermanos

General Stores.

(Wholesale and retail.)

Joaquin Flores
Juan Manuel Flores
G. Canales
Guillermo Garza
E. Guitierrez Garza

Porfirio C. Garza
Emeterio Gonzalez
Anastacio Gutierrez
Encarnacion Gutierrez
Juande Dios Gutierrez
Cadena Gutierrez
Victor Salazar
Justino Sada
I. Saldaña
Manuel Ramirez Vela
Erasmo Villa

Hardware, Housefurnishing, Etc.

Marcelo Chavez
D. M. Hughes
I. Saldaña
Juan de D. Gutierrez.

Hotels.

Erasmo Martinez

Jewelers.

Agustin Gonzalez
Gillermo Garza

Mining Engineers.

Luis Gorand
Teodoro Santa Cruz

Photographer.

Rafael V. Garza

DURANGO,

STATE OF DURANGO.

Population, 86,000.

Bankers.

Maximiliano Danum
Doorman y Ca.
Juambeltz Hermanos
Stanlknecht y Ca.

Commission Merchants, General.

Francisco Alvarez y Ca.
Juan Belz Hermanos
Julio Doorman y Ca.
Viuda y Hijos de Grimaldo
Gurza Hermanos y Ca.
Guillermo Moller
Pedro del Rio y Ca.
Salcido Hermanos

Druggists, Retail.

" Del Cármen "
" Del San Agustin "

" Universal "
Manuel de Avila
De Guadalupe
Eusebio de Ostolaza
Cárlos Leon de la Peña
Jesus de San Martin
Manuel Santa Maria
Arcadio Tabison

Dry Goods and Groceries.

Juan Alvarez
Andrés Bastera
Bose y Schmidt
Toribio Brancho
J. Castillo
C. Clarke
M. Damin
Doorman y Ca.
Hengeler y Deras
Julia Hildebrand
Jambelz Hermanos

MEXICO.

Dry Goods and Groceries - *continued.*
Lowre Hermano
Juan B. Olagaray
C. Rodrigues
Stahlknecht y Ca.

Flour Mills.
Francisco Alvarez y Rafael
Gavielan y Guerrero

Foundries.
Juan N. Flores
Cerro del Mercado
Compañia Americana

Lithographers.
Francisco Flores
Miguel Gomez

Merchandise, Brokers.
Benito Arritda
Julio Delino
Francisco Fernandez
Jacinto Gomez
Luis Mijaris
Jesus Vazquez

Merchants, General.
Maximiliano Danum
Juan Belz Hermanos
Julio Doorman y Ca.
Viuda y Hijos de Grimaldo
Anezaga y Ca.
Bengoechea y Ca.
Gurza Hermanos y Ca.
J. Hildebrand y Ca.

J. Lopez Rangel
Guillermo Moller
Jambelz Hermanos
Stahlknecht y Ca.
D. Arguelles
Fernandez Hermanos
Gallegos
Clementi Garcia
Faustino Gomez y Ca.
M. Jaquier
Francisco Ortigosa
Parra
Vargas Hermanos
Vazquez y Dias

Mining Engineers.
A. Luis Lavie
J. Patoni

Physicians.
Librado Castillo
Felipe Gavilan Perez
Mariano Herrara
Francisco A. Lazalde
Juan A. Loneza
Juan de Dios Palacios
Ambrosio Sanchez
J. Contreras
José Reyes
Jesus San Martin
Cárlos Santa Marina
Fernando Sarraga
David Rios

Printers.
Cárlos de la Mariposa Gomez
Guadalupana
José S. Rocha

GUYAMAS,
STATE OF SONORA.

Population, 6,000.

Agricultural Implements.
(See General Merchants.)

Booksellers and Stationers.
Tauzi y Ca.

Bookbinder and Printer.
Miguel Castelan

Commission Merchants.
V. M. Gray
Ricardo Laborin
Sandoval y Hijos
Matias Tamayo

Druggists.
A. Wallace, 94 Principal
Luis G. Dávila, 86 Principal

Dry Goods and Notions.
Selner y Von Borstel

Jewelers and Watchmakers.
J. Selner
Felide Misa

Merchants, General.
Aguilar, Sucesores
Dominiciano Baston
W. Iberri
Kiesnelback, Moller y Ca.
G. Sandoval y Hijo
Seldner y Von Borstel
Camon Hermanos

Physicians.
Casca y Garcia
Priciliano Figueroa
Agustin A. Roa
Tomas Spencer

GUADALAJARA,

STATE OF JALISCO.

Population, 100,000.

Ales and Beer Dealers.

Placido Guerrero
Juan Ohoner
Benito Rebollon
A. Coiffier
Miguiel Gutierrez

Arms and Ammunition.

(See Hardware, Etc.)

Architects and Builders.

Antonio Arroniz
David Bravo
Gabriel Castanon
Castañeda Hnos
Manuel Gomez
Jesus Lomeli
Manuel Quevedo

Boots and Shoes.

José Maria Arias
Espiridion Arrieta, Loreto
Silvestre Castro
Petronilo Gomez
Alberto, Nava y Ca.
José Maria Portillo
Antonio Rodriguez
Viuda de Rodriguez
Ciriaco Torrez
Jesus Gomez

Commission Merchants, General.

Castañeda Hermanos
Emilio Ascher
Jesus Alvarez del Castillo
Julian Camarena
Evaristo Iniquez
Rafael Lopez
Dionisio Mead
Ramon de la Mora
Enrique de la Pena
Ignacio Rasura
Vudriffed Hermanos
Renito Barroso
Chavez y Guido
Juan Galvan
Gustavo Gravenhorts
Placido Guerrero
Francisco Infante
José M. Infante
Luis Infante
Edurado Iturbide
Salvadore Maconzet
Loreto Martinez del Campo
Atansio Mier
Manuel Montano
Santiago Ortiz
Epifanlo Oseguera
Gabino Oseguera
Ramon Ramirez
José J. Retana
Nemesio Ruiz

Ignacio Solorzano
Pablo Torres
Vallejo Hermanos
Juan Vallejo
Ramon Villareal

Dentists.

Francisco Mendez Padilla
Francisco Ponce de Leon
Guillermo H. Rigger
Francisco P. Leon
Felix Castillo
Pablo Comacho
José M. Rones

Druggists.

Manuel Arreola
Jesus Cortis de Ocampo
Alejo Garcia Conde
Antonio Esteves Gutierrez
Jacinto Montano
Jesus Montano
Etiquio Murillo
Vicente Ochoa
Lorenzo Ornelas
Cárlos Perez
Lazaro Perez
Nicolas Puga
José Maria Romo
Nicolas Tortolero
Vidal Torres
Enrique Weitenauer
Cárlos Zulnaga
Juan Montano
Lazaro Perez y Hijo
Fernando de los Rios
Jesus Ascenio
Torres y Tapia

Dry Goods and Notions.

Jesus C. Arce
Julio Jurgensen
Viuda y Hijos de Lacroix
Mauricio Rohde
Juan D. Muñoz
Runchaldt y Rose
Antonio Alcarez
Aracio y Ca.
F. Arévalo
José Juan Babadilla
Bannafoux, Fortoul y Chapuy
Casadevant y Garselon
Francisco Celso
Feliciano Corona
Corona y Ca.
Cogordan Gas
José Gasibe
Ignacio Gomez
Amado Gonzalez
Vicente Gonzalez
Honoraf, Pelester y Saldini
Lagnette y Brihuega
Lebre, Barriére y Ca.

MEXICO. 71

Dry Goods and Notions—*continued.*
Cayetano Melendez
Santiago Mendoza
Juan D. Muñoz
Nestor Navarro
Pedro Navarro
Canuto Romero
Julio Rosse
Eduardo Romero
Ramon Ugarte
José Maria Zuloaga

Express Company.
Wells, Fargo & Co.

Flour Dealers.
Canedo y Valdivieso
Apolonio Garcia
Matias Gomez
F. Simon del Llano
Torres, Morfin y Hermano
Maximiano Valdovinos

Furniture.
Octaviano Aldava
José Cano
José Procopio Cassillas
Miguel Cassillas
Antonio Garciadiego
Teodoro Gomez
Antonio Orozco
Bonifacio Romero
José Maria Cano

Gas Companies' Agents.
Santiago Alvarez
Nabor Gallegos
Lucio Robles
Rafael Sanchez
Francisco Valencia

Groceries and Provisions, Wholesale and Retail.
José Felix Agraz
Santiago Alvarez
Angel Arch
Florentino Badial
Lucas Barron
Castillo y Zuñiga
Jesus Chavez
Apolonio Cedeño
Donaciano Corona
Celso Cortes
José Isabel Cortes
Antonio Covarrubias
Tomás Cruz
Dernongin y Victor Hermano
Ambrosio Diaz
Librado Escamilla
Fernandez y Ca.
José G. Fernandez
Ochoa J. Gallardo
Joaquin Garcia
Ramon Garibay
Ignacio Garibay
Francisco Garibay
Miguel Garibi
José Maria Gomez
Felipe Gomez
Polomar B. Gonzalez
Ramon Gomez
Ignacio Gudino
Julian Gutierrez
Priciliano Hernandez
Alberto Jiminez
Evaristo Moncayo
Tomas Molina
Hiliano de la Mora
Ignacio Navarro
Jacobo Navarro
Valerio Nuñez
Mariano P. Oruelas
Abraham Oseguera
Conrado Osegeura
Gonzalez de Perez
Pedro Quiroz
Rafael Rios
Robles y Vizcaino
Mauro Rodriguez
Antonio Romero
José Maria Romero
Felipe Romero
Ponciano Ruiz
Metamoros Portal
Manuel Sainz
A. Aldama Sanchez
Ignacio Valdez

Hardware, Cutlery, Etc.
Agustin Bontholly
Benito Gonzalez Palomar
Julio Jurgensen y Ca.
Adolfo Niemann
Mauricio Rohde
Juan Zuluaga
Mauricio Rohde
Augustin Blume

House Furnishing, Tinware, Etc.
Ignacio Aranda
Hipolito Granados
José Maria Guerrero
Sebastian Mariscal
José Sandoval

Jewelry, Watches and Silverware.
Andrés Beha
Leal Hermanos
Nicolas Sanchez Aldana
Jacinto Torres
Juan B. Torres
Eustasio Ulloa
Francisco P. Vallasta
Antonio Winterhalder
Sabino Aguilar

Lithographers.
Anciray Hermano
José Maria Iguinig
J. Antonio Izaguirre
Alberto Rodriguez

Lumber Merchants.
Octaviano Aldapa
José Cano
José Casillas
Miguel Casillas
Antonio Garciadiego
Theodoro Gomez
Antonio Orozco

Machinery Depots.

Emilio Hachar
Wm. Jameson y Hermano
Juan Kip
Juan N. Bautista
Rosalio Briseno
Pedro Carillo
Francisco Leon
Felix Martinez
Antonio Valovinos

Merchants, General Wholesale.

Alfonso Heyman
Antonio Alverez del Castillo
Blume y Ca.
Castañeda Hnos
Eduardo Colignon y Ca.
Manuel Corcuera y Hijos
Manuel Fernandez del Valle
Fernandez Somellera y Ca.
Agustin Gil
Miguel Hermosillo
Teodore Kuhnhardt
Rafael Lopez
Nicolas G. Lemus
Francisco Martinez Negrete
Ramon Miravete
Moreno y Palomar
Oetling y Ca.
Palomar Hermanos
Lazaro Perez y Hijo
Genaro Sanchez
Somellera Fernandez y Ca.
Francisco Ugarte
Santiago Camareno y Ca.
Librado Escamilla
Gonzalez Olivarez y Hermano
Negrete F. Martinez
Pablo Navasotlo
Francisco Grande
Gustavo Gravenhort
J. Maconzet y Hermano
J. Morellon y Ca.
L. Oruna y Hermanos
Manuel Solorozano

Perfumery and Toilet Articles.

Ventura Diaz
Viuda de Lacroix
Viuda de Paez
Cruz Ramrez

Photographers.

Cárlos A. Barriere
Ramon G. Fuentes
Pedro Magallanes
Octaviano de la Mora
Espalda y Portal
Refugio Ibarre de Diaz

Physicians.

Abundio Acevez
Teofilo Alvarez
Crispiniano Arce
Fortunato Arce
Antonio Arias
José M. Benitez
Perfecto G. Bustamante
José M. Carmarena
Salvador Camarena
Jesus Castillo

José M. Castillo
Carlos Z. Dieznez
Juan S. Escobedo
Espinosa Monroy
José Maria Frenoso
Salvador Diego Garcia
Silverio Garcia
Ignacio Godinez
Manuel Guemez
Luis Hernan
Eduardo Ibarra
Jesus Larios
Rafael Mendez
Lopez Miguel Mendoza
Emigdio Nuno
Juan Oliva
Martin Polanco
Topete Justo Pastor
Manuel Rey
José Maria Reynoso
Gregorio Rubio
Raul M. Serrano
Vidal Torres y Tapia
Juan Zavala
Carlos Zulunga
Francisco M. Padilla
Ficolas Puga
Fausto Uribe
Julio Cordova
Jesus Avelar
Bonifacio Morales
Mariano Cortes
Mucio Cortes
Reyes G. Flores
Gutierrez J. Macias
Antonio Ornelas

Pianos and Organs.

Ed. Cullignon y Ca.
Mauricio Rohde
Claro Tome Villasenor

Printers.

Francisco Arroyo
Federico Echeverria
José Maria Iguinig
Loreto Ancira y Hermano
José Cabrera
Suarez Martinez
José Maria Robles
José Maria Vargas

Publishers and Booksellers.

Francisco Ahedo
Cárlos Bouret
Neveriano Galvan
José Gomez Daniel Garcia
Francisco Nigrete Martinez
Moreno y Mora
Cármen Muñoz
Nicolas de Pena
Josefa de Cortes Rubio
Eusebio Sanchez y Ca.

Sewing Machines.

Emilio Hachar
Alfonso Heymann
Julio Jurgensen
Dionisio Meade
Mauricio Rohde
Julio Rose

Tanners and Leather Merchants.

Vincente Banales
Viuda de Carmona
Sixto Monteon
Emilio Peinado
J. Fernando
Manuel Stampa
Maximiano Valdovinos

Undertakers.
(See Furniture.)

Wholesale Dealers in Native Products.

Pablo Comacho
Santiago Camarena, Sta. Teresa
Felix Castillo
Florencio Chavez
Cárlos Garcia Sacho, 29 Aduana
Gonzalez Olivares Hermano, 2 Degellado
Albino Martin
Marcelino Morfin
Clemente Munguia
Liberato Munguia
Pablo Navarrete
Francisco Padilla
Exiquio Ponce
Jesus Maria Rubio
Domingo Salcedo
Ricardo Villegas

GUANAJUATO,
STATE OF GUANAJUATO.
Population, 65,000.

Agricultural Implements.
(See Hardware Merchants, General.)

Ales and Beer Dealers.
Antonio Camacho
Ernesto Ruger
Juan Irigaray

Arms and Ammunition.
(See also Hardware,)

Narciso Nunes
Francisco Manriquez
Castulo Villegas

Assayers and Chemists.
Dario Abanez
Leoncio Lobato
Abraham Lozano
Eugenio Lozano
Roberto Philipo
Francisco M. Sardaneta
José Velez
Pedro Belounzaran
José Marsa Cantero
Ildefonso Gomez
Oca de Montes
Miguel Pezquera
Gabriel Montes de Oca

Banks.
Banco Mercantil
Banco Nacional Mexicano

Billiards.
José Gilbert y Ca.
Rosalio Lara
Trinidad de la Torre

Blacksmiths.
Ignacio Gomez
Francisco Manriquez
Castulo Villegas

Bookbinders.
Eugenio Corono
Pedro Parres
Augustin Serrano

Books and Stationery.
Cárlos Bouret
Pedro de la Fuente
Pedro Ripollez

Boots and Shoes.
Jesus Alvarado
Margarito Arias
Enrique Bernard
Emetrio Duarte
Francisco Heredia
J. Maria Machuca
Felipe Madrid
Ceferino Pedroza
Francisco Rodriguez
Catarino Rodriguez
N. Soria
Francisco Vilannueva

Brokers.
Magdaleno Dominguez
Feliciano Guzman

Commission Merchants.
Fuentes y Romero
Enrique Meyerberg
Narcisco Nuñez
Manuel Reinoso

Copper Goods.
Ramon Alvarez
Antonio Bonifacio

Crockery and Glassware.
Diego Abascal
Santos Acostas
Caloca y Ca.
Luis Caudra

Crockery and Glassware—*continued.*
J. Fuentes
Felipe Gomez
Hermanos Obregon
Monico Ortego
Enrique Palasson
Francisco de P. Pedrosa

Dentists.
Espiridion Martinez

Druggists.
Felipe Aragon
B. Arreguin
Jesus Gasca
Elias Villafuerte
Tomas Fonseca
Gasca y Ca.
Leal y Ca.
Francisco Lopez
Marquez y Ca.
Sirio Maicote
José Ruoda
Vincente Salcedo
Cárlos Sotura
Ignacio Vazquez
Villanueva y Ca.

Dry Goods, Wholesale.
Luis Goerne
Enrique Langenscheidt
Hermanos Osante
Alcazar Stalfort y Ca.

Engineers, Architects & Builders.
Agustin Ajuria
Julian Antillon
Ponciano Aguillar
Miguel Bravo
Pedre Belauzaran
Juan N. Conteras
Luis Campa
Juan N. Garcia
Francisco Glennier
Anda Luiz Gutierrez
Ignacio Ibarguengoitia
Enrique Martinez
Francisco Manriquez
Vicente Mana
A. Mendoza
Luis Muro
Severo Navia
Pablo Orozco
Manuel Ortiz
Pedro Otero
Joaquin Parres
Francisco Reinoso
Guadalupe Reinoso
Ignacio G. Rocha
Francisco Sardaneta
Miguel Septien

Flour Mills.
Antonio Anaya
M. Coz
Pablo Zepeda

Furniture.
Antonio Bonifacio
Juan Jaunoud
Obregon y Hermano

Gas Manufacturer.
Juan M. Conteras

Groceries and Provisions.
Florencio Arteaga
Manuel Valadez
Francisco Zarrate

Hardware, Cutlery and Tools.
Diego Abascal
Alcazar y Ca.
Luis Goerne
Enrique Laugenscheidt
Hermanos Osante
Rodriguez y Ca.

House Furnishing Goods and Tinware.
Alfonso Damen
Enrique Palasson
Pablo Duran
Hilario Flores
Hilario Flores
Tiburcio Delgado
Antonio Moron
Narciso Flores
Ricardo Reina
Ignacio Vazquez
Bruno Alvarez
Modesto Frias

Hotels.
Hilario Gaidan, Guanajuato
Magdalen Garcia, Meson Santonio
Concepcion Gimenez, Alonso

Ice Dealers.
Roman Navarro
Bartolo Peñaflor

Importers and Warehousemen.
M. Ajuria
Alcazar y Ca.
Luis Goerne
Enrique Langenscheidt
Narciso Muñoz
Cipriano Rodriguez y Ca.

Jewelry and Watches.
Gabellon Galacion
Alejandro Hernandez
Antonio Perez
Antonio Villalpando
Federico Wieland
Hernandez y Hijo
Luis Laux
Federico Gerilant

Lithographer.
Faustino Laureto

Lumber Merchants.
Sucesores de Benito Herrera
Trinidad Lopez
Rafael Alvarado
J. M. Anda

Merchants, General, Wholesale.

Abascal y Ca.
Miguel Arvizer
Caire Andriffred y Ca.
Caloca y Ca.
Margarito Castro
Luis Cuadra
Antonio Cuellar
Amado Delgado
Alfonso Denne
Victorino Espinosa
Ignacio Fernandez
Fuentes y Romero
Luis Goerno
Felipe Gomez
Ventura Gomez
Jesus Gonzalez
Lino Gutierrez
Juan Herrera
Luis Hugelstein
Francisco Lara
Pascual Marmol
Muñoz Torres Hermanos
Obregon y Hermano
Palasson Hermanos
Francisco Pedraza
Roman Robles
Juan Romero
José Velazquez
Evaristo Villaseñor y Ca.
Pablo Zepeda
Florencio Alferez
Aguerre Hermanos
Oton Bollmeyer
Guillermo Brockmann
Juan B. Cassaneve
Modesto Cos
Oetling Droege y Ca.
E. Palasson
Stallforth, Alcazor y Ca.
Manuel Gonzalez
José Hernandez
Romulo Lopez
Antonio Macias
Manuel Mena
Vicente Mena
Ambrosia Olivares
Francisco Roblés
Vicente Salcedo
Francisco Salgado
Abraham Santabanez
Andrés Telles
Indalecio Wario
José Wesleyr Herrera
Manuel Moreno
José Palacios
Manuel Ruiz
Trevino Ruiz
Andrés Tellez
Ortega Hernandez

Paints and Varnishes.

Geronimo Hijar
Antonio Santoyo
Flopencio Arteaga
Manuel Valdez
Francisco Zorate

Perfumery.

Hermano y Obregon

Photographers.

Vicente Contreras
Iñigo y Ramirez

Physicians.

Manuel Arraya
Eduardo Armendariz
José Bribiesca
J. M. Bribiesca
Tomas Cásillas
Tomas Chavez
Jesus Chica
Alfredo Duges
Dimas Flores
Vicente Gomez

Pianos and Organs.

Enrique Langenscheidt
Enrique Meyerburg
Antonio Villapando

Printers.

Francisco Onate
Justo Palencia
Francisco Rodriguez
Joaquin Hérnandez
José Palencia

Sewing Machines.

Margorito Castro
Jesus Herrara
Enrique Palasson
David Wininburg.

Ship Chandlers' Goods.

Manuel Castro
Santos Cepeda
Refugio Morales
Lorenzo Rodriguez

Telegraph Companies.

El Federal
Jalisco

Undertakers.

(See Furniture.)

Wall Paper.

(See Stationers.)

Warehousemen.

M. Ajuria
Alcazar, Stalfort y Ca.
Arango Bros.
Jesus Flores
Narciso Muñoz
Capriano Rodriguez

HERMOSILLO,

STATE OF SONORA.

Population, 6,000.

Agents, General.

Luis Rodriguez
Eduado Castañeda
José M. Eucisas
Leonado Euciso
Florencio Velasco
Manuel Escalante
Cristobal Serrano

Merchants, General.

Ramon Ayon
E. Goblentz y Ca.
José M. Miranda
Juliana Noriega
Eduardo Duran
A. Majocchi
Gaudara Hermanos
José Porto
Rafael Ruiz
Manuel Mascareñas
Ricardo Diaz
Juan N. Castro
Carlos Nanetti
Antonio Calderon y Ca.
Filomeno Loaiza

Carmelo Echeverria
R. Rodriguez
Vicente V. Escalante
Juan Marcos

Druggists.

Botica Alemana
Botica Mexicana
Botica Nueva

Physicians.

Eugenio Pasqueira
Gabriel Monteverde
Fernando Aguilar
Alberto C. Carbo

Printers.

Roberto Bernal
Imprenta del Gobierno

Boot and Shoe Dealers.

L. Boido
J. E. Yepez
Salviano Sainz

IRAPUATO,

STATE OF GUANAJUATA.

Population, 12,000.

Ales and Beer.

Miguel Almanza
Pedro Dumas
E. Sanchez

Agricultural Implements.

Juan Vargas y Hermanos

Billiard Halls.

Juan A. Gaytan
Mariano Perez

Bookseller.

Nicolas Hernandez

Commission Agents.

Vicente Aguilerd
Manuel Bocanegra
Librado Lopez

Crockery and Glassware.

Genaro Acosta
Trinidad Betancourt

Druggists.

Aguirre Gondalez
Ignacio Canal
S. Galvan
Miguel Orozco
Apolinar Revea
E. Sanchez

Dry Goods.

Vincente Diaz
Antonio Flores
Gabriel Vega

Express Company.

Wells, Fargo & Co.

Flour Mill.

Agustin Moussier.

Hardware and House Furnishings.

Genaro Acosta
Gabriel Vega
Antonio Rangel
Guadalupe Alvarado

EL CÉLEBRE **ARADO** ENFRIADO Y MEJORADO DE BISSELL.

EL ARADO

mas perfeccionado en el mercado.

Fuerte y durable. Permutable y perfecta en todas sus partes. Cerrojos que no sueltan, y no son experimentos. Arados en tres tamaños, 7, 8 y 9 pulgadas. Pídase catálogo. Dirigirse,

THE BISSELL CHILLED PLOW WORKS,
SOUTH BEND, IND., E. U. DE A.

THE
Joseph Schlitz Brewing Company's
WORLD FAMOUS
"MILWAUKEE LAGER BEER,"
MILWAUKEE, WIS., U. S. A.

HERCULES
POWDER

STRONGEST AND SAFEST DYNAMITE EXPLOSIVE KNOWN TO THE ARTS for all Mining, Railroad Work, Rock and Stump Blasting.

FUSE, CAPS, BATTERIES AND ELECTRIC MINING GOODS.
Hercules Powder Co., 40 Prospect St., Cleveland, O.
J. W. WILLARD, Gen'l Manager.

GEORGE W. TIFFT, SONS & CO.

MAQUINAS Y CALDERAS DE VAPOR,

de todas clases y tamaños, y á precios muy bajos. Mas de 9,000 de nuestra máquinas en uso. Pídanse catálogos. Dirigirse,

GEORGE W. TIFFT, SONS & CO.
BUFFALO, N. Y., E. U. de A.

VALENTIN BLATZ,

Milwaukee, Wis., E. U. de A.,

Cervecero, Embotellador y Exportador

de laa

CÉLEBRE CERVEZA

MILWAUKEE

"LAGER,"

DE LAS MARCAS

"Pilsener," "Tivoli," "Wiener" y "Private Stock."

EMBOTELLADAS EXPRESAMENTE PARA LOS MERCADOS TRÓPICOS.

Ha recibido los primeros premios por todo El Universo.

SE SOLICITA CORRESPONDENCIA.

VALENTIN BLATZ,

Milwaukee, Wis., U. S. A.,

BREWER, BOTTLER AND EXPORTER OF HIS CELEBRATED

"MILWAUKEE LAGER."

CORRESPONDENCE SOLICITED.

MEXICO. 77

Hotels.

Eduado Guerrero
Vargas Hernanas

Mechanical Engineers.

Ignacio Gonzales
Manuel Magallanes

Mineral Water Factories.

Francisco A. Gonzalez
Ignacio Chagogan
Alejandro Fajardo

Music Store.

Jacobo Marmolejo

Photographers.

Francisco Fajardo
Lanuza y Lanuza

Physicians.

E. Betancourt
Francisco Arroyo
Francisco Montenegro
Miguel Orozco
Enrique Reynoso
Antonio Retana

Pianos and Instruments.

A. Cosio
Simeon Gonzalez

Printers.

Miguel Castro
Vicente Cervantes

Wholesale Warehouses, General.

José Barquin
Genaro Acosta
T. Betancourt
Nieves Castro
Nicolas Fernandez
José Rivera
G. Ramirez

JIMENEZ,

STATE OF CHIHUAHUA.

Population, 6,000

Merchants, General.

Torres y Subia
Carlos Flores y Hijos
J. P. Baca y Hermanos
Matias Balderrama

Hotels.

Hotel Mexicana

Physician.

Manuel Ramos

JALAPA,

STATE OF VERA CRUZ.

Population, 15,000.

Agents and Attorneys.

Pedro Dominguez
Enrique Zimenez
Joaquin Aguilar
Angel Rivera
Mariano Rivadeneyra

Chemists and Druggists.

Perez y Redondo
Antonio Crespo
M. Gutierrez Lozada
Juan Pozo
Señoritas Martinez
Virginia Pastrana
Idelfonso Trigos
Manuel Quiroz

Cigar Factories, Wholesale.

Ignacio Betancourt
Carlos Florida
Manuel Rocha

Dry Goods, Haberdashery, Etc.

Luis Cordero
Carlos Bonchez
Sucesores de Milan
J. A. Rodriguez

General Stores, Retail.

Francisco Pastorisa
Francisco Guevara
Vinda de J. Franchechi
Mariano Romero
José Maria Teran
Ramon Zubieta
" La Favorita "
" La Estrella de Oro "
Escribano y Co
Juarez y Nieto
Aragon y Martinez
Angel Cordera
" La Diana "

General Stores, Wholesale.

Francisco J. Guevara
Francisco Pastoresa
José Maria Teran
Ramon Sulueta
Escobar Hermanos

Hotels.

Pedro Baez
Juan Pasalgas

Machinery Warehouses.

Carlos Bonchez
Luis Cordero

Manufacturers of Preserves, Etc.

" El Dique," Agustin Cerdan
" Lucas Martin," Carlos F. Garcia
" La Providad," M. Emelio y Ca.
Antonio Sayago

Mechanical Engineers.

José A. de la Peña
Juan A. Perez

Soap Factories.

Pedro Luelmo
José Maria Rech

LEON,
STATE OF GUANAJUATO.
Population, 12,000.

Agricultural Implements and Machinery.

Jorge Heyser
Luz Alvarado

Ales and Beer, Dealers.

Roberto Huitch
Julio Cornu
Roque Verneuil

Arms and Ammunition.

B. Rembez
Ramon del Olmo
Eufemio Berumen.

Billiard Saloons.

Juan Aranto
Pedro Espinosa
A. Guerroro
Louja Mercantil

Bookbinders.

Cardona Hermanos
José M. Monzon
Zeferino Rocha

Booksellers.

Portillo y Guemes
Jesus Izquierdo
Rafael Villalobos.

Boots and Shoes.

Valente Barbora
Juan Maldonado
Agustin Jaqueres
Teodaro Ruiz
Lauro Segura

Cigar Factories and Tobacconists.

Amado Delgado
Baltasar Gonzalez
Manuel Malacara
Miguel Segura
Norberto Trueba

City Railway Company.

Epigmenio Yedra, director

Clothing, Etc., Retail.

Bessonart y Apesteguy
Angel Bustamente
Santiago Barbier
Echeagaray y Ca.
A. de Leon Garcia
Gonzalez y Ca.
Carlos Obregon
Lorenzo Thommé
José Muñatones
Rafael Villalobos
Sabino Mena

Clothing, Hats, Etc.

Sebastian Avila
Cárlos Carpio
José Chavez
Amado Delgado
Baltasar Gonzalez
C. Hernandez
Lopez y Hermano
Ildefonso Lopez
Santiago Manrique
Manuel Malacara
Serapio Manguia
E. Muñoz
Victoriano Ramirez
Pascual Salgado
Fernando Puente Salas
Jesus Segura
Norberto Trueba
Pablo Aldana
Juaquin Flebe
Luis Haglestein

Commission Brokers and Agents.

Hernandez y Alvarez
Salvador Zimenez
J. de la Luz Alfaro
Juan S. Lopez
Miguel F. Segura

Crockery and Glassware, Lamps, Etc.

Bittrolff y Manini
Serapio Munguia
J. A. Perez
Fernando Martinez y Hermano
Juan P. Rico
Jesus Seguara
Fernando Puento Salas
Ramon Olino
José Perez

Dealers in Native Produce.

Fuentes y Piña
Echeagaray y Ca.
Manuel Madrazo
Santiago Manrique
Bezaury Rembez
Jesus Valazquez.

Dentists.

Patricia Padilla
Felipe Gonzalez

Dry Goods, Clothing, Etc.

Antonio Oller
Lopez de Nava y Ca.
Fisch y Bischoff
Fernando Martinez y Hermano
Polhs y Guedea
Portilla y Guemes
Juan P. Rico
Fernando Puente Salas

Druggists.

Juan N. Castro
Pedro Acosta
Miguel España
Antonio España
Luis Gonzalez
Francisco Aguerro Gonzalez
Leal y Ca.
Petronillo Ruiz
José Ortiz

Express Company.

Wells, Fargo & Co.

Fancy Goods, Laces, Haberdashery, Etc.

Fuentes y Piña
Pedro Esteves
Echeagaray y Ca.
Amado Hermosillo
De Nava Lopez y Ca
Antonio Oller
Pohls y Guedea
Portillo y Hayser

Flour Merchants.

Santiago Manrique
J. M. Gonzalez
Julio Reynaud
Manuel Sierra
Elulalio Torres

Flour Mill.

Jorge Gray

Furniture Dealers.

Fuentes y Pina
Ramon Olmo
Rembez y Bezaury

General Commission Merchants.

Fisch y Bischoff
Fernando Martinez y Hermano
Fuentes y Piña
Luz Alvarado
Hernandez y Alvarez
Francisco C. Garza
Juan Savedra Lopez
Miguel Gomez Luna
Cleto Mena
Miguel Segura
S. Munguia

Hardware, Cutlery, Etc.

Fernando Martinez y Ca.
Bittrolff y Manini
Ramon Olmo
Felipe Robles
José Perez

Hotels.

Lopez de Lalande
Santiago Aranjo
Pascual Hourcade

Pianos and Musical Instruments.

Ramon Del Olmo
Juan P. Rico
Pohls y Guedea
Rauron Olmo
Bittrolff y Mauini

Photographers.

Elias Castillo
José Maria Pacheco

Physicians.

Juan N. Castro
Pedro Acosta
Francisco Aranjo
Octaviano Galvan
Felipe Gonzalez
Velasco Rosendo de Gutierrez
Jesus Soto
Angel Trujillo
Ezequiel Torres
Garcia Saavedra
José Ortiz
Francisco Leal
Jesus Jimenez

Printers.

Daniel Camacho
Gomez y Hijo
José M. Munzon
Jesus Villalpando

Theater.

"El Dablado"

Watches and Jewelry.

Luis Long
Rembez y Bezaury
Pascual Barroso
Francisco Gray

Wool Exporters.

Diego Manrique
Ramon Munoz
Francisco Cortina Garza
E. Munoz
Antonio Oller

METAMOROS,

STATE OF TAMAULIPAS.

Population, 13,000.

Druggists.
V. E. Brayder
Eduardo Bremer
C. Braider

Dry Goods, Notions, Etc.
José A. Cardenas
Jacobo Berhein
Burchard y Hermano
Francisco Fernandez
Lorenzo Garibay

Groceries and Provisions, Retail.
Antonio Davila
Juan Gamboa
Francisco Davila
G. Garcia
M. F. Garcia
A. Gonzalez Garza
Montemayer y Ca.
Tiburcio Punente
Manuel Salazar
N. Torres

Hardware and Tools.
A. Doulet
Miguel Madrazo
Marcelino Rougier
Juan Sansat

Jewelry, Watches and Silverware.
José A. Hinojosa
Belemberg y Quast

Merchants, General.
Diego Abad
Adolfo Alarez y Ca.
Francisco Amendariz, Sucs
José M. Amendariz

Francisco Bali
Bahnsen y Ca.
Barreda y Liaña
Bremer y Scholtz
Ambrosio Cantu
Manuel Cantu
José Maria Cardenas
Rafael Crespo
José de la Mora
Antonio M. Erhard
Julio Eversmann
José Fernandez y Ca.
Manuel F. Fernandez
José Gutierrez
Santiago Iturri
W. Junco
J. Lira
Eduardo Longoria
Manuel F. Fernandez
Lopez de Lara y Ca.
Gaspar A. Lynch
Adolfo Mar
Tomas Marquez
Daniel Milo y Ca.
Antonio Mireles
Leocadio Muñoz
H. Nilson
Federico O'Boile
Antonio Prado
Octaviano Reyna y Hermano
Manuel Sierra
Julio Smag
Francisco A. Soni
Melquiades Torrez
Enrique Trevino
Manuel Trevino
H. E. Woodhouse y Ca.
Julio Zander
Ramou Zepeda

Physicians.
Ponco Fernando
W. Welsh

MERIDA,

STATE OF YUCATAN.

Population, 30,000.

Agricultural Implements.
(See Hardware and Tools.)

Ales and Beer.
(See Groceries and Provisions.)

Bookbinder.
Felipe Montilla

Boots and Shoes, Retail.
Muñoz C. Arestegui
Pedro Camara
Juan Gonzalez Carvajal
Basilio Carrillo
Benito Carrillo
Espejo Ciriaco
Euladio Cayoe
Juan de D. Hernandez
Mateo Hernandez

MEXICO.

Boots and Shoes, Retail—*continued*.
Guadalupe Mendoza
Joaquin Preng
Lucas Rubio
Castillo Ruiz
Domingo Ruiz
Martin Salazar

Cotton Mills.
Juan A. Urcelay

Dentists.
J. M. Gilkey
Eduardo Rodriguez

Druggists.
Santiago Aguilar
El Refugio
José Font
La Catedral
La Mejorada
Parque Central
Cárlos Perez
Pedro Troncoso
Eduardo Casares
Medina
Francisco Negron
Patron
P. P. Pinto Perez
Abelardo Ponce
W. Ponce
Rivera y Ca.
Miguel Villamil

Engineers, Mechanical.
José A. Ensenyat
Evia Alfonso Lopez
Leopoldo Perdones
Cárlos Ramirez
Gonzalo Ruiz
Juan Villamil

Furniture and Cabinet Ware.
Leopoldo Alberto

Groceries and Provisions.
Manuel Almeyda
Juan Aragon
Daniel Argona
R. Atocha y Ca.
Faustino Avila
Adolfo Bolio
Hermanos Bolio
Joaquin Camps y Hijo
G. Canto
José C. Carrillo
Magdaleno Carrillo
Juan B. Castillo
Pedro Castillo
Cervera y Ca.
Miguel Concha
Espinosa y Ca.
Bartolome Fuentes
Fuentas y Ca.
Francisco Fuentes
Manuel J. Gallareta
Francisco Gonzalez
José de Hidalgo
José Millet Hubbe
Gabriel Lujon

Melquiades Mena
Isidro Mendiento
Gregorio Milon
Tiburcio Mota
Ortiz y Ca.
Palma y Hermanos

Hardware, Tools, Etc.
Crasemann y Ca.
Ricardo Gutierrez
Gregorio Diego Ayroa
L. Gutierrez
Gutierrez y Ca.
German Ravonburg
Leopoldo Albertos
Alveraz y Ca.
Manuel Donde
Antonio Esenat
Ramon P. Juanes
Nicolin Hermanos

House Furnishing Goods and Tinware.
José D. Burgos
Bosénito Rivas
José Ruz Sanchez
Domingo Valencia

Ice Merchants and Manufacturers.
El Pabellon Mejicano
M. Almedia.

Jewelry, Watches and Silverware.
Luis Claudon
Enrique Dellemberg
Paulino Aragon
Barcelo y Mateo
Joaquin Basulto
Juan E. Basulto
Euladio Cabrera
Loreto Carrillo
Cárlos Dominguez
Tiburcio Flores
Juan C. Monforte
Elgio Quen
José D. Ramirez
Policarpo Rosel
Francisco Rodriguez
Saturnio Rodriguez
Mateo Sanchez

Lithographers.
Santiago Bolio Quijano
Ricardo B. Caballero

Merchants, General, Importing and Commission.
Marcelino Gandarillas
Luis Gutierrez
Ricardo Gutierrez
Haro y Concha
Haro y Pena
Hoffman y Dominguez
Ibarra y Ca.
Miguel Laviada
Pedro Seal
F. Lizarraga y Ca.
Gregorio Milan
Sergio Padron

Merchants General, etc.—*continued.*

Palma y Hermanos
Alfredo Peon
Perez y Ca.
Ponce y Ca.
Viuda y Hijo de Regil
Pedro Rotger y Ca.
Manuel Rucio
Celestino Ruis del Hoyo
Francisco Ruis del Hoyo
Viuda de Toledo y Ca.
Manuel Zapata y Hijo
Luis Bros.
Rodolfo G. Conton
Francisco Alvarez
Agustin Alcina
Nicanor Ancona
Benito Azzar
Aznar, Perez y Ca.
Eduardo Bolio
Camilo Camara y Hijos
P. Camara y Ca.
Amado Canton
Pedro Cicero
S. Crasemann y Ca.
Manuel Donde Camara
E. Escalante y Hijo
Dario Galera
Miguel Laviada
Felipe Molina
Duarte Gonzalez
Solis Guzman
Severo Lara
Leocadio Lara
Francisco Garcia Lopez
Francisco Loza
Joaquin Maldonado
Feliciano Mauranilla
Duarte Manuel Medina
Braulio A. Mendey.
Francisco de P. Montalvo
Luis Augusto Molina
Castulo Palma
José D. Patron
José Conterras Peon
Federico Pedrera
Galvez Perez
Maranda Perez
Cisneros Ramos
Juan Rio Manzano
Figueroa Rivero
José Maria Roca
Francisco Rubio
Pastor Solis
Francisco Valencia
Fabian Vallado
Aniseto Villalobos
Sabas Vega
Juan Pablo Zapata

Photographers.

Pedro Guerra
Guzman y Ca.

Physicians.

Juan P. Aguliar
Manuel Arias
Waldemazo G. Canton
Marcial Cervera
Manuel Donte Preciat
Juan Pio Manzano
Eugenio Milan
Florencio Narvaez
Juan Nicoli
Agustin O. Horan
José Talomequi
Patron Dolores
Joaquin Rendon
J. Ricardo Sauri
José Maria Tappan
Estabara Vargas
Rafael Villamil
Joaquin Alcevedo
Domingo Amabilis
Rafael Andrade
Clotilde Bagueiros
Manuel Bolis
Gregorio O. Buenfil
Manuel Barrero
Roberto Buenfil
Alvarez Capetillo
Fernando Caceres
Gerardo Castillo
José J. Lopez Castro
Vargas Esteban Cirio
Domingio Evia
Elias Febles
José Maria Zappan
Severaino Gongora

Printers.

Gil Canto
Del Comercio
N. Rubio
De la Libreria Meridana
Eraclio G. Canton
De la Libreria del Estado
Espinosa y Caballero
Heredia Erguelles
J. F. Molina
Guzman y Hermanos
" La Revista de Merida "
Alfonso Lopez
" El Eco del Comercio "

Paints and Varnishes.

(See Merchants General, and Druggists.)

Saddlery and Harness.

Nestor Castillo
Antonio Flores
Pedro A. Lavadores
Casimiro Mendoza
Juan de D. Pindo
Juan Antonio Pinzon
Mateo Rosado

Tanneries.

Cervera y Ca.
José Cobá
Selverio Coba
Leonido Culloch
Francisco Gengota
Marcelino Perez
Angel Zolozar
Marcos Zalazar

MORELIA,

STATE OF MICHOACAN.

Population, 30,000.

Agricultural Implements.
(See Hardware.)

Boots and Shoes.
Jesus Garcia
El Botin de las Damas
La Urgencia Michoacana

Bookbinders.
Jesus Calderon
Vicente Manjarrez
Pedro F. Rodriguez

China, Crockery and Glassware.
Victor J. Morera
Epifanio Oseguera

Dentists.
Q. Lorenzoeria
Izquierdo Ortiz

Druggists, Retail.
Manuel Montano
Juons Vallejo
Teodora Arrega
Merando Burgos
Andres Cervantes
Ciraco Gonzalez
Anastasio Mier
Nicanor Ortiz
Genaro Padilla
Silviano Martinez
Ricardo Angondar
Miguel Otiz y Cano
Miguel Gutierrez
Silviano Martinez
Manuel Montano
Juan Vallejo

Dry Goods, Notions, Etc.
F. G. Alba
Bose, Garcin y Hermanos
Castaneda y Ca.
T. Cortes y Ca.
Infante Pelat y Ca.
Pedro Quiros
M. Villagomez

Furniture.
Juan Velez

Hardware, Cutlery, Tools, Etc.
Epifanio Oseguera
El Mosaico, Juan Rangel
El Ferro-carril
El Topocio
La Jalapena, Loreto Martinez
La Palma, Pládido Guerero
La Paz, Burgo y Ca.
Las Rovedado, Ponce de Leon y Ca.

Hides and Leather.
Juan Bermudez
Antonio Garcia
José M. Ibarrola
Nicolas Ortiz
Agustin Sachez
Ignacio Tapio
Ausencio Breña

Ice Dealer.
Bernabé Vazquez

Jewelry, Watches and Silverware.
Onesimo Humbert
Felix Goyzueta
German Goyzueta
Onesimo Humbert
Antonio Marquez
Mariano Ramirez

Merchants, General.
L. Diezde Bonilla
Herculano Ibarrola
Juan B. Lozano
Sacramento Murguia
Carlos Solorzano
Jesus Villarreal
Ramon de la Vega
José Maria Zapien
Antonio Colimote
Pedro B. Chavez
Antonio R. Garton
Francisco Hidalgo
Loreto Martinez
A. Ocequera
G. Paramo
R. Perez
Tomas Puente
Salvazar Cruz
Francisco Silva
Ferando Sosa
Hilario Tapia
Gustavo Gravenors
Angel Velez
Andiffred Hermanos
Benito Barroso
Basagoiti y Ca.
Izidoro Burgos
Chavez y Gnido
Dueñas Luis Espino
Juan Galvan
Gustavo Gravenhorst
Placido Guerreso
Francisco Infante
José Maria Infante
Luis Infante
Eduardo Iturbide
Agustin Luna
Salvador Macouset
Loreto del Campo Martinez
Antanasio Mier
Ramiro Manuel Montaño

Merchants, General—*continued*.

Santiago Ortiz
Gabino Oseguero y Epifanio
Gil José Maria Perez
Ramon Ramirez
José J. Retana
Nemesio Ruiz
Ignacio Salorzano
Arroyo Pablo Torres
Valejo Hermanos
Juan Vallejo
Ramon Villareal

Photographers.

R. Manriquez
Gutierrez y Ca.

Physicians.

José Arevalo
Angel Carreon
Eduardo Carreon
Faustino Cervantes
G. Domingo
Mateo Gonzalez
Francisco Iturbide
Luis Iturbide
Rafael Montano
Antonia P. Moto
Antonio Perez
Antonio Puente
Z. Ruperto
Francisco Torres
José C. Marquez

Gustavo O. Farrill
Victor Blay
Miguel Cruz y Cano
Miguel Arriaga
Manuel Ramirez
Floriencia Flores
Amado Brule
Mariano Carrillo

Pianos and Organs.

Felix Alba
Manuel Cardenas
Joaquin Estrado
Alberto Gomez
Manuel Lozano
José Maria Novoa
Ramon Ramirez
Ignacio Reynoso
Mucio Espinosa

Printers and Stationers.

Ignacio Arango
Octaviano Ortiz
Del Gobierno
De Aranjo
Jesus Calderon
Vicente Manjarrez
Pedro F. Rodriguez

Saddlery and Harness.

Francisco Navarete

Undertaker.

Juan Velez

MONTEREY,

STATE OF NEUVA LEON.

Population, 42,000.

Bankers.

Wells, Fargo & Co.
Patricio Millmo
Francisco Martinez
V. Rivero
Pedro Maiz

Billiards.

A. Vilarax

Bookseller and Stationer.

Francisco Grim

Boots and Shoes.

Allegro y Ca.
José Maria Franco
Thomas Ortiz
Francisco Z. Treviño

China and Glassware.

V. Laustroff y Ca.
Ancira Hermanos
R. Dressel y Ca.

Clothing, Etc., Jobbers.

P. Doud y Ca.
Arvele y Olivier
Elizondo y Fox
Mariano Garcia
Carlos Holke
Hernandez Hermanos
Valentin Rivero
Hilario Rodriguez
Cardenas Martinez y Hermanos
Fernando Martinez y Hermanos

Clothing, Hats, Etc., Retail.

Hesselbart y Ca
Arvele y Olliviere
Patricio Doud
Fernando Garza
Elizondo y Fox
Hernandez y Hermanos
Hilario Rodriguez
Lorenzo Gonzalez
Lozano y Ca
Jacinto Galindo
Bernardino Garcia
Praxedes Garcia

Clothing Hats, Etc., Retail—cont'd.

Juan B. Gonzalez
José Gutierrez
Martinez Cardenas
Patricio Milmo
Pederico Palacios
Emilio Pautrier
Esteban Roel
Francisco Treviño
Zambrano Hermanos y Ca.
Francisco Armendais
Roque Barrios
José Calderon
Digatan y Garcia
Elizonda y Ca.
S. Jamie
Desiderio Jiminez
Pedro Maiz
Valentin Rivero
Francisco Oliver
Silvestre Treveño y Ca.
Roque Varrios

Druggists.

Bremer y Ca.
Franciso Bello
Joaquin Cortazar
Agustin Cantu
Ramon Garcia Perez
Felipe G. Gonzalez
Antonio Lafon
Lazeano y Ca.
José O. Margain
Mean y Hermanos
Juan H. Mears
Ramon G. Perez
Manuel Seda
Jesus Sanchez
Vicente Sepulveda
Antonio Garcia
Tomas Hinojoso
Emilio Lafont
Eusebio Rodriguez
Martinez y Echartea

Dry Goods and Notions.

D. Brainard y Ca.
Rudolfo Drenel
Cárlos Ayala y Ca.
Inocencio Lozano
E. Pautrier
David Rios
Juan Reyes
Salvador Jarrier
Ayala y Ca.

Express Company.

Wells, Fargo & Co.

Hardware and Tools.

Ancira Hermanos
R. y C. Dressel y Ca.

Hotels.

El Iturbide

House Furnishing Goods.

Ancira y Ca.
Prudencio Trujillo

Jewelers, etc.

Carlos M. Ayala

Lumber Dealers.

Fernandez Martinez y Hermano

Merchants, General Wholesale.

Boot y Royt
Brach Sconfield y Co
Victoriano Castro
Clausen y Ca.
L. G. Coindran
Degatan y Dose
Viuda de Farnava y Ca.
Guilbeau, Hermann y Ca.
Salvador Jarie
Ramon Lafon
Madera y Ca.
Patricio Milmo
José Morrell
Tomas O'Farrell
Oliver y Hermanos
Palacio Arguelles
Rivero y Ca.
Schonian y Dressel
Weber y Ulrick
José Calderon
P. Maiz y Ca

Merchants, Wholesale Commission, General.

Bruno Ayala
Reynaldo Bernardi
Adolfo Cantu
Francisco Artichi
Elizondo y Ca.
Martinez y Hermanos
Pedro Maiz

Mining Engineer.

Francisco Leonides Mier

Photographers.

Nicolas Mauro Rendon
Lagrange Hermanos
Nicolás Rendon

Physicians.

Carlos Ayala
Antonio Garcia
J. Eleuterion Gonzalez
Tomas Hinojosa
A. Lafon
José Maria Lozano
D. Martinez
E. Martinez
José Martinez Ancira
Eusebio Rodriguez
Juan de D. Trevino
E. Zamora
José A. Martinez
Lorenzo Sepulveda
Bernado Sepulveda
C. Villareal
Epitacio Ancira
José J. Mears
J. MacMaster

Pianos and Organs, Dealers in.

Zambrana Hermanos y Ca.

Printers.

Lagrange Hermanos
" Literaria "
" Del Gobierno "

Warehousemen and Wholesale Agents.

Davalos y Hermanos
Mariano Garza

Marin Perez
Ramos y Hermanos
Zambrano y Ca.

Watches and Jewelry.

Viuda de Ayala
Bogue Varrios
Valintin Rivero
Martinez y Hermanos

MAZATLAN,

STATE OF SINALOA.

Population, 5,000.

Bankers.

Melchers y Echeguram, Sucesores

Business Agents and Attorneys.

Angel Bonilla
Antonio Canalizo
José Maria Iribarren
Pedro Padrilla
Albino A. Pulido
Daniel Arce Pérez
Jesus Rio
Francisco Salcedo
Jesus Maria Tavisou

Druggists.

Luigi Canobbio
Dionisio Canobbio
Angel Podesta
Federico Köerdel
Benjamin D. Restes

Hotels.

La National
El Hotel Sinoloense
Hotel Iturbide

Merchants, General.

Bartning Hermanos y Ca.
Farbet y Meyer
Francisco Piña
Calisher, Charpentier y Renaud

Jesus Escobar
Gallick, Goldsmith y Ca.
Haas y Almada
Heymann y Ca.
Hernandez, Mendia y Ca.
Melchers, Peña y Ca.
Somellera Hermanos
Tames y Elorza
Vega Hermanos

Photographers.

Guillermo L. Zuber
Bevan y Mondaea

Physicians.

J. W. Rogers
Fortunato Randich
A. H. McHatton
Benjamin Carman
Juan J. Valades
Mariano Ruñiga
Felipe S. Martinez
Vicente Tonseca

Printers.

Miguel Retes
Campuzano y Ca.
Ira Valades

Warehousemen.

Ramon Alvarez
Abraham Ibarra
Florencio Lopez
Urbano Bonsigner
Miguel Estravillo

OAXACA,

STATE OF OAXACA.

Population, 10,000.

Commercial Agents.
Antonio Falcon.
Santiago Cruz
José M. Castro
José Guerrero
Antonio Prado
Juan T. Bravo

Druggists.
José A. Alvarez
Ramon Bolaños
Pedro Bustamente
Amado Zurita
Amado Santaella
Estate of Francisco Loaeza
Estate of Juan J. Vasconcelos

Hotels.
Hotel Nacional
Hotel de la Paz
Hotel Diaz Ordaz

Physicians.
Ramon Bolaños
José A. Alvarez
Francisco Rinçon
Francisco Hernandez
José Palacios
Agustin Dominguez
Aurelio Barsalobre
Leonides Castellanos
Manuel Gornez
Jesus Campos
Manuel Ramos
Fernando Sologuren
Manuel de Esesarte

José A. Alvarez
Aurelio Valdivieso
Constancio P. Idiaquez

Principal General Merchants.
Constantino Ricars.
Enrique Hinricles
Juan N. Jimenez
José Larrañaga
Manuel Peralta
Ignacio Esperon
Allende y Sobrino
Quijano y Ca.
José Zorilla
Gustav Stein y Ca.
Viuda de Trapaga Lopez
Julian Gonzalez
Manuel Caballero
Felix Marquez
Mariano Esperon
Camilio Tolis
Pascual Portillo
Juan Cabo de la Peña
Gregorio Fuentes
Vicente Gallado
Ramon Ibañez
Vicente Osorio
Frieben Hermanos
Luis Herrera
José B. Camacho
M. Orozco
Lorenzo San German

Printers.
Gabino Marquez
Juan T. Bravo

NATURAL PRODUCTS—Gold, silver, copper, lead, iron, quicksilver, etc. Also, cotton, rice, cocoa, sugar cane, and various kinds of grain.

ORIZABA,

STATE OF VERA CRUZ.

Population, 26,000.

Agricultural Implements.
(See Hardware, Tools, etc.)

Ales and Beer.
Carense y Ca.
Cárlos M. Argumedo
Diego Espinosa
Donacaino Morales

Arms and Ammunition.
Primitivo Llanos
Juan B. Ruffier

Banks and Bankers.
Mazon Hermanos
Agencia del Banco Nacional

Billiards.
Valentine Fernandez
Adernas Lay

Bookbinders.
Francisco Cabo
Juan Gonzalez Cenon
Demetrio Rangel

Boots and Shoes.

Anastasio Camiro
Francisco Cruz
Crescencio Jimenez
Francisco Muñoz
Francisco Gaston
Guadalupe Ramos
Vicente Ramirez
José de Jesus Saldaño
Cipriano Gaetan

Commission Merchants.

Tiburcio Gomez
Facundo Sota
Adolfo Verea
Berea Hermanos

Commission Agents and Brokers.

Diego Espinosa
Tiburcio Gomez
José M. Laredo
Vicente Roman
Facunda Sota
V. Eulogio

Coffee and Tobacco Broker.

Plutaro Rodriguez

Copper Merchants.

Bonifacio Blanco
Juan Brando
Juan Mercadanti
Francisco Teilhe

Dealers in Hides.

E. Cerilla
Ignacio Cueto
Mariano Saldana

Dentists.

Luis Azcarate
Eduardo Pablos
M. Roberto
Fructuoso Tellez
H. F. Timm

Druggists.

Miguel Mendizabal
Viuda de Anaud
A. Bustamente
J. E. Bustillos
J. Mendizabal
Leopoldo Rinçon
Rontas
Ismael Talavera
Juan Diaz
José Bustamente
José M. Isagurri
Rafael Potas
J. Manuel Valverde
Carrillo Cartabuena Joachin

Dry Goods and Notions.

S. Bustillo
Enrique Escudero
C. Fernandez
P. Garragori

Gomez Sota
Soberon
Villa y Ca.
Estevas Vivance
José Fondevila y Ca.
Teofilo Gross
Rafael Islas
Sigori y Ca.
Ricardo Rogna

Flour Mills.

Francisco Flores
N. Guevera
José Sanz
Francisco Sota
Isidoro Sota
Severino Sota
Gabriel Torre y Ca.
Torres y Ca.
Luis Guevara

Furniture Warehouse.

Teofilo Grosse

General Merchandise Brokers.

Cárlos Argamedo
Ramon Baturoni
José Bravo
Diego Espinosa
N. Mendizabal
Agustin Morillo
José M. Naredo
Manuel Rodriguez
Ramon Pimentel
J. M. Penasco
Facundo Sota
Ambrosio Tejada
Ramon Valverde
Eulogio Victorino
Castillo Coss y Ca.

Groceries and Provisions.

José Antonio O. Gomez
Ignacio Orosco
Agustin Alvarez
Pascual Aguilar
Tomas Alvarado
Ignacio Baldvia
Francisco Campos
Timoteo Castillo
José Dominguez
Maximo Espinola
José Maria Garces
Antonio Gimenez
Cortes Ismael Gomez
Tiburcio Hernandez
Pedro Lopez
Julian Porras
Basilio Rivera
Pedro Riquelme
Sabino Rivera
Rojina y Ca.
Plutarco Rodriguez
Angel Toledano
Antonio Vivanco
José Aguerrela
Maximo Espindola
Ramon Garcia
Merodio Pedro Diaz
Joaquin Romero

Hardware, Tools, Etc.

José M. Avila
Patricio Carmona
Epitacio Lopez
Rafael Merino
Juan Minchaque
Encarnacion Ojeda
Felipe Perez
Hermanos Carrillo
Rafael Islas
José Sanchez Vega

Hotels.

Manuel Calleja, Puente de la Border
Juan Manpome, Puente de la Border
Viudade Stuvembol, Puente de la Border

House Furnishing Goods, Etc.

Luis Buendia
Abraham Mañon
Amado Rosette

Ice Dealer.

J. J. Limon.

Lithographer.

Juan O. Gonzalez

Machinery and Foundry.

Vivanco y Estevez
Teofilo Grosse
Ligori y Ca.
Miguel Hernandez
Pedro Fougeras
L. Pimental

Lumber Dealers.

Antonio Castillo
Maria Guadalupe Cortez

Merchants, General Wholesale.

Camarillo y Teller
Castro Fernandez
Mazon y Hermanos
Juan Aguilar
Isidoro Sota
E. Vitorero
Gabriel Bárranco
Jaramillo Ismael

Paper Manufacturer.

Escandon Hermanos

Paints and Varnishes.

(See Hardware and Merchants, General.)

Photographers.

Manuel Castillo
Lucio Diaz

Physicians.

Marcario Ahumada
Ernesto Arzamendi
Francisco Carrillo
Nicolas Diaz
Manuel M. Fernandez
Manuel Jofre
Juan Kremeser
Miguel Kubieza
Francisco Marron
Gregorio Mendizable
Roberto Meredy
Luis Meza
Leopoldo Pedroza
Ismael Talavera

Printers.

Juan Aguilar
J. Zenon Gonzalez
Margarita Rosete

Saddlery and Harness.

Antonio Martinez
Miguel Cerrilla
Ignacio Cueto
Manuel Perez
Anastasio Solis

Sugar Merchants.

José Maria Bringas
Gargollo y Parra
M. Guevara

Watches and Jewelry.

Andrés A. Arenjo
José Maria Mayor
Felix Palacios

Undertaker.

T. Grosse.

PASO DEL NORTE,

STATE OF CHIHUAHUA.

Population, 6,000.

Banks.
Miner's Bank of Chihuahua

Commission Agents.
Dusing y Ca.
Joaquin D. Chichester
Ketelsin y Degetan
Klien Hermanos
O. Maheary
Kalin y Oliver

Druggists.
G. Witte
E. Alexan

Express.
Wells, Fargo & Co.

General Merchandise.
Francisco Armendias
José Maria Flores
Manuel Lucero
Inocente Ochod
Jesus Perez
E. Provencio
Flores y Alarcon
A. Gonzalez
Mariano Samaniego
Enrique C. Creel
Luis Terrazas

Physicians.
Mariano Samaniego
Emelio Alexan

PACHUCA,

STATE OF HIDALGO.

Population, 24,000.

Agricultural Implements.
(See Hardware.)

Ale and Beer Dealers.
Marguivar & Co.
J. Larrañaga
Juan Alegre
Carlos Greenfield
José Renaud

Arms and Ammunition.
(See Hardware, etc.)

Bankers.
Trinidad Aguirre
Adelberto Gomez
Jaime Jari
Wells, Fargo & Co.

Billiards.
Cárlos Grenfield
José Reynaud
A. Maciel
Pedro C. del Castillo
Cruz Ortez
J. Scoble

Booksellers.
Earisto Pastrana
El Instituto Literario
José Zuverano

Bookbinders.
Jesus Chavez
Vicente Ortiz

Boots and Shoes, Retail.
Carmona de Badillo
Gumersindo Corchado
Lorenzo Garcia
Vicente Garcia
Grisanta Hermosillo
Soteral Hidalgo
Antonio Maldonado
Pablo Maldonadó
Trinidad Mugés
Vicente Ponce
Antonio Rodriguez
Sostenes Zepeda

Dentists.
Mariano Laracilia
Pastrana Ibañez
G. Pastraña

Druggists.
Felipe Guerrero
Angel Conteras
Fernando Lescalle
Norberto Moreno
Elizondo Martinez
"El Refugio"
José Montenegro

El Famoso Cerveza,
"MILWAUKEE LAGER BEER,"
DE EL
Joseph Schlitz Brewing Co.,

EMBOTELLADO

y

EMPAQUETADO

CUIDADOSO

ESPRESAMENTE

PARA

LOS MERCADOS

TRÓPICOS.

LA CAPACIDAD

de

ESTE CÉLEBRE

Fabrica de Cerveza

es como

600,000 BARRILES

AL AÑO.

MILWAUKEE, WIS.,
E. U. de A.

THE CONTRACTORS' PLANT MFG. CO., Buffalo, N. Y., E. U. de A.

Poseedores de patentes y Fabricantes de cabrestantes que funcionan por medio de fuerza de sangre para uso de **constructores de ferrocarriles y puentes, canteros y trabajos de minas.** Es máquina **sencilla de poco peso, compacta, duradera, de facil manejo y gran resistencia,** estando construida enteramente de hierro y acero si exceptuamos la mesa de apoyo. Basta un solo operario para hacer funcionar las palancas. Se engrana y desengrana miéntras esté en movimiento. **No se usan garras en ella.** Es cabrestante bastante poderoso para elevar un cubo ó peso de 700 libras setenta y cinco piés por minuto, miéntras que el tambor tiene la capacidad de 500 piés para arriba de cuerda de acero de ⅝ pulgadas de diámetro.

Se enviará el catálogo ilustrado "gratis" á los que lo deseen.

AGENTES PARA LA VENTA EN MÉXICO:
Los Sres. MAXIMO A. PHILIPP y CIA., 137 Apartado, México.

La máquina se desarma con la mayor facilidad, bastando mulas para su transporte.

DELMAR'S
CLASSIFIED BUSINESS DIRECTORY
OF
SOUTH AND CENTRAL AMERICA,
CUBA AND PUERTO RICO.

PUBLISHED IN 1887.

Can be had on application to E. H. DELMAR, care of Messrs. Belford, Clarke & Co., Chicago, Ill.

PRICE, $10.00 PER COPY.

N. B.—The new edition of the above work will be issued in 1892.

Bullock Diamond Drills
FOR PROSPECTING AND DEVELOPING MINERAL AND COAL LANDS.

Holes bored at any angle to any required depth, taking out a CYLINDRICAL CORE showing the EXACT CHARACTER of all STRATA PENETRATED.

We make 15 sizes and styles of Drills, from Hand and Horse Power Machines to the Largest Well-Boring Machine. Also **LANE'S BAND FRICTION HOISTS AND DRUMS** from two feet to thirty feet in diameter.

BULLOCK CORLISS ENGINES
Fifty to 2,000 Horse Power.

Write for Circulars and Prices.

M. C. BULLOCK Manfg Co.,
138 Jackson Street, Chicago.

Clothing and Tailoring.

Fernando Escudero
Imbert y Mauriso
Juan Langier
Mecheyer y Hermanos
Mariano Aguilar
José Martinez Castro
Valentin Chavarria
Antonio Gonzalez

Dry Goods and Notions.

Fernando Escudero
Alejandro Garcia
Mercheyer Hermanos
Sangier y Ca.
Ramon Alfaro
Maurice Bloch
Bonavit Hermanos
Francisco Gutierrez

Engineers, Mining and Mine Owners.

Juan B. Blasquez
Ramon Almurez
Arcadia Ballesteros
Antonio Caso
José Maria Cesar
Juan Cuátaparo
Antonio Dominguez
Joaquin Gonzalo
Antonio Domingo Gutierrez
Manuel Icaza
Atilano Manriquez
Miguel Montafar
Rodolfo Muñoz
Luis Lozano Murillo
Ignacio Ortuno
Felipe N. Parrés
Angel Romero
Guillermo Seguro
José Serrano
Manuel Palacios
Juan Fleury
Manuel R. Veytia

Furniture, Dealers in.

Felix L. Hernandez
Felix Herrera
Jesus Guerrero
Gregorio Rivera

Flour Dealers.

Albino Hernandez
Refugio Leon
Albino Garcia

General Stores, Retail.

Tomas Alfaro
Reyes Alvarez
G. Anaya
Trinadad Carmona
Guadalupe Carmona
Morales y Santin
M. Rangel de Osorio
Paula Perez
Martin Reyes
Francisco E. Tellez
Felipe Vazquez
Jesus Arias
Alvarado y Rayon

Juan Andrade
Trinidad Angeles
Manuel Bustamente
Moises Canejo
Ciprano Garcia
Dolores Guevara
Pilar Esparza
Feliciano Escobar
Simon Campo
José P. Campo
Luciano Gomez
Rafael Gomez
José Luis Islas
Antonio Islas
Jesus Islas
Marcial Islas
Ignatio Viente Islas
Luis Lara
Luciano Romo
Francisco Rosales
Isaac Palaez
Jesus Ordaz
Morales y Ramon Santin
Felipe Ramos
Juande Dios Samperio
Manuel Torres
Benito Trejo
Maricano Velez
Julio Zarco

Groceries and Provisions, Wholesale.

Viuda de Antonio Boule
Aranzabal y Gueidi
Reyes Alvarez
Francisco Cacho y Ca.
Jacinto Gonzalez
José Gonzalez
Maquivar y Ca
Antonio Tafolla
Gabriel Urquijo

Hotels.

Domingo Altenori
Hotel S. Carlos
Hotel Diligencias
Hotel Baños
Hotel Refugio
Hotel Itabide
Hotel El Paraiso

Jewelers and Watchmakers.

Fernandez Gonzalez
Arelio Andrade
Luis Cervantes
Francisco Peña
Vidal Reina
Julian Soria

Lumber Merchants.

Rodriguez Diaz
Mateo Hidalgo
Franciso Rozales

Merchants, General.

Alvarado y Raynon
Juan Andrade
Trinidad Angeles
Jesus Arias
Manuel Bustamente

Merchants, General—continued.

José P. Campo
Simon Campo
Feliciano Escobar
Pilar Esparza
Cipriano Garcia
Luciano Gomez
Dolores Guevara
José Luis Islas
Jesus Islas
Antonio Islas
Jesus Islas
Marcial Islas
Vicente Ignacio Islas
Luis Lara
Morales y Ramon Santin
Jesus Ordaz
Rangel de Osorio
Isaac Pelaez
Felipe Ramoz
Luciano Romo
Francisco Cacho y Ca
Reyes Alvarez
Aranzabal y Guridi
Jacinto Gonzalez
Maquivar y Ca.
Antonio Tafola
Antonio Boule (Viuda)
Gabriel Urquijo
Francisco Rosaleses
Juan de Dios Samperio
Manuel Torres
Benito Trego
Mariano Velez
Julio Zoreo

Millers.

Castillo Garcia
Luciano Ortiz

Mining Companies.

El Progreso
La Providencia
La Purisima Chican
La Luz

Paints and Varnishes.

Cárlos P. Garnica
Justo Pastor Nava
Antonio Robles
Luis Seguri

Physicians.

Andrade Nemorio
Joaquin Alatriste
Nemesio Andrade
Angel Contreras
Edurado Corral
Francisco Guerrero
Elizondo Martinez
Rodrigo Ramirez
Santiago Robles
Manuel Roman
Fernando Ponce
Miguel Varela
Cenobio Viniegra
Fernando Lescalle
Felipe Rangel
Francisco Martinez
José Montenegro
N. Rosano
Agustin Navarro
Manuel Luna

Pianos and Organs.

I. Aguilar
I. Montenegro
M. Rodriguez

Printers.

Refugio Camacho
Imprenta del Gobierno
Guillermo Pascoe

Railroads.

There are two railroad companies, one city and suburban, and one to Hidalgo.

Saddlery and Harness.

Roman Carpintero
Refugio Espinola
Luis Lopez

Undertakers.

(See Furniture.)

Watches and Jewelry.

Fernando Gonzalez
Julian Soria
Aurelio Andrade
Luis Cervantes
Francisco Peña
Reina Vidal

PUEBLA,

STATE OF PUEBLA.

Population 72,000.

Agricultural Implements.

(See also Hardware and Tools.)
D. Valdés
Acedo y Hijos

Ale and Beer Dealers.

M. Gumesindo
Eduardo Financio
Mateos y Gatoir
J. Poyoulet y Ca.

Arms and Ammunition.

Glockner y Ca.
Nicolas Leon
Donaciano Ruiz
Manuel Morroquin

Banks.

Banco Nacional, Agency of
Banco Mercantil
Banco Nacional de Monte de Piedad

Bankers.

Bauer y Ca.
Berkembuch Hermanos
Contollen y Ca.
E. Fernachon
L. Garcia Teruel
A. Hernandez
José Maria Saldivar
E. Velacio

Billiard Rooms.

A. Bouvet
S. Magloire y Ca.
Sabino Mugica
Miguel Quiñones
Ignacio Ramirez
Juan Bordegaray y Ca., 4 Carniceria
Francisco Limon, 18 Victoria
Juan Oyhenaset, C. del Teatro
José Maria Peralta, 16 Mesones
Juan Traslosheros, 6 Zaragoza

Blacksmiths and Wheelwrights.

Antonio Espinosa, 5 Sta. Teresa
Bernardo Galindo, 15 Carros
Juan Lecony, 3 Dean
J. M. Leon, 23 Sta. Catalina
José Maria Manzano, 8 Dean
Juan Polo, 1 Coralillo
José De Jesus Romero, 23 Sta. Catalina
José Maria Mazano, 8 Dean
Juan Polo, 1 Corallillo
José De Jesus Romero, 2 Sta. Catalina
Donaciano Ruiz, 11 Porfirio Diaz
Francisco Sanchez, 16 Raboso
Isidoro Sosa, 3 S. Judas
Antonio Tapia, 3 Cruz de Piedra

Bookbinders.

Benjamin Lara
Joaquin Rodriguez
Miguel Tello
Miguel Villegas
Antonio Galicia
F. Viralo
Antonio Camacho
Joaquin Rodriguez
Miguel Tello
Miguel Villegas
Antonio Galicia

Books and Stationery.

Alberto Angulo
Nacriso Baslois
Ramon Lainé
Mateo Tagle
José Villegas
Manuel Espino Barros
Enrique Beguerissa
Pantaleon Lara

Boots and Shoes, Retail.

Doroteo Arce, 9 S. Pedro
Arnaud y Saller, 5 S. Pedro
José de Jesus Diaz, S. Luis
José Madrid, 6 Porfirio Diaz
Francisco Paz y Puente, 1 Cuarta de S. José
Ignacio Rodriguez, 2 S. Pedro
Santiago Sosas, 8 S. Pedro
Guadalupe Baes
Isidro Corro
Pedro Domerq
Alejandro Franco
Nicholas M. Gomes
Hilario Manzano
Luis C. Mateos
Rafael Ochoa
Perez y Ca.
Luis Ramirez Gonzaga
José de la Luz Urico

Carriages, Buggies and Wagons.

José de Jesus Angulo, Ce de Alatriste
J. M. Brito, 2 Huertas
Cecilio Camacho, Solar de Castro
Mariano Delgado, 12 Belen
Eleuterio Golzarri, 2 Solar de Castro
Antonio Rodriguez, 7 Belen
Valenzuela y Ca., 2 Monton

Commission Merchants.

Manuel Thomas y Teran
Gustavo Arrioja
M. M. Calderon
Mariano Fernandez y Ca.
Luis Tesnel Garcia
Antonio S. Miera
Barbollu Ortiz
Salazar Perez
Librado Rosales

Commission Merchants—*continued.*

Guillermo Turnbull
M. Thomas y Teran
Doroteo Vazquez
Von der Beck y Ca.

Coppersmiths.

José Bello, 1 Cholula
Juan Bifano, 4 Cruces
Rafael Mercadante
Antonio Caraneo, 20 Muradores
Miguel Esparragora, 1 Iglesias
José Panza, 1 Miradores

Crockery and Glassware.

Miguel Banuelos, 4 Sta. Clara
Antonio Palacios, 6 Segunda de la Merced
Miguel Toguera, 4 Zargoza
Fernandez y Ca.
Eduardo Colombres
Cenobia Fernandez y Ca.
Mariana Oropesa
Manuel Rojos
M. Oropeza

Dentists.

C. Portillo, 7 Mercaderes
Alejandro Besse, 6 S. Pedro
Valadie Benne, 3 Herreros
Miguel Larracilla, 7 Cruces
José M. Cabrera, 12 Victoria

Druggists.

Romulo Castillo
Gregorio Encinas
Placido B. Diaz
M. San Martin
Delfino Arrioja, 10 Moreles
Joaquin Arrioja, 11 Segunda de Sta. Teresa
Maria de J. Andifred, S. Luis
Paulino Bautista, 8 Sto. Domingo
Pedro Beguerisse, 2 Carniceria
Santiago Beguerisse, 4 S. Pedro
Botello y Ca., 8 Compañia
Vibiano Carrasco, Hospital de San Pedro
Guadalupe Coriche, 8 Miradores
Luis Crespo, 7 Guevara
Antonio Fernandez, 22 Herreros
Pascual Gonzalez, 33 Aduana Vieja
Joaquin, Ibanez y Lamarque, 8 Carniceria
Luis Inchaguaregui, 11 Sto. Domingo
Manuel Mena, 5 Obispado
Angel Rangel, 8 Zaragoza
Rafael Rodriguez, 7 Guevara
J. Ibanez
G. Lamarque
Marcus Cal
Luis Campos
L. Crespo
R. Gomez
Mariscal y Ca.
José M. Barrios, 8 Miradores
Antonio Gil
Vicente Inchaurregui, 10 Portal Morelo
Manuel M. Maldona
José Reinal
Aguiles Rojano
José Maria de la Torre
Cárlos E. Barros
Deodora Suarez
Jesus Toquero

Dry and Fancy Goods, Wholesale.

Cárlos Charles, 2 Hidalgo
Dichel y Ca., 2 Guevara
P. Garcia
Guthiel y Ca., 1 Carniceria
A. Lopez
Hernando Perenz y Ca., 3 Hidalgo
Antonio Rosales, 13 Primer de Mercaderes
Villaret y Duttner, 7 Primera de Mercaderes
Manuel Teruel
Velasco Hermanos
Ignacio Rivero
Alberto Quijano
Santos L. Lopez
Juan Matienzo
Rafael Mora
Borpillo Ortiz y Huos
Manuel Peon
Felix Perez
Ballo y Cabrera
Benitez y Hermanos
Manuel Conde
Gavito y Hijo
Gutierrez y Palacios

Engineers, Architects & Builders.

N. Aguado y Jesina
Ismael Alvarez, 6 Porfirio Diaz
Juan Blazquez
Angel Cabrera, 3 Sto. Domingo
Luis Careaga, 11 Sta. Teresa
Miguel Espino
N. Kassian, Sacrista de Capunhinas
Antonio Lorenz, 6 Miradores
Juan Meza, 8 América
Eduardo Morales, 8 Raboso
Juan Pardo, 10 Chihuahno
Ignacio Ramirez, Calera de Ramirez
Emilio Rodreguez, 7 Cuarta de San José
Herculano Santa Maria, 29 Carros
Pedro Senties, 8 Cruces
Feliciano Tello, 2 Guadalupe
Eduardo Valie, Colegio del Estado
Manuel Carrasch
Joaquin Cora
Guillermo Hay
José Domiauguez Iglesias
Alberto Ibañez
José Maria Pacheco
Cárlos Revilla
Refugio Rodriguez
Eduardo Tamaria

Fancy Goods and Notions, Jobbing and Retail.

J. de Arrioja
M. Arce
E. Arrioja y Valverde
B. Azla
Cardoso Hermanos
Chaiz Hermanos
Lions y Ca.
Moreno y Ca.

Flour and Corn Mills.

Cárlos Baez y Ca., S. Diego
Miguel Benitez, Molino de Huezotitla
Berges de Zuniga, Sto. Domingo
M. Garcia Teruel
Florencio Gavito y Hijo, Sta. Cruz.
Juan Haquét, Molino de S. Antonio

Flour and Corn Mills—*continued.*

Tomas Larie, Molino de Sta. Barbara
A. Leblanc, Molina del Volcan
Clemente Lopez, Molino del Carmen
Mauret Hermanos, S. Mateo
Sebastian Miez, Molino de San Francisco
S. Pardo
Juan Perez, Molino del Puente
Francisco Amaniscar
José de J. Tuta
Hernandez Gil
Laureano Islas
P. Vellegas
Tomas Furlong
Emilio Benitez, Hnixotitla
Francisco Condé, Santo Domingo
Francisco Diaz, San Francisco
P. M. Gonzalez, Costado de San Agustin
Tomas Latorre, Santa Barbara
A. Montiel, Esquina de Marquez
José Rafray, San Antonio
Francisco de la Rosa, 13 Huertas

Flour Merchants.

Manuel Macias Calderon
Becerra Manuel Calderon
Mariano Charles
Francisco Diaz
Pascual Lara
Trinidad Beyes
Luis Torija
Miguel Toquero

Foundries.

Fauesto Acedo, 5 Estanco de Hombres
Miguel Esparragoza, 1 Iglesias
Tomas Marshall, 11 Sta. Ana
Jesus Toquero, 8 Segunda de Tepetlapa

Furniture Warehouses.

Juan Leroux, 3 Dean
José Maria Manzano, 8 Dean
Francisco Sanchez, 3 Porfirio Diaz
Gabriel Alvarado, 7 Cruces
M. de la Luz Arana, 6 Santa Teresa
J. de L. Baces, 14 Estanco de Mujeres
Vicente Cano, 11 P. de Santa Cativina
Francisco Denetro, 5 Correo Viejo
Anastosio Domingo, 10 Santa Domingo
Andrés Gomez
J. de J. Guevara
Santiago Gutierrez
Jesus Huesca
Francisco Lara
Jorge Rosano
Luis Rosano
Claudio Valdéz
Joaquin Arraiga
José Costo
Ignacio Sanchez
Rafael Sanchez
Juan Pablo del Rio
José Maria Aguilar
José Baez
Andrés Gonzalez
Jesus Gueverra
Francisco Gueverra
Luis Rosano
Jorge Rosano
Claudio Valdes
Jorge Rosario

Gas Fixtures, Etc.

José Bueno
Juan Castillo
Francisco Fernandez
Miguel Fajardo
A. Martinez
José Maria Mendez
Albino Lopez, Pl. de S. Pablo
Guadalupe Medina, 21 Zambrano
Juan Ramos, S. Antonio
Francisco Reyes, 17 Rinconda

Glass and Crockery.

Miguel Palacios, 19 Pte. de Belen
Javier Paluisee, Tecali
José de J. Santillana, 2 Canoa
Van den Bussche y Ca., 12 Corralillo
Cenobio Fernandez
Miguel Banuelos
Miguel Toquero
Mariano Oropeza
Manuel Rojas
G. de M. Fuentes

Groceries and Provisions, Wholesale and Retail.

Rafael Anaya
José Aldas
Agustin Becerra
Ponce y Muñoz
José Caldena
Ramon Cortina
Rubin Diaz
Perez Diaz
Antonio Maria Dominguez
Juan Escobar
Francisco Fernandez
Garcia Hermano y Ca.
Mucio Hernandez
Hernandez Hijos y Ca.
Manuel Labarcas
José Maria Mendez
Manuel Maria Mendez
José Naval
José Nieva
José V. Olivares
Vicente Olivares
Luis Ochoa
José Pastor
Cirio Perez
Manuel Diaz Perez y Hermano
José de Jesus Ponce, 2 Mesones
José Maria Portillo
Adolfo Quevedo
Quevedo y Hernandez
Rafael Quintana
Joaquin Rosete
José Maria del Rio
Pedro Hoyo del Ruiz
Rivero Ismael y Ca.
Sabinon y Rivas
José de la Luz Sosa
Valentin Toraya
Eduardo Valverde
José Tanez
Josefa Calderon
Eara Cárlos Fernandez
Jesus Hernandez
Adolfo Montiel
José Maria Osorio
Ana Torreblanca
Viuda Hernandez y Hijos

Hardware, Cutlery and Tools.

Paz Garcia, Porfirio Diaz
Gutheil y Ca., Carniceria
Antonio Lopez, 1 Pte. del Toro
Manuel Martinez
Glockaer y Ca., 9 Primera Mercaderes
Francisco Traslosheros, 2 Carniceria
Miguel Ruiz
Antonio Rosales
Blumenkron y Bravo
Cárlos Charles

Hides, Wholesale.

R. Acho
Franciso Arrioja, 7 Aduana Vieja
Leonardo Barriga, 4 Cruces
Teresa Domerge, 2 Carniceria
Furnbull, Strybos y Mora
Garcia Beiran
Nicolas Gomez y Ca., 3 S. Pedro
Bernabe Martinez, 4 Coliseo Viejo
José Maria Montiel, 1 Santisima

Hotels.

Del Roncal
Del Cristo
Diligencias
Español
Jon Juan Nepomuceno
Universal

House Furnishing Goods.

José Maria Carcago, 3 Molina
Rafael Cisneros, 5 Santisima
Agustin Cisneros, 9 Lafragua
Manuel Cueto, Santa Teresa
J. Medina, Estanco de Hombres
Francisco Reyes, San Pedro

Ice Dealers.

José Maria Barranco
Franca Castillo

Jewelers and Watchmakers.

Julio Gauthier, Segunda de Mercaderes
Cárlos Herchman, 2 Sta. Clara
Rodolfo Jacobi, 9 Guevara
Andrés Shiverer, Primera de Mercaderes
Bravo Blumenkron
Glackner y Ca.
Manuel Marroquin
Mendivil y Ca.
Juan Ochoa
Rafael Otañes
Eduardo Patiño
Nestor Rangel
Feliciano Ruiz
Rafael Anzurez
Francisco Carretero
José Maria Liar
Miguel Palacios
Feliz Guerrero y Hijo
Miguel Beristain
Manuel Espinosa
Ignacio Soriano
Jesus Guerrero
José Mora
José Ochoa
J. Ruiz

Lumber Merchants.

Jorge Berkemburchs, 9 Sta. Catalina
Francisco Fernandez, 13 Sta. Catalina
Gabriel Ferrer, 3 S. Agustin
Eduardo Friera, 7 Alguacil Mayor
Eduardo Garcia, 23 Chiquero
Justo Leon, 1 S. Luis
Teodoro Palafox
Manuel Pastor, 5 Porfirio Diaz
Ibarra Fernandez, 13 Porfirio Diaz
Francisco Traslosheros, 12 Porfirio Diaz

Manufacturers' Agents.

Agustin Lamy, Sta. Clara
Manuel Marroquin, 5 Primera de Mercaderes
Manuel Rojas, 17 Compañia
Ramon Alvarez, 12 Infantes
José Maria Anaya
Pedro Arcos, 1 Carniceria
Gregorio Avalos, 16 Gallos
José Blanco
Alejandra Fajardo
Luis Gomez, 4 Cholula
Paz Gomez, 12 Dean
Mariano Manzano, 8 Estanco de Hombres
Agustin Melendez, 6 Sto. Domingo
Andrian O'Farril, 6 Torreblanca
Miguel Olivares, 5 Infantes
Joaquin Perez, 3 Romero
Mateo Porras, 6 Capuchinas
Miguel Zamora
Monica Zapata

Machinery Depots and Dealers.

Gutheil y Ca.
Rosales y Doremberk
Domingo Valdes

Merchants, General, Wholesale.

Ramon Acho
Arnan Salles
Adolfo Arrioja
Luis Bello
Francisco Cabrera
José Caloca
Manuel Conde
José Maria Contoline
Chaix y Ca.
José Diaz
Diehl y Ca.
Luis Garcia
Manuel García
Florencio Gavito
H. Gomez
Hernandez y Ca.
Ramon Laine
J. B. Lyons y Ca.
Marroquin y Gauthier
Mier y Conde
Felix Perez
Antonio Rosales
Francisco Traslosheros
Dionisio Velasco
J. Buttner
C. Charles
José Rubio Diaz
Ligero M. Gomez
A. Gutheil y Ca.
Apolonio Hernandez
Antonio Lopez
Felix Perez

MEXICO. 97

Merchants, General, Etc.—*continued.*
Eugenio Reyes
Rueda y Ca.
M. Soquero
Cárlos Vonderbeck y Ca.

Native Produce.
R. Ajura
Alani y Ca.
Angullane
N. Bastida
M. Bermudez
Carral Carrillo y Ca.
G. Encina
José Salgado Sota

Paints and Varnishes.
Castulo Padilla, 1 Chito Coetero
Cayetano Padilla, 11 Correo Viejo
Francisco Morales, 8 Raboso
José Andrés Lopez
Luis del Carmen Lozada
Ignacio Peralta

Photographers.
José Barreal, 1 Sta. Teresa
Lorenzo Beccerril, 3 Mosones
Benito Gerciu, Sto. Domingo
Joaquin Martinez, 3 Santa Clara
Jesus Pacheco, 5 Estanco de Hombres
Del Monte, Hermanos
Abraham Cabrera

Physicians.
Francisco Arrioja, 7 Aduana Vieja
Joaquin Arrioja
Placido Barriga
José M. Calderon
Jesus Diaz
Manuel Diaz
Pedro Espindola
Cárlos de Ita
Esteban Lamadrid, 3 Aduana Vieja
Francisco Marin, 5 Sta Clara
Samuel Morales
Manuel Neva
Miguel Ramirez
Ignacio Rivadeneyra
Miguel Salas
Luis Zaragoza
Cárlos Amezcua
Delfino Arrioja
Aurelio Avalos
Francisco Bello
Jesus Botello
Pedro Blasquez
Juan Calderon
Manuel Calva
Leonardo Cardona
Eduardo Ceron
Daniel Chavez
Gonzalez Dias
Francisco Dias
Placido B. Dias
Miguel Durango
Jesus de Espindola
Joaquin Ibañez
José Ita
José Justo Jofre

José M. Marin
Manuel Noriega
Alberto O'Farrill
Gustavo O'Farrill
Miguel Arenas
Rafael Ohea
Cárlos Orosco
Francisco Sanchez
Agustin P. Salazar
Domínguez A. Salazar
Secundino Sosa
Ignacio Rivadeneyra
Baltazar Uriarte
Ignacio Gil Gomez
Manuel Ceron
Calva y Zamudio
Guillermo Davila
Antonio Dominguez

Pianos and Organs.
José M. Romero
José Cuevas
Felipe Gracidas
Felix Olmedo
Francisco Velazquez
D. Espinosa
Agustin Polo

Printers.
J. Gonzales
Joaquin Martinez
Ignacio Moncdo
Dario Ortiz
Isidro Romero
M. Boetar
Pedro Alarcon, 22 Carros
Miguel Corona
Ismael Macias, 5 Sto. Domingo
José Maria Osorio, 6 Sta. Clara
Miguel Pastor, Carniceira
Francisco Ruiz, Bovedas de la Compañia
Tamariz Hermanos, 12 Mesones
Tomas Neve, 3 Sta. Clara
Alberto Angulo
Isidoro Bochler
José de J. Franco

Saddlery and Harness.
Antonio Dovantes
Herlindo Franco
Juan J. Juarez
Esteban Lopez
Ignacio Sanchez
Alberto M. Turnbull

Sewing Machine Agents.
Antonio Rosales
Guillermo Corn y Ca.
Agustin Gutheil y Ca
Rafael Anzurez
Clokner y Centurion
Antonio Lopez
Manuel Marroquin

Sugar Merchants.
M. Colosia
Rafael Illescas, 11 Herreros
Marron y Ca.
R. Ramora

Trunks, Bags, Etc.
Teresa L. Domeneck
Nicolas M. Gomez
Lorenzo J. Osorio

Undertakers.
(See also Furniture.)
Juan Pablo del Rio

Wall Paper.
(See Stationers.)

QUERETARO,
STATE OF QUERETARO.

Population, 36,000.

Ales and Beer.
Ignacio Galeanco
Victor Morgenthaler

Banks.
Banco National
Banco Mercantile
Banco Monte de Piedad

Billiards.
Guerro Ignacio Gomez
Fermin Casino Rodriguez

Bookbinders.
Federico Espinosa
Epifanio Garcia
Manuel Jiminez
Trinidad Santelices

Books and Stationery.
Antonio Chavez
Gonzalez y Ca
Ricardo Plageman

Boots and Shoes.
Ignacio Ballandra
Alberto Dominguez
Hilarion Diaz
Antonio Saldaña
Manuel Flores Muñoz

China and Glassware.
Manuel Alday
Andrés Arias
Antonio Gonzalo
Kosendis Desiderio y Ca.
José Maria Rivera
José M. Mendez

Clothing.
Arnaud y Martel
Teófilo Irdrac
Dionisio Marcel
Mendez y Hijos
Mayrant y Richaud

Commission Merchants.
Andrés G. Arias
Luis MacGregor Rivera
José Maria Rivera

Dentist.
Alfonso Maria Brito

Druggists.
Bonifacio Carmona
Gabriel Carrillo
Manuel Cabo
Aurelio Diaz
Alberto Guerrero
F. de Jauregui
Miguel Arnulfo
Juan Septien
Estéban Vera

Engineers, Mining.
Cárlos Alcocer
Adolfo Casperovi
Francisco G. Cosio
Mariano Gorraez
Adolfo Isla
Eduardo Isla
Mandel Pastor y Cevallos
Alonzo Mariscal
José Maria Romero
Antonio J. Septien

Jewelers and Watchmakers.
Julian Richarte
Nemesio Manilla
Mariano Altamirano
Sinecio Monfont
Pedro Pereira

Merchants, General.
Demetrio Aguilar
Amando y Martel
Bernardo Borja
N. Escudero
José Garcia
Gonzales y Legarreta
Fernando Olvera
J. Plagemann
José Maria Rivera
Rivera y MacGregor
Cárlos Rubio
Gregorio Vargas

Native Products.
Andrés G. Arias
Antonio Loyola
Dionisio Maciel
Baltazar Ugalde

Paints and Varnishes.
Sevilla Reyes

Paper Box Maker.
Cárlos Bremer

Photographers.
Teodoro Balvanera
J. Gomez
Ignacio Flores Muñoz
Antonio Ruiz

Physicians.
Antonio Aguirre
José Maria Bocanegra
Bonifacio Carmona
José Esquivel
Ponciano Herrera
Luis Serafin Jimenez
Ricardo Nandin
Manuel Septien
José M. Suirob
Manuel Jiminez

Antonio Maldonado
José Puente
Santiago Torres
Geronimo Torres

Perfumery.
Vicente Bastida
Melchor Olivera
Nicolas Torres
Arnaud y Eartel
Manuel Alday
José M. Mendez
José M. Rivera

Pianos and Organs.
M. Arcos
Trinidad Mendoza
Manuel Mosquera
Miguel Romillo

Printers.
Gonzalez y Ca.
Frias y Soto
Frias y Herrera

SALAMANCA,
STATE OF GUANAJUATO.

Ales and Beer.
Camila Medal
Mánuel Portusac

Bankers.
Asuncion Martinez
Altagracia Calzada

Billiard Halls.
Juan Sanchez
Marcos Herrera

Boots and Shoes.
Rivera y Ca.
Crescencio Mares
Serapio Nuñes

Cigar Factories and Dealers.
Eduardo Hernandez
José M. Rivera
Tomas Solache
Jesus Rojas

Clothing and Tailoring.
Epitacio Garcia Refugio Farfan
Santana y Medina
Marcos Garcia
Anecedo Rangel

Commission Merchants, General.
Ismael Domezain
Manuel Portusac

Druggists.
De la Salud
De San José
De Guadalupe
De la Union

General Merchants, Retail.
Juan Medrano
José Jayrne
Antonio Gamiñio
Zarandena y Pacheco
Regino Gamiño
Tomas Solache
Ramon Granados
Mariano Granados
Luis Rojas
Francisco Rojas
Eduardo Flores
Z. M. Martinez
Epigmenio Rojas
Rafael Arredondo
Antonio Puente
E. Figuroa
Jorge Sanchez
Andres Perez
J. Dolores Gonzalez
Modesto Castillo
José M. Patiño
Thofilo Chavez

Hotel.
Tomas M. Moreno

Kid Glove Factories (*Quite Famous.*)
Modesto Gomez
Luis Freyre
Manuel Aboytes
Miguel Campos
José M. Andaluz
Antonio Vidal

Machine Shop.

Esteban Castillo y Hijo

Photographer.

Luciano Roa

Physicians.

Diego Reynoso
Julio D. Vera

Eduardo Partida
G. de la Gruyere
Carlos Santander
Ricardo T. Garza
Florentino Lopez

Printers.

Ismael Domenzain
La Penetenciaria

SALTILLO,

STATE OF COAHUILA.

Population, 25,000.

Agricultural Implements.

(See Merchants' General.)

Bank.

Banco Comercial

Bankers and Brokers.

Valeriano Ancira
C. Francisco Puentes
Juan José Rodriguez, agente del Banco Nacional Mexicano
Pedro Aguero
Eusebio Moye
Francisco Muarras
Franquilino Ortiz

Booksellers and Stationers.

Antonio de la Fuente
C. Bouret

Bookbinders.

Salvador Jove
Luis Letona
Simon de la G. de Pen
Pricilliano de la Rosa

Billiard Rooms.

Faustino Cepeda
Fritz Gerard
Augustin Gonzalez
Hausen y Michlean
Felipe Rodriguez

Brickmakers.

Jesus T. Montes
David Montes
Damaso Rodriguez

Boots and Shoes

Antonio Aguirre
Juan Garcia
Ascenio Molina
Felix Salinas
Porfirio Valdéz
Juan Sanches

Druggists, Retail.

Hilario Hernandez
F. de Pena
Jesus Rodriguez
Sostenes de la Fuente
Mauricio G. Barreda
J. D. Carothers
José I. Figueroa
M. Warremosch

Flour Merchants.

Arispe y Ramos
Gabriel Flores
Guillermo Paurcell
Juan Valdes

Flour Mill.

Ramon de Leon y Aragon

Furniture.

Blumenthal y Cordt

Hardware and Tools.

Eusebio Moya
Francisco Muarras
Franquilino Ortiz
Antonio Valverde
A. Berlanga
José Cardenas
Manuel Myjica
Timotheo Hernandez

Hotels.

El Filopolitano, Calle Juarez
San Estéban, Calle Victoria

House Furnishing Goods.

Jesus Agirre
Juan Alvarado
Geronimo Cenicero
Felipe Ortiz
Simon Charles
Damosa Rodriguez
Felix Maria Salinas

Jewelers and Watchmakers.

Juan Castilla
Rosa Peña
Venturo Urbina
Cárlos Camacho
Cárlos Flores

Lithographers.

La del Gobierno

Lumber Merchants.

Jesus Maria Martinez Ancira
Marcellino Garcia
Pablo A. Lopez

Printers.

Mariano Cardenas
Severo Fernandez
Francisco G. Fuentes

Simon Pena y Hno

Merchants, Wholesale, General.

E. Davila y Ca.
Marcelino Garza
Romulo Garza
Florencio Llaguno
Cárlos Martinez
Mazo Hermanos
José Negrete
Porth y Sieber
Guillormo Purcell
Jose Maria Ramos
Bernardino Rendon
Damasco Rodriguez
Francisco Rodriguez
Jos Juan Rodriguez

Merchants, Wholesale, General.

Daniel Salas
Juan Sanches y Hermanos
B. F. M. Seixas
Eusebio Calzada
Mariano Grande
Bernado Sota

Paints and Varnish.

Aujel Martinez y Hijos

Physicians.

José Maria Barreda
Mauricino G. Barreda
R. H. Bibbi
Ramon Davila
José T. Figueroa
Dionisio Fuentos
Jesus Fuentes
R. Logan
Ismael Salas
Santiago Smith
J. Wadsworth
Atanasia Carrillo
Jesus Maria Gill
Mauricio Garcia
Matias Porth

Pianos and Organs.

Casimiro Medrano
Villaneuva y Francesconi

Sewing Machine Agents.

E. Blumenthal
Estorey y Hayes
Hermanos Mazo

SAN JUAN BAUTISTA,

STATE OF TABASCO.

Boots and Shoes.

Reyes y Heredia
Jimenez Aguilar y Hermano
Bernadino Espindola
Geronimo Flores

Clothing, Hats, Etc.

José Maria Diaz
Esteban Sanque
José Miralda
José C. Garcia
Augustin Perez Leon
R. Alvarez
Francisco Nieto

Dentist.

C. del Portillo

Druggists.

Fernando Mendez y Ca.
Manuel Pons

General Merchants.

Romano Hermanos
Salvador Serralta
Bulnes Hermanos
M. Barteaga y Ca.
Mosquera y Ca.
Ruiz de la Peña Hermanos
Graham y Vidal
Jamet y Sastre
Maldonado y Hijos
Oliver Hermanos
A. Barranco y Ca.
J. Pulido y Hermans
Juan Piña
Isadoro M. Diez

Hotels.

La Reforma
Calderon Buenaventura
Antonio Penaro

Lumber Merchant.

Policarpo Valenzuela

Physicians.

Francisco Pulido
Adolfo Castañares
Felipe Cherizola
Fernando Formento
Manuel Mestre
Antonio Soler

Watches and Jewelry.

David Hunter
Elias Nelson
M. Pellecer

SALVATIERRA,
STATE OF GUANAJUATO.

Ales and Beer Dealers.

Clemente Aguilar
Pio Gama
G. Zamudio

Bookbinder.

Francis L. Rivera

Booksellers and Stationers.

Francisco L. Rivera
Juan de la Fuente

Cigar Factories and Tobacconists.

Juan Taledo
Jesus Ramirez
Tomas Gomez

Clothing, Hats, Etc., Retail.

Jesus Bolaños
Rafael Nieto
Hilario H. Carrera
Leandro Escobedo
Lucas Lira
Maximo Miranda
Adolfo Fabre

Commission Merchants.

Jesus Saldaña y Ca.
Encarnacion Ramirez
Casildo Capetillo
Jesus Arias
Primitivo Estrada

Druggists.

Antonio Ceballos
Alberto Gomez
Luis Anaya
Trinadad Sanchez
José Leal Moreno y Ca.

Flour Merchants.

Juan D. Argumedo
Santiago Scanlan

General Merchants, Retail.

José Maria Calderon
Francisco Guzman
Juan de la Fuente
Rafael Diosdad
Trinadad Campos
Lucas Lira
Guadaloupe M. Rivera
Viuda de B. Capetilio
Prudenciano Ramerez

Francisco Rodriguez
Francisco Paramo
Rafail Nieto
Almanza Cayetano
Mariano Abanto
Francisco Barriga
Manuel Cruz
Gabriel Castillo
Ignacio Calderon
José Dios
Francisco Lira
Apolonio Martinez
Pablo Mendez
Nicolas Muñes
Camilo Niño
Francisco Rodriguez
Felipe Ruiz
Jesus Soto
José Maria Toledo
Manuel Valesco
Antonio Villalobos
Ignacio Izaraga
José M. Castañeda
Jesus Sotomayor
Tedoro Avila
Ignacio Hernandez
Jesus Barajas

Hardware and House Furnishing.

José M. Guisa
Eugenio Balandra

Hotels.

Francisco Dias Barriga
Casildo Capetillo

Jewelry.

Antonio Reyes
Pasenal Guisa
Penasal Coria

Lumber Dealers.

Vicente Aragon
Maximo Miranda
Juliano Esparza

Mills.

Santiago Scanlan (sugar)
Aniceto Soriano (sugar)
Juan D. Argumede (flour)
Francisco Campos (flour)
Luis Ayala (chocolate)
Jesus Soto (chocolate)
Manuel Maldonado (sugar)

Physicians.

Vicente Aragon
Francisco L. Paramo
Benito Soriano
Ramon Ruiz

Printers.

Temoteo Ruiz
Francisco Balandra

Sewing Machine Agencies.

J. Leal Morens y Ca.
G. M. Rivera

SAN LUIS POTOSI,
STATE OF SAN LUIS POTOSI.

Population, 47,000.

Agricultural Implements.
(See Hardware, Etc.)

Ales and Beer Dealers.
Lexfond
José Otahegui
Pedro Pons
Nicolas Zapedt

Arms and Ammunition.
(See Hardware, Etc.)

Banks and Bankers.
Banco Mercantil
Banco Monte de Piedad
Banco Nacional
Banco Enrique Aristi y Hermano
Banco Ignacio Muriel
Banco Saberon M. Hernandez

Billiards.
Santiago Couttolene
Francisco Fabre
Manuel Muno
Agustin Ondarza
Feliciano Palacios

Bookbinders.
Antonio Cabrera
Diego Fonseca
Cárlos de los Rios

Booksellers and Stationers.
Cárlos Bouret
Antonio Babrera
Cástulo James

Boots and Shoes, Retail.
Pascual Berrones
David Borrego
Nemesio Garcia
Andrés Gonzalez
José Lopez
Pomposo Ramirez
Manuel Reyes

China and Glassware.
Aguerre y Ca.
Santiago Deliz
German Gedovius
Felipe Gonzalez

Agustin Gutheil y Ca.
H. de Lara Manrique
Philip A. Max
Antonion Reyes

Commission Merchants and Agents.
Cruz Hermanos
Eduardo Dauban
José Maria Grande
Ronnaldo Anaya
Ildefonso Armida
Juan Diaz Barriga
Fernando Bolado
Felipe Cortes
Lorenzo Galvan
P. Gallardo
S. Garcia
Marcelino Gomez
R. Gonzalez
Froilan Guerrero
Daniel Lazo
José Marmolejo
José Maria Nieto
Isabel Reyes
Urquidi & Boleaga
Viramontes Hermanos
Aristi y Hermano
Hermanos Farias
Joaquin Heredia
Soberon M. Hernandez
Larrache y Ca., Sucesores
Marty y Vegambre
Meade y Hermano
Pittman y Ca.
Varona y Ca.

Copper Goods.
Domingo Bueno
Ramon Vasquez

Dentists.
Manuel Sierra
H. V. Warner

Druggists.
Mariano Hermosillo
Francisco Limon
Nicolas Mascorro
Antonio Mena
Severiano Vega
J. M. Villasenor
Luis G. Crespo
Antonio Lopez
N. Outanon

Druggists—continued.

Otero y Altamirano
Rafael Rodriguez
Ismael Salas
José M. Valdes
Julio Mauro
Dr. Alejo Monsivaio
Muñoz y Fonnegra
J. Salas

Dry Goods and Notions, Jobbers.

Aristegui y Ca.
Casanova y Muñoz
Cosio y Herreria
Hernandez Soto
Laguera, Muriedas y Ca.
Michel y Foustoul
Nacero y Ca.
Rucabado y Ca.
L. Poagori
Varona y Otaria
Agustin Gallardo
Carolina Leanteaud
Julian Tolsa
Vida de Salazar

Engineers, Mining and Civil.

Adrian Aguirre
Aguirre y Fierro
Francisco Avalos
Camilo Bros.
Luis Gonzalez Cuevas
Espinoza y Cervantes
Espinoza y Cuevas
Rafael Espinosa
Campo del Gomez
Herrara y Lazo
Miguel Mayora
Eduardo Meade
Antonio Rayon
Jacobo Urtetegui

Flour Merchants.

Anastasio Alcocer
Domingo Bustamente
Julia Davila
Francisco Goribar
G. Meade y Hermano
José Maria Otahegui
Manuel Othon
Cayetona Parra

Furniture Dealers and Importers.

Miguel Lazo
Cruz Lopez
Jesus Rojas
G. Godovieu
Agustin Gutheil
Philip A. Max

General Manufacturers' Agents.

Tomas Caloca y Ca.
Manuel Castello y Ca.
Dili y Lavin
Larcos y Ca.
Mijares y Diaz
Felix Muriel
Ignacio Noriega
Gregorio Perez
Apolino Rangel

Ulabarri y Bustamante
Villegas y Ca.

Groceries and Provisions, Wholesale and Retail.

Caledonio Alva
Balmori Hermano
Ramon Calvillo
Chavez y Pazzi
Leon Desidero de Diaz
Santiago Dilis
Clemente Hermosillo
Herculano Lara
Francisco Lascos
Hilario Nieto
Eugenio Nuñez
Antonio Ortiz
Apolonio Rangel
Antonio Reyes
Rivero Cantolla y Ca.
Jesus de la Torre
Francisco Viramontes

Hardware, Cutlery and Tools.

Elcoro Lopez y Ca.
German Gedovius
Felipe Gonzalez
Nestor Gonzalez
Leffman y Hijos
Anastasio Alcocer
Aristi y Hermano
Barrenechea Hermanos
Larache y Ca.
Emetrio Lavin
Manuel Macias
Marti y Vegambre
Pitman y Ca.
E. Shroeder
Zorzoza Hermanos
Felipe N. Gonzalez
Gutheil y Ca.
Angel Argueta
Dimas Castañeda
Ricardo Gomez

Importers and Warehousemen.

Bahnsen y Ca.
Juan Barajas y Ca.
F. Cabrera
Chabot Hermanos
Davies y Ca.
Gedorius y Langenscheidt
Miguel Gonzalez
Federico Gresser
Gutierrez Castillo y Ca
Matias Hernandez Saberon
T. Labadie
Fernando Larrache
Mayor de Parra y Caloca
Martinez Hermanos
Blas, Preda y Ca.
Pitmar y Lynch
Ruiz, Perez y Ca.
R. Santos de Aguirre
Simpson y Pitman
Stephan y Ca.
Jacobo Ulibarri

Iron Merchants.

Elcon y Ca.
Francisco Valladolid

Jewelers, Watchmakers and Silversmiths.

G. Gedovius
A. Gutheil
Ernesto Heffter
Francisco Mougarez
Simon Aviles
Nicolas Lopez
Muriedas y Ca.
Antonio Reyes
Lieña Rivero
Arcadio Narvaez
Miguel Gutierrez Sanchez

Lithographers.

Esquivel y Salas
Ramon Muñoz

Lumber Merchants.

Cruz Lopez
Marcelino Muriel
Pedro S. Navarro

Machinery Dealers.

Farias Hermanos
Jacobo Ulibarri

Manufacturers of Brick.

José Maria Grande
Enrique Winfield

Merchants, General Wholesale.

Aristi y Ca
J. H. Bahnsen y Ca.
Balmori y Ca.
Lounzo Campa
Campos y Gomez
Cárlos Danne
José M. Davalos
Juan Eguillor
Gastinel Auber
Geodowins y Ca.
Macedonia Gomez
A. Gutheil y Ca.
J. Heredia
Herculano M. de Lara Hermanos
Sucesores de Larrache
Lavin y Dilig
Marti y Bede
Moro y Tena
Muriedas y Ca.
Manuel Noriega y Ca.
Ignacio Noriega
J. M. Otahegui
Juan José Ottermin
Caledonio Perez
Pittmon y Ca.
Pons Hermanos
José Rodriguez
Matias H. Soberon
Tena y Galindo
Varona y Ca.
Aguerre Hermanos
Artolozaga y Ca.
Caire y Texier
Antonio Renteria Delgado
Gedovius y Ca.
Macedonio Gomez
Ceferino Navarro
Andrés Salinas
Matius H. Soberon

Paints and Varnishes.

(See Hardware, and Merchants, General.)

Pianos and Organs.

Aguirre Hermanos
Felipe Gonzalez
Max y Ca.
Sixto Espinasa
Antonio Leija
Eduardo Sierra

Photographers.

Mariano Nieto
Alberto Orozco

Physicians.

Gregorio Barroeta
Juan Cabral
José M. Coca
J. M. Davila
Juan N. Diaz
Francisco Estrado
Francisco P. Gallardo
Ignacio Gama
José Gama
Buenaventura Paz
Joaquin Lopez
Manuel Lopez
Estéban Olmedo
Buenaventura Paz
Flaviano Romero
M. Schaffner
Antonio Soso
Alberto Hermosa Lopez
Gustavo Hermosa Lopez
Juan N. Losa
Boca F. Martinez
Jesus Monjarás
Alejo Monsivais
Miguel Otero
Gustavo Pagentecher
Ventura Paz
Ricardo Salinas
Leon Villaseñor

Printers.

José Maria Dávalos
Secundio Gáudara
Escuela de Artes para Hombres
Escuela de Artes para Mugeres
Bruno Garcia
Silverio Velez

Sewing Machines.

Aguirre y Ca.
David Borrego
Clements y Clark
German Gedovius
Nabor Macias
Ernesto Thiss

Stationery.

Cárlos Bouret
G. Gedovius

Undertakers.	Wall Paper.
Cruz Lopez N. Sanchez	G. Gedovius. Felipe Gonzalez Gutheil y Ca.

TOLUCA,

STATE OF MEXICO.

Population, 17,000.

Agricultural Implements.
(See Hardware and Tools.)

Ale and Beer Dealers.
Santigo Graff
Telesforo Valdes
Mariano Avilo

Billiard Halls.
Fernando Rosenberger
Hotel de la Gran Sociedad
Ramon Diaz
Jesus Rivas
Telesforo Valdes

Bookbinders.
Roberto Alba
Juan Mirando

Books and Stationery.
Gordillo Gonzalez
Fernando Salazar
José Velazquez

Boots and Shoes, Retail.
José Barbosa
Pascual Legorreta
Juan Maya
Justo Oca de Montes
Jesus Moreno
Jesus Rivas
Gil Robles
Mariono Goroztieta

China and Glassware.
José Lopez
Ignacio Urbina
Antonio Pliego y Cruz

Copper Goods.
Ambrosio Gratecat

Dentists.
H. Carrillo
Cecilio Garcia
Adolfo Morales

Druggists.
M. G. Jiminez
Ignacio Urbino
Alberto Gutierrez
Calixto Morales

Luis Ortiz
Arevalo Palomares
Juan Rodriguez
Agustin Vargas
Fernando Fernandez

Dry Goods and Notions, Retail.
Ramon Ballina
Caviedes Hermanos
Cienfuegos Hermanos
Tomas Navas
Francisco Pichardo
Benigno G. Rojas
Antonio Lopez

Flour Dealers.
Cresanto Avalo
Gonzalez Dias
Fernando Garduno
Pedro Mondragon
Luciano Richardo

Furniture Dealers.
Anacleto Nava
José Cortina

Groceries and Provisions, Jobbers and Retail.
Jesus Barrera
Joaquin Cortina y Hermanos
Andrés Garcia y Hermanos
Santiago Laiseca
José Lopez
Benigno Rojas
Davio Valdés
Joaquin Alaniz
Blas Dias
Fermin Garcia
Tomas Gutierrez
Jacinto Sanchez

Hardware, Cutlery, Tools, Etc.
G. Ballysteros
Agustin Ayala
José Gallegos
José Lapoz
Adolfo Stein
Santo Almeida
Abundio Betancourt
Vicente Heras
N. Vazquez
Gonzalez y Benavidez

Hotels.

Francisco Colon
Fernando Rozenzweig
Gargollo y Ca.
Manuel Pelaez
L. Pliego

Ice Dealers.

Mariano Avila
José M. Sanchez

Jewelry, Watches, Etc.

José Maria Carrasco
Jesus Almazan
Luis Frausto
Pascatio Mena
Juan Olmedo
Jesus Barron
Ramon Santin
Agustin Monteil
M. Quiros

Lithographers.

Felipe Renteria
Pedro Martinez

Lumber Merchants.

Babiano Gastro
Pascual Castano
Sostones Vilches

Photographers.

Daniel Alva
Torres y Mejia

Physicians.

Emelia Arenas
Juan N. Campos
Cárlos Chairx
Ramon Espejo
Gonzalez Diaz
Urbina F. Gonzalez
Alberto Gutierrez
Antonio Hernandez
Mariano Hernandez
Nicolas Iñigo
Miguel Licea
José Ramos
Juan Rodriguez
Isaac Vazquez
Manuel Villada
Enrique Villela
Santiago Zambrano
J. Estrada
Eduardo Navarro

Pianos and Organs, Dealers.

Cresencio Inclan
Cruz Medina
José Montalvo
Mariano Orcoz
Guadalupe Rodriguez

Printers.

Pedro Martinez
Benito Quitano
Juan Quitano
Fenando Salazar

Saddlery and Harness.

Antonio Petiño
Ramon Vieyra

Sewing Machines, Agents.

José Lopez
Adolfo Stein
José Gallegos
Augustin Ayala

Tanners.

José Cortina
Pedro Trevilla
Eugenio Plata
Treville Hermanos

Wall Papers.

Pascual G. Gonzalez
José M. Velazquez

Undertakers.

(See also Furniture Dealers.)

F. Fernandez
Ignacio Guadarrama

VERA CRUZ,

STATE OF VERA CRUZ.

Population 15,000.

Agricultural Implements.

(See Hardware, Etc.)

Ales and Beer.

(See also Merchants, General.)

Jesus Elvisa

Bankers.

Esteban, Bencke y Ca., 12 Tercera del 5 de Mayo
H. D. Oleire y Ca., 569 Flores
Neron Hermanos, 563 Primera de San Juan
Manuel Oliver, 4 Benito Juarez
R. C. Ritter y Ca., 29 Independencia
Torres y Fisher, 228 Cuarta de la Playa
Velasco Hermanos, 128 Principal
Villa Hermanos, 221 Segunda de la Playa
Wetinez y Ca., 264 Primera San Juan
Cos, Castillo y Ca., 10 Independencia
A. Doussine y Ca., 9 Benito Juarez
Landero, Pasquel y Ca., 31 Navas
C. A. Martinez y Ca., 11 S. de la Playa
J. F. Muñoz y Ca., 11 Independencia
F. M. Priela, Sucesor es de 10 Navas
Watermeyer y Ca., 11 S. de la Playa
Zaldo Hermanos y Ca., 20 Salina

Billiards.

Damaso Ballejo
Joaquin Loera

Book Stores and Stationers.

J. Carredano
Paso y Ca.
Rafael Rodriguez

Boots and Shoes.

Serapio Aguero, 20 Arista
Paulino Carbonell, 48 Independencia
Juan Cuneo, 9 Zaragoza
Julian Diaz, 95 Independencia
Francisco Font, 78 Independencia
Juan Lopez, 28 Independencia
José D. Gonzalez, 57 Cinco de Mayo
Bernardo Horro, 38 Independencia
Juan Lopez, 28 Independencia
Bedro D. Mantecon, 25 Vicario
J. M. Moll, 44 Independencia
Blas Ramos, 8 Plaza del Triguero
Basilio Roque, 23 Vicario
Alejandro Sanchez, 42 Cinco de Mayo
Guadalupe Valdes, 28 Cinco de Mayo

Commission Merchants, Importing and General.

Aladres y Ca., 5 de Mayo
Codes y Ca., Pl. del Muelle
Pedro Cortina, Vicario
Pedro del Paso
Vicente Reyes, Salinas
Rivas Hermanos, Independencia
Zaldo Hermanos, Salinas
Jorge Barnet, 277 Segunda de la Compañia.
Bonne, Ebert y Ca. 560 Primera de S. Juan
Brehn y Ca., 509 Segunda de San Agustin
Busing Metengs y Ca., 112 Primera del 5 de Mayo
Calleja Hermanos y Ca., 117 Segunda de la Caleta
Salvador Carran, 138 Segunda de la Parroquia
F. Civert, 577 Pescaderia
Lorenzo Codez, Garcia y Ca., 661 Segunda del Dicario
Cos, Castillo y Ca., 211 Segunda de la Caleta
D. Oleria y Ca., 569 Portal de Flores
During y Ca., 131 Pl. de Armas
Fernandez y Ca., 465 Segunda de la Pastora
Galaimena y Ca., 235 Primera de la Compañia
Gassier y Reynaud, 562 Primera San Juan de Dios
Gomez Velasco, Martinez y Ca., 126 Principal
M. Guilaron y Ca., S. Agustin
A. Gutheil y Ca., 127 Principal
José Rafael Herrera, 481 Primera de Nava
A. Hoffman, 205 Primera de la Pastora
Jauffred y Oliver, 120 Segunda de Caleta
L. Jon Blanc, Playa
Kröncke y Ca., 568 Portal de Flores
R. S. Lamadrid, 206 Segunda de la Compañia
Landero, Pasqual y Ca., 474 Primera de Nava
Julio Levy y Ca., 122 Priméra de la Pastora
Markoe y Ca., 514 S. Francisco
C. A. Martinez y Ca., 220 Segund de la Playa
Menendez y Ca., 18 Tercera del 5 de Mayo
Meson y Hermano Wittinez y Ca., 563 Primera de S. Juan de Dios
Pedro G. Millan, 606 Maria Andrea
Leon Minvielle, 616 Primero de la Alhondiga

Francisco J. Muñoz y Ca., 617 Primera de la Alhondiga
Manuel Oliver, 129 Principal
Palomo Fernandez y Ca, 622 Plaza de Armas
Pedro A. Paso y Troncoso, 784 Salinas
Francisco Maria de Prido, 489 Segunda da de Neva
R. C. Ritter y Ca., 204 Principal
Rivero y Hijo, 273 Merco
Juan Manuel Sevilla, 483 Premera de Nava
Stucke y Ca., 516 S. Francisco
Torre, Fincher y Ca., 228 Pl. del Muelle
Velasco Hermanos, 128 Principal
Viya Hermanos, 221 Segunda de la Playa
Watermeyer, Wichers y Ca., 125 Tercera de la Caleta
Wittenez y Ca., 264 Primera de San Juan
Zaldo Hermano y Ca., 675 S. Vincente
Guillermo Busin y Ca.
A. Cantero
Cos, Castillo y Ca.
H. L. Desmarets
Salvador Diez
Formento y Ca.
Garcia y Ca.
Grimaud y Ca.
Alberto Hackmack
R. Laine
Llarena Hermanos y Ca.
Leon Mineville
Luciano Muñez
J. de Olizaga
Ollivier y Ca.
R. Sierra Aermanos
C. Temprana
Torres Fisher y Ca.
Wells, Fargo y Ca.
Fernandez y Ca.
Fernando Garcia
Garcia de la Lama y Ca.
Garcia Wolf y Ca.
Rafael Garcia
Gomez y Ca.
Hoyos Braulio
P. I. Izazola
Luciano Joublane
Luciano Leycegui
Manuel Oliver
Manuel Pastor y Valdes
Petit, Juan Porte
Torres Vincente Reyes
Gil Rico
Yendrell y Villerave
Wittenez, Villa y Ca.
Francisco J. Ultuarte.

Dentists.

Paulino Arrondo, Meson del Buza A.
Manuel Emilio Isaac, Independencia
Desiderio Rojo, Zamora

Druggists.

Daniel Alandi, 114 Primera de Caleta
Ramon T. Alverez, 475 Pescaderia
Luis Campos, 97 Cuarta del 5 de Mayo
José Capdevila, 133 Primera de la Parroquia
Jaime Capellero, 290½ Quinta de la Compañia
José Diaz, 287 Primera de la Alhondiga
L. Arnaul
José Manuel Carrilo Zamora
Adolfo Follenveire, 650 Vicario
Luis Hoyos, Zaragoza

Druggists—continued.

Landero y Ca., Independencia
Cárlos Mariscal, 629 Maria Andrea
Muller Vicario
A. Perez Redondo, 199 Principal
J. Valdes y Ca., Belen
Antonio Verela y Ca., Independencia
Carrillo y Ca., 24 Zamora
Guillermo A. Esteva y Ca., Independencia
Cárlos Mariscal 33 Zamora
Miguel Reyes Marquez, Cinco de Mayo 77
Artuso del Rio, Marced 26
Gonzalo Sanchez, Independencia 42
Rafael Rossel
Sanchez y Ramos

Dry Goods and Notions.

Ader y Ca.
Brien Hermanos
Codes y Ca.
J. Herrera
J. Larroni
Larrinaga y Gorostega
Eugenio Marque
Muriel Ulibarri y Ca.
Victor Rivera y Ca.
Socasa y Ca.
B. Vandesoel Salde

Engineer, Mechanical.

Enrique Diaz del Pino

Furniture Dealers.

J. I. Izazola
José J. Zarate

Groceries and Provisions, Wholesale.

M. Guilleron y Ca.
Martin Garcia y Ca.
Martinez y Gonzalez
R. Sierra y Hermano
Maximo Dorantes
Enrique Fince
Rafael Gonzalez
Juan Ortega
Joaquin Ruiz

Glass and China Ware, Lamps, Etc.

Segundo Alonso, 571 Pescaderia
J. Palomo
R. C. Ritrer y Ca., 204 Principal
Zeriner y Ca.
Francisco Ribera

Gunsmiths.

Enrique Lanoy
Benito Mirayes

Hardware, Etc.

Dallhaus y Ca., 197 Primera de Sto. Domingo
Duering y Ca., 131 Pl. de Armas
Agustin Gutheil y Ca., 127 Principal
German Kroncke y Ca., 568 Portal de Flores
R. Varela y Ca., 613 Primera de Maria Andrea
Rodriguez y Lopez

Hatters.

José Avila, Vicario
Murrillo y Barros, Bohorges
Rebattu y Ca., 126 Principal
Eugenio Samara
M. Valdes, Independencia
Warnholtz y Ca., Portal de Flores

Hides.

Cuervo Mantecon y Ca., Independencia
Juan Diaz, de Mayo
Gabrial Mantecon, Independencia
Joaquin del Paso y Ca., Independencia

House Furnishing Goods.

D. Hurri
M. Hernandez
J. Lorenzana
Victor Rendon
Santisteban
J. M. Tenorio
Sabas Zetino
Luis Acosta
Aniceto Alcade
Emilio Brousset
Lazaro Cabrera
Gregorio Leon
Antonio Lestrade
Angel Montero
Juan B. Roldan

Ice Dealers.

J. Fizmosis
Llarena Hermanos

Jewelry and Watches.

Luis Melendez, 140 Primera de Sto. Domingo
Cárlos Huguenin, Independencia
Manuel Miron, 19 5 de Mayo
Constantino Werle, 576 Portal de Flores
Ramon Barcaz
Julian Fuentes
B. Guerolo
Manuel Cosio
José Medina
Juan Vidal

Leading Cigar Manufactories.

"La Prueba," R. Balsa y Hermanos
"La Union," J, Fuente
"La Nacional," F. Rendon y Ca.
"La Union Nacional," Blanco y Ca.
"El Arte," Cappa de Villa
Gabarrot y Ca.
C. Benito y Ca.

Lumber Merchants.

Felipe Abascal, Extamuros
Madrazo y Ca.
H. Rodriguez, ex-convento de San Agustin

Merchandise Brokers.

Ascobe
J. Aspe
J. Canals
Diaz Miron
Dousine Fernandez
Maurice Fixt
J. Font

Merchandise Brokers—*continued.*

C. Gomez
C. O. González
T. Cardillo Hidalgo
Isidro Incera
J. Leon
Martinez Hermanos
Montero de Castro
B. Penelas
M. Perea
F. Prida
Ortiz Rodriguez
Sinseco y Mas
M. Salas
Soto y Ramos
J. Uriarte

Merchants, General Wholesale.

Julio Ascorbe
R. Balza
H. Ritter y Ca.
Viuda de Carredano
Castillo y Ca.
J. Cuseinera y Ca.
During y Ca.
Ficher y Ca.
Galainena y Ca.
Gomez y Ca.
Guillaron y Ca.
Kronte y Ca.
Landero y Pasquel
Landero y Ca.
Pasquel y Ca.
Luis y A. Hoyos
Madrayo Hermano y Sucesores
Markoe y Ca.
Martinez y Ca.
Del Paso
M. Robert y Ca.
Torre y Ca.
Velasco y Ca.
Villa Hermanos
Weber y Rojo
Witenes, Vila y Ca.
J. Abocal
Daniel Alundi
Bernardino Barros
Brunet y Ca.
Cipriano Bueno
Ciriaco Calleja
Guillermo Cano
Jaime Capallera
Miguel Carreño
Emeterio Cuesta
Manuel J. J. Font
Garcia Martin y Ca.
Giminez y Ca.
Juan Masa Gomez
M. Guilleron y Ca
Manuel Hernaiz
Laisequilla y Ca.
José Lopez
Martinez y Gonzalez
Martinez Macho y Ca.
Victor Niño
Antonio Nouriega
Victor Palacio
Francisco Pelaez
Manuel Pelaez
José Verduga Perez
José Ponso

Toedoro Ruiz
José Sanchez
José Sanchez y Ca.
José Santiesteban
Sierra y Hermano
José A. Soler
Sordo y Ca.
Tocarranza
Torres y Ca.
Manuel Villamia

Musical Instruments.

C. Dahlhaus y Ca., 197 Primera de Sto. Domingo.
Viuda de Carredano, 201 Principal

Photographers.

A. G. Alexander

Physicians.

Rafael Artigas, 780 Salinas
Manuel Cabrera, Independencia
M. Egowesch
José A. Gamboa, 522 Juarec
Manuel Garmendia, 614 Maria Andrea
Rafael Gomez, 5 de Mayo
Cárlos Heinemann, 824 C. de Flores
Miguel Heras, Playa
Anastasio Iturralde, 625 Maria Andrea
R. Zacarias de Molina, 22 5 de Mayo
Antonio Mosquera
Vicente Ordozgoiti, 6 5 de Mayo
José De la Pinta
Ignacio Pombo. 675 Segunda del Vicario
M. Reinoso
M. Roldan
Daniel Ruiz, Independencia
José Sanfelin y Bernal, 484 Nava
José Maria Sellallo, 173 Segunda de la Merced
Ignacio Vado, 674 Vicario
Alfred Velasco
Domingo Avil
Peña Garcia
Ernesto Hegeroisch
Enrique Palazuelos
Juan F. Rio
Narciso Rio

Printers.

J. M. Blanco
Juan Carredano
F. B. Jordan
José Ledesma, 784 Salinas
J. Sanchez
Rafael de Zayas, S. Francisco
Manuel G. Mendez

Perfumery and Toilet Articles.

A. Carral y Ca.
Delpaso y Ca.
B. Dominguez
Martinez y Diaz
Perenz del Molino
F. Rivera
Nicolás y Ca.

Saddlery and Harness.

Rio Riveia
Victornino Torres

MEXICO. 111

Seed, Grain and Plant Dealers.
Bazanes y Martinez
Fernandez y Gomez
Gallareta y Ca.
Garcia Hermanos y Ca
Guillaron y Ca.
Masolives y Ca.
J. U. Remmec
Zoerilla y Ca.

Steamship Agents.
Guillermo Busing y Ca.
Calejas Hermanos

Cos, Castillo y Ca.
A. Fournier
Llarena Hermanos y Ca.

Trunks and Bags.
Cuervo y Ca.
Cuesta, Conjeo y Ca.
Luis Salvador Diaz
Gabriel Mantecou

Undertakers.
Tomas Castro
Andrés Mendez

VALLE DE SANTIAGO,
STATE OF GUANAJUATO.
Population 10,000.

Commercial Agents.
Rafael del Rio
Antonio Guerrero
Juan Garcia Maravilla

Druggists.
R. Alvarez del Castillo
Pascual Bravo

Flour Mill.
Cárlos Deseloche y Hijos

Physicians.
Andres Ortega
Francisco Brebiesca
Ignacio Rangel

Principal Merchants, General.
Ramon D. Ropero
C. Saavedra
Demetro R. Gomar
Alvarez del Castillo

VILLA LERDO,
STATE OF DURANGO.
Population, 11,000.

Agricultural Implements and Machinery.
R. Dresel y Ca.
Goodman y Schmidt
H. Franke y Ca.

Ales and Beer Dealers.
P. Villalobos
Aguilar y Melendez

Banks and Bankers.
Banco Nacional (agency)
H. Franke y Ca.
Hernandez Angel
Francisco Aguilar
Wells, Fargo & Co.

Billiard Halls.
Manuel Dominguez
Sebastian Vera
José Gutierrez

Biscuit Bakery.
Gregorio Sanchez

Books and Stationery.
Luis G. Alva
Cresoforo Garcia

Carriage Makers and Dealers.
José Alanes
Albino Gandara
Magdaleno Garcia

Clothing, Hats, Etc., Retail.
Calderon y Leal
Jesus Calderon
Garcia y Calderon
Goodman y Schmidt
Gaspar Gutierrez
Angel Hernandez
Martin Martinez
Pedro Calderon
Mariano Odriozola
Vicente Reyes

Commercial Agents.
Aguilar y Melendez
Franke y Ca.
Santiago Gonzalez

Commercial Agents—continued.

Miguel Alva
Carlos Bravo
Luis Gamboa
Francisco G. Alvarez

Crockery and Glassware.

Martin Martinez
Victor Michaud.

Dealers in Native Products.

Pedro Calderon
Jesus Calderon
H. Franke y Ca.
Fuentes y Piña
Goodman y Schmidt
Hernandez y Ca.
Victor Michaud

Druggists.

Manuel Avila
Casimero A. Hernandez
Viuda de J. Reyes
J. E. Underwood
M. Gonzalo Jimenez

Dry Goods, Etc.

Rodolfo Dressel y Ca.
Fuentes y Piña
Rosendo Peña
Victor Michaud

Express Company.

Wells, Fargo y Ca.

Flour Mills.

H. Franke y Ca.
Francisco Favela
Manuel Manso
Gabino San Miguel

Foundry.

Roman Perez

Furniture Dealers.

H. Franke y Ca.
Goodman y Schmidt
Fuentes y Peña
Victor Michaud
Trinadad Urguiza
Leandro Urrutia

General Dealers, Retail.

Antonio Baez
Guadaloupe Alva
Pedro Calderon
Juan Bajar
J. Sancedo
Crescencio Soria
Antonio Cano
Gregoria Garcia
Crisoforo Garcia
Canuto Gamboa
Antonio Lopez
Martin Martinez
Mariano Odriozola
Vicente Sanchez
Juan Tajan
Antonio Valles

Casimero Gonzalez
Rafael Reyes
S. Arellano
Miguel Mancilla

General Merchants, Wholesale.

H. Franke y Ca.
Francisco Alvarez
Aguilar y Melendez
Jesus Calderon
Goodman y Schmidt.
A. Hernandez
Martin Martinez
Victor Michaud

Hardware and House Furnishings.

Pedro Calderon
Rudolfo Dressel y Ca.
Fuentes y Piña
Francisco Reyes
Francisco Aguilera
Albino Gandara
Cecilio Herrera
Juan Villa
Miguel Herrera
Luis Ortega

Hotels.

El Comercio
Hidalgo
Progreso

Insurance Agents.

Rudolfo Dressel y Ca.
H. Franke y Ca.

Perfumery, Etc.

Victor Michaud
Luis Jimenez

Physicians.

Agustin Vegara
Valeriano Gonzalez
José Reyes
Federico Fischer
J. E. Underwood
Maria G. Jimenez

Picture and Picture Frames.

Rafael Gonzalez
Abraham Aguado
Hipolito Gallado
Abraham Oviedo
Antonio Cano
Guillermo Wranga y Ca.

Printers and Publishers.

E. Parga
El Boletin de la Gendarmeria Fiscal
El Iriciador
El Tlahantilo

Saw Mills.

Abraham Aguado
Angel Coronel

Sewing Machine Agencies.

Jesus Calderon
Rodolfo Dressel y Ca.
H. Franke y Ca.
Angel Hernandez

Goodman y Schmidt

Watches and Jewelry.

Miguel San Miguel
Juan Garces

ZACATECAS,

STATE OF ZACATECAS.

Population, 64,000.

Agricultural Implements.
(See Hardware, Etc.)

Ales and Beer, Dealers.

Martin Diaz
Antonio Castellanos
Jacobo Wiltman
Domingo Perez

Banks.

Banco Nacional
Banco Mercantil

Billiards.

C. Gregoire
Domingo Perez

Bookbinders.

Pablo Carra
Eugenio Castillo
Severo Moreno
Luis G. Zubillaga

Booksellers and Stationers.

Cárlos Bouret
Tomas Cortina
Godoy Hermanos
Manuel Rodriguez

Boots and Shoes.

Bernardo Alvarez
Juan Busson
David Mercado
Esteban Vazquez

Dealers in Native Produce.

Aguero y Elisondo
Arteaga Hermanos
Campuzano y Ca
Martin Diaz
Escobedo Hermanos
Antonio Frias
Muñoz y Peral
M. Parra
M. Silva
José Maria Torre
Manuel Veyna

Dentists.

Manuel Alfaro
L. Carbo
N. T. Herwin

Druggists.

Hipolito Bovis
P. Carrillo
Ignacio Hierro
C. de la Caja
Adrian Larre
Rafael Villalpando
C. de la Arribu
Agustin Alvarez
Luis Gonzalez
Basilio Moreno
Pedro Ponce
Adolfo Scholtz
Guillermo Valle
Lorenzo Villa

Engineers, Mining, and Mine Owners.

J. A. Bonilla
Hermenglido Campillo
Luis G. Cordoba
Luis Correa
Pedro Espejo
Lorenzo Floreci
Ignacio Hierro
Rivero J. Lorenzana
José A. Noriega
Agustin Preciado
Luis Pozo
Miguel A. Rico
Enrique Wist
Francisco Zarate

Flour Merchants.

Alberdi y Ca.
Perfecto I. Aranda
Corvera y Hijos
Juan Fernandez
Inocencio Isasi
Julien Ibarguengoita
Benigno Soto

Furniture Dealers.

Simon Acosta
Albino Aldama
Felix Aldama
Cayetano Carilla
Pedro Rodriguez

General Dry Goods Merchants.

Campuzano y Ca.
S. Armida
Cayetano Castaneda
M. Juanchuto
Marcias y Ca.

General Dry Goods—*continued.*
Maderia y Ca.
Silvely Echegaray
Alberto Thio y Ca.
Escobedo Hermanos
Muñoz y Peral
M. Silva

Groceries and Provisions, Wholesale.
Alberdi y Camacho
Arena Pio y Ca.
Julian Ibarbuengoita
Oscar Lorenzent
Ramon Ortiz
Benigno Soto

Hardware and Tools.
Sras. Bustamente
Leonidas Tenorio
Frieben y Ca.
Krieglestein y Ca.
Cárlos Storck
Schoeder

Hides and Tallow, Wholesale.
Santa Ana Benitez
Gabriel Esparga
Pedro Mora
Antonio Salazar
Jesus Valdes
Julian Zesati

Hotels.
Comercio
Diligencias
Nacional
Zacatecano

House Furnishing Ware.
Ramon Azuna
Matilde Diaz
Camilo Macias
Dionisio Macias
José Maria Macias
Matias Macias
N. Macias

Jewelry, Watches and Silverware.
Guillermo Brunet
Desiderio Lebre
Guillermo Bruchner
Rodriguez Hermanos
Tomas Gonzalez
Rafael Perez
N. Amador
Tirso Arteaga
Julian Davalos
Cárlos Folte
Ignacio Godina
Severo Olague
José Maria Villa Senor

Lithographer.
Nazario Espinosa

Merchants, General, Importing and Commission.
Alberdi y Pilon
Alexander y Ca.
Higino Cevallos
Genaro de la Fuente
Antonio Gomez
Guadalupe Gomez
Julian Ibarguen
Ramon C. Ortiz
Oscar Llorente
Mariano Llaguno
Anacleto Escobedo
Cayetano Escobedo
Daniel Escobedo
José Maria Escobedo
Esteinn Hermanos
Genaro de la Fuente, Sucesores
Antonio Gomez
Julian Ibarguengoytia
Oscar Lorenno
Juan Olivier
Roman, Ortiz y Ca.
Julian Petit
Petterson y Hermanos
Kimball y Alverdi
Tellezere y Ca.
Viadero y Ca.
Alejandro Aguilar
Juan B. Alatorre
José Campuzano
Mariano Diaz
Ignacio Dominguez
Miguel Dominguez
Benigno Elias
Elisondo Hermanos
Cayetano Escobedo
Tomas M. Escobedo
Gorcia y Cabasas
Marcos Garcia
Gonzalez y Gonzalez
Gilverino Lopez
G. Lopez y Hermanos
Manuel Munoz
Tiburcio Munoz
Apolonio Salas
Vicente Salinas
Segura y Larran
Cosme Torre
V. Chacon
Manuel D. de la Serna Diaz
Manuel Guerra
Cruz Diaz
Pascual L. Velarde
Andrés Lopez
Tomas Martinez
Vicente Martinez
E. Parra
Mariano B. Real
José Solorzano
José M. T. Escalante

Photographers.
Agustin Barraza
Manuel Orozco
Manuel Velasco

Pianos and Organs.
Fernando Kerber
Jesus G. Vazquez

Physicians.

I. Aviles
Ismael Bonilla
M. Brena
M. Espinosa
I. Hierro
Luis G. Gonzalez
J. Lares
Luis Mora
A. Padilla
J. Pani
V. F. Ponce
F. Solis
J. Torres
M. Torres
Rosario Torres
Jesus Hayos
Castillo de Mora

Printers.

Del Gobierno
Mariano Mariscal
Nestor de la Reva

Canute A. Tostado
Mariano R. Esparza
Nazario Espinoza
Tomas Lork
Mariano Mariscal
Norberto Raigosa
Francisco Villagrana

Sewing Machines.

Agustin Dávalos
Ernoulf y Ca.
Enrique Krieglestein
Ricardo Meade
Juan Petit
Rodriguez Hermanos
Rodriguez M. Sanchez

Undertakers.

Felix Aldama
Simon Acosta

Wall Papers.

(See Stationers.)

THE CLASSIFIED

TRADES DIRECTORY

OF

CENTRAL AMERICA.

1889-90.

COSTA RICA.

CITY OF SAN JOSE.

Population, 54,000.

Agricultural Implements.
(See Hardware and Tools; also General Merchants.)

Ales and Beer Dealers.
(See General Merchants.)

Banks and Bankers.
Banco Anglo-Costariense
Banco Nacional
Banco de la Union
Le Lacheur, Dent y Ca.
Tinoco y Ca., see heading "*Coffee Planters*"

Books and Stationery.
Guillermo Molina
Morrell y Ca.

Coffee Planters and Exporters.
Bonilla Hermanos
John Brealey
Bruno Carranza
José Maria Castro
Alfonso Cavit
Compañia Frankfort de las Paves
Echaudi Bros.
Esquivel Hermanos
Ramon Herran
Francisco Marfa Iglesias
Francisco Montealagre
Mariano Montealagre
Saens y Montoya
Tinoco y Ca.
Leoncio de Vars
E. Tarrer
William Witting
Rafael Berrocta
Remigio Quizos
P. Saborio
José Maria Orozco
Antonio de Jesus Soto
J. Soto
José Duran
Francisco Echeverria
Fernandez y Tristan
Jaime Guell
Demetrio Iglesias
Francisco Iglesias
Alijo Jiminez
Pedro Manan y Ca.
T. N. Millet
Francisco Peralta
Otto von Schroter y Ca.
Tinoca y Ca.
A. M. Velasquez

Druggists and Chemists.
J. Bansen
Bruno Carranza
José Maria Castro
Moises Castro
Durau y Nunez
Lordly y Wemen
Juan Padilla
J. A. Pinto
Francisco Quesada
J. Saenz
Juan Ulloa
J. Valverde

Furniture Dealers.
(See General Merchants.)

Groceries and Provisions.
Manuel Carazo
Alfonso Carit
F. Chacon
Esquivel Hermanos
Piza, Maduro y Ca.
Morel y Mason
Juan Serrano
F. Pinto
Tourette y Ca.
Alfaro y Dent
Duprat, Allard y Ca.
Jaime Guell
Andrés Marsicano

Hardware, Tools, Etc.
M. Arguello
Manuel Carago
Morell y Ca.
José Muños
Dent y Ca.

Hotels.
Hotel Frances
Hotel Montané
Hotel de Roma
Hotel Victor
Hotel Villanave

Ice Dealers.

Juan Aguerro
José Chaves

General Merchants, Wholesale and Retail.

Alfaro y Dent
Piza, Maduro y Ca
M. A. Robles
F. Soto
Alberto Verdean y Martin
E. Soto
Manuel Arguello
Carazo Beche
J. R. Carazo
Manuel Carazo
Alfonso Carit
M. A. Adolfo Carit
Bruno Carranza
Jaime Carranza
M. Carranza
F. Chacon
Dent y Ca.
José Duran
Juan Echevarria
M. D. J. Veuta Epinde
Aniceto Esquivel
Esquivel Hermanos
Tomas Farrer
Fernandez y Hijos
Joaquin Fernandez
Garcia Hermanos
Guillard, Naute y Ca.
F. Hernandez
Huffer y Grytzel
Juan T. Jorge
Adolfo Knohr
Juan Knohr
Juan Federico Lahmann
Lelacheur y Ca.
Isidro Leorico
J. Mamneck
Alvarado Marsilio
Montealegre e Hijo
Montealegre y Salazar
Mateo Mora
Arturo Morrell
Morrell y Mason
J. Naucelt
Francisco Peralta
Concepcion Pinto
F. Pinto
Jaime Pyle
F. Robert y Ca.
Schrenta y Ca.
Juan Serrano
Mompon, William y Ca.
Tinoco y Ca.
H. Tournon y Ca.
Tourette y Ca.
Van Dyke y Ca.
Van Nuffel y Ca.
Leoncio de Vars y Ca.
Von Shroter y Ca.
José de Ycasa
Juan Acasta
Mariano Acosta
T. Alfaso y Ca.
David Alpizar
Maurillio Alvarado

Merchants, General.

George André
Cruz Brenes
F. R. Brenes
Brenes y Echandi
Juan Castro
Theodosio Castro
Caatro y Andrés
Rafael Dengo
Juan Dent
Duprat, Atlard y Ca.
Carlos Echeverria
Fernandez y Tristan
Juan Hernandez
Otto Hubbe
Alfred Lawenthal
Pedró Manan y Ca
F. M. Millet
Mariano Monje
Otto von Schroter y Ca
Esteban R. Smyth
Pedro Terrez
Thompson y Ca.

Newspapers and Printers.

"El Correo Español"
"El Ferrocarril"
"La Gaceta"
"La Replica"
"The Reporter"

Physicians and Surgeons.

Cruz Alvarado
J. Bansen
Juan Bonnefil
Bruno Carranza
José Maria Castro
Moises Castro
N. Duran
R. Heine
F. L. Lordley
N. Michand
J. Nuñez
Juan Padilla
J. A. Pinto
J. Saenz
J. Rucavad
Juan Ullra
J. Valverde
Leopoldo Wesner

Printers.

De Carranza
Nacional
La Paz
Imprenta del Istmo
Imprenta del Pueblo

Sewing Machines, Agencies.

G. Molina
Manuel Arguello
Piza Maduro y Ca.

Undertakers' Supplies.

(See General Merchants.)

ALAJUELA.

Population, 12,000.

Banks.
Caja de Ahorros
Caja de Descuentos

Druggists and Chemists.
Francisco Padilla
F. Soto
José M. Toledo

General Merchants, Wholesale.
Mariano Acosta
Alfaso y Ca.
J. Fernandez
Garcia y Ca.
H. Tinoco y Ca
Miguel Lopez
Eustaquir, Perez y Ca.

Piza, Madulo y Ca.
Manuel Sandovel
Filadelfo Soto
Trijos y Ca.
Zamora e Hijo

Physicians and Surgeons.
Francisco Padilla
J. Toledo
E. Uribe

Planters and Exporters.
Piza, Eaduro y Ca.
Pedro Sabario
Jesus Soto
José Maria Soto

GUATEMALA.

CITY OF GUATEMALA.

Population, 55,000.

Ales and Beer Dealers.
Cerveceria Alemana
Cerveceria Francesa

Agricultural Implements.
(See General Merchants.)

Banks, Bankers and Importing Merchants.
Banco Colombiano
Banco Internacional
Banco Nacional
Bamaso Angelo y Ca.
I. Francisco Aguirre
Luis Asturias
Braulio Novales
Ramon Asturias
Antonio de Aguirre
Pedro S. de Tyada
Angel Peña
Juan F. Aguirre
G. Angulo y Ca.
Pedro Barros
Benito y Ca.
Pablo Blanco y Ca.
O. Bleuler
José M. Escamilla
Braulio Novales
J. M. Samayoa

Booksellers and Stationers.
F. Alpirez
Bertrand y Ca.
Emilio Goubaud
Antonio Partegas
F. Matheu
Sanchez y Ca.
Norbeto Ziza
Juan Capella
Marchado, Irigajen y Ca
Adriano Paez

Bookbinders.
Tranquilino Dorante
Genaro Fuentes
Mariano Solare

Boots and Shoes, Wholesale and Retail.
Toribio Alvarado
Felix Aristondo
Bernardo Bargas
Salvador Bersian
Victor Brau
Simeon Cabrera
Mariana Cordova
Daniel Coronado
Jaqier Coronado
Martin Paz
Domingo Diaz
Pedro Escobar

Boots and Shoes—*continued*.

Liberato Farfan
Salvador Fernandez
Cupertino Flores
Simeon Franco
Anselmo Galvez
Casimiro Garcia
Cárlos Gonzalez
Francisco Granados
Manuel Guzman
Manuel Lafuente
Tomas Larquet
Anastacio de Leon
Juan C. Lopez
Juan Marroquin
Florencio Meono
Andrés Mendoza
Eugenio Mendoza
José Maria Milan
Fernando Morales
Alejandro Naiarro
Baltasar Ortiz
José Pepio Farfan
Mariano Perez
Leopoldo Pulle
Vicente Ramirez
Dioniosio Rendan
Camilio Rosales
Juan Rosales
Saturnio Salazar
Cleto Sanchez
Esteban Saro
Braulio Silva
Ignacio Ariola
Juan Silva
Rafael Silva
Sebastian Trejo
Santos Vazquez
Jorga Vega
José Maria Valezquez
Mecario Aguilar
Pedro Arrazola
Agapito Ayala

Coppersmiths.

Pedro Berduo
Domingo Contreras
José Maria Chinchilla
Barbaro Garcia
Cornelio Garrido
Ignacio Granado
Vicente Herrera
Pedro Iriarte
Higino Lopez
Pantaleon Marroquin
Serapio Minera
Juan Ortega
Manuel José Palomo

Dentists.

D. Castillo
José Diaz
J. B. Triersen
Felipe Banaza
Francisco Corso
Luis Estrada
F. Ucles

Druggists and Chemists, Retail.

Vicente Aravalo
Eduardo Bendfeldt
Domingo R. Castillejo
Ladislao Cordero
Secundo Diaz
José Maria Escobar
José Maria Galvez
Pedro Galvez
Rafael Gallardo
Francisco Garcia
Ramon Garcia
F. C. Herbruger y Ca.
Celestino Hernandez
Vicente Herrera
Mariano Lara
Juan Losa
David Luna
Leopoldo Mancilla
Cárlos Molina J
Manuel Monge
Manuel M. Montenegro
Federico Morales
Manuel Orellana
Jacinto Pacheco
Manuel Quevedo
Anastasio Rodriguez
Domingo Samoya
Miguel Sanchez Moreno
Salvador Saravia
Isaac Sierra
Joaquin Solares
José Maria Vides
Salvador Arevalo

Dry Goods, Notions, Haberdashery, Etc., Retail.

Valentin Aceytuno
Antonio Avila
Ladislao Avila
Manuel Avila
Clemente Aviley
Francisco Barrera
Juan Barrera
Ciriaco Beteta
Florencio Bobadilla
Marcelo Borrajo
José A. Castro
Miguel Castro
José Maria Caballos
Luis Corado
Francisco Flores
Concepcion Galvez
José Angel Galvez
José Maria Galvez
Pablo Galvez
Leandro Garcia
José Maria Garrido
Dorateo Gonzalez
Terero Guzman
Catarino Lara
Eugenio Lara
Juan Leiva
Vicente de Leon
Albino Lopez
Justo Lopez
Secuadino Lopez
Juan Lima
J. Megin
Magdalena Megicano
Domingo Menco
Julian Molina
José Maria Mérales
Gregorio Ortiz
Gregorio Penagos

GUATEMALA.

Dry Goods, Etc.—*continued.*
Francisco Pena
José Maria Perez
Pedro Quintero
Eustaquio Reynosa
Rosalio Reynosa
José Rodriguez
Santiago Rodriguez
Rosalio Roja
Feliciano Ruiz
Juan de Dios Salvatierra
Manuel A. Solares
Juan Tobar
Manuel Tobar

Fireworks Dealers.
Gerónimo Aldana
Manuel Barrientos
Lucio Garcia
Manuel Garrientos
Jacinto Guerra
Teodoro Guerra
José Maria Mendez
Lazaro Monzon
Remigio Quinones
Pedro Ramirez
Juan Robles

Foundries and Machinists.
Benbenuto Archila
Miguel Archila
Rafael Bautista
Manuel Carrillo y Hnos
Lanreano Enrique
Casimiro Espiñoso
José Maria Figueroa
Domingo Flores
Aquilino Garcia
G. W. Eernando Goez
Manuel Gomez
Ruperto Gonzalez
José Maria Menco
Manuel Mendoza
Manuel Ortiz
Trinidad Osaeta
Cárlos Schmidt
Teodoro Useda
José Maria Villalobos
José Maria Villatoro
Gregorio B. Vela

General Merchants, Wholesale.
Manuel Cardenas
Duran y Ca.
Pedro J. Barrios
Julian Batres y Hijos
Batres y Hermanos
Francisco Camarcho y Ca.
Compañia de Agencias de Guatamala
Eduardo y Ca.
Eduardo Hall
F. C. Herbruger y Ca.
Hockmeyer y Ca.
Goethos y Vendepute
José Thomas Lanahondo
W. Friedman y Ca.
Martinez y Ca.
Jorge Prado
Rafael Quiñones
Juan Rodriguez
Juan Aparico

E. N. Bolander
F. Duran
Enrique Fisher
P. Barros
Benito y Ca.
Betran y Ca.
Gustavo y Bernardo Haas
G. Kler
T. Mattheu
Ocitz y Hermanos
Bosner y Ca.
Sanchez y Ca.
A. Sinibaldi
M. Sirigier Suarez
Uruella y Hermanos
T. Valenzuela

General Merchants, Wholesale and Retail.
Antonio Agurre
Juan Francisco Aguirre
Manuel Aguirre
Ramon Aguirre
Francisco Alvarez
Luis S. Andreu
Rafael Angulo
Salvador Arevalo
Pedro Anechea
M. Arroyo
Raymundo Arroyo
E. Ascoli y Ca.
Luis Asturias
Rafael Asturias
Xavier Asturias
Augener y Cassebohm
Manuel S. Ayau
Mercedes M. de Ayau
Rafael Aycinena
Pedro J. Barros
Julian Batres y Hijos
Luis Batres y Hermanos
Vicente Beltranena
Benito y Ca.
Bertrand y Ca.
Pablo Blanco
Jorge Bramma
Francisco Camacho y Ca.
Juan Capella
Ildefonso Castellanos
H. Chiguero
Cristobal Cifre
Miguel Coloma
Compañia de Agencias de Guatemala
Eduardo David y Ca.
Leona David
José Descalzi y Ca.
A. E. Donelly
H. Domer y Ca.
Xavier Du Fiel
J. M. Escamilla
Valentin Escobar
Vicente Fonseca
Eduardo Geering
Goethoes y Vendpute
Emilio Goubaud
José Guardiola
Eduardo Hall
Emilio Herbruger
F. C. Herbruger y Ca.
Manuel Herrera
Hockmeyer y Ca.
Jorge Klee

General Merchants, Wholesale and Retail—*continued.*

Buenaventura Baubrir
Lara, Pavon y Zollikofer
José Tomas Lanahondo
Julio Lowenthal
Joaquin Macal
Antonio Machada
Machado, Irigyen y Ca.
Manuel Machado
G. E. Magee
J. Magee
Federico Matheu
Juan Matheu
Matheu y Ca.
S. McNieder
Juan Mejicano
J. Minondo
Manuel M. Monge
José Monteros
Manuel Monziols
Ulisses Monziols
Braulio Morales
Ramon Murga
W. Nelson y Ca.
Luis Noverto
Francisco S. Orrellano
Manuel Ortega
F. Ortiz y Ca.
Manuel Ortiz
Antonio Partegas
Pedro Ramas
José Revelo
Juan Rhimer y Ca.
Rittscher y Ca.
Rivero y Valerdi
Francisco Rohrmoser
Rafael Romaña
Rosenberg y Hennings
Juan M. Ruiz
Viviano Salvatierra
Domingo Samayoa
Doroteo Samayoa
José M. Samayoa
Dionisio Sanchez
M. Sanchez y Ca.
Pedro N. Sanchez
Salvador Saravia
Henry Scholfield
Isaac Sierra
Alejandro M. Sinibaldi
Dolore C. de Sinibaldi
Julian Sinibaldi
Rafael Sinibaldi
S. B. Storms
Rafael Teran
Hormanos Tielman
Miguel Tinoco
Horacio Ubico
Francisco Urruela
Gregorio Urruela
Hermanos Urruela
José Urruela
Juan Francisco Urruela
Miguel Urruela
Salvador Urruela
Felipe Neri Valdez
Hermanos Valentine
José Valerdi
J. Vasquez y Jaramillo
Vasquez y Ulrico
Pablo Vazen
José A. Vega
Manuel Vega
E. Widmer
Frederico Widmar
A. Zadickz y Ca.
Vicente Zebadua
Miguel Zepeda
Norberto Zinza
Antonio Zirion
Juan Aparicio
E. N. Bolander
Hermanos Bramma
Manuel Cárdenas
Duran y Ca.
Enrique Fisher
W. Friedman y Ca.
Casimiro Guillard
Juan Pablo Maldonado
Martinez y Ca.
Hermanos Meyer
J. Nimanda y Ca.
Jorge Prado
Rafael Quiñones
Guillermo Rodriguez
Juan Rodriguez
E. Rosenberg y Ca.
Cárlos Schultz
Jacobs, Wolfe y Ca.

Hotels.

Gran Hotel
Hotel de Europa
Hotel del Globo
Hotel de Guatemala
Hotel Nicolé
Hotel del Teatro

House Furnishing, Tinware, Etc.

Estanislao Aragon
Mariano Gonzalez
Gregorio Iriondo
Juan Iriondo
Pedro Lopez
Ramon Molida
Eufrasio Moran
Pedro Moran
Ramon Poggio
Alberto Rivera
Nazario Rivera
Valeriano Santa Cruz
Francisco Sta. Maria
Sebastian V. Storm
Pedro Villalobos

Iron Foundry.

Juan Klee

Jewelers and Silversmiths.

Marcelo Argueta
Antolin Cáceres
Bartólome Castilla
Fulgencio Estrada
Santiago Estrada
Gregorio Grageda
Asencion Jardin
Salvador Minera
Dolores Munis
D. Madero
José Maria Sosa
Miguel Mancilla
Federico Widmer

Lithographers.

José Cividanes
Bibiano Salvatierra

Military Goods.

Manuel Alvarez
Casimiro Estrada
Manuel Gomez

Newspapers and Printers.

" El Guatemalteco "
" El Horizonte "
" El Médico Cirujaáno Centro-Americano "
" El Progreso "

Paints, Varnishes, Oils, Etc.

Cayetano Arroyo
Francisco Bertonin
Felipe Caballeros
Sinforosa Caballero
Julio Cestilla
Paulino Ceballos
Adolfo Chenal
José Maria Diaz
Pedro Gallardo
Cárlos de Leon
Rafael de Leon
Antonio Letona
Manuel Letona
Francisco Monterroso
Ramon Morales
Felix Ovando
Felix Rogel
Bibiano Salvatierra
Cecilio Soto
Santiago Valenzuela

Perfumery and Fancy Goods.

Rafael Aranda
William Beecher
Adolfo Grace
Mariano Guerra
Fernando Morales
Salvador Morales
Francisco Ortiz
Luis Ory
Julian Paz
Tomas Sanchez
Francisco Santa Cruz
Alejandro de Sevilla
Isodro Villalobos
Felix Zavala

Pianos and Sewing Machines.

Rafael Aranda
Manuel Maroquin
Gabriel Velenzuela
M. Guerra

Photographers.

Emilio Herburjer
Feliz Muniz
Bibiano Salvatierra
M. H. Somelliani
N. J. Zaguirre
F. Herburger
Wolfenstein y Libes

Physicians.

Francisco Abello
José Antonio Acebedo
Nicolas Andrade
Luis Andrino
Nicolas Angulo
Manuel Aparicio
Cárlos Aragon
Felipe Arana
Camilo Arevalo
Segismundo Arriaga
Manuel Arroyo
Gregorio Avalos
Teodore Avila
Eligio Baca
Felipe Barrasa
José Berchtinger
Enrique Bermudez
Francisco Bogran
Cárlos Bonilla
Juan Brau
Manuel Carranza
Francisco Castellon
Cárlos Castro
Moises L. Castro
Victor Colon
Simeon Contreras
Esteban Cruz
Rafael Cruz Meani
Joaquin Diaz
Miguel Diaz
Remigio Diaz
Eduardo Estrado
Manuel Estrada
José Maria Estupinian
José Farfan
José Maria Gallardo
Manuel Gallardo
Francisco Gemera
Ramon Garcia
Juan German
Dario Gonzalez
Ramon G. Gonzalez
Juan Jener
Buenaventura Lambuz
Luis Laso
José Cuna
Simon Magana
Dario Mazariegos
Edurado Mendoza
Cárlos Molina
Jacinto Molina
Julio Molina
Pedro Molina
Manuel Molina Milla
Cornelio Moncada
Alejandro Montalvo
José Menteros
José Maria Montes
Francisco Nunez
Bernardo Nunez
Juan Crollano
Juan Ortega
Valentine Ortiz
Otto Stoll
Agustin Pacheco
Juan Padilla
Mariano Padilla Matute
N. Pagaoga
Apolonio Palma
Fernando Palomo

Physicians—*continued.*

José Maria Palomo
Augustin Pasos
Luis Perez
Basilio Pineda
Juan Quitoua
Raul del Pino
Francisco Roquero
Manuel S. Samayos
Maximo Santa Cruz
Juan Climaco Solares
Enrique Soto
Francisco Tejada
Nicolas Tiferiano
Nazario Toledo
Salvador Trequeros
Fabrico Uribe
Manuel Valdes
Valentin Fernando
Trinidad Valladares
Mariano Valle
David Vazques
José de T. Velazques
José Maria Vides
Joaquin Yela
Rafael Zaldavar

Planters.
(Local Address.)

Ramon Aguirre
Luis Astunás
Anstides Bertliolin
J. M. Escamilla
Manuel Gonzalez
José Guardiola
M. M. Herrera

Emilio Lopez
Ricardo Lopez
Vitalino Lopez
Guillermo Rodriguez
Juan Rodriguez
Domingo Samayoa
J. M. Samayoa
Doroteo Samayoa
J. M. Samayoa
José Vega

Printing Establishments.

Tipografia "El Progreso"
Tipografia de Abraham F. Padilla

Steamship Lines and their Agents.

Campagnié Génerale Transatlantique, A. Bertiolin
Pacific Mail Steamship Co., Benito y Ca.

Stoves.
(See Furniture, also Hardware.)

Wholesale Merchants and Importers, General.

A. M. Sinibaldi
Matheu y Ca.
Frederico Matheu y Ca.
Hockmeyer y Ca.
T. Kriemler y Ca.
Betránd y Ca.
Benito y Ca.
P. N. Sanchez
M. Urruela y Ca.
R. Aguirre y Ca.

QUEZALTENANGO.

Bank.
Banco Internacional de Guatemala

Dentist.
G. A. Frierson

Druggists.
M. Aguilera
José Ramos
Doroeta Cayás

Jewelers.
José Leon
Gabriel Oltramare

General Merchants, Wholesale.
José Aguilar
Pomposo Castro
Mariano Enriquez
Doroteo Gutierrez
Bernardino Herrate
Martin de Leon

Cinilo Lopez
Geronimo Martinez
Tadeo Pacheco
Hermanos Paganini
Manuel Pelaez
Francisco Sanchez y Hijos
Roman Villagran
Whitney y Hawley

Physicians.
Francisco Cayás
Alberto C. de Castro
José M. Martinez

Printing Establishments and Newspapers.
Tipogrofia de la Industria
"El Bien Publico"

Sewing Machine Agents.
La Compañia Fabricante "Singer," Eudecia Diaz, Agent

REPUBLIC OF HONDURAS.

COMAYAGUA.

Population, 10,000.

Merchants, General, Wholesale and Retail.

Jacob Baez y Ca.
Victarino Berlioz
Castillo y Hermanos
Fiallos y Hermanos
Trinidad Hernandez
J. M. Inestrano
Raimundo Valenzuela
Pedro Abadie
Pedro Leitzeler
Bernhard y Hijo
Manuel Denis & Co.
Pedro Leizeler
Pedro Morris Jule y Ca.
Arias y Bustillos
José Maria B. Valenzuela
Juan Ramon Valenzuela

TEGUCIGALPA.

Population, 15,000.

Druggists and Chemists.

J. Aguelera y Ca.
M. Angulo
S. Angulo
Pedro Arias
E. Bernard
Dias y Morales
Manuel Vijil Molina
M. Streber
J. Ucles

Hardware, Tools, Etc.

Julio Balette
José Mari Reyna
José Lazo Sotero
Zelaya Hermanos

Merchants, General, Wholesale.

Jacob Baez y Ca.
Geo. Bernard
Catillo y Hijos
Diaz Hermanos
T. Figueroa
R. Streber
Zelaya Hermanos
Agurcia y Soto
Vicente Ayestas
Felix Bonilla
Francisco Castillo
Cordova y Quiñones
Florencio Cuellar
Remijo Diaz
Francisco Planas
Marcial Molina
Salvator Diaz
Jacob Estrada
Jesus Estrada
Benito Fernandez
J. J. Fernandez
Jesus Fiallos
Juan Fiallos
Dionisio Galinda
Ramon Jerez
Samuel Laines
Luis Laddizabal
Lazo y Ca.
Doula Loanzo
Enrique Midence
Ramon Midence
Perez y Lazo
Pio Ucles
Leopoldo Servilla
R. Streeber
Marrin Ucles
Tomas de Ugarte
Ugarte y Hermanos
J. Zelaya
Zelaya y Hermanos
Miguel Zuniga
Rafael Camilo Diaz y Hijos
Martin Ucles
Fortin y Bonilla
Ramon Vigil
Julian Fiallos y Hijos
Gutierrez, Lopez y Ca.

Newspapers and Printers.

" La Gazeta "
" La Paz "
" La Republica "

Physicians and Surgeons.

A. Bernard
Joaquin Diaz
Estavan Ferrari
Manual Juan Fiallos
Vijil Manuel Molina
E. Toledo
J. Ugarte

Printing Establishments.

Nacional Tipografia

YUSCARAN.

Merchants, General.

Daniel Fortin
Alecio Fortin
Monico Cordova, padre

Santiago Moncada
T. Gradiz

TRUJILLO.

Merchants, General.

J. Font
Binney, Melhado y Ca.
P. Castillo

José Julio
Juan Lafitte

AMAPALA.

Merchants, General.

Pedro Abadie
Bernard Hermanos
Manuel Denis y Ca.
J. P. Gattorno y Hijo
E. Herran
A. Dubon

P. Juhl y Ca.
Pedro Leitzelar y Ca.
Morris y Ca.
Remigio Padella
The Ampala Co. (Limited.)
José Rossner

JUTICALPA.

Merchants, General.

M. Guegllin
J. M. Zelaya
F. Calis
S. Meza
Juan Castell
M. Vega de Cedros
P. Inestroza

T. Malute
T. Zelaya
G. Gardela
Torrez y Hernandez
P. Bertrand
C. Fortin

PUERTO CORTEZ.

Merchants.

Debrot Hormanos
Gedirico Debrot

A. Ruiz
W. Merilees

SAN PEDRO SULA.

Merchants.

Parting y Ca.
Ph. Arnoux y Ca.

F. Girbal
P. Vidaureta

PRINCIPAL MINING COMPANIES OF HONDURAS.

Yuscaran Mining Company
   Address, Yuscaran
Santa Eleana Mining Company
   Address, Yuscaran
Gibraltar Mining Company
   Address, Yuscaran
Rio Chiquito Mining Company
   Address, Santa Lucia
San Antonio Mining and Milling Co.
   Address, San Antonio
Paraiso Reduction Company
   Address, Yuscaran
Honduras Mining Co.
   Address, Yuscaran
Santa Lucia Mining and Milling Co.
   Address, Santa Lucia
(N. B.—For New York address of the foregoing companies see New York City Directory.)
New York and Honduras Rosario Mining Co.
   Address, San Juancinto
Zelaya Mining Company
   Address, Tegucigalpa
Santa Cruz Mining Company
   Address, Santa Cruz
Platero Mining Company
   Address, Yuscaran
Los Angeles Mining Company
   Address, Valle de Los Angelos

REPUBLIC OF NICARAGUA.

MANAGUA.

Population, 15,000.

Bankers, Etc.

Francisco Gomez Rivas
Hirchen y Ca.

Druggists and Chemists.

Rafael Cabrera
Gomez L. D. Luciano

General Merchants, Wholesale.

Antonio Cabrera y Ca.
Cabrera Delgadillo
Gabriel Espinoso
Francisco Gomez Rivas
D. J. Hirchen y Ca.
S. D. Mozia
Ascension Rivas
D. Rodriguez
M. D. Sanchez
James Simpson
Federico Solorzano
J. B. Thomas
Tiserino Hermanos
J. C. Bengoechea
F. y S. Bermudez
Calesto Cesar
F. Chamoro
J. de la Paz Cuadra
Teodoro Delgadillo
Miguel Espinoza
Daniel Frixione
L. Gomez
H. E. Low y Ca.
Viuda de Martinez
José A. Robleto
F. Solorzano
Salvador Solano

Newspapers and Printers.

" La Nacional "
" El Porvenir "
" El Semanal "
" Gaceta Oficial "

RIVAS.

Population, 8,000.

General Merchants.

Narciso Arguello
Hutago de Bustos
A. Cardenas
Pedro Chamorros
G. W. Cole
H. Goodman
Leonidas Guerra
A. B. Hurtado
Lopez y Maliaño
J. Maliaño y Hijos
M. Maliaño y Hermanos
Francisco Martinez
L. y N. Martinez
M. L. de Runnels
Francisco Torres
José Vicente Urcullo

LEON.

Population 25,000.

Ales and Beer.
(See also General Merchants.)

José J. Palacios

Agricultural Implements.

(See Hardware and Tools.)

Bankers.

Coronada A. de Morin
Justo Midence
Espiridion Orosco
Manuel Perez

Boots and Shoes.

Federico Aguero
Modesto Balladares
Antonio Bustos
Francisco Carbajal
José M. Cortez
Nicolas Chacon
Ramon Chavarra
Francisco Delgadillo
Cipriano Delgado
Juan Fonseca
Marcelino Giron
Clemente Iglesias
Pastor Macias
Boque Medina
Juan Medrano
José Melendez
Trinidad Melendez
Bernardo Mendez
Manuel Montes
Tomas Pantoja
Rosendo Pineda
Rafael Puintana
Benito Ramirez
Antonio Saenz
Cipriano Salgado
Alejan Sequeira
Rafael Syto
Toribio Soto
Francisco Valle
Vicente Vaquero
Pedro Vargas
Manuel Zapata

Commission Merchants.

Pedro E. Aleman
Carmen Belladares
Deshon y Murazan
Martin, Gutierrez y Ca.
M. Salazar y Ca.

Druggists and Chemists.

Julio Castro
Luis Cruz
Cosme Chevez
Teodoro Fassmer
Basilio Marin
Desiderio Pablais
Tomas Telleria

Foundries and Machine Shops.

Pastor Lindo
Vicente Osorno

General Merchants, Wholesale and Retail.

Almeda y Ca.
Pedro E. Aleman
Simon Altamirano
Frederico Alvarado
Pedro Alvarado
Elioloro Arana
Carmen Balladares
Lino Balladares
Manuel Balladares
Francisco Boquin
Salvador Cardenal
Mariana J. Castellon
B. Condhur y Ca.
Luis Cruz
Emilio Chesnay
Ramon Chica
Luis Debayll
Deshon y Morazan
Gabriel Dubon
Salvador Dubon
Florke, Notter y Ca.
Miguel G. Granera
Guerrero y Montenegro
Camilo Gutierrez
Estéban Gutierrez
Alberto Herdocia
Gordiana Herdocia
Rosa Icara
Gabriel Lacayo y Hijos
Narciso Lacayo
Panfilo Lacayo
Coronado A. de Marin
S. B. Marin, Gutierrez y Ca.
Fulgencio Mayorza
Midence y Ca.
Manuel J. Montealegre
Mariano Montealegre
José F. Muñez
Navarro, Villa y Ca.
Vicente Navas
Juano Ocampo
Desiderio Pallias
José Pineda
Prado y Arguello
Mariano Salazar y Ca.
Domingo Salinas y Ca.
Norberto Salinas
José Sania
Benitio Sarria
Otto Schiffman
Schubert y Paten
Alejandro Sequeira
J. R. Sevan
Thomas Telleria
Manuel T. Teran
Manuel Zuñiga
Aguilar y Sanchez
Aleman y Salzar
David Arguillo
Ignacio Aguillo
Pedro Arguillo y Hijos
Juan Bapes
Juliano Buitraga
Ramon Chica
B. Conduhr y Ca.
Eduard R. Deshon
J. J. y F. B. Deshon
P. Eisenstuck y Ca.
Guillermo Federich
Concepcion Garcia
Eduardo Garcia
Castullo J. Gurdian
Hazera y Ca.
Leonardo Lacayo
Alejandro J. Manning
Apolonio Marin
Salvador Marin
Luiz de Viuda Marin
Cleto Mayorga

General Merchants, Etc.—*continued.*

Rafael Mayorquin
M. J. Midence
Geo. A. Morris
S. D. Pallais
Cayetano Peralta
Dolores Ramirez y Ca.
José de J. Rojas
Macario Romero
Rafael Salinas
John R. Swann y Ca.
A. H. Teller
J. R. Teran
James Thomas

Hardware and Tools.

Benito Ardila
Gregorio Banegas
Trinidad Calderon
Leopoldo Cisne
Luciano Leon
Salvado Mungua

Hides and Leather.

Paula Balladares
Desiderio Baneto
Sebastian E. Escorcia
Felipe Granera
Salvador Gutierrez
Coronado Mayorga
Venancio Montalban
Vicente Oseps
Sinforoso Valle

Hotel.

Leon de Oro

Paints and Varnishes.

Demetrio Molina
Manuel Zapata

Photographers.

Manuel Godoy
Alejandro Lazarenco
Roman Perez
Samuel Sedilez

Physicians.

Antonio Aguilar
Juan F. Aguilar
Luis Aguilar
Santiago Arguello
Trinidad Palladares
Julian Castellon
Julio Castro
H. Fassmer
José Guerrero
Miguel Guerrero
Rodolfo Herdocia
Rafael Icasa
Leocadio Juarez
Timoteo Juarez
Francisco M. Lacayo
Juan Lacayo
Julian Lacayo
Basilo Marin
Juan Midenque
Venancio Montalban
Francisco Montenegro
Desiderio Pallais
Roberto Sacasa
Manuel Sedilez
Tomas Tolleria

Printers.

Constantino Gross
J. C. Gurdian
Benito Hernandez
Antonio Orue
Joaquin Ruiz

Sewing Machines.

(See Commission Merchants.)

Stoves.

(See Hardware.)

Tinware and House Furnishing.

Antonio Breneo
Sinforiana Robelo
Nazario Soliz

Undertaker's Supplies.

(See Commission Merchants.)

CHINANDEGA.

Merchants, General.

Señor I. T. de Callejas
Callejas y Callejas
Francisco Cardenal
Antonio Casineli
Julio Cesar
Emilio Chesnay
J. B. Gorlero Hermanos
J. B. Gorlero y Hijo
Juan de Dios Guerra
Camilo Gutierrez

Alberto Herdocia
Cárlos Halmann
M. Montealegre
Mariano Montealegre
Francisco Morazan
G. A. K. Morris
Angel Navarro
Pantaleon Navarro
Francisco Orrico
Hermanos Zeferino

GRANADA.

Population, 25,000.

Agricultural Implements.
(See General Merchants.)

Bankers.
Salvador Arana
Chamorro y Zabala
Santiago Morales
Manuel Urbina
Juan Vargas

Druggists and Chemists, Retail.
Francisco Alvarez
Alfonso Guerrero
Horacio Guzman
Alberto Lacayo
Agustin Pazos
J. Ignacio Urtecho
Pedro Vargas

General Merchants.
José Arguello y Ca.
Luis Arguello
Mariano Arguello
Agustin Aviles y Ca.
Bermijillo y Ca.
José I. Bermudez
Fernando Chamorro
S. H. Hamburger
Jesel de Leslie
F. y M. Lacayo
Panfino Lacayo
F. Lacayo y Ca.
Gabriel Lacayo y Hijos
Pastora Lacayo y Hijos
Federico Marena Hermanos
Manuel Mejia y Ca.
Luis Mejia Hijo
C. y J. Quadra
Ascension Rivas
Felix Romero
Hilario Selva
Marcos Tefel
Teodoro Tefel
Rosario Vivas
Rosario E. Vivas Hijo
Juliana S. de Abaunza
José Arce Arguello
Arguello y Avilez
Benard y Vivas
David Castrillo
Chamorro y Zavala
Juan M. Ciambrino
J. L. Costigliolo
Costigliolo y Guevara
Costigliolo y Guzman
Costigliolo y Zavala
Exequiel Cuadra y Salvador
Manuel Cuadra y Hermano
V. Cuadra y Joaquin
R. Espinola y Ca
Gonzalo Espinoza
Sebastian Espinoza
Daniel Lacayo
Fernando Lacayo
J. Lacayo y Ca.
Pánfilo Lacayo
L. Palazio
Roberto Lacayo, Sr.
F. A. Pellas
Quiros Hermanos
P. R. Ramirez y Ca.
M. Salazar y Ca.
Benjamin Sandoval
Concepcion Sequeira
F. de Abaunza Silva
Eduardo Teran
Juan Vargas
Serapio Vela
Leandro Zelaya

Hotels.
Hotel de los Leones
Hotel Sirena

Physicians.
Francisco Alvarez
Joaquin Arguello
Alfonso Guerrero
Horacio Guzman
Virgilio Gurzman
Alberto Lacayo
José Lejarza
I. Morales
Agustin Pasos
Pedro Vargas
A. Falla
N. Guerrero
G. Guzman

Planters, General.
Faustino Arellano
Rito Baez
Agustin G. Berard
Costigliolo y Zalala
Fernando Guzman
Daniel Lacayo
Fernando Lacayo
Vicente y Joaquin Quadra
Leandro Zelaya

Planters, Sugar.
Costigliolo y Zabala
Espinola y Ca.

Planters, Cocoa.
José Arguello
Chamorro Hermanos
E. Menier
C. y J. Quadra

Planters, Coffee.

A. Aviles
José T. Bermudez
Hermanos Brown
Francisco Espinola
Daniel Lacayo
F. y M. Lacayo
Tomas Lacayo
Desiderio Roman
Vagnan y Hermanos
Juan Vega

Printers.

José de Jesus Cuadra
Anselmo H. Rivas
Miguel Romero

Watches and Jewelry.

Martin Chamorro
P. Ramirez y Ca.
Roberto Lacayo
Felipe Ryas
José Lacayo

UNITED STATES OF COLOMBIA.

BOGOTA.

Population, 80,000.

Agricultural Implements.
(See also Hardware, Tools, Etc.)

Ferreteria de Pacho
Pereira, Gamba y Ca.
Isaac Diaz

Ales and Beer, Dealers.

A. Alford
A. B. Cuervo
Cayetano Cuervo
M. Montoya
Pizarro y Restrepo
Salvador Reias
Octavio Sayer

Banks and Bankers.

Banco de La Armistad, Norte 27 Occidente
Banco de Bogota al Occidente, Calle 3 Num 90
Banco Caja de Propietarios
Banco Columbia Oriente 151 Norte
Banco Credito Hipotecario
Banco Nacional
Banco Popular (Banco Hipotecario)
Banco Prendario
Banco Union

Bookbinders.

Daniel Boada
Valerio Cabrera
Evaristo Encisco
Indalecio Gomez
Adolfo Gonzalez
Ismael Gonzale
Manuel Gonzalez
Antonio Samudio
Francisco Torres Amaya

Books and Stationery.

Antonio Miguel Caso
Lorenzo Chavez
Pimitivo Delgadillo
Nicolas Esquerra
Garcia Rico Vayas y Ca.
Libreria Americana
Rafael G. Mogollon
Frederico Patino
Lázaro Maria Perez
Fidel Pombo
Manuel Pombo
Hermanos Ruiz Ramos
Saldevila y Curriols
Hermanos Zalamea

Boots, Shoes, Trunks and Leather Goods.

Jose Alvarez
Agustin Alva
Higinio Bunch
Angel M. Gomez
Federico Pardo y Ca.
Hermanos Pardo
Pedro Preciado
José M. Quintero
José M. Scavedra
Buenaventura Foleso
José M. Vega

Cabinetmakers and Furniture Dealers.

Rafael Archili
I. Bastida
Julio Charles
Antonio Clopatoski
Cárlos Duirne
Aldemar Dosenville
Rafael Espinel
E. M. Gavisia y Ca.
Teodosio Leon
Francisco Paniagua
Cruz Sanchez
Ramon Torres

Commission Merchants, General.

Comancho Roldan y Tamayo
N. Esquerra y Ca.
Francisco Groot
Rufino Gutierrez
Lazaro Maria Perez
M. W. Quintero
Restrepo y Arteaga
R. Silva y Hijo

Coppersmiths.

Florido y Ca.
Gregorio Foreso

Crockery and Glassware Dealers.

Roman Acero
Rita Caballero
J. Leocadio Comacho
Carmage y Ca.
J. Cubillos
Simon Huertas
Jesus Jimenez
Nicolas Leiva
Aurelio Moncada
Frederico Montoya
Eusebio Olaya
Luis Pardo

Crockery and Glassware—*continued.*

J. Paul y J. de Brigard
Gregorio Riano
Nepomuceno Ricon
Luis Ulises
Luis Umana
José de Jesus Fonseca
Posada y Diaz
Gregorio Salas

Dentists.

Manuel Abello
Julio C. Buitrago
R. J. Cabrales
Carazo Lancano
Rafael J. Corrales
G. V. Craper
G. Crowther
N. Chaguceda
G. Chambero
Francisco Escobar
Ignacio Gomez
Juan B. Velila Arango
Ricardo Berraza
J. A. Hermida
Indalecio Losada
Moreno y Vermaya
Francisco Quintero
R. Roa Ospina
Frederico Rosas
Marco M. Rozo
A. Salcedo
Rafael Lamayo

Druggists and Chemists, Wholesale.

R. M. Acero y Ca.
A. Aparacio
L. Barreto
Carlos Contreras
Hugo Biester
Bigot, Prada y Ca.
Buendia Herrera y Ca.
J. D. Herrera
Lombana y Ca.
Medina Hermanos
Osorio y Castaneda
P. Pizarro
Antonio Samper y Ca.
Uribe St. Croix
Ignecio Carrizosa
Mariano Gaviria
Miguel A. Madero
Ramon Pereira

Druggists and Chemists, Retail.

Ricardo M. Acero
Arroyo y Maldonado
Ignacio Berberi
Leoncio Barreto
Hugo Biester
Bigott, Prada y Ca.
Botica Alemana
Botica Militar
Buendia y Herrera
H. Buster
R. Canales
C. Contreras
Rafael Franco
Rodolfo A. Froez
J. David Herrera

Alejandro Lezaca
Medina Hermanos
L. Mendez
Jesus Glaya L.
Osorio Castañeda
Ospina Hermanos
M. C. Pena
G. E. Perdomo
Policarpo Pizarro
E. de J Roca
Rodriguez y Valez
Martiniano Rodriguez
Frederico Rosas
M. M. Rueda
Nemesio Sotomayor
Uribe y St. Croix
Francisco Barreto
Buendia, Rocha y Garcia
P. P. Cerrantes
Samuel Fayardo
David Herara
Santos Lezaca
Pizarro y Asparicio
Putnam y Ca.
Cárlos Quijano

Engineers, Architects and Builders.

Elsi Castro
Lorenzo Codazi
Luis Lleras
Francisco Olaya
Manuel H. Peña
Manuel Pons de Leon
Nepomuceno Santamaria
Julio D. Vallasino

Flour Merchants, Wholesale.

Roberto Bruce
Juan Caldos
Pompilio Lozano
Aurelio Moncada
Emilio Moncada
Genaro Osorio
Manricio Quijano

Flour Mills.

Molino de Campuzano
Molino de Sarmiento
Molino de Quijano

Foundries.

Jorge Bunch
Samaca de Fundician
Manrique y Codazi

Glass and Glassware.

Compañia Vildriera
Benjamin Garay
Elias Garay
Gregorio Salas
Thorin Hermanos

Hardware and Tools.

Isaac Diaz
Ferreteria de Pacho
Ferreteria de la Predera
Ferreteria de Samaca
Gonzalez Benito Hermanos
Jorge Vergara
Rafael Paris Nieto

Hardware and Tools—continued.

Pereira, Gamba y Ca
Ramon Salgar
Hermanos Thorin
Hermanos Zalamea

Hotels.

El Afanador
Cardenas
Virginia Fernandez
E. Gracia
Gran Hotel
Hotel Bogotano
Hotel Columbia
Hotel Cundinamarca
Hotel Frances
Hotel Panama
Hotel La Paz
Hotel Malakoff
Hotel Victoria
Hotel Violet
Filomena Lozano
Ana Joaquina
Eduvigis Vanegas
Hotel Bolivar
Hotel Santander
Jockey Club

Iron Merchants.

Isaac Diaz
Gonzalez Beurlto Hermanos
Periera, Gamba y Ca.
Antonio Samper y Ca.
Jorge Vergara y Ca.

Jewelers and Watchmakers.

Francisco Alvarez
Mariano Alvarez
Pablo Baquero
Julio Dardelin
A. Hidalgo
Francisco Alvarez
Santiago Baur
Enrique Bradock
Nazario Galindo
Rafael Nieto Paris
Domingo Ortega
E. Piechacon
Francisco Plata
Leon Rosez
Alfredo Rossez
Basilio Saenz
José M. Hidalgo
Kirkpatrick Brothers
Antonio Llaña
Quintin Navarro
Rafael Paris Nieto
X. Ortega
Alexandro Pizarro
Demetrio Rey
Manuel B. Rodriguez
Madero Hermanos
Diego Madero
Emeterio Madero
José M. Madero
M. Ortiz
Luis Maria Peña
Ricardo Quijano
Gumersindo Pozo
Rafael Torres

Leather and Findings.

Calndio Alba
Hermogenes Duran
Gazon Gaviria
José Maria Rosas
Jorge Santamaria

Lithographers.

Daniel Ayala
Demetrio Paredez
Julio Rascines
Antonio Rodriguez
Leon F. Villoveces

Machinery Depot.

J. M. Callejas
Rafael N. Paris
Pereira, Gamba y Ca.
D. Predratrita

Merchants, General, Wholesale and Retail.

Abadia y Ca.
Isaias Abadia
Enrique Acosta
Aepli Eberbach y Ca.
Elias Aguedelo
Antonio M. Angel Hijo
Ana V. de Aranjo
Aranjo y Hijo
Francisco de Arboleda
Cárlos Balen
Felipe Bonet
Bengoechea y Lopez
Valerio Berrio
Paulina Billy
Bonnet y Ca.
José Bonnet
Cárlos Borda
Luis M. Borda
Juan de Brigard
Cleofe Buenaventura
Carlota Caloo
Cárlos Camacho y Ca.
Camargo y Ca.
G. de Caicedo y Ca.
Joaquim Campuzano
Genoveva Cardenas
Gregoria Cardenas
Antonio Caarasquilla
Carlotta Carrasquilla
Nicolas Casas
Castrillon Gregorio
Concepcion Cervantes
A. Collar
A. Collar
de G. Elena Corena
Marie Cortes
German, Cubillos
Lorenzo Cuellar
Primisto Delgadillo
Carlos Deumue
Isaac Diaz
Laura Diaz de G.
Santos Diaz
Juan de M. Duarte
Dumaine y Dubois
Francisco Duque
Gonzalo Duque
Mariano Duque y Ca.

Merchants, General—*continued.*

Duran Cuellar y Ca.
Guillermo Escobar
Antonio Espinosa
Mariano Ester
Nicolar Fajardo
Eugenio Fernandez de C.
Emilio Ferguson y Ca.
J. M. Forsegas y Ca.
Leopoldo Torero
Benjamin Garay
José T Garbrois
Cecilio Garcia
Theodoro Gaste
Gavuria y Hijos
M. Gomez Calderon
Gomez Saiz Hermanos
Gomez Benito Hermanos
Felix Gonzalez
Luis Gonzalez
Narciso Gonzalez L.
Segundo Goinalez
Santiago Gooanzae
Leopoldo Guevaro
Bartolome Guiterrez
Jesus Maria Guiterrez
Rufino Guzmas
Heckle y Treese
Juan Heller
Hermine Kuhne
Nicolasa de P. Herrera
Janant y Fajardo
Emiliane Jaramillo y Ca.
Ruperta Gimenes
G. Kilpatrick
Koppel y Schrader
A. Knoppel y Ca.
Koppel y Schloss
S. Kranochmar
Marcelino Laurens
Theodosio Leon
Idalecio Lievano
Victoria Lopez
Luis Babin Fety y Ca.
Tadeo F. Macharaviaya
Dolores Maldodado
Mallarino y Perez
Medina Hermanos
José M. Mejia
Mendez y Tobar
Primitivo Molano
Frederico Montoya
José Maria Murcia
P. Navus Muero
Agustin Nieto
Francisco Noguera
Luis D. Noguera
Sebastiano Obregon
Alejandro K. Osorio
Juan C. Otalora
Padilla y Ca.
Demetrio Padillo
Palan Corrales y Ca.
Emilio Pardo
Manuel M. Pardo y Hijos
Santiago B. Pardo
T. Paredes
Pa. is y Ca.
Alejo Patino
Luis Patifio
Pedro Patino

F. F. Paul y J. de Brigard
Perez y Ca.
J. Joaquim Perez
Lazaro Maria Perez
M. Antonio Perez
Leonidas Posada
Uldisiao Posada
Posse y Silva
Leon, Posse y Salas
Antonio Pulezio
Manuel Quesada
Trinidad, Recaredo
Restreppo Eusse y Silva
Felix Riano
Luis Maria Robles
Faustino Rodriguez
Francisco Rodriguez
José Maria Rozas
Patrocinio C. de Rozas
Eduvigio Rubio
Francisco Saenz
J. N. Salamanca
Anna Maria Slaazar
Antonio Samper y Ca.
A. Saumer
Joaquim Serrano
Silva y Ca.
R. Silva y Hijos
Carlos Tanco
D. Telu
Thorin Hermanos
F. Torres Ancaya
Ucros Hermanos
Gabriel Ujueta
Guillermo Uribe
Juan de Dios Uribe
Luciano R. Uribe
Manuel Uribe Toro
Carlos Vallarino
Vargas Hermanos
Francisco Vargas y Hermanos
Isidros Vargas e Hijo
Marcelino Vargas
Vicente Vargas
Antonio E. Velez
Braulio Velez
Jorge Vergara y Ca.
Wilson, Caidedo, Munoz y Ca.
Julio Yerles
Zalamea Hermanos
Antonio Zapata
Aguirro y Ca.
Antonio D. Alvarez
Hermanos Alvarez
Nepomnceno Alvarez
Antonio Maria Angel
Aquilino Angel
Manuel Antonio Angel
Araujo y Hijo
Daniel Arboleda
Gonzalo Arboleda
Luis M. Azcuenja
Luis Bermudez
Francisco de Prula Borda
Ricardo Borda
Elias Gomez Caceres
Gomez Manuel Calderon
Sinforso Calro
Roldan Hermanos Camecho
Hermanos Carrizosa
Carrizosa y Parda
Castellanos y Carral

Merchants, General—*continued*.

Edmundo Gasuello
Castello y Kopp
C. Castro y Valencia Hermanos
Chastel y Maguine
Casonare de Cia
San Martin de Cia
Cortéz y Suarez
Currea é Hijo
Evaristo Delgardo
M. A. J. Demme
A. Debois
José Diaroni
Dordelly y Varjas
Hermojenes Duran
Lizandro Duran y Ca
Elutesio Echeverria
Nicholas Esguerra y Ca.
Fajardo y Mora
Eladio Ferro
Joaquin B. Ferro
Valentin B. Ferro
Juan J. Fonnegra y Ca
Juan Maria Fonnegra
S. M. de Francisco
José Maria Garzon
Bestrepo Gomez é Hijos
Francisco Groot
Francisco Gutierrez
Pantaleon Gutierrez
Herran Mendez y Ca,
Bernardo Herrera é Hijos
Herrera y Ca.
Holguin y Arboleda
Nenceslas Ibañez
V. Jaramillo é Hijos
Indalecio Lievano
Fajardo Lozano y Ca.
Lorenzana y Montoya
Bruno Maldonado
Hermanos Manent
Guillermo Marco
Cárlos Martin
Basilio A. Martinez
Antonio José Mejia
Guzman Rafael Mogollon
Luis Moret
Marcellino Murrillo
Hermanos Nieto
Paris Rafael Nieto
J. A. Obrojon y Ca.
Antonio B. Ortega
Ortega y Castello
Osorio y Castello
Osorio y Castoñeda
Hermanos Ospina
Rafael G. Padilla
Joaquin Paramo
Eugenio Parado
Felix Maria Pardo
Hermanos Pardo
J. Ma. Pardo
Pardo Velez
Frederico Patiño
Miguel José de Paz
Gamba, Pereira y Ca.
José Piard
Flavio Pinzon
Pinzon y Saeuz
Hermanos L. Pomba
Rafael y Antonio Portocarreso
Ricardo Portocarreso
Benito G. Posado
Posado y Diaz
Quitana y Cebazos
Miguel W. Quintero
Hermanos Ruiz Ramos
Cárlos B. Rash
Aparicio Reballedo
Euse y Silva Restrepo
Julio Restrepo
Ruperta Restrepo y Hijos
A. y Manuel Ricaurte
Felix Ricaurte
Luis G. Rivas
Antonio Rivera
Ridriguez Ugarte y Ca.
Jacinto Maria Puiz
Ramon Salgar
Alejandro Salcedo
Eustacio Santamaria
Ferro José Maria Seravia
J. A. Schlesinger
Otero Hermanos Silva
Ricardo Silva
Soldevila y Curriols
Juan Sordo
Vellamizar y Ca.
Leopoldo Panco
Mariano Panco
Hermanos Loro y Ca.
Fustaco de la Torre
Francisco de la Torre
José Maria de la Torre
De la Torre y Rivas
Cárlos y Alejandro Ucros
Diego Uribe
José Pablo Uriba
Uribe y Hijos
A. y P. Velanzula
Hortensia A. de Vasquez
Roberto Vela
Gabriel Vengoechea
José Vallafranca
Patricio Wills y Hermanos

Newspapers and Periodicals.

" El Anolador "
" El Bien Social "
" El Cachaco "
" El Debate "
" El Deber "
" El Diario de Cundinamarca "
" El Diario Oficial "
" El Pasatiempo "
" El Relator "
" El Reportorio Columbiano "
" El Zipa "
" La Discusion "
" La Justicia "
" La Mujer "
" La Reforma "
" La Situacion "

Paints and Varnishes.

Vicente Bastida
José Maria Espinosa
Genaro Figueroa
Santos Figueroa
Ramon Jimenez
José Larramendi
Pantaleon Mendoza
Cipriano Rubiano

Paints and Varnishes—*continued.*

Julian Rubiano
Alberto Urdaneta

Perfumery and Toilet Articles.

Buendia Herrera
Osorio Castañeda
Adolfo Collas
Echevarria y Hijo
Gilede y Ca.
Lopez Vengoechea
Medina Hermanos
Luis Moret
Lazaro Maria Perez
A. Lampere y Ca.

Photographers.

Ricardo Silon
Aquilino Casas
A. Faccini, Pl. de Bolivar
Emilio V. Mendoza
Osuna Hermanos
Demetrio Paredes
Julio Racines
E. Garcia
Rosa de la Vorgas

Physicians.

Abraham Aparicio
Leoncio Barreto
Francisco Bayon
José Maria Buendia
R. Enrique Camacho
Roberto Canales
Juan de Dios Carrasquila
Gabriel Casteñeda
Saturnio Castillo
Pedro Pablo Cervantes
Angel Maria Céspedes
Julio F. Convero
Daniel E. Coronado
Rodrigo Chacon
J. Tomas Enao
Bernardo Espinosa
D. Amico Florez Arteaga
Luis Fonegra
José Gomez
Aosias Gomez
Aristides V. Gutierrez
Alajnadro Herrara
Juan David Ferrara
Pacafico Lara
Guillermo Leon
Domingo Lopez
Joaquin Maldonado
Bernardino Medina
L. Jesus Olaya
Cristobal Ortega
Nicolos Osorio
Enrique Pardo
Manuel C. Peña
Guillermo Perdomo
Vicente Perez Rubio
Policaroo Pizarro
Manuel Plata Azuero
Cárlos Putman
Elberto de J. Rocha
José F. Rocha
Daniel Rodriguez
Juan de la Cruz Santamaria
Nemesio Sotomayor

J. Vicente Uribe
Jorge Vargas
Antonio Vargas Vega
Pedro Vera
José Antonio Vergara
Liborio Zerda
Francisco Barberi
Francisco Barreto
Julio Francisco Convers
Samuel Tajardo
P. Gomez
Santos Pegaca
Antonio J. Muños
Ignacio Pereira
Pio Renjifo
Rafael C. Rocha
Chacon Rodrigo

Printers.

H. Andrade
Ignacio Borda
Capallero y Paniague
Liborio Cantillos
Caro Hermanos
Castro Peralta
Echevarria Hermanos
José Benito Gaitan
A. M. Galan
Luis Gonzalez
La Lux
M. Merchon
Agustin Nuñez
Ochoa y Ca.
Ricardo Ordonez
Nicolas Ponton
Quintaña y Ca.
La Reforma
Medardo Rivas
Silvestre y Ca.
Francisco Torres Amaya
Zalamea Hermanos
Gomes Amaya
Federico Ferro
J. Mantilla
Fernando Ponton
N. Salamea

Railway Companies.

Compania De Antioquia
Compania De Bolivar
Compania Del Cucala
Compania De El Dorado
Compania De Giradot
Compania Del Magdalena
Compania De Panama
Compania De la Sabana
Compania Del Cacua

Saddlery and Harness.

Pascuel Castillo
David Obando
Pascual Rodriguez
Antonio Sanchez

Sewing Machine Agencies.

Domestic Sewing Machine Co.
Rafael Nieto
Nicolas Pereira
Remington Sewing Machine Co.
Ramon Salgar
Singer Machine Co.

Sewing Machine Agencies—continued.

Ucros Hermanos
White Sewing Machine Co.

Stationery and Wall Paper.

E. Castro Peralta
Rafael Chavez
P. Delgadillo
Gomez Calderon
Manuel Pombo
El Portico
F. Pombo
Torres Caicedo
Deositeo Vargas
Pacifico Echevarria
Emilio y Ca.
Elias Garay
Benito Gonzalez y Hermano
Koppel Schloss
T. Lievano
Salustiano Obregon
Alejandro Osorio

Stoves.

(See Furniture, also Hardware.)

Tinware and House Furnishing Goods.

Rafael Amaya
Ramon Barriga
Pablo Cevova
Abelardo Cuellar
Lino Espinosa
Sebastian Espitia
Miguel Gaitan
Laureano Mayorga
Juan Neiro
Andres Noval
Francisco Propice
Indalecio Reina
Emeterio Rodriguez
Felipe Rosillo
Cipriano Rubiano
Fermin Torres

Trunks and Bags.

Genára Gómez

Wall Paper Dealers.

Pacifico Echeverria
Elias Garay
Indalecio Lievano

CARTAGENA.

Population, 20,000.

Banks.

Banco de Bolivar
Banco de Cartagena

Druggists and Chemists.

Julian Aguirre
Vincente A. Garcia
Roman e Hijos
Villarel e Hijos

Merchants, General.

Alardete Simon y Ca.
Antonio Amador
Eduardo Amador
Fernando Aranjo
Joaquin Aranjo
Santiago Aranjo
José Maria Arrazola
Benjamin Baena
Francisco Xavier Balmaseda
Enrique Benedetti
Juan P. Benedetti
R. y S. Benedetti
S. W. Benedetti
N. Bonolial y Ca.
Rafael del Castillo
E. C. Delvalle
Juan Eckart
L. V. de Emiliani
Gabriel de la Espriella
Justo M. de la Espriella
Eladio Ferrer
F. y A. Franco
Vicente A. Garcia
Manuel Gomez y Ca.
Juan Manuel Grau
Jorge Henriquez
Henriquez y Garcia
G. Manuel, N. Jimenez
Blas de Leon
Bernarde B. Lopez
Marcia y Hijo
Bossio Bartolomé Martinez
Bossio Manuel E. Martinez
Alberto Mathiu y Ca.
Manuel G. Merlano
J. V. Mogollon
Francisco A. Morales
Pedro A. Navarro
Manuel A. Nuñez
Luis M. de Ochoa
F. S. Paz y Hijos
José Ignacio de Pombo
José Joaquim de Pombo Jr.
Fernando Porras
Eduardo Roman
Ricardo P. Roman
Federico Romero
Ramon Leon Sanchez
Fulgencio Segera
Juan Stevenson
Federico Terrill
Aureliano Velez
Velez y Hijos
Joavuim F. Vilez
Manuel I. Vilez
Pedro Vilez
J. Villa del Carmen
Manuel Villa del Carmen
Manuel Villa
Nicholas Zubiria

Physicians and Surgeons.

Rafael Calvo
J. A. Gomez
Froilan Manjarres

Printers.

Antonio L. Araujo
Donaldo Grau
Hernandez y Hijos
Ruiz y Hijos

MEDELLIN.

Population, 30,000.

Agricultural Implements.

(See Hardware and Tools.)

Ales and Beer Dealers.

A. R. Cuervo
Constantino Martinez
Ospina Hermanos
Restrepo y Arango
Vicente y Pastor Restrepo
Charles Wright

Banks and Bankers.

Banco de Antioquia
Banco de Medellin
Banco Popular
Banco del Progreso
Botero, Arango y Hijos
Restrepo y Ca.
Vicente Villa y Hijos

Blacksmiths and Wheelwrights.

Jesus Davila
Gabriel Garcia
Marcelino Rendon
Alejandro Villa

Coppersmiths.

Higinio Acevedo
Francisco Restrepo
Emilio Roynel
Gregorio Tabares

Dentists.

Felipe B. Gomez
Jesus Lopez
Lorenzo Marquez
Frederico Martinez
Eduardo Perez
Fernando Retrespo
Luis G. Restrepo
Elias L. Uribe
Victorino Velilla

Druggists and Chemists.

Escobar y Uribe
J. P. Gallo y Hijos
Isaza y Escobar
Frederico A. Pena
Perez y Hijo
Piedrahita, Villegas y Ca.
Andrés Posada Arango
J. J. Quevedo
Retrespo y Pelaez
Uribe y Delgado
Pedro Antonio Uribe
Enrique Villa

Rodolfo Zea
Camilio Botero
José Maria Escobar
Jenaro Gutierrez
Pedro Herran
Justiano Montoya
Julio Ospina

General Merchants, Wholesale and Retail.

Alonso Angel
Jorge Angel
Arango y Fernandez
Leocado Maria Arango
Botero y Hijos
José Maria Botero
Luis Botero
Jorge Bravo
Cordova y Arango
Corral y Toro
Rudesindo Echevarria y Hijos
Echevarri Llano y Ca.
Francisco Echevarri
Clestino Escobar
Justiniano Escobar
Etienne y Heiniger
Julio F. Fernandez
Teodoro Gast
Juan A. Gavira y Hijos
Jaramilo Zapate y Hijos
Gabriel Lalinde y Hermanos
Alejandro Lopez y Hijos
Manuel Maria Melguize
Lope Montoya y Hijos
Teodosio Moreno y Hijos
Olarte y Lince
Bartolme Perez y Hijos
Piedrahita Villegas y Ca.
Retrespo y Ca.
Restrepo Hermanos
Eduardo y Francisco Restrepo
Fernando Restrepo y Hijos
Marcelino Restrepo y Hijos
Santamaria y Lalinde
Alejo Santamaria y Hijos
Manuel Santamaria y Hijos
Toro y Jaramillio
Victor Todo
Uribe Hermanos
Lisandro Uribe y Hijos
Manuel Uribe
Mariano Uribe y Hijos
Tomas Uribe
Julio Uribes
Del Valie Hermanos
Eduardo Vasquez
Manuel Maria Velez y Ca.
Villa y Hernandez

General Merchants, Etc.—continued.

Villa y Toro
Indelacio Villegas
C. Amador
Francisco Botero y Hijos
Cesareo Z. Castro
José Miguel Cordova
I. M. Diaz y Hijos
Felipe Etienne
Zapata Zarmillio y Hijos
Tomas W. Jaramillio
Hermanos Lopez y Ca.
Juan de J. Martinez
Luis ma Mejia
Modesto Molina
Montoya y Hijos
Abraham Moreno
Athanasio Restrepo y Hijos
Fernando Restrepo y Hijos
Manuel O. Restrepo y Hijos
Restrepo y Pelaez
Vicente Restrepo y Pastor
Victoriano Restrepo
Manuel Barrientos Santamaria
Hermanos Toro y Ca.
Uribe y Gavira
Mariano Uribe y Hijos
Manuel A. Valencia
Miguel B. Vasquez
Vincente B. Villa y Hijos

Gold Mining Companies.

Compañia del Zañendo y Savaletas
Compañia de Sitioviejo y Titiribi
Compañia Minerva Antioquia

Gold and Silver Assayers and Reducers.

Ospina y Hermanos
Restrepo y Escobar
Julian Vazquez y Hijos

Hardware Goods, Etc.

M. Molina
A. Restripo y Hijos
Y. M. Cordoba
Tomas Jaramillio

Jewelers and Watchmakers.

Garcia y Navarro
José Maria Calle
Manuel Escobar

Felipe Etienne
Rito Gomez
Daniel Salazar
Victoriano Vellia

Mining and Mechanical Engineers.

Estaban Alvarez S.
Enrique Haensler
Luis Johnson
Gandido Molina
Joaquin Pinillos
José Maria Villa

Physicians.

Francisco A. Arango
Ramon Arango
Rafael Campuzano
Joaquin Castella
Julian Escobar
Ricardo Escobar
Pedro D. Astrada
Frederico A. Pena
Rafael Perez
Andres Posado Arango
José Ignacio Quevado
Tomas Quevado
Alejandro Restrepo
Julio Restropo Arango
Manuel Vicente de la Roche
Ricardo Rodriguez
Avelino Saldagarriaga
Angel Manuel Uribg
Francisco Antonio Uribe
Juan de Dion Uribe
Rodolfo Zea

Photographers.

Gonzalo Gavria
Emiliano Mejia
Mesa y Latorre

Printers.

Angel Maria Diaz
Imprenta del Estado
Imprenta de la Libertad
Imprenta Republicana
Nazario A. Pineda

Undertakers.

Wenceslao Naranjo
J. Fernando Respreto
Meliton Rodriguez

PANAMA.

Population, 22,000.

Ales and Beer Dealers.
(See Groceries and Provisions.)

Agricultural Implements.
(See Hardware and Tools.)

Arms and Ammunition.
Alfaro Hermanos
Pedro Aguero
Salmon y Ca.
G. Casadeval

Bankers.
Planas, Kelly y Arango
Henry Ehrman
Piza, Piza y Ca.
Samuel Piza y Ca.
Juan B. Paylo

Boots and Shoes.
Ramon Arias
Hermanos Alfaro
Camprubi y Cucalon

Crockery and Glassware.
Alfaro Hermanos
Nicanor Obarrio
D. Bertina

Dentists.
Erastus Wilson
N. Henriquez

Druggists, Wholesale.
Guenero De Amador
Domingo Lopez Lindres
Preciado Mora y Ca.
Roman E. Reicher
Hartung y Ca.
D. W. Waidelin

Druggists, Retail.
Coroalles, Amador y Ca.
B. Manuel Espinosa
F. Fernandez y Ca.
Arturo Kohpeke
Pedro del Oro
Preciado Mora y Ca.
B. Vallarino y Ca.

Furniture Dealers.
Fedbrico Boyd y Ca.
L. A. Fernandez y Hermanos
S. L. Isaacs y Asch
E. N. Martinez
Vallarino y Zubeieta

Gas Company.
Director, Adolfo Stefans

General Merchants, Wholesale and Retail.
E. Alfaro
Ascoli Hermanos
Aepli, Salmon y Ca.
Pedro Aguero
Alfaro Hermanos
Aquilino Alvarado
Amador Guerrero Hermanos
Ramon Arias
Arritola y Ca.
Florencio Arosemena
Arosemena Hermanos
Rosendo Arosemena
José Batalla
Beruarchina y Reiter
S. Bernascosi
Boston Ice Co.
F. Boyd y Ca.
John Brakemier
Pablo Brauca
Brandon Bros.
Juan Bravo
Camprubi y Cucalon
Juan Casselly y Ca.
M. J. Cucalon
Santiago, Dellatore y Ca.
J. B. Delvalle y Ca.
S. B. Delvalle
Dias Bertina
Eugenio M. Dias de Jovane
Pedro A. Diaz
Duque Hermanos
Henry Ehrman
L. A. Fernandez Hermanos
J. Fidanque y Ca.
Furth y Campbell
Luis Galbrois
D. Goldsmith
Leonardo Gonzalez
Guardia Quelquejen
Heliot y Ca.
Henrique y Ca.
Pedro Higuero
M. Heurtematte y Ca.
S. L. Isaacs y Asch
Manuel Jean
F. Javier y Ca.
Leona de Leon
G. Lervis y Ca.
R. Linares Estor
Alfredo, Lindo y Ca.
Lunan y Guardia
Maduro y Hijo
Juan Mazola
Ramon Medrano
Menotti Hermano
Noreiga de H. Florencio
Obarris y Ca.
Nicanor de Obarris
Samuel Piz y Ca.
J. B. Poylo
Preciado y Mora
Preciado, Mora y Ca.
J. N. Recuero

General Merchants, Etc.—continued.

Teresa Perez Recuero
Julian Ribbio
R. Rivera y Ca.
Manuel Rivera
Robles y Lindo
Felipe Rosa
Federico Sampson
F. Sanchez y Hijo
Sasso y Hijo
Manuel Sosa
Vallarino y Zubieta
José Vazquez Alvarez
Villalaz Hermano
Wing Wo Chong y Ca.
Zumbine, Lyming y Ca.

Groceries and Provisions, Wholesale.

Begatini y Brunca
Carlos Borbua
Isaac Brandon
Brilli y Ferrari
Tomas Carranza
S. Dellatorre y Ca.
Domingo Jiminez
S. L. Lansbury
Tomas Piñon
J. M. Recueso y Hemanos
W. de Roux
Julio Ruiz
Teodore J. de Sabla
Francisco Sanches y Hijo
H. Schuber y Hermano
Manuel Tallafero

Hardware and Tools.

Aepli Salmon y Ca.
E. Lyonsy Ca.
Henry E. Cooke
E. N. Martinez
Juan Casselly y Ca.

Hotels.

Grand Central Hotel, Shuber y Hermano
Hotel de Francia y Inglaterra, C. Dumele
Hotel Hispano Americano, Natalia Vitalia
Hotel del Universo, S. Menotti
Grand Hotel
Cosmopolitan House
Jardin del Paraiso
La Independencia
Valparaiso Hotel

Lumber Dealers.

Fero R. Arias
Federico Boyd
Francisco A. Hurtado
Nicanor Obarrio

Naval Stores and Ship Chandlery.

Hermanos Arosemena
Guelfus y Fink
J. McCook

Newspapers.

" El Cronista "
" El Hispano-Americano "
" El Precusor "
" Gaceta de Panama "
" Star & Herald "

Paper Warehouses and Paper Hangings.

Preciado Mora y Ca.
Nicolas Remon

Physicians.

M. Amador Guerrero
Juan A. Cantero
M. B. Castellanos
Manuel Corvalles
Antonio D. Haucourt
A. D. Gallol
Rodolfo Halstead
C. C. Hoheb
A. Cárlos Icasa
José Kratohwill
Giovani Lombardi
Quintin Miranda
N. Montalva
Manuel —. Mora
Santiago Moya
Nelson Welfred
W. Daniel Quijano
G. Burchard
Mateo Iturralde
Manuel Jose Paredes
Bernardo Vallarrino

Photographer.

Otto Limeon

Printers.

Aquilino Aguirro
Star and Herald Company
M. R. de la Torre y Hijos

Telegraph Companies.

Centraz y South American Telegraph Co.
West Indian Panama

Watches and Jewelry.

E. M. Diaz
Marcus A. Asch
Oreste Padron
Eugenio Coulin
Julio J. Diego
Hermanos Menotti
Duque Hermanos.
Henry Ehrman

SOCORRO.

Population, 12,000.

Druggists and Chemists.

Hugo Biester
Hermanos Billafrade
Jacinto Leon
Matthews y Enciso

Merchants, General.

Telesforo Acevedo
Narciso Cadena
Santos Alejandro Gomez
Antonio Moreno
Domingo Moreno
Leon Mujica y Ca.
Luis Otero
Wilches, Vargas y Ca.

Physicians and Surgeons.

Rodrico Chacon
A. Encisco
Pablo Gonzalez
Guillermo Leon
Jacinto Leon

REPUBLIC OF SAN SALVADOR.

CITY OF SAN SALVADOR.

Population, 35,000.

Agricultural Implements.
(See Hardware.)

Ales and Beer.
(See Groceries and Provisions.)

Banks and Bankers.

Banco Internacional
Blanco y Trigueros
Banco Lozano
Miguel Lagos
Pilor Lagos
José Rosales
Emeterio Ruano

Booksellers and Stationers.

M. Anguelo
Anselmo Cousin
Manuel Herrara y Ca.
Mathias Hermanos

Boots and Shoes, Wholesale.

Aguilar y Serrano
Cirino Morales
Jose Sagrera y Ca
Preto, Hermanos y Ca.

Carriage and Wagon Manufacturer.

Catrolier de Sera

Commission Merchants.

Blanco y Lozano
Blanco y Trigueros
Carlos Cromeyer
M. Cohen y Ca.
G. C. Duke
Dorantes y Ojeda
Gallardo y Orosco
Miguel Lajos
Gustavo Müller
J. M. Fernandez
Neebecker y Ca
M. J. Morales
Roberto Schoenemberg
Daniel Domingues y Hermanos.

Dentists.

Artistides Arango
Aleandro Cromeyer

Druggists and Chemists.

M. Arguyo
Cárlos Bonilla
Felicito Duena
Manuel Berrera
Ambrosios Mendez
José M. Vides
Otto Von Nievecker
Antonio Liébano
Ambrosio Mendez
Daniel Palacios
Manuel Rivera y Hermanos

General Merchants, Wholesale and Retail.

J. M. Alcarte
Daniel Anguelo
Angulo y Salazar
Emilio Ballettee y Goens Belismelio
Augusto Boineau
Pablo Bousquet
M. M. Cohen y Ca.
Anselmo Cousin
Gustavo D. Aubuisson
Deltour y Salinas
Dorantes y Ojeda
A. Liberti y Ca.
Manning Moffatt y Ca.
Matheu Hermonas
C. G. Mathies y Ca.
Rafael Montis y Ca.
Gustavo Müller
Isidro Rodriguez
Sagrero Hermanos
Roberto Schoenemberg y Ca.
Blanco y Lozam
Blanco y Merlos
Blanco y Trigueros
M. Bustarnente Hermanos y Ca.
Juan Carazo
Cárlos Cromeyer
Dorautes y Ojeda
Gauricio J. Duke
Gallardo y Orosco
M. y B. Haas
Korn, Adams y Ca.
Miguel Lagos
Pilar Lagos
Encarnacion Mejia
Manuel E. Melendez
Dionisio Mendoza
Antonio Peralta
J. M. Peralta
Aguilar y D'Amduisson
Aguilar y Serrano
Francisco Bozen
Orturo Bustamento
Felix Dardano

General Merchants, Etc.—continued.

José Maria Fernandez
Gustavo Lozano
Manuel J. Morales
Neebecker y Ca.
Luis de Ojeda
Emeterio Reuna y Ca.
Joaquin Salazar
Prieto Hermanos y Ca.
José Rotales

General Merchants, Wholesale.

Ruano y Aguilar
J. M. de Vrioste
Yudice y Ca.

Groceries and Provisions, Wholesale.

Antonio Agacio
Daniel Anguelo
Bustarneute, Hermanos y Ca.
Prieto, Hermanos y Ca.
Aguilar y Serrano
Alberto Adeler
Constantino Ambroji
Juan Badice
Euardo Bogen
Francisco Casas
Perez y Párraga
Fedenco Prado
Andrés Puig
José Sagrera
Erasmo Salazar
Serrano y Aguilar

Hardware, Cutlery, Tools, Etc.

Francisco Aguilar
Sullo Kalette
D. Aubuisson y Ca.
Dorantes y Ojeda

Hotels.

Hotel Aleman
Hotel de Europa
Teodora Kreitz

Mail Steamship Companies.

Royal Steam Packet Co.
Pacific Mail Steamship Co.

Planters, General.

Manuel Aguilar
Emilio Alvarez
Francisco Boguen
Bustamente Borgia
A. Cellier
Felix Dárdano
Rafael Zaldivar
Dorantes y Ojeda
Cruz Lozano
Emetrio S. Ruano
Cruz Ulloa

Physicians.

Emilio Alvarez
Camilo Arevalo
Manuel Bertis
Francisco Guevara
Julio Interiano
Rafael Izaguirre
José Maria Pena
Francisco Sagrini
Salvador Trigueros
José M. Vides
Francisco Bonilla
Francisco A. Garcia
N. Leiba
José M. Trabanino

Photographer.

Agustin Somelian

Newspapers and Printing Establishments.

Imprenta Comercio
Imprenta de la Juventad
Imprenta Nacional

Stoves.

(See Hardware, Etc.)

Watches, Jewelry, Etc.

Cárlos B. Gazati
Marcos Glaser y Ca.

SAN MIGUEL.

Population, 8,000.

General Merchants.

Francisco Arguelara y Ca.
José M. Melendez
G. M. Duke
José Arguello
Marcelino Arguello
J. J. Auerbach
Brizuela y Charlaix
Mertilla Duke de Bucaro
M. Bustamente, Hermanos y Ca.
Manuel Calvo
Ambrosia Canesa
Cayetano Canesa
Cuellar y Padilla
Pedro Dárdono
Luis Duke
Hugentobler, Haltmayer y Ca.
Jacinto Mendoza
Merino, Imbert y Ca.
José Molina
Cárlos M. Prieto
Feliz J. Quiros
D. Rosales
Luis Schlesinger
Juan Schonenberg
Simon Sol
Cipriano Suay

SANTANA.

Population, 8,000.

General Merchants.

Marcos Aguilaz
Maria Alvarez
Daniel Angulo y Ca.
Emilio Belismelis
Narcisco Aviles
Bertrand Matheu y Ca.
P. J. Escalon
Elias Cienfuegos
Manuel Cabrera
J. M. Gutierrez
H. Interiano
A. Liberti y Ca.
Dolores Lopez
Francisco Martinez
Matheu Hermanos
C. G. Mathies y Ca.
Tomas Medina
Joaquin Medina
F. Pena y Ca.
Rafael Quñiones
Romos Hermanos
Miguel Ramos
Carlos Segui
Urvela Hermanos y Ca.
José Valle y Andres
José Antonio Zaldivar
Virginio Quinteros

Steamship Companies.

Hamburg American Steam Packet Co.

Sewing Machines.

Marcos Glaser y Ca.

//
ISLAND OF CUBA.

HABANA.

Population, 300,000.

Agricultural Implements.

(See also Hardware Dealers.)

Abrau, Malza y Ca., 74 Oficios
Martinez y Hijos, 16 Obrapia
Planas, Petirona y Ca., 20 Govellanos
Alfonso y Millet, Marianao
José Alvaro, 48 San José
José B Diaz, 25 San Nicholsa
Garraido y Montero, 90 Coneortia
Vega y Flores, 70 Galiano
S. Martinez, 150 Comportela
Francisco L. Quinoñes, 83 Obispo

Ale and Beer Dealers.

(See also Groceries and Provisions, Wholesale.)

Bustamente y Hermanos, 157 C. de Monte
Tenville, Hermanos y Ca., 527 C., del Cerro

Architects and Builders.

Nicomedes Adam, 4 Chacon
E. Arteche, 297 Jesus del Monte
Tomas Bartalot, 21 Luz
Luis Bardot, 50 San Ignacio
J. Baeza, 65 Mercaderes
José Blanco, 78 O'Reilly
Juan Benite, 166 Lealdad
Clemente Bretones, 200 Jesus del Monte
Miguel Bustamente, 97 Mercaderes
Vicente Calderon, 4 Perseverancia
E. Castilzo, 80 San Rafael
Manuel M. Campos, 35 Mercaderes
Claudio Catala, 1 Lucena
Manuel Civera, 37 Calon
José Cali, 11 Sumaritana
Santiago de la Cruz, 18 Jesul del Monte
S. Crespo, 39 Alambique
Bernardo Delones, 97 Jesus del Monte
Rafael Diaz, 22 Alcarantilla
Jorge Desarge, 160 San Miguel
Antonio Dolz, 159 Ancho del Norte
Emelio Dolz, 194 Corciles
Pedro Dominguez, 90 Sitios
Juan Dominguez, 68 Alambique
Adrien Camolin, 31 Mercaderez
Diego Downing. 53 Amargura
Luis Engel, 73 Zulueta
Leandro Fabels, 51 Bernaza
Daniel Fernandez, 156 Compostela
José Fernandez 84 Factoria
Francisco Ferran, 81 Habana
José Ferreira, 21 Alcantarilla
Francisco Fonseca, 57 San Nichola
C. Felchere, 106 Amistad
Antonio Garrido, 182 Vives.
Antonio Garduna, 22 Zanja
A. M. Glynn, 34 San Isidro
José Gomez, 51 Merced

Andalio Gomez, 85 Jesus Maria
Maximo Gomez, 25 Amistad
Carlos Gonzalez, 178 San Nicolas
Bamon Izquierdo, 3 Jesus Perizerino
Adolfo M. Dago, 105 Suarez
Bruno Lavielle, Ancha del Norte
Manuel Lopez 116 Rapo
Lopez y Gomez, 47 Obrapia
Francisco Marcotegui, 155 Aguila
Manuel Marques, 52 Dragones
Antonio Martinez, 68 Revslfazizedo
Eduardo Martinez, 30 Merced
F. Martorell, 14 Santa Clara
E. Masino, 11 Neuva del Cristo
Antonio Medero, 24 Amistad
A. Madrano, 30 Sitioe
Santiago W. Mellor, 12 Mercaderes
Juan Mora, 344 Ppe. Alfonso
Benito Navarro, 142 Ancha del Norte
Lazaro Neilson, 12 Rastro
José Ocampo, 133 Reina
Oliva Pedro, 49 Blanco
Olivera Agustin, 102 Maloja
Paradela Francisco, 155 Ancha del Norte
Pardo C. y Moreno, 6 Zanja
Pardinas Jose, 28 Nueva del Cristo
Paz Juan, 22 Alcantarilla
Parez Ramon, 55 Penalver
Peña Andres, 128 Ancha del Norte
Peddomo Felipe, 212 Ppe. Alfonso
Perez Roman, 74 Merced
Pimienta Eugenio, 59 Aguila
Pina N., 72 Ancha del Norte
Perez Juan, 106 Lealtad
Piñon Jose, 187 Compostela
Pita Ramon, 7 Refugio
Pouchin Maurico, 50 San Ignacio
Pujals Jose, 22 Anto Recio
Quintana Salvador, 57 Villegas
Quinones Francisco, Placido, 76 Luyano, Jesus del Monte
Rodriguez Bernabe, 52 Virtudes
Rodriguez Miguel, 295 Aguila
Rosello Jose, 103 Habana
Francisco Sampera, 146 Ancna del Norte
Miguel Sanchez, 4 Colon
Juan Torrens, 9 Concepcion de la Valla
Andres Vailla, 40 Revilagigedo
José Varela, 57 Alambique
Santiago Vazquez, 30 Alcantarila

Arms and Ammunition.

Blas Obiolo, 264 Ppe. Alfonso
Agustin Regalado, 11 Zanja
Rosendo Rivas, 93 Teniente Rey
J. Sabau, 103 Egido
Llano y Castellanos, 176 Calzada
Francisco Matori, 22 Sol
Tomas Merino, 69 Belascoain

Arms and Ammunition—continued.

Francisco Montero, 5 Estivez
Manuel Caparo, 115 Vives
Angel Costales, 19 Tenerife
Gardner, Martinez y Ca., 124 Amistad
Francisco Arroyo, 192 Ancha del Norte
Ignacio Bigas, 469 Ppe. Alfonso
Antonio Blanco, 123 Esperauza
Francisco Borras, 21 Obrapia
Francisco Cuxart, 123 Monserrete
Lucio Diaz, 104 Salud
S. Dominguez, 23 Prado
Pedro Espada, 85 Merced
Juan Espinosa, 60 Ancha del Norte
J. Fernandez, 14 Arsenal
Juan Guijarro, 2 Monserrate
José Martinez, 73 Monserrate
Martorell y Pena, 14 Santa Clara
Antonio Perez, 89 Habana
Pedro Peluqui, 114 Aguila
S. Pinedo, 106 Merced
Francisco Portero, 33 Egido
José Rosello, 103 Habana
Sellen y Bosch, 103 Habana
Torrello y Ca., 42 San Ignacio
Florentino Vento, 55 Fernandina
Francisco Zarazua, 108 Aniuas
Ignacio Vigas, 469 Ppe. Alfonso
Joaquim Royo, 65 Aguacate

Banks and Bankers.

Banco del Commercio, 36 Mercaderes
Banco Español de la Isla de Cuba, 81 Aguiar
Banco Industrial, 3 Amagura
Banco y Almacenes de Santa Catalina, 22 Mercaderes
Banco Territorial Hipotecario de la Isla de Cuba, 1 Amagura
J. M. Borjes y Ca., 2 Obispo
J. A. Bances, 21 Obispo
J. Balcells y Ca., 43 Cuba
Juan Conill y Hijo, 60 Teniente-Rey
Narciso Gelats y Ca., 108 Aguiar
Luciano Ruiz, 6 O'Reilly
Hidalgo y Co., 35 Obrapia
.H. Upmann y Ca., 64 Cuba
Todd, Hidalgo y Ca., 25 Obrapia
Lawton Bros., Mercaderes

Bookbinders.

Horoson y Heinen, 11 Obrapia
José Domingo Frias, 29 Teniente-Rey
Viuda de Escariz, 49 Cuba
C. Fernandez, 37 Obispo
Francisco Garcia, 88 O'Reilly
Tomas Howson, 19 Obrapia
Viuda de Merelo y Hijos, 36 Empredado
T. Navarro, 119 Salud
Ramon Pardo, 168 Habana
Antonio Serrano, 49 Obrapia
Federico V. Hernandez, 85 Obispo
Torroella, Perez y Ca., 27 San Ignacio

Booksellers and Stationers.

Alvarez R., 55 Ricla
Artiaga Luis, 8 Neptuno
Aso y Alvarez, 5 C. del Monte
Castro y Gutierrez, 78 San Ignacio
Chao A., 54 O'Reilly
Molinas y Juli, 30 Rayo

José Turbiano, 50 O'Reilly
Abraldo Jose Maria, 63 Obispo
Alarcia Anselmo, 44 Ricla
Baraudiaran, Hermano y Ca., 29 Mercaderes
Chao Alejandro, 54 O'Reilly
Cueto Anselmo, 43 Obispo
Fernandez Arango José, 49 Ppe. Alfonso
Fernandez y Ca., 34 Obispo
Garcia Francisco y Vazquez, 48 Obispo
Guitierrez Baldomero, 84 Obispo
Gutierrez José y Ca., 2 Salud
Gutierrez y Naredo, 89 Ppe. Alfonso
Heinen H. E., 11 Obrapia
Lopez Santiago, 67 Ppe. Alfonso
Merckel Leopoldo, 106 Obispo
Merino José, 137 Obispo
Navarro Toribio, 14 San Rafael
Pozo Eduardo de, 9 Bernaza
Poso José, 84 Aguiar
Rueda Bustamante José, 1 Ppe. Alfonso
Soler Vuida de y Ca,, 40 Ricla
Voldepares José, 61 Ricla
Villa Miguel de, 50 Obispo
Wilson Tomas, 43 Obispo

Boot and Shoe Dealers, Wholesale.

Bernado, Alfonso y Hermano, 113 Habana
Antonio Aedo, 19 Lamparilla
Alonso y Ca., 36 Tineente-Rey
H. Delinan y Ca., 115 Habana
Ferran y Hermano, 31 Ricla
Finestas, Bordoy y Ca., 25 Amagura
Fontanals, Llampallas y Ca., 23 Lamparilla
Gelats Hermanos, 108 Aguiar
Antonio Gutierrez, 28 Amagura
Juan Marino y Pau, 104 Aguiar
Ramon Martinez, 80 Cuba
Martinez y Suarez, 78 San Ignacio
Palacio, Garcia y Ca., 46 Teinente-Rey
Pons y Ca., 34 Amargura
Quintana y Suarez, 63 Aguaeate
Soldevila Hermanos, 21 Lamparilla
Vidal Hermanos, 65 Cuba

Boots and Shoes, Retail.

(☞ *Names here reversed, surnames given first.*)

Alonzo Manuel, 124 Ppe. Alfonso
Alverez José, 379 Ppe. Alfonso
Ambizear Isidore, 112 Obispo
Barnes Cristobal, 57 Escobar
Bori Adolfo, 77 Ricla
Cofino Barrera y Ca., 88 Aguiar
Canea Juan, 35 Reina
Canoura y Hernandez, 87 Galiano
Cardenas y Piris, Ricla
Cardono y Perez, 1 Ricla
Carranza Julian, 102 Compostela
Cruz Antonio de la, 37 Salud
Cuervo Fernando, 128 Galiano
Diaz Robustiano, 2 Oficios
Diaz y Hijo, 83 Neptuno
Duena Garcia Antonio, 6 Salud
Durano J. y Ca., 62 Aguiar
Escandon Servanda, 192 Real Mariano
Estranay Hermanos y Ca., 91 Ricla
Ferran y Hermanos, 81 Ricla
Ferrer y Hermanos, 73 Aguiar
Fontanals, Llampallas y Ca., 85 Aguiar
Garcia Alonzo Juan, 4 Ppe. Alfonso
Garcia Bonifacio, 79 Neptuno
Garcia José, 39 Teniente-Rey

Boots and Shoes, Retail—*continued.*

Garcia Palacio y Ca., 46 Teniente-Rey
Girones Wenceslao, 39 Mercaderes
Gomez y Pelaez, 5 Bernaza
Gonzalez Nicolas, 62 Sol
Gonzalez Manuel y Ca., 16 Salud
Guerra José, 122 Ppe. Alfonso
Gutierrez Alonso Manuel, 124 Ppe. Alfonso
Gutierrez Francisco, 6 Ppe. Alfonso
Hevia Silverio, 128 Compostela
Jiminez Francisco, 70 M. de Colon
Junco Domingo, 104 Industria
Lopez Fernando, 89 Galiano
Lopez Salvador, 37 Cuba
Llieteras y Ferrer, 201 Aguila
Malda Ceferino, 89 Ppe. Alfonso
Marino Juan, 85 Neptuno
Martin Fabian, 261 Aguila
Martinez Ramon, 52 O'Reilly
Martinez Severino, 83 Jesus Maria
Martinez Ramon y Ca., 7 Bazar Habanero
Martinez y Suarez, 78 San Ignacio
Masens, Boada y Ca., 213 Aguila
Maurin Manuel, 82 Crespo
Medino Lucio, 79 Belascoain
Migolla Francisco y Ca., 40 Compostela
Olivella Juan, 22 Obispo
Ortiz José, 90 Aguiar
Ortiz y Ca., 35 Ricla
Pascua Eusobio, 42 Neptuno
Pila José y Ca., 213 Aguila
Polo Diego, 127 Neptuno
Prat y Pica, 16½ Ricla
Quintaña y Suarez, 81 Ricla
Rodriguez Ramon, 14 Ppe. Alfonso
Sanchez Mariano, 48 Dragones
Santa Moriana José, 13 Ricla
Terreda Mariano, 53 Manserrate
Varrano José, 182 Real, Mariano
Verdu y Martinez, 37 Obrapia
Victorero Manuel, 76 Ricla
Vidal y Ca., Carlos, 221 Aguila

Carriage and Wagon Makers.

Antonio Bello, Oquedus
Juan Rabionet, 254 C. del Monte
Juan Sallaberry, 18 Belascoain
Dominquez y Diaz, 150 San Rafael
L. Belthoise y Ca., 150 San Rafael
J. Biscayard y Ca., 131 Industria
Pedro Casamayor, 24 Belascoain
Simon de Frau, 10 Salud
Juan Peniche, 89 San Jose
Santiago Polo, 161 Real Mariano
Agustin Regalado, 2 Geneval Casas.
Manuel M. Sanchez, 16 Real
Atanasio Soto, 679 Cerro
José M. Berris, 104 Aguila
Juan P. Bonoza, 254 Ppe. Alfonso
Antonio Ferrer, Oquendo
F. Navarro, 391 Ppe. Alfonso
S. Paz, 266 Ppe. Alfonso
Ramon Soler, 278 Ppe. Alfonso
Venta y Ca., 413 Ppe. Alfonso
Juan German, 97 Industria
Angel Llanos, 385 C. del Monte
Rosello y Ca., 98 Zanja
Antonio Polo, 125 San Jose
E. Santiuse, 32 Belascon

China, Glassware, Lamps, Etc.

Alonzo Abascal y Ca., 38 Obispo
C. Canedo, 57 Galiano
Martin Diaz, 49 Reina
Juan Felin, 37 O'Reilly
Garcia y Gomez, 21 Reina
Gomez y Ca., 85 Ricla
Hermoso y Ibarra, 33 Obispo
M. Martin, 113 Obispo
Maruri y Ca., 17 Obrapia
Antonio Muñoz, 81 Escobar
Ortiz y Hermano, 113 Ppe. Alfonso
Pages y Ca., 24 Mercaderes
Ignacio J. Sainz, 134 Ppe. Alfonso
P. Sirven y Ca., 25 Mercaderes
Ignacio J. Sainz, 134 Ppe. Alfonso
Torres y Gutierrez, 12 San Rafael
Oscar de Castro, 81 Escobar
Ibarra, Hoyo y Ca., 35 O'Reilly
Lombide y Ca., 26 Tacon
Carlos Martinez, 58 Galiano
Enrique Mesino, 49 Aguiar
Noriega y Hijo, 37 San Ignacio
Manuel C. Ortiz, 113 Monte
P. Ortiz y Ca., 107 Ricla
Luis Pardo, 15 O'Reilly
Pareda y Ca., 85 O'Reilly
Victoriano Pajizo, 24 Mercaderes
Pedraja y Planilla, 16 Mercaderes
José Sanz, 75 Galiano
Isidoro Solla, 115 Obispo
Zabalar y Ca., 19 Ricla
Zulta, Pereda y Ca., 123 Galiano

Cigar Manufacturers, First Class, and their Principal Brands.

(☞ *Names here given are reversed from our regular order, the surnames being given first.*)

Acosta J. y Ramirez, "La Huelvana," 147 Campanario
Alonso Valentin, "Alonso Fernandez," 39 Mercaderas
Alvarez José, 19 Fjuras
Alvarez Casimiro, 67 Macias, Santiago de las Vega
Alvarez Julian, "Henry Clay," 9 O'Reilly
Alvarez Gercia y Ca., "Romeo y Julieta," 87 Rafael
Allones Antonio, "El Rey del Mundo," 27 Gervasio
Allones R. y Ca., "Flor Extrafina," 129 Animas
Amat M. y Ca., "La Gloria," 110 Lealtad
Arango Francisco, 7 Aguila
Arango Rasael. "La Hija de Cuba," 17 Salud
Arango Valentin, "La Cautiva," 20 Factor'i'
Armand E. y Ca., "Flor de Joaquim Ortiz," 69 Ppe. Alfanso
Azcano Sebastian, "Flor de Sebastian Azcano," 75 Sitios
Bancells J. y Ca.. "Florinda," 72 Sierra, Santiago de las Vegas
Bances Francisco G., "La Mejor," 8 O'Reilly
Bances y Ca., "Flor de Tabacos de Partagas," 160 Industria
Bances y Suares, "La Carolina," 100 Animas
Bango Ramon, "La Dalia," 142 Salud
Bacelo y Bowey, Sierra, Santiago de las Vegas
Barruete Beonicio, "La Flor de Fumar," 41 Dragones

Cigar Manufacturers, First Class, and their Principal Brands—cont'd.

Bastarrechea Leonarda, "La Flor de Bastarrechea," 88 Merced
Beci M. y Harmanos, "La Antoñica," 51 San Ignacio
Bejar Ulpiano, "La Ultamariana," 190 Campanario
Bajar y Alvarez, "El Rio Sello," 178 Neptuno
Bengochea y Fernandez, "La Comercial," 101 San Rafael
Bock y Ca., "Aguila de Oro," 85 Lagunas
Boher y Hermano, "La Barcelonesa," 15 Teniente-Rey
Busto Celestino del, "El Meteoro," 152 Estrella
Busto y Ca., "La Veguera," 68 Maloja
Cabal F. y Cabal, "Flor de Cabal y Cabal," 42 Lealtad
Cabanas y Carbajal Hijo de, 4 Dragones
Carbajal y Ca., 22 Obrapia
Carbajal Leopoldo, 320 Ppe. Alfonso
Caruncho Antonio, "La Intimidad," 34 Belascoain
Catellaños M. y Hernandez, "La Montana," 70 Calzada de Arroyo Naranjo
Castro Marcos de, "La Dulzura Cubana," 14 San Ignacio
Celorio Benito, "La Oportua," 93 San Rafael.
Codina Hijos de Jaime, "La Odalisca," 53 Estrella
Codina Jaime, "El Cinto de Orion," 19 Estrella
Conill Juan, "Flor de las Vegas," 71 Teniente-Rey
Cortina y Suarez, "Estrella," 39 Tenreife
Corujo Luis, "Flor de Corujo," 34 San Nicolas
Costales Bernardo, "Flor de Mayo," 6 Amargura
Cuervo y Hermano, "La Republica," 129 Revillagigedo
Dias Antonio, "No me Olvides," 135 Gervasio
Dias Lazo Luis, "Modelo de la Antiguedad," 32 Compostela
Fernandez Fernando, 2 Dragones
Fernandez Garcia Antonio, "Guardian," 4 Belascoain
Fernandez Muri Antonio, 168 Maloja
Fernandez Rafael, Compostela
Ferreira Francisco, "La Election," 71 Zanja
Garbalosa Juan, Amargura
Garcia Gumesindo, "Flor de Manuel Garcia Alonso," 40 Refugio
Garcia José Antonio, "La Ingenudad," 28 Rayo
Garcia Pefecto de Jesus, "Las Bervas," 39 Merced
Gonzalez del Ralle Hermano Martin, 4 Dragones
Gonzalez José, "La Paz," 292 Escobar
Gonzalez Perfecto, "La Africana," 26 Manrique
Genzalez Riaó y Ca., "La Granadina," 64 Dragones
Gutierres y Fernandez, "La Isleña," 117 Sitios
Inclan Francisco, "Flor de Inclan," 25½ Concordia
Jane M. y Ca., "La Mojagua," Prado
Lopez Antonio, "La Paz de China," 159 Neptuno
Lopez Manuel, "La Corona," 93 Galiano
Libre Miguel, "La Favorita," 39 Obrapia
Marinas Manuel, "Flor de Marinas," 144 Gervasio
Martinez y Ca., 95 Habana

Maté P. y Campo, "Pureza de Mato," San de las Regas
Menendez Francisce, "El Indio," 113 San Miguel
Menendez y Suarez, "Flor el Todo," 118 Manrique
Morales y Ca., "Flor de Morales," 127 Galiano
Moreira Francisco, "Flor de Moreira," Tenreife
Mosqueira Domingo, "La Renus," 1 Concepcion
Murias P. y Ca., "La Meridiana," 53 Corrales
Obeso y Cueto, "Flor de Naves," 31 Maloja
Olmo Ignacio, "El Comercio," 6 Angeles
Ortiz Joaquin, "Flor de Joaquin Ortiz," 69 Ppe. Alfonso
Oseguera Pablo, "La Voz de Cuba," 188 Manrique
Parea y Ca., "Punch," 138 Gervasio
Perez del Rio y Ca., "La Legitimidad,"
Perez F. y Ca., "El Gil Blas," 64 Amargua
Perez y Perez, "La Igualdad," 152 San Nicolas
Perez y Relez, "El Brillante," 11 Sitios
Piñera Rosendo y Hermano, "La Resolucion," 129 Salud
Queipo José, 67 San Rafael
Queipo Campillo y Ca., "La Industria," 70 San Rafael
Ravell R. y Ca., 37 Amargura
Rivero Oyarzabal y Ca., "Por Larrañaga," 58 San Miguel
Rodriguez Andres, "Flor de San Juan y Martinez," 39 Dragones
Rodriguez Antonio, "B. B. B.," 35 Estrella
Rodriguez Antonio Lopez, "La Sociedad," 138 Manrique
Rodriguez José Antonio, "La Infancia," 70 Jesus Maria
Rodriguez Rosendo, "Flor de Rosendo Rodriguez," 1 Carmen
Roger P. y Ca., "Flor de Pepilla," 9 San José
Romero Juan B., "La Española," 88 Prado
Sanchez y Hermanos, "La paz de España," 6 Egido
Soto Emilio, "El Mapa-Mundi," 52 San Nicolas
Sosa José Alfonso, "El Unico," 47 Macias
Unanue, Hermanos, "Arroyo-Hondo," 76 Consulado
Upmann y Ca., "H. Upmann," 85 San Miguel
Vall y Ca., "Flor de Cuba," 96 Virtudes
Valle J. y Hermano, "Flor de Murias," 1 Zanja
Vega José, "La Abundacia," 155 Malojo
Vidal Viuda de, "La Perfeccion y Guerrarabella," 39 Maloja
Viejo, V. y Ca., "La Integridad," 104 Campanario
Vilaro Valentin, 33 Sol
Villar, Viuda y Villar, "Villar y Villar," 174 Industria
Zumalacarregui, Juan M., "Flor de Zumalacarregui," 20 Oficios

Cigar Manufacturers, Second Class.

Alfonso Agustin, 4 Picota
Alvarez, Manuel L., 85 Suarez
Alvarez Pedro, 378 Jesus del Monte
Amat Manuel, 116 Lealtad
Arango Valentin, 20 Factoria
Azcano Sebastian, 75 Sitios
Balbin J. y Ca., 21 Neptuno
Barcañela, Eusebio, 106 Compostela
Bamp, Bernado, 48 Zanja
Barreute, Leonce, 6 Mercaderes

Cigar Maufrs, Second Class—continued.

Bastarrechea, Leodardo, 88 Merced
Boher Francisco, 141 Obispo
Cáceres y Ca., 537 Teniento-Rey
Camps Francisco, 82 Compostela
Carrillo Pedro, 214 Real Marianao
Castillo R. Rafael, 550 Jesus del Monte
Castillo Ramon, 65 Luyano
Chamorro y Ca., 6 Inquisidor
Diaz Ildefonso, 409 Jesus del Monte
Diaz Ramon, 389 Jesus del Monte
Dozal Martin, 141 Neptuno
Espanogas Loreto, 9 Colon
Fernandez Fernando, 176 Industria
Fernandez Manuel, 100 Compostela
Fernandez Pedro, 102 Estrella
Figuéredo José, 101 Boina
Fuentes José, 126 Aguila
Galuzo Leon, 13 Oficios
Garcia E. y Brito, 118 Salud
Garcia Julian, 209 Salud
Gerard Jose J., 69 Maloja
Gonzalez Eusebio, 6 Factoria
Gonzalez Marcelino, 171 Campanario
Gonzalez Miguel, 80 Consulado
Gonzalez Rafael, 7 Industria
Hernandez Tobar José, 2 Herrera Puentes Grandes
Hernandez Juan, 65 Lagunas
Iber Vicente, 33 Corrales
Igesias José, 24 Indio
Jordan Antonio, 197 Ancha del Norte
Lopez Cecilio, 97 Real Marianao
Lopez José, 90 Gervasio
Lopez y Garcia, 9 Sitios
Lucas Ramon, 118 Sitios
Luango Antonio, 253 Jesus del Monte
Luna Domingo, 101 San Nicolas
Martinez José, 7 Carcel
Menendez Julian, 125 Escobar
Mato Juan, 32 Colon
Maza José de la, 25 Obispo
Menendez José, 109 Salud
Minilia Domingo, 137 Habana
Pastrana Ignacio G., 45 Perseverancia
Paulin Pedro, 69 Estrella
Palaez Manuel, 20 Obrapia
Perullero Jacinto, 54 Velascoain
Pico Hermenegildo, 2 Picota
Pons Pablo, 40 San Isidro
Presmane Juan, 5 Esperanza
Quintero Francisco, 24 Salud
Renducles Manuel, 1 Teniente-Rey
Rivero Manuel, 180 Manrique
Rey Julian, 77 Mercedes
Rodrigues Nazario 66 San Isdro
Rodrigues Rafael, 317 Ppe. Alfonso
Rojo José, 49 Jesus del Monte
Rubio Antonio, 76 Cienfuegos
Ruiz Regino, 86 Corrales
Sanchez Francisco Gabriel, 154 Manrique
Salcedo Pedro M., 53 Lealtad
Sotelongo Mauricio, Ppe. Alfonso
Suarez Juan Hermanos, 14 Sol
Torre Jose Maria, 52 Animas
Trasancos Manuel, 40 Acosta
Valdes Josefa, 1 Industria
Valenzuela Zacarias, 21 Egido
Valerie Florentino, Inquisidor
Valledares M., 36 Tenerife
Valle Jose Fermin, 58 Emperado
Varele Agustin, 149 Ppe. Alfonso
Varela Joaquin, 39 Virtudes
Vega Antonio, 183 Compostela
Villari A. y Villar, 174 Industria

Coopers and Cooperage.

Arocha y Ca., 102 Vives
José Cañero, 142 Ppe. Alfonso
Juan Gion, 220 Ppe. Alfonso
Manuel Guell, 50 Jesus Peregrino
Juan Llano, 235 Ppe. Alfonso
Juan Solor, 152 Ppe. Alfonso

Crackers and Biscuit.

(See Groceries and Provisions.)

Custom House, Merchandise and Railway Ticket Brokers.

Ezequiel Anja, 89 Galiano
Victoriano Calatayud, 84 oficios
Angel Castro, Ppe. Antonio 41
José B. Diaz, 114 Animas
Justo Echevarria, 89 Reina
Serafin Gallado, 501 Jesus del Monte
J. Gomez y Ca., 16 Mercaderes
Lucas de la Guardia, Paradero de Villanueva
Ricardo Ibañez, 1 Concordia
Federico Lopez, 101 Sal
Antonio Macia, 40 Lealtad
Pablo Macia, 112 Aguacate
Fermin Marquiaran, 25 Obispo
German Martin, 20 San Carlos
Felipe Martinez, 364 Jesus del Monte
Aniceto Mendezabal, 241 Archa del Norte
Mesa y Chamorro, 39 Obispo
Ramon Montiel, 59 Tejadillo
Francisco W. Pulgaron, 14 Dragones
Candido Ramos, 19 Oficios
Gellermo Roch, Paradero de Villaneuva
Victoriano Suarez, 11 Cuba
Francisco Urutia, 59 Zanja
Gaspar Valledor, 14 Obrapia
José Villazon, 113 Concordia

Dentists.

Adolfo Betancourt, 108 Aguacarte
F. Rey, 107 Habana
Jose Valdez y Malina, 98 Reina
Arturo Beaujardin, 50 Neptuno
M. Calvo, 34 Lamparilla
Juan V. Garcia, 23 Zulenta
M. Arino, 122 Aguiar
Carlos Baron, 37 Habana
Z. Emelio Barrena y Zajas, 96 Aguila
Pedro Calvo, 55 Obrapia
F. Chaguaceda, 110 Aguiar
F. de P. Chaguaceda, 10 Ayuntamento
Florencio Cancio, 99 Obrapia
Ramon Echegaray, 18 Luz
Francisco N. Justiniani, 46 Salud
F. P. Nunez, 110 Habana
Jose Francisco Pair, 08 Luz
Jose A. Valdez, 7 Galiano
J. Warner, 90 Habana
Francisco P. Rodriquez, 113 Manriqe
Ramon Rodriquez, 230 Corales
Ramon C. Valdez, 57 Galiano
Ignacio Rojas, 74 Lamparilla
Miguel R. Vieta, 55 Obrapia
Andrew G. Weber, 44 Obrapia
Erastus D. Wilson, 94 Habana

Dentists—continued.

Cirilo A. Yarini, 88 Campauario
M. Gutierrez, 55 Rafael
José V. Rabell, 45 Sol
R. Valerio, 75 Aguacarte

Druggists, Wholesale.

Antonio C. Gonzalez, 106 Aguiar
Alam y Ca., 47 Reina
José Gordano y Ca., 60 Dragones
A. Lobe y Ca., 33 Obrapia
José Sara y Ca., 41 Teniente-Rey
Domingo Yungsug, 91 Teniente-Rey

Druggists, Retail.

Antonio M. Aguilera, 64 Dragones
Martin Arnanto, 66 Ricla
Ramon Botet, 13 Reina
José Brunet, 31 Ppe. Alfonso
Pedro Consuegra, 280 Jesus del Monte
Viuda de Valintin Catala, 27 Obispo
Pedro N. de Castro, 181 Ppe. Alfonso
Anselmo Castells, 28 Empedrado
José Diaz, 412 Ppe. Alfonso
José C. Estevez, 62 Suares
Francisco A. Figueroa, 16 Lealdad
Ricardo Fina, 37 Animas
Julio Z. Formel, 11 San Rafael
A. Gonzalez, 106 Aguiar
Antonio C. Gonzalez, 44 Ppe. Alfonso
José Cordaño y Ca., 34 Industria
Felix Hernandez, 99 Salud
Ramon M. de Hita, 71 Salud
Rafael de Leon, 18 Mercaderes
Agustin Leon, 14 Galisno
José Alacan, 435 Jesus del Monte
Francisco Alvarez, 101 Galiano
Arturo Barinat, 12 Sol
C. Bonald, 99 Ricla
Alfredo Bosque, 86 Drajones
Benjamin Brito, 344 P. Alfonso
B. Domas, Maloja
Rafael R. Ecay, 53 San Ignacio
Joaquin Fraile, 448 Jesus del Monte
José L. Marquez, 145 Neptuno
Justo L. Martinez, 75 Ricla
Ildefonso de la Maza, 44 Amagura
Eduardo Palu, 52 San Rafael
Alfredo Perez, 233 Neptuno
Viuda de Ruiz, 4 Bernanza
José Rovera, 67 Amistad
De la Peña Sainz, 34 Industria
Miguel de la Maza, 307 Ca. Del Monte
Marin M. Perez, 212 Neptuno
Ricardo Reyes, 161 Salud
D. R. Rodriguez, 53 San Ignacio
José Sarra, 41 Teniente Rey
Tirso Valdez, 14 Belascoain
Eligio Natalio Villavicencio, 24 Salud
Frias y Cintra, 17 Tacon
M. Johnson, 3 Obispo
Antonio Torralbas, 138 Ppe. Alfonso
Belen Valdéz, 47 Maurique
Manuel Villiers, 125 S. Rafael
D. Yungsug, 10 Teniente-Rey
Juan Zamora
Ricardo Consuegra, 280 C. del Monte
Felipe Fontanills, 18 C. del Monte
Julio Formell, 11 San Rafael

José Z. Gardaño, 34 Industria
Juan M. Gomez, 33 O'Reilly
Domingo Hernando, 215 Ancha del Norte
Juan T. Jimenez, 7 Picota
Francisco Luis, 38 Perseverancia
Tomas Martinez, 91 Neptuno
Miguel Montejo, 37 Lagunas
Jorge L. Nuñez, 7 Aguacarte
Mariano Pruna, 38 Tejadillo
Abelardo M. Rodriguez, 161 Compostela
Miguel Romen, 111 Gloria
Ricardo Saez, 4 Estevez
Manuel Guzman Sell, 44 P. Alfonso
Ernesto Suarez, Lealtad
Agustin Tremolada, 19 Belascoain
A. Tremols, 115 Industria
Carlos Ulrici, 103 S. Miguel
Maximo Zardozo, 24 Alcontarilla

Dry Goods and Notions, Wholesale.

A. Alvarez y Ca., 128 Aguacate
Angel, Arcos y Co., 46 Obispo
Argumosa, Gutierrez y Ca., 19 Amagura
V. Antram y Ca., 6 Amagura
Bolivar Vina y Ca., 26 Mercaderes
Barbon, Hermanos y Ca., 26 Amagura
Balbin, Martinez y Ca., 78 San Ignacio
Benito Bustamente, 863 C. del Cerro
Bustamente, Guel y Ca., 42 Mercaderes
Casamityana, Hermanos y Ca., 93 Aguir
Benito Castro, 150 Amistad
Juan Casusa, 82 Compostela
J. M. Casuso y Ca., 37 Mercaderes
A. G. Cavanzon y Ca., 11 Ricla
Clarke y Ca., 38 Mercaderes
Cubria y Gonzalez, 59 Cuba
A. Docarrete y Ca., 55 Cuba
Del Val y Ca., 5 Amagura
Diaz, Garcia y Ca., 16 Ricla
Falk, Rohlsen y Ca., 96 Cuba
Z. Fargas, 4 Amagura
Fernandez, Arenas y Ca., 96 Cuba
Fernandez, Junxuera y Ca., 73 Cuba
Fernandez, Martinez y Ca., 76 Cuba
Fuentoville y Ca., 11 Teniente-Rey
Galan, Cuesta y Ca., 35 San Ignacio
Galinde, Sobrinho y Ca., 33 San Ignacio
Garcia Legundo, 07 Aguiar
Garcia, Sobrino y Ca., 12 Teniente-Rey
Garcia Villasuso y Ca., 82 San Ignacio
Gilledo, Cabañas y Ca., 33 Mercaderes
José Gomez y Hermano, 76 San Ignacio
F. Gonzalez, 44 O'Reilly
Gutierrez, Sobrino y Ca., 50 Ricla
Aders Alberto y Ca., 10 Mercaderes
Aluarez y Hermano, 39 Ricla
José Bustamente de Rueda, 37½ Mercaderes
Calvo Francisco, 20 Blanco
Corujo y Sobrino, 112 Compostela
Corujo Francisco, 09 Compostela
Dudic Miguel, 103 Obispo
Dufau L. y Ca., 31 Obispo
Espinosa A. y Ca., 10 Ricla
Faez Lopez y Ca., 72 San Ignacio
Fernandez Arenas y Ca., 96 Cuba
Garcia Corjedo Hermanos y Ca., 28 Ricla
Garcia Luis, 115 Compostela
Gonzalez y Alvarez, 58 Ricla
Illa Pujol y Ca., 32 Mercaderes
Izquierdo y Ca., 124 Aguiar
Jimenez Musset y Ca., 9 Teniente-Rey

Dry Goods, Etc., Wholesale—continued.

Lacazette Seraan y Ca., 40 Obispo
Martinez Ablaneda, 03 Ricla
Maseda Pedro, 102 O'Reilly
Monte Guilermo del, 102 Villejas
Placio Tarracena y Ca., 61½ Cuba
Sanz y Peinado, 32 Ricla
Serrapiana y Canela, 99 Aguiar
Saurez Ramon y Ca., 68 San Ignacio
Herrera Cosme y Sobrino, 14 Teniente-Rey
Herrera José V. y Ca., 39 Mercaderes
Hurtado José y Ca., 72 San Ignacio
Jimenez Musset y Ca., 9 Teniente-Rey
Lenzano Cobo y Ca., 70 San Ignacio
Lopez F. y Ca., 14 Amargura
Lodero Pedro y Ca., 27 Ricla
Lucius y Ca., 66 San Ignacio
Maribona Suarez y Ca., 34 Mercaderes
Maristany Rosendo y Ca., 38 O'Reilly
Martinez Galan y Ca., 61 Cuba
Masferá y Ca., 72 San Ignacio
Nazabal Ocha Perez y Ca., 56 San Ignacio
Orden Roig y Ca., 23 Ricla
Osorio y Herrera, 71 Ppe. Alfonso
Paez Manzanedo Antonio y Ca., 45 Mercaderes
Paz Juan A., 1 Amargura
Peña y Sobrinos, 19 Ricla
Perez Cespa y Ca., 77 San Ignacio
Prendes y Ca., 62 San Ignacio
Regalado Pedro, 70 Compostela
Rendules Manuel y Ca., 40 Amargura
Rodriguez Alvarez y Ca., 40 Mercaderes
Rodriguez Forencio, 101 Compostela
Rodriguez Hermanos M., 12 Amargura
Rodriguez Solis J., y Ca., 14 Amargura
Ruiz V. y Ca., 5 Inquisidor
Saiz, Miguel y Ca., 41 Mercaderes
Salas y Ca., 10 Amargura
Sanchez y Ca., 13 Teniente-Rey
Santos Villaverde, 33 San Ignacio
Sobrado y Ca., 33½ San Ignacio
Soliz Martinez y Ca., 67 Cuba
Suarez Castañeda y Ca., 72 Ricla
Sueyras Pedro y Ca., 8 Amargura
Ulcia Francisco, 18 Ricla
Ulcia Sebastian, 13 Ricla
Ubarri Ignacio y Ca., 12½ Ricla
Valdés Alvarez y Ca., 7 Ricla
Valle José de y Ca., 54 Ricla
Valle y Rivera, 68 Cuba
Rillalba Feliciano, 2 Cárdenas
Rillalba T. y Ca., 15 Amargura
Zabala Hermanos y Ca., 74 San Ignacio
Xamora Heredores de Gonzalo, 43 Cuba
Zarraluqui J. M. y Ca., 31 San Ignacio

Electrical Apparatus.

Francisco Girard, 30 Obrapia
F. Moure, 23 Obrapia

Foundries and Machinists.

Escobar y Cisneros, 63 San Isidro
Tomas J. Bartalot, 36 Peregrino
José Mandurell, 135 Vives
Juan J. Orbea, 7 Vedado
Francisco A. Sauralle, 26 Regla
Vandewater y Ca., 99 Ancha del Norte
Zuleuta y Sobrino, Casa Blanca
Ambrosio Tomati, 8 Industria

Furniture, Wholesale.

Florenteno Castillo, 118 Galiano
Juan Rigal, 89 Galiano
N. Perez, 11 Bernanza
Antonio Armentero y Ca., 47 Ppe. Alfonso
Mariana Gonzalez, 136 Habana
Bahamonde, Barballa y Ca.

Furniture Dealers, Retail.

Antonio Armentéro, 47 Monte
Alvarez y Ca., 9 Ppe. Alfonso
Cárlos Betancourt, 42 Bernaza
Juan Baquila, 29 Galiano
José M. C. Diaz, 47 Galiano
F. Fernandez, 67 Corrales
Bartolome Garcia, 20 Bernaza
F. Garcia, 66 Villegas
Huerta y Blanco, 65 Galiano
Antonio Masuet, 5 Industria
J. Maxencha, 33 Reina
Vicente Pardo, 109 Galiano
Antonio Rivera, 224 Jesus del Monte
José Saloria, 62 Galiano
José Comas, 33 Galiano
Juan C. Fernandez, Bazar Habenero
Cayon y H. Fernandez, 52 Galiano
Francisco Fernandez, 89 Villegas
P. de la Presa Fernandez, 113 Habana
Gaudara y Ca., 88 Cuba
J. Hourcade y Ca., 54 Galiano
Esteban Hundain, 67 C. del Monte
George L. Lay, 50 Obispo
Lavaru y Ca., 100 Galiano
Ricardo Lopez, 21 Galiano
Nemesio Perez, 39 Bernaza
F. Quintana y Ca., 63 Concordia
Jaime Riera, 33 Galiano
Juan Rigol, 91 Galiano
Inocencio Sanchez, 3 Ppe. Alfonso
Pardo y Hoyo, 94 Galiano
Manuel Suarez, 111 Compostela
Victorio Tuero, 84 Sol
José Vidal, 114 Galiano
Miguel Albo, 103 Concordia
Francisco Alonzo, 247 Ppe. Alfonso
José Alvarez, 90 S. Nicolas
Ramon Callon, 62 Galiano
Manuel Fernandez, 15 Reina
Pedro Fernandez, 132 Amistad
Benito Fuero, 37 Neptuno
Miguel Garcia, 94 Galiano
Gomez y Ca., 53 Obrapio
Juan Lourcade y Ca., 54 Galiano
Nicolas Rodriguez, 71 Corroles
Salorio y Gonzalez, 76 Galiano
Sanchez y Calleja, 81 Sol
Inocencio Sanchez, Bazar Habanero
Manuel M. Suarez, 122 Compostela
Bernardo Tuera, 84 Sol
Francisco Vazquez, 21 Neptuno
Andres Zapata, 125 Galiano

Groceries and Provisions, Wholesale.

M. G. Abello y Ca., 1 Baratillo
Perez Aballi y Ca., 4 Oficios
Acdo y Ca., 19 Oficios
Juan Aguirre, 265 Ppe. Alfonso
Salvador Aguirr, 21 Obrapia
Miguel Aleman y Ca., Justiz
Benito Alonso, 177 Ancha del Norte

Groceries, Etc., Wholesale—*continued*.

Francisco Alonso, 29 Obispo
Vicente Alonso y Ca., 41 San Ignacio
Almirall y Ca., 19 Obrapia
Luis Alvarez y Ca., 82 San Ignacio
Fernandez H. Alvarez, 5 Ricla
Maning Alvarez, 2 San Pedro
Nicolas Alvarez, 87 Sol
Alvarez y Fernandez, 42 Belascoain
Revuelta Arcé y Ca., 56 Ricla
Aresta y Hermano, 2 Baratillo
Goicochea Arechaga y Ca., 6 Enna
Arroyo y Ca., 4 Sol
Nemesio Asto y Ca., 845 Ppe. Alfonso
Baguer y Hermanos, Ricla
H. de Mendy Beche y Ca. 22 O'Reilly
Dionisio Bedoya, 121 Ricla
Berenguer y Hermano, 25 Obispo
Bosch y Ca., 5 Obrapia
Nonell Brunet y Ca., 38 Oficios
Solder Brunet y Ca. (en liquid), 10 Lampailla
Francisco Busquet, 11 Concordia
Alejandro Bustamante, 40 Dragones
Marcelino Arango, 121 Ricla
M. Averhoff, 2 Empredado
J. Blanco y Sobrinho, 94 Lamparilla
Rodriguez Bencochea y Manticon, 2 San Pedro
Benilla y Ca., 86 Obrapia
Bibiano Bustillo, 10 Bernaza
S. Capella y Ca., 298 Aguila
Careaga, Zubiaza y Ca., 12 Oficios
Coll y Ca., Baritillo
Coro, Quesada y Ca., 17 Obrapia
E. Echezarreta y Ca., 1 Lamporilla
Pedro Fargas, 19 Obrapia
L. de Gabanche, 2 Obrapia
Pasenal Galvez, 9 Teniente-Rey
Abello Garcia y Ca., 1 Baratillo
Cué Garcia y Ca., 5 Oficios
Garcia y Gutierrez, 8 Oficios
Gili, Cuadrena y Ca., 28 Oficios
Giral y Ca., 32 Oficios
Gonzalez y Abalti, 95 Consulado
Benigno Guerendian, 24 O'Reilly
Gutierrez y Ca., 55 O'Reilly
Alej Hernandez, Neptuno
Herrara y Ca., 79 Oficios
Garcia Isizar y Ca., 207 Poseo Tacon
Lauza, Polanca y Ca., 9 Baritillo
Larrea, Eguidazu y Ca., 6 Teniente-Rey
B. Lesoja, 105 Ricla
Dosa, Perez y Ca., 6 Baratillo
J. Loredo y Ca., 97 Sol
Marcos y Ca., 40 Oficios
J. Mataró y Ca., 8 Lamparilla
Mauri y Ca., 180 C. del Monte
A. Mende y Ca., 22 O'Reilly
Menendez y Mujica, 5 Teniente-Rey
Mesana y Ca., 18 Oficios
Miró y Otero, 27 Obrapia
Morelo y Ca., 84 Ricla
Nonell, Labrada y Ca., 35 Oficios
Otamendi, Amiel y Ca., 26 Mercaderes
Antonio Perez y Ca., 5 Obrapia
L. Piñan y Ca., 96 San Ignacio
Pino, J. L., 109 Ricla
Pumarieja y Gonzalez, 134 C. del Monte
S. Rahasa y Ca., 1 Obispo
Romillo, Hermano y Ca., 5 Obispo
M. Sanchez y Ca., 54 Oficios
Suarez y Perez, 77 Miguel
Tabermilla y Sobrino, 1 Inquisidor

L. Varela, 9 Amazura
Villaverde y Ca., san Ignasio
Vice y Moncalian, 38 Amagura

General Commission and Importing Merchants.

E. Aguilera y Ca., 26 Obrapia
Alberti y Dowling, 22 Sta. Clara
C. E. Beck, 28 Obrapia
E. Balencourt, 52 S. Ignacio
B eselmann y Schroder, 18 Lamparilla
A. Boving 78 Cuba
Faustino Cabrera, 16 Oficios
F. Caine, 28 Obrapia
Juan Fatges, 36 Obrapia
Ramon Garcia, 69 Aguiar
Samuel Giberga, 7 Baratillo
M. Gonzalez y Ca., 2 Mercaderes
Hamel y Ca., 2 Mercaderes
Hings y Ca., 9 Baratilla
George Hyatt, 23 Cuba
Lawton Bros. (American House), 35 Mercaderes
Lange y Ca. 10 Amagura
H. Leonhardt, 37 Cuba
Enrique Liron, 4 Vedado
Antonio Lopez, 37 Obispo
Lopez y Ca., 92 O'Reilly
Antonio Marcias, 20 Obrapia
Malvido Hermanos, 108 Habana
José R. Marquette, 120 Cuba
Rafael Menendez, 12 Cuba
H. Millinton, 50 S. Ignacio
Rafael B. Pegudo, 2 Tacon
Rafael S. M. Perez, 16 Obispo
Ricardo Perkins, 37 S. Ignacio
Pons, Orta y Ca., 1 Empedrado
A. Richtering y Ca., 1 Mercaderes
Ross, Asman y Schnyder, 10 Mercaderes
Rodrigo Saabedra, 16 Mercaderes
Gustavo Salomon, 57 P. Alfonso
Schival y Filonal, 18 Amargura
Schmidt y Ca., 3 Mercaderes
J. Seidel, 4 S. Ignacio
Leoncio Serrano, 19 Sr Clara
Someillan y Hijo, 21 Obispo
Juan Tapia, 10 Mercedes
Traite y Ca., 84 S. Ignacio
H. Upman y Ca., 64 Cuba
A. Verastigui, 50 S. Ignacio

Hardware, Cutlery, Stoves, Tools, Etc., Wholesale.

V. Alvarez y Ca., 55 Reina
H. Alonso y Ca., 20 Lamparilla
Araluce y Uresandi, 32 Lamparilla
F. De Arriba, 15 O'Reilly
Fernando Blanco, 225 Aguiar
Alvarez y Santillana, 20 Obrapia
Gabriel de Antenabar, 18 Oficios
Ignacio Alvarez, 33 San Ignacio
Aguilera, Garcia y Ca., 27 Mercaderes
Cañarto y Ca., 13 Obrapia
Ignacio Escalante, 21 Damparilla
Jorge Ferran, 8 Barratillo
A. Gutierrez y Ca., 7 Lamparilla
S. Luna y Iturralde, 30 Mercaderes
Mariño, Laca y Ca., 5 Lamparilla
Viuda de Martinez Aija, 16 Obrapia
Domingo Martinez y Ca., Pontales de Luz
Viuda de Mencia, 17 San Ignacio
Mendiguren y Sobrino, 32 Lamparilla

Hardware, Etc., Wholesale—*cont'd.*

Olaquibel y Lopez, 76 Oficios
Orbea y Ca., 45 Obrapia
Pedraya y Planellas, 52 San Ignacio
Ricardo Perez, 21 San Ignacio
Ramos y Castillo, 18 Obrapia
Rodriguez y Ca., 25 San Ignacio
Soto y Ca., 80 San Ignacio
Tijero, Hermano y Ca., 17 Mercaderes
Jorge Toulet, 1 Marquez Gonzales
S. Uribarri y Ca., 21 Mercaderes
F. Zapata, 117 Obispo
Zarrolegui, Quintana y Ca., 95 Ricla
Benguria y Fernandez, 32 Galiano
Builla y Ca., 11 Lamparilla
Casus y Ca., 11 Teniente-Rey
José M. Cabezon, 102 Habana
Carlos M. Carrillo, 67 Ricla
Conejo y Velis, 503 C. del Monte
Diaz y Ca., 511 Jesus del Monte
Dominguez y Ca., 20 Obrapia
George Ferran, 7 Baratillo
Gáneara y Primo, 30 San Rafael
Francisco Gonzalez, 120 O'Reilly
Larrazabal y Ca., 97 Ricla
Morino y Cagigal, 18 Oficios
Francisco de la Maza, 369 del Monte
Maning Muiño y Ca., 5 Lamparilla
R. Ortiz, 36 Belascoain
Pardo y Hoyo, 104 Galiano
R. Palacio, 16 Tacon
José F. Pazos, 25 Mercaderes
Perez, Inchausti y Ca., 46 Galiano
Presa y Torres, 10 San Pedro
Prieto y Ca., San Ignacio
Quintana y Ca., 95 Ricla
Jose Tarno, 12 Belascoain
Uresandi, Diaz y Ca., 3 Monte
Urquiola, Diaz y Ca., 7 Lamparilla
Urinte y Ca., 15 Mercaderes
S. Urquijo, 27 Teniente-Rey
Gregorio Uludaja, 107 Neptuno
Maning Vila y Ca., 117 Galiano
Martin Zapata, 193 C. del Monte
Urribarri Isasi y Ca., 21 Mercaderes

Hotels.

"America," Aliart Maria del Rosario, Monserrate y 20 Teniente-Rey
"Arbol de Guernica," Aguirre Garcia y Lozano, 45 Mercaderes
"Aurora," Narviso Portas, 1 Dragones
"Buena Vista," Abril S. y Galcerán, 37 Cuba
"Cabrera," Severto Portos, 10 Ppe. Alfonso
"Cubano," Bolsino Ramon, 15 Teniente-Rey
"Europa," Manuel Souto, 2 Lamparilla
"Inglaterra," Márcos y Parrondo, 123 Prado
"Lisa," Gomez Joaquin La Lisa, Marianao
"La Mascotte"
"Navarra," Caracedo M., 74 San Ignacio
"Paris," Julio M. Maulini, 136 Industria
"Passajes," Linares, Manuel, Prado
"Pas," Rosa Aliart, 2 Egido
"Perla de Cuba," Rodriguez Alvarez y Ca., 137½ Armistad
"San Cárlos," Castañeda Muhoberas J. M., 35 Oficios
"Telégrafo," Batet J. y Morel, 136 Armistad
"Union La," Barcia Manuel y Ca., 63 Lamparilla
"Villanueva," Arias y Blanco, 12 Dragones

"Vascongada," Capetillo Manuel, Mercederes y Obispo
"Habana," Teniente-Rey
"Hispano-Americano," 112 Prado
"New York," 102 Galiano
"Luz," 35 Oficios
"Neuvitas," 7 Dragones
"Flor Catalana," 75 Teniente-Rey
"La Saratoga"
Alberdi y Lastra, 27 Mercaderes
Bernardo Alvarez, 222 Monte
Marina y Cajigas, 18 Oficios
Martinez, Diaz y Ca., 3 P. Alfonso

Ice Dealers, Wholesale.

Frederico Dubos, 142 Consulado
Felipe Suarez, 9 Dragones
Juan Zorrilla, 86 Cuba
Compañia Habanera, Infanta y San José

Jewelry, Watches and Silverware, Jobbers.

Borbolla y Ca., 54 Compostela
Esteban, Dufan y Ca.. 31 Obispo
Gustavo Jensen y Ca., 11 Mercaderes
W. F. Grumbach, 77 Cuba
Martinez, Calan y Ca., 61 Cuba
Hierro y Ca., Obispo
Ignacio Misa y Hermanos, 121 Habana
Enrique Schochlin y Ca., 10 Mercaderes
Ortiz y Ca., 36 Belascoain
P. Roman, 43 Concordia
Palacio, Taracena y Ca., 74 Obispo
Joaquin Sanchez, 37 Muralla

Jewelry, Etc., Retail.

Alonzo y Ca., 57 Compostela
Bahamonde, Borbolla y Ca., 56 Compostela
Miguel Carmona, 22 Muralla
Manuel A. Cores y Hermano, 69 San Miguel
Mario Fernandez y Ca., 24 Obispo
Pedro Fernandez, 114 Manrique
Ramon Guerra, 135 Habana
Juan Irben, 120 Ppe. Alfonse
Enrique Luengo, 36 Obispo
Marinas y Hermanos, 16 Obispo
Aurelio Maruri, 66 Obispo
Pedro Masedo, 192 O'Reilly
Vicente Moreno, 78 Ppe. Alfonso
Juan B. Prentice, 40 Amargura
Joaquim M. Sanchez, 37 Ricla
F. Alvarez y Ca., 15 O'Reil'y
Alvarez y Masson, 1 Teniente-Rey
Gabriel M. Callaco, 86 San Miguel
José Y. Dopico, 15 Bernaza
Vicente Fernandez, 76 O'Reilly
Enrique Fischer, 12 Mercaderes
José Garard, 15 Mercaderes
Cueva M. Fernandez, 13 Teniente Rey
M. Hierro, 27 Neptuno
Ibern y Brito, 120 Ppe. Alfonso
Roberto Kamer, 115 Obispo
Alberto Lamerano, 53 Obrapia
Tomas Lancha, 100 Aguir
Oviedo de Santa Cruz, 49 Luz
G. Springel, 28 Teniente-Rey
Francisco Valles, 60 Obispo
Manuel Gil, 199 Aguila
Pablo Gonzalez, 233 Ppe. Alfonso
F. Gimenez, 17 Mercaderes

Jewelry, Etc., Retail—continued.

F. Gomez y Ca., 121 Obrapia
K. Rainer, 105 Obispo

Lamps and Gas Fixtures.

Juan Dominguez, 128 Aguila
Frederico Dorado, 69 Habana
A. P. Ramirez, 75 Amistad
Rio y Perez, 26 San Rafael
Cabellero y Hernandez, 39 Concordia
Pedro Alfonseca, 95 Lealtad
D. Antunen, 6 Romay
Manuel Baloira, 100 Obispo
Francisco Cabellero, 37 Concordia
Garcia y Sanz, 105 Neptuno
Pio Garcia, 495 Ppe. Alfonso
Antonio Gili, 99 Neptuno
Gonzalez y Rodriguez, 615 C. del Corro
Lopez y Alvarez, 45 Bernaza
Manuel Marquez, 50 Dragones
Enrique M. Masino, 49 Aguiar
José Papiol, 71 O'Reilly
José Pardiñas, 44 Compostela
Juan Pariagua, 238 Ppe. Alfonso
José Portas, 26 San Rafael
Pedro A. Ramirez, 75 Amistad
Dolores Ruffin, 79 O'Reilly
S. Subirana, 40 Teniente-Rey
Manuel C. Valnerde, 66 Empedrado
Charles P. Weeks, 90 O'Reilly
Villadoniga y Castrillon, 105 Aguiar

Lithographers.

Jacinto Abello, 128 Amistad
Marcellino Abello, 89 Compostela
Abadens y Colso, 12 Reinca
Jacinto Trello, 128 Amistad
J. V. Cuseta, 40 Obrapia
Guerra y Rodriguez, 50 Mercaderes
Ricardo Hernandez, 132 Aguila
A. Lagriffoul, 35 O'Reilly
E. Lamy y Hermanos, 11 Mercaderes
Lastra Hermanos y Ca., 87 Obispo
Lastra y Barrera, 37 Mercaderes
A. J. Morn y Ca., 124 San Nicolas
Ricardo Caballero, 14 Mercaderes
C. J. Guerra y Ca., 35 O'Reilly
Moré Garcia y Ca., 124 San Nicolas
D. Azopardo, 138 Consulado
José Cinta, 122 Aguila
Diaz, Alvarez y Ca., 234 P. Alfonso
Manuel Estevez, 93 Monserrate
Santos Fernandez, 101 Monserrate
Francisco Lanza, 113 Monserrate
Patricio Laurido, 3 Corrales
S. G. Lopez, 79 Ppe. Alfonso
Salvador Molus, 54 Neptuno
Moncunil, Sola y Ca., 12 P. Tacon

Lumber, Lime and Building Material.

José Albazzi, 87 Prado
Barreras Antonio, 83 Prado
Crespo y Ca., 361 P. Alfonso
Garcia y Longo, 19 Carcel
Guell y Ca., Calzada de Cristina
Juan Cristobal, 200 Ppe. Alfonso
Lando y Ca., 113 Prado
B. Ortoll y Ca., 8 Lacena
Pons Francisco, 5 Romay
Pons Ignacio y Ca., 4 Egido

Rio y Perez, 73 Prado
Telleria A. C. 61 Prado
Vila Antonio, 75 Belascoain

Photographers.

Delgado y Toro, 37 O'Reilly
José Calvet, 67 Reina
S. A. Conner, 62 O'Reilly
Fredricks y Daries, 108 Habana
Antonio Herrera, 111 Jesus Maria
Rafael Lopez, 49 O'Reilly
Esteban Mestre, 63 O'Reilly
Narcisco Mestre, 19 O'Reilly
Petit y Mestre, 45 O'Reilly
J. A. Suarez y Ca., 64 O'Reilly
N. E. Maceo, 75 O'Reilly
F. Pumariega, 63 O'Reilly
José Soroa, 80 Prado

Physicians and Surgeons.

(☞ *Names here are surnames first*)

André Claudio, 89 Jesus Maria
Agilera Manuel, 30 Villegas
Aragon Gustavo Luis, 220 Real, Mariana
Arango José Francisco, 40 Campanario
Argumosa José, 1 Maloja
Arrufat Eduardo, 26 Maloja
Arteaga Serapio, 109 Villegas
Bango Manuel, 56 San Isidro
Beato J. y Dolz, 33 Jeses Maria
Beltran J. A. 232 Real, Marianao
Brito P. Maria, 127 Animas
Bueno Rafael, 17 Inquisidor
Burgess D. M., 23 Obispo
Caballero Domingo, 106 Merced
Caballero Pedro, 479 Ppe. Alfonso
Cabrera Hernandez Domingo, 86 Jesus del Monte
Cabrera F. y Sanchez, 95 Cuba
Camara Pedro de la, 6 Ricla
Cañtzares Manuel, 158 San Miguel, Vedado
Carbonal F. y Rivas, 16 Teniente-Rey
Castañedo Valentin, 66 Oficios
Castell José Francisco, 81 Salud
Castro R., 129 Industria
Castaño y Polo, 336 Ppe. Alfonso
Chaple Ramon L., 185 Manrique
Chaple Ramon Mazario, 111 Concordia
Chavez Manuel, 111 Sol
Chiappa Juan, 128 Suarez
Cisneros Luis, 118 Manrique
Clairac José, 82 Estrella
Comoglio José de la Luz, 26 Aguacate
Córdoba Frederico, 77 Campanario
Córdoba Julian, 42 Cárdenas
Córdoba Luis, 103 Merced
Córdova Ramon, 68 Sol
Cowley Luis Maria, 125 Cuba
Cowley Rafael, 47 Aguiar
Diaz Albertini Antonio, 111 Habana
Diaz Albertini Jorge, 108 Manrique
Diaz M., 207 Ppe. Alfonso
Donoso Cárlos, 145 Cuba
Doran Juan, 551 Animus
Echarte E. y Alfonso, 84 Cuba
Escarras J. Ricardo, 37 Bompanario
Espada Montanos Juan, 29 Lamparilla
Fernandez Cubas Domingo, 60 Reina
Fernandez de Castro Manuel, 17 Luyano, Jesus del Monte.
Fernandez Francisco, 64 Acosta

Physicians and Surgeons—*continued.*
Fernandez Pedro, 129 Suarez
Figueredo Felix, 157 Neptuno
Finlay Carlos, 65 Obrapia
Figueroa Bernardo, 64 Prado
Fleitas R. y Lamos, 306 Ppe. Alfonso
Franca M. y Mazor-a, 60 Prado
Frias Francisco, 883 Cerro
Freixas Patrocinio, 45 San Miguel
Gandul Manuel, 36 Salud
Garcia Juan de D., 32 Neptuno
Garganta R., 10 Amargura
Gaston Ricardo, 41 Ancha del Norte
Gavalda Enrique, 33 Inquisidor
Giralt Felix, 87 re Pado
Gomez de la Maza Francisco, 7 Emprorado
Gonzalez Antonio, 106 Aguiar
Gonzalez del Valle Ambrosio, 120 Aguacate
Gonzalez de la Torre Ricardo, 128 Consulado
Gonzalez Fernando, 8 Villanueva
Gordillo, Miguel, 10 Estrello
Guardia, Vicence, 62 Prado
Gutierrez, Nicolas J., 64 Oficios
Hernandez, José de la Luz, 22 Neptuno
Hernandez, Pedro, 27 Apodaca
Herrera, Pablo, 324 Jesus del Monte
Hoya, Tomas de la, 32 San José
Landeta, Adolfo, 59 San Miguel
Landeta, Juan Bautista, 37 Campanario
Lopez, Jose, Joaquim, 166 Companario
Machado J. Pantaleon, 128 Manrique
Marill, Francisco, 59 Salud
Marquez, Juan E., 82 San Nicolas
Martinez, P. y Sanchez, 38 San Nicolas
Meneses Rafael, 115 Escobar
Menocal, Raimundo, 45 Amistad
Mestre, Antonio, 26 Jesus Maria
Montalvo, J. R. 18 Virtudes
Montaner, Luis, 67 Prado
Montemar, Cárlos, 95 Teniente-Rey
Morales, Julian, 116 San Nicolas
Muñoz, Francisco de Paula, 66 Acosta
Noriega Narciso, 13 San Isidro
Nuñez, Emiliano, 11 Galiano
Nuñez, Miguel, 116 Consulado
Obregon, F. y Mayol, 9 Galiano
Obregon, F. y Serra, 107 Cuba
Penichut, Francisco, 304 Ppe. Alfonso
Perez, de Utera Antonio 77 Teniente-Roy
Perez, F. Betancourt 64 Estevez
Plá, Eduardo, 109 Campanario
Plasencia, Ignacio, 83 Galiano
Plasencia, Tomas, 29 Aguiar
Ponce, J. y Abrante, 47 Rayo
Porto, Enrique M. 123 Compostela
Prendes, Faustino, 50 San Ignacio
Pujol, Juan B., 74 San Nicolas
Puledo P. José, 226 Aguila
Quesada Francisco, 98 Aguila
Rainery Francisco, 59 Campanario
Raimirez J. M. y Fabor, 210 San Nicolas
Ramos, José, 123 Manrique
Redondo, José, 39 Amargura
Redondo, Pedro, 163 Virtudes
Regueira, Francisco, 132 Campanario
Reyes, Manuel de los, 70 Virtudes
Rodriguez, Ecay A., 53 San Ignacio
Rodriguez, Segundo, 37 Industria
Ruiz, San Romain Emtlio, 46 Luyanó, Jesus del Monte
Saaverio, Anastasio, 69 Compoztela
Santos, Fernandez Juan, 62 Neptune

Sirvens, Faustino, 7 Damas
Torralbas, José I., 44 San Nicolás
Torrellas Francisco, 82 Mision
Torrens, Pedro, 28 Trocadero
Torres M., 108 Aguacate
Trujillo, José, 114 Aguacate
Valdespino, Andrés, 3 San Nicolás
Valdespino, José, 70 Campanario
Valencia, Pablo, 58 Neptuno
Valera, Alfredo, 126 Estrella
Vilardell, Gerardo, 61 Merced
Walling, Guillermo, 19 Crespo
Yarini J. Leopoldo, 55 Ppe. Alfonso
Zayas, Francisco, 29 Real Puentes Grandes
Zayas, Juan Bruno, 24 Reina
Zuñiga, Julio, 97 Aguila

Pianos and Musical Instruments.

Tomas J. Curtis, 90 Amistad
Esperez y Hermano, 127 Obispo
Avelino Pomares, 113 Habana
Carlos Ackerman, 11 Tejadillo
Federico Aspiazu, 32 Cuba
Carlos Bordas, 16 Aguacarte
Carlos G. Champaigne, 68 O'Reilly
Juan Noriega, 76 Aguila
Bahamonde, Borbilla y Ca., 56 Compostela

Preserved Meats, Canned Goods, Etc.

J. Cano y Ca., 19 Oficios
Barraque y Ca., 48 Oficios
Freixas, Pratt y Ca., 6 Lamparilla
Frederico Giraud, 9 Obrapia
Mayner y Ca., 7 Obrapia
Otamende y Ca., 36 Oficios
J. Pedro y Ca., 2 Amagura
F. Sanchez y Ca., 54 Oficios
Tapia, Eguilor y Ca., 15 San Ignacio

Machinery, Importers Of.

H. Alexander, 19 San Ignacio
Arnat y La Guardia, 74 Cuba
Cail y Ca., 13 San Ignacio
J. B. Cotiart, 15 San Ignacio
George W. Hyatt, 25 Cuba
Kragewski y Pesant, 92 Aguicar
Lawson Bros., 35 Mercaderes
James Smith, 69 Cuba

Paper, Stationery, Etc., Wholesale.

Alvarez, Gonzalez y Ca., 55 Muralla
Barandiaran, Hermanos y Ca., 29 Mercaderes
Castro, Fernandez y Ca., 23 Muralla
P. Fernandez y Ca., 17 Obispo
Ramon Gomez, 14 Mercaderes
J. Hernandez Gonzalez, 100 Habana
Howson y Heinen, 9 Obrapia
Miguel Costas, 9 Obrapia
Pahiras, Gutierrez y Ca., 28 Mercaderes
M. Ruiz v Ca., 18 Obispo
Thomas Wilson y Hijo, 45 Obispo

Printers and Newspapers.

Imprenta del Gobiernio, 23 Teniente-Rey
Viuda de Barcina, 6 Reina
J. Cerda, 20 Obispo

Printers, Etc.—continued.

Rosendo Espina, 34 Rayo
H. E. Heinen, 11 Obrapia
Pedro A. Martinez, 90 Villegas
Federico de Armas, 366 Ppe. Alfonso
A. Calvet, 140 Neptuno
Fernando de Casanova, 23 Lamparilla
Z. Casona, 34 Obispo
"El Egercito," 20 Rayo
José Doroteo, 106 Lamparilla
Juan Guerrera, 28 Mercaderes
"The Havana Weekly Report," 10 Empederado
Rafael Lasua, 61 San Miguel
N. Lopez, 100 Amistad
Saturnino Martinez, 58 Ppe. Alfonso
Victor Perez y Ca., 24 Obrapia
"La Correspondencia de Cuba," 24 Obrapia
José Pulido y Ca., 30 Amazura
José M. Ruiz y Hermano, 29 San Ignacio
José Simon Sanchez, 77 Amazura
Alvarez Saler, 40 Muralla
N. Torre, 61 O'Reilly
Carlos J. Valdez, 63 Estrella
Salvador Videl, O'Reilly
José Villa, 149 Manrique
"Avisador Comercial," 30 Amazura
"Baletin Comercial," 10 Empredado
"Diario de la Marina," 89 Ricla
"El Eco Mititar," 20 Cuba
"El Español"
"Gaceta de la Habana," 23 Teniente-Rey
"La Lucha," 24 Obrapia
"El Pais," 39 Teniente Rey
"El Popular," 92 Habana
"El Radical," 28 Zulueta
"The Havana Herald"

Saw Mills.

Julian Ferrer, 2 Universidad
M. Gonzalez, Puente Grande
Juan M. Lafon, 34 Puente Grande
Diaz y Alvarez, 234 Monte
Juan Maria Lafont, 74 Real
Ortoll, Alegret y Ca., 8 Lucena
Antonio Vila, 76 Belascoain
Rio y Ca., 99 Calzada de Vives

Sewing Machine Agencies.

Alvarez y Hinse, 123 Obispo
Juan Mazon, 51 O'Reilly
José Gonzalez, 74 O'Reilly
José Sopeña y Ca., 112 O'Reilly
Felipe E. Xiquez, 106 Galiano
L. Salares, 98 Ricla
José M. Garcia, 19 Ppe. Alfonso

Stoves.

(See Hardware, etc.)

Stationery, Wall Paper, Etc.

Barandiaran, Sobrinos y Ca., 29 Mercaderes
Barcena y Ca., 45 Ricla
R. Gomez, 15 Mercaderes
Castro Hermano y Ca., 35 Mercaderes
H. Arvier y Ca., 16 Mercaderes
Arturo Codezo, 134 Aguiar
Bernardo Duran, 59 O'Reilly
Guerra y Rodriguez, 28 Mercaderes
B. Gutierrez, 83 Obispo
José Gutierrez y Ca., 2 Salud

Gutierrez y Naredo, 89 Ppe. Alfonso
Benito Izaguirre y Ca., 30 Obispo
R. Mascuñana 23 Bernaza
Mario Menendez, 4 Reina
Leo Merchel, 106 Obispo
P. Rodriguez y Ca., 15 Mercaderes
José de B. Rueda, 1 Ppe. Alfonso
M. Ruiz y Ca., 18 Obispo
N. Torre, 18 O'Reilly
Uriarte y Ca., 78 San Ignacio
Thomas Wilson, Obispo
Cerda y Ca., 22 Obispo
C. Fernandez y Ca., 17 Obispo
Miranda, Diaz y Ca., 74 San Ignacio
Juan Rivero, 43 Ricla
José Torralba, 30 Obispo

Steamship Companies and Ship Agents.

French Mail Steam Packet Company; J. H. Durruty y Ca., 23 San Ignacio
New Orleans, Florida and Havana Mail Steamships; Lawton Hermanos, 35 Mercaderes
New York and Havana Direct Mail Line; McKillar, Luling y Ca., 76 Cuba
New York and Cuba Steamship Company; Lawton Hermanos, 13 Mercaderes
North German Lloyd; H. Upmann y Ca., 64 Cuba
Spanish Mail Steamers de A. Lopez y Ca.; M. Calvo y Ca., 28 Oficios
Spanish Mail Steamers de R. de Herrera; Ramon de Herrera, 63 Oficios
Spanish Steamers (between Habana and Spain); J. Demestre y Ca., 88 Cuba
West India R. Mail Steamships (between Havana and Southampton); G. R. Ruthven, 16 Oficios
José N. Baró, 10 Paula
Victoriano Cusi, 24 Inquisidor
Dávila y Ca., 66 Oficios
N. Deulofeu y Ca., 48 Oficios
Llanderal, Avendaño y Ca., 24 Inquizidor
Mata G. L. de la, 50 San Ignacio
Menendez y Ca., 82 San Ignacio
Soler y Ca., 48 Oficios

Tobacco Leaf, Wholesale Merchants..

(☞ *Names here are the surnames first, Christian names following.*)

Suarez Hermano, 101 Principe Alfonso
Tabares, Bustamenta y Ca., 117 Ppe. Alfonso
Tarapa, Mas y Ca., 106 Estralla
Alfonso, Francisco, 176 Ppe. Alfonso
Arco, Juan del, 225 Ppe. Alfonso
Arduengo, Felix, 167 Ppe. Alfonso
Argudin, Manuel, 110 Dragones
Arguelles Ramon y Ca., 46 Ppe. Alfonso
Bacallas, Antonio, 12 Trocadero
Bances, J. A., 11 Figuras
Bárcena Nicolás, 32 Ppe. Alfonso
Bedoya y Rodriguez, 122 Aguila
Bejar y Alvarez, 168 Neptuno
Bengocheo José, 54 San Miguel
Colero, Juan Bautista, 84 Estevez
Carbajal, Leopoldo, 318 Ppe. Alfonso
Cosals, Jose, 38 Ppe. Alfonso
Casanova A. y Padron, 4 Empedrado
Castiñeiras y Sobrinos, 59 Ppe. Alfonso

Tobacco Leaf, Wholesale Merchants—continued.

Celaya y Rodriguez, 74 Ppe. Alfonso
Cernuda y San Julian, 154 Ppe. Alfonso
Coll, Freixas y Ca., 128 Amistad
Conill, Juan, 69 Teniente-Rey
Diaz y Suarez, 20 Ppe. Alfonso
Fojo, Ramon, 45 Suarez
Fernandez, Gabino, 136 Ppe. Alfonso
Fernandez, Isidro, 142 Lealtad
Fernandez, Cadenava y Ca., 50 Ppe. Alfonso
Font Luis, 6 Ppe. Alfonso
Fontanillas Pablo, 227 Aguila
Fontanillas y Gonzalez, 133 Ppe. Alonso
Franchi Juan Bautista, 111 Ppe. Alfonso
Garbaloza, Domingo, 199 Ppe. Alfonso
Garcia, Francisco, 71 Empedrado
Garcia, Modesto, 57 Ppe. Alfonso
Garcia F. y Cuevas, 164 Ppe. Alfonso
Garcia y Medel, 27 Estrella
Gonzalez Busto Benito, 25 San Rafael
Gonzalez, Diaz Ramon, 116 Ppe. Alfonso
Gonzalez y Fernandez, 23 Ppe. Alfonso
Grau J. y Hermano, 32 Bernaza
Huelguero, Manuel, 106 Ppe. Alfonso
Ibarrondo, Ramon, 83 Nueva del Cristo
Lopez, José, 53 San Miguel
Luege, Manuel, 277 Ppe. Alfonso
Mantecon y Ca., 94 Ppe. Alfonso
Martinez, Antonio, 7 Barcelona
Martinez y Hermano, 114 Ppe. Alfonso
Menendez, Manuel, 223 Ppe. Alfonso
Menendez y Ca., 36 Ppe. Alfonso
Miranda B. y Ca., 168 Ppe. Alfonso
Muñiz José, 229 Ppe. Alfonso
Muñiz, Prendes y Ca., 100 Aguila
Muñiz y Ca., 227 Ppe. Alfonso
Oteiza, José Antonio, 22 Ppe. Alfonso
Palicios, Gregorio, 14 Eserella
Pascual, Enrique, 56 San Miguel
Perez Hermano, 105 Ppe. Alfonso
Puente J. de la y Fernandez, 203 Ppe. Alfonso
Ricardo Vesi, 232 Manrique
Rivero Hermanos, 17 Revillagigedo
Rodriguez Puentes José, 211 Ppe. Alfonso
Roig Juan, 172 Ppe. Alfonso
Salazar Vicente, 98 Galiano
Sanchez Benito, 140 Ppe. Alfonso
Serra Enrique, 22 Tenerife
Suarez Blás, 171 Ppe. Alfonso
Suarez, Celaya y Ca., 74 Ppe. Alfonso
Suarez, Genaro y Ca., 139 Ppe. Alfonso
Suarez Manuel, 39 Figuras

Theaters, Etc.

Albisu Theatre, Comedies and Light Opera
Cervantes Theatre, Variety and Ballet
Tacon Theatre, Grand Opera and Drama
Plaza de Toros, Bull Fights
Circo de Gallos, Cock Fights

Besides the above, there is in Havana a Base Ball Park and several concert halls.

Undertakers and Funeral Supplies.

Manuel Campos
Viuda de Barbosa, 63 Aguacate
Roman Campos, 54 Revillagigedo
Tomas R. Giralt, 129 Anchadel Norte
Ramon Guillot, 72 Aguiar
Carlos Hernandez, 33 Concordia
Matias Infanson, 79 Zanja
Serafin Lopez, 110 Zanja
Leandro Lozano, 184 Habana
Adolfo Ramos, 48 Estevez
Dorotea Ramos, 95 Estevez
José de los Reyes, 30 Sol
T. Rodriquez, 52 Neptuno
Camilio Suarez, 102 Suarez
C. Urrutia, 108 Zanja
Rafael Urrutia, 111 Zanja
Felicia Villagas, 109 Zanja

Surveyors.

José Alamo, 132 Lealtad
Francisco de la Cueva, 34 Arimas
Juan Guillardo y Imberuo, 6 Concordia
N. Ortega, 31 Nueva del Cristo
Esteban Pichardo, 104 Merced
José F. Rodriguez, 228 San Nicolas
Rafael Rodriguez y Rodriguez, 228 San Nicolas
Domingo Saavedra, 94 San Miguel
José Salazar y Hernandez, 21 Concordia
Simon Valdez de la Torre, Animas

Warehousemen.

Santiago Abascat, 2 San Ignacio
José Ramon Ariza, 152 Neptuno
Juan Casasu, Vendodo
Enrique y Ordoñez, 22 San Ignacio
Pascual Galvez, 9 Teniente-Rey
Pedro Garcia, 26 Galiano
Güell y Ca., 1 Calzada de Cristina
Francisco Miro, 11 Oficios
Perez y Ca., 5 Obrapia
Marcelo Ruiz, 4 San Ignacio

CARDENAS.

Population, 20,000.

Agricultural Implements.
(See Hardware, Tools, Etc.)

Ales and Beer Dealers.
(See also, Grocers, Wholesale.)

Manuel Anduiza
A. S. Mendez
E. Howeta y Ca.
Francisco P. Carbonell

Architects, Builders & Surveyors.
B. E. de Biart, 137 Laborde
José Martinez Lopez, 140 Laborde
Salvador Vidal

Arms and Ammunition.
Alberto Giralt, 85 Obispo
Domingo Hernandez

Banks and Bankers.
Surcusal del Banco Español
Juan Martinez
Rojas y Bacot

Booksellers and Stationers.
José Alvitos, 43 Real
A. Triay, 23 Real
J. Serra y Capdevila, Jenez
José Soler, 44 Calvo
Bernardo Suarez, 104 Ayllon
V. Suarez y Puerta, 132 Jenez
Julio Tonley, 83 Coronel Verdugo
Juan Turró, Plaza de Mercado
Turró y Toledo, 136 Calvo
Urbistondo y Hermano, 91½ Ayllon
Benito J. Valdés, 154 O'Donnell
José Villar, 150 Vires
José Zabala, 452 Janez

Boots and Shoes, Wholesale and Retail.
Juan Basilio, 69 Ayllon
Pedro Casañas, 103 Ayllon
Benito Castro, 24 Ruiz
José Fonnodona, 49 Real
Paudencio Gauneta, 88 Industria
Francisco Achedo Gomez 12 Salud
Domingo Gonzalez, 25 O'Donnell
Vega Gonzalezy, 12 Ayllonz
Juan Gordillo, 166 Real
Viuda de Juan Hardiria, 167 Ruiz
Rodriguez Antonio Hernandes, 186 Calvo
Alejandro Lopez
Viuda de Martinez, 12 Real
Fuire y Paz, 94 Coronel Rerdugo
Anselmo del Pino y Ca., Laborde
Federico Rivas, 77 Real
J. Vicens, 73 Real

Coal Merchants.
M. V. Lezcano, 62 Pinillos
José Portilla, 197 Espriu

Crockery and Glassware.
M. Gonzalez y Ca., 71 Real
Elizondo, Orihuela y Ca., 33 Real
Lizonda, Laurnaca y Ca., 20 Real
Francisco Llaca, 75 Real

Dentists.
Ramon Beldady, 73 Ayllon
José M. Carreño, 37 Real

Druggists, Retail.
Francisco Barrinat, San Juan de Dioz, 93 Real
Juan Figueroa y Padre, Ntra. Sra. de Regla., 34 Real
Carlos José Quin, Nueva de San Agustin, 133 Real
Ramon Leon Ruiz, La Marina, 42 Real
B. Herrero, 89 Real

Dry Goods, Retail.
A. Alonso, 126 Ayllon
Manuel Alvarez y Ca., 128 Real
G. Fernandez
Hilaño Fernandez, 96 Real
Fernandez y Ca., 185 Real
J. Garcia y Alvarez, 109 Real
Gemez Calleyá, 159 Ruiz
Gutierez Ca., Coronel Verdugo
Lloniz y Ca., Coronel Verdugo
Loredo y Ca., 79 Real
Mazo y Hijo 12 Ayllon
Fernandez, Pelaez y Ca., 76 Real
Villasante Ruiz, 119 Real
Nicolas Sanchez, 141 Laborde
Felipe Garcia Suarez, 78 Real
Severino Suarez, 114 Real
Suarez y Ca., 79 Real
Suarez y Hermano, 88 Real
Dionisio Torre, 220 Real
M. Vivanco y Ca., 84 Real

Fancy Goods.
Altuzarra y Bastranica, 102 Real
German F. Bujan, 29 Real
Maria del Rosario Bustamante, 143 Real
Pedro Dama, Laborde
Diaz y Conijo, 80 Real
Lopez y Ca., 56 Real
J. Pagés y Hermano, 46 Real
Luis Pagés, 74 Real

Furniture.
J. Artigas, 95 Laborde
A. Madruga y Freire
Tomas Magin
Villa Rivas y Ca.
N. Bahamonde

General Merchants, Wholesale and Retail.

Bazco Aedo, 56 Princesa
Antonio Aguilera, 48 Cossio
Folgueras Pedro Alvarez, 32 Obispo
Garcia Faustino Alvarez, 143 O'Donnell
Juan Alvariño, 175 Jenez
Andiarena a Ca., 40 Ayllon
Saevedra Andrés, Concha
Antonio Garcia Arua, 70 Laborde
Francisco Bargés, 55 Industria
F. Cabarcos y Hermanos, 156 Real
L. Cambo y Piñeira, 118 Ruiz
Santos del Campos, 127 Calvo
Castilla y Diaz, 189 Real
Cobrelias y Ca., 95 Real
M. Collia y Estrada, 225 Ruix
Coló y Ca., 18 Laborde
Benito Dávio, 97 Ruiz
Francisco Diaz, 38 Laborde
José Diaz, 187 Real
Benigno Duran, 282 Jenez
J. Fernandez y Hermanos, 105 Ayllon
Pedro N. Flaquer, 61 O'Donnell
Juan Nadad Flaquer, 225 Ayllon
Manuel Flores, 227 Ruiz
B. Font y Roselló, Navarro
Dionisio Fragas, J2 Cossio
F. Fuèrro y Gonzalez, 91 Velazquez
Galan y Gonzalez, 109 Jenez
Andrés Garcia, 81 Aranguren
Perez Garcia, 570 Real
Garriga y Gay, 18 Héctor
Joaquim Jimenez Gomez, 9 Espriu
Leopoldo Gomez, 170 Real
Gomez y Corral, 20 San José
Pedro Llera Herrera, 32 Raal
Evarista de la Incera, 40 O'Donnell
Antonio Garcia Inclau, 135 Vives
Jamet y Hermano, 78 Ruiz
Janetti y Ruiz, 8 Plaza de Mercado
A. Junco y Otero, 33 Vives
Angel Laborde, 124 O'Donnell
Gerónimo Llano, 149 Vives
Francisco Larranz y Ca., 29 Laborde
A. Ledo y Garcia, 14 O'Donnell
José Buch Llort, 203 Jenez
José Rodriguez Lopez, 9 Hector
Magin y Rosch, 55 Real
Francisco G. Manzo, 37 Anglona
Bartolo Marquez, 272 Laborde
F. Martonell y Roca, 9 Anglada
Juan Rico Fernandez, 293 Laborde
Juan Pascual Miro, 59 Obispo
Mitzaus y Cruts, 143 Laborde
F. Montelo y Perez, Plazo de Mercado
Montes y Gallico, 69 O'Donnell
Moya y Hermano, 152 Jenez
Muñiz y Rivero, 48 Ruiz
J. Niella y Sola, 27 Laborde
Sebastian Rodriguez Olivera, 166 Calvo
Frederico Torriente Palacio, 182 Real
José Cristóbal Perez, 20 Jenez
A. Piñero y Viña, 58 Pinillos
Antonio Plá, 15 Laborde
Luis F. Prats, 12 Jenez
J. Pruneda y Gafort, 29 Laborde
José A. Pulido, 85 Calvo
José Casellas, Rabassa, 198 Real
Maria Fernando Rios, 22 Ruiz
Antonio Roan, 70 Laborde
Juan Ronca Roca, Nazareno
Vicenta Gonzalez Rodrigues, 7 Soumerville
L. Rodriguez y Martinez, 199 Ayllon
Rodriguez y Ca., 17 Obispo
Silverio Rubiera, Plaza de Mercado
Segundo Saez, 9 Cristina
S. Salas y Gali, 50 Pinillos
José Salviejo, 132 Calvo
Francisco Gomez Sanchez, 19 Calv
Sebastian Sanchez, 82 O'Donnell
Santos y Lastre, 18 Laborde

General Commission Merchants.

J. Balsells, 16 Real
G. Cazimajon, 4 Ayllon
Crabb y Tria, 82 Pinillos
A. Gon y Ca., 6 Real
Pedmonte y Ca., 88 Pinillos
Rabel y Ca., 18 Real
Rojas y Pacot, 24 Real
Tellado, Barrera y Ca., 70 Pinellos

Ice Dealer.

Juan B. Hamel, 72 Real

Groceries and Provisions, Wholesale and Retail.

Bermudez, Braga y Ca., 108 Pinillos
Alzugaray y Ca., 13 Laborde
Roig, Arango y Ca., Pinillos
Arechabalay y Pillar, 72 Pinillos
Arena y Ca., 90 Pinillos
Bardia y Ca., 84 Pinillos
Ferro, Bermudez y Ca., 28 Real
Bustamante y Ca., 18 Real
Coto y Ca., 18 Laborde
Ometa, Diaz y Ca., 11 Laborde
Enrique Dima, Coronel Verdugo
Vidal, Garcia y Ca., 102 Pinillos
Mederos, Gomez y C., 94 Pinillos
Bernardo Llano, 140 Real
Echenique, Llerandi y Ca., 102 Pinillos
Domenech, Mendizabal y Ca., 102 Pinillas
Perdemante y Ca., Ayllon
Francisco Otero Peñeda, 113 Real
Roca y Ca., 78 Pinillos
Segrera y Ca., 2 Real
Manuel G. Soto, 16 Pinillos
Ruiz, Suarez y Ca., 1 Real
Alonso Valle, 69 Obispo
Bermudez, Suarez y Ca., Pinillos

Hardware, Tools, Etc.

Cabezon, Cobo y Ca., 13 Real
Gregorio Fuentes, 130 Real
Larrauri Larrousoe y Ca., 3 Real
M. Linares Martinez, 86 Pinillos
Agesta Maribona y Ca., 12 Real
M. Torre y Ca., 104 Pinillos
Torre y Framil 76 Real

House Furnishing Goods.

Luis Garcia, 23 Ruiz
Agustin Sanchez, 62 Real
Salvador Vidal, 145 Real
Francisco Gafa, Real

Jewelry and Silverware.

S. Pineda, 81 Real
Aguayo y Ca., 102 Real
Matias Bourgeois, 131 Real
Secundino Cesta, 97 Real
Altuzarra y Cambronero, 102 Real
José Carol, Ayllon
V. Riesta y Gallego, 81 Real
Enrique C. Salvart, Nerdugo
José Soler, 77 Ayllon
Antonio Vidal, 97 Real
J. Matteos, 145 Real
Agustin Mota, 109 Coronel Verdugo

Lumber and Steam Saw Mills.

E. Guerendian y Ca., Héctor
Vicente R. Vila, O'Donnell

Machine Shops.

F. Rico Alvarez, 72 Calvo
Juan M. Corzo, 96 Princesa
F. Petit, 53 O'Donnell

Oil, Lamps, Etc.

Manuel Martinez
Rodriguez y Olivera, 30 Cossio

Paints and Varnishes.

(See Hardware and Druggists.)

Photographer.

Juan Busto, 211 Laborde

Physicians and Surgeons.

Francisco Aday, 24 Ayllon
Manuel Alvarez Laborde
Antonio Mir Barrinat, 72 Laborde
Alejandro Biast, 137 Laborde
Enrique E. Casabuena, 155 Jerez
Juan Mir Codina, 109 Coronel Verdugo
Ramon Elcid, Ayllon
Valentin Alcaraz Fernandez, 120 Ruiz
Gutierez y Quiros, 32 Daniel
Antonio Hay de la Puente, 41 Ruiz
Engenio N. Herrero, Aranguren
Lorenzo Hévia, 58 Obispo
Fernandez Menendez, Coronel Verdugo

Ciriaco Navarro, 12 Ayllon
Antonio José Pacetti, 75 Laborde
Dionisio Saez, Real

Theaters, Etc.

Teatro Otero
Teatro Asiatico

Printers.

José Puig, 60 Real
Tomas Dais y Nuñez, 116 Real
Enrique Trujillo
J. Puente, 15 Princessa
" Diario de Cardenas "
" La Cronica"

Saddlery and Harness.

Tomas Delgado, 157 Real
José Hernandez, 44 Real
Manuel Mederos Hernandez, 151 Real

Sewing Machines.

Bastarrica y Cendoya
Alberto Giralt
Nadal y Ca.
Domingo Viti
R. Villaneva

Trunks, Bags, Etc.

Abajas y Ca., 68 Real
Castilla y Ca., 117 Real
Alejo Diaz, 108 Real
Diaz y Ca., 108 Real
Suarez Diaz, 102 Ayllon
Sanchez Fernandez y Ca.
Manuel Gonzallez, 109 Real
Serra Gran y Ca., 60 Real
A. Lopez y Gutierrez, Plaza del Mercado
Prieto y Albajas, 68 Real
Silva Ruiz y Ca
Villanueva, Vetti y Ca., 83 Real

Undertakers.

Hipólito Cabezola, Verdugo
Juan Madruga, Ayllon
Juan Rivas, 93 Labode
José Bernal Rodriguez, Industria

CIENFUEGOS.

Population, 21,000.

Arms and Ammunition.
(See also Hardware.)

Luis Diaz
Andres Grandilla

Agricultural Implements.
(See Hardware and Tools).

Banks.
Sucursal del Banco Español, 29 Santa Clara
S. Fernando

Billiard Halls.
Jesus E. Alvarez
Manuel Borrato
G. Castellanos
Jose J. Cienfuegos
Fernández y Cruz
Herrera y Gonzalez
Juan B. Hormoza
Vidal y Serra

Bookbinders.
Anselmo Garcia, Arguilles
Muñiz y Hermano, Santa Isabel

Boots and Shoes, Retail.
Cruz José Aguero, Horruitinier
Antonio Ayona, La Capitana
Bergo y Hernandez, Santa Cruz
J. Cauteña y Hermano, D'Clouet
Carreras y Tutzo, D'Clouet
Alejandro Caralá, Arguelles
Domingo Cruz, Castillo
Ferrer y Garcia, S. Fernando
Magin Fonts, D'Clouet
José Guel, S. Carlos
Caridad Niebla, Cuartel
José Quintero, Santa Cruz
J. Rodriguez y Salas, Dolores
Gabriel Roselló, Marcillan
B. Vargas, Castillo
J. Sans y Acebedo, Santa Cruz
Salvodor Sorbonet, Dolores

Building Materials.
Gil Cano y Ca., Castillo
Miguel Colon, Castillo
J. Fernandez y Fernandez, Castillo
Francisco Lorenzo, Castillo
José Maria Meñica, Castillo
Francisco de Virella Paula y Ca., Castillo
Perez y Ca.
Juan Roig, Castillo
Gomez y Ca., Castillo

Carriage and Cart Manufacturers.
Felix Calderon
Joaquim Angel, San Fernando

Juan Tenorio Rodriguez, Vires
Pagola y Ca.

Coppersmiths.
B. Panza y Maimon, Castillo
Nicholas Schittino, Castillo

Crockery and Glassware.
Lorenzo Perez, Arguelles
Felipe Quesada, 10 D'Clouet

Dentists.
Adolfo C. Betancourt
Enrique Grau
Diego Lopez

Druggists and Chemists.
Isidro Castiñeira
José F. Ferry
Figueroa y Velis
Fernando Frias
Ramon Novoa
Saler y Mendez
R. Figueroa y Marti, Nuestra Sra. de Regla
Frias y Cintras, La Central
Francisco G. Gonzalez, San Anacleto

Dry Goods.
José M. Alonso, San Fernando
Lorenzo Alvarez, San Cárlos
D. Aya y Fernandez, San Fernando
Janer Blanco, San Fernando
Campa y Hermano, Castillo
José Campoamor, 27 D'Clouet
Castrillon y Hermanos, Castillo
Braulio, Coteron y Ca., San Fernordo
Grazés Conceyro y Ca., 13 Santa Isabel
F. Diaz de Villegas y Arce, San Cárlos
Antonio J. Fernandez, 102 San Cárlos
Angel Forcelledo, 30 San Cárlos
José Gutierrez, 26 Santa Isabel
José Maria Menendez, 21 Santa Eleua
Hermanos Posada, San Fernando
Manuel Rivero y Ca., 26 San Fernando
F. Rodriguez y Ca., D'Clouet
Sanchez y Ca.
Trerilla y Ca., San Fernando
Laureano Villa, Santa Isabel

Exchange Brokers.
Felix Ballina
Muruelo y Trelles

Electrical Apparatus.
Manuel Solis

Furniture Dealers.
Hipolito Larcada
Jacinto Manticon
José D. Martinez
Carlos Sardiña
Villapol y Fernandez

General Commission Merchants.

Aviles y Leblanc, 6 Dorticos
Fowler y Ca., Dorticos
Federico Hunihe, La Mar
Cardona, Hart y Ca.
Castañoy Intriago
G. Castillo
Garcia y Ca.
Gustavo Gravan
Ricardo Hoya
Minendez y Ca.
Tomas Terry y Ca.
Hermanos Torriente

Groceries and Provisions, Wholesale.

Gandara y Hermano
Manuel Menendez
Planas y Sanchez
Manuel Traviesa
Alvarez, Llano y Ca.
Garcia y Ca., D'Clouet
Granda y Ca., San Fernando
Pons y Ca., Santa Isabel
Sanchez y Ca.
Cardona, Artarancacz y Ca.
Castaño Intriago, Manuel Mendez

Hardware, Tools, Etc.

Perez y Hermano
Perez y Olascoaga
Arrucharrena y Trujillo, D'Clouet
Lloivo y Ca., San Fernando
Lorenzo Perez, Santa Isabel
A. Copperi y Ca.

House Furnishing, Tinsmiths, Etc.

Sabino Abello y Ca., Castillo
Josefa Campo, Castilla
E. Fernandez, Santa Isabel
D. Lamoglia, Castillo

Lamps, Oils, Etc.

Eduardo Muñoz
José Romero, D'Clouet
I. Romero
Lorenzo Perez
Perez Hermanos

Lumber and Brick Dealers.

A. Cabezo Garcia y Ca., Paseo de Arango
Hermanos Garriga y Nuro, Paseo de Arango

Photographers.

Jacinto Cotera, 37 San Carlos
J. Carbonell, 4 Chamat, San Fernando

Physicians and Surgeons.

Manuel Aguiar, San Carlos
Isidoro Castiñira, San Fernando

Ramon Mazzarredo, Santa Clara
J. Pertierra y Albuerne, San Luis
Rafael Saboride, Santa Cruz
Juan A. Vila, Arguelles
Antonio Balbañia
Lorenzo Acevedo
Jacinto Cotera
Manuel Ferreyro
José Frias
N. Vieta Garcia
Juan Hildalgo
Gabriel N. Lauda
Joaquin P. Marti
Federico Mazarredo
Octavio Ortiz
Luis Poma

Printers and Lithographers.

J. José Andreu, Santa Isabel
Nicolas de Gamboa, Horruitinier
Manuel Muñiz, Santa Isabel
A. Muir, La Aurora San Fernando
V. Vila

Sewing Machine Agents.

José Alonso
Q. Capalleza

Surveyors and Architects.

Manuel Torre O'Bourke
José A. Alvarez, Santa Cruz
Nicolas de Gamboa, Horruitinier
Rey y Barro

Trunks, Leather Articles, Etc.

Aedo y Hermano, Castillo
Antonio Bernes, Santa Cruz
Juan Bustamante, D'Clouet
Carreras y Touso, D'Clouet
J. Miranda, 18 Santa Cruz
Cristina Clarilla, Santa Cruz
R. Gener, D'Clouet
Francisco Martinez, D'Clouet
José Quirós, 18 San Cárlos
A. de la Torre y Harmano, 28 San Fernando

Undertakers.

Juan Oriol, Santa Cruz
J. Rabassa y Verges, Santa Isabel

Watchmakers and Jewelers.

Juan Amat, Santa Isabel
Carlos Basset, Horruitinier
Luis Fino, D'Clouet
Gestlry U. Fritz, San Carlos
Tomas Martin, Santa Cruz
Yrarolra Meras, D'Clouet
Saturnino Ortega, D'Clouet
A. Rigot, D'Clouet
Manuel Solis, D'Clouet

GIBARA.

Population, 25,000.

Agricultural Implements.
(See Hardware.)

Ales and Beer.
(See Groceries and Provisions)

Arms and Ammunition.
(See Hardware Dealers.)

Boots, Shoes and Leather Goods.

Victoriano Martinez, Gloria
Ramirez M. Toledo, Fortaleza
Miguel Torres, Fortaleza

Druggists and Chemists.

Juan Gomez, "San José"
Castor del Moral, "Fortaleza"
Eduardo Gonzalez

Dry Goods.

Bolivar y Ca., Fortaleza
Sartorio Fernandez y Ca.
Benito Langoria, Fortaleza
Demetrio Langoria, Fortaleza

Furniture.

Victor L. Casamora, San Isidoro
Joaquin Pomposo, San Isidoro

General Merchants.

Hermanos Garrido, Fortaleza
Antonio Gutierrez, Fortaleza
Gutierrez y Beltran, Cementerio
Manuel Aja Martinez, Fortaleza
Mendez y Alvarez, Espana
Francisco Montadas, Cementerio
Muñiz y Garcia, España

Garcia Rebelgo y Ca., España
Sainz y Hermano, Fortaleza
Torre Necino y Ca., Fortaleza
Vidal y Hermanos, Felices
Anguela y Driggs, Mariana
Padiemo, Garcia y Ca., San German
Hidalgo, Gueri y Ca., San German
Munilla, Longoria y Ca., Mariana
Amat Manus y Ca., Fortaleza
Juan Martinez, Mariana
Riancho, Federica y Ca.,
Rodriguez, Silva y Ca., Fortaleza
Torre, Vecino y Ca., Fortaleza

Groceries and Provisions.

Rufino del Rusal, Rosario
Agustin Barciela, Fortaleza
José Naval Diaz, Gloria
Modesto Lopez, Fortaleza
Francisco Montada, Clarin

Jewelers, Etc.

Lafont y Lambret, Fortaleza
A. Marquez, Fontaleza
Rafael G. Vicedo, Fontaleza

Physicians.

Antonio G. Avia, Mariaño
Lucas Calderon, Fontaleza
Peña Garcia, Calixto
Ricardo G. Longaria, Mariño
Calixto G. Peña, Herman Cortes

Printers.

Rafael Lopez Cuesta, San Marmeto

Undertaker.

Francisco Rodriguez, San German

GUANABACOA.

Population, 25,900.

Ales and Beer Dealers.
(See also Groceries and Provisions.)
Ayats y Romaguera
Rafael Anedo, 30 Cardenas

Agricultural Implements.
(See Hardware Dealers.)

Arms and Ammunition.
(See Hardware.)

Boots and Shoes, Retail.
José Arce y Remus, 220 Corral Falso
Andrés Cabrera, 191 Corral Falso
José Carreras, 169 Corral Falso
Joaquin Espinosa, 93 Palo Blanco
José Carvajal Fernandez, 32 Ppe. Antonio
José Ferreiro y Maril, 207 Corral Falso
Eusebio Borges Farcio, 205 Corral Falso
Candido Gomez, Ppe. Antonio
Pedro Guach Martin, Concepcion
Cristóbal Villarosa, 4 Concepcion

Builders.
Ramon Cueto
Juan Castellá, 79 Vénus
Aleman Hernandez y Francisco, 82 Santo Domingo
José Jurado, 52 Calzada Regla
Francisco de la Piedra, 66 Campo Santo
J. Rico y Alvarez, 75 Delicias
Domingo Vilela, 73 Concepcion
Agustin Martinez

Dentists.
Luis Aguera
E. Dalman, 13 Candelaria
Tomas Bello

Druggists and Chemists.
Juan T. Figuerra
F. Josar y Hernandez
Espinosa y Sardina, 200 Corral Falso
Antonio E. Gonzalez, 10 Candelaria
Ramon Fuentes, 43 Concepcion
Juan Suarez, 65 Palo Blanco
Suarz y Miranda

Dry Goods, Retail.
Manuel Camén, 26 Candelaria
Manuel Cañedo, 9 Pepe Antonio
Maximino Cañedo y Ca., 34 Pepe Antonio
Rafael Coñedo, Pepe Antonio
Manuel Diaz, 14 Animas
Juan Arenas Fernandez, 30 Polo Blanco
Antonio Fons, Concepcion
Feliciano Garcia, Animas
Felix Salas Gonzalez, 13 Pepe Antonio
Melchor Gurdiel, 6 Real
Manuel Luzarraga, 212 Corral Falso

José Ruiz, 30 Pepe Antonio
Dionisio G. Solaris, 167 Corral Falso
Mariano Urieta
Gumersindo Venero, 29 Candelaria

Furniture.
Ramon y Francisco Cueto, 14 Real
Ramon Guanche

Groceries and Provisions, Wholesale and Retail.
Jaime Adue
Beraza y Ca., 18 Candelaria
Matilde Acosta, 54 Santa Maria
José Adue, 25 Palo Blanco
Antonio Adroe, 2 Corona
Felix Alberti, 25 Pepe Antonio
Braulio Alberno, 79 Real
Albuerno y Ca., 32 Obispa
Francisco Alfonso, 5 Santa Maria
Camilo Alvarez, 113 Corral Falso
Solis A. Alvarez, 34 Gleria
Ignacio Amaya, 25 Palo Blanco
Miguel Ayats, 9 San Antonio
Maria José Babeda, 181 Corral Falso
Manuel Barroso y Ca., 104 Palo Blanco
Marcelino Batalon, 14 Division
M. Bello y Tamago, 9 Delicias
Beraza y Ca., 18 Candelaria
Antonio Blanco, 58 Cerreria
Manuel Bóbeda, 57 San Antonio
José Bulfill, 47 Division
José Cayon, 98 Real
Juan Campos, 36 Fuente
José Carrió, 2 Candelaria
Juan Casariego, 77 Venus
José Castillo, 77 Molinos
Cañas y Ca., 25 Palo Blanco
Corbera y Soto, 46 Concepcion
Antonio Crosas y Ca., 15 Samaritana
José Cuanda, 16 Jesus Maria
Pedro Cuerdo, 109 Concepcion
Cuervo y Garcia, San Antonio
Juan B. Cueto, 42 Delicias
José Diaz, 133 Joaquim
Juan G. Diaz, 80 Amargura
J. Esuvir y Ramos, 18 Candelaria
Domingo Fernandez, 2 Santo Domingo
Eusebio Fernandez, 107 Venus
Antonio Mayor Fernandez, 110 Concepcion
J. Mayor Fernandez, 7 Corrales
M. Fernandez y Hermano, 41 Corrales
Ramon Fernandez, 36 Soledad
José Fortuni, 43 San Antonio
Francisco Gally, 67 Cereria
Francisco Garcia, 56 Palo Blanco
José R. Garcia, 32 Juan José
Juan Garcia, 23 Beguer
Rafael Garcia, 44 Real
Ramon Garcia, 7 Padilla
Benito Gomez, 351-2 Real
Vicente Ganez, 45 barreto
Juan Gonzalez, 80 Amargura

Groceries and Provisions, Wholesale and Retail—*continued*.

Ramon Gonzalez, 33 Obispo
Grana y Ca., 15 Cardenas
Felipe Guiño, 22 Santa Maria
Pedro Herrera, 215 Corral Falso
Divisio Infiesta, 12 Camarera
Ignacio Binares, 184 Corral Falso
Sebastian Llorens, 75 San Joaquin
Manuel Mahr, 31 Amenidod
Juan Martinez, Pepe Antonia
Manuel Maseda, 61 Real
José Medio, 20 Luz
Medio y Hermano, 55 Corral Falso
Francisco Menendez, 35 Animas
M. Moner y Pi, 42 Jesus Maria
Manuel Montaoer, 84 Division
Santos Nieto, 181 Corral Falso
Benito Nogué, 75 Corral Falso
Juan Noriega, 1 Real
Joaquin Pasper, 16 Santa Andrés
Juan Perez y Ca., 11 Cadenas
Lucas Perez, Plaza de Justiz
Claudio Perqué, 75 Corral Falso
Félix Presas, 98 Concepcion
Joaquin Piñera, 82 Caniposanto
Modesta Piñeiro, 13 Lebredo
Agustin Pujol, 69 Concepcion
José Pujol, 31 Cadenas
Manuel Puerna y Ca., 115 Palo Blanco
Ramon Ramis, 57 Amargura
Francisco Real, 12 Animas
Cefernio Rodriguez, 35 Asuncion
Fernando Rodriguez, 108 Corrales
José Rodriguez y Hermano, 15 Plaza Vieja
Manuel Rodriguez, 28 Pepe Antonio
Rodriguez y Ca., San José
Antonio Ribot, 80 Cereria
Claudio Rivas, 92 Corral Falso
Pastor Sains, 70 Animas
Jamie Salas, 40 Delicias
Servio Salas, 20 Santo Domingo
Miguel Soler, Cruz Verde
Juan Suarez, 41 Lebredo
Manuel Suarez, 195 Corral Falso
Salvador Surida, 22 Cruz Verde
José de la Torre, 51 Joaquin
Manuel de la Torre, 42 Samaritana
Ramon Vazquez, 19 Real
Vazquez y Machado, 19 Real
Jaime Vidal, 42 Cocos
Jamie Vila, 44 Aguacate
Miguel Vila y Ca., 41 Animas
Jacinto Villamil, 24 Padilla
Mariano Yaño, 55 Palo Blanco
Antonio Yolasano, 63 Cruz Verde
José Muñiz, 7 Corral Falso
Antonio Neida, 42 Luz

Hardware, Tools, Etc.

Enrique Casas.
Serafin Alio, 42 Pepe Antonio
Baltasar Arronte, Versalles
José Jurado
Francisco Piedra
Rico y Alvarez
Juan Trujillo

Lamps, Oils, Etc.

Juan Bada
Domingo Vilela, 73 Concepcion

Physicians and Surgeons.

Mariano Domenech, 37 Animas
Enrique G. Gonzalez, 871-2 Corral Falso
José Antonio Párraga, 56 Concepcion
Juan Manuel Prieto, 41 Concepcion
Francisco Rivero, 19 Pepe Antonio
José Gutierrez
Francisco M. Hector
T. Moreno Ceballos
Ricardo Morillas
Francisco Vidal
Rufino Vidal

Printers.

Belisario Garceran, 28 Real
José Huguet y Belarza, 18 Pepe Antonio
Juan Manro, 79 Concepcion

Saddlery and Harness.

Francisco Sirra, 139 Corral Falso

Sewing Machines.

(See Dry Goods.)

Trunks, Leather Goods, Etc.

Serafin Alió, 42 Pepe Antonio
Evaristo Zabala Diaz, 16 Animas
Bernardo Gonzalez, 124 Cárdenas
Manuel Serra Migolla, 140 Corral Falso
Manuel Noriega, 40 Palo Blanco
Francisco Sanchez, 6 Real
Pablo Vila, 48 Concepcion

Undertakers.

José Casado, 50 Division
Felix de la Cruz y Ca., 60 Palo Blanco
Carlota Molina, 16 Verte Marte
Cirilo Chassagne

GUANTANAMO.

Population, 7,000.

Agricultural Implements.
(See Hardware Dealers.)

Ales and Beer.
(See Groceries and Provisions.)

Arms and Ammunition.
Prospero Gamir
Prospero Juanneau
Salvador Perez

Bankers.
J. Baro y Hermano
Brooks y Ca.
J. Bueno y Ca.

Billiards.
Francisco Conovaca, 24 Concha Baja
Lesaum y Ca., 23 Vorgas Baja
Vincente Mico, 7 Real

Crockery, Glassware, Lamps, Etc.
Callico y Ca., 2 Valdes Alta

Dentists.
Ernesto Martin
Sebastian Lacavaliere

Druggists and Chemists.
José Lacavalerie y Ca., 4 Valdés
Ambrosio Quintana, 27 Valdés
Esteban Jierra

Dry Goods.
Bertran Arará y Ca., 15 Concha
Brunet, Carreras y Ca., 28 Valdés
Mestre y Gorgas, Real
Padrol y Ca., P. de Arnias
José Pascual, P. de Arnias
Roldós y Ca., 9 Concha
Hermano Rosés y Ca., Real

General Merchandise, Wholesale.
Bertran, Arará y Ca., 15 Concha
Hermanos Rosillo Arce, 12 Maujon
Bertran y Hermano, Santa Catalina
Bertran y Mirel, 15 Concha
Callico y Ca., 12 Valdés
Brunet, Carreras y Ca., 28 Valdás
Bandillo Gallart
Agustin Hernandez, 6 Maujon
José Jacas y Ca., 1 Concha

José Castro
Miguel Collantes
Francisco Dubos
Vincente Ereña
Ramon Gonzalez
Francisco Iglesias
Mestre y Ca.
José Mompó
Pedro Monte
Antonio Puente
José D. Seis
P. Soler y Ca.
Vestú y Ca.
Mestre y Gorjus, 34 Real
Mariano Mila, 26 Santa Catalina
Morlote y Solcines, 26 Maujon
Hermano Rosés y Ca., Real

Jewelers and Watchmakers.
José Gaulhiac
José Polanco
Daniel C. Aimable
Garcia y Ca.
Florencio Valero

Merchants, Commission.
G. Branet y Ca., 36 Real
Brooks y Ca., 47 Real
Bueno y Ca., 44 Valdés
Emilio Sanchez

Physicians and Surgeons.
Joaquin Botey, Real
Manuel Granda, Concha
Faustino Garcia
N. Sobrino, Hotel Comercio
Luis M. de Castro
Joaquin Ros

Printers and Newspapers.
"La Voz del Ganso"
Francisco Castellanos
Mendoza y Ca.
"El Echo del Comercio"
Luis Lamarque

Saddlery and Harness.
Juan Bautista Carrey, 27 Valdés
Cosme Forment, 23 Valdés
Eduardo Jalonasky, 2 Santa Catalina
Jorge Lalonne, 2 Campana
Maria Luisa Mena, Campana

MANZANILLO.

Population, 18,000.

Ales and Beer.
(See Groceries and Provisions.)

Agricultural Implements.
(See Hardware Dealers.)

Boots and Shoes.
Zacarias Arenal, Real
José Carbonell, 65 Angel
Wenceslao Castro, Real
M. Fernandez y Hermano, 22 Comercio
Gonzalez y Ca., 17 Comercio
Emilio Vigas, 20 Comercio

Dentists.
Elario Aguilera
Calisto Betancourt, 30 Cristina
N. Herman

Druggists and Chemists.
Pedro Tomas Cespedes, 26 Cristina
Ramon Sanchez, 51 Comercio

Dry and Fancy Goods.
Silverio Cangas, 45 Real
Ramon Garcia, 23 Cristina
Perez Nuñiz y Ca., 51 Zeal
Riega y Ca., Real

General Merchandise, Provisions, Etc.
Almiral y Llopis, Angel
Castro, Boeras y Ca., 25 Real
Eusebio Camino, 46 Real
Fuentes y Sanchez
Jabel y Ca.
Luis Matas, P. de San José
Saturnino Mennendez, 36 Real
Antonio Morales, 42 Real
J. Nuñiz y Ca., 19 Comercio
Pedro Pardias, Real
Planas y Hermanos, 65 Real
M. Rabentós y Ca., Santa Ana
Riera y Ca., 8 Santa Ana
J. Sanchez y Ca., 53 Iglesia
Feliciano Sisa
Solis y Ca.
M. Suan y Ca.
Tabel y Ca.
Vallejo y Ca.
José Tasis, 25 Iglesia
Vallejo y Ca.
José Velasquez, 29 Real

Hardware, Tools, Etc.
José Bruneli, 13 Cristina
A. Riera y Ca., 56 Santa Ana

Treserra y Ferrer, San Pedro
V. Roca y Hermanos, 20 San Pedro

Merchants, General, Wholesale.
Sebastian Comas, Santa Ana
Mari Ferrer y Ca., 18 Comercio
Ferrer y Ca., 5 San Juan
Ramirez y Oro, 15 Marina
Roca y Ca., 55 Iglesia
C. Rovira y Ca., 20 Marina
Treserra y Ferrier, 14 San Pedro
José Venecia, 68 Sariol

Paints and Varnishes.
(See Hardware, also Druggists.)

Photographers.
Ramon Garcia, 38 Christina
Elias Ibañez, Balmaseda

Physicians and Surgeons.
José Badia, 4 Salas
P. Francisco Codina, Iglesia
Joaquin Espinosa, 16 San Juan
Antonio Maria Lastres, 16 Sariol
Francisco Muñoz, Comercio
Góngora S. Rodriguez, Salas
Diego Tamayo, Santa Ana
Manuel F. Forment, 17 Salas
Victor A. Zugaste

Printing Establishments.
Martin y Ca., 10 Real
Francisco de B. Bertol, 61 Santa Ana
Alberto R. Segrera, 10 Sierra

Provisions, Etc.
(See Merchants, General.)

Saddlery, Trunks & Leather Goods.
Juan P. Espinosa, 23 Comercio
J. Arenal, 14 Comercio
Vicente Comas, 53 Real
Hernandez y Hermano, 22 Comercio
Gonzalez y Ca., 17 Comercio
Emilio Vigas, 20 Comercio
Bonifacio Celsis, 19 San Juan

Saw Mill.
V. Roca y Hermano

Sewing Machines.
(See Dry Goods.)

MATANZAS.

Population, 35,000.

Ales and Beer Dealers.

(See, also, Wholesale Grocers and Provisions.)

Acebal y Ca., 14 Azuntamento
José Gonzalez, 27 Borde
Robert A. Finlay, 18 Contreras
Pablo Hernandez, 50 Terry
Manuel Mascarrieto, 15 Cuba

Arms and Ammunition.

(See, also, Hardware.)

José Maria Mon, 7 Manzaneda
Antonio Rodriguez, 26 San Senerino

Banks and Bankers.

Branch of Banco Español de Cuba
Belleo Bea y Ca.

Boots, Shoes and Leather Goods.

Alonzo y Corrales, 55 Ricla
M. Alvarez y Ca., 69 Ricla
Antonio Anés, 18 Dos de Mayo
C. Borges y Horta, Ricla
Comas y Cañellas, 48 Ricla
I. Garcia y Ca., Contreras
Eloy Haedo, 37 Ricla
Juan Parera, 351 Contreras
Juan Pagés, 23 Dos de Mayo
Aedo Preciado y Ca., 87 Ricla
Justo Rodriguez, 61 Ricla
Eduardo Sanchez, 18 Dos de Mayo
Margarita Serra, 5 Oña,
Berros I. Solis, 40 Ricla
Antonio Sotolonga, 34 Tirry
Francisco Suarez, 16 Ricla

Booksellers and Stationers.

Luciano Carreño, 19 Ricla
" La Aurora," 28 Medio
" La Primera," 26 Ricla
Adolfo Estevez, 9 Azuntamiento
Sedana y Hernandez, 41 Ricla

Brokers, Money and Exchange.

Llama y Ca., Bajo Palacios
Isidor Ojoda, 60 Gelabert
Vidal Hermano, 41 Gelabert

Carriage and Wagon Makers and Dealers.

Juan B. Browert, 44 Sta. Isabel
Harbouro y Hermanos, 18 Tirry
José Lascano, 68 Esteban
Carricaburo y Hermanos, 20 Jovellanos
Juan Borga, 22 Tirry
Jose Guardiola, 11 Ayllon
Antonio Mon, Saborde

China and Glass Ware.

Ampudia y Fuentes, 10 Ricla
Ampudia y Marones, 88 Ricla
Menendez y Ca., 24 Ricla
Rivas y Ca., 30 Ricla

Cooperage.

J. F. Almirall y Ca., 4 Comercio
Simon Capó, 3 Comercio
Itumalde y Ca., 6 Refugio
Ledesma y Ca., 16 Zaragoza
Sainz y Ca., 6 Comercio

Dentists.

Isadoro Bonelli Zayas, 25 Contreras
José D. Anieva, 63 Contreras
Alfredo Carnot, 65 Gelabert
Ricardo Gordon, 70 Gelabert
Victor Normand, 76 Medio
Carlos W. Ruffo, 42 Contreras
Manuel B. Trelles, 98 Gelabert

Druggists and Chemists.

Artis y Zanetti, 15 Ricla
E. Alvarez y Ca., 51 Gelabert
Bartolomé Casañas, 25 Oña
Antonio Betancourt, 94 Daviz
Juaquin Boffil y Felin, 23 Sta. Teresa
Pedro Ginoulhiac, 42 O'Reilly
Juan Michelena, 121 Ricla
Rafalde Vargas Ruiz, 11 San Vicente
Eugenio Ginonlhiac, 40 O'Reilly
Domingo Lecuona, 123 Ricla
Diego Marchena, 35 San Jeande Dios
Miguel Montego, 115 Cuba
Ernesto Triolet, 49 Gelabert

Dry and Fancy Goods, Wholesale.

Bango y Menendez, 9 Ricla
Garcia, Garcia y Ca., 3 Ricla
Helguera y Nova, 49 Ricla

Dry Goods and Notions, Retail.

Aguirre y Arrastia, La Brisa, 5 Ricla
Alsina Joaquin, Juanita, 130 O'Reilly
Alvarez Juan, La Primavera, 16 Cuba
Alvarez Selzo, La Diana, 22 Cuba
Angulo y Gil, Andrés, La Central, 32 S. Ambrosio
Barquin Juan, La Primera, 90 Tirry
Bazar Parisien, 70 Medio
Belarmiro Antonio, Temblor, 6 Oña.
Blanco y Barquin, 122 y 124 Manzano
Caos y Ca., Manuel, El Niagara, 113 Manzano
Cortés Basilio, El Número Uno, 30 Tirry
Cubillas Manuel, Principe Alfonso, 8 Sto. Tomás
Cuervo Ventura, La Mar, 4 Santo Tomás, frente al
Delaz José Maria, La Quemazon, 30 Dos de Mayo
El Pasaje, Villa del Rey. Campos Servando

Dry Goods, Etc., Retail—*continued*.

Fernandez Rosendo, La Fisica Moderna, Medio, esquina'á Ayuntamiento
Fuente Marcelino de la, 144 O'Reilly
Garcia Bernardo, Flor de Cuba, 72 Tirry
Garcia Juana, Angel, 19 Cuba
Gaspar y Ca., El Bazar, 70 Ricla
Gomez Ramon, La Cubana, 33 San Vicente
Haza José de la, Ea Oriental, 43 y 89 Ricla
Haza y Murillo, Precios fijos, 9 Ricla
Helguera y Nova, La Norma, 49 Ricla
La Mia, 10 Sto. Tomás
Lamadrid Ruviera y Ca., La Marquesita, 144 O'Reilly
Lombana, Canellas y Ca., El Boulevars, 48 Contreras
Longar Evaristo, El Huracan, Plazo de Santo Tomás
Luis Domingo, Los Locos, 58 O'Reilly
Llanes Remigio, El Recreo, 9 Santo Tomás, y frente al, 4 y 5 El Trovador
Llorian Fonseca y Ca., Las Novedades, 61 Ricla
Hachin Hermanos y Ca., L. Gallo de Oro, 52 Ricla
Menendez Manuel, El Clavel, Plaza Santo Tomás
Menendez Manuel, La Numancia, 24 Dos de Mayo
Menendez Grande José, La Primavera, 146 O'Reilly
Montoto Ramon, Mi Esperanza, 16 Dos de Mayo
Muñiz y Ca., La Filosofia, 67 Gelabert
Nuñez Emilio, 141 Ricla
Pajares Manuel, 65 Tirry
Perez Ramon Diana, 20 Cuba
Perez Bernardo, El Vesubio, 23 San Antonio
Piñon José, El Fuego, 12 Magdalena
Quizá Cárlos, La Sultana, 16 Cuba, y Aguila de Oro, 146 O'Reilly
Riego Feliciano del, La Lealtad, 11 Ricla
Riego Laureano del, El Uracan, 6 Sto. Tomas, frente al
Riego Nicanor del, La Villa de Madrid, 110 O'Reilly
Rivas Almirall José, Cruz Verde, 33 Tirry
Rodriguez José, 1 y 2 Sto. Tomas
Rodriguez y Ca., Tomas R., La Primera, 104 Ricla
Ruiz Pedro, La Perla Cubana, 36 Ricla
Samper Blanco, L. Boulevard, 48 Contreras
Sanchez Hermano y Ca., 15 Gelabert
Tamargo y Ca., Gumersindo, El Cielo Cubano, 7 America
Valladares y Ca., Ricla
Venero Casimiro, La Hija del Pueblo, 55 Tirry

Furniture Dealers.

Alvarez y Martinez, 64 Ricla
Bethancourt y Hermano, 17 Gelabert
Marcial Rosell, 51 Ricla
Servia Hermano, 82 San Juan
Valentin Villa, 92 Ricla

Gas Company.

Matanzas Gas Light Company

General Commission Merchants.

G. Diaz, 39 Ricla
Beracierto y Pancorbo, 40 Gelabert
Vicente Foruo, 13 Versailles

Juan Oliva y Raya, 17 Contreras
Pancorbo, Vega y Ca., 59 Ricla
Riradulla y Castañeda, 194 Contreras
José A. Rodriguez, 19 Gelabert
Julio Yarini, 18 Manzano
Fredrick Drinkwater, 4 Contreras
I. Gonzalez, 42 Ricla
Juan Mir, 3 Pavia
Eduardo A. Sanchez, 9 Magdalana
Dally y Ca., San Ambrosio
Juan Hernandez, 117 Ricla
Jaime Marzol, 5 Ayllon
Fedrico Pereda, 1 Ayuntaments
Francisco Fernandez, 13 Manzano
J. Fernandez, 18 America

General Importing and Exporting Wholesale Merchants.

Peralta Almirall y Ca., 4 Commercio
Amezaga y Ca., 19 Ricla
G. Amezaga y Ca., 12 Tirry
Bellido Bea y Ca.,
Brinkerhoff y Ca., 17 Contreras
Joaquin Castañer, 8 Comercio
F. Castello y Ca., 1 Caminar
E. Crespo, 35 Gelabert
J. M. Clark, 19 O'Reilly
John J. D'Acosta, 18 Contreras
L. Deetgen y Ca., 20 Matanzas
Robert A. Finlay, 18 Contreras
A. Galindez y Aldama, 1 Recurso
Garcia, Bangoy & Ca., 3 Ricla
Heidegger y Ca., 30 Contreras
Melville y Ca., 24 Contreras
Mir y Ca. Muelle
Pablo Purcalla y Argui, 4 Tirry
J. Sainz y Ca., 5 Comercio
J. Suris y Ca., 14 Ricla
S. T. Tolon y Ca. 4 Contreras
A. B. Zanetti y Ca., 15 Ricla
Zanetti, Dubois y Ca., 5 Contreras

Groceries and Provisions, Wholesale.

Amezaga y Ca., 17 Ricla
Bea, Bellido y Ca., 30 Gelabert
L. Cancela y Ca., 2 Matanzas
Gomez y Ortiz, 112 O'Reilly
Grande y Ca., 294 O'Reilly
La Perla del Pueblo, 76 Tirry
Larragoiti, Ugarte y Ca., 33 Contreras
Martinez, Burel y Ca., 105 Ricla
Juan Martinez, 1 Pavia
Martinez, Perez y Ca., 1 Ricla
G. Suris y Ca., 14 Ricla

Hardware, Cutlery and Tools.

Hipolito Alvarez, 12 Ayllon
Alegria y Hermano, 3 Matanzas
Bea, Bellido y Ca., 28, 30 Gelabert
Pedro de la Fé, 2 Ricla
Francisco Fernandez, 18 Cuba
E Iturraide, 8 Dos de Mayo
"La Campana," 28 Tirry
Candido Mancebo, 103 Ricla
J. Oti y Ca., 7 Ricla
Juaquin Peña, 9 Ricla
Urrechaga y Alonzo, 58 Ricla

Hotels.

El Louvré
Hotel Frances
La Glorieta
El Caballo Blanco
La Lonja

Housefurnishers, Tinware, Etc.

Salvador Amigo, 133 Ricla
José Blanco, 22 Ricla
O. P Fernandez, 18 Cassillas
C. Martines, 140 Sta. Rita
Pedro Martoret, 117 Campostela
Pablo Saladrigas, 221 Animas

Ice Factories and Dealers.

Agustin M. Fernandee, 77 Ayuntamento
Enrique Mendes, Embareadero Blanco.
Luis Velasco, 13 Ayuntamento

Lumber and Building Materials.

Amezaga, Garcia y Ca., 12 Tirry
Galindez y Aldama, 2 Caminar
Fernando Malberti, 28 Medio
Pablo Percalla, 6 Tirry

Lamps, Oils, Etc.

Antonio Campos, 39 Gelabert
Domingo Cejas, 22 Ricla
Andrés Fernandez, 11 Ayuntamiento
Frederico Loredo, 91 Ricla
Antonio Ordoñez, 72 Gelabert

Musical Instruments, Pianos, Etc.

(See also Importing Merchants.)

Bea, Bellido y Ca.
Diego J. Martinez, 5 Ricla
José Figueras, 92 Contreras
Manuel Hervia, 22 Tirry

Newspapers and Periodicals.

Dcario de Matanzas (daily)
Boletin Oficial de Matanzas (daily)
La Comercial (daily)
El Ferro Carril (weekly)
La Aurora del Yamuri (weekly)
La Pluma de Oro (weekly)
La Propaganda Literaria (weekly)

Machinists and Machinery.

Juan Apolinario, 158 Merced
John Dally, Sta. Teresa
Carlos Hughes, 9 Tirry
Marques, Noriga y Ca., 14 Tirry
J. Marot y Sabrino, 44 Sta. Isabel

Paints, Oils, Varnishes, Etc.

(See Importers and Druggists.)

Photographers.

Molla y Menendez, 65 Ricla
C. Ruiz de Castro, 47 Contreras

Physicians and Surgeons.

Severino Abascal, 11 Ricla
Julian R. Baracean, 5 Jovellanos
José B. Betancourt, 31 Contreras
Benito Bordas, 127 Gelabert
José M. Camejo, 82 Ricla
José M. Caraballo, 97 Gelabert
B. Carbonell y Padilla, 85 Gelabert
Pedro M. Cartaya, 42 Gelabert
V. Casalins, 132 Ricla
E. Collado, 129 Ricla
Antonio Ferrer Sanchez, 15 Ricla
Antonio Fons, 95 Ricla
Santiago Garay, 28 Zaragoza
Ricardo Garcia, 18 Sta. Teresa
Miguel Guitart
Florencio Hernandez, 69 Navia
José E. Lopez Jimenez, 83 Gelabert
Adolfo M. Llorach, 94 Ricla
Domingo L. Madan, 15 Contreras
Roberto Mandan, 24 Contreras
Juan Mas, 62 Sta. Rita
Emelio Naranjo, 110 Ricla
Julio Ortiz, 36 Contreras
Octavio Ortiz, 21 O'Reilly
A. del Portillo, 50 Manzaned
Elijio J. Puig, 81 Tirry
Prudencio Querol, 70 Manzano
Julio M. Rodriguez, 37 San Juan
Manuel Q. Sanchez, 143 Manzano
Alberto Schmeyer, 39 Rio
Vicente A. Tomas, 92 Gelabert
Luis D. Tapia, 74 Contreras
Andres Ulmo, 119 Daoiz
Antonio Utrilla, 34 Espirito Santo
Felix Vera, 100 Contreras
Justo Verdugo, 81 Gelabert
Manuel N. Zambrana, 94 Manzano

Printers.

Diario de Matanzas, 1 Matanzas
Pedro Fullá, El Ferro Carril, 93 Ricla
Estebau Labastida, El Nacional, 69 Gelabert
Pio Campuzano, 6 Gelabert
Sedano y Hernandez, 53 Ricla

Saddlery and Harness.

José Artili, 114 O'Reilly
Manuel Dacosta, 26 O'Reilly
Eduardo Estin, 83 O'Reilly
Juan Soler, 60 O'Reilly
José Trémol, 102 O'Reilly

Sewing Machines.

Simon Castañedo, 18 Dos de Mayo
Antonio Fernandez, 72 Ricla
Manuel Salguiro, 79 Ricla
J. Venero y Ca., 67 Ricla

Ship Chandlers and Naval Stores.

Francisco Fernandez, 13 Mauzano
Bea, Bellido y Ca, 7 Ricla
Juan Fernandez, 18 America

Veterinary Surgeons.

Rafael Abril, 77 San Luis
Juan Balber, 1 Tirry
Juan Cariszueta, 18 America
Juan Carreres, 22 San Luis
Salvador Casanovas
Francisco Condon
Bonifacio Gomez
Basilio Izquierdo
Bonifacio Martinez
Ramon Perez
Adolfo Perez
Salvador Ramirez

Watches, Jewelry, Etc.

Francisco Cabral, 22 Dos de Mayo
Agustin Calderon, 52 Dos de Mayo
Simon Castañedo, 18 Dos de Mayo
Rufino Alvarez, 45 Ricla

Ramon Caballero, 63 Ricla
Camesañas y Rodriguez, Dos de Mayo
M. Fernandez y Ca., 36 Gelabert
Jimenez Becera, 42 Ricla
Justo Perez, 71 Gelabert
José Illas, 15 Ayuntamiento
Simon Rodriguez, 42 Dos de Mayo
Juan Templeman, 19 Ricla
N. Vuilleumier, 26 Ricla

Wall Papers.

(See Stationers.)

Undertakers.

Ricardo Arrais, 65 Daviz
José Perez, Sta. Teresa
Solano, 30 Ayuntamento
Valderrama y Quibus

NUEVITAS.

Population, 6,000.

Ales and Beer.

(See Groceries and Provisions.)

Agricultural Implements.

(See Hardware Dealers.)

Boots and Shoes.

Cárlos Anglada, Sol
Eugenio Cabral, San Francisco
Gil Quizada, San Francisco
Juan Sellen, Bonora
Tomas Varona, San José

Druggists.

Américo Silva, San José
Antonio Maja, 6 San José

Dry Goods.

Huerto, Alvarez y Ca., San José
Justo Alzago, Jan José
Marsella y Ca., San José
Mazuri y Hermano, San Fernando
Baldomero Miranbell, San José
Francisco Ruiz, 24 Marina
Ramon Suarez y Ca., San José

Furniture Dealers.

Miguel Bonora
Juan Borreo
Bartolome Ferrer
José M. Formosa

General Merchants.

Eduardo Aluija, 2 Marina
Santiago Arias, Bonora
Antonio Barran, San Francisco
Felix Berenguer, Paradero
Francisco Berenguer, Sol

Castro y Besoley, Marina
Aua Dinuendigo, San Fernando
José Antonio Fleites, Mariana
Juan Formosa, San Francisco
Pimo Gispert, Sol
Marano Lernio, Concepcion
Enrique Masjuan, San Francisco
Juan Mateu, San Miguel
Felix Pons, San Francisco
José Rabentós, San Francisco
Salvador Sabatella, Concepcion
Andrés Soririlla, 24 Marina
Agustin Torres, San Francisco
Ricardo Gibbs y Ca., Marina
Ruperto Cazares, 30 Marina
A. Roberts y Ca., 7 Marina
Rodriguez, Martinez y Ca., 26 Marina
Hijos de Sanchez Dolz, 5 Marina

Groceries and Provisions.

Andrés Arguelles, San José
Ruperto Casares, 30 Marina
Formosa y Ca., 7 dan Fernando
José Hipolit, Bonora
Juan Hiriart, Marina
Robert y Ca., 16 Marina

House Furnishing Goods.

Ramon Cordori, Concepcion
Angel Hernandez, Marina

Physician.

Gregorio Aguro

Trunks and Leather Goods.

Baudilio Cordori, Concepcion
Angel Hernandez, Marina

Undertaker.

Bartolo Ferrer, San José

PINAR DEL RIO.

Population, 6,000.

Ales and Beer.

(See Grocers and Provisions.)

Bankers.

Ricardo Fernandez y Ca.
José Maria Gil y Ca.
Juan Gonzalez, Hermanos y Ca.

Billiards.

Ricardo Fernandez y Ca.
Juan Gon
Jales y Hermanos

Booksellers and Stationers.

Marcos Mijares
S. Fornaqueros

Cigar Factories.

Alea y Fuentes
Francisco Alvarez
Miguel Ascuy
Bernabe Gonzalez
José Nieto
Sordo y Ca.

Dentists.

Ramon Muiña
Manuel Rey
Garedes Velez
Alberto Sales

Druggists and Chemists.

Dominguez y Legoburo
M. Rodriguez y Ca.
Tito Vila

Dry and Fancy Goods, Etc.

Guerra, Costales y Ca.
Ramon Buergo
Manuel Gonzalez
Ambrosio Muñoz
L. Sanchez

Furniture.

Manuel Alonso
G. Diaz
Gonzales, Hermano y Ca.
Francisco Urrutia

Groceries and Provisions.

Augustin y Patricio
Manuel Alea
Avendaño y Hermano
José Blanco
Dominjo Bosch
Cabo y Ca
Primo Campo y Ca.
Carriles, Cabo y Ca.
Jaime Cervera
Ramon Colvado
Juan Carona
Manuel Cortina
Manuel Escobar
Daniel Estelles
Agustin Fernandez
Fernandez, Guerra y Ca.
Marcelino Fernandez
Ramon J. Fernandez
Ricardo Fernandez y Ca.
Julian Galeterrera
Carlos Garcia
José M. Gil y Ca.
Gonzalez, Hermanos y Ca.
Ignacio Iglesias
Lopez y Ca.
Nicolas Lopez
José Martinez
N. Mazon
José Mendez
Daniel Mijans
Manuel Naveda
Nieto y Castillo
Esteban Ovaya
Bernardo Portilla
Recasens y Rodriguez
Ruiz, Sanches y Ca.
Sanchez Hermanos
Salarez y Ca.
A. Sordo y Ca.
Viquera y Ca.
J. Zabalo y Ca.

Hardware, Tools, Etc.

Jaime Barba
Juan B. Baylac
Demetro Martinez
José Puig
Francisco Seres

Hotel.

La Nueva Reforma

Physicians.

Agustin Anton
Guillermo Dolz
Cárlos Fortera
Juan A. Gandara
Eduardo Mont-Ros
Francisco Ramos
Antonio Rubio
José de la Trinchera

Surveyors.

José Comba
Marquez y Rivas
José Salazar

PUERTO PRINCIPE.

Population, 40,000.

Agricultural Implements.
(See Hardware Dealers.)

Ales and Beer.
(See Groceries and Provisions.)

Arms and Ammunition.

Juan Baylac Recres
Baltasar S. Quiñones, 43 Estéban
Antonio Ruiz, 22 Soledad
Manuel Solis, 5 Comercio
Ramon Villamyl, 50 Veina

Boot and Shoe Dealers.

Francisco Aleman, 74 Santa Ana
Higririo Agaudo, 23 Comercio
Pedro Cammaño, 74 Santa Ana
Sebastian Cassi, 13 Candelaria
Francisco Cueto, 36 Soledad
Cárlos Guerra, 110 Reina
Martin Iriarte, 67 Reina
Liberio Lazo, 146 Reina
Ramon de Quesada, 19 Soledad
Joaquin Raspall, 46 Soledad
Julian Vasquez, 15 Mayor
Luis de Zayas, 34 Soledad
Gonzallez, Morena y Ca., 29 Comercio
José Herrera, 10 Comercio

Dentists.

Alfredo Batista, 17 San Diego
Diego y Betancourt, Candelaria
Emilio Batista Escobar, 5 Cristo

Druggists and Chemists.

S. Mendes, 84 San Ramon
Enrique Herrera, 20 Comercio
Fernando Betancourt, 33 Soledad
Pedro N. Marin, 32 Santa Ana
Jose Nicolás Rodriguez, 43 San Juan
Ernesto Suarez, 23 Soledad
Manuel Valdez, 63 San Juan
Emilio Xiques, 37 San Diego
Francisco Ramirez, 56 Reina
R. Valdez, 22 Comercio
S. Varona, 23 Soledad
Manuel Xiques, San Diego

Dry Goods and Notions.

M. Alvarez y Ca., 19 Comercio
Flores Alvarez y Ca., 8 Comercio
Vicente Alvarez, 28 Comercio
Constantina Argudin, 22 Comercio
Lorenzo Arrazalain, 5 Soledad
Bernardo Espinosa y Ca., Comercio
S. Garcia, 79 Reina
Alvarez Garcia, 10 Comercio
Manuel Parnas y Ca., 24 Comercio

Domingo Perez, Comercio
Manuel Revilla, 24 Candelaria
Revilla y Lotorre, Soledad
Arsemode la Hoz, 2 Comercio
Bernardo Menendez, 29 Candelaria
Garcia Riego, 79 Reina
P. Sarundona, 29 Candelaria
M. Suarez, 10 Comercio

Furniture.

Vincente Barreto, 66 Santa Ana
Buenaventura Salia, 33 Candelaria

Groceries and Provisions, Wholesale.

Alegria y Ca., 51 Soledad
Belas Cazares, 7 Santiago
Carreras y Ca., 14 Comercio
Celis Juan Gonzalez, 39 Santa Ana
Mersella Gonzalez y C., 60 Reina
Juan Mandri y Ca., 27 Soledad
M. Esvas, 25 Soledad
Leucia Hermanos
M. Mas
José R. Vidal
Isaac Rodriguez, 70 San Diego
S. Serra y Ca., 26 Candelaria
Antonio Valladres, 10 Astillero
Juan Vanquez, 71 Caridad
Vilardell, Rovira y Ca.

Hardware, Tools, Etc.

Melliton Castelló, Candelaria
Corejuéla y Ca., 5 Comercio
E. Garcia y Ca., 19 Soledad
Marcella Gonzalez y Ca., 58 Reina
Marti y Pagés, 21 Candelaria
Obregon y Ca., 2 San Ignaci
Jose Rodriguez y Hermano, 18 Comercio
Silverio Valez, 22 Comercio

House Furnishing Goods, Etc.

Miranda Teópilo Acosta, 76 Candelaria
Pedro Esquirel, o Candelaria
Miguel Estrada, 3 San Ignacio
Alvaro Marin, San Ignacio
José Maria Marin, Reina
Justo Olazábal, 114 Reina
Bartolmé Pinarez, 38 San Ramon
Ignacio Porro, 45 San Fernandez
Anrique Rodriguez y Rodriguez, 29 Soledad
Calixto Sebada, 65 Santa Ana

Hotels.

"Cuatro Naciones"
"El Telegrafo"
Manuel Flores

Jewelers, Silversmiths and Watchmakers.

Antonio Barios
Lafon y Ca., 20 Comercio
Manuel Seijó, 17 Comercio
Enrich José Fabrésch, 23 Comercio
Aguiles Delatre, 6 Comercio
Leonardo Sonnier, 2 Comercio
José A. Vilaseca
José Ferres, 23 Comercio
Andrés V. Perez, 9 Comercio
Francisco Chames
Angel Gorrita
José Moret

Paints and Varnishes.

(See Druggists.)

Pianos and Music.

S. Machado, 21 Soledad

Photographers.

Rafael Delmonte, San Diego
Antonio Naranjó, Candelaria

Physicians and Surgeons.

G. Z. Aguero
Juan Arteaga, 10 Pobres
Melchor Bernal
Anacleto Betancourt, 52 Candelaria
Joaquin Roura
Antonio Fernandez, 35 Mayor
José S. Diaz
Juan Guzman
Esteban Moreto
Miguel Ramirez

Printing Establishments.

Montolier y Ca.
Luis Perez, 6 Candelaria
Puerta Rafael Zaldivar, 13 Mercederes

Saddlery and Harness.

José Argudin, 16 Comercio
Juan E. Bastian 13 Comercio
Blay y Ca., 10½ Comercio
Manuel Cardenas, 3 Santa Rita
Antonio Criado, 131 Reina
Juan Dulon, 20 Santa Ana
Melchor Guerra, 64 Reina
Fidel Lazo, 7 Ignacio
Sebastian Saez, 14 Comercio
Manuel Socarres y Ca., 11 Comercio

Sewing Machines.

(See Dry Goods.)

Trunks and Traveling Articles.

José A. Alonso, 70 Reina
A. Chavaney, 30 Comercio
Garcia y Gomez, 20 Soledad
José F. Miranda, 29 Candelaria
Rodriguez Hermano, 18 Comercio
Sanchez y Crespo, 23 Candelaria
Julien Vasquez, 15 Mayor
Silveiro Velez, 22 Comercio
José Alvarez
M. Cabada y Ca.
Covada y Hermano
Juan Dolon
Moreno y Hermano
Rijes, Papes y Sanchez
Lorenzo Torres

Undertakers.

E. Bourge
Ramon Beltran, 24 Santa Ana
Cláudio Cotifla, 23 San Diego
José Rodriguez Espinoso, 2 San Pablo
Luciano Gonzalez, Santa Ana
Ramon Gonzalez, 75 San Francisco
Estéban Hidalgo, 144 Reina
Manuel Hidalgo y Losada, 51 Contaduná
Libores Lazo, 24½ San Martin
Juan de Mata y Lastre, 21 Soledad
Agustin Ramirez y Ca., 80 Santa Ana
Buenaventura Salis, 23 Candelaria
Bruno Noriega

SAGUA LA GRANDE.

Population, 19,000.

Agricultural Implements.
(See Hardware Dealers.)

Ales and Beer.
(See Groceries and Provisions.)

Bank.
Agency, Banco Español

Billiards.
Arronte y Ca.
Lopez y Ca.
Gonzalez y Cardenas
Faruoso y Alonso
José Fernandez
Angel Noriega
Andres Pita
Manuel G. Pumariega
Juan A. Uriarte

Boots, Shoes and Leather Goods.
Pedro Gelabert, 23 Estrella
Pons, Magins y Ca., 55 Colon
Ripoll y Ca., 3 Gloria
Rivas y Ca., 1 Ramirez
D. Tomasion, 74 Colon

Carriage Manufacturers.
Pedra Biscaisac
Luis Maria Alfonso
Felix Maria Arenas, Progresa
Hilario Gañellen, Colon
Daniel Nuret, Ramarez
Juan Uriarte, Tacon

Cooperage.
Guardiola y Tejedor, 18 Colon
Joaquin V. Lavié, Linea Férrea
Ajuria Moré y Ca., Isabela de Sagua
Oña Moré y Ca., Isabela de Sagua
Joaquin R. Pita, Isabela de Sagua
Soniellan y Ca., Isabela de Sagua

Dentists.
José Arcadio Ausley, 84 Colon
Fernandez J. Guizola, 16 Oriente

Druggists and Chemists.
Alfredo Figueroa
F. Gutierrez
Abraham H. Iglesias
Luis F. Lopez
Machado Roa

Dry and Fancy Goods.
Manuel Alonso, 25 Plaza del Mercado
Anido y Hermano, Gloria
J. Gomez y Ca., 30 Estrella

José A. Lopez, 10 Gloria
M. Martinez y Ca., 99 Real
Menendez y Ca., 22 Gloria
Fariciano Pulido, Estrella
Indaiecio Ramos, 19 Estrella
Miguel Ramos, Estrella
Ramos y Hermanos, 71 Colon
Alvaro Rodriguez, 29 Estrella
Eugenio Rodriguez y Ca., Gloria
Martinez, Sarria y Ca., Colon
Somonte y Ca., 101 Colon
Villamil y Lamadrid, 68 Colon
Fernandez, Valdéz y Ca., 63 Real
Manuel Alenso, Mercado
Juan Buenrostro, Mercado
José Cabeza, Mercado
Florencio Elola, Mercado
Manuel Gonzalez Mercado
Infiesta y Ca., Colon
Tomas Lopez, I Ramirez
Rafael Montero, Marcado
Falriciano Pulido, Amistad
José M. Pulido, Mercado
Modesto Sastres, 70 Colon
Claudio Vidal, Mercado

Furniture.
Pedro Carreras, 8 Gloria
José Font, 3 Progreso
Pedro Rivas, 6 Estrella

Groceries and Provisions, Wholesale.
Blanco, Fort y Ca.
A. Menendez y Ca.
Tanset, Arenas y Ca.
M. Fernandez y Ca., 8 Cruz
Uriarte y Mijares, Gloria

Hardware, Tools, Etc.
Antonio Bustello
José E. Alba
E. Dieste y Ca.
Pedro Carbonell, 15 Estrella
Lopez y Castillo, 52 Gloria
Juan Toscano

Jewelers and Watchmakers.
Ramon Asing
M. Cancier y Hermano, 17 Gloria
Eduardo Pola, Estrella
Luis Willenmier, 4 Gloria

Jewelry, Etc.
José Diaz y Alvarez
Enrique Llunot

Lumber and Brick Dealer.
Llacuna, Pratt y Ca., 40 Merced

ISLAND OF CUBA. 181

Merchants, Wholesale.
Maribona, Laya y Ca.
Mora, Oña y Ca.
Moré, Ajuria y Ca.
Sordo, Huertas y Ca.
Vilar, Castellanos y Ca.

Merchants, Wholesale, Commission, Etc.
Amezaga y Ca.
Larrondo y Ca.
P. Lopez y Ca.
Diego Llacuna
Francisco Machado
Lopez y Castillo, 52 Gloria
Rodriguez y Hérmanos, 44 Gloria
Uriarte y Mijares, Gloria

Paints, Oil, Varnishes.
(See Druggists.)

Photographers.
E. Alvarez
J. Villa Lopez

Physicians and Surgeons.
Nicolas P. Bustillo
Nicolas Ealo
Manuel Manero
Francisco Martinez
J. G. Bisbal, Colon
Jaime Bonet, 50 Colon

Pedro Garcia, Isabela de Sagua
Manuel Iglesias, Esperanza
N. Manant, Cruz
Joaquin Planas, Colon
Antonio Zamora Reyes, 33 Amistad
E. F. Rodriguez, Calabasa

Printing Establishments.
Francisco Ballester, " El Comercio," Colon
Guardado y Pozo, " La Illustracion," 67 Amistad
M. Martin, 2 Cruz
Miguel Ramos, " La Armonier," 20 Estrella

Saddlery and Harness.
Artolo y Hermano, 18 Gloria
Francisco Fernandez, 8 Estrella
Manuel Lopez, 46 Colon
Guardiola y Tejédor, 78 Colon
Joaquin V. Lavié, Linea Férrea
Laureano Pequeño, Caraliatas
Someillan y Ca., Isabela de Sagua

Sewing Machines.
M. Carnicer, 25 Estrella

Trunks and Travelers' Articles.
(See Boots, Leather Goods, Etc.)

Undertakers.
Chavez y Parayuelos
Tomas Praderas
C. Zayas Vagas

SAN JUAN DE LOS REMEDIOS.

Population, 15,000.

Agricultural Implements.
(See Hardware Dealers.)

Ales and Beer.
(See Groceries and Provisions.)

Boots, Shoes, Trunks and Leather Goods.
Bernardo Bidegaray, Jesus Nazareno
Bidegaray y Ca., 20 Gloria
Ramon S. Hernandez, 20 Gloria
Meliton Veti, Amargura
Villa-Hermano y Ca.
Adolfo Palacio y Ca.
José Robasti y Ca.
Abraham Perez
Andres Garzon
Ramon Garzon
Ramon Hernandez
M. Torres

China, Glass and Lamps.
A. Noriega, 41 San José
Palacios y Ca.

Dentists.
E. M. Garcia
Amador Morales, 53 Amagura

Druggists and Chemists.
Esteban Paget
Luis Laredo Escobar, 43 Mercaderes

Dry and Fancy Goods.
Juan Madrid
José Moran
Penabad, Riego y Ca.
Pertierra Hermanos
Adolfo Quintana

Jewelers, Etc.
Ramon Fernandez
Francisco Marin
B. Perez

Furniture.
Juan Nariega
Antonio Perez, San José
Antonio Villa, San Juan de Dios

Groceries and Provisions, Wholesale.

Alvarez y Pando
José Maria Gomez, 26 Mercaderes
Fraga y Rey
José Piedra
Seigle y Hermano
Casimero Alvarez
Manuel Alvarez
Couto y Ca.
Rafael Duyos

Hardware, Tools, Etc.

Juan B. Noriega, 41 San José
José Gonzalez y Sobrino, P. De Armas
Rodriguez y Ca., 1 San Juan de Dios

Hotels.

Lorenzo Duyos
Juan Fernandez
Juan Piñeiro

Photographers.

Abelardo Barcedo, Sol
Miguel Seigle, Amargura

Physicians and Surgeons.

M. Bru y Gras, 1 Pastora
Paul Elizalde, 1 Aurora
Oria Rojas, 30 Gloria
Juan J. Dominguez
Fernando Gonzalez
D. Lagomasino
José H. Martinez
José M. Nuñes
F. Ramos
José Rojas

Sewing Machines.

(See Dry Goods.)

Undertakers.

Alejandro Testar, Jesus Nazareno
Testar y Evers

SANTA CLARA.

Population, 20,000.

Agricultural Implements.

(See Hardware Dealers.)

Ale and Beer Dealers.

(See Groceries and Provisions.)

Boots, Shoes, Trunks and Leather Goods.

Santiago Ote
José Maria Caribero, P. Mayor
P. Fernandez y Hermano, Santa Elena
Isidro Subirano, Santa Elena
D. Clacia y Hijos

Crockery, Glassware and Lamps.

Arias y Hermanos, Santa Elena
Pablo Bestard, Santo Espiritu
Bengochea y Ca., 6 Calon

Dentists.

Florencio de la Barreia, 1 Cuba
M. V. Lopez
Damian Silva

Druggists and Chemists.

Francisco Cañizares
José F. Acosta
J. N. Cristo, "La Salud" P. Mayor
Rafael Fleites, Santa Elena
Rafael Silva, "Santa Clara," 57 Santa Elena

Dry and Fancy Goods.

Amador Alday, 49 Santa Elena

Aramburo y Landaluze, Santa Elena
Mariano Campos, Cuba
Duñet y Ca., Carmen
Manuel Gari, Santa Elena
José Ibaceta, Santa Elena
Inclan y Ca., 2 Colin
Martinez y Ca., Calvario
Natalio Melendez, Calvario
Rafael Solar, Santa Ana
Isidro Subirano, 35 Santa Eleana
Victorlano Torre, Santa Elena
José Usal, Colon
Antonio Anido, Santa Elena
Florentino Muro, Calvario
Indalecio Muro, Santa Elena
Santiago Oti, Calvario

Furniture.

Manuel Primo Arias y Ca.
P. Castellanos
B. Perez
Moras y Ca.
Santos Suarez

General Merchandise, Retail.

Maria Alarcon, Santa Blena
Santiago Abarracin, Calvario
Salvador Aleman, San Agustin
Francisco Alvarez, Carmen
Modesto Alvarez, San Francisco Javier
M. Alvarez y Cueto, Santa Clara
Manuel Arias y Hermano, San José
Ramiro Armayor, Colon
Juan Arilta, Santa Rosalia
Sebastian Bello, Santa Elena
Francisco Carta, Condada
Ramiro Casonova, San Juan Bautista
Frederico Castellon, San Francisco Javier

Gen'l Merchandise, Retail—*continued.*

Aquilino Castro, San Isidro
Genaro Cayo, Sancti Spiritus
Santiago Chamorro, Union
José Corteguera, Condado
Sabina Coya, 11 Santa Clara
Theodoro Diaz, Santa Elena
Antonio Diepa, Union
Dominguez y Pedraza, San Francisco Javier
Perfeceo Duran, Condado
Mariano Farias, Conyedo
Juan Fernandez, San Miguel
Luis Fernandez y Hermano, Santa Elena
Eulogio Fuentes, San Francisco
José Gari, Colon
Desiderio Garcia, Condado
Filomeno Garcia, San Francisco
Gaibno Garcia, Calvario
José Garcia, 1 P. Mayor
Martias Garcia, Condado
Pola José Garcia, San Miguel
Garcia y Sixto, San José
Sebastian Sato, Santa Rosa
Cipriano Gonzalez, Santa Rosalia
Estanislao Gonzalez, Colon
Ramon Gonzalez, Colon
Gonzalez y Ca., San Francisco Javier
Bernardo Hernandez, Cuba
G. Hernandez Garcia, Colon
Hoz y Ca., San Francisco Javier
J. de Leon y Fleites, Santa Clara
Pedro Lleros, San Francisco
Cárlos Lopez, San Juan Susau
Manuel Lopez, San Agustin
Eduardo Machado, Sancti Spiritus
Juan Marréo, Condado
Benita Marti, Cuba
Faustino Martinez, San Juan Bautista
José Mendez, Condado
J. Muñiz y Garcia, San Miguel
Ceferino Muñoz, San Agustin
Juan Olma, San Mateo
Manuel Ortiz, San Francisco
José Pagés, Sancti Spiritus
Miguel Polacio, San José
Saturio Peguero, Cuba
M. Pozo y Valdez, Colon
Gabino Pupo, Cuba
Antonio Quintana, Sancti Spiritus
Antonio Quiñones, Cármien
M. Rodriguez y Gonzalez, San Miguel
Ramon Rodriguez, 2 Mayor
J. Ruiz y Perez, Santa Rosalia
J. Sanchez, San José
Matias Sastre, San Francisco
Manuel Serrana, San José
Ramon Vidal, San Miguel

Paints and Varnishes.

(See Druggists.)

Hardware, Cutlery, Tools, Etc.

Gregorio Bauguelo
Ignacio Lima
Alejandro Rodriguez

Jewelers and Watchmakers.

Valentin Charro, Santa Elena
Fernando Lama, del Busto, Calvario
Fernando Camas
José Solar, San Juan Bautista
José Maria Tobio, San José

Photographers.

Antonio de Leon
José Antonio Rojas
José Hernandez
Jesus Quiñones
B. Velero

Printers and Newspapers.

Antonio Bacaro
Dominguez Hermanos
Manuel Pichardo
P. Bestard y Dánla, Santo Espiritu
" Boletin Oficial " San Jose
" Eco de las Villas " Santa Ana
" El Orden " Calvario
Manuel Muñiz, San José
Manuel de Sed, San Francisco Janier

Physicians and Surgeons.

Francisco Aday
José Cornides
Arturo Ledon
Rafael Tristá, 16 Santa Clara
Rafael Martinez
Gabriel Pichardo

Saddlery and Harness.

Gabriel Ayala, San Juan Bautista
Mariano Demonech, Calvario
Florencio Muro, Calvario
Isidro Subirá, Santa Eleda
Plá Valdés, Diego

Undertakers.

B. Perez, San Francisco Javier
Teresa Perez, San Francisco Javier

Wall Paper.

Antonio Anido, Santa Elena

SANTIAGO DE CUBA.

Population, 42,000.

Agricultural Implements.
(See Hardware Dealers.)

Ales and Beer.
(See also Groceries and Provisions.)
Crori y Mestre

Arms and Ammunition.
José Duran
Pedro Galiano, 4 Gallo
Juan Moumas, 2½ Gallo

Bank.
Sucursal del Banco Español de la Habana

Bankers.
Bosch y Ca.
Brooks y Ca.
José Bueno y Ca.
J. F. Ferrer
Mas y Ca.
E. Ross y Ca.
Claudio G. Saenz y Ca.
Schumann y Ca.

Billiard Tables.
Sebastian Mestre, 84 Pazo del Rio

Booksellers and Stationers.
Juan Perez Dubrill
Torres y Ca.
B. Carona

Boots and Shoes, Wholesale.
Marabent y Ca.
Espina y Ca., 13 San Francisco
Flaquer y Ca., 12 Santa Tomás
Rio y Hermanos, 5 San Juan Neponuiceno

Bricks, Cement, Etc.
Alfonso Dugnesse
Angel Girandy
Martin Leon
P. Martinez
Tomas Vega

Coal Depots.
Estenger, Mesa y Galiego
S. L. Ros y Ca., 24 Mariana
Schumann y Ca., 31 Marina

Cooperage.
Emilo Hereau, Barracones
Felipe Ugas, 55 Enramadas

Crockery, Glassware, Lamps, Etc.
Font y Ca., Calvario

Cutlery.
Juan Beisert, 11 Gallo

Dentists.
Nicolas Armado
Ignacio de Arce, 24 Enramadas
Idelfonso Bravo, 9 Fermin
Demingo Ferrer, 41 San Geronimo
Eugenio G. Flamaud, 5 San Felix
E. Nicolae, 1 Trinadad
Tomas Ortiz, 50 San Francisco
Antonio Pizarro, 12 San Pedro
Nicolas Sanderval

Druggists and Chemists.
Luis Cárlos Bottino, 43 Marina
Frederico Arce, 2 Enrimadas
Miguel Millan, "La Trini'd," San Francisco
Jaime Padro, "Ros Dolores," 29 Enramadas
Tomás Padro, 65 Santo Tomás
Theobaldo Trenard, "La Reunion," 26 Marena
Causse y Ca., Santo Tomás

Dry Goods, Wholesale.
Sanchez, Hermanos, 9 San Francisco
Herrera, Rodriguez y Ca.
Hill y Casas
Serradel y Ca.

Dry and Fancy Goods, Retail.
Miguel Baringola, 67 Santo Tomás
José Bastard, 41 Gallo
Batlle y Hermano, 15 Santo Tomás
R. Cadilla y Hermano, 2 Providencia
Rafael Gener, 2 Barracones
Antonio Glas, Providencia
Pedro Macary, 15 San Pedro
Mas y Casanovas, 5 Santo Tomás
Mirabent y Sobrino, 11 Providencio
Montané y Hermans, 768 Santo Tomás
Musons y Primos, 67 San Pedro
J. Pagés y Ca., 9 San Juan Neponuiceno
Pagés y Via, 15 San Tadeo
Planas y Coll, 41 San Tadeo
Francisco Robert, 2 Enramadas
José Robert, 3 Santa Rita
Rafael Robert, 3 Santo Tomás
Juan Rossés, 74 Santo Tomás
Manuel Socias, 35 Gallo
J. Soler y Boscli, 9 Providencia
M. Soler y Boschi, 76 San Felix
Soler y Pimo, Enramadas
Vives y Felin, 4 Santo Tomás
Angelino Burges, 3 Gallo
Ana Codina, 55 San Francisco
F. Janer y Ca., 3 Enramanda
Agustin Lopez, 18 Gallo
Bartolome Mestre, 4 Santo Tomás
Juan Mestre, 11 Santo Tomás
Francisco Montané, 18 Gallo
Juan Roses, 74 Santo Tomás
Tomas Sagué, 51 Gallo
Schumann y Ca., 2 San Gerónimo
Paulino Seguin, 25 Gallo
Engenio Solá, 6 Enramadas

Furniture Dealers.

La Barcelonesa
Santiago Valet

Groceries and Provisions, Wholesale.

Abascal y Ca.
Almirall y Ca.
Antonio Bruna
José Berenguer
Cristobal Bory
José Maria Eguillor
M. Ferret
Jaime Font
Lluhi y Ca.
Mas y Ca.
Manuel Planas
Saenz y Ca.
Sala y Fornells
Vinas y Ca.

Hardware, Tools, Etc., Wholesale.

C. Branet y Ca.
Arturo Inglada y Ca.
J. Llovet y Ca.
Marques, Hermanos y Ca.
Sarda y Ca.

Hotels.

Hotel del Telegrafo
Hotel Hispano Americano

Ice Factory.

Alfredo Reaud

Jewelers and Watchmakers.

Antonio Armas
Bernado Calvo
Mariano Peña
José Rey
Pedro Casadesus, 14 San Tadeo
Daniel Gramatages, 19 Enramadas
Luis Anders
Johanes Otto
Pedro Yeras

Paints and Varnishes.

(See Druggists.)

Photographers.

Antonio Desquiron, 68 San Geronimo
Miguel Serra

Physicians and Surgeons.

Enrique Caminero, 7 Catedral
Federico Carbonell, 7 Euramada
Urbano Guinera, 9 San Garónimo
Filipe Hartman, 5 San Basilio
José Ortis Ramirez, 6 Carniceria
Eduardo P. Ros, 24 Marina
Luis Ros, 35 San Pedro
Magin Segarra, 14 P. Dolores
Manuel Yero, San Basilio
D. Vera y Arnaz
José Maria Aviles
José Bishe
Antonio Campiña

Joaquin Castillo
Silvestre Castillo
Ernesto Defaix
Federico S. Garcia
A. Portuondo Grillo
Pedro Echavarria
Manuel Jiminez
Miguel Migares
Eduardo G. Padro
Luis F. Portuondo
Manuel Salazar
Girado Vilardell

Printers and Newspapers.

"Bandera Española," Marina
Antonio Maria Casañnas, San German
Gabriel Dias, 31 Enramadas
"El-Boletin Eclesiastico"
"El Constitucional," 8 San Gerónimo
"El Progreso," 25 Enramades
Bernardo Martinez, 25 San German
C. Mestre, 14 Santo Tomás
Ravelio y Hermano, 1 Santo Tomás

Machinery and Machinists.

Manuel Aragon
Cardona Hermanos
Manuel Cespedes
Marcos Madariaga

Railways.

Ferro-Carril Del Cobre
Ferro-Carril de Juragua Iron Company
Ferro-Carril de Sabanilla y Maroto

Sewing Machines.

Rio Hermanos
Ricardo Valiente
Teresa Padreu, 18 Enramedas

Shipping and Commission Merchants.

C. Branet y Ca.
Brooks y Ca.
José Bueno y Ca.
Estenger, Messa y Gallego
Mas y Ca.
L. Ros y Ca.
Saenz y Ca.
Schumann y Ca.

Steamship Agency.

Bueno y Ca.

Sugar Dealers.

Galope y Hermanos, 3 Cristina
Antonio Norma, 37 Jaguey

Undertakers.

Casamor y Ca., 11 San Félix
Luis Felipe Ruiz
Francisco A. Bravo

Wall Paper.

Torres y Ca., 11 San Francisco
Juan E. Revello, 13 Enramadas

PLANTERS AND PLANTATIONS OF CUBA.

(The names here are arranged with the surnames first.)

A.

Name of Owner.	P. O. Address.	Name of Plantation.	Jurisdiction.
Abad José	On the estate	Santa Olalla	Sagua
Aballa (heirs of Francisco)	Mantanzas	Maria	
		San Francisco	Matanzas
Abreu Francisco N.		Buenavista	Cienfuegos
Abreu Manuel	Remedios	Soberano	Remedios
Abreu Juan G.	Havana		
Abreu y Leon José A.	"	Santa Rosalia	Jovellanos
Abreu y Montes de Oca		Perseverancia	
		Velloceno	Alacarenes
Acea Nicolas S.	Cienfuegos	Dos Hermanos	Cienfuegos
Acebedo José Antonio	Cardenas	Esperanza	Cardenas
Adam y Arteaga Luis	Puerto Principe	Uraho	Puerto Principe
Agramonte Francisco		San José	Cuba
Aguiar Francisco A.	Habana	Mercedes	Jarunco
Aguiar Tomas Francisco		Convenio	San Antonio
Aguilera Gabriel		Carmela	Villaclara
Aguirre Juan Santiago	Habana, Oficios	San Agustin	
		San Claudio	Guanajay
Alamo de Mojardin Josefa	Manrique	Perseverancia	Guantanamo
Alberini Herederos de Salvador			
Albir de Sarria	Animas	Rosario	Cienfuegos
Albornez Juan	Habana, Consulado		
Albuerne Tristan		Loma	Cardenas
Alcalde y Morrondo		San Isidro	Holguin
		Armonia	Alacranes
		Concepcion	Mantanzas
Aldama Miguel de Mercaderes, Estate of	Habana	Santa Ana	San Antonio
Alentado José Prudencio,	Ingenio	San José	Jaruco
Ales y Aldecoa Agapito	Matanzas,	Julia	Matanzas
Alfonso de la Guardia, de M Herederos	Habana, Prado	San Miguel	
Alfonso de Moliner Julia	Habana, Cerro	Julia	
Alfonso Anacleto		Tres Palmas	Bahia Honda
Alfonso, Herederos de Gonzalo	Amargura	San Silvestre	
Alfonso Herederos de Ricardo	Carmelo	Guayabo	Villaclara
Alfonso Herederos de Rosario	Habana	Esperanza	Villaclara
Alfonso y Madan Joaquin	Habana, Cuba	Resultas	
		Dorado	Habana
Alfonso Herederos, de Julian	Cuba		
Alfonso Rafael			
Aljaza, Herederos de José M.			
Almagro Juan Antonio	Habana, Lamparilla	Almagro - Cochinata	Bahia Honda
		Pepilla, Avalos	Jovellanos
Almeida Manuel		Prueba	Sagua
Almendares Herrera	Habana	Antilla	Colon
		San Jose	Habana
		Serafina	Colon
		Union	Habana
Alonso de Farres Herederos de Josefa	Habana	Horizonte	Colon
Aloy de Sarria Maria del Rosario		Soledad	Cienfuegos

ISLAND OF CUBA. 187

Name of Owner.	P. O. Address.	Name of Plantation.	Jurisdiction.
Altes y Baille Federico	Cardenas, Garnica	Mra. Sra. del Carmen	Colon
Alum Luis		San Jose Graibacoa	San Antonio
Alvarez Benito		Manaca Iznaga	Trinidad
Alvarez Cordoba Jose	Guanajay	Ntra. Sra. del Pilar	Pinar del Rio
Alvarez Herederos de Ana J.	Habana Cerro	Santa Ana	Alacranes
Alvarez Isabel	Ingenio	Monasterio	Sagua
Alvarez Pedro	Habana, Concordia		
Alvarez Robles	" "	Villegas	Santiago
Alvarez Sanchez Dolores	" Reina	Gnacamayo	Pinar del Rio
Alvarez Sardena y Ca.		San Francisco	Jovellanos
Alvarez y Campos		Perla	Matanzas
Alvarez y Guillen Lucas		Nueva Felicia	Cardenas
Amaro Ramon	San Antonio	Armonia	San Antonio
Amoros Crego y Ca.	Matanzas	Palma	Matanzas
Amoros Herederos de José	Matanzas, Contreras	San José de Bagaez	Nueva Paz
		Felicia	Sa. Ma. del Rosario
Amoros y Alemany	Matanzas, Contreras	Carmen	Matanzas
Andren José	Habana Real, 17 Marianao	Panchita	Colon
Angulo Antonio y Herederos de Amoros	Matanzas, Contreras	Diamante	Matanzas
Apodaca e Hijos Isabel de	Habana, Bnos Aires 41 Cerro	San Francisco de Asis	Sagua
Arango Domingo y J. Kiessel	Habana, Cuba 123	Teresa	Guines
Arango Herederos de Felix I.		Penas Altas	Jaruco
Arango Julian	Habana, San Francisco	Semillero	Colon
Araoz y Ca. Herederos de Miguel	Habana Tejadillo	Palmarejo	Trinidad
Araoz y Rodriguez	Sagua, Colon	Triunvirato	Sagua
Aranjo A. G. y N. Hernandez		Firmeza	Cardenas
Arcosy Herederos de Manuel de Leon, Marques de	Habana, Aguila 123 y S. Rafael	Progreso Jesus Maria	Guines
Arche Manuel	Isabela	Santa Julia	Sagua
Arguelles Dias Carlos	Habana, Cerro	Destino	
		Santa Isabel	Cardenas
Ariosa Agustin	Habana, Amargura	San Agustin	
Ariosa Gutierrez	Habana, Amargura	San Fe	Remedios
Armas Agustin y Florencio	Ingenio	Flora	Alacranes
Armas de Plasencia Socorro	Socorro	Socorro	
Armas y Cabrera José		Santa Rosalia	Colon
Armas y Hermanos		San Miguel de Caobas	Matanzas
Armenteros Francisco de	Habana, Peña Pobre	Margarita	Sagua
Armenteros y Castillo Pedro	Habana, Manrique	Emilia	Madruga
Armildez de Toledo Condesa	Ansente, Aguiar	Tinguaro	Jovellanos
Arozarena Herederos de Maximo	Galiano, 105	Mercedes	
	Habana, Mercederes	Merced la	Bahia Honda
Arrastia Viuda de Juan de	Habana, Sol, 54	Dos Hermanas	Pinar del Rio
Arrechea Simon		Cacaiban	Trinidad
Arriaga Virragarse y Ca.	Cienfuegos	San Esteban	Cienfuegos
Arrieta Francisco	Habana, Ptes. Grandes	Flor de Cuba	Colon
Arroyo y Ca.	Habana, Sol, 4	San Lorenzo	Matanzas
Arteaga y Cervantes Isidoro	Habana, Chacon, 19	Fraternidad	Cardenas
Arruerabena Francisco		Santa Rosalia	
Arruerabena y Trujillo		Donostilla	Cienfuegos
Asca y Terry		Esperanza	
Aveille Concurso de Pedro	A. Sagua	Delta	Sagua
Arerhoff Herederos de Mariana	Habana, Prado, 94	Providencia	Guanajay
Aviles y Loblac	Habana, Dorticos		
	Cienfuegos	Encarncion	Cienfuegos
Ayme y Hermanos		Resignacion	Cardenas
Azcuy Manuel de Leon		Jesus Maria	Neuva Paz

B.

Name of Owner.	P. O. Address.	Name of Plantation.	Jurisdiction.
Baez Manuel	Ingenio	Lucesita	Sagua
Bages Juan		El Corojal	Puerto Principe
Bango N.		San Pablo	Matanzas
Bango y Avellanal		San Francisco	Alacranes
Bannatyne y Astrils Roberts		Gamborino	Matanzas
Balsinde Ramon	Habana, Prado	Conchita	Mariel
Baralt Joaquin	Habana, Aguila 104	San Marcos de Jagua	Cuba
Barberia de Lasa Rita	Habana, Ppe. Alfonso	Casnalidad	Matanzas
Barberia José Ramon		Sirena	
Bardaji Julian	Habana, Po. de Tacon	Santa Barbara	Guanajay
Barnadas G. y Muro R.		San Francisco	Colon
Baro y Blanchart Salvador Ignacio	Matanzas	San Miguel	Remedios
Barreto Conde de Casa Herrera	Habana, Oficios 76	Rio Hondo	
		Salvador	Sa. Ma. del Rosario
Barroso Fabian		Ecuador	Bejucal
		San Vicente	Jovellanos
Barroso y Amaro		Andorra	Cardenas
Barroso y Sanchez	Ingenio, Central	La Caridad	Nuevitas
Bassave Pedro R.	Habana Salud	Nieves	
		Trinidad	Mantua
Batista José Santos		Santa Margarita	Matanzas
Bauza Estraton Luis y Manuel	Habana	Jagney	Remedios
Bauza Francisco G.	Ricla 6, Cuba 28	Concepcion	Colon
Belanstegoitia Domingo	Habana	Juguetillo	Matanzas
Bell Sucesion de J. Alejandro		Perseverancia	Cuba
Benitez Concurso de Antonio		San Laureano	
Benitez y Hermanos	Habana, Cerro 627	Fenix, El	Matanzas
Beranes Juan		Reforma	Cuba
Berenguer Antonio		La Pastora	Villaclara
Bernal y Sanchez M. y J. E.		El Congreso	Puerto Principe
Betarte y Arenas	Sagua, Colon 54	Vista Hermosa	Sagua
Buenza y Cartaya		Urbasa	Remedios
Biard Beauregard Juan	Cardenas	Virginia	Jovellanos
Bishoff y Compania	Caibarien	Prudencia	Remedios
Blanco Manuel		Rosalia	Cienfuegos
Blanco Quiebra de Pedro	Habana	Salvador (a) Bottino	Matanzas
Bocalandro José Francisco		Desempeno	Guines
Bofill Magdalena		Buenaventura	
		Occano	Matanzas
Bofill y Setien		Iberia-Reforma	Remedios
Boher, Menendez y Ca.	Habana, Reina	San Lorenzo	
Bolanos	Habana	Rosario	Jaruco
Bolivar y Ca., J. M.	Mercaderes	Felicia y Puenta Felipe	Sagua
Bombalier Carlos y J. Brito		Dolores	Matanzas
Bonifax Ramon		San José	Villaclara
Boril de Fabre Antonia	Habana, Habana	Sileno	Cuba
Borme Herederos de Luis vi		San Rafael	San Antonio
Borrego José Aurelio		Industria	Gibara
Borrell Federico y Eloy		Guaimaro	Trinidad
Borrell Ramon	Habana, Oficios	San Isidro	Santiago
Borron Hermanos Silvestre	Ingenio	Dos Amigos	
Borruci Francisco		Central Recuerdo	Sagua
Borzon, Gazmui y Hermano		Apolo	
Bou y Marill Herederos de	Habana, Aguiar	La Paza Molas	Matanzas
Boyd Herederos de		Florida	Cardenas
Bravode Castillo Antonia		San Rafel	Cuba
Brooch, Hermanos y Ca.		Soledad	Guantanamo
Brook y Ca. Herederos de Teodoro		San Sebastian	Cuba
Brunet Conde		San Nicolas	Cienfuegos
		Occitania	
Brunet de Hemely y Ca., Catalina C		San Pedro	Trinidad
Brunet y Ca., C		Palmarito	Colon
			Guantanamo

Name of Owner.	P. O. Address.	Name of Plantation.	Jurisdiction.
Bruzon Dolver, Viuda de Portillo	Habana, Cuba	Santa Rita	Sagua
Buchpalal y Soler		Merced	Cuba
Bueno Sucesion de José D.	Habana, Monserate	Belloza	
		California	
		Confluente	Guantanamo
Bueno y Ca., Juan		San Miguel	Cuba
Biudes Herederos de Ramon	Habana, Monserate	Adelaida	
		Europa	
		Santa Rita	Colon
Bulver Manuel G.		Santa Rita	Bejucal
Burgness é Hijos B.		Prudencia	Remedios
Bustamante G. y Herederos de Eguiler	Habana	Corolina	Cardenas

C.

Cabanilla Carmen		Manacas	Cienfuegos
Cabello Felix	Habana, S. Nicolas 55	Luisa y Antonia	Sagua
Cabrera Dionisio G		Amparo	
Cabrera Ramon C.		Donacion	Cienfuegos
Cabrera y Hernandez	Habana, Principe Alfonso 322	Cristalina	
Caurez Zacarias		Leandra	Matanzas
Cairo Andres	Habana, Aguacate 125	San Vicente	Sagua
Caithness Maria	Habana, Oficios	Santa Catalina	Colon
Calero Sebastian P.		Santa Teresa	Cienfuegos
Calichs José	Aguacate 42	Libano	Sagua
Calvo Aguirre Manuel	Habana, Aguiar 98	Portugalete	Jaruco
Calvo Fernando		Pasiego	Sagua
Calvo Herederos de Catalina		San Luis	Matanzas
Calvo Ignacio	Habana, Cerro 613, Oficios 19	Empresa	Colon
Calvo y Herrera Pedro	Habana, Cerro 625	Dolores	Matanzas
Calvo y Laserie	Sagua, Progreso 2	Flor de Sagua	Sagua
Camacho Mercedes	Ingenio	Triunfo	Sagua
Cameron Herederos de Pedro	Matansas, Santa Teresa	San Sebastian	Matanzas
Camino Eduardo del		Constancia	
		Laberinto	Cienfuegos
Caneda Pedro A.	Ingenio	San José	Cardenas
Canal Herederos de Campanyá Salvador		Constancia	Pinar del Rio
		Santo Tomas	Gibara
Campo Alegre Conde de	Habana, Oficios 13	San Lorenzo	Jaruco
Campo-Florido Marques de	Habana, Paula 2	Encarnacion	Guines
		Tivotivo	Jaruco
Campo Manuel Maria		Encarnacion	Colon
Campo Santo Marques de Vizconde de la Torre		Concordia	Guines
		Encarnacion	Colon
Campos Antonio Maria	Habana, Habana 200	San Francisco	Nueva Paz
Campos y Francisco		Dolores	Bejucal
Campos y Diez José Maria	Blanco 36	Casa Blanca	Gibara
Campos y Marroqui Damso del	Habana, San Francisco 3	Delirio	Cardenas
Campos y Rivas Domingo		Santa Maria	
Carboy Canto José	Remedios	Santa Catalina	Remedios
Carbonell Antonio y E. Sierra		Sitges	Cienfuegos
Carbonell José		Adela	Guantanamo
Carbonell Herederos de Josefa - Depositario M. C. Blanco		Trinidad	
		Santisima	Habana
Cardenal Manuel		Galope	San Cristobal
		Reforma	Matanzas
Cardenas Herederos de Isabel	Habana, O'Reilly	Candelaria	Guanajay
Cardenas Herederos de Josefa de	Habana, Cuba, Dominguez 4	Toro	
Cardenas Herrera Francisco		Angiula	Cardenas

Name of Owner.	P. O. Address.	Name of Plantation.	Jurisdiction.
Cardenas Luis		Alegria	Cienfuegos
Cardenas Nicolas de	Calzada del Cerro 480	Dos Hermanos	Bejucal
Cardenas Simon de y E. Diago	Calzada, Cerro 546	Fermina	Jovellanos
Cardenas y Ortega Nicolas	Calzada, Trocadero	San Rafael	Guines
Carol y Artigas Jose		Santa Rita	Cardenas
Carrera Hijos de Jose J.	Habana, Oficios 74	Concordia	San Antonio
		Gratitude	Jovellanos
Carret y Hermano Jose		San Pablo	Trinidad
		Boca Chica	Cienfuegos
Carrillo Andres	Habana, Pena Pobre 20		
		Vega	Colon
Carrion Joaquin de		Mercedes	Guanajay
Cartaya, Herederos de Catalina		Encarnacion	Remedios
Cartaya Micaela	Cardenas, Real	San Vicente	Cardenas
Carrajal y Cabanas Francisco	Marianao 70		
	Sto. Domingo	Cabanas	Santiago
Casa Calderon Marques de	Habana, Oficios 70	San Juan de Dios	Jaruco
Casalcos Ramos Miguel		Mercedes	Alacranes
		Antonia	Cardenas
Casanova Antonio	Habana, Hotel Inglaterra	Fantes	Cienfuegos
Casanova Inocencio	Ansente	Armonia	Jovellanos
Casanas Antonia, y J. R. Escobar,		Antonia	Cardenas
Casanas Frederico y Bartolome	Matanzas, Contreras 9	Dos Rosas	Cardenas
Casas y Ca. Julian F.	Habana, Ancha del Norte,	Central Victoria	Colon
Castaneda Luis Miguel	Ingenio	Candelaria	Bahia Honda
Castaner Salvador	Matanzas, Gelabert 56	Luisa	Cardenas
		Santa Rosalia	Alacranes
Castaner y Ca.	Ingenio	Jicotea	Guines
Castill-Florit Marquesa de	Habana, San Pedro 14	Santa Elena	Matanzas
		Sobrante	Matanzas
Castro y Amerhazurra		Central San Juan	Cardenas
Castro y Arguelles	Cardenas, Ayllon	Trinidad	Jovellanos
Castro y Rabasa, Ignacio	Habana, Escobar 105	Santa Elena	Guanajay
Catasio Hermanos y Ca.		Rio Grande	Cuba
Caturla José de	Remedios, Pl. de Armás 2		
		Dolores	Remedios
Cause, sucesor de Juan Bautista		Cujabo	Caney
Cavarroca Felix	Matanzas, O'Reilly 20	Domingo	Sagua
Cejas Leandro		Joséfita	Jovellanos
Cejero Serajiro	Ingenio	Panchita	Sagua
Cespedes Clara	Habana, Prado 94	Guayacan	Gibara
Cespedes Emilio		Carmen (a) Jardin	Cardenas
Cespedes Emili y Rosa	Habana, Buenos-Aires	San Salvador	Sagua
Civico Domingo		San Juan Nepomarceno	Jaruco
Clemente Manuel		Maravilla	San Cristobal
Colome Herederos de Juan A.		Baracoa	Santiago
Compte y Sule	Habana, Enna 2	Luciana	Remedios
Confligny y Ortiz Hermanos	Matanzas, O'Reilly 41	Santa Catalina	Cardenas
Contreras Rosa Viuda de Pedro N. Abrue	Matanzas, Prado 72	Dos Hermanos	Villaclara
		San Francisco	Cienfuegos
Coppringer Cornelio C	Cerro 871	Santa Teresa	
Cordoba Bernardo	Habana 68	Jaspre	Sagua
Corlina y Aldera Juan M		Algoita	
		Enregueta	Cardenas
Crespo de la Serna J. Luis	Matanzas, Gelabert 35	Dolorita	Cardenas
		San Juan	
		Teresita	Matanzas
Crespo y Calva		San Vicente	Sagua
Crespo y Laborde		Constancia	San Antonio
Crullas Miguel		Tomas de Barreto	Gibara
Cruz Francisco de la		Santá Elena	Caibarien
Cruz Juana Vin de la Roldan		Santá Clara	Holguin
Cuesta Hermanos Bonifacio	Habana, Aguiar 101	Mercedita	Guanajay

Name of Owner.	P. O. Address.	Name of Plantation.	Jurisdiction.
Cuesta y Terga, Pedro de la		Vega	Matanzas
Cullen José Diego		Manuelita	Neuva Paz
Culloda Juan		Trinidad	Sagua
Cutting Roberto		San Juan de Wilson	Cardenas
Chacon Juan de	Habana, Cerre 795	Encarnacion	Colon
Chamberlain Francisco	Sagua	Dos Rios	Sagua
Chapman Guillermo		Colombia	
		Santa Maria	Gibara
Chappotin Francisco	Habana, Ancha del Norte 34	Concepcion	Guanajay
Chavez Maria Regla y Dolores G		San Francisco de Asis	Cardenas

D.

Dardallo y Matos		Aljovia	Bejucal
Davalos y Garcia Nicolas		Virgen Maria	Bejucal
Davalos y Maza	Matanzas, O'Reilly, 1	Gabriela	Matanzas
Delcourt Teodoro y Agustin		Reunion Deseada	Matanzas
Delgado Ciriaco	Sagua Progreso	San Francisco	Sagua
Delgado Enslaquio	Santo Domingo	Panchita	"
Delgado e Hijos Ramon		Carmen	Cardenas
Delgado Felipe A.	Cardenas, Garnica	San Felipe	Colon
Delgado Francisco	Habana, Acosta 78	San Antonio	Sagua
Delgado Herederos de Baldormero	Habana, Justiz 3	Maria Josefa	"
Delgado José de Jesus	S. Miguel 51	San José	Cardenas
Delgado Lorenzo	Matanzas, Gelabert 20	Santa Lucia	Matanzas
Delgado Luis	Ingeno	Santa Emilia	Sagua
Delgado Urbano Francisco		Dolorita	Jovellanos
Delgado y Hernandez R.		Santa Gertrudis	Cardenas
Depestre Herederos de Edmundo	Ingenio, Luisa	Julia	Remedios
Depestre y Hermano	Sagua	Luisa	Sagua
Deschapelles Elena B.		Eden Park	Colon
Deville Eduardo	Matanzas, Galabert	Arcadia	Matanzas
Diago Ramon y Enrique A.	Habana, Compostela, 20	La Paz	Jovellanos
Diaz Antonio	Sagua la Grande	Socorro	Sagua
Diaz Antonio G. y Teodosio		San José	Matanzas
Diaz Marcos J.		San Pedro	
Diaz Mariano		Tartesio	Sagua
Diaz Piedro Francisco	Habana, Prado 47	Andrea	Bejucal
Diaz Suiza Francisco		Jesus Maria	
Diaz Urzurun Luis	Habana, Empedrado	Arco Iris	Alacranes
Diaz Villegas J. Sucesores de Diaz de y Ca., J.		Josefa Magnaraya	Cienfuegos
Diaz y Ca., J.		Jicarita	Alacranes
		Asturias	Villaclara
Diaz y Ramos			
Dihigo y Juan Pedro			Cardenas
Dihigo y Mestre	Habana, San Ignacio 110	Santa Rosa Dominicos	Matanzas
Dols Jacinto		San Lorenzo	Remedios
Dominech y Ca., Manuel Maria		Ntra. Sra. de Regla	Colon
Dominguez Alfonso Eugeno	Matanzas, Gilaberto 100	Santo Domingo	Bejucal
		San José	Matanzas
Dominguez Bernardo	Habana, Prado 35	Maria	Remedios
Dominguez Francisco J.		San Francisco	
Dominguez y Fumero		Nueva Esperanza	Matanzas
Dominguez y Lacalle		Caridad	Matanzas
Dorticos Pedro E.		Flora	Cienfuegos
Dos Hermanos Marques de	Habana, Aguiar 59	Nazareno	Bahia Honda
Drake y Hermano Carlos		Saratoga	Matanzas
Duany Calixto y Octaviano		S. Geronimo de Jagua	Cuba
Duany Condesa de		El Carmen	Cuba
Duarte Bernardo		America	Villaclara

Name of Owner.	P. O. Address.	Name of Plantation.	Jurisdiction.
Duarte Herederos de Antonio	Habana, Cerro San Elias 12	Ruley	Guanajay
Duarte Ignacio	Calzada del Cerro	Diminuto	Villaclara
Duarte y Betarte	Zaragoza, 23 Cerro	Macagua	
Du-Bouchel Herederos de Blas	Tacon 2	Destino	Colon
Ducoman Quiebra de		Jatinicu	Cuba
Duenas José y Concepcion		Tentativa	Jovellanos
Duenas y Ca., Juan		San José de Caridad	Colon
DuQuesne Marques de	Habana, Habama 198	Alberro	Sta. Maria Rosario
DuQuesne Rita	Habana, Habama 198	Casnalidad	
		Admiracion	Cardenas
		Capitolio	
Duran y Borras Arturo	San Nicolas 118	San Antonio Alegre	Bejucal
		Antonio	Jaruco
Duranona Herederos de Francisco	Habana, Oficios 36	Dos Adelas	Guanajay
	Habana, Marianao Rey 3	Pilar	Jaruco
		San Francisco	
		Toledo	Habana

E.

Echarte Dolores	Habana	Atenas	Sagua
Echegoyen Hanchol Pedro		Helvecia	Cardenas
Echenique y Ca.	Cardenas	San José Valiente	Sagua
Echevarria y Martinez Domingo	Habana, Paula	Cuatro Pasos	Matanzas
Elizalde Juan Bautista	Habana, Vedado	Guerrero	
		Paz	Colon
Elizalde y Hermanos Salvador	Matanzas, O'Reilly	Elizalde	
Elgnea Francisco	Ingenio	Arbolde Guernica	Sagua
Elosegui Pedro		San José	San Antonio
Emard Juan y Gonzalo Molina		Amelia	Bejucal
Emerson Herederos de	Sagua	Palma	Sagua
Escarza Sotero	Habana, Ancha del Norte	Portugalite	Cienfuegos
Esnard Herederos de Juan		Isabel	Colon
Espino Herederos de Juan y Vegamer	Habana, Cuba 98, y Acosta 21	Vegamar	Sagua
Espinosa Dolores	Ingenio	Bella Vista	
Espinosa José de la O.		Sociedad	Alacranes
Espinosa Remigio		Reglito	Sagua
Espinosa y Hermano	Sagua, Gloria 26	San Fernando	Sagua
Espinosa y Nocedo		San Cristobal	Colon
Estevez Herederos de Juan Bautista		Recurso	Cienfuegos

F.

Fabio y Hermano		Central Batalla	Colon
Fabre Eugenia		Prosperidad	Guantanamo
Fabregas Joaquin	Sagua Amistad 53	Diamante	Villaclara
Fanjul Juan		Petrona	Matanzas
Farebo Juan		Altamira	Cienfuegos
Fanra Sucesion de		Santa Fé	Guantanamo
Febles y Flores, José y Juan		Jan José y Animas	Matanzas
Fernandez Castellano Fernando		Pastora	Matanzas
Fayta José		La Ceiba	Trinidad
Fernandez Criado y Gomez Antonio	Habana	Anton	
Fernandez Criado y Gomez Hermanos	Habana 66	Ntra. Sra. de Neda	Colon
Fernandez de Castro Pedro	Habana, Aguiar 108½	Ntra. Sra. del Carmen	Jaruco
	Habana, Prado 90		San Antonio
Fernandez de Lara Joaquin	Habana, Aguacate 122	Victoria	

Name of Owner.	P. O. Address.	Name of Plantation.	Jurisdiction.
Fernandez Delgado José R.		Lucrecia	Matanzas
Fernandez Herederos de José Belen	Habana, Paula 3	Santa Ana	Remedios
Fernandez Herederos de J. Santos		Atrevido	Alacranes
Fernandez Herederos de Victor	Ingeno	Caridad	Sagua
Fernandez José		San José	"
Fernandez Lopez	Sagua, Gloria 42	Jagua	Villaclara
Fernandez Manuel I.	Habana, Companario 131	Las Charcas	Sagua
Fernandez Mederos José Maria		Caney	Colon
		Colombia	Colon
		Laberinto	Jovellanos
		Resolucion	
Fernandez Mercedes		Palma Cubana	Cardenas
Fernandez Mourat F.		El Salvador	
		San Miguel	Henra Paz
Fernandez Pastora		Mercenas	Colon
Fernandez Pedro Lamberto	Habana, San Ignacio 50	Union	Jovellanos
Fernandez Piloto Francisco	Cardenas, Ayllon	Conquista	
		Dos Hermanas	Cardenas
Fernandez Rafael	Sagua	Socorro	Sagua
Fernandez Rubalcaba José	Ingenio	Socorro	Sagua
Fernandez Tomas		Mayaguara	
		Saira Familia	Trinidad
Fernandez Valentine		La O.	Villaclara
		San Antonio de Padua	Remedio
Fernandez Vallin Antonio		Ofo de Agua	Matanzas
		Vista Hermosa	Madruga
Fernandez y Valdes		Central Destino	Colon
Fernandina, Herrera Garo José Maria Condede	Habana, Mercaderes, 4	Angosta	Guanajay
		Santa Teresa	Colon
Ferranz Francisco, Lorenzo y M. Pulido	Baratillo	San Pedro	Sagua
Ferreira Jose Maria	Lealtad 106	Merceditas	Cuba
Ferrer Benigno		Mariel	"
Ferrer Casto		Quemado	"
Ferrer Castulo		Borgita	
Ferrin Juan	Cardenas	Palestina	Jovellanos
Fiol Juan Agustin	Habana, Tejadillo	Jesus Maria	Guanajay
Flaquer Antonio	Sagua, Gloria 107	Manuelita	Sagua
		San Antonio	"
Flores Apodaca Roman	Habana, Galiano 122	Caridad	Colon
		Desquite	
Flores Hernandez, Dolores		Loteria	Jaruco
Fouriner y Cases		San Jose	Guantanamo
		Belencita	Remedios
Font Herederos de Juan			
Font Ramon	Habana, Salud 28	Pasora	Sagua
Font y Suris Jose		Trinicu	Sancti-Spiritus
Forcade Gabriel	Habana, Cuba 52	Porvenir	Colon
Fornaris y Corral Felipe	Habana, San Nicolas 122	Jésus Maria	Guanajay
Fornaris y Corral Manuel	Habana, Tacon 2	Garro	Santiago
Fortun Jose Maria			
Marques de Placetas	Remedios	San Andres	Remedios
Fowler Guillermo		San Tranguilimo	Cardenas
Fresneda Manuel	Habana, Campanario	Merceditk	
Fresneda Mercedes	Habana, Amistad 54	Nueva Empresa	Guines
Freville H de		Nieves	
Fritze y Ca.		Buena Vista	Trinidad
		Las Breas	
Fuente Lazaso		Perla	Matanzas
Fuentes José			San Antonio Bejucal
Fumero Josefa	Habana, Galiano 26	S. José de la Caridad	Bejucal
Fumero Juan Bautista		San Rafael	Matanzas
Fumero Pablo	Matanzas S.	Santa Teresa	Jaruco
Fumero y Hermanos Jose A.	Juan de Dios 66	San José	Alacranes

G.

Name of Owner.	P. O. Address.	Name of Plantation.	Jurisdiction.
Gaitan Emilio	Habana, Habana	Deleite	Cardenas
Galainena Herederos de Carlos	Ingenio	Movimiento	Bahia Honda
Galan, José		Carambola	Jovellanos
		Concepcion	Cardenas
Galarraga Matias	Habana, Tulipan 16 Cerro	Confianza	Matanzas
Galofre Pablo y Juan		Ponuco	Cuba
Galvez y Hermano	Matanzas, Gilabert 92	Dos Mercedes	Alacranes
Galvez y Zanetti Jesus Benigno	Habana, Aguacate 128	San José de Cannabo	Matanzas
Gallart José Nicolas	Igenio	Felicia	Sagua
Gandara y Lomba Ramon		Santa Elena	Cienfuegos
Garay y Ca., Santiago	Matanzas, Contreras 56		
		Santa Cristo	Matanzas
Garcia Angarica Joaquin		Desemperro	Colon
		San Antonio	Alacranes
Garcia Antonia			
Garcia Barbon Luciano	Habana, S. Ignacio 76	Fortuna	San Antonio
		San Luciano	Colon
Garcia Carlos	Habana, Aguila 60	San Rafael	Bejucal
Garcia Cartaya José Belen		Piedad	Matanzas
Garcia Chavez Francisco	Matanzas, Gelabert 24	Luz	Matanzas
Garcia Chavez Hermanos	Matanzas, Contreras, 59	Dolores	Cardenas
Garcia Fabian	Ingenio	Gerona	Sagua
		Santa Rita	Alacranes
Garcia Francisco Antonio	Isabela	Na. Sa. de los Dolores	Sagua
Garcia Herederos de Fulgencio		Tiempo	Matanzas
Garcia Milian Lorenzo	Matanzas, Contreras, 50		
		San Ramon	Cardenas
Garcia Milian Pablo Maria		San Florencio	Alacranes
		Mercedes	Matanzas
Garcia Oña Enrique y A.	Matanzas, O'Reilly 34	San Luis	Colon
Garcia Ona Recardo	Matanzas, Gelabert 47	Cuavalejos	Cardenas
Garcia Pablo Maria		Central	Matanzas
Garcia Sardina Ignacio		San Juan	Jovellanos
Garcia Sardina Pantaleon		Santa Facunda	Colon
Garcia Sebastian		Juanita	Cienfuegos
Garcia y Ca., Beatrix		Ntra. Sra. del Rosario	Cardenas
Garcia y Garcia, Enrique	Habana, Prado 47	San José	Jovellanos
Garcia y Hermano, J. Belen	Habana, Bartillo	Santo Domingo	Colon
Garcia y Hermanos		Buena Vista	Cardenas
		Santa Ana	Cardenas
Garcia y Hermanos		El Tiempo	Colon
Garralde Viuda de Pedra		Algaba	Trinidad
Garri y Fernandez, Angel	Habana, Ancha del N. 104		
		Angel de San Antonio	Sagua
Garrido y Hermanos		Delicias	Villaclara
Gatke I. Larraque Viuda de E. F.	Habana, Cuba 26	Angerona	Guanajay
Gay Francisco de Paula	Habana, Cuarteles 42	Ntra. Sra. de la Luz	Cardenas
Gay Josefa Calderon de	Habana, Cuba	Santa Rosa	Cuba
Gerome de Mora Maria	Habana, Merced 16	San Antonio	Cardenas
Gil Herederos de José	Baracoa	Cagnasey	Baracoa
Gilledo N.	Habana, Merced 16	Mundo	
Gualt y Madrazo José	Habana, Chacon 3	El Doctor	Santiago
Girard Succesion de Gustavo		San Agustin	Cuba
Giraud Mercedes Viuda de Lleo	Habana, Amistad 98	Luisa	Sagua
Gleam Francisco R.		Panchita	Sagua
Gobel y Hermanos Mariano	Habana, Lamparilla 78		
		Aurora	Jovellanos
Godinez Francisco G.	Habana, Cerro 442	Triunfana	Colon
Goicoechea N.		San José	Remedios
Goicoechea Pascual	Habana Principe, Alfonso 45		
		Providencia	Guines

ISLAND OF CUBA. 195

Name of Owner.	P. O. Address.	Name of Plantation.	Jurisdiction.
Gomez Aranjo Antonio		Nena	Colon
Gomez Mederos y Ca.		Por Fuerza	Cardenas
Gomez y Cepero Martin		San Abraham	Colon
Gomez y Hermano Julian	Matanzas, Ricla 31, Contreras 34	Reforma	Matanzas
		San Andrian	
		San Antonio	Cardenas
		San Cayetano	
		San Miguel	Matanzas
Gon. Francisco		Luz	San Antonio
Gonzalez Abun Diego		El Rubi	
		La Quinta	Villaclara
Gonzalez Abun Herederos de Eduardo	Habana, Amistad 104	Santa Catalina	Cienfuegos
Gonzalez Abun Herederos de Francisco	Villaclara	Guaimarito	Villaclara
Gonzalez Abun Juan y Rafaela	Habana, Prado 68 y 70	Dolores	Remedios
Gonzalez Abun Vincente		San Antonio	Santa Clara
Gonzalez Carballo R.		Central	} Cardenas
Gonzalez de Larrazabal A.		San Manuel	
Gonzalez G., Conde de Palatino y L. Alda	Habana, Cerro 795	San Miguel Rosario	Pinar del Rio
Gonzalez Herederos de Antonio		Caridad	Alacranes
Gonzalez Herederos de Guillermo		Industria	Habana
		San Nicolas	Jaruco
Gonzalez José Maria		Central Perla	Colon
Gonzalez Lara José	Habana, Merced 45	Luisa	Cardenas
Gonzalez Larrinaga, Herederos de B.	Habana, Reina 63	Begona	Pinar del Rio
		Julia	} Jaruco
		Purisima Concepcion	
Gonzalez Manuel		Nazareno	Pinar del Rio
Gonzalez Rodiles José		Nueva Luciana	Colon
Gonzalez Rosa Maria Ruiz de		Purisima Concepcion	
Gonzalez Rosario	Habana	San Luis	Sagua
Gonzalez Sebastian		Cuprey	Cuba
Gonzalez y Arango Francisco	Habana, S. Indalecio 17	El Cristo	Bejucal
Gonzalez y Bolanos Herederos de		Unica	Cardenas
Gonzalez Dominguez J.		Fenix	Cardenas
Gonzalez y Quinonez Higinio		Rosario	Colon
Gonzalez y Ramos Vinda de Hilario	Habana, Merced 26	Purisima Concepcion	Jaruco
Gorostiza Barberia y Ca.		El Pan	Matanzas
Govin y Dominguez Felix		Central Louisiana	Habana
Govin y Pinto Felix	Habana, Manrique	Maravilla	Alacranes
		Niagara	Colon
Goytizolo y Lizarzabun Agustin		Purisima Concepcion	
		San Austin	Cienfuegos
Gran Azucarera en liquidacion	Habana, Oficios	Echeverria	
		San Martin	Cardenas
Granda, Cantero y Ca.		Santa Rita	Villaclara
Gran y Junco		Rioja	Cienfuegos
Groso de Anido Natalia		Rosa	Villaclara
Guardado y Hermano Herederos de	Ingenio	Palma	Sagua
Guell y Rente		Acana	Matanzas
Guerra Laureana		Mamey	Jovellanos
Guerrero Marqueti Vicente	Habana Cerro 552	Santa Maria	Matanzas
Guillo y Restoy	Ingenio	Florentina	Sagua
Guma Gregoire y Antonio	Matanzas Magdalena	{ Angelita	Habana
		{ San Ramon	Cardenas
		{ Santa Sofia	Jovellanos
Gutierrez y Casal Concurso de	Habana, San Pedro 2	Panchita	Sagua
Gutierrez y Hermanos Herederos de Jose	Santo Domingo	Casnalidad	"

H.

Name of Owner.	P. O. Address.	Name of Plantation.	Jurisdiction.
Hatton y Soran		Chuchita	Colon
Haza y Cubellas Jose		Tres Hermanos	Jovellanos
Hermennay y Batt			
Herederos de	Estados Unidos	San Jorge	Sagua
Herrera Herederos de Francisco y Leonor	Habana, Cerro 480	Libano	Cardenas
Herrera Jose Mariano		Luisa	Habana
Herrera Juan Francisco	Aguacate 112	Destino	Pinar del Rio
Herrera Leonor y Miguel de	Teniente-Rey 39	San Francisco	Pinar del Rio
Herrera Maria Francisco		San José	Pinar del Rio
Herrera Maria Josefa	Habana, Salud 79	Encarnacion	Pinar del Rio
Herrera Melgares Herederos de T.	Tacon 2	Atrevido	Colon
		Belfast	Jovellanos
		San Luis	Cardenas
		Santa Maria	Colon
Herrera y Carter Miguel Antonio	San Ignacio	Concepcion	San Antonio
Herrera y Cardenas L. Maria		Galope	San Cristobal
Hernandez Armas José		San José	Nueva Paz
Hernandez Capote Manuel	Habana, S. Miguel 108	Charcas	Sagua
Hernandez de Hernandez A.	Habana, Galiano	Audax	Cardenas
Hernandez de la Cruz y Hermano J.	Matanzas, Gelabert 74	Santa Catalina	Matanzas
Hernandez Dominguez E.		Maria Louisa	San Antonio
Hernandez Herederos de Belen		Santa Ana	Remedios
Hernandez Herederos de Dgo. y Mo.	Habana, Ancha del N. 122	Aurora	San Antonio
Hernandez Herederos de Eusebio	Amistad 56	Santa Ines	Alacranes
		San Rafael	Jaruco
Hernandez José		Reglita	Cienfuegos
Hernandez Josefa	Ingenio	San José	Sagua
Hernandez Marcos		Victoria	Cienfuegos
Hernandez Maria Gregoria		Santa Isabel	Cardenas
Hernandez Morejon Herederos de F.	Matanzas, Santa Teresa 21	San Francisco	Matanzas
Hernandez Morejon Herederos de P.	Matanzas, Ricla 71	Carmen	"
Hernandez Otero y Hermano Isidoro	Matanzas, Burriel	Trinidad	"
Hernandez Piloto Juan		El Carmen	Cardenas
Hernandez Rafael	Ingenio	Socorro	Sagua
Hernandez Rodriguez F.	Matanzas, Contreras 26	San Fernando	
		San Juan	Cardenas
Hernandez Rodriguez S.	Cardenas, Industria	Santa Rosa	Matanzas
Hernandez Serapio	Matanzas Isabel, I. Versalles	Escorial	Jovellanos
Hernandez Tomas	Sagua, Colon 45	Santa Clara	Sagua
Hernandez Trinidad		San José	Cardenas
Hernandez y A. G. Aranjo N.		Firmeza	Cardenas
Hernandez y A. Montes E.		San Rafael	Madruga
Hernandez y Gonzalez N.		Dos Cecilias	Matanzas
Hernandez y Giuria		San José	"
Hernandez y Rios Pablo	Matanzas, O'Reilly	Mercedes	Colon
		Osado	Cardenas
Hernandez y Rios Pastor	Matanzas, O'Reilly 23	Santa Rosa	Colon
Heria Roma y Pedro Cerro	Habana 618, Mercaderes, 12	Santisema Trinidad	San Antonio
Heria S. y J. P. Abren	Habana Sol 87	Triunfo (a) Concepcion	Cardenas
Hidalgo José Maria		Amalia	Cienfuegos
Hoyos de Perez Hijolita		Preciso	Cardenas

I.

Name of Owner.	P. O. Address.	Name of Plantation.	Jurisdiction.
Ibanez Francisco F., Conde de Casa Ibanez	Habana, Cuba 5	Chumba	Guanabacoa
		Montana	Bahia Honda
		San Joaquin	Colon
		Socorro	Sagua
Ibarra y La Guardia, Rita y C.	Habana, Prado 87	San Ignacio	Alacranes
Iglesias y Hermanos	Sagua, Esperanza 14	Santa Tomas de Alba	Sagua
Illa y Ruiz		Ntra. Sra. Remedios	Bahia Honda
Illareta Joaquin		Lola	Villaclara
Innevarich Santiago	Remedios	Floridano	Remedios
Isasi Marques de	Habana, Justiz 2	Magdalena	
		San Ignacio	Matanzas
Izaba y Fernandez Hilario	Sagua, Gloria 42	Aurelia	Villaclara
Izaguirre Ildefonso	Habana, Oficios 62	Empresa	San Cristobal
Iznaga de Acosta Natividad	Amargura 23, A. del N. 221	Maipo	Sancti Spiritu
		Natividad	"
		San Fernando	"
Iznaga de Cantero Herederos de M.		Corojal	Trinidad
Iznaga de Riquelme Barbra		Aracas	"
		Mainicu	"
Iznaga de Sanchez Maria C.		Delicias Magnas	"
Iznaga Juan A.		Conchita	Cienfuegos
Iturralde Juan		Libano	Sagua

J.

Name of Owner.	P. O. Address.	Name of Plantation.	Jurisdiction.
Jenks José Matias	Matanzas, Magdalena 15	Concepcion	Colon
Jibacoa Conde de	Habana, Jesus Maria 6	San Ignacio	Guines
Jimenez Francisco		Buena Vista	Cardenas
Jimenez Rojo Isidro		Reunion	San Antonio
Jimenez y Ayla	Habana, Virtudes 2	San Francisco de Asis	Guanajay
Jimenez y Eslevez Ramon	Matanzas, Contreras 38	Nueva Cecilia	Matanzas
Jimenez y Mahy Leon		Conte	Cardenas
Jimenez Fuentes J. M. y F.	Matanzas, Contreras 34	Granja	Cardenas
Jorrin Gonzola	Habana, Cerro Principe, Alfonso	San Rafael	Alacranes
		Vista Hermosa	Cardenas
Jova y Hermanos Federico	Tacon, 46 Sagua	Chubasco	Sagua
	Santo Domingo	Mercedes	Cienfuegos
	Marianao	Natalia	Sagua
		San Jacinto	Santa Clara
Jova Ricardo		San Ildefonso	Guantanamo
Jovellar y Cardona		Aurora Zayas	Jovellanos
Jover Herederos de Juan		San Gabriel	Guantanamo
Juda José		Lima	Matanzas
Junco Guadalupe		Divertido	Cienfuegos
Junco Leandro del			
Junco Morejon y Hermano W.	Matanzas, Gelabert 10	Mercedes	Matanzas
Junco y Morejon Gabino	Matanzas, Burriel	San Vicente	Jovellanos
Jurda José		Santa Rosalia	Remedios
Justiz Manuel		Bolanos	Cuba

K.

Name of Owner.	P. O. Address.	Name of Plantation.	Jurisdiction.
Kessel Emilio	Habana, Empedrado 16	Redencoin	Bahia Honda
Kinderland y Ca., Juan		Palmorepo	Cuba

L.

Name of Owner.	P. O. Address.	Name of Plantation.	Jurisdiction.
Labarrere Mateo J.	Habana, Empedrado 3	Bramales	Guanajay
Laferte Goitia Francisco		Merced	Cardenas
La Guardia de Ponce Merced	Habana, Prado	Merced	Matanzas
Landa Gabriel Maria	Habana, San Miguel 62	Afan	Cardenas
Landa Martin	Habana, Mercaderes 11	Santa Rosa	Sagua
Landa y Ca., F.	Habana, Mercaderes 11	Armonia	Colon
Lanz Herederos de Juan Bautista	Habana, Compostela 158	Chucha	Jovellanos
Lara Roque de		San Carlos (a) El Quemadero	Cardenas
Lara de Cantero Monserrate		Guina de Soto	Trinidad
Larrondo Ignacio	Sagua, Colon 87	Manuelita	Sagua
Larrondo y Ca., Ignacio	Sagua, Colon 87	Constancia	Sagua
Lasa Carlos de		Tinaja	Mariel
Lasaga Virgilio y Recio Morales José		Correderas	Jaruco
Lasarte Manuel	Ingenio	Santa Maria	Sagua
Lastra Maria de la Cruz		Janlas	Bejucal
Lastra Ramon	Igenio	Santa Rosa	Guines
Lastre y Ginart, Joaquin	Habana, Habana 35	Asuncion	Matanzas
Lavin Domingo		Resolucion	Guines
Lavin Ildefonso		Jobo	"
Lavin Juan	Cardenas Pinillos 86	Meteoro	Cardenas
Lavin Juan y C. Herrero	Cardenas, Real 24	Conchita	Colon
Lavin Juan, en Concurso y Santiuste N.		Guamutitas	Cardenas
Lawton Herederos de Jaime	Habana, Mercaderes 13	Santa Rosa	Sagua
Ledesma R. U. y J. Bardaji		Monte Sano	Guantanamo
Leonard Herederos de Juan Bautista		Amalia	Jovellanos
Leon y Ceballos		Santa Leocadia	Alacranes
Limonta Sucesor de M. y E. Brooks		Isabel	Guantanamo
Linares Dolores	Cifuentes	Trinidad	Sagua
Lombard y Hermano		Conformidad	Cardenas
Lombiel Tomas	Habana, Consulado		"
Lombillo Jose, Conde de	Habana, Empedrado	Fraternidad San Gabriel	Bahia Honda
Lopez del Campillo y Hermano D		California	Cienfuegos
Lopez J A		Arratia	Colon
Lopez Lage y So. Manuel	Habana, Reina 119	Santa Ana	San Antonio
Lopez Silverio Elias	Habana, Ancha del N. 153	Santa Lutgarda	Sagua
Lopez Silverio Rafael		Laberinto	Santa Clara
Lopez Trigo Ignacio	Habana, Vedado	Ntra. Sra. del Carmen	Cardenas
Lopez Tringo y Ca.		Jesus Maria (a) Ramos	Guanajay
Lopez Villavicencio Teofilo		San Claudio	Matanzas
Lopez y Farragut	Igenio	Panchita	Sagua
Lopez y Hermanos Demetrio		San Rafael	Colon
Luire y Alberdi Herederos de Diego	Sagua, Colon 179	Ceiba	Sagua
Lugo Vinas Nicasio	Sagua, Santa Domingo	San Andres	Sagua
Llanos Viuda de Cespedes	R. de Matanzas, Ricla	Buen Suceso	Matanzas
Llera y Rodriguez	Igenio Destino	Destino	Santa Clara
		Juanita	Sagua

ISLAND OF CUBA. 199

M.

Name of Owner.	P. O. Address.	Name of Plantation.	Jurisdiction.
Mac Culloc Herederos de Juan Macia	Estados Unidos	Unidad	Sagua
Macias Herederos de José		Girafa	Cardenas
Machado Eleuterio		Socorro	Matanzas
Machini Hermano Manuel		Santa Ana	Remedios
Madan Cristobal F.	Habana, Cuba 80	Santa Maria	Villaclara
Madan de Alfonso Herederos de A.	Habana, Cuba 84	La Rosa	Cardenas
		Antonio	Matanzas
		Triunvirato	Matanzas
Madan de la Guardia Rosa	Habana, Prado 62	Hatney	Colon
Madan Guillermo y Avelino		San Antonio	Cienfuegos
Madrazo y Hermano Narcisco		Luisa	Cardenas
Malpica Felipe	Habana, Prado 101	Caridad	Colon
Mallet Maria		Santa Ana	Colon
Mantecon N.		Santa Rita	Colon
Manrique Roque	Habana, Oficios 16	Panchita	Colon
Maragliano Benito		La Benita	Alacranes
Marcellan Herederos de Andres		Santa Isabel	Cienfuegos
Marcos José	Matanzas, Santa Teresa	San José	Jovellanos
Mariscal del Holjo Rafael	Sagua, Tacon 80	San Rafael	Sagua
Marquetti Herederos de J. y A. M. C.	Habana, Obrapia	Santisima Trinidad	San Antonio
Marquetti y Gonzalez	Habana, San Miguel	Central Dolorita	Cardenas
Marquez Antonio	Igenio	San Miguel	Sagua
Marquin Fermin N.		Caridad	Gibara
Marroquin Cajigas y Ca.	Habana, Barcelona 8	S. Francisco de Paula	{ Guines
Martiartu Leon	Habana, San Ignacio	Dolores	} Nueva Paz
Martinez Catalina		Santa Catalina	Colon
Martinez Herederos de Antonio		Caridad	Remedios
Martinez Isabel Viuda de Pablo Perez Zamora		Tauro	Las Vegas
Martinez Jose Antonio Abad	Habana, Salud	Ana	Sagua
Martinez Juan Manuel		Caridad	Villaclara
Martinez Martin		San José	Gibara
Martinez Campos Mercedes	Paris, Christofle Colomb.	Serbabo	Bejucal
Martinez Campos Serefina	Chateaubriand	Santa Rita	Guanabacoa
Martinez Mesa y Ca.	Sagua, Amistad	Reforma	Sagua
Martinez Rafael		Vista Hermosa	Jaruco
Martinez Rico José	Habana, O'Reilly	Ntra. Sra. del Carmen	Guanajay
Martinez Rico Heroderos de Manuel		{ Santa Teresa { Santisima Trinidad	Matanzas Cardenas
Martinez Valdiviose Herederos de N.	Habana, Habana	{ Aurora } Monserrate { San Antonio	} Matanzas
Martinez Valdiviose Josefa		San Isidro	
Martinez y Hermanos	San Ignacio	Dos Hermanos	Jaruco
Martinez y Sobrino Francisco		Perseverancia	Cardenas
Masforroll, Trenard y Ca.		Union	Cuba
Masvidal y Ca. Nuevitas		Central Redencion	Nuevitas
Maten Antonio		San Antonio	Bejucal
Maurin Herederos de José		San Isidro	Las Vegas
Mayner Jaime	Habana, Obrapia	Mercedes a Aurrera	Cardenas
Mayor y Ca.		San José	
Maza Evaristo		Lanzarote	Jovellanos
Maza José		Central Anita	Cardenas
Maza Munoz Juan de la	Habana, Inquisidor	Dolores	Jaruco
Maza y Hermanos	Habana, Empedrado	Apuros	Bahia Honda
Mazorra Herederos de José Pio	Habana, Dominguez	Clarita	Bejucal
		Santa Clara	Sagua
Medina Antonio	Remedios	Falcon	Remedios
Medina Ramon H.		Estrella	Cienfuegos
Medina y Montero		Carmen	Jaruco
Melgares N.		Atrivido Sta. Maria	
Mena Agustin J.		Magnolia	Cardenas
Mena Bernardo		Juanita	Jovellanos

Name of Owner.	P. O. Address.	Name of Plantation.	Jurisdiction.
Mena Maria Francisco		Oriente	Jovellanos
Mena Meneses Juan		San Juan	Manzanillo
Mendez Herederos de		Buenaventura	Jovellanos
Mendez Valladares Rafael		San Juan Bautista	Alacranes
Mendive Herederos de		Altura	Bahia Honda
Menendez Ramon		San Jóse	Cardenas
Menendez Teresa	Habana, Oficios 16	Santa Isabel	Cardenas
Menendez y Sobrino		Santa Rosa	Colon
Meres Herederos de Josefa Madrona		Victoria	San Antonio
Mesa Herederos de		Dos Felices	Alacranes
Mesa y Herederos de Galarraga Luisa	Habana, Tulipan 8 Cerro	Guasimal	Cardenas
Mesa y Compánia Antonio	Sagua, Amistad	Union	Sanga
Mildestein Guillermo	Igenio	Amjaro	Sanga
Milian de Garcia Herederos de Petrona	Mantanzas, Gelabert 42	Petrona San Narcisco	Matanzas Matanzas
Mitjaros Concurso de Bartolome		Guacamayo	Pinar del Rio
Molina Fernando	Habana, Compostela	Santa Teresa	Bejucal
Molina Ignacio y Ricardo	Habana, Cerro 10	Mina	Cardenas
Moliner y Hermanos Adolfo	Habana, Tulipan 9 Cerro	Luisa	Colon
Mons D'Orbigny Herederos de Luis de		Santa Victoria	Guines
Montalvos Dolores R. De		Concepcion	Cienfuegos
		San Lino	Cienfuegos
Montalvos Encarnacion	Habana, Campanario 127	Encarnacion	Colon
Montalvos y Cablvo Herederos de Ignacio Conde de Casa	Habana, Habana 198	Jesus Maria Merced Penon	Cardianes Cardianes
Montalvo y Calvo Herederos de Ramon	Cuba, 40	Desquite	Matanzas
Montalvo y Rodriguez Lino	Habana, Amargrua	Andreita	Cienfuegos
Montelo Herederos del Marques de	Habana, Baratillo Matanzas, Arpentamiento	La Rosa San Cayetano San José	Matanzas " "
Monterro e Hijos Francisco	Habana, Bernaza, 29	San José de las Ciegas	Colon
Montes Lorenzo y Hernandez Antonio	Guines	Nombre de Dios	Habana
Montes de Oca y Torres Manuel	Guines, Carmelo	Alianza	Guines
Montes Victor	S. Antonio, Real 47	Penalver	San Antonio
Mora Agustin S.		Adelaida	Cienfuegos
Mora Conc. de José y A. Maria	Habana, San Ignacio	America San Joaquin	Sagua Cardenas
Mora Cullado Pedro		Victoria	Sagua
Mora de Arangurer Dolores	Habana, San Ignacio	Victoria	Cardenas
Mora e Hijos Vicenta de		Pejilla	Sagua
Mora Gabriel		Sacramento	Cienfuegos
Mora Jacinta		San Jacinto	Sagua
Mora José Maria	Hab'na, San Celestino	Alejandria	Guines
Mora Justa Vinda de Palacio		San Isidro	Cienfuegos
Mora Mamerto		Benigna	Sagun
Mora Oha y Ca.	Sagua, Merced 47	Armonia	"
	Habana, Merced, 49	Manuelita	" ,
Morales Alejandro Conde de	Habana, Cuba	Indarra	Colon
Morales Armentero Herederos de Pro	Habana, Salud	Rosario	Jaruco
Morales Armenteros Vidal	Habana, Galiano	Telegrafo	Cardenas
Morales Guerra Antonio		San Rafael	Villaclara
Morales Herederos de Ramon	Habana, Compostela	Santa Teresa	Sagua
Morales Manuel A. R. Marques de la Real Proclamacion	Cuba	Alegre Luisa Ntra. Sra. de las Mercedes	Cardenas Santiago Guines
More Ajuria y Hermano		San Isidro	Sagua
Morey Ajuria	Habano, Obispo	Indio Labrador	" "

Name of Owner.	P. O. Address.	Name of Plantation.	Jurisdiction.
More y Ping Manuel B.	Habana, J. del Monte	Purisima Concepion	Cardenas
Morejon Ambrosio		Gonzalo	Alacranes
Morejon Herederos de P.	Matanzas, Ricla	Carmen	Matanzas
Morejon Manuel	Habana, Zaragoza	Martilde	Santiago
Morcero Pumariega y Compa		San Joaquin	Santiago
Morell Carlos	Remedios	Louisa	Remedios
Muis e Hijos		Dulce Nombre	Colon
Muller Eduardo Maria		El Bamo	Jaruco
Munoz Heredero de		San Ramon	Manzanillo
Munoz Izanguirre y Hermano		Pajayal	Bahia Honda
Munoz San Clemente Herederos de		Concordia	Guines
Munoz y Ca. Juan J.		Santa Susana	Jovellanos
Munoz y Hermanos		San Joaquin	Bahia Honda
Muro Rosario y G. Barradas		San Francisco	Colon
Muro Sainz y Ca.	Cardenas, Garnica	Dulce Nombre	Colon

N.

Name of Owner.	P. O. Address.	Name of Plantation.	Jurisdiction.
Naranjo Jesus		El Rosario	Manzanillo
Naranjo Marcelina		Piedad	Matanzas
Navarrete de Rodrigues Teran	Habana, Aguacate	Carla	Villaclara
Navarro, Casas y Ca.	Sagua, Colon	Estrella	Sagua
Navarro y Pedraja Bernardo	Matanzas, Contreras	Conga	Matanzas
		Recurso	"
Ninninger Herederos de Juan	Habana, Oficios	San Isabel	
Nicolas José y Baro Herederos de Amalia	Habana, Prado	Matilde	Remedios
Nicolas Juan José	Matanzas, Jovellanos	Santa Isabel	Alacranes
	Matanzas, Jovellanos	Victoria	"
Nicolas y Frennor José R.		Josefina	Mantanzas
Nodalas Eusebio		Casanlidad	Remedios
Norma Antonio		San Luis	Cuba
Noreiga, Olomo y Ca.	Habana, Cuba	Andrea	Colon
		Noriega	Remedios
		San José R. Gomez	Santiago
Nunez Benito	Matanzas	Olallita	Sagua
Nunez Fernando	Sagua, Merced	Juanita	"
Nunez, Herederos de Juan J.		Rita	Madruga
Nunez Juan	Ingenio	San Juan	Sagua
Nunez Manuel	Sagua, Amistad	Santa Clara	"
Nunez Rita Micaela y Juana	Sagua, Intendente, Ramirez	Manuelita	"
Nunez Vega José Manuel		Nueva Empresa	San Antonio
Nunez y Ca., Domingo		Guadalupe	Guines
Nunez y Hermanos Bernardo	Matanzas	San Francisco	Sagua

O.

Name of Owner.	P. O. Address.	Name of Plantation.	Jurisdiction.
Ocampo y Arredondo	Habana, Industria	Luis O. Je Rita	Sagua
O'Farrill Herederos Josefa	Habana, Salud	San Luis	Jaruco
O'Farrill José Ricardo	Habana, Cuba	Cayajabos	Habana
		Concordia	"
O'Farrill José Ricardo	Habana, Cuba	San Antonio	
		San Rafael	Sagua
O'Farrill Ricardo R.	Habana, Colon	Esperanza	Habana
		Limones	Matanzas
O'Farrill Vicente		San Ignacio	Villaclara
Olano y Molina José	Matanzas, O'Reilly	San José	Alacranes
Olivera Hermanos y Ca.	Matanzas, O'Reilly	Catalina	Cardenas
Olivera Manuel		Buen Amigo	Alacranes
Olmo Frade y Ca.		Josefita	Jaruco
O'Nagten y Orozco Juan	Habana, Compostela	Desengano	Colon
Oramas Lucas		Santa Lucia	Villaclara
O'Reilly Conde de	Habana, Oficios	Bufon	San Antonio
Orta Juan	Sagua la Grande	Tenerife	Sagua
Orta y Lleria		Esperanza	Jovellanos
Ortiz Antonio	Remedios	Artemisa	Remedios

Name of Owner.	P. O. Address.	Name of Plantation.	Jurisdiction.
Ortiz Cabana y Ca.		San Antonio Polo	Villaclara
Otamendi Baltasar		Santa Isabel	Pinar del Rio
Otero de Tolon Dolores		San José Valiente	Alacranes
Owens Herederos de Tomas	Matanzas, O'Reilly	Santa Barbara	Jovellanos
Oxamendi Vicente		Union	Cardenas

P.

Name of Owner.	P. O. Address.	Name of Plantation.	Jurisdiction.
Padron Justo y Herederos de Canal		Constancia	Penar del Rio
		Paso Real	
Palacios Herederos de Lazaro		Paso Real	Trinidad
Palatino Gregorio Gonzalez Conde de	Habana, Cerro, P. Grandes	Balbanera	Pinar del Rio
		Desengano	"
		Nueva Empresa	"
		Recurso	Habana
Palma y Nieto	Sagua, Gloria	San Rafael	Sagua
Pallimonjo y Sobrino	Cardenas, Princesa	San Pablo	Cardenas
		San Vicente	Cardenas
Parera de Sotolongo Aurora	Habana, Aguacate	Carmen	Jaruco
Pasalobos Damaso		Armantina	Cienfuegos
Pascual Enrique		Merceditas	Guines
Pasinal Maria		Santa Rosa	Santa Clara
Pedro Herederos de Francisco	Habana, Amargura	Menocal	Mariel
Pedro José		Mercedes	Matanzas
Pedro Lorenzo	Habana, Industria	Buen Hijo	Guanajay
Pedro y Roig Juan	Habana, San Ignacio	Asuncion	Pinar del Rio
Pedroso Maria Luisa y A. Rodriguez	Habana, Amargura 21 y 23	Luisa	Habana
		Des Hermanas	Colon
Pedro y Echevarria Herederos de J.		Santa Gertrudes	Cardenas
		San Joaquin	Colon
Pedroso y Hermanos Carlos	Habana, Bernaza	Ntra. Sra. del Rosario	Jaruco
Pedroso y Pedroso Francisco	Habana, I. del Monte Compostela	San Cayetano	Cardenas
		San Gabriel	Pinar del Rio
Pelayo Matilde G. Viuda de		Esperanza	Cardenas
Pelayo Vigil Francisco	Remedios	San Joaquin	Remedios
Pella y Caso		Congreso	Matanzas
Penalver Concepcion	Habana, Tejadillo	Santiago Canas	Pinar del Rio
Penalver Sebastian de	Habana, Tacon	Macasta	Santiago
Penalver y Sanchez Herederos de J.	Habana, Sol	San Gabriel a Zayas	Pinar del Rio
Penate José	Sitio, Grande	San José	Sagua
Pequeno y Ca. L.	Habana, Acosta	L. Pequeno	"
Peraza Francisco	Sagua, Colon	San Lorenzo	"
Peraza Juana		Central Granja	Jovellanos
Peraza Manuel	Habana, Escobar	Maria Teresa	Cardenas
		San Juan	"
Perera José		Paz	Colon
Perez, Aguin y Ca.	Ingenio	San Ramon	Sagua
Perez Candida		Palafox	San Antonio
Perez Carballo Francisco		Andrea	Cardenas
Perez Felipe	Habana, San Ignacio	Arnonia	Habana
Perez Herederos de José Rafael J.		Concepcion	Matanzas
Perez Teran y Hermano C.	Cardenas, Princesa	Jesus Maria	Cardenas
Perez Tomas		Cuba	Sagua
Perovani Elvira Viuda de Torre	Habana, Ricla	San Andres	Cardenas
		Santa Elvira	"
		Union	"
Perez Herederos de		Maria S. J. de Dios	Bahia Honda
Pers Gabriel	Habana, Paula	Reserva	Colon
Pezuela e Hijo Jacobo de la		San Luis	Jaruco
Pichardo e Hijo Rafael	Sagua, San Valentine	Concepcion	Sagua
Piedra Andreas Viuda de Diaz		Bella Amistad	San Antonio
		Santa Ana	San Antonio
Piedra Bartolome		Minerva	Pinar del Rio
Piedra Juan Antonio		Atrevodo	San Antonio
Piedra y Ca.		El Felix	Alacranes
Pineira y Tapia Adriano	Habana	Elisa	Sagua

Name of Owner.	P. O. Address.	Name of Plantation.	Jurisdiction.
Pla Julio		Concepcion Santiago	Bejucal
Pla e Hijo José	Habana, Oficios	Descanso	Matanzas
		San Manuel	Matanzas
Planas Sucesion de José		Cubana	Cuba
		Lagunitas	Cuba
Plazarola Ureta Fernando	Habana, Cuba	Vizcaino	Bejucal
Poey Herederos de Juan	Habana, Compostela	Canas	Alacranes
Polo Francisco V.		El Siglo	Santiago
Polledo Joaquin	Matanzas, Magdalena	Asturias	Jovellanos
		San Ramon	Cardenas
Pombert Elias		Carmen	Villa Clara
		Hormiguero	Villa Clara
Ponce Marcial		Maria	Colon
		Santo Domingo	Colon
Ponce Patricio	Habana	Dolores	Matanzas
Ponce y Hermanos	Tejadillo	San Blas	Cardenas
Pons Fernando		Santa Maria	Guantanamo
Pons Gabriel		La Perseverancia	Trinidad
Portila, Jose de Jesus	Habana, Cerro	Santa Matilda	Jaruco
Portilla Herederos de Jose de la		La Palma	Matanzas
Portillo, Isabel		Juanita	Alacranes
Portillo y Bermudez, Manuel	Matanzas, Gelabert	El Molino	Matanzas
Portuondo y Barcelo, Manuel		{ Quemado { Santa Cruz	{ Cuba {
Prado Ameno y Herederos de Maria Isabel de Cardenas Marques de	Habana, Aguiat	Isabel	Guanajay
Prendes y Fernandez Juan	Matanzas, Daoiz	Sta. Catalina	
		Ramoncito	Colon
Primilles, Juan Manuel		La Fortuna	Nuevitas
Puente y Toledo		Santa Rosalia	Cardenas
Puig y Sanchez, Juan Jose		Confianza	Alacranes
	Habana, Maloja		
Puig Luis	Habana, Reina	Caridad	Sagua
Puig y Amigo Manuel	Habana, Cuba	Socorro	Bejucal
Pulido Mamerto	Habana, Aguair	San Antonio	San Antonio
Pumaldo Jose Maria		San Jose	Gibara
Pumareda y Compania Eduardo		Central Oriente	Cardenas
Pumariega Juan		Julia	Colon

Q.

Querol y Bello Vicente		Retribucion	Cardenas
Quevedo e Hijos Francisco		Dos Hermanas	Cienfuegos
Quevedo y Ca.		San Antonio	Alacranes
Quiam José Maria	Cardenas, Real	Estrella	Cardenas
Quintana de Frias Bernardo	Sagua La Grande	Dichoso	Sagua
Quintana F. Marques de Robrero	Ingenio	Otono	Cardenas
Quintero Gabino y Antonio	Habana, Cuba	San Antonio	Matanzas
Quintero José	Sagua La Grande	Santa Rosalia	Sagua
Quintero y Coloma	Madruga	S. Juan Nepomuceno	Madruga
Quintero y Hermanos Concurso de	Guanabacoa	Mantua	Sagua
Quinones Ana Joséfa		Santa Ana	Colon
		San José	Jovellanos
Quinones de Alfonso Concepcion		Dolores	Cardenas
Quinones Manuel	Habana, Animas	Vigia	Bahia Honda

R.

Name of Owner.	P. O. Address.	Name of Plantation.	Jurisdiction.
Ramirez Estenoz Juan	Habana, Gervasio	Dos Hermanas	Bejucal
Ramos Izquierdo Manuel en Concurso		San José	Jaruco
Ramos Laureano		San Juan Bautista	Matanzas
Rancolo Juan		{ San Carlos { San Vicente	Guantanamo
Rancell Hermano y Ca.	Habana, Habana	Gratitud	Sagua
Real Proclamacion Marques de la		Ceres	Cardenas
Rebolledo Agustin		Central Loreto	Colon
Recio de Morales Manuel A.	Habana, Paula	Moralite	Jaruco
Redo L. y A. Lescaye		San Antonio	Guantanomo
Redondo Manuela	Habana, Cerro	{ Capricho Carmen { Progreso	Sagua
Rud y Ca.	Mercaderes	Central Redencion	Puerto Principe
Reguera Francisco y Antonio	Prado	Gabriola	Guanajay
Reguera Javier		Manuelita	Cienfuegos
Rinaldo e Hidalgo Pedro		El Triunfo	Cardenas
Rendon Marques de		Nieves	Matanzas
Reunion Conde de la	Habana, Aguiar	Dos Hermanos	Guanajay
Rivella y Calvo		Pasiega	
Rey Sucesion de Antonio R. del		Caridad	Cienfuegos
Reyes Bacallao Belen y A.	Habana, Cerro	Paz de San Juan	Colon
Reyes Miguel		Guerro	Colon
Riancho Federico G.		Victorio	Gibara
Ribalta Herederos de Pablo		Santa Marta	Cienfuegos
Ribalta Tomas		Santa Teresa	Sagua
Rionda N.	Matanzas	China Central	Jaruco
		Elena	Matanzas
Rio Roque del		San Juan	Cardenas
Rios Gonzalez José T.		Las Nieves	Sagua
Rios Manuela		Esperanza	Sagua
Rios Miguel		Bejucal	Bejucal
Rios y Hermanos		Delicia	San Cristobal
Risech Jaime		Destino	Cienfuegos
Rivero Castillo José		Flora	San Cristobal
Robreno y Delgado	Ingenio	San Pedro	Sagua
Roca Carlos de la		Isabel	Colon
Roca Manuel Antonio	Sagua, Colon	Bella Luisa	Sagua
Roca y Compania	Sagua, Malpaez	Belencita	Sagua
Rodriguez Ana		D. Pelayo y J. Miguel	Villaclara
Rodriguez Cantera Maria de los Angeles		Encarnacion	Cardenas
Rodriguez de Arenas Teresa	Sagua la Grande	Vigilancia	Sagua
Rodriguez Francisco		Refugio	Guanajay
Rodriguez Lopez y Hermano José	Habana, Prado Sagua, Gloria	Angles Santa Rita Tres Hermanos	Sagua " "
Rodriguez Lopez Santiago	Habana, Prado	Flor de Cuba	"
Rodriguez Manuel		San Antonio	Jovellanos
Rodriguez Maria del Rosario		Reyes	Gibara
Rodriguez Ricardo	Ingenio	Bella Rosa	Sagua
Rodriguez Silva Concepcion		Dichoso	Alacranes
Rodriguez Somante Manuel		Cometa San Manuel Pelayo	Cienfuegos
Rodriguez y Ca., Laureano	Sagua, Tacon	Oriente	Sagua
Rodriguez y Grande	Matanzas, Ona	Santa Ana	Alacranes
Rodriguez y Hermanos C.	Sagua, Viana	Esperanza	
Rodriguez y Hermanos, Ramon	Igenio	San Ramon	Sagua
Rodriguez y Villar	Sagua, Tacon	Recurso	
Rojas Manuel y José de	Sauga, Samaritana	San Rafael	Remedios
Rojo Francisco	Sagua, Indte Ramirez	Guadalupe	Sagua
Rojo Herederos de Sixto	Habana, Colon, 107 y 109	Laberinto	Sagua

Name of Owner.	P. O. Address.	Name of Plantation.	Jurisdiction.
Rojo Nicolas		Santi Rita	Sagua
Rolando Herederos de Francisco G.		Recurso	Jovellanos
Roldan Antonio	Habana, Justiz	Santa Rita	Colon
Romay, Pedro y José	Habana, Cuba	San Luis	Nueva Paz
Romay y Navarrete Herederos de C.		Asentista	Guanajay
Romero Conde de Casa	Habana, San Ignacio	Esperanza	Guines
Roque de Casuso Julia	Habana, Dragones	Julia	Bejucal
Roque Gonzalo		Rancho Veloz	Jovellanos
		San Gabriel	"
Roque y Ca. Viudade			Colon
Rosa y Vede, C. de la y Herederos de Angel Hernandez		San Pablo	Colon
Rosell, Sucesion de Manuel		Silverita	Cienfuegos
Rosell y Malpica	Habana, Baratillo	Aguedita	Colon
	Habana, Cuba	San Salvador	Colon
Ruas José de la	Habana, Cerro	Jecarita	Guines
Rueda Gertrudis Dominguez de	Habana, Mercedes y Obispo	Caridad	Jovellanos
Ruiz Coboz Manuel		San Juan	Colon
Ruiz de Rodriguez Josefa	Cifuentes	Josefita	Sagua
Ruiz Francisco J.	Matanzas, Gelabert	Paloma	Matanzas
Ruiz Herederos de E. y Ca.		Eugenia	Cardenas
Ruiz Herederos de Martin		San Miguel	Villaclara
Ruiz y Hermano	Cardenas, Hector	San Blas	Cardenas
Ruiz y Hermanos José E.		Dos Amigos	Remedios
Ruiz y Hermano Modesto	Remedios	Panchita	Remedios
Ruiz y Perez Felipe	Habana, Principe Alfonso	Fajardo	San Antonio

S.

Name of Owner.	P. O. Address.	Name of Plantation.	Jurisdiction.
Saez Herederos de Santiago	Habana, Cuba	Jagua	
		Recuerdo	} Sagua
		Santa Fe	
		San Juan	Bahia Honda
		San Rafael	Guanajay
Salas Alejo		Esperanza	Isla de Pinos
Salas Pedro	2do. Guines, Santa Gertrudis	Recurso	Sagua
Salazar y Echevarria Vicente	Cuba	Caridad	
Salazar y Justiz Juan Francisco	Cuba	Ulloa	} Cuba
	Cuba	Arroyo de Agua	
Salom y Garcia	Habana, Aguiar	San Francisco	Nueva Paz
Salva Munoz Manuela		San Antonio	Santiago
Sama Viuda de Garcia Munoz Emilia	Habana, Cuba		
	Habana, 1 y Chacon	Buenaventura	Alacranes
Sanchez Benitez y Alfonso	Habana, Virtudes 111	Santa Lutgarda	Sagua
Sanchez Diego J.		Caledonia	Cienfuegos
Sanchez Dols Pedro	Habana, Oficios	Desengano	Nuevitas
Sanchez Ferriera Miguel		Campo Alegre	Cardenas
Sanchez Herederos de Rafael L.		Santa Lucia	Cuba
Sanchez Luisa		Concepcion	Pinar del Rio
Sanchez Pedro R.		Combate	Colon
Sanchez Salvador Teodoro		Santa Sofia (a)Coloso	Cardenas
Sanchez Toledano José M.		Piedra Blanca	Holguin
Sanchez Toledo Juan	Habana, Ancha del N.	Recurso	San Antonio
Sanchez Chavez Martin	Habana, Salud	Santa Rita	Matanzas
Sandoval Marquis de	Santa Clara	Dos Hermanos	Pinar del Rio
	Inquisidor	Gauges	San Antonio
		Recuerdo	San Antonio
		San Jacinto	Pinar del Rio
San Ignacio Herederos del Conde de	Paseo Tacon	Gerardo	Pinar del Rio
		Neptuno	San Cristobal
		San Ignacio	Pinar del Rio
		Santa Teresa	Pinar del Rio

Name of Owner.	P. O. Address.	Name of Plantation.	Jurisdiction.
San Miguel Marques de	Habana, Cuba	Intrepido	Colon
Santa Cruz de Oviedo Herederos de	Inquisidor	Esperanza	Alacranes
		Jesus Maria	Matanzas
		San José	Jaruco
Santa Cruz Herederos de Dolores de		Candelaria	Cienfuegos
Santiago Condesa de		Santiago	Pinar del Rio
Santos y Fonseca	Habana, San Ignacio	Santa Teresa	Colon
Santovenia Conde de		Monserrate	Colon
Sardina Alejo	Cardenas, Hector	Desquite	Colon
Sardina Cesareo y Prospero		Reglita	Colon
Sardina Felix		Dos Hermanos	Colon
Sardina Marcos		Santa Petrona	Colon
Sarria Joaquin		San Ignacio	Cienfuegos
Sarria Jose Manuel		José de Jabacoa	Cienfuegos
Sarria y Albis Domingo		Regla	Camarones
Satorre e Hijos Jose		Aventador	Matanzas
Sanvalle Carlos	Santa Cruz de los Pinos	Balestina Rangel	Pinar del Rio
Schmith Guillermo		Canamabo	Trinidad
Scull Herederos de Rosario	Habana, Mercaderes	Armonia	Nueva Paz
	Habana, Prado	Bancos	
		Santa Teresa	Habana
Scull y Marcel José Francisco	Habana, Mercaderes	Conclusion	Colon
Secada Francisco G.	Cardenas Ruiz y Cossio	Pedro Lorenzo	Cardenas
		Soledad	Jovellanos
Selden de Morgan Maria Luisa		Santa Agustina	Cardenas
Sentelles Juan	Matanzas Vera Versalles	San Francisco	Jaruco
Serra Seriva y Gonzales		San Francisco	Alacranes
Serra y Ca. Apolinar		Cataluna	Bejucal
Serrate Herederos de José		San Antonio	Matanzas
		Josefa	
Servia y Hermanos Manuel		Cataluna	Colon
Setien y Hermano	Matanzas, O'Reilly	Ignacio	Matanzas
Sewart Guillermo H.		Carolina	Cienfuegos
Siere y Bottino Pedro		Ambrosia	Cardenas
Sierra y Toscano	Ingenio	San Leon	Habana
Silva Francisco		Conyedo	Villaclara
Silveira y Quintana Francisco	Matanzas, Gelabert	Adriana	Matanzas
Smith Juan H.		Asuncion	Remedios
Smith Sucesion de Ricardo D.		San Ricardo	Cardenas
Smith y Ca. Liquidacion de E. G.		Santa Ana	Cuba
Socarras Francisco	Ingenio	Las Pozas	Bahia Honda
Sola Francisco		Cienfuegos	Cienfuegos
Soler Juan	Habana, Cuba, Esquina a Luz	Santa Filomena	Colon
Soler y Hernandez Juan		Diana	Colon
Soler y Morell Juan		Manuelito	Alacranes
Soler Leandro	Habana, Cuba	Santa Rita	Jovellanos
Solis Manuel		Reglita	Villaclara
Solier y Ca., José S.	Sagua, Sebastopol	San Fernando	Sagua
Sonceric Eduardo		Aurora	Remedios
Soto Andres	Habana, Aguiar	Andrea	Sagua
Sotolongo Desiderio de		Carmen	Habana
Sotolongo Herederos de Tomas	Habana, San Ignacio	Morenita	San Antonio
Sotolongo Mateo		San Mateo	Bejucal
Sotolongo y Abren Francisco	Habana, Oficios	Satelite	Jovellanos
Sotolongo y Ca., Lorenzo		Teresa	Habana
Sotolongo y Zas Agustin		Nino Jesus	Habana
Stockes Luis F. S.	Sagua le Grande	Santa Rita	Sagua
Suarez Argudin José Antonio	Habana, Mercaderes	Angelita	Cienfuegos
		Nueva Teresa	Bahia Honda
Suarez Chaveaux Angela		San Juan Bautista	Guanajay
		Rosario	San Antonio
Suarez del Villar Herederos de J. R.		La Nina	Cienfuegos
Suarez Herederos de José Ildefonso	Habana San Ignacio	Suriman	Habana

Name of Owner.	P. O. Address.	Name of Plantation.	Jurisdiction.
Suarez Vigil Miguel	San Ignacio, Ricla	Emila	Habana
		Mariel	Pinar del Rio
Suarez y Gonzalez		Armantina	Cardenas
Suarez Ruiz de Villa		El Siglo	Puerto Principe
Surias Francisco y R. Celaya		Resolucion	Jovellanos

T.

Name of Owner.	P. O. Address.	Name of Plantation.	Jurisdiction.
Taltvull José P.		Caridad	Cienfuegos
Tapia Eguillor y Ca		Conquista	Cardenas
Tapi Pablo		Resolucion	Sagua
Taylor Herederos de		Santa Amalia	Cardenas
Tauler y Ca. José		Esperanza	Holguin
Tejada de Torrijos Irene	Habana, Bnos-Aires 7 Cerro	Manacas	Cuba
Tejedor Gregorio	Habana, Consulado	Carmen	Nueva Paz
Tellechea Jeronimo		Limpios	Colon
Tellechea Viuda de	Habana	San Dionisio	Sagua
Terry Andres	Habana, Cuba	Cayajabos	Guines
Terry Tomas	Cienfuegos	Caracas	Cienfuegos
		Reparador	"
		Teresa	"
		Vivijagua	"
Thorndike Herederos de Israel	Sagua la Grande	Santa Ana	Sagua
Thompson Herederos de Ana	Estados Unidos	Capitolio	"
Thompson y Macomb		Victoria	Matanzas
Tintore Herederos de Francisco	Sagua, Colon	Amalia	Sagua
Tirso de Rodroquez Maria		Esperanza	Alcranes
Tora Josa Ricardo		La Merced	Villaclara
Torices y Ca., Rafael R.	Habana, Habana	Ponina	Colon
		San José	Villaclara
Torre Caridad y Mariana di la	Habana	San José de Ramos	Cuba
Torres Agustin	Sagua, Colon	Carmen	Sagua
Torres Antonio	Sagua la Grande, Ensenada	Concepcion	"
Torres Vendrell Jaime		Sonora	Bejucal
Torriente Celestino di la	Habana, Carlos III, 119	Central Maria	Colon
Torriente Francisco Maria di la	Habana, Ancha del Norte	Buen Suceso	Jovellanos
Torriente Herederos de Cosme de la	Matanzas, O'Reilly	Cantabria	Colon
		Elena	Matanzas
		Isabel	Jovellanos
Torriente Herederos de J. G. de la		Progreso	Cardenas
Torriente Herederos de Francisco de la		Laura O. Tosca	Cardenas
Torriente Hermanos Sucesion de	Matanzas	Santa Maria	Villaclara
		Vueltas	Cienfuegos
Torriente Juan A. de la	Habana, Habana	Carlota	Jovellanos
Torriente		Isabel	"
Torriente	Cardenas	Amistad	"
Torriente	Camarioca	Puray Liupia	
Toscano Isabel Blain Va. de So. Tomas 7, Cerro	Habana, S. Ignacio	Santa Isabel	Cardenas
Trenard y Pesant Simon		Santa Cecilia	Guantanamo
Triana y Hermanos Benigno		Santa Elena	Villaclara
		San Rafael	"
Troncoso y Ca. N.	Habana, Mercaderes	Clavellina	Sagua
		Mercedes	Matanzas
Truffin y Ulmo	Habana, Contreras	San Juan	Sagua
Trujillo Cabrera José		Santa Rosa	Guines
Trujillo José R	Habana, Contreras	San Antonio	Cienfuegos
Tucro Antonio		San José	Remedios

U.

Name of Owner.	P. O. Address	Name of Plantation.	Jurisdiction.
Uggate, Bardia y Ca.		San Carlos	Colon
Uggate Claudio	Habana, San Nicolas	Victoria	Jovellanos
Ugarte de Sotolongo Dolores	Habana, Oficios	Buen Amigo	Matanzas
		San Miguel	Jaruco
Ugarte Herederos de Jose Rafael		Platano	Sa. Ma. Rosario
Ugariza y Ca. Jose Maria		Santa Rita	Sagua
	Habana, Ricla	Amistad	Cardenas
		Arroyo	"
Ulacia Sebastian		Carolina	"
		Favorito	"
		San Rafael	Matanzas
Ulloa Jose de Jesus		Bella Vista	Bahia Honda
Urbizu Joaquin	Habana, Amargura	San Antonio	Guines
Ureta Tomas y Herederos de Duenas		Santa Lucia	Bejucal

V.

Vaillant Mariano		Hatillo	Cuba
Vaillant y Sucesion de J. Colas M.		Victoria	"
Valdes Alvarez y Ca.	Habana, Ricla, Esqa. a Inquisidor	Alpes Australia	Colon
Valdes José y Emilia		San Jose	Jaruco
Valera Ernesto		Herculano	Habana
Valera Galvez y Zayas		San Antonio	Matanzas
Valera y Cano José Maria	Matanzas, O'Reilly	Paraiso	"
		San Juan	"
Valera y Cano Nicolas	Matanzas, Ayllon	Combate	"
Valero de Urrutia Marques de	Habana, Compostela	Santiago	Colon
Valladares Herederos de José	Marianao, San Francisco	San Agustin	Alacranes
Valle Antonio Maria del	Habana, Aguiar	San Francisco	Jaruco
Valle Miguel del		San Miguel	Habana
Valleliano Conde de	Habana, Cerro	Lutgardita	Sagua
Varela Herederos de Manuel		Industria	Alacranes
Vega Claudio de la	Matanzas	Caridad	Guines
Vega de Alzugaray Casimira		Esperanza	Cardenas
Vega Juan		El Corojal	Puerto Principe
Vega Nieves de la		Nieves	Jovellanos
Vega y Corripio Manuel	Habana, Cerro Zaraga. y Atocha	Nueva Luisa	Habana
Veguer y Flaquer Juan	Habana, Oficios	Amistad	"
Venecia José		Demajagua	Cuba
		Esperanza	"
Vergara José		Adela y Convenio	Remedios
Vergara Ramon		Vista Alegre	Cienfuegos
Veitia y Zayas Antonio	Habana, Amistad	Recompensa	Guanajay
Vila y Torrens Francisco	Santa Clara	San Francisco	Sagua
Villagelin Jacinto		Carmen	Jaruco
Villaitre Marques de		Vega Grande	Cuba
Villaba y Ayllon Marquez de	Habana, Mercaderes	Angelita	Cardenas
Villar Gabriel del		Recreo	Cardenas
Villiers F. M. de y Sanchez I.		Palma Sola	Cienfuegos
			Santiago
Vinent y Gola Santiago		Sabanilla	Cuba
Vives Pablo		Vestio Hermosa	Cienfuegos

W.

Welsh S. y W.	Estados Unidos	Pario	Sagua
Wilson Augusto		Guaninicum	Caney

Y.

Name of Owner.	P. O. Address.	Name of Plantation.	Jurisdiction.
Yanez Manuel	Sagua, Colon	Begona	Sagua
Yera y Rodreguez		Destino	Santa Clara

Z.

Name of Owner.	P. O. Address.	Name of Plantation.	Jurisdiction.
Zabala José		San José	Matanzas
Zaldivar y Pedroso Julian	Habana		
	Consulado	San Pablo	
Zambrana de Chorros Juana	Matanzas	Dolores	Cardenas
Zanolletti José	Habana	Andalucia	Cienfuegos
Zayas Fernando A.	Matanzas O'Reilly	Pura y Limpia	Alacranes
Zayas Herederos de Martin	Marianao, Real	San Francisco Javier	Matanzas
Zayas y Dominguez		El Pilar	"
Zayas y Zayas, Herederos de J.	Habana, Cerro	San José	"
Zequeira Socorro	Habana, San Ignacio	San Felipe	"
		Paula	Jaruco
Zozaya y Ca.		Caridad	Remedios
		San José	Remedios
Zuaznavar Benito	Habana, Obrapia	Urumea	Colon
Zuaznavar Herederos de Fidel	Habana, Amargura	Recompensa	Colon
Zulueta Concurso de Salvador		Santa Elena	Trinidad
Zulueta Herederos de Julian de Marques de Alava	Habana, Aguiar	Alava	Colon
		Espana	Jovellanos
		Habana	Colon
		Mercedes	Remedios
		Vizcaya	Colon
		Zaza	Remedois

ANTIGUA, W. I.
(British.)
Population of the Island, 35,000.

NAMES OF BUSINESS MEN AND OTHERS.

Agricultural Implements.
A. J. Comache & Co.
McDonald & Co.
Geo. M. Bennett & Co.
D. W. Ramier & Co.
Geo. Davis
Manuel Gomes
James McDonald

Ale and Beer Dealers.
Murdoch & Co., wholesale and retail
Wm. Forrest " "
Wm. H. Moore " "
A. J. Comache & Co., wholesale and commission
Geo. W. Bennett & Co., wholesale and commission
Manuel Gomes, wholesale and commission
McDonald & Co., " "
James McDonald, " "

Banks and Bankers.
Colonial Bank, Limited

Billiard Rooms.
Globe Hotel
Recreation Co., Limited

Booksellers and Stationers.
John Bridger
W. W. Malone

Boot and Shoe Dealers.
Murdoch & Co.
Delos Martine
Madswick & Co.
W. H. Moore
John Bridger
Louisa Thibon
A. McAdam
Warnford & Co.
Gardner Bros.
S. Galbraith
Wm. Forrest
Robert Pigott
Thomas Pigott

Carriage or Wagon Dealers or Makers.
Henry White, maker and repairer
C. P. St. Luce " "
Geo. W. Bennett & Co., dealers in commission
McDonald & Co. " "

Coal Merchants.
Geo. W. Bennett & Co.
A. J. Comache & Co.
Manuel Gomes

Druggists.
Samuel Taylor
John Bridger

Dry Goods Dealers.
Murdoch & Co.
Delos Martine
Madswick & Co.
Wm. H. Moore
Louisa Thibon
A. McAdam
Warnford & Co.
S. Galbraith
Wm. Forrest
Thomas Piggott
Robert Piggott

Furniture Dealers.
A. McAdam
Wm. H. Moore
Murdoch & Co.

General Merchants, Wholesale Importing.
Archer & Co.
James McDonald
A. J. Comache & Co.
Geo. W. Bennett & Co.
Manuel Gomes
Jeremiah Gonsalves
De Lusa Jardine Bros.
McDonold & Co.
A. R. Mendes

Groceries and Provisions.
Murdoch & Co.
Wm. H. Moore
Delos Martine
Louisa Thibon
John Bridger
A. McAdam
Wm. Forrest
Thos. Faussett
Mrs. T. Thibon

Hardware and Tool Dealer.
Murdoch & Co.
Delos Martine
A. McAdam
Wm. Forrest
A. J. Comache & Co.
Manuel Gomes
Geo. W. Bennett & Co.
Geo. Davis
Scotland, Lucas & Co.
D. N. Ramier & Co.

Hotels.
Globe Hotel
Holliday's Hotel

Ice Merchants.
Globe Hotel

Iron Merchants.
A. J. Comache & Co.
Manuel Gomes
Geo. W. Bennett & Co.

Jewelry and Watches.
John Bridger
S. Galbraith
Wm. Forrest

Lumber Merchants.
A. J. Comache & Co.
Geo. W. Bennett & Co.
Manuel Gomes
McDonald & Co.
D. N. Ramier & Co.
Geo. Davis
Scotland, Lucas & Co.

Machinery Dealers.
Geo. W. Bennett & Co.
A. J. Comache & Co.

Musical Instruments.
S. Galbraith
Wm. Forrest
Warnford & Co.
John Bridger

Newspapers.
Antigua Standard
Antigua Observer
Antigua Churchman
The Colonist

Physicians.
Wm. H. Edwards
A. E. Edwards
A. G. McHattir
G. Gabriel
John Freeland
A. A. Mackir
F. Pierez

Photographer.
Thos. Faussett

Planters.
S. Sedgwick
T. D. Foote
Geo. Holborow
C. A. Shard
E. G. Lane
John Freeland
Victor Gaffroy
James Burns
H. O. Bennett
A. J. Comache

James Maginly
John Maginly
Alex. McAdam
James Rocke
W. H. Edwards
Leeward Islands Produce Co.
Wm. H. Moore
Wm. Goodwin
James Goodwin
J. Sutherland
Sir Oliver Nugent
Oliver Nugent, Jr.
T. Romney Guiness

Saddlery and Harness.
Geo. W. Bennett & Co.
D. N. Ramier & Co.
Manuel Gomes
G. McAdam
Wm. Forrest
Murdoch & Co.

Schools and Colleges.
Antigua Grammar School
Antigua Wesleyan School
Antigua Girls' School

Sewing Machine Dealers.
S. Galbraith
Wm. Forrest
Delos Martin

Sugar Estate Stores, Dealers in.
Geo. W. Bennett & Co.
A. J. Comache & Co.
Manuel Gomes
D. N. Ramier & Co.
Geo. Davis
Scotland, Lucas & Co.

Telegraph and Telephone Company.
West India Telegraph Co.

Trunks and Travelers' Outfits.
Murdoch & Co.
W. H. Moore
Delos Martine
A. McAdam
Wm. Forrest

Undertakers.
John James

Wall Paper Dealers.
Wm. Forrest
A. McAdam
John Bridger
Murdoch & Co.
Wm. Moore

DEMARARA.
(British Guiana.)

Population of the Territory, 340,000.

Attorneys at Law.

Abraham E. A. V.
Belmonte J. B. C.
Dalton E. H. G.
Hinds G. W.
Alton M. P.
Abraham F.
Cameron U. S.
Forshaw G. A.
Murdoch J. A.
Parnell C. G.
Woolford J. B.

Banking Institutions.

British Guiana Bank—Directors: B. V. Abraham, chairman; R. J. Kelly, B. Howell Jones, G. A. Forshaw, J. W. Davson, I. M. Garnett. Manager, G. L. Davson; accountant, E. J. N. Thomas.
Colonial Bank—Manager, M. R. O'Maley; accountant, E. M. Sanderson.

Barristers at Law.

Belmonte B. E. C., LL. D.
Clark Wm.
Davson C. S., Crown solicitor
De Groot R. J. V. R., New Amsterdam
Hutson D. M.
Lynch E. F. N.
Payne C. L.
Brandon David
Dargan P.
De Sonsa L.
Lewis W. E.
McKinnon N. R., New Amsterdam
Neblett R. B.
Phillips T. W.

Chemists, Druggists and Tobacconists.

Alty & J. D.
Cendrecourt C.
Coronel & Co.
Hannays G. E. L.
Kerr W. B.
Lobo Isaac
Mathews H. T.
Newsam W. R.
Van Norten & Co.
Amson H.
Cendrecourt H.
Davis H.
Jordan & Co. J.
Klien & Co. Joseph
Main Street Dispensing Co.
Max & Co. E. L.
Scott & Co.
Virtue & Co.

Chinese Merchants.

Hing Cheong & Co., fancy goods, Chinese groceries, etc.
Kwong Tai Lung & Co., general Chinese merchandise and tobacconists
Lee & Yhap, dry goods
Wo Lee & Co., merchants and importers

Contractors and Builders.

Bugle Michael
Evelyn J. D.
Evelyn J. T.
Hannays G. H.
La Penitence Woodworking Company
McDavid W. A.
Pratt R. B.
Mussenden H. C.
Sharples & Co. J. B.
Smith & Oldfield
Sproston H. & Son

Cooperages.

Applewhite John
Gaskin & Co.
Booker Bros. & Co.
Richards H.

Dentists.

Dr. James Spaight
Dr. W. C. Horne

Dry Goods and Clothing.

Bethencourt & Co., G.
Collier & Son, wholesale and retail
Currie & Co., Donald
Fogarty & Co., wholesale and retail
Kaufman & Co., R. T., drapers and fancy warehousemen
McGowan & Co., D. H., proprietors Grand Central Clothing and Notion Depot
McGowan & Co., R. J., proprietors "Granite Stores"
D'Oliveyra E., wholesale and retail
Playfair & Co., general dry goods and variety store
The Caledonian Warehouse, dry goods and clothing. Robert Crawford, proprietor
The Guianese Cash Store, dry goods and millinery

Foreign Consuls in Georgetown.

France—Henri Ledoux, Vice-Consul
German Empire and Portugal—Arthur Weber, Consul
Netherlands—Elias D'Oliveyra, Consul
Sweden and Norway—Jacob H. de Jonge, Consul
United States of America—Major W. T. Walthall, Consul; James Thomson, Vice-Consul
Venezuela—M. L. R. Andrade, Vice-Consul

Fire and Life Insurance Agencies.

Barbados Mutual (life)—Agents, Ramsey, Hill & Co.
Commercial Union (fire)—Agents, George Little & Co.
Equitable Life Assurance Society of the United States of America—Agent, Jacob A. de Jonge.
Guardian (fire)—Agents, Sandbach, Parker & Co.
Liverpool, London & Globe (fire)—Agents, Sandbach, Parker & Co.
London Assurance Corporation—Agent, A. Barr.
London and Lancashire (fire)—Agents, George Little & Co.
Mannheim Marine Insurance Company—Agents, A. W. Perot & Co.
Marine Insurance Company—Agents, Garnett & Co.
Marine and General Mutual (life)—Agents, Garnett & Co.
New York Life Insurance Company—Agent, J. Thomson.
North British and Mercantile (fire)—Agent, A. Barr.
Northern Assurance Company (fire and life)—Agents, Davson Bros. & Co.
Norwich Union Fire Insurance Society; agents, H. Ledoux & Co.
Phœnix Fire Office; agents, Sandbach, Parker & Co.
Queen of Liverpool (fire); agents, George Little & Co.
Royal Insurance Company (fire and life); agents, Booker Bros. & Co.
Standard (life); agent, G. A. Forshaw
Sun (London) Fire; agents, Garnett & Co.
The Imperial (fire); agent, Thomas H. Glennie
Underwriting and Agency Association, Limited, of London; agents, J. Tengely & Co.

Foundries.

Demerara Foundry; R. Buchanan & Co., proprietors. B. J. Godfrey, attorney; R. Allan, engineer
Demerara Railway Foundry; S. R. Starage, engineer
Sproston Dock and Foundry Co.; A. Sproston & Son, proprietors

General Merchants, Importers and Exporters.

Abraham B. V., merchant
Birch & Co., commission and general merchants, importers of live stock and lumber, and ice contractors to the government
Bagot Walter, merchant and estates' town agent
Booker Bros. & Co., merchants, importers and exporters and estates' agents; general wholesale and retail dealers
Cameron D. C., estates' attorney and town agent
Cameron Wm., commission merchant and ship broker
George Chapman, ship broker and commission merchant
Colonial Company, limited, merchants and town agents; T. H. Glennie and R. J. Kelly, attorneys
Conrad H. & Co., general merchants and importers, dealers in china and glassware
Currie & Co., Donald, importers and commission merchants
Davson Bros. & Co., estates' and insurance agents and commission merchants
DeFreitas & Co., J. F., provision merchants and dealers
DeJorge & Smith, general merchants; agents for Thom & Cameron, of Glasgow Scotland
Demerara Crushed Feed Co.; James Watson, manager
D'Nobrega M. F., general provision merchant
Farnum & Culpeper, estates' attorneys, town agents and commission merchants
Fernandez Joas, heirs of, wholesale provision and liquor dealers; J. G. Henriques, attorney
Garnett & Co., estates' attorneys and town agents, commission merchants and agents for the Royal Mail Steam Packet Company
Gonsalves & Co., M., general provision merchants and grocers, wholesale and retail
La Penitence Stores, estates' supplies and agencies; manager and attorney, A. Barr
Le Drux & Co. H., ship brokers and commission merchants
Macquarrie C. J., wine and cigar merchant and importer
McLeod Edwin, shipping and commission merchant and importer
Park & Cunningham, importers of and dealers in hardware and house-furnishing goods, and cabinet makers.
Perot & Co., A. W., general commission merchants, and shippers of colonial produce
Pitman & Grant, estates' town agents and merchants
Ramsay, Hill & Co., general commission merchants and agents
Rodriguez & D'Amil, provision merchants and dealers
Sandbach Parker & Co., general merchants and estates' town agents
Smith Bros. & Co., importers of, and wholesale and retail dealers in, dry goods, hardware and general provisions
Teugely & Co., J., commission merchants and ship brokers
White, E. T., commission agent, and importer of breadstuffs and provisions
Wieting & Richter, general commission merchants and importers. Proprietors Demerara steam bakery
Wakefield, Conrad & Co., commission merchants
Geo. Little & Co., general merchants and provision dealers

Government Medical Practitioners.

(Georgetown.)

Dr. F. H. Anderson, city health officer.
Dr. F. C. Fisher, surgeon to Almshouse, also private practitioner.
Dr. W. F. Law, assistant resident surgeon Colonial Hospital.
Dr. A. T. Ozzard, supernumerary medical officer Colonial Hospital.
Dr. J. R. Reid, supernumerary medical officer Colonial Hospital.
Dr. E. D. Rowland, resident surgeon Colonial Hospital.
Dr. A. D. Williams, medical inspector, British Guiana.

Goldsmiths, Watchmakers and Jewelers.

Abraham J. & B. V.
Fraser G. A.
Green L. G.
Peppiette & Co. C. W.
Archer R.
Gale C. Harold
Jacelon C. F.
Schuler & Sons J. A. W.
Small Richard

Hotels and Boarding Houses.

Mrs. Baynes, Boarding House, Murray street
J. B. Buttery, Grand Central Hotel
S. H. Clarke, Criterion Club
Mrs. Forbes, Boarding House
Town Hotel, Mrs. Isador C. Murray, Proprietress
Victoria Hotel, Mrs. Spooner, Proprietress.

Insurance Companies.

The Hand-In-Hand Mutual Guaranteed Fire Insurance Company of British Guiana, Limited—Chairman of board of directors, B. V. Abraham; secretary, F. A. Conyers; assistant secretary, Æneas D. Mackay; inspector, F. A. R. Winter.
British Guiana Mutual Fire Insurance Company, Limited—Chairman, R. P. Drysdale; manager and secretary, John S. Hill; assistant secretary, James A. Hill; Berbice agent, Wm. Ingall.

Land Surveyors.

Anderson C. M., Crown Lands Department
Chalmers W.
Hill Luke M., Town Superintendent
Perkins H. I. Crown Land Department
Thomson Wm. F
Chalmers E.
W. J. Fowler, sworn
McQuirk Michael Kalacoon, sworn
Prass J. P., sworn
Wight T. G., Crown Surveyor

Licensed Auctioneers.

De Jonge Jacob H.
Jacobs Joseph
Macquarrie C. J.

Livery Stable Keepers.

Birch & Co., High Street Stables
Gonsalves A., Werk-en-Rust Stables
Wieting & Richter, Georgetown Stables

Manufacturers of Aerated Waters.

Alty & Co. J. D.
Fernandes, executors of Joao
John Virtue & Co.

Miscellaneous Corporate Institutions.

Georgetown Gas Company, Limited—Principal office, London, England; director at Georgetown, R. P. Drysdale; manager, T. B. Younger; secretary, F. A. Conyers.
Georgetown Tramways Company. Limited—Chairman G. A. Forshaw; manager, W. F. Nunn; secretary, C. S. Davis.
Demerara Railway Company—Principal office, London. Demerara directors : Fred A. Mason, A. J. Pitman, M. Garnett, W. H. Sherlock, J. J. Dare. General manager, F. A. Mason ; goods superintendent, G. C. Collins ; assistant, A. Phillips.
British Guiana Building Society, Limited—G. A. Forshaw, chairman ; James H. Jones, secretary and accountant ; David Smith, surveyor.

Municipal Officers City of Georgetown.

Mayor and president of Town Council, James Thomson; town clerk, J. C. R. Hill; assistant town clerk and bookkeeper, P. P. Fairbairn; town superintendent, Luke M. Hill; clerk of markets, W. T. Binnie; engineer of Water Works and assistant town superintendent, J. B. Craig; superintendent of fire engines, N. Cox; senior inspector of police, W. C. Harrigin.

Newspapers and Other Publications.

"Argosy," weekly newspaper; J. Thomson, editor and proprietor
"British Guiana Blue Book," annually by authority
"British Guiana Directory," annually; C. K. Jardine, publisher
"Catholic Calendar," monthly; printed by the "Argosy" press
"Daily Chronicle;" C. K. Jardine, proprietor; R. Offord Sherrington, editor
"Echo," weekly, Plaisance Village; W. H. Hinds, editor and proprietor
"Mercantile Intelligencer and Price Current," semi-monthly; Baldwin & Co., publishers.
"O'Portuguez," weekly; J. M. Pacheco, editor and proprietor
"Official Gazette," bi-weekly; by C. K. Jardine, government printer
"Royal Gazette," daily; Thos. Watt, editor and proprietor
"Timehri," semi-annually, journal of the Royal Agricultural and Commercial Society; J. J. Quelch, editor; James Thomson, publisher.

Piano Dealers and Tuners.

Barnard W. F., tuner
J. S. Belasco, dealer and tuner
T. Browne, dealer and tuner
Colbeck W. R.
Strong H., piano dealer and importer

Photographers.

Siza Julia A.
Siza Henrique
Stevens & Co. U. H.
Read H.

Private Practitioners.

Dr. U. Brebner
Dr. J. E. London
Dr. M. M. Gonsalves
Dr. Pereira
Dr. J. Teixeira

Sail Makers.

Chambers J. A.
Green F. A.
DeVillier W.
Phillips W. E.
Wilson E.

Saw Mills.

Bugle M. & Son
Georgetown Saw Mill Co.
Kingston Saw and Planing Mill, Georgetown
La Penitence Wood Working Co.

Ship Chandlers.

Bayley B. S.
Smith A. J.
Smith Bros. & Co.
Smith & Oldfield

Stationery, Bookbinding and Job Printing Establishments.

Baldwin & Co.
Guiana Church Book Depository
Thomas Watt, *Royal Gazette* Establishment
Crombie & Ashton
Jardine, C. K., Public Printer
James Thomson

Sugar Estates.

Adelphi—Canje Creek, Berbice County; proprietors, non-resident ; attorney, A. Barr; town agents, S. Davson & Co.
Albion—Corentyne Coast, Berbice ; proprietors and town agents, The Colonial Company
Annandale—Demerara ; attorney and town agent, W. Bagot
Anna Regina—Essequebo ; attorney and manager, A. R. Gilzean; town agents, Booker Bros. & Co.
Aurora—Essequebo ; proprietor and attorney, W. Craigen ; town agent, William Smith
Bath—Berbice ; proprietors, A. & T. M. Hunter ; town agents, S. Davson & Co.
Bel Air—Demerara; proprietor, Bel Air Company ; attorney and town agent, A. Barr
Belle Vue—Demerara ; attorney and manager, Wm. Elliott ; town agents, J. P. Farnum, Jr., and S. A. H. Culpeper
Blairmont—Berbice County ; proprietors, Davson Bros.; attorneys and town agents, Davson Bros. & Co.
Blankenburg—County Demerara ; attorney and town agent, M. Garnett
Blenheim—Leguan Island ; town agent and part proprietor, A. Barr
Caledonia—Wakenaam ; town agent, A. Barr
Canefield—Canje Creek, Berbice; attorney, P. H. Nind; town agents, Brooker Bros. & Co.
Cane Grove—Demerara;proprietor, J. McConnell (non-resident); town agents, Booker Bros. & Co.
Chateau—Margot; Demerara, attorneys and town agents, Pitman & Grant
Clonbrook—Demerara; proprietor and attorney, J. B. W. Clementson; town agent, W. Bagot
Coffee Grove—Essequebo ; proprietor and manager, B. Winter
Cornelia Ida—Demerara County; proprietors, Cornelia Ida Estate Company; attorneys, W. Craigen and W. Smith; town agent, W. Smith

Cove and John—County Demerara; proprietor and manager, Hon. C. J. Bascom; town agent Wm. Smith
Cuming's Lodge—Demerara; proprietor, the Bel Air Company; town agent, A. Barr.
De Kinderen—Demerara; proprietors, A. T. Stokes and Q. Hogg; attorney and town agent, A. Barr
De Willem—Proprietors, non-resident; attorney, Hon. J. J. Dare; town agents; Booker Bros. & Co.
Diamond—Demerara; proprietors, non-resident; town agents, Sandbach, Parker & Co.
Dunoon—Demerara; proprietor, B. A. Robertson; town agents, A. W. Perot & Co.
Enmore—Demerara; attorney, J. J. Dare; town agents, Booker Bros. & Co.
Enterprise—Demerara; proprietors, non-resident; attorneys, E. J. Borman and J. J. Dare; town agents, Booker Bros. & Co.
Enterprise—Leguan Island; proprietor. H. McN. Greene; town agent, D. C. Cameron
Farm—Demerara ; proprietors, non-resident; town agents, Sandbach, Parker & Co.
Friends—County Berbice; attorneys, R. J. Kelly, and T. A. Glennie; town agents, Colonial Company
Friendship—Wakenaam Island; proprietress, Mrs. Mary Cameron; attorney and town agent, D. C. Cameron
Goedverwagting—Demerara; attorney and town agent, Alex Barr
Golden Fleece—Essequebo; proprietors, non-resident; attorney and town agent, A. Barr.
Good Success—Wakenaam Island; part proprietor and Manager, John Pendleton; town agent, Wm. Smith
Greenfield—Demerara; proprietors, J. A. Booker and J. J. Dare; town agents, Booker Bros. & Co.
Hague—Demerara; attorneys and town agents, Pitman & Grant
Hamburg—Essequebo; attorney, and manager, Henry R. W. Greig; town agents, George Little & Co.
Hampton Court—Essequebo ; attorneys, R. J. Kelly and T. A. Glennie; town agents, Colonial Company
Helena—Demerara; attorney and manager, Edwin Morgan; town agents, George Little & Co.
Herstelling—Demerara; attorney, Wm. Craigen; town agent, Wm. Smith
Highburg—Berbice; town agents, Garnett & Co.; attorney and manager, Andrew Miller
Hope—Demerara; attorney, B. Howell Jones; town agent, F. Grant
Houston—Demerara River; proprietors, B. Howell Jones and others; town agent, F. Grant
Industry—Demerara; proprietors, The Belair Company; attorney and town agent, A. Barr
Johanna Cecelia—Essequebo ; attorney and town agent, A. Barr
La Belle Alliance—Essequebo; attorney, A. R. Gilzean; manager, H. S. Humphreys
La Bonne Intention—Demerara; attorney, J. J. Dare; town agents, Booker Bros. & Co.
La Jalousie — Demerara; attorney and town agent, A. Barr
La Penitence—Demerara; proprietors, Bel Air Company; attorney and town agent, A. Barr
Leonora—Demerara; proprietor, non-resident; town agents, Sandbach, Parker & Co.

Sugar Estates—*continued*.

Lochabar—Berbice; attorney, P. H. Hind, town agents, Booker Bros. & Co.
Lusignan—Demerara; town agent, A. Barr; proprietor and manager, Hon. W. A. Wolseley
Mara—Berbice; proprietors, Colonial Company; town agents, Colonial Company
Ma Retraite—Berbice; attorneys, R. J. Kelly & T. H. Glennie; town agents, The Colonial Company
Maryville and Bellefield—Leguan; attorneys, Hon. B. H. Jones and Wm. Cameron; town agents, Farnum & Culpeper
Melville—Demerara; attorney, J. J. Dare; town agents, Booker Bros. & Co.
Met-en-Meerzorg—Demerara; attorney and manager, F. E. James, Jr.
Mon Repos—Demerara; attorney and manager, A. Brand; town agents, A. Ledoux & Co.
Montrose—Demerara; attorney, P. H. Nind; town agents, Booker Bros. & Co.
Nismes—Demerara; attorney, Carl Wicting; town agents, Wieting & Richter.
Nonpariel—Demerara; proprietor, Quintin Hogg; attorney and town agent, A. Barr
Peters Hall—Demerara; proprietors, Colonial Company; attorneys, R. J. Kelly and T. A. Glennie
Philadelphia—Demerara; manager, D. A. Ainge; attorney and town agent, D. C. Cameron.
Port Mourant—Berbice; attorney, J. J. Dare; town agents, Booker Bros. & Co.
Providence—Demerara; proprietors, non-resident; town agents, Sandbach, Parker & Co.
Reliance—Essequebo; attorney and town agent, A. Barr
Rose Hall—Berbice; town agents, Booker Bros. & Co.
Ruimveld—Demerara; attorneys and town agents, Sandbach, Parker & Co.
Schoon Ord—Demarara; attorneys, B. H. Jones and Wm. Cameron; town agents, Farnum & Culpeper
Skeldon—Berbice; attorney, Hon. J. J. Dare; town agents, Booker Bros. & Co.
Smythfield—Berbice; attorney, Wm. Ingall (New Amsterdam); town agent, Wm. Ingall
Spring Hall—Demerara; town agent, Walter Bagot

Success—East Coast; Demerara; proprietors, Colonial Company; town agents, Colonial Company
Success—Leguan; proprietors, A. Sproston & Son; planting attorney, D. C. Cameron; town agents, Sproston Dock and Foundry Company
Taymouth Manor—attorneys and town agents, Pitman & Grant
Turkeyen—Demerara; proprietors, The Bel Air Company; attorney and town agent, A. Barr
Uitolugt—Demerara; proprietors, non-resident; town agents, Booker Bros. & Co.
Versailles—Demerara; attorneys and town agents, Pitman & Grant
Vive-la-Fource—Demerara; proprietors, Hon. Thos. Mulligan and F. A. Mason; town agents, Booker Bros. & Co.
Vriesland—Demerara; attorneys, M. Garnett and T. Mulligan; town agent, M. Garnett
Vryheids Lust and Better Hope—Demerara; attorney, P. H. Nind; town agents, Booker Bros. & Co.
Windsor Forest—Demerara; proprietors, The Colonial Company; attorneys, R. J. Kelly and T. A. Glennie; town agents, The Colonial Company

Tailors.

Applewhite
Lord G. N.
Playfair & Co.
Rieck estate of M. N.
Robinson J. S.
Thompson Saml.
Wallace & Paul

Weighers.

Croal C. C.
Hart H. F.
Neblett J. E.
Thorpe G. A.
Gaskin K. M.
Howard J. A.
Keese J. C.
Whitehead J. C.

ISLAND OF JAMAICA, W. I.

(British.)

Population of entire Island, 380,000.

Agricultural Implements.

Emanuel Lyons & Son, Kingston
Arnold L. Malabre & Co., Kingston
David Henderson & Co., Kingston
I. W. Middleton & Co., Kingston
Martin & Spicer

Ales and Beer Dealers.

West India Brewing Company, Kingston
I. Wray & Nephew, Kingston
Peter Desnoes & Son, Kingston
Daniel Finzi & Co., Kingston
Simon & Co., Kingston
I. E. Kerr & Son, Montego Bay
A. L. DaCosta, Port Maria
I. E. Kerr & Co., Port Maria
M. Solomon & Co., St. Ann's Bay
I. H. Levy, Brown's Town

Banks and Bankers.

Colonial Bank, Kingston
People's Discount and Deposit Co. (Limited), Kingston
Government Savings Bank, with branches throughout the Island, Kingston
Penny Savings Bank, Kingston
Colonial Bank (branch), Sav-la-Mar
Colonial Bank (branch), Montego Bay
Colonial Bank (branch), Falmouth
Colonial Bank (branch), Annatto Bay
Penny savings banks are now being established throughout the Island

Billiard Rooms.

Commercial Billiard Rooms, Kingston

Booksellers and Stationers.

Aston W. Gardner & Co., Kingston
De Cordova & Co., Kingston
Arthur Hylton, Kingston
Justin McCarthy & Co., Kingston
McCartney & Co., Kingston
Rouse & Co., Kingston
Wesleyan Bookstore, Kingston
Mortimer C. de Souza, Kingston
I. W. Kerr & Co., Kingston
Alfred F. Aarons, Kingston

Boot and Shoe Dealers.

John Cassis, Kingston
J. C. Silburn, Kingston
Nathan & Co., Kingston
Alfred Pansey, Kingston
Wm. Malabre & Co., Kingston
Pinnock & Bailey, Kingston
Parks & Burrows, Kingston
R. Recivero & Co., Kingston
Dick & Abbott, Kingston
Ellis & Co., Kingston
Henry Lindo, Kingston
Ellias C. Dazevedo, Kingston
A. H. Morales, Kingston
Jacob Brandon, Kingston
Joseph Burrow, Kingston
John Milo Burke, Kingston
Joseph Bewley, Kingston
Daniel J. Motta, Kingston
Hepburn, McCarthy & Co., Kingston
Charles Millingen, Kingston
Thomas Largood, Kingston
Leoniel M. Mordecai, Port Antonio
David S. Gideon, Port Antonio
J. H. Levy, Brown's Town
M. Solomons & Co., St. Ann's Bay.
Robt. Nunes, Falmouth
Leyden & Farquharson, Black River
Neilson & Co., Sav-la-mar
Nathaniel Henriques, Annatto Bay
A. L. Da Costa, Port Maria
I. J. Mordecai & Co., Morant Bay

Carriage and Wagon Makers and Dealers.

G. I. de Cordova, Kingston
Reginald de Lonza, Kingston
Alfred Brent, Kingston
Martin and Spicer, Kingston
Turnbul, Mudon & Co., Kingston
Wales Bros., Kingston
G. Goring, Kingston
A. Hunt, Kingston

Coal Merchants.

Sontar & Co., Kingston
J. H. McDowell, Kingston

Dentists.

F. A. Dunand, Kingston
Comer & Miller, Kingston
John A. Carpenter, Kingston
Reginald W. Bird, Kingston
Ernest Sturridge, Kingston
D. L. Levett, Kingston
B. H. Dias, Kingston
F. A. Duannie, Kingston

There are no dentists in the interior parts. Several of the above dentists make regular tours throughout the Island.

Dry Goods Dealers.

Pinnock, Bailey & Co., Kingston
Turnbul & Co., Kingston
Finke & Co., Kingston
Frederick Alexander & Co., Kingston
W. G. Young & Co., Kingston
Jacobsen & Anderson, Kingston
Wm. Schiller & Co., Kingston
Wm. Malabre & Co., Kingston
W. R. McPherson & Co., Kingston
Nathan & Co., Kingston
Jacob Brandon, Kingston

Dry Goods Dealers—continued.

Joseph Bewley, Kingston
Alfred Pansey, Kingston
D, J. Motta, Kingston
Ellias C. Dazevedo, Kingston
Dick & Abbott, Kingston
Henry Lindo, Kingston
Maduro, Brandon & Co, Kingston
Ellis & Co., Kingston
Parks & Burrows, Kingston
Joseph Burrows, Kingston
A. H. Morales, Kingston
Thomas Sargood, Kingston
John Milo. Burke, Kingston
Hepburn, McCarthy & Co., Kingston
E. A. Ledward, Kingston
S. M. DaCosta & Co., Kingston
Charles Millingen, Kingston
Judith Aarons, Kingston
Hyman Cohen, Kingston
Chas. S. Barrow, Kingston

Druggists.

E. D. Kindkead, Kingston
Alfred Pansey, Kingston
J. M. Croswell, Kingston
W. G. McPherson & Co., Kingston
P. E. Anveay, Kingston
L. M. Mordecai, Port Antonio
David L. Gideon, Port Antonio
A. Escoffrey, Port Antonio
I. J. Mordecai & Co., Morant Bay
Cresser & Co., Morant Bay
R. W. Crawford, Port Morant
Carter & Co., Port Morant
F. C. Henriques, Annatto Bay
A. L. Da Costa Port Maria
Goffe & Co., Port Maria
A. L. Sweetland, Port Maria
Bravo Brós. & Co., St. Ann's Bay
M. Solomon & Co., St. Ann's Bay
Silvester Cotter, St. Ann's Bay
Solomon Isaacs, St. Ann's Bay
I. H. Levy, Brown's Town
E. P. Delgado, Brown's Town
Robert Nunes, Falmouth
Delgado Bros., Falmouth
I. E. Kerr & Co., Montego Bay
G. L. P. Corrinaldi, Montego Bay
Neilson & Co., Sav-la-mar
Leyden & Co., Sav-la-mar
Herbert Jones & Co., Sav-la-mar
I. S. Segree, Sav-la-mar
Leyden & Farquharson, Black River
Lionel Isaacs, Mandeville
R. B. Braham, Mandeville
Robert Beverland, Dry Harbor
Nash & Co., Dry Harbor
Santfleben & Co., Lucea

Furniture Dealers.

Alexander Berry & Son, Kingston
Turnbull, Mudon & Co., Kingston
Thomas H. Aguilar, Kingston
Mark C. Hendricks, Kingston
George L. Facey, Kingston

General Merchants, Wholesale and Importing.

Lascelles de Mercado & Co., Kingston
F. Correosso & Co., Kingston
Davidson Colthirst & Co., Kingston
Solomon Ashenheim & Co., Kingston
Archibald Munro, Kingston
John C. Fegan & Co., Kingston
Henry H. Iles, Kingston
G. I. de Cordova, Kingston
A. Mordecai & Co., Kingston
Moses M. Alexander, Kingston
Hermann Stern, Kingston
Gomes, Casseres & Co., Kingston
Thaddeus J. Alexander, Kingston
Bravo Bros. & Co., St. Ann's Bay
J. H. Levy, Brown's Town
Kerr & Co., Montego Bay

Groceries and Provisions.

Pinnock, Bailey & Co., Kingston
Andrew Delisser, Kingston
S. M. Da Costa & Co., Kingston
Uriah Delapenha, Kingston
J. Watson Scott, Kingston
Alfred Morrice, Kingston
Richard White, Kingston
Joseph Millingen, Kingston
Charles Grant, Kingston
J. J. G. Lewis, Kingston
H. W. Cody, Kingston
A. McMillan, Kingston
E. D. Kindkead, Kingston
John M. Croswell, Kingston
W. G. McPherson, Kingston
P. E. Amray, Kingston
Delgado & Co., Kingston
D. Stevenson & Co., Kingston
Moses Levy, Kingston
A. B. Hart, Kingston
Horatio Abrahams, Kingston
George A. Campbell, Kingston
Fred. L. Myers, Kingston
G. Eustace Bevike & Bros., Kingston
Emanuel X. Leon, Kingston
D. P. C. Henriques, Kingston
G. Boetcher & Co., Kingston
G. C. H. Lewis, Kingston
Charles Levy & Co., Kingston
John J. Hart, Kingston
Lascelles de Mercado & Co., Kingston
I. J. Cunningham, Port Antonio
I. C. Dias, Annatto Bay
J. E. Kerr & Co., Port Maria
A. L. Da Costa, Port Maria
J. B. Goffe & Co., Port Maria
Marchalleck & Co., Morant Bay
Robert Nunes, Falmouth
J. H. Levy, Brown's Town
C. P. Delgado, Brown's Town
M. Solomon & Co., St, Ann's Bay
L. L. Fraser, St. Ann's Bay
J. E. Kerr & Co., Montego Bay
Herbert Jones & Co., Sav-la-mar
Hendricks & Co., Black River
Melhado Bros. & Co., Old Harbor
Delgado & Co., Old Harbor
Browne & Co., Lucea

Hardware and Tool Dealers.

Emanuel Lyons & Son, Kingston
D. Henderson & Co., Kingston
Arnold L. Malabre & Co.
J. W. Middleton & Co., Kingston
Martin & Spicer, Kingston

Hotels.

Park Lodge, Kingston
Myrtle Bank, Kingston
Brook's Hotel, Mandeville
There is a company formed who are building hotels on a large scale; they are called the American Hotels Company in Jamaica
There are many private lodgings throughout the Island

Ice Merchants.

Kingston Ice Making Company, Kingston

Iron Merchants.

Emanuel Lyons & Son, Kingston
Arnold L. Malabre & Co., Kingston
David Henderson & Co., Kingston
J. W. Middleton & Co., Kingston
Martin & Spicer, Kingston

Jewelry and Watches.

J. H. Milke, Kingston
J. O. Milke, Kingston
Martin & Spicer, Kingston
John Millholland, Kingston
Chas. T. Burton, Kingston
J. W. Whitbourne, Kingston
Frederick Alexander, Kingston

Lumber Merchants.

Arnold L. Malabre & Co., Kingston
Alexander Fuertado, Kingston
Emanuel Lyons & Son, Kingston

Machinery Dealers.

Emanuel Lyons & Co., Kingston
David Henderson & Co., Kingston
Arnold L. Malabre & Co., Kingston
I. W. Middleton & Co., Kingston

Musical Instruments.

Louis Winkler & Co., Kingston

Newspapers.

"Daily Gleaner," De Cordova & Co., Kingston
"Tri-Weekly Gleaner," De Cordova & Co., Kingston
"Tri-Weekly Budget," C. L. Campbell, Kingston
"Colonial Standard," George Levy, Kingston
"The Electric Messenger," J. Maynier & Ross, Kingston
"Gall's News Letter," James Gall, Kingston
"The Evening Express," W. B. Hannan, Kingston
"The Jamaica Gazette," Government, Kingston
"The Police Gazette," Government, Kingston
"Jamaica Christian Chronicle," Revd. J. Roberts, Kingston
"Jamaica Prices Current," De Cordova & Co., Kingston
"Methodist Messenger," Revd. W. C. Murray, Kingston
"Jamaica Churchman," Revd. Wm. Simms, M. A., Kingston
"The Baptist Reporter," Revd. D. J. East, Kingston
"The Jamaica Witness," Revd. Alex. Robb, D. D., Kingston
"The Wesleyan Chronicle," I. C. Carver, Kingston
"The St. Michael's Magazine," Revd. P. G. Ambrose, Kingston
"The Jamaica Post," J. W. Kerr & Co., Kingston
"Monthly Journal of Commerce," Chas. E. de Mercado, Kingston
"The Trelawny," H. G. Delisser. Falmouth
"The Falmouth Gazette," J. W. Henry, Falmouth
"The Nineteenth Century," D. A. Corinaldi, Montego Bay
"The St. Elizabeth Messenger," A. G. Levy, Black River
"The Record," Revd. E. J. Worthy, Port Antonio

Pianos.

Louis Winkler & Co., Kingston
John C. Fegan & Co., Kingston
Alexander Berry & Son, Kingston
Martin & Spicer, Kingston

Photographers.

I. B. Valdes & Co., Kingston
I. N. Marby, Kingston
O. Bavastro, Kingston
I. W. Cleary, Kingston

There are no photographers at any other point of the Island.

Physicians.

C. B. Mosse, C. B., M. R. C. S. Eng., Kingston
F. H. Saunders, M. R. C. S. Eng., Kingston
W. H. Strachan, L. R. C. P. Lon., M. P. C. S. Eng., Kingston
I. Leslie Cox, L. R. C. P. Edin. L. R. C. S. Edin., Kingston
A. B. Ewart, M. B. C. M., Kingston
G. E. Cheyne, M. R. C. S. Eng., Kingston
M. P. C. McCormack, L. R. C. S. Edin., Kingston
I. W. Anderson, M. D., Kingston
C. Gayhard, M. R. C. S. Eng., Kingston
James Scott, M. R. C. S. Eng., Kingston
James Olgilvie, F. R. C. S. Edin., Kingston
J. C. Phillipps, M. D. Edin., Kingston
A. R. Saunders, M. R. Lon. F. R. C. S. Eng., Kingston
E. E. Bronstorph, L. R. C. P. Lon., Kingston
G. F. A. da Costa, B. M. M. S. Aber., Kingston
Henry Knaggs, army medical staff, Jamaica, Kingston
James Neish, M. D. Port Royal
John Breakey, inspector general hospital R. N., Port Royal
J. Cargill, M. D., L. R. C. P. Lon., St. Andrew
G. C. Henderson, M. D. Lon., M. R. C. S., M. R. C. P. Eng., St. Andrew
Y. T. G. Moore, L. R. C. P., St. Andrew
G. T. Martin, M. R. C. S. Edin., Spanish Town
H. J. Minchinton, M. R. C. S. Eng., L. R. C. P. Edin., Spanish Town
J. A. Wegg, M. D., Ohio, Spanish Town
J. H. Peck, L. R. C. S. Edin., Linstead
T. M. Drummond, M. D., St. John's
C. R. Gillard, M. R. C. S. Eng., Old Harbor
J. E. W. Holwell, M. D., Old Harbor

Physicians—*continued*.

R. C. Gibb, M. R. C. S. Eng., L. R. C. P. Lon., Vere
H. L. Clare, M. B., Vere
B. M. Beckwith, M. D., Mile Gully
S. M. Logan, M. D., New Port
George Cooke, L. R. C. S. Irld., Mandeville
E. L. Grant, M. B. C. M., Siloah
J. H. Clarke, L. R. C. S., M. R. C. P. Edin., Santa Cruz
J. A. Calder, M. B., M. R. C. S. Edin., Black River
J. Adolphus, M. R. C. S. Eng., Black River
R. C. Harvey, M. D., Sav-la-mar
R. S. Harvey, M. D., Sav-la-mar
Z. Mennell, L. L. A. London, Sav-la-Mar
John Delcon, M. R. C. S. Eng., Lucea
E. H. Cooke, M. B., Lucea
F. A. Sinclair, M. D., Montego Bay
I. Wilson, M. D., Aber., Montego Bay
A. G. McCatty, M. D., Montego Bay
M. D. Hart, M. D., Montego Bay
S. T. Vine, M. D., Good Hope
S. P. Madden, M. D. Falmouth
C. T. Dervar, M. D., Swanswick
A. W. T. Steer, M. D., Ulster Spring
W. H. Miller, M. D., Brown's Town
J. C. E. Roberts, M. D., Moneague
H. S. Mannsell, M. B., M. R. C. S. Irld., St. Ann's Bay
V. F. Mullen, M. D., Port Maria
J Pringle, M. B., Belfield
T. Clarke, M. D., Edin., Annatto Bay
L. Gifford, M. B., Annatto Bay
D. M. McPhail, M. D., Buff Bay
C. A. Mosely, M. D., Port Antonio
Keitch, M. D., Port Antonio
L. E. Delmege, L. R. C. S. Irld., Manchioneal
A. C. Neyland, M. D., Bath
E. W. Major, M. R. C. L. Eng., Bath
J. L. Gerrard, M. R. C. L. Eng., Morant Bay
Thos. Manners, M. R. C. L., Moran Bay
W. I. Calder, M. B. Edin., Malvern

Planters.

M. C. Morgan, St. Andrew
D. I. Davis, St. Thomas
James Harrison, St. Thomas
Richard Evans, St. Thomas
Charles Hode Levy, St. Thomas
C. E. Scudamore, St. Thomas
W. L. Richards, St. Thomas
R. Valdes, Portland
W. B. Epnet, Portland
G. W. Middleton, Portland
H. Edwards, St. Mary
I. C. Melville, St. Mary
F. H. Barker, St. Mary
W. Macdonald, St. Mary
Henry Braham, St. Mary
Wilmot Westmoreland, St. Mary
John Cameron, St. Ann's
Joseph Shearer, St. Ann's
H. P. Thompson, St. Ann's
Richard Todd, St. Ann's
Richard Young, St. Ann's
Wm. Cover, Jr., St. Ann's
I. Sine, Trelawny
Wm. Gentles, Trelawny
W. Kerr, Trelawny
F. R. Coy, Trelawny
W. Ogilvy, Trelawny
G. R. Dewar, Trelawny
L. C. Shriley, Trelawny
George Robertson, Trelawny
H. I. Kerr, Trelawny
J. W. Parkin, St. James
D. B. L. Heaven, St. James
I. W. Fisher, St. James
John Lawrence, St. James
George Robertson, St. James
C. D. Willingham, St. James
A. C. Fouchen, St. James
C. W. Sterling St. James
I. McFarlane, St. James
G. L. Phillips, St. James
A. Charley, St. James
Wm. Ewen, St. James
Dutton Trench, St. James
A. E. Cooks, Hanover
John Hodson, Hanover
I. M. Mills, Hanover
Fred. Topper, Hanover
D. T. Mudie, Hanover
H. Davies, Hanover
J. H. Clark, Hanover
E. J. Sadler, Hanover
Wm. Farquharson, Hanover
H. Davidson, Hanover
H. A. Vickers, Westmoreland
H. Clark, Westmoreland
J. Hudson, Jr., Westmoreland
Thos. Cridland, Westmoreland
Wm. Hill, St. Elizabeth
I. M. Farquharson, St. Elizabeth
John Calder, St. Elizabeth
Arthur James, Clarendon
J. W. McKenzie, Clarendon
Q. Logan
R. C. Gibb, Clarendon
H. T. Ronaldson
Thos. Ellis, Clarendon
J. Dingwall, Clarendon
J. Fox, Clarendon
John McGregor, Clarendon
E. C. Elliott, Clarendon
W. Jurmp, Clarendon.
John Scully, Clarendon
J. W. Kemp, Clarendon
J. Grinan, Clarendon
W. G. Ramsay, St. Catherine
F. R. Hall, St. Catherine
John McPhail
E. C. Bather, St. Catherine
D. Campbell, St. Catherine
Wm. Gles, St. Catherine
J. Scarlett, St. Catherine

Printers and Publishers.

Mortimer C. De Souza, Kingston
J. W. Kerr & Co., Kingston
W. B. Hanan, Kingston
C. L. Campbell, Kingston
De Cordova & Co., Kingston
James Gall, Kingston
George Levy, Kingston
Aston W. Gardner & Co., Kingston

Railway Companies.

Jamaica Government Railway, extending to Spanish Town, branching off into Porus (Manchester), a distance of 50 miles, and into

Railways—continued.

Ewarton in another direction, a distance of 34 miles. An American syndicate are now in treaty for the purchase of this railway.

STATIONS.

Kingston
Spanish Town
Old Harbor
Linstead
Ewarton
Porus
May Pen
Four Paths
Clarendon Park
Hartlands
Bog Walk
Bushy Park
Grange Lane
Cumberland, Penn.

Saddlery and Harness.

John McDonald, Kingston
Henry Sinclair, Kingston
T. Agton, Kingston
M. P. DaCosta, Kingston

There are many small shops at different points of the country where harnesses may be repaired.

Schools and Colleges.

St. Mary's Industrial School, Kingston
Gunvale College, Kingston
Lady Mico's Charity, Kingston
Wolmer's Free School, Kingston
Calabar College, Kingston
St. George's College, Kingston
Mary Villa College, Kingston
Middle Grade School, Kingston
Grammar School, Kingston
Church of England High School, Kingston
Divinity School, Kingston
Jamaica High School, St. Andrew
Wesleyan High School for Boys, St. Andrew
Wesleyan High School for Girls, St. Andrew
Jamaica Female Training College, St. Andrew
Trichfield Free School, Port Antonio
Moerwick's Charity, Buff Bay
Moravian Female Training College, Bethabara
Moravian Training School, Fairfield
Ludford's Bequest, St. Catherine
Buckford & Smith's School, St. Catherine
Vere and Manchester Free Schools, Alley
Munro & Dickinson's Free School, St. Elizabeth
Rusea's Free School, Hanover
Manning's Free School, Sav-la-Mar

Sewing Machine Dealers.

Gomes, Casseress & Co., Kingston
Maduro, Brandon & Co., Kingston
R. Recuero & Co., Kingston
Nathan & Co., Kingston
Bravo Bros., St. Ann's Bay
L. M. Mordecai, Port Antonio
J. H. Levy, Brown's Town
J. E. Kerr & Co., Montego Bay
Neilson & Co., Sav-la-Mar
Leyden & Farquharson, Black River
A. L. DaCosta, Port Maria

Steamship Companies.

Royal Mail Steam Packet Company, A. de Montagnac, Acting Agent
Atlas Steamship Company, W. Peploe Forwood
West India and Pacific Steamship Company, James H. McDowell
Anchor Line, Leonard Wiley and Chas. Hannay
Clyde Line, E. A. H. Haggart
Honduras and Central American Steamship Co., Solomon Ashenheim & Co.
Caribbean Line, Davidson, Colthir & Co.
Royal Mail Company, Davidson Colthirst & Co.
Kerr & Co's Line, I. E. Kerr & Co.
Bell Line, Jamaica Fruit & Co-operative Co.
Hart Line, Jamaica Fruit & Co-operative Co.
Several chartered Steamers calling here principally for fruit for the U. S.

Telegraph Companies.

West India and Panama Telegraph Company, Kingston
Post Office Telegraph, with offices throughout the Island

Telephone Company.

West India Telephone Company, Kingston

Wall Paper Dealers.

John Milo Burke, Kingston
Nathan & Co., Kingston
W. R. Macpherson & Co., Kingston

Walls are generally painted or calcimined in this country; therefore the importation of wallpaper is very small.

Undertakers.

Alexander Berry & Son, Kingston
Thomas N. Aguilar, Kingston
Turnbul, Mudon & Co., Kingston
Marck C. Hendricks, Kingston

CITY OF NASSAU AND ISLAND OF NEW PROVIDENCE.

(British.)

Population of the Island, 40,000.

Ale, Beer and Wine Dealers.

Adderley Geo. B.
Alfred John
Farrington R. W.
George J. S. & Co.
Henry C. S.
Henry W. J.
Roker Joseph
Someillan & Co.
Weech W. J. & Son

Agricultural Implements.

The General Hardware Co.

Bank and Bankers.

(None. Public Bank failed in 1883.)

Billiard Rooms.

Alfred John
Royal Victoria Rooms
Someillan & Co.

Bookseller and Stationer.

Moseley Percy J.

Boots and Shoes.

Holmes A. T.

Builders and Contractors.

Aranha Francis J.
Bascom N. J.
Cox John A.
Dorsett Thomas
Dupuch Jos. E.
Johnson Enoch
Styles Thomas

Cigar Manufacturers.

Clark Isadora
Gomez Henry
Pierce W. F.
Saudo & Bros.

Coal Merchants.

Darling T. & Co.
Rahrning H. T.

Dentists.

Cheesebrough A. H.
Russell Herman T.
Webb Edwd. Y.

Druggists.

Albury Jos. B.
Bahamas Dispensary.
Bannister Robt. H.
Sears R. J.
Public Dispensary

Dry and Fancy Goods.

Armbrister W. E. & Co.
Armbrister A. S. & Co.
Burnside & Brother
Brice D. A.
Bullard Francis
Culmer & Russell
Curry W. H.
Depot General Merchandise, B. M. Smith, manager
Hall E. S.
Harris B.
Higgs & Brother
Higgs Geo. R. & Co.
Holmes & Son
Jones Emeline A.
Kemp Edwd. C.
Kemp Mary E.
Knowles C. C.
Knowles M. C.
Knowles Theodore
Lightbourn J. H.
Lofthouse T. H. C.
Mac Donald D.
Mac Donald D. J.
Menendez & Son
Menendez W. J
Menendez Brothers
Moore Thos. P.
Musgrove R. N.
Necks Eliza F.
Perpall C. R.
Pyfrom Wm. R.
Pyfrom R. W.
Rattray J. S.
Rivers Mrs. H.
Russell Effie
Sands Chas. T. & Co.
Sands Robt. T.
Sands W. P.
Saunders Henry R
Sturrup B. P. & Bro.
Thompson J. A. & Co.
Turtle & Sands
Weech, W. J. & Son
Whitehead P. M.
Young & Higgs

Furniture Dealers.

Fitzgerald F. A.
Johnson J. S.
Bascom N. J.
Elliott N. S.
Lightbourn Wm.

General and Commission Merchants.

Darling T. Co.
Rahming H. T. & Co.
Johnson & Brother
Sawyer R. H. & Co.

Groceries and Provisions.

Albury Hilton C.
Albury W. F.
Alfred John
Brown J. H.
Bosfield & Brothers
Christie Geo. F.
Dupuch J. E.
Fitzgerald F. A.
Grist John F.
Henry Copeland S.
Henry Wilmore J.
Johnson Geo. H.
Johnson T.
Lightbourn Henry W.
Malcolm Alfred
Malcolm W.
McCulloch Alfred
Pinder Saml. G.
Pritchard Brothers
Rae S. H. C.
Roker Joseph
Sands Jas. P. & Bros.
Saunders Mrs. J. B.
Saunders Pembroke
Smith Henry T.
Sweeting J. A. & Sons

Hardware Dealers.

George John S. Co.
Rae C. S., manager of The General Hardware Co.

Hotels.

Corson House, S. F. Corson proprietor.
Curry House, R. H. Curry, proprietor
Royal Victoria Hotel, S. S. Morton, proprietor.
American Hotel, Mrs. M. Wall.

Ice Merchants.

Nassau Ice House, J. H. Brown, proprietor.
Pritchard Brothers
Sands Jas. P. & Bros.

Jewelry and Watches.

Brown & Musgrove
Demeritt John
Minns A. C. J.
Minns A. T. S.
Thompson H. J.

Livery Stables.

Charlew J. R.
Grist J. F.
Johnson James
Maura W. J.
Nicolls J. W. B.

Lumber Dealers.

Hall Edwin S.
Rohrning H. T. & Co.
Lawyer R. H. & Co.
Dupuch J. E.

Newspapers.

The Nassau *Guardian*, P. J. Meseley, propr.
The Nassau *Times*, C. H. Kemp, propr.
The *Freeman* S. Theus Smith, propr.

Physicians.

Albury J. B.
Jackson W. J.
Kemp G. T. R.
Maclure, W. M. G.
Mill William
Robinson William

Photographer.

Sweeting Richard

Planters.

Brown John
Johnson Joseph S.
Lightbourn Henry C.
Nicolls J. W. B.
Roker Joseph
Sands Charles T.
Burnside Alfred
French N. J.
Fitzgerald, Chas. T.

Shell Dealers and Manufacturers.

Camplejohn G. C., Jr.
Evans Mrs. R. H.
Florance G.
Edgar E.
Thompson H. J.
Saunders S. P. & Son
Thompson Thos. H.

Shipbuilders.

Aranha Francis J.
Bethel Albt. J.
Brown J. R.
Cooper S. A.
Evans G.
Fernander Philip
Higgs G. W., proprietor of "Marine Railway."
Ramsay John
Rodgers J. A.

Soda and Bottling Works.

E. N. Murphy, proprietor

Sponge Dealers.

Adderley G. B.
Brown J. B.
Hall E. S.
Higgs Geo. W.
Johnson & Brother
Lightbourn H. W.
Saunders S. P. & Son
Sawyer Robt. H. & Co.
Treco P. A.
Young & Higgs
Dupuch Jos. E.

Undertakers.

Bridgewater J. A.
Hall W. L.
Jonson W. E.
Lightbourn Wm.
Pearce R. A.
Bascom N. J.
Elliott, N. S.

ISLAND OF PUERTO-RICO.

(Spanish West Indies.)

Population of the entire Island, 750,000, of which 450,000 are whites.

SAN JUAN.

(The Capital of the Island.)

Population, 25,000.

Agricultural Implements.

(See General Wholesale Merchants, also Hardware.)

Ales and Beer.

(See Wholesale Merchants, also Groceries.)

Banks and Bankers.

Banco Credito Mercantil
Cabrera Hermanos
Sabrinos de Ezquiaga
Fedderson y Ca.
Mullenhorff y Korber
J. Sala y Ca. (successors of)
José T. Silva
Vijande y Ca.

Billiard Halls.

Juan Carreras
Francisco Ferrer
Luis C. Labrador
Pablo J. Lopez
Ramon Quintana Miyar

Biscuit Bakers.

Jaime Barcelo
Juaguin Pacheco
Pedro Ramon

Bookbinders.

José J. Acosta
J. Anfosso y Ca.
Francisco Furnaguera
Gonzalez y Ca.
José Gonzalez
M. A. Lynn
José M. Villilla

Boots and Shoes, Wholesale.

Bordoy y Ca.
Peza Hermanos
Sierra, Martinez y Ca.

Chocolate Factories.

Carbonell, Ribas y Ca.
José Balmes
Dorado y Ca.
Juan Esoler

Cigar Factories.

Ballesteros y Ca.
Miguel Amilibia
Beneto Baquero
Guillermo Bausa
Antonio Cauvet
Pedro Carré
Jaime Cervera
José Córdovo
Andres Cueto
Diaz y Lavandera
Francisco Font
José R. Fuentes
Gandara Hermanos
José Garcia
Gomez Hermanos
José Maria Gonzalez
Gonzalez y Ca.
José Pacheco Gonzalez
Gonzalez y Perez
Pedro J. Jaca
Landran Hermanos
J. Lopez y Ca.
Manuel Luengo
E. Martinez
Mendez, Vegueta y Ca.
Novella y Ca.
Francisco Novella
Andres O'Reilly
Padin Hermanos
Felix Pardo
Domingo Perez
Miguel Pons
Portela y Lomba
Renta y Rodriguez
Cecilio Rodriguez
Juan Rivera
Eusebio Rodriguez
Manuel A. Sanchez
Paulino Somahano
Manuel Sordo
Alejandro Storer
Fidel Jenajero
Francisco Trapaga
M. Vidal y Ca.
José E. Vidal
Celestino Villamil
Manuel Villamil
Paulino Villamil
Mullenhoff y Kober
Orcasitas (successors of)
Palacios y Ca.
Joaquin Peña
Piza Hermanos

Cigar Factories—*continued.*
C. Pratto y Ca.
Eulogio Rivera
M. Roman y Ca.
Rubert y Hermanos
Claudio G. Saenz y Ca.
Sainz, Cerra y Ca.
J. Sala y Ca.
Serra y Ca.
Silva, Ferrer y Ca.
B. Simonet y Ca.
Vicente G. Troncoso
Vicente y Ca.
Vijande y Ca.
Zalduondo y Valle

Clothing and Tailoring.
M. Audrillon
Jacinto Coco
P. Gonce
Moneny y Ca.
Angel Carmides
S. Catalan
Manuel Cerda
Agustin Cordoba
Francisco Diaz
Luciano Esturio
Ramon Figueroa
Julio Lopez
J. D. Menendez
P. Nieto y Ca.
José Provisi
José Rodriguez
Jaime Tomás

Commission Merchants.
Aguilar, Delgado y Ca.
Cerecedo, Hermanos y Ca.
Mullenhoff y Korber
Bernado Ponce
José T. Silva
Vijande y Ca.

Crockery and Glassware.
Francisco Armas
Ramon Gardon
Antonio Jauregui
Manuel Roman
B. Simonet

Dentists.
E. D. Mangara
E. Martinez
Jacinto Naranjo
J. Luis, Salierup
Prisco Viscarrondo

Druggists and Chemists.
José M. Blanco
Juan B. Daubon
F. Guillermetz
Gallardo y Ca.
Ledesma Hermanos
Juan E. Saler
Pedro del Valle

Dry Goods, Hosiery, Textiles, Etc.
Arrabal y Ca.
Ahumada y Ca.
Chavarry y Ca.

Chavarry y Mendizabal
Echevaria y Ca
Elizalde y Guerro
Feddersen y Ca.
Font Vidal y Ca.
Hernaiz y Ca.
S. Melon y Ca.
Oreasitas y Ca.
Juaquin Peña
A. Raynat y Ca.
Sainz, Cerra y Ca.
José Siges
Zalduondo y Ville

Furniture Dealers.
Masjuan y Ca.
Noa y Valle

General Wholesale Merchants.
(Importers and Exporters.)

Alonso Hermanos
José J. Acosta
Armas y Jimenez
F. Arrabal y Ca.
Arrillaga y Ca.
Ateca y Ca.
Severo Baston
G. Bolivar y Ca.
Bozzo y Canevazo
Cabrera Hermanos
Caldas y Ca.
M. Campoamor
Castillo y Ca.
Cerecido Hermanos
Crosas y Finlay
Chavarri y Ca.
Chavarri y Mendizibal
Evaristo Chevremont
Dorado y Ca.
Elezalde y Guerero
Ezquaga Sobriños de
Faura y Ca.
Feddersen y Ca.
Font, Vidal y Ca.
José R. Fuentes
Ramon Gardon
José Q. Gonzales
Hermaiz y Ca.
Iriarte, Hermanos y Ca.
Antonio Jauregui
Latimer y Fernandez
Lopez, Villamil y Ca.
V. Luiña
Llaneras, Uria y Ca.
A. Mayol y Ca
S. Melon y Ca.

Groceries and Provisions, Wholesale.
Castillo y Ca.
Cerecedo Hermanos y Ca.
Faura y Ca.
R. Gonzalez y Hermano
Lopez, Villamil y Ca.
Alejo Mendez
Oliver y Ca.
Andres O. Kelly
Narciso Ribot
Rodriguez y Ca.
Suarez y Troncoso
Vidal y Ca.

Gas Company.

Mullenhoff y Korber, general agents

Hardware, Tools, Etc., Wholesale.

Evaristo Chevremont
José Quixano
Miñon Hermanos
Francisco Ramirez
Rodriguez, Mareno y Ca.
M. Roman y Ca.
B. Simonet
Armas y Jimenez
Julian Martienzo

Hotels.

El Universo
Hotel de San Juan
La Nueva Estrella

House Furnishing Goods, Tinware, Etc.

Alejandro Barlela
Tomas Diaz
Pablo Fuentes
Gregorio Laguna
Jenaro Lippo
Domingo Reyes

Ice Dealers and Manufacturers.

Gioco y Ca.

Jewelry, Watches and Silverware.

N. Alberti
Boschetti y Schira
José Claudio
Lentine y Ca.
Victor Atroyo
Enriqui Dominguez
D. Esturio
Vicente Furiati
Juan Palma
C. Ramon
Angel Rivera
Blas Sechini
Facundo Tizol
Enrique Kerman
Evaristo Laloma
José M. Roig
Tinaud y Ca.

Lamps, Oils, Etc.

B. Fernandaz
Santos Filippi

Lithographers.

A. Morris Lynn (successors of)
Herman Rodeck

Lumber Dealers.

Crosas y Finlay
Daubon y Ca.
Latimer y Fernandez
R. Margary y Ca.

Machine Shops.

Francisco Abarca
Portilla y Ca.

Merchandise Brokers.

Eugenio Corton
Bernado Ponce
Segundo Sety
Francisco M. Turull
Javier de Zequeira

Military Equipments.

José Claudio
Juan Matens

Millwrights and Mill Supplies

J. Perez
Armas y Jimenez

Native Products.

Santiago Echeveste
Esmoris Hermanos
Bernado Ponce

Newspapers and Periodicals.

El Boletin Commercial (daily)
El Boletin Eclesiastico
El Boletin Mercantil (daily)
El Buscapie
El Clamor del Pais
El Creterio
La Draga
El Eco del Comercio
La Gaceta Oficial
La Instruccion Publica
La Integridad Nacional
La Nacion
La Opera
El Ilustrado Puerto Rico
La Revista de Agricultura

Paper and Stationery, Wholesale.

José J. Acosta
F. Anfosso y Ca.
Gonzalez y Ca.
José Font Gonzalez
A. Moris Lynn (successors of)

Photographers.

Feliciano Alonzo
Pedro Catinchi
J. R. Ingles
Eduardo Lopez

Physicians and Surgeons.

José M. Baralt
José C. Barbosa
José Maria Cueto
Gabriel Ferrer
E. Cabrera Garcia
Pedro G. Goico
José B. Gomez
Juan Hernandez
Ricardo Hernandez
Emelio Lazaro
Fernando Z. Nuñes
A. D. Paniagua
Antonio Font y Pastor
Pedro Puig
Ricardo Rey
Calixto Romero
B. Robert

Physicians, Etc.—*continued.*
José Casenave Saldaña
Pedro Salicrup
José J. Tizol
Francisco del Valle

Pianos and Musical Instruments.
José Agullo
Pedro Delgado

Plantation Superintendents.
Heraclio Cordero
Bernardo Ponce

Printers.
José J. Acosta
J. Anfosso y Ca.
A. Cordova
Manuel Fernandez
Gonzalez y Ca.
José F. Gonzalez
Imprenta Militar
A Moris Lynn
Francisco Valderramas

Railway Companies.
Compañia del Oeste, José Peñade Chavari, Prest.
Compañia de San Juan á Rio Piedras, Pablo Ubarri, Prest.

Sewing Machines.
S. Melon y Ca.

Viuda de Rodriguez
Julian Silva

Ship Agents and Brokers.
Sobrinos de Esquiaga
Feddersen, Wildink y Ca.
Menendez y Ca.
Mullenhoff y Korber
C. Pratt y Ca.
Sala y Ca.
J. T. Silva
Vijande y Ca.

Ship Chandlers and Naval Stores.
Crosas y Finlay
Latimer y Fernandez

Steamship Agents.
Larrinaga y Ca., Catalan Steamship Co.
Ezquiaga Sobrinos, Lopez line to Cadiz
José T. Silva, French Transatlantic line
Rubert Hermanos
Iriarte Hermanos, Caracena y Ca.

Submarine Telegraph.
The West India and Panama Telegraph Company (Limited).

Undertakers.
Tomas Aquino
Carambot L. Llanger
Mesa, Moreno y Ca.

AGUADILLA.

Population, 7,000.

Agricultural Implements and Machinery.
(See General Merchants.)

Coffee Merchants and Exporters.
Antonio C. Arana
Felipe Arana
Sebastian Colon
Serapio Feo
Gillermo Frontera
Pablo Luigi
Miguel Marqué
Oliver y Delgado
Antonio Delgado
Domingo Paoli
Santiago Torres
Viella Hermanos

Coffee Cleaners.
M. Marquez y Ca.
Suan y Ca.
Vilella Hermanos

Druggists and Chemists.
Jorge M. Navas
Iturrino Hermanos
Salvador Picornell

Furniture Dealers.
Juan Belfors
José B. Call
Antonio Morales

General Merchants, Wholesale and Retail.
V. Acevedo y Ca.
Juan Arbona
Canals, Coll y Ca.
Agustin Carbonell
Juan Castañer
Garbino Garcia
Felipe Gonzalez
Tomás Gonzalez
Nicolas Lacaroz
Marquez y Ca.
Miguel Marquez
Braulio Martinez
Mayol y Suan
Aurelio Mendez
Justo Mendez
Ramon Novoa
Pedro Rios
Suan y Ca.
Juan Torres
Pablo Vidal
Vilella Hermanos

General Stores, Retail.

V. Acenedo
Pedro Aramburo
Juan Arbona
Ines Castro
Sebastian Calon
Antonio Collazo
G. M. Cordova
Francisco Enseñat
Garbino Garcia
Aurelio Mendez
Justo Mendez
Miguel Marguez
Mayol y Suan
Ramon Novoa
Manuel Palenpue
Santiago Torres
Francisco Vergara

Hotel.

Santiago Robles

Jewelry, Etc.

Luis Gonzaga
Pedro Aramburo

Physicians.

Francisco Blanes
Juan Vicente Gonzalez
Pedro M. Yordan
Salvador Picornell

ARECIBO.

Population, 20,000.

Agricultural Implements and Machinery.

(See General Merchants.)

Druggists and Chemists.

Cárlos Hijalmarson
Manuel Perez
José Ramon Rivera
Rafael Gabino Silva

General Importing Merchants.

Benigno Balseyro y Ca.
Ahumada y Ca.
Bahr y Ca.
G. Ledesma y Ca.
Ruperto Muro
Nones y Ca.
Roses y Ca.
M. Rupert y Ca.

Groceries and Provisions, Wholesale.

Galanes y Garcia
Francisco Ledesma
José Morales
Pericas y Ca.
M. Rupert y Ca.
Ramon Villamil

Hotels.

La America
La Castellana

Ironmongery, Etc.

Estelban Castro
José Martinez

Printers.

Agustin Cambell
Alejandro Salicrup

Physicians and Surgeons.

Cayetano Coll
Francisco Perez
Rafael del Valle
L. Zeno

Ship Chandlery and Naval Stores.

Ahumada y Ca.
Nones y Ca.
B. Balseyro y Ca.
Ruperto Muro

Tobacconists.

Juaquin Gonzalez
José Angel Pereira
Juan B. Perez
Christino Rojas
Juan Soler

Undertakers.

José Lopez
Juan Pereira

GUAYAMA.

Population, 12,000.

Agents for Plantation Estates.
José Pratts
Maximo Saunion.
Juan Vieta

Agricultural Implements, Etc.
(See General Merchants.)

Ales and Beer Dealers.
(See Groceries and Provisions.)

Bankers.
Amoros Hermanos
Cano y Ca.

Billiards.
Nicholas Graner

Booksellers and Stationers.
Castillo y Luzunares
José Capo

Bookbinders.
Castillo y Luzunares

Cooperage.
Mateo Amoros
Cano y Ca.
Juan McFarland

Druggists and Chemists.
Carlos Bruno
Julio S. Bruno
Nicolas Bruno
C. Dominguez
Tomas Dominguez
Juan B. Massanet

Dry Goods, Hosiery, Etc.
Tomas Balbas.
Juan Ignacio Capo
Manuel Cevedanes
José Enseñat
Rafael Fuster

General Importing Merchants.
Tomas Cano y Ca.
Jenaro Cantiño
Vicente Fernandez
Antonio Grau
Manuel Lopez

Morazani Hermanos
José Sanguinety

Groceries and Provisions.
Francisco Bernier
Antonio Berrios
Nicolas Colon
José Esteve
Jose Figueroa
Juan Franco
Mateo Fulladosa
Cayetano Fuster
Gaya y Ca.
Dionisio Gely
José Moreta
Santiago Nieto
Juan Ortiz
M. Vazquez

Hardware, Tools, Etc.
Juan Caussade
Girod y Ca.
Francisco Rovira

Hotels.
Hotel Español

Ice Factory.
Ignacio Diaz

Physicians.
Juan B. Blondet
Eugenio Grau
Francisco Rendon
Joaquin Sabater.

Printers.
Castillo y Luzunares.

Sugar Merchants and Shippers.
Juan Ignacio Capó
Luis P. Cabassa
El Conde Garcia de la Palmira
Gual Hermanos
Francisco Lopez
Julian Lopez
Felix Massó
Clemente Moret
Jesus Maria Texidor
Rafael Vazquez
Jauquin Villodas
Pedro Virilla
Juan Vives

MAYAGUEZ.

Population, 12,000.

Agricultural Implements and Machinery.

(See General Merchants.)

Ales and Beer Dealers.

(See Groceries and Provisions.)

Bankers.

M. Badrena y Ca.
F. Bages y Ca.
Barahona, Blaines y Ca.
Cuyar, Pratts y Ca.
Boothby & Co.

Bookbinder.

E. Viñas

Booksellers and Stationers.

Mantilla y Ca.
Enrique Dick

Chocolate Factories.

Antonio Gomila
Oliver y Rulan
Eugenio Peltaint
Victori, Pelegri y Ca.

Clothing, Hats, Etc.

F. Bages y Ca.
Jaime D. Barbena
Francisco Blanes
Cancio y Lopez
S. Castañer
Cuyar, Pratts y Ca.

Dealers in Native Produce.

M. Ahedo y Peña
José R. Castro
Mendes Vigo
Cuevas y Grappe
G. Homar
Martinez Hermanos
Mendez Vigo
Miguel Quiñones

Dentists.

Alfredo Cristi
José G. Garcia

Druggists and Chemists.

Manuel Manzano
Gatell y Ca.
Carlos Monagas
Gillermo Mulet
Saliva Hermanos

Dry Goods, Hosiery, Etc., Wholesale.

Miguel Ahedo y Peña
F. Bages y Ca.
Jaime Barbena
Cancio y Lopez
Sebastian Casteñer
Jacinto Caco
Pablo Gonze
Ramon Martinez
Pablo Pietri
Pedro Ramirez
Revera y Rodriguez
Sancho, Sard y Ca.
J. Sitjes y Ca.

Furniture Dealers.

Pablo Berga
José Castro

General Merchants, Importing and Exporting.

J. Aduana
Boothby y Ca.
Bages y Ca.
M. Badrena y Ca.
C. Barahona
Blanes y Ca.
Francisco Blanes
Cuyar, Pratts y Ca.
Esmoris Hermanos
Fernandez y Ca,
Antonio Gomila
Francisco Molina Guio
Haws y Ca.
Felix Infanzon
Kraemer y Ca.
Lopez, Gonzalez y Ca.
Moral Gonzalez y Ca.
Guillermo Mulet
P. Nieva y Ca.
Pluja y Bravo
Adolfo Roberts
Sancho, Sard y Ca.
Schultz y Ca.
J. Torrabells y Ca.
Victori, Pelegri y Ca.

Groceries and Provisions, Wholesale.

M. Bengoa y Ca.
Martinez Hermanos
Guillermo Homar
Miguel Quiñones
José Garcia Rodriguez

Hardware, Tools, Etc.

Blanes y Ca.
P. Nieva y Ca.
Mendes Vigo

Hotels.

Sandalio Dalmann
José Gonzalez
Rudolfo Gautier

Ice Factory.

Lopez, Besosa y Ca.

Insurance Agencies.

Alfredo Falbe
Jacobo M. Monsanto
Moral, Gonzalez y Ca.
Manuel Sama

Jewelry, Silverware and Watches.

Antonio Rivera
Tomas Grau

Lithographers.

H. Rodek

Lumber Dealers.

P. Fornabels y Ca.
Isidro Vidal

Newspapers and Periodicals.

El Anunciador Comercial (daily)
El Imparcial
El Liberal
El Progreso
La Unidad Nacional

Photographers.

Rudolfo Alonso
Eduardo Lyon

Physicians.

Fernando Ruiz
Martin Travieso
T. Vazquez y Rivera
Julio Andinot
Francisco Basora

Salvador Carbonel
José de la Cruz
I, de J. Dominguez
Agustin Feliū
B. Gaudier Texidor
Adolfo Martinez
Jesus Monagas
Miguel Pons

Printers.

Domingo Arecco y Hijos
Martin Fernandez
Antonio Jimenez
Benito Monje
Tió Segarra

Steamship Agents.

Playa y Bravo

Tobacconists, Etc.

Felipe Arias
José Fuentes Rodriguez
M. Sojo
Carlos Capré
José Carrero
Pedro Luna
Manuel Moncayo
Federico Neuadich
Juan Ortiz
Roberto de Santana
M. M. Sajo

Undertakers.

Andres Berga y Ca.
José Gutierrez y Ca.
José Marcias y Ca.

PONCE.

Population, 21,000.

Agricultural Implements, Etc.

(See General Merchants.)

Ale and Beer Dealers.

(See Groceries and Provisions.)

Architects and Builders.

Lorenzo Vizcarrondo
Adolfo Runger
Francisco Valls
Ramon Coll
B. Pericas
Hilarion Vigo

Banks and Bankers.

Caja de Ahorros
Armstrong y Ca.
Gandaria, Brigaro y Ca.

Billiards.

Casino de Ponce
Centro de Recreo

Booksellers and Stationers.

Olimpio Otero
Manuel Lopez
José Melendez

Bookbinders.

A. Campius
Luis Revera

Brick Makers and Dealers in Building Material.

Narciso Arabia
Salvador Bigay
U. Gonzalez
Salvador Pigen

Carriage and Wagon Makers.

Graham y Ca.
Francisco Perez
Querejeta Hermanos

Chocolate Factories.

Francisco Barnes
Isidoro Arroyo
Cortara y Ca.
Pedro A. Puig
A. Simonpretri

Coffee Cleaners and Shippers.

Ramon Cartada
Gandaria, Bregaro y Ca.
E. P. Salazar y Ca.
Sauri, Subira y Ca.

Commission Merchants.

Armstrong y Ca.
Lazaro Martinez
Salazar y Ca.
Gandarias, Bregaro y Ca.
Pedro Hedilla
Mayoral y Ca.
Sauri, Subira y Ca.
H. Geradino
T. Laguna
Eugenio Vivas

Dentists.

A. Arrastia
Roberto Ponte
Gaudia Ruiz
Emelio Toro
A. Valdes

Druggists and Chemists.

Ferrer y Reyes
Francisco Giol
Ferrer y Sobrino
José Henna
José Pon
J. Porras Ruiz
N. Rodriguez
Balbino San Antonio
Monge, Arrillaga y Ca.
Ferrer y Rulan
Francisco G. Texidor
Juan B. Pon
Rodriguez y Gonzalez
Cancio Valle

Druggist, Wholesale.

Arillago, Monge y Ca.

Electrical Apparatus.

J. Vidaurre y Ca.

Foundry and Machine Shops.

Graham y Ca.
(2) Querejeta Hermanos

Furniture Dealers.

Pedro Carreras
Miguel Coda
B. Pericas
Vigo y Rivera

General Merchants, Wholesale.

Armstrong y Ca.
Gandaria, Brigaro y Ca.
Pedro Hedilla
Juan Mayaral y Ca.

Salazar y Ca.
Sauri, Subira y Ca.
P. Batistin
A. Luchetty
J. O. Otero
Pellegrini Hermanos
H. Rivera
Francisco Lagroña
Schuck y Ca.
R. Toro
Torres y Hijos
Valdecilla y Ca.
Mirandes Hermanos
A. E. Molinas y Ca.
Simon Pierluicci
José Pujadas
Vidal y Ca.

Groceries and Provisions, Wholesale.

Fernando Angulo
José Canto
Codo y Ca.
Mayal Hermanos
Leon y Garcia
M. Morales

Hotels.

Hotel de America
Hotel de Marina
Hotel del Leon de Oro
Hotel Isabel Castro

Ice Factory.

Otto Hoffmann

Insurance Agencies.

E. Salazar
Eduardo Asensio

Jewelry, Silver, Watches.

Pedro Ventura
A. Ludwig
José Melendez
Pedro Guberne

Lumber Merchants.

Perez, Guerra y Ca.
Hedella y Ca.
Porrata, Doria y Ca.

Pianos and Musical Instruments.

M. Aspiroz
P. G. Carreras
Pedro Castiner
O. Otero
José Forns

Physicians.

Martin Corchado
Luis Aguerrevere
E. Carronas
Juan Genebrieras
Manuel Iglesias
Eduardo Lacot
Elias Lamonte
Gustavo Moret
Miguel Pagani
M. Portero
Rafael Pujals
N. Reveron
Esteban Vidal

Photographer.

M. Molina

Printers and Publishers.

El Comercio
El Vapor
L. R. Velazquez
Manuel Lopez

Ship Chandlery and Naval Stores.

Gandarias, Bregaro y Ca.
Salazar y Ca.

Tobacconists.

F. Bustamente

Rodriguez y Fuentes
U. Casals

Wall Papers.

(See Stationers.)

Veterinary Surgeons.

Eusebio Molina
Roman Nieto

Undertakers.

Pedro G. Carreras
Antonio Santa Maria
Antonio Toro

THE ISLAND OF SANTA CRUZ OR ST. CROIX.

(Danish.)

Population of the Island, 20,000.

F. G. Phipps, provision dealer and estate supplies
Armstrong & Co., provision dealers and estate supplies
Bartram Bros., provision dealers and estate supplies
Jas. W. Roche, provision dealer and estate supplies
W. A. Creagh, provision dealer and estate supplies
C. R. Jacobs, provision dealer and estate supplies
W. H. Heyliger, hardware
Branch of McDougal & Co., of St. Thomas, hardware

Thos. Moore, hardware
H. B. Stubbs, dry goods
C. Gautier & Co., dry goods
W. B. Woods, dry goods
H. Iwersen, dry goods
A. Paladan-Muller, drugs
L. Faber, drugs
Russell Bros., fancy goods
R. G. Bell, groceries
P. E. Kalmer, physician
L. Neumann, physician

SANTO DOMINGO.
(Spanish Negro Republic.)
Population of town and district, 12,000.

PUERTO-PLATA.

Agricultural Implements.
Heinsen & Co.

Ale and Beer.
Cosme Batlle
C. Klüsener & Co.
Diego Loinaz
G. Chiodi & Co.
Ginelra Hermanos
Manuel Cocco

Banks.
El Banco de la Compania de Credito

Bookseller and Stationer.
Manuel Castellano

Boots and Shoes.
B. R. Puyans
Ginelra Hermanos
G. Chiodi & Co.
M. G. Amabile
Vives & Caballero
C. Simpson

Dentists.
Virgilio Barranco
G. W. Jones

Druggists.
C. A. Fraser
Botica San José
T. G. Levy
Botica del Mercado

Dry Goods.
C. Klüsener & Co.
Cosme Batlle
B. R. Puyans
Barrera Hermanos
G. Chiodi & Co.
Ginelra Hermanos
M. G. Amabile
Vives & Caballen

General Merchants.
Cosme Batlle
C. Klüsener & Co.
G. Choidi & Co.
Ginelra Herm.
Manuel Cocco

Groceries and Provisions.
Barrera Herm.
B. R. Puyans
Cosme Batlle
C. Klüsener & Co.
Diego Loinaz
E. Piola & Co.
Felipe Mir
Genelra Hermanos
G. Chiodi & Co.
H. J. Manecke & Co.
J. H. Colson
J. M. del Canto
Manuel Cocco
M. G. Amabile
M. Piola & Co.
Vives & Caballero

Hardware and Tools.
Heinsen & Co.
G. Chiodi & Co.
Genelra Hermanos
Vives & Caballero

Newspapers.
Journal of Commerce
Porvenir

Physicians.
P. M. Garrido
U. Lellundi

Planters.
Lithgow Bros., "Central Santa Maria"
Genelra Herm., "La Yndustria"
H. Shultz, "La Rosa"
F. Barranco, "La Ubaldina"
Manuel Boitel, "La Aurora"

Printers.
Manuel Castellano
H. A. Taylor

Sewing Machine Dealers.
C. Klüsener & Co.
B. R. Puyans
Ginelra Hermanos
Cosme Batlle
G. Chiode & Co.
M. G. Amabile
Vives Caballero

Soap Manufacturer.
J. L. Compart

Telegraph Company.
Compania Telegrafica de las Antillas. M. Rousell, agt.

Trunk Manufacturer.
Y. Mella Brea

ST. THOMAS, W. I.

(Danish.)

Population of the Island, 15,000.

Banks.
Bank of St. Thomas
Colonial Bank
St. Thomas Savings Bank

Bookseller and Stationer.
Charles E. Taylor

Boots and Shoes.
L. Gomez & Co.
R. D. Senior

Cigars and Tobacco.
F. Drejer & Co.

Dentist.
James Gordon

Distiller of Bay Oil.
R. M. Hassell

Druggist.
A. H. Ruse

Dry Goods, Wholesale and Retail.
W. Broüdsted & Co.
Thomas Pearson & Co.

Dry Goods, Retail.
M. Fidanque
G. Beretta
Carty & Co.
A. Gaspard
J. Müller & Co.
R. Senior & Co.
Dd. B. Delvalle
J. H. Beverhoudt
Fratelli, Copello & Co.
J. Levin
William White
M. Van Eps & Co.
W. B. Castello & Co.
Delvalle & Co.
J. H. Souffront

Gas Company.
St. Thomas Gas Company

General Provision Merchants, Wholesale and Retail.
J. H. Fechtenburg & Co.
Klingberg, Krebs & Co.
D. G. Fonseca

Hardware.
McDougall & Co.
Cameron & Co.
Jos. Levi and Sons

Hotels.
Hotel Turco
Commercial Hotel

Ice and Wholesale Provision Dealers.
Raven & Co.

Jewelry and Watches.
A. de Lagarde

Money Brokers.
J. B. M. Monsanto
B. Bornn

Newspapers.
Daily Bulletin
St. Thomas Tidende

Panama Hats.
Ch. Delinois & Co.

Photographers.
A. Giglioli
Fraas

Physicians.
C. Krebs
F. Erichsen
J. H. Wissing
R. Villavicencio
N. Auguste

Provisions and Groceries, Retail.
A. Burnet
O. Ffrench & Co.
A. Vance & Co.
J. Fidanque & Co.
David Pretto & Co.
S. H. Toledano
L. Delinois
A. Lugo & Co.
Louis Berg & Co.
Russell Bros
H. Michelsen
H. Toussaint

Ship Brokers and Commission Merchants.
G. W. Smith & Co.
Lamb & Co.
Jas. T. Abbott & Co.
Bache & Co.
J. F. D. Jurgens & Co.
J. Sala & Co.

Ship Chandlers.
Wharam & Co.

Steamship Companies.
United States and Brazil Mail
West India and Pacific Mail
Harrison S. S. Co.
Don Ramon de Herrera
Hamburg American Packet Co.
Royal Mail S. S. Co.
Compagnie Generale Transatlantique

Telegraph Company.
West India and Panama Telegraph Company.

ISLAND OF SAINT LUCIA, W. I.

(British.)

Population of the Island, 30,000.

General Commission Merchants.
Wiewall & Co.
Ch. Aug. Brewer

General Merchants.
Agostini A. G., Castries, architect and land surveyor
Augier John, Castries and Soufriere, ale and beer dealers
Augier Jules, Castries, dry goods merchant
Barnard, Peter & Co., Castries, Soufriere, Choiseul and Vieux Fort, dry goods, provision, wine and spirit, lumber and general merchants, shipping agents and steamship owners, importers and dealers in coal
Belmar C., La Curieux, Soufriere, dry goods merchants
Belmar & Sons, Castries, dry goods merchants
Castries Club, Castries, G. Grof, secretary
Chastanet Chs., Castries, Vice Consul for France
Chastanet E., Castries, dry goods dealer
Celestin Pelage. Dumery, provision dealer
Clavier Fernand L., Castries, dry goods dealer
Clavier & Co., Castries, grocers and druggists
Colonial Bank, Castries, Alexr. Richard, manager; London office, Bishopsgate St., within London, E. C.
Dennehy Dr. Chas., Castries, colonial surgeon
DuBrulay & Co., Castries, dry goods merchant
Edmund W. H., Dennery, wine, spirit and provision dealer
Eudoxie Luc, Castries, ale, beer, grocer and provision dealer
Galgey Dr. Otho, Castries, assistant colonial surgeon
Gordon T. D., Castries, schoolmaster Lady Mico Schools
Gouin Mde. A., Castries, billiard saloon and hotel-keeper
Granger Paul, Castries, billiard saloon and hotel-keeper
Houry C., Castries, chemist and druggist
Laugellier Athenase, Castries, tobacco dealer
Lastic R. & Co., Castries, ale, beer, wine and spirit merchant
Lawrence Frederick, wine and spirit merchant, Castries
Lestrade Dr. C., Dennery
Macfarlane Junior & Co., Castries, Soufriere, Choiseul, Laborie y Vieux Fort, provision, lumber and general merchants and shipping agents
Macfarlane, Moffatt & Co., Castries, Soufriere and Vieux Fort, dry goods, hardware and general merchants, ale, beer, wine and spirit dealers
MacHugh R. G., Castries, printer and publisher
Margaud Eugene, Castries, dry goods and provision dealer
Margaud Robert, Anse La Raye, provision and general dealer

Marius F. W., Castries, druggist and dry goods dealer
Meagher C. I., C. E. Castries, architect and surveyor
Medouze W., Laborie, grocer and provision dealer
Minville & Chastanet, Castries and Soufriere, dry goods, hardware and general merchants and shipping agents, ale, beer, wine and spirit dealers
Moffatt John D., Castries, Vice-Consul for Germany
Monplaisir Adolph, Castries, general dealer
Myers Mde. Chas., Castries, hotel keeper
Norton Dr. H., Castries
Osborne Samuel, Castries, builder and undertaker
Peter Frank, Consul for the Netherlands and Consul for Venezuela
Peter William, Castries, Consular Agent U. S. A. and Consul for Sweden and Norway
Proctor Dr. S. F., Soufriere
Quinlan W. C., Soufriere, school master, Lady Mico School
Quinlan J. C., Castries, architect and land surveyor
Rabier Victor, Dennery, ale and beer dealer
Roger, Langellier & Co., Castries, dry goods, hardware and general merchants, ale, beer and wine and spirit dealers.
St. Lucia Ice Factory Co., Ld., Castries; R. G. MacHugh, secretary
St. Lucia Steam Conveyance Co., Ld., Castries, steamship owners; Charles Chastanet, managing director
Troja Julien, Castries, printer and bookbinder
"Voice of St. Lucia," Castries; R. G. MacHugh, editor
Williams Dr. S., Vieux Fort
Zepherin Mark G., Castries, provision dealer

Planters.
Agard E., la Rosiére Estate, Castries
Alphonse A. Belle, Veu Estate, Laborie
Ambrosio Laurent, Cuinbar Estate, Vieux Fort
André Mde. V., Foyeaux Estate, Vieux Fort
Angel L., Pipe Rois Estate, Micoud
Auguste J. M., Calbasier Estate, Micoud
Azor René, Esperanco Estate, Vieux Fort
Baptiste W. Jean, Moreu Laure Estate, Micoud
Barnard S., Sans Soucis Estate, Castries
Bernard Edwin, Hope & Beausejour Estate, Vieux Fort
Blanchard A., Belle Vue Estate, Micoud
Blanchard D., Greuno Estate, Vieux Fort
Bonnie F. Louis, La Rochelle Estate, Gros Islet
Cadet L., Jalousie Estate, Laborie
Charles A. J., Valmont Estate, Vieux Fort
Charles J., Morue Bay Estate, Micoud
Chastanet, Chs., Ann Galet Estate, Soufriere
Clavier Fernand L., Guixlin Estate, Gros Islet
Constable Jno. A., Beauchamp Estate, Micoud
Cooper Justin, La Blanche Estate, Laborie

Planters—*continued.*

Cooper Pascal, Hélène Estate, Micoud
Dacretin E., Rivière Mitant Estate, Gros Islet
Darcheville, Mdc. A. Malgré Ca. Estate, Choiseul
DeBreltes Charles, Union Vale Estate, Soufriere
DeBreltes, Mrs. H. Cap Estate, Gros Islet, and Palmiste Estate, Soupriere
DeCharleroy A., Mont Lizard Estate, Choiseul
DeGaillard Jno., Beausejoin Estate, Laborio
DeLanbenque Joseph, Malgretout and Jalousie Estate, Soufriere
DeLanbenque Leon, Ruby Estate, Soufriere
Deligny Mde. P., Beranger Estate, Laborie
Dennery Factory Co., Dennery; A. Mathieu, manager.
Devaux E. Morne, Courbaril Estate, Soufriere
Devaux Henry, Reduit Estate, Gros Islet and Fond Doux Estate, Soufrere
DuBoulay Alexr., Troumassée and Mondesir Estates; Micoud and Pearl and Diamond Estates, Soufriere
DuBoulay, Mrs. B., Dauphin, Robert and Soufriere Estates, Soufriere and Anse Ivrogue Estate, Choiseul
DuBoulay Jules, Anse Mamin and Anse Mahaut and Mont Plaisant Estates, Soufriere
DuBoulay, Mackay & Co., trustees of Canaries Estate, Soufriere
Dunoyer Mdc. C., Morue Doudon Estate, Castries
Elliott Francis, Belle Vue Estate, Vieux Fort
Etienne E., Ratoon Estate, Laborie
Fadlin Auge, Belle Vue Estate, Laborie
Fontenelle A., Garnier Estate, Laborie
Gabriel Jacques, Prosperity Estate, Laborie
Gillespie A. M. & Co., trustee of Cannelles Estate, Micoud
Giraudy Chas., St. Urbain Estate, Vieux Fort
Glace Mde. Chas., Morue Vert Estate, Laborie, and Industry and Esperance Estates, Choiseul
Goodman Mrs. J., Reunion and Fond Estates, Micoud
Goodman J., heirs of Chateau Belair Estate, Soufriere
Guillette Mde Chas., Cardinal Estate, Gros Islet
Hippolite Felix, Delandreau Estate, Choiseul
Hunt J., La Choisiers Estate, Micoud
Husselin P., Gentilly Estate, Laborie
Irmise Mathurin, Felin Estate, Laborie
Isaie Civil, Providence Estate, Choiseul
Jeremie J., Morue Doudon Estate, Castries
Joseph A., La Grace Estate, Laborie
Joseph Flavieu, Moulin à Veut and Fayole Estates, Gros Islet
Joseph Fontenelle, Le Riche Estate, Choiseul
King Mrs. L., Belle Plaine Estate, Soufriere; and Belle Vue Estate, Vieux Fort
Lartigue L., Belle Air Estate, Castries
Laure Mde. J. F., Justin Estate, Laborie
Laurencin A., Marquis Estate, Micoud
Lewis A. E., Reunion Estate, Choiseul
Lloyd Alex., Cafeyer, Riviere Doric, Desgatiers, Laforgue, and DeBreuil Estates, Choiseul
Lynch Mrs. H. E., Pare Estate, Choiseul, Tourney Estate, Vieux Fort and Fond and Volet Estates, Micoud
Lynch Mrs. L., Point Sable Estate, Vieux Fort
Macfarlane Jas., Balembouche Estate, Choiseul
Macfarlane, Junior & Co., Mont Paisible Estate, Castries
Mallet J., Fond La Toque Estate, Castries
Marcel M., Belle Vue Estate, Laborie
Marie Leon, Jr., Fonds Estate, Laborie
Marucheau F., Retraite & Resourse Estates, Vieux Fort
Marucheau P., Belle Vue Estate, Vieux Fort
Melville Mrs. S., Savannes, Black Bay, and Anse Noir Estates, Vieux Fort, and Monplaisir, Japhir, and Herelle Estates, Laborie
Michel Edmond, Beausejour Estate, Gros Islet
Minvielle & Chastanet, Marquis Estate, Gros Islet
Modeste Auguste, Valois Estate, Choiseul
Modeste C., Chouvallier Estate, Vieux Fort
Moffatt L. M., Bois d'Orange Estate, Gros Islet
Molinard Fils & Cie., Anse Canot Estate, Dennery
Montoute E., Belle Vue Estate, Gros Islet
Nelson Alfred, Vigil Estate, Micoud
Newton Lawrence, Union Estate, Castries
Pambar B. Mde., Daly Estate, Gros Islet
Pascal Edward, Mont Jean and La Penseo Estates, Choiseul
Peter A. G., Delcer Estate, Choiseul
Pibot Reine, Beranger Estate, Laborie
Puiel A., Labot Estate, Laborie
Puiel F., Delomel Estate, Micoud
Puiel Xavier, Petit Morue Estate, Micoud
Rosiete Louis, Belle Vue Estate, Laborie
Salmon J. T., New Field Estate, Choiseul
Sedwen J., Sedwen Estate, Castries
St. Helen Mde. Ve., Belle Vue Estate, Laborie
St. Jean Daniel, La Clairie Estate, Castries
St. Louis Louisy, Gentilly Marguerite Estate, Laborie
St. Lucia Central Sugar Factory Co., Ld., Grand Cul de Sac Bay; Theo. Rousselot, manager
St. Lucia Nimes & Estates Coy., Ld., Roseau and Vieux Fort; E. du Boulay, manager
St. Prix A., St. Prix Estate, Gros Islet
Verneuil A., Mouripos Estate, Laborie
Verneuil Mde. C., La Rochelle Estate, Laborie

ST. VINCENT. W: I:

(British.)

Population of the Island, 42,000.

Banks.

Colonial Bank

Builder and Contractor.

John G. Nauton

Commission Merchants and General Agents.

Jno. I. Hughes & Sons, agents of the London Fire Insurance Corporation
Wm. E. Hughes, resident consular agent of the London Fire Insurance Corporation, chairman of the Standard L. A. Company, Edinburgh
Weston James Shearman, Consul resident of Venezuela, agent Whittington L. A. Company, London

Commission and General Agent and Proprietors of Sugar Estates.

Jno. H. Hazen, Sons & Co., agents Barbados Mutual L. A. Society; agents Northern Fire Insurance Co., London

Commission and General Agents, Dealers in Sugar Plantation Supplies, Lumber, Etc.

C. J. Simmons & Co., agents Royal Insurance Co., London

Dentist.

H. D. Croney

Druggists.

J. B. Proudfoot
W. J. Durrant
B. K. Biddy
D. A. Abbott

Dry Goods Dealers.

W. C. Dalrymple
H. A. Hazen & Co.
Thos. Lawlor & Co.
Glover Bros.
B. K. Biddy
J. B. Proudfoot
Eliza Moss
Arthur Sheppard
Thomas F. Linby, Jr.

Engineer.

John Young

General Dealers and Importers Sugar Plantation Supplies, Lumber, Etc., Proprietors Sugar Plantations.

D. K. Porter & Co., agents Lloyd's direct line of steamers, London and West Indies; Sun Fire Insurance Co., London; Standard L. A. Co., Edinburgh

Ice and Billiard Saloon.

R. H. Romney

Newspaper.

Sentinel, Weekly.

Provision Dealers and Grocers.

W. C. Dalrymple
Corea Bros.
Soachim Corea
G. B. Corea
Julien Learmond
John Sardine
Antonio Despassos
A. S. Benyun
H. A. Hazen & Co.
Samuel Boxice
J. A. Van Romoudt

Physicians and Surgeon.

Wm. F. Newsam, colonial surgeon and Mexican practitioner.
Geo. Finlay
J. V. Young
John Kirkpatrick
Martin O. Canoe
Sanford Arnott

Planters, Sugar Growers and Shippers.

Wm. Smith
Geo. Smith
Alexr. Smith
C. E. Cloke
Henry King
B. T. King
E. A. Hadley
Geo. Roberston
Jas. R. Waith
C. Cowie
Frank Coull
Wm. Hutchinson
Wm. Parsons

TRINIDAD, W. I.

(British.)

Population of the Island, 160,000.

Ales, Beer and Porter.

Campbell, Hannay, Campbell & Co., St. Vincent wharf, Port of Spain
Clairmonte & Co., Marine square, Port of Spain
Schorner & Co., South Quay, Port of Spain
Turnbull, Stewart & Co., West End, Port of Spain
Gordon, Grant & Co., St. Vincent wharf, Port of Spain

Auctioneers.

F. I. Scott & Son, St. Vincent street, Port of Spain
W. Norman, Marine square, Port of Spain
Andrew Hamilton, St. Vincent street, Port of Spain
A. I. Eckstein, Abercrombie street, Port of Spain
W. E. Tyrer & Co., Almond walk, Port of Spain
James Drennan, San Fernando, San Fernando

Bankers.

The Incorporated Society of the Colonial Bank, Port of Spain and San Fernando

Barristers and Advocates.

Hon. S. H. Gatty
Hon. M. M. Philip
Hon. George Garcia
A. W. Anderson
Robert Guppy, M. A.
L. E. Agostini
I. B. Hutton
I. F. A. Farfan
Vincent Brown
L. J. Lamy
H. A. Alcazar
L. M. Power
R. A. Archer Warner, B. A.
A. E. Hendrickson
L. A. Wharton
W. F. Chaver, B. A., LL. B.
A. I. L. Maingot
Eugene E. Coryatt
D. de Freitas de Silva
J. R. Warner

Blacksmiths.

William Games, Tragerete road, Port of Spain
J. Young, Richmond street, Port of Spain
Farr Bros., St. Joseph road, Port of Spain
L. Brice, Corbeau Town, Port of Spain
A. McComie, Corbeau Town, Port of Spain
J. Williamson, St. Ann's road, Port of Spain

Breadstuffs and Commission Merchants.

A. Cumming & Co., Marine square, Port of Spain
Campbell, Hannay & Co., St. Vincent wharf, Port of Spain
Gordon, Grant & Co., St. Vincent wharf, Port of Spain
Schoner & Co., South Quay, Port of Spain
Julian H. Archer & Co., Marine square, Port of Spain
Schjolseth & Holler, South Quay, Port of Spain
Jules E. Attale, Lowery Hy. street, Port of Spain
Jas. Atwell, Marine square, Port of Spain
Futriner & Ramsay, Marine square, Port of Spain
M. H. Smith, Lower Hy. street, Port of Spain
Rodriguez Sons & Co., Marine square, Port of Spain
Turnbull, Stewart & Co., West End, Port of Spain
W. Norman, Marine square, Port of Spain
Singuineau & Co., Almond walk, Port of Spain
Eugene Boissiere, Almond walk, Port of Spain
J. M. Ortiz, Almond walk, Port of Spain
Jules Cipriani, Almond walk, Port of Spain
W. S. Robertson, San Fernando, San Fernando

Bookbinders.

Harry Spooner, St. Ann's road, Port of Spain
E. Luce, Henry street, Port of Spain

Boots and Shoes.

Wilson & Co., Marine square, Port of Spain
G. Goodwille, Marine King street, Port of Spain
Galt & Co., Frederick street, Port of Spain.
H. Monceaux, Frederick street, Port of Spain

Carriage and Wagon Makers.

Alfred Court, Steam Works, West End, Port of Spain
Farr Brothers, St. Joseph Road, Port of Spain
P. St. Laurent, Frederick street, Port of Spain
Henry Court, Queen street, Port of Spain
Joseph Bouis, Cumberland street, Port of Spain

Chinese and Japanese Goods.

Lu Lum & Co., Charlotte street, Port of Spain
Quang Lee, corner of Charlotte and Queen streets, Port of Spain

Cocoa Merchants.

Leon Centeno, Lower Charlotte street and S. Quay, Port of Spain
Llanos & Co., St. Vincent street, Port of Spain
Edward Louis & Co., Henry street, Port of Spain
Charles Fabien & Son, Henry street, Port of Spain
W. Kernahan, South Quay, Port of Spain
C. Leotaud, Marine square, Port of Spain
Houghton & Co., St. Vincent wharf, Port of Spain

·Cocoa Merchants—*continued.*

Anduzi & Co., St. Vincent wharf, Port of Spain
C. Prada & Co., King's wharf, Port of Spain
Ganteaume, Tinoco & Co., Marine square, Port of Spain
Jose Drago & Co., Marine square, Port of Spain
Borde Bros., Columbus square, Port of Spain
Cipriano Ponjados, Columbus square, Port of Spain
Leonard Carry, Almond walk, Port of Spain

Cocoanut Estates.

Cucasa Valley, W. Tucker
Hicar, I. Alfred
Constancio, F. Agostini
Chautevelo, J. S. C. Bernard
Columbia, S. B. Waith
Carlisle, A. Wupperman
Irvis, C. F. Wallmeyer
Carlisle, A. Wupperman
Nariva, Brought Council
St. Joseph, F. A. Gauteaunne
St. Bernard, F. Urich & Son
P. J. Pierre, Plaisance

Cocoa Estates and Owners.

La Reunion, L. Centuro
Mon Repos, L. Centuro
San Juan, L. Centuro
San Joaquin, L. Centuro
El Retiro, L. Centuro
Verdant Vale, C. Cleaver
Willow Vale, C. Cleaver
La Chaguramas, L. Centuro
La Soledad, L. Centuro
La Nives, L. Centuro
Mores, L. Centuro
Hermitage, L. Centuro
La Victoria, A. V. Gomez
Caroni Farm, H. Borde
Forest, F. Hernandez
El Carmen, A. Basso
L'Hermitage, E. Winnett
Montrose, Geo. Fitt
Phillipine, E. Prean
San Pablo, Cipriani
San Pedro, Dabadi
San Salvador, G. Fitt
San Jose, L. Joyeau
San Juan, F. Agostine
Solo Consuelo, A. Schuelt
El Retiro, J. Eligon
El Corazol, D. Brice
Tortuga, L. a de Verteuil
Esperanza, L. a de Verteuil
Maraval, J. Devenish
El Reposo, B. Devenish
La Carmelite, P. Rolingston
Santa Clara, J. Ponce
El Dorado, J. A. Peschier
San Philip, D. Brice
El Paraioso, P. Gonzales
La Victoria, Labastido
La Gloria, du Putron & Booth
San Fernando, L. Centuro
San Antonio, L. Centuro
San José, L. Centuro
La Trinidad, L. Centuro
Torricella, F. Strickland
San Bartholemy, F. Klanos
Spring Bank, G. Francis

Ortinola, C. Tennant
Trafford, A. M. Moller
La Reconnaisance, Elida La Coste
San Francisco, I. P. Zepero
San Juan de Cerro, I. A. Priets
Las Cuevas, A. Augeron
El Carmen, C. Fabien & Son
El Calvario,   "   "
La Soledad,   "   "
La Maravilla,   "   "
San Souci, G. W. Houghton
Santa Barbara, C. Fabien & Son
St. John,   "   "
Mon. Plaisir   "   "
Cumana, Mrs. C. Pautin

Commission Merchants.

T. A. Finlayson & Co., St. Vincent street, Port of Spain; Tennants agency, San Fernando
Colonial Co., Limited, South Quay, Port of Spain; Turnbull, Ross & Co., San Fernando
C. Schock & Co., St. Vincent street, Port of Spain; Leoland Knox, San Fernando
George Alston & Co., Marine square, Port of Spain
W. S. Ross, Edward street, Port of Spain
E. J. Wainwright, Queen street, Port of Spain
Robert Stiven, St. Vincent street, Port of Spain
G. Lambie, St. Vincent street, San Fernando

Contractors and Builders, Etc.

Turnbull Stewart, West End, Port of Spain
N. F. Graham, Corbeau Town, Port of Spain
Carl Saurmann, Belmont, Port of Spain
J. J. Johnston, Park street, Port of Spain
J. Worrell

Dentists.

Charles Daly, corner of Queen and Abercrombie streets, Port of Spain
H Archer, corner of Frederick and Queen streets, Port of Spain
A. Grausant, Park street, Port of Spain
J. Ramsay, Brunswick square, Port of Spain
C. Penida, Abercrombie street, Port of Spain

Dressmaking, Etc.

Misses Cotton, La Violette, Port of Spain
Mdlle. Anais Merlen, Frederick street, Port of Spain

Dry Goods and General Dealers.

Wilson, Son & Co., King street, Port of Spain
Wilson & Co., King street, Port of Spain
George Goodwille & Co., King street, Port of Spain
Smith Bros., Frederick street, Port of Spain
James Miller, Frederick street, Port of Spain
James S. Keoch, Frederick street, Port of Spain
Johnston & Co., Frederick street, Port of Spain
Delorme & Co., Frederick street, Port of Spain
Perreira & Co., Frederick street, Port of Spain
Paul Innis, Frederick street, Port of Spain
Lafargue Bros., Brunswick square, Port of Spain
E. Watronville, King street, Port of Spain
Jules Lamy & Co., King street, Port of Spain
Boissieré & Park, corner of Henry and King streets, Port of Spain
Arnold Lamy, King street, Port of Spain

Dry Goods, Etc.—continued.

J. M. Blanc & Co., King street, Port of Spain
J. G. D'Ade & Co., Frederick street, Port of Spain
Galt & Co., Frederick street, Port of Spain
Cunningham, Thompson & Co., San Fernando, San Fernando
L. Geoffroy, King street, Port of Spain
J. Alcazar, King street, Port of Spain

Foundries and Machine Shops.

James Wishart, Corbeau Town, Port of Spain
C. Malcomie, Corbeau Town, Port of Spain
Patrick Este, Frederick street, Port of Spain
I. Read, Chacon street, Port of Spain

Glassware and Crockery.

James Todd & Sons, Frederick street, Port of Spain
Traveno & Perez, Frederick street, Port of Spain
Arnold Knox, Frederick street, Port of Spain
J. E. Deiroses, Marine square, Port of Spain
H. Bourdon, Charlotte street, Port of Spain
Leon, Mathieu & Co., Henry street, Port of Spain
E. Borherg, Frederick street, Port of Spain
L. Doyon, cor. Henry and Queen streets, Port of Spain

Groceries.

C. L. Haley & Co., corner of King and Abercrombie streets, Port of Spain
Muir, Marshall & Co., King street, Port of Spain
J. A. Rapsey, Frederick street, Port of Spain
McGruer & Vuille, Brunswick square, Port of Spain
Arnold Knox, Frederick street, Port of Spain
Frank Brown, Abercrombie street, Port of Spain
Querino Baptista, King street, Port of Spain

Hardware.

F. Urich & Son, South Quay, Port of Spain
F. Zurcher & Co., South Quay, Port of Spain
Gerold & Sherer, South Quay, Port of Spain
George Fitzwilliam & Co., Marine square, Port of Spain
Leon Mathieu & Co., King street, Port of Spain
P. B. André, South Quay, Port of Spain
Arnot & Co., King street, Port of Spain
L. Nestor, corner of Queen and Frederick street, Port of Spain

Hides and Horns.

F. Zurcher & Co., Port of Spain
F. Urich & Son, Port of Spain

House Furnishing Goods.

J. G. D'Ade & Co., Frederick street, Port of Spain
D. Monceaux, Frederick street, Port of Spain
James Todd & Sons, Frederick street, Port of Spain
James Miller, Frederick street, Port of Spain
Arnold Knox, Frederick street, Port of Spain
Perreira & Co., Frederick street, Port of Spain

Jewelry, Etc.

James Todd & Co., Frederick street, Port of Spain
Traverio & Perez, Frederick street, Port of Spain

Alexander Donnetieu, Marine square, Port of Spain
Alexander Decle, Frederick street, Port of Spain
Barcaut Bros., Frederick street, Port of Spain
Leonidas David, Frederick street, Port of Spain
M. Aumatre Beaupatre, Marine square, Port of Spain
Charles Renaud, Frederick street, Port of Spain
J. B. Marcano, Frederick street, Port of Spain

Journalists and Printers.

T. R. N. Laughlin, Chacon street, Port of Spain
Joseph Lewis, Abercombie street, Port of Spain
Philip Rostant, Chacon street, Port of Spain
Samuel Carter, San Fernando, San Fernando
W. E. Tyrer & Co., Almond Walk, San Fernando

Local Companies, Etc.

Tramways Co., Limited, St. Vincent street, Port of Spain
Trinidad Chocolate Manufacturing Co., St. Vincent street, Port of Spain
Trinidad Ice Manufacturing Co., St. Vincent street, Port of Spain
Trinidad Telephone Co., Frederick street, Port of Spain
Trinidad Tucker Valley Estate Co., South Quay, Port of Spain
Trinidad Match Manufacturing Co. Limited, Marine square, Port of Spain
Trinidad Belmont Chocolate Manufacturing Co., Belmont, Port of Spain
Trinidad J. G. B. Siegert & Sons (Angostura Bitters), King street, Port of Spain
Trinidad Sr. Batala e Hijos, Armago, George street, Port of Spain

Lumber Mills.

Turnbull, Stewart & Co., West End, Port of Spain
N. F. Graham, Dorbeau town, Port of Spain
Government Mills, St. Joseph road, Port of Spain

Medical Practitioners.

Thomas Murray, M. D.
Henry Mitchell, M. D.
L. A. D. de Vertiuel, M. D.
Richard Mercer, M. D.
J. V. de Boissierè, M. D.
J. H. Inwey, M. R. C. S.
E. J. Hammond, M. R. C. S.
R. Knaggs, M. R. C. S.
Thomas Murray, jr., M. R. C. S.
I. Leonard Crane, M. D.
I. F. Chittenden, R. M. C. S.
R. Francis Black, M. R. C. S,
Jas. A. de Wolff, M. D.
Charles F. Knox, M. R. C. S.
N. Claude Burgoyne, Pasley, M. R. C. S.
Arthur Woodlock.
Louis Fabien, M. R. C. S.
Domingo Monthrun, M. D., M. R. C. S.
F. A. de Vortiuel, M. R. C. S.
Alex. W. Wight, M. R. C. S.
Albert Boucaud, M. B.
Rob. Hy. Edward Knaggs, M., R. C. S.
John C. Cleaver, M. D., M. R. C. S.
James Wilson Eakin, M. B.
H. McCaul Alaton, M. B.
Gervase R. Percy, M. D.

Medical Practitioners—*continued*.

Joseph L. Boussingnac, M. R. C. S.
Edward Inskip Read, L. R. C. P.
George Sam'l Lescombe, M. R. C. S.
J. Edgar Joseph, M. R. C. S.
Sam'l Campo, M. R. C. S.
R. C. Bennett, M. B.
J. B. Gravely, M. R. C. S.
Sam'l Weeks Fitt., M. R. C. S.
Beaven Neave Rake, M. D.
Ed. A. Doyle, M. R. C. S.
H. M. Kelly, M. R. C. S.
P. L. de Montbrun, M. R. C. S.
D. A. de Montbrun, M. R. C. S.
G. D. Knox, M. R. C. S.
Edgar Sicaro, L. S. A.
Aldric, Perez
J. Darwent

Merchant Tailors.

M. H. Herbert, King street, Port of Spain
George Goodwille, King street, Port of Spain
James Miller, Frederick street, Port of Spain
Philip Gonzales, Henry street, Port of Spain

Pianos and Musical Instruments.

H. Monceaux
Perreira & Co.
J. G. D'Ade & Co.
James Todd & Sons
H. Strong

Photographers.

J. Morin, Brunswick square, Port of Spain
C. Cazabon, Brunswick street, Port of Spain
L. Micheaux, Queen street, Port of Spain

Shipbuilders.

H. W. Armstrong, Corbeau Town, Port of Spain
William Thwaites, E. Wharf Improvement, Port of Spain
James Harvey, E. Wharf Improvement, Port of Spain
J. Tronchin, E. Wharf Improvement, Port of Spain
J. Charbonier, Corbeau Town, Port of Spain

Sugar Estates and Owners.

Bonaventure, Tennant, Sons & Co.
Brechin Carblo, Gregor Turnbull
Camden & Exchange, J. Cumming
Caracas, J. Henderson
Concord, C. Tennant Sons & Co.
Edinburgh, L. Latour
Endeavour, B. de Verteuil
Esperanza, W. F. Burnley
Felicite, A. C. Miles
Caroni, Gregor Turnbull
Milton, C. Tennant. Sons & Co.
Mon Plaisir, F. Zurcher
Mon Salonic, Q. Kelly
Mount Pleasant
Forest Park & Cedar Hill, A Devenish
Orange Field, L. Peraw
Perseverance, A. C. Miles
Perseverance, I. Cumming
Petersfield, J. Rugros
Phœnix Park, W. F. Burnley
St. Clair, F. Zurcher
St. Helene, Gregor Turnbull
Adela, J. E. Coryatt
Trafalgar, Ambard & Cadet
Waterloo, J. Cumming
Reform, J. E. Coryatt
Aranguez, A. Blasán
Barrataria, A. Blasán
Champs Elysées, Dr. de Boissière
Duisley, T. C. Pile,
El Socoro, Colonial Company
Garden & Bonavi, A. McLean
Golden Grove, F. W. de Blanc
Lavantille, J. E. Coryatt
Laurel Hill & Cane Farm, F. Zurcher
Macoya & Eldorado, A. McLean
Orange Grove, W. F. Burnley
Paradise, Campbell Hannay
River & Cascade, W. F. Brunton
St. Agustin & Cheatham Lodge, Leon Agostine
St. Claire, I. R. Olton
Valsayn, Paul Guiseppi
Woodbrook, W. F. Burnley
Bellevue, C. Tennant, Sons & Co.
Benlomond, C. Tennant. Sons & Co.
Bronte, M. Lennon & Shine
Broomage & Buenintendo, C. Tennant. Sons & Co.
Cedar Grove, James Lamont
Concord, Mrs. de Verticul
Corial, Price Brothers
Craiguish, G. Lichllelow
Cupar Grange, M. Lennon
Esperance, Paul Vessing
Fairfield, Gregor Turnbull
Garth, Thompson, Hawkey & Co.
Glenroy & Malgretonto, C. Tennant Sons & Co.
Harmony Hall, Colonial Co., Limited
Hermitage, C. Tennant, Sons & Co.
Hope, Peter McIntosh
Hindostan, C. O. McLean
Inverness, C. Tennant, Sons & Co.
Jordan Hill, M Lennon
La Resource, Gregor Turnbull
Lothians, Gregor Turnbull
New Grant, C. Tennant Sons & Co.
Palmille & Caanan, James Lamont,
Paradise, Mrs. Gomes
Philipine, James Lamont
Plen Palais, W. L. Johnson
Plaisance, Gregor Turnbull
Elswick, J. Palmer
La Fortitudo, Price Bros.
Reform, T. A. McQuaid
Retrench, Robt. Wilson
Santa Margarita, F. Brash
Taruba, Col. Coy., Limited
Guion & Marabella, A. P. Maryatt
Wellington & Picton, J. Cumming
Williamsville & Brothers, Col. Co., Limited
Sr. Madden, Col. Co., Limited

Trunks, Etc.

Edward Guy, Belmont, Port of Spain
I. Louisy, Charlotte street, Port of Spain

STEAMSHIP LINES

FROM THE

UNITED STATES

TO THE

COUNTRIES NAMED IN THIS DIRECTORY.

FROM NEW YORK.

PACIFIC MAIL STEAMSHIP COMPANY, for Central, South American and Mexican ports, *via* Isthmus of Panama, every Monday.

NEW YORK AND CUBA MAIL STEAMSHIP COMPANY, for Havana, Matanzas and Sagua, Cuba, and Vera Cruz, Mexico. Sailing days, Wednesdays and Saturdays.

ATLAS STEAMSHIP COMPANY, for Jamaica and Hayti, connecting with steamers for all West India ports, sailing every Saturday.

QUEBEC STEAMSHIP COMPANY, for St. Kitts, Antigua, Dominica, Martinique, St. Lucia, Barbadoes, Grenada and Trinidad, sailing every Thursday.

COMPANIA TRANSATLANTICA ESPAÑOLA, for Havana, Cuba; Puerto-Rico, Vera Cruz, and Progresso, Mexico, and ports in Central America, sailing every two weeks.

NEW YORK AND JAMAICA STEAMSHIP CO., for Jamaica, sailing every fortnight.

FROM NEW ORLEANS, LA.

MORGAN STEAMSHIP CO., for Havana, Vera Cruz and Central American ports, sailing every two weeks.

FROM FLORIDA.

PLANT STEAMSHIP COMPANY, for Havana, Cuba, *via* Tampa and Key West, every Monday, Wednesday and Saturday, from November 1st to May 1st, and every Monday and Thursday, from May to November.

FROM SAN FRANCISCO, CAL.

PACIFIC MAIL STEAMSHIP COMPANY, for Pacific ports of Mexico and Central America, every week.

DELMAR'S

MERCANTILE MANUAL

AND

BUSINESS GUIDE

IN RELATION TO TRADE WITH

MEXICO,

CENTRAL AMERICA AND WEST INDIES.

HOW TO SELL GOODS IN MEXICO AND SPANISH AMERICA.

Many very intelligent and successful American and English merchants commit the grevious error in supposing that business can be conducted pretty much the same way in all parts of the world.

To suppose that a plan or system which they have followed with marked success at home, should be equally successful abroad, is, to say the least, expecting rather too much.

Every country has its own ways and customs, commercial as well as social, and more particularly is this noticeable in Spanish-American countries.

The Spanish race everywhere is deeply wedded to old customs, habits and ways, and it requires considerable time, patience and perseverance to effect any radical change from their ancient, time-honored customs, to our more modern, progressive ideas.

With these facts before us, the merchant who desires to open successful trade or commercial relations with the people of Mexico and Spanish-America, will do well to abandon some of his own ideas and defer to the advice of those who have had extensive practical experience with these people; and, by following the advice and plain course of sailing which we respectfully submit for your information and guidance, we think you will be sure to consult your own best interests in the premises.

ADVANTAGES IN MAILING CIRCULARS AND PRICES.

In the first place, and as a preliminary step, we cannot too strongly urge the necessity and importance of mailing circulars, catalogues and price-lists (always in Spanish) to those merchants in Mexico, Central America, Cuba and Porto Rico who deal in or handle your goods.

A great many commission, export and shipping houses, especially those in New York, will advise, even urge you, not to follow our advice in the above respect. Some of these foreign commission houses go so far as to *strictly forbid* American manufacturers mailing or even inclosing circulars, catalogues and price-lists in the packages containing goods which they have purchased of you for shipment abroad.

The reasons for these arbitrary restrictions must be patent and very apparent to any intelligent mind. These commission middlemen wish to retain all the foreign trade in their own control, and monopolize this valuable business to the exclusion of the manufacturers and direct producers.

For nearly one hundred years the immensely profitable import and export trade between this country and Spanish America, Brazil and the West Indies, has been monopolized by a limited number of shipping and commission houses, mainly in New York, Boston and Baltimore, all of whom have realized immense fortunes out of the business.

The policy of all these commission houses has been to put every obstacle in the way of *direct trade* between the merchants and manufacturers of the United States and the people of Spanish America. By this means these export commission houses have maintained the exclusive monopoly of this valuable trade, and consequently have limited our commercial relations and intercourse with the people of Spanish America.

By mailing your circulars, as we suggest, you not only introduce your goods, but also your house; and thereby pave the way for more intimate and profitable future commercial relations.

Be assured that, in mailing your circulars, catalogues, etc., *direct* to buyers abroad, you are wasting neither time, printing nor postage, for the merchants of Mexico, Central America and the West Indies, are always pleased to receive price lists direct from the manufacturer or first hands, and these they carefully preserve for future reference.

SENDING OUT COMMERCIAL TRAVELERS.

Having made your business and your goods known to the trade abroad, as suggested above, and having received some direct orders or inquiries in relation to your goods, it may prove advisable and profitable for you to send out an agent, or commercial traveler, to represent your house and take orders by direct solicitation.

It is very easy to decide upon sending out an agent, but not quite so easy to decide upon or secure the services of a competent, qualified man to represent your business successfully in those countries. Your best, most experienced and most successful salesman, if he has never before visited Spanish America and cannot speak the Spanish language fluently, will prove anything but a flattering success in those countries.

The traveling agent who attempts to sell goods in Spanish-America, without having had any previous experience with the ways, manners, customs and language of the people with whom he expects to trade, will encounter more obstacles, and meet with more reverses, than he anticipates, and he is liable to "throw up the sponge," even before he has fairly begun his work.

Your representative, being unfamiliar with the country, the people and the language, as before stated, fails to secure many orders, and leaves the country in disgust, after involving his firm in a heavy bill for expenses, besides fines and other penalties. The result is, the manufacturers and merchants of the United States put the people of those countries down as swindlers, as never intending to pay for goods ordered, when it is really the fault of the manufacturers, or their representatives, in not first informing themselves as to the law and customs and points necessary before shipping the goods. Then, again, many American manufacturers, after such an experience as above described, become disgusted and dissatisfied with their first venture, and declare that the South American trade is a fraud, and that all the brilliant promises held forth by press and public regarding the value of that trade are but a "delusion and a snare."

To do business in Spanish America properly and successfully, the American merchant or manufacturer must first advertise his goods by means of circulars through the mails, then secure the services of an experienced commercial traveler, who is thoroughly familiar with the language, customs and country, and who has had several years' practical experience trading with the people of South America. A German, or an Englishman, who enjoys the advantages above enumerated, is by far the best man to employ. After your representative has traveled the country thoroughly for one season, and thoroughly introduced your goods to the people, then your next step is to establish a permanent branch house or agency of *your own*, in some centrally located city of the country, where you propose selling your goods. Try the above plan one year, and it will be found to pay.

BUSINESS OPPORTUNITIES IN CUBA.

There are excellent business opportunities in Cuba for enterprising merchants and capitalists, that many Americans know but little of. Besides an active demand for goods of American manufacture, there are many openings for the safe investment of American capital and the employment of American skill and enterprise. Notwithstanding the high tariff exacted by the Spanish government on most goods imported from countries other than Spain, there is a steady and constantly increasing demand for certain kinds of American goods, such as provisions, tools, cutlery, fire-arms, builders', carriage makers' and shelf hardware, nails, lumber, clothing, printing paper and ink, shovels, spades, hoes, rakes, sewing machines, railway rolling stock, fire extinguishers and apparatus, machinery, especially for sugar plantations, canned goods, paints, oils and varnish, kerosene and lubricating oils, pianos, organs, and musical instruments, books, such as reprints in Spanish, carriages, patent medicines and medicinal specialties, patented novelties, trunks and valises, harness, and windmills. By the introduction and general adoption of improved American machinery, a more careful, economic and scientific cultivation of the sugar estates is now being developed. Cuba to-day is, therefore, enabled to outrival all other lands in the quantity, quality and price of sugars. But there are thousands of acres of the most valuable sugar lands of the world yet undeveloped, which, if taken up by enterprising capitalists, employing skilled labor and labor-saving machinery, would readily pay 100 per cent annually on the investment.

ABOUT SAMPLES OF MERCHANDISE.

In the first place, it is best to carry as few samples as possible, especially those of a heavy or bulky nature, and try to confine your samples to *one* ordinary traveling trunk.

There are hundreds of small cabs in Havana, but no local baggage wagons, or "baggage transfer" companies. Your baggage is conveyed to your hotel, if of small dimensions, in your cab; if too large for the accommodation of the cab, you must hire a dray, and wait the pleasure of the drayman to deliver it at his convenience, if delivered at all.

If you carry but a limited amount of samples, and carry such in an ordinary traveling trunk (not a huge sample case), you will have no difficulty in passing your baggage, samples included, at the Custom House.

If you carry several sample trunks, more than is usually carried as ordinary personal baggage, you will be required to enter such baggage, and declare the samples on the manifest of the steamer on which you are a passenger, and you will be required to enter the same at the Custom House as merchandise, giving bonds for the re-shipment of such merchandise, and a guarantee that such merchandise or samples are not to be sold in the country.

By arranging your samples in limited quantity and compact form, as before suggested, so as to carry them easily, as *personal baggage*, you will avoid all the trouble and annoyance above described.

The purser of the steamer on which you journey to Havana will ask you to make a declaration as to the nature and character of your luggage and belongings. It will be as well to tell him you have nothing but your personal effects; say nothing about samples.

Where you carry samples of heavy goods, such as hardware, tools, etc., you will, perhaps, find it the best plan to carry such samples in a separate package, and not in the trunk with your personal effects. Trust to chance that the Custom House officers will pass such samples without trouble; you will find the chances in your favor.

Never offer a bribe to the Havana Custom House officers, or, in fact, to any Spanish official — unless the occasion demands that the bribe should be a *large* one. You can employ a $5 or $10 fee to good advantage in *Mexico*, on almost any occasion; but don't try it on at Havana. The consequences may be annoying. In the latter city, every official is a sort of spy on his brother official; and, if you once begin the bribery business, you may have to go through the entire list, from high to low, otherwise you may find yourself in an embarrassing position, to draw it mildly.

SELLING GOODS.

As a rule, the merchants of Cuba, or, in fact, any Spanish country, will rarely call at your hotel to examine your goods. While they are always polite and courteous to agents calling on them, they, as a class, not being afflicted with any remarkable degree of energy, or anxious for any unusual effort outside of their own places of business, prefer that you wait upon them rather than that they should be put to the trouble of waiting upon you.

Before offering your goods or attempting to make sales, you should first call on the trade and politely introduce yourself and your business, then make a regular business appointment, specifying the day and hour when you will call and show your goods. Always recollect that you cannot successfully transact business in Spanish-American countries as expeditiously as you can at home. The Spanish race are never in a hurry, and you must consult *their* convenience and time, besides cultivating a considerable degree of patience, if you would succeed with them.

If you strike a Spanish merchant with the right goods at the right time, and you succeed in making a favorable impression, you can sell him readily, and he will buy largely.

After making out a memorandum of the names and addresses of the merchants you desire to interview, get your samples ready and call a cab. For such occasions be careful to engage your cab by the hour *(por hora)*, the tariff being $1.50 per hour in local paper money (called "*Billettes*"), equivalent to about fifty cents American money, at the present rate of exchange. You need not understand Spanish to direct your cabman. They are usually intelligent fellows. Write the name of street and number plainly on a slip of paper, and give it to the cabby; he'll carry you straight enough. In all Spanish countries the *number* of the house always *follows* the name of the street, as "Obispo 51," instead of 51 Obispo street. The word street, or "*Calle*," is never used.

"DRUMMERS'" SAMPLES IN MEXICO.

The same rule and advice for commercial men which we recommend for the observance of those visiting Cuba on business, apply also to Mexico, only more so. The custom house regulations of Mexico, as regards travelers' baggage and samples of merchandise, are usually more stringent than those in Cuba.

We would suggest that commercial men should try to get along with as few samples as possible, and those should be carried in very compact form, avoiding bulk and weight, where the nature of the goods will allow, and use as few sample cases or trunks as you conveniently can.

We would recommend commercial travelers to carefully read what we have to say regarding "Samples of Merchandise," in Cuba, which will be found elsewhere in this Commercial Guide.

ABOUT PASSPORTS.

Passports are no longer required in visiting Mexico, Central America, Cuba or any place in the West Indies. At the same time it will do no harm for one to provide himself with a passport, simply as a matter of identification, and, in case of need, a possible protection.

According to a royal decree of 1887, the passport system, once very annoying, onerous and expensive, was abolished as regards the Spanish Islands of Cuba and Porto Rico. But, while no passport is required to *land* in Cuba, you are not permitted to *leave* the Island without a consular certificate.

The new regulations provide that every foreign citizen, wishing to leave the Island of Cuba, and also that of Porto Rico, must apply to his consul, who will provide him, free of cost, with a certificate setting forth his nationality, profession or occupation and general respectability. This consular certificate must be presented, in person, to the civil governor of the town from whence you take your departure, who will indorse the document (on payment to him of thirty-five cents specie) when you may go your way rejoicing.

PACKING AND SHIPPING GOODS.

There are two highly important matters to be considered, and which should never be neglected, in shipping goods to Mexico or any South American market. Firstly, the styles, patterns and quality of the goods shipped should conform strictly with the kind ordered, and, secondly, great care should be taken in manifesting and in packing the goods to be shipped.

One of the reasons why the English have succeeded in establishing a large and prosperous trade with the countries of Spanish-America is due, in no small degree, to the fact that they make themselves thoroughly acquainted with the wants and tastes of the people, and, as a rule, keep faith with their customers in those countries. They are frequently advised, by resident agents, as to the condition of the markets there, and they usually send just such goods as are ordered. Americans too frequently send goods quite different, in quality and style, from those ordered, because they happen to have such other goods on hand, thinking a different article will suit or answer the purpose quite as well as the kind ordered. But it should be remembered, that, if people down there ordered *painted* goods, they don't want to receive *varnished* goods instead. They know just what they want, and order it, and, when something different is sent them — no matter how trifling the difference — they feel disappointed and cheated.

The following amusing story, related by an experienced South American merchant, will illustrate how ridiculous are the prejudices of some of the ignorant natives:

"We were in the habit for years of shipping out what we call soft tallow candles, 'dips.' The only purpose for which they were used was to grease the niggers' heads; a nigger would step into the store and buy one of these dips, and then go out and rub it over his head and body. That is all they were used for. Well, we bought these candles for years from one manufacturer, and they always had on the boxes a yellow label, giving the manufacturer's name in Spanish, and all about it. Finally he got out of labels, and had a new batch made, and he altered the color, and had the labels made blue. Our next shipment went out with blue labels, and every single lot was thrown on our hands, and they said, as the labels were blue, the candles were bogus. All we could do was to have a lot of yellow labels made, like the former, and sent out there, and pasted on the boxes, and then they were sold."

When we say that it is absolutely necessary to conform to the tastes and usages of the natives in selecting, packing and shipping goods to South America, we refer to staple goods, such as provisions and all kinds of eatables, laundry articles, hats, shoes, cotton and woolen fabrics, toilet articles, etc. In the matter of machinery, agricultural implements, tools, patented articles, pianos, organs, etc., they, of course, must and do conform to our ideas.

One of our largest shipping merchants complains of the careless manner in which some of our manufacturers pack their goods for foreign markets. He says: "They pack their goods here very carelessly, as if goods were going to be shipped on a train a short distance, whereas they are handled several times, getting aboard the steamer and getting off the steamer, and then on the train or mule backs, and the goods arrive in a damaged condition."

Speaking of the importance of invoicing goods correctly, an old shipping merchant remarks: If the United States could have an influence upon the Government of Mexico to so alter its custom-house regulations, it would not be so difficult for our merchants in filling orders for that country. Every shipment made to Mexico requires an enumeration of the articles in detail, three copies to be made. Then, if there is an erasure or a blot, there is a possibility of a fine in the custom-house. If there is a mistake in the weight or in the figuring, although it may not be of any importance, there is a fine for that.

In regard to the matter of packing boxes used by American shippers, the same merchant says:

"They (the American shipper) do not care; they go to work and knock up a box with boards an inch thick, and they will fill it with nails, and put all kinds of heavy cleats and straps on it, and that box will weigh very heavy. The English have an advantage over us in that respect; they use a wood over there that is a finer wood; they can make a box out of one-half or one-quarter inch stuff that is stronger than our stuff which is an inch thick. They use a different quality of nails from what we do; they use a round nail made of wire; the French use them very much, too. Then they use much lighter wood than we do."

As Mexico and many of the South American governments levy duty on the gross weight of the package, it is very important that the package should be made up as light as possible, consistent with proper strength, and care should be taken to give the correct weights and numbers in applying for a consular invoice. Says one merchant on this subject:

"You take for instance, Carthagena, in the United States of Colombia They have a tariff with about six clauses in it, divided into six clauses, and there is a different duty levied on each clause, but it is on the gross weight. Now, we are obliged here to make out what we call a consular invoice; every case has got to have a number on it, and, without a number, we are liable to a fine. We have to describe, in that invoice, the kind of goods that are in the case, then to give the gross weight of each case, and then, the total gross weight of all the cases, and this has to be reduced to kilograms. That is all right; it is a right of the country to demand consular invoices, indicating the contents, and stating that the goods are what they purport to be. But, getting their duties as they do on gross weights, they exact a fine for every 10 per cent. difference gross weight on arrival and the gross weight as expressed in the invoice. Well, you can readily see that, in the hurry of getting off our goods, errors will creep in. We go round to the different houses here and buy a lot of goods, and want the gross weight of those goods; the young man in the store weighs the goods, and the goods may weigh 250 pounds, and they put it down 150; we take their weights and make out our invoices, and, when it gets out there, there is a variation of 10 per cent., so they fine the receiver of the goods for having made mistakes in the United States."

While the manufacturer here has little or nothing to do with the tariff and duties in South American ports, as such matters pertain to, and are arranged by, the consignee or buyer, yet our people would greatly facilitate and increase our trade relations with Spanish America if they were to aid and assist the buyers for and in those countries, by conforming to the commercial rules and usages of those countries, as above related.

AMERICAN TRADE WITH CUBA.

Perhaps no portion of Spanish-America is so well and so favorably known to Americans as the " Ever Faithful Isle " of Cuba, with its population of 1,800,000 souls.

The great wealth and natural resources of Cuba are proverbial. The natives are highly educated and intelligent, and they are as industrious and enterprising in business as they are advanced in intelligence and culture.

The three great products and sources of wealth of Cuba, namely, sugar, tobacco and cigars, find a ready and advantageous market in this country. Probably nearly two-thirds of the entire product of Cuba is sold in our markets, and in return the Cuban merchants invest very liberally in our manufactures. And, were it not for the existing onerous Spanish tariff, and the many trade restrictions imposed by Spain, there is little doubt but that the Cuban merchants (especially the natives) would, as a matter of preference, purchase in our markets nearly everything that they are now compelled to buy in Europe.

Our exports of domestic manufactures and commodities to Cuba are usually very considerable, exceeding in value the combined amount which we export to all the other West India Islands.

Recently there has been a considerable falling off in the amount of our export trade to Cuba, which is accounted for by reason of the unsettled state of the market, caused by the unsatisfactory condition of the commercial relations now temporarily existing between our government and the government of Spain, owing to the failure of Spain to live up to her treaty agreements and commercial stipulations as regards trade with her West India colonies.

There is little doubt but that the Spanish government will see the necessity of soon renewing the commercial treaty of 1884, and grant to Americans even better and more advantageous trading facilities with Cuba and Porto Rico. This country affords such an advantageous and profitable market for the sale of all the products of Cuba and Porto Rico that Spain can hardly afford to quarrel with us, and maintain, for any length of time, the onerous trade restrictions which have, for a short time, somewhat impeded our business relations with Cuba. The Cubans absolutely need our markets, and they also need our goods. One is as indispensable to them as the other, and it will always be so.

MEXICAN CIGARS—A COMPARATIVELY NEW INDUSTRY.

The manufacture of cigars from native tobacco as a regular commercial industry in Mexico, is now beginning to assume considerable national importance and proportions; and, from present indications, this industry bids fair to become, at no distant day, quite a formidable rival to the Havana cigar trade.

The manufacture of cigars in Mexico for export, is at present confined to the city of Vera Cruz, where it has flourished, more or less, for the past twenty years. The trade began to attract foreign attention and gain in commercial importance in 1879, in which year the Havana tobacco crop was bad, and the output of Havana cigars comparatively small.

There are now some twenty cigar manufactories in Vera Cruz, which give employment to nearly 3,000 skilled operatives, mostly Cubans.

The Mexican cigars compare favorably with the medium grades of Havana, while the prices are much lower. Besides the cigar factories above alluded to, there are in Vera Cruz several extensive cigarette factories. Both products are extensively shipped to England and France.

THE REPUBLICS

OF

CENTRAL AMERICA.

CENTRAL AMERICA.

The Central American States, or those Spanish-American countries lying south of Mexico and north of Venezuela, comprise the Republics of Guatemala, Spanish Honduras, Salvador, Nicaragua, Costa Rica and the United States of Colombia.

Taking these Republics in point of territorial size, they may be enumerated in the following order: Guatemala, United States of Colombia, Honduras, Nicaragua, Costa Rica and Salvador, the smallest.

All the Central American Republics are extremely rich and prolific in mineral and agricultural resources. In point of fact, the undeveloped wealth of these rich and fertile countries is almost fabulous, and only awaits the pleasure of enterprising Americans and Europeans to develop this latent wealth, and reap a rich reward for their enterprise and trouble.

With the exception of small portions of lowland territory (*tierra baja*), or that laying contiguous to rivers, the climate of all the Central American countries is generally healthy and salubrious. The temperature is uniform and agreeable, being neither cold nor excessively hot, the thermometer ranging from 70° to 90° all the year round.

The Central American Republics are now, and have been for some time past, in a comparatively pacific and progressive condition politically and commercially, and life and property is about as safe in those countries as in most other communities. To quote the language of Señor Don Miguel Velascory Velasco, minister resident of Salvador to the United States: "The Republics of Central America, being free from degrading despotic governments, have entered into a new life and prosperity effective in every respect."

The staple agricultural products of the Central American States are coffee, cocoa, indigo, tobacco, rubber, cotton, sugar, dye-woods, hard woods, medicinal plants and fruits. All of these articles find a ready cash market in this country and in Europe. The three first-mentioned articles, namely, coffee, cocoa and indigo, are the prime and most valuable staples, and upon which depends the main commercial wealth of these countries.

Gold and silver abounds in almost all portions of these countries, and, with proper modern appliances, can be mined in greater and better paying quantities than in any part of the United States.

These Central American countries are being rapidly developed in their agricultural, mining, and commercial resources. Railways, telegraphs, telephones and modern appliances and improvements of every description, are being introduced in every section, and emigration, and capital from Europe and the United States, is flowing rapidly toward these most promising "El Dorados." The most important and most valuable estates, as well as most of the internal improvements now in progress, are mainly owned and controlled by the English, French, Americans and Germans. These settlers are very hospitable, live well, and, as a rule, are possessed of considerable wealth, which they have made in the country.

With enterprise, energy and a small capital, almost any of the Central American Republics offers very tempting inducements for Americans who desire to "grow up with the country."

A TREATY OF FRIENDSHIP AND COMMERCE BETWEEN THE CENTRAL AMERICAN STATES.

The Central American Diet, recently held in Guatemala, agreed to a treaty of friendship and commerce between the five Central American Republics. The citizen of any one of the five Republics will hereafter be a citizen of all, no matter in which of them he may have been born. This convention provides for the fullest liberty of commerce and navigation between the different States, for the friendly intervention of all in any political disputes, and the observance of strict neutrality in the event of armed contests between the different States. Provision is also made for joint action in any case in which any one of the States should find itself involved with a foreign power. Arrangements are also made for the adoption of similar weights and measures, and a common civil and criminal code, the abolition of the death penalty, and the assimilation of constitutional principles, such as that which declares the necessity of periodical changes of all officials. Lastly, it contains a basis for the re-establishment of the Central American Union.

THE
WEST INDIA ISLANDS.

THE WEST INDIA ISLANDS.

As our readers are probably aware, the Islands of the West Indies embrace or include as many as eight different nationalities, as follows: English, Spanish, French, Danish, Dutch, Haytien (French negroes), and Dominican (Spanish negroes). The most important in point of size, population and commercial greatness, are the Spanish Islands of Cuba and Puerto Rico. Next in commercial importance, population and progress are the British Islands of Jamaica, Trinidad, Barbadoes, Antigua, Dominica, Tobago, St. Kitts, St. Lucia, Bermuda, Turks Island, New Providence, and numerous small Islands in the Bahama group.

Then come the French islands of Martinique and Guadeloupe, the former of which is of considerable commercial importance, being in a high state of cultivation, while its inhabitants are very intelligent, industrious and progressive. Saint Pierre, the capital of Martinique, is a very attractive and delightful little city, and its people are highly cultivated and most agreeable entertainers.

The Dutch (Hollanders) control the rich and prosperous Island of Curaçoa; the Danes are masters of the Islands of St. Thomas and St. Croix, while the large and fertile Island of Santo Domingo, divided into the two negro Republics of Hayti and Dominica, is of very little agricultural, commercial or political importance under its present rulers.

Owing to limited population, and consequently limited consumption, circumscribed territory, more or less national prejudices, and, last but not least, a lack of regular and systematic business canvassing or "drumming," our trade with the West India Islands — with the important exception of Cuba — has never been as large and important as it should and could be.

All the islands of the West India group procure the bulk of their provisions and breadstuffs from the United States, while but a limited amount of hardware, tools, machinery, furniture, shoes, woolen and cotton fabrics, of American manufacture, find a market in those small but prosperous communities.

This is all wrong, and entirely at variance with the laws of trade and the geographical contiguity of these Islands to the United States. They find a ready and usually a profitable market with us for the bulk of their product, and there is no good and substantial reason why we should not supply them with anything and everything in manufactured articles that they require.

The only plausible reason that can be assigned for this disparity of American trade with the West Indies is due mainly to the fact that but few American merchants and manufacturers have sought *direct trade*, while those merchants or traders, resident in the United States, who represent, or affect to control, the trade between the United States and the West Indies, are foreigners imbued with strong national prejudices against Americans and everything American, except American dollars.

The writer has traveled extensively throughout the West India Islands, and has had considerable business relations with the people of those Islands, and we can assure our readers that there are no more intelligent, ready, reliable, responsible and honorable merchants, as a rule, in any part of the world, than can be found in the British and French West Indies (Hayti excepted). In those Islands a merchant must be eminently responsible and reliable or he must go under and leave the place. His business peers and associates will not tolerate a man who is or who may become a reproach to the honored credit of the place. As a consequence, you are pretty sure to get your pay for all goods you may sell in the British or French Islands of the West Indies.

Mail your circulars and price lists direct to the merchants of the West Indies, then follow it up by sending out a competent agent, or commercial traveler, and you will soon be satisfied that there will be found a good and profitable market for your goods.

COMMERCIAL DATA.

As this book is purely a commercial work, designed only for the purpose of affording merchants such commercial information and data as will prove useful and advantageous in their business, we do not propose taking up the time of our patrons and confuse them with any further unnecessary platitudes and essays regarding the beauties of the countries and matters under consideration, but, instead, we shall proceed direct and to the point, by giving such commercial data as will prove most interesting and useful.

With the foregoing object and purposes in view, we now place before our readers the latest official tables, prepared by the Bureau of Statistics of the United States Treasury, which will show the extent, importance and value of the trade between the United States, Mexico, Central America and the West India Islands, the countries under consideration in this volume.

MEXICAN MONEY.

Table showing the equivalent of foreign coins with the Mexican dollar, which is the monetary unit of the Republic.

COUNTRIES.	COIN.	METAL.	Equivalent in Mexican dollars and cents.
Argentine Republic	Peso	Gold and silver	$1 00
Austria	Florin	Silver	40
Belgium	Franc	Gold and silver	20
Bolivia	Boliviano	Silver	90
Brazil	Milreis	Gold	55
British North America	Dollar	Gold	1 00
Central America	Peso	Silver	90
Chili	Peso	Gold and silver	95
China	Tael	Silver	1 25
Colombia, United States of	Peso	Silver	90
Cuba	Peso	Gold and silver	1 00
Denmark	Crown	Gold	27
Ecuador	Peso	Silver	90
Egypt	Piaster	Gold	5
France	Franc	Gold and silver	20
Great Britain	Pound Sterling	Gold	5 00
Greece	Drachma	Gold and silver	20
German Empire	Mark	Gold	25
Hayti	Gourde	Gold and silver	1 00
India	Rupee	Silver	40
Italy	Lira	Gold and silver	20
Japan	Yen	Silver	1 00
Netherlands	Florin	Gold and silver	40
Norway	Crown	Gold	27
Paraguay	Peso	Gold	1 00
Peru	Sol	Silver	90
Portugal	Milreis	Gold	1 08
Puerto Rico	Peso	Gold	1 00
Russia	Rouble	Silver	70
Saint Thomas	Dollar	Gold and silver	1 00
Sandwich Islands	Dollar	Gold	1 00
Spain	Peseta	Gold and silver	20
Spain	Peso	Gold and silver	1 00
Switzerland	Franc	Gold	20
Turkey	Piaster	Gold	5
United States, N. A.	Dollar	Gold and silver	1 00
Uruguay	Patacon	Gold	1 00
Venezuela	Bolivar	Gold and silver	20

Foreign Weights and Measures, with United States Equivalents.

Denomination.	Where used.	United States equivalent.
Almude	Portugal	4.422 gallons.
Ardeb	Alexandria	7.6907 bushels.
Arratel, or libra	Portugal	1.011 pounds avoirdupois.
Arroba	Portugal and Brazil	32.38 pounds.
"	Spain and Buenos Ayres	25.36 pounds.
"	Spain (wine)	4.26 gallons.
Artal	Morocco	1.12 pounds avoirdupois.
Baril	Argentine Republic and Mexico	20.0787 gallons.
Candy	Bombay	560 pounds avoirdupois
"	Madras	500 pounds avoirdupois.
Cantar	Turkey	124.7036 pounds avoirdupois.
Catty	China	1.333 pounds avoirdupois.
"	Japan	1.31 pounds.
"	Java, Siam, Malacca	1.35 pounds.
"	Sumatra	2.12 pounds.
Centner	Bremen	127.5 pounds.
"	Brunswick	117.5 pounds.
"	Darmstadt and Zollverein	110.24 pounds.
"	Denmark and Norway	110.11 pounds.
"	Nuremberg	112.43 pounds.
"	Prussia	113.44 pounds.
"	Vienna	123.5 pounds.
Fanega	Mexico	1.54728 bushels.
"	Peru	140 Castilian pounds.
Gramme	Metric	15.432 grains avoirdupois.
Hectoliter	"	26.417 quarts.
Kilogram, or kilo	"	2.2046 pounds avoirdupois.
Kilometer	"	0.621376 miles.
Last	Belgium and Holland (dry)	85.134 bushels.
"	England, for dry malt	82.52 bushels.
"	Prussia	112.29 bushels.
Libra	Castilian	7,100. grains troy
"	Chili	1.014 pounds avoirdupois.
Liter	Metric	1.0267 quarts.
Livre	Guiana	1.0791 pounds avoirdupois.
Maund	Bengal	82.285 pounds avoirdupois.
"	Bombay	28 pounds avoirdupois.
"	Madras	25 pounds avoirdupois.
Meter	Metric	39.37 inches.
"	Metric (cubic)	1.308 cubic yards.
"	Metric (square)	1,550.0 square inches.
Oka	Egypt	2.7235 pounds avoirdupois.
"	Hungary	3.0817 pounds avoirdupois
"	Turkey	2.83418 pounds avoirdupois.
Picul	Borneo and Celebes	135.64 pounds.
"	China and Sumatra	133½ pounds.
"	Japan	130 pounds.
"	Java (Batavia)	135.10 pounds.
"	Hemp of Manila, Philippine Islands	139.45 pounds.
"	Sugar of Manila, Philippine Islands	140 pounds.
Pie	Argentine Republic	0.9478 feet.
"	Castilian	0.91407 feet.
Pik	Turkey	27.9 inches.
Quarter	England	8.252 bushels.
Quintal	Brazil	130.06 pounds avoirdupois.
"	Buenos Ayres	101.42 pounds avoirdupois.
"	Castile, Chili, Mexico, Peru	101.61 pounds avoirdupois.
"	Metric	220.47 pounds.
Taci	Cochin-China	590.75 grains troy.
Tonde (ton)	Denmark	3.94783 bushels.
Vara	Castilian	0.914117 yard.
"	Curaçoa, Cuba and Peru	33 375 inches.

No. 1.—STATEMENT SHOWING THE QUANTITIES AND VALUES OF THE PRINCIPAL AND ALL OTHER ARTICLES OF IMPORTS INTO THE UNITED STATES FROM, AND OF EXPORTS FROM THE UNITED STATES TO, MEXICO, THE CENTRAL AMERICAN STATES, BRITISH HONDURAS, THE WEST INDIES, AND SOUTH AMERICA, DURING EACH OF THE YEARS SPECIFIED BELOW.

MERCHANDISE.

MEXICO, 1861–1888.

IMPORTS OF MERCHANDISE.

Year ending June 30—	Breadstuffs and other farinaceous food.		Coffee.		Copper: Pigs, bars, ingots, old, and other unmanufactured.		Chemicals, drugs, dyes and medicines.			Hides and skins, other than furs.	Hair unmanufactured.	India rubber and gutta-percha, crude.		Jute and other grasses, unmanufactured.		Lead: Pigs, bars, and old	
	Corn.	All other.					Cochineal and indigo.	Dyewoods in sticks.	All other.								
	Dollars	Dollars	Pounds	Dollars	Pounds	Dollars	Dollars	Dollars	Dollars	Dollars	Dollars	Pounds	Dollars	Tons	Dollars	Pounds	Dollars
1861	19,612	8,445	461,416	59,805	....	1,320	91,645	115,757	411	267,527	2,264	....	....	382	35,607	57,482	1,150
1862	....	6,399	7,175	1,036	12,958	1,734	49,564	91,976	....	171,905	11,535	....	252	286	33,537	....	....
1863	....	15,048	935,594	122,665	85,796	14,081	91,151	48,094	10,830	383,530	912	....	....	898	44,647	295,136	13,988
1864	....	9,818	11,736	2,927	129,810	21,401	123,434	136,299	12,622	563,978	2,140	....	201	143	63,455	4,609	297
1865	....	6,337	505	109	114,761	16,528	132,959	136,341	7,127	547,109	1,665	....	20	333	36,496	648	61
1866	....	....	524,777	84,478	40,299	5,629	96,362	69,350	40,722	325,186	3,196	....	214	889	116,455	25,152	1,509
1867	9,975	5,183	138,005	18,468	20,497	3,091	139,154	108,754	39,024	368,817	2,848	....	228	862	110,455	....	....
1868	34,269	29,509	882,521	112,159	29,536	5,123	144,144	187,337	38,526	411,905	2,613	2,554	610	1,513	237,803	79,504	2,799
1869	71,163	53,149	203,045	22,262	57,820	7,326	144,974	207,859	64,510	745,550	1,728	34,842	8,648	2,906	469,235	523,043	22,211
1870	79,321	48,551	110,607	13,223	21,497	2,304	192,836	244,932	28,380	833,743	4,997	98,656	23,594	3,870	631,090	450,516	14,677
1871	104,534	68,613	526,495	56,454	161,711	18,648	117,745	30,648	53,206	714,489	6,442	93,056	33,055	3,328	606,041	725,211	23,261
1872	74,297	43,114	1,858,301	218,032	2,168	218	104,772	39,660	266,781	1,186,082	15,940	106,417	34,792	4,244	781,829	461,274	14,653
1873	54,547	62,720	2,035,540	334,317	39,774	3,120	55,239	27,753	163,745	1,023,387	55,220	184,551	63,269	3,597	635,254	802,440	19,394
1874	63,048	37,720	2,930,285	624,611	14,028	2,161	16,974	70,090	158,379	1,561,830	18,625	72,263	23,710	4,867	691,251	807,579	41,978
1875	61,081	31,620	2,691,889	485,189	4,611	620	54,519	63,958	247,427	2,077,156	28,784	115,447	35,650	6,185	542,756	325,643	16,286
1876	45,249	49,622	3,941,229	711,833	23,050	2,490	10,736	59,413	270,993	1,812,567	79,239	39,835	11,803	6,846	654,716	889,698	43,253
1877	25,701	33,411	6,794,693	1,205,970	67,703	7,017	423,196	72,452	284,135	1,529,702	29,217	43,314	13,825	7,278	809,261	1,336,041	68,218
1878	12,321	34,339	6,307,063	1,082,272	68,556	7,782	50,726	112,482	199,017	1,565,516	41,720	47,494	11,364	9,161	930,396	1,136,453	50,245
1879	33,497	56,432	8,397,040	1,371,079	18,443	3,302	62,683	96,877	166,706	1,675,777	31,274	17,500	4,432	10,197	1,324,075	497,276	20,839
1880	85,240	65,198	9,818,505	1,523,658	226	19	68,315	149,651	263,642	1,951,918	36,964	607,026	44,435	14,086	1,034,215	....	....
1881	57,840	43,441	13,911,920	1,737,288	55,740	6,625	20,973	158,734	198,222	2,111,750	39,820	646,742	315,959	17,153	1,639,029	630,997	27,164
1882	58,648	41,352	7,902,669	817,584	3,962	494	5,813	211,714	....	1,525,197	36,886	325,206	164,447	19,358	2,713,088	1,182,064	44,865
1883	22,072	50,192	8,578,533	1,114,594	22,924	8	63,869	158,823	119,681	1,568,645	52,985	290,935	123,484	25,065	2,763,435	1,191,225	26,919
1884	4,383	19,971	9,975,426	1,205,156	....	2,169	44,497	156,851	492,536	1,600,157	52,546	241,478	145,068	36,411	2,263,205	(c)	(c)
1885	7,757	1,815	10,201,434	979,538	3,431	300	43,265	129,664	193,832	1,650,135	59,154	133,784	52,568	24,547	3,102,009	(c)	(c)
1886	8,517	2,314	15,764,024	1,389,538	63,249	3,098	41,306	156,291	198,656	1,851,138	51,806	91,035	89,637	36,098	3,607,156	(c)	(c)
1887	16,313	3,702	14,657,005	1,837,450	5,825	82	7,136	169,301	1,001,666	1,871,824	52,786	313,048	141,117	36,078	3,607,156	(c)	(c)
1888	20,159	2,696	14,125,523	2,111,130	64,475	4,023	11,137	176,397	1,297,020	1,560,908	48,611	395,755	131,224	35,207	5,394,132	(c)	(c)

a Cochineal only.   *b* All indigo.   *c* Not separately stated.

No. 1.—IMPORTS INTO, AND EXPORTS FROM, THE UNITED STATES FROM AND TO MEXICO, ETC.—Continued.

MEXICO, 1860-1888—Continued.

IMPORTS OF MERCHANDISE.

YEAR ENDING JUNE 30—	Animals.	Precious stones.	Salt.	Spices of all kinds.	Sugar and molasses.	Wool, unmanufactured.		Wood, unmanufactured.	Other merchandise.	Total imports of merchandise.
						Pounds.	Dollars.			
	Dollars.	Dollars.	Dollars.	Dollars.	Dollars.		Dollars.	Dollars.	Dollars.	Dollars.
1860	....	....	22,555	642	55,309	....	15,151	101,392	819,105	1,003,431
1861	....	....	12,206	1,835	23,333	....	1,641	102,711	141,120	886,112
1862	....	....	16,138	1,551	10,886	....	3,560	51,415	a289,510	730,988
1863	....	....	49,871	3,959	45,576	31,209	155,450	69,014	b4,684,068	3,943,882
1864	....	....	36,247	22,873	12,019	1,226,820	96,503	62,342	c4,987,889	6,128,445
1865	....	....	6,452	10,836	816	702,676	45,490	83,921	d5,188,606	6,220,874
1866	....	....	12,326	30,920	79,904	....	18,667	82,968	770,268	1,726,092
1867	....	....	13,645	19,041	1,693	....	377	106,921	127,392	1,071,936
1868	....	....	21,368	40,324	29,735	69,493	4,386	72,973	217,404	1,590,667
1869	....	....	13,716	33,841	65,197	716,068	51,838	126,345	225,821	2,336,164
1870	....	....	30,235	104,476	28,123	656,459	49,829	107,868	377,916	2,715,665
1871	....	....	29,600	124,403	39,877	865,999	68,907	176,724	908,268	3,209,688
1872	188,558	32,449	20,984	10,396	52,007	1,182,481	128,375	279,020	263,941	4,002,920
1873	147,512	330	6,905	1,613	11,818	1,182,414	129,475	171,554	550,070	4,276,165
1874	134,701	102,048	9,841	2,100	17,682	1,173,099	112,226	324,520	379,557	4,346,364
1875	81,439	156,690	8,201	1,882	104,547	1,095,282	119,534	346,923	756,226	5,174,594
1876	108,050	63,329	6,803	1,520	164,567	838,798	85,887	247,833	735,763	5,150,572
1877	129,807	6,355	7,196	5,481	227,543	1,405,983	119,708	133,690	533,176	5,204,264
1878	132,971	1,540	6,768	1,650	155,700	835,487	72,216	257,853	580,051	5,251,502
1879	132,873	3,927	6,138	3,760	76,992	819,784	66,300	224,925	529,001	5,493,221
1880	175,395	5,416	8,419	9,040	232,655	1,321,874	144,875	408,754	889,136	7,209,593
1881	314,272	21,657	7,178	5,219	124,535	1,009,376	99,479	329,295	974,452	8,317,802
1882	455,917	76,241	862	8,428	104,374	191,666	18,037	499,776	1,212,601	8,461,899
1883	661,245	56,176	973	10,775	64,520	1,775	257	441,083	1,244,549	8,177,123
1884	959,467	62,670	3,959	9,690	25,286	438,401	37,648	742,462	720,297	9,016,486
1885	636,684	58,790	923	3,750	18,881	1,662,763	122,594	459,702	1,094,876	9,267,021
1886	750,196	13,671	1,425	7,737	33,640	2,384,654	186,277	315,929	2,769,600	10,687,972
1887	469,083	20,795	1,692	6,461	16,936	1,862,758	150,410	438,153	4,729,233	14,719,840
1888	406,261	13,775	2,411	8,172	14,748	82,406	7,098	537,600	5,951,987	17,329,889

a Of this amount $60,497 was the value of unmanufactured cotton.
b Of this amount $1,790,615 was the value of unmanufactured cotton.
c Of this amount $4,859,725 was the value of unmanufactured cotton.
d Of this amount $1,128,875 was the value of unmanufactured cotton.
e Of this amount $117,197 was the value of unmanufactured cotton.

TABLES. 277

No. 1.—IMPORTS INTO, AND EXPORTS FROM, THE UNITED STATES FROM AND TO MEXICO, ETC.—Continued.

MEXICO, 1860-1888—Continued.

EXPORTS OF DOMESTIC MERCHANDISE.

YEAR ENDING JUNE 30—	ANIMALS.		BREADSTUFFS.				Chemicals, drugs, dyes and medicines.	Cotton, unmanufactured.	
	Sheep.		Corn.		Wheat and wheat flour.	All other.			
	Number.	Dollars.	Bushels.	Dollars.	Dollars.	Dollars.	Dollars.	Pounds.	Dollars.
1860	....	....	80,329	78,063	247,206	8,247	63,727	9,043,377	1,076,150
1861	....	....	13,577	9,993	169,033	10,920	48,710	1,410,659	153,995
1862	....	....	18,304	14,017	282,810	34,915	75,194	....	....
1863	....	....	268,653	263,849	777,122	379,727	118,604	....	....
1864	....	....	187,014	256,924	855,772	50,730	166,741	417,497	331,199
1865	280	740	181,462	347,464	1,089,016	90,238	326,075	....	....
1866	33	590	158,624	121,553	584,012	66,227	89,690	50,317	17,611
1867	543	2,800	14,218	16,874	547,965	117,066	68,137	3,310,842	934,458
1868	3,156	2,253	7,292	9,051	343,205	10,938	85,635	8,228,598	1,319,685
1869	(a)	(a)	72,216	72,439	278,111	10,923	73,572	2,042,224	458,405
1870	27,841	18,189	62,359	65,292	209,371	11,911	113,105	6,609,707	1,412,863
1871	36,347	32,837	173,585	169,350	225,718	14,069	96,245	11,309,495	1,586,517
1872	27,228	25,843	21,039	27,233	218,279	35,166	93,734	957,229	128,186
1873	57,217	59,935	104,146	99,166	110,525	22,310	107,436	559,639	74,352
1874	111,445	110,290	55,851	40,049	96,660	25,449	126,437	2,289,501	322,507
1875	112,553	133,222	9,862	9,092	102,173	21,532	112,877	1,395,276	184,186
1876	95,215	104,865	93,487	75,945	108,952	26,580	111,348	6,972,575	890,574
1877	161,549	144,908	64,776	55,658	88,913	23,756	79,799	3,966,812	462,902
1878	153,065	158,217	288,109	267,623	171,450	51,885	123,069	3,422,162	357,210
1879	89,689	103,789	126,613	95,802	129,971	50,001	127,756	9,848,129	912,583
1880	115,265	120,817	85,702	68,743	69,072	44,126	145,331	9,851,543	1,176,067
1881	108,886	118,498	352,510	240,182	93,757	60,198	212,477	13,386,186	1,494,101
1882	81,338	112,421	410,263	332,642	103,528	91,475	288,824	12,537,650	1,447,522
1883	235,585	364,866	476,453	394,751	178,408	118,744	265,220	20,577,771	2,217,259
1884	218,950	359,323	1,094,776	1,403,213	174,067	102,381	202,119	11,184,207	1,195,396
1885	192,873	261,811	2,058,037	1,371,318	120,595	69,465	202,799	5,877,000	613,251
1886	139,865	154,430	1,263,953	728,630	123,544	52,437	176,091	10,517,415	1,015,759
1887	90,960	131,078	894,496	488,423	142,408	72,645	197,540	5,075,330	573,288
1888	113,152	160,522	216,468	121,313	136,752	86,983	264,987	5,707,174	566,191

a Classed under the general heading "Animals, living, all kinds," total $156,773.

No. 1.—IMPORTS INTO, AND EXPORTS FROM, THE UNITED STATES FROM AND TO MEXICO, ETC.—Continued.

MEXICO, 1860-1888—Continued.

EXPORTS OF DOMESTIC MERCHANDISE.

YEAR ENDING JUNE 30—	COTTON, MANUFACTURES OF.					Glass and glassware.	GUNPOWDER, AND OTHER EXPLOSIVES.		Iron and steel, and manufactures of.	LEATHER, AND MANUFACTURES OF:		All other.
	Cloths, colored.		Cloths, uncolored.		All other.		Gunpowder.	All other explosives.		Boots and shoes.	All other	
	Yards.	Dollars.	Yards.	Dollars.	Dollars.	Dollars.	Dollars.	Dollars.	Dollars.	Dollars.	Dollars.	Dollars.
1860	1,049,621	149,569	....	....	641,870	5,981	66,523	....	329,326	8,929	4,291
1861	755,338	102,254	....	....	312,695	5,763	25,775	....	255,327	4,552	6,395
1862	559,411	84,387	3,718	1,049	157,874	14,486	4,906	....	265,225	9,676	4,067
1863	500,156	66,185	45,383	9,915	1,784,531	43,224	6,115	....	704,944	289,543	112,334
1864	277,032	35,357	407,619	68,023	717,622	40,670	6,244	....	1,165,541	373,146	67,404
1865	569,855	62,724	(a)	(a)	2,222,410	126,447	....	....	1,423,571	1,119,848	166,203
1866	141,780	29,186	(a)	(a)	58,663	23,515	1,750	....	420,034	32,131	35,114
1867	397,472	51,828	601,927	76,127	356,163	16,813	16,957	....	770,150	21,533	21,639
1868	(a)	(a)	1,451,727	162,934	387,610	27,010	26,573	66,774	784,897	61,227	23,874
1869	1,210,286	111,351	1,335,630	156,537	341,593	27,076	20,968	37,003	811,384	95,590	18,430
1870	6,255,489	513,488	1,258,921	155,657	106,373	21,217	26,220	39,817	654,298	116,761	11,591
1871	10,104,048	746,301	1,086,883	155,057	94,366	18,995	24,274	29,594	698,296	91,070	16,970
1872	7,663,001	509,255	1,019,997	104,668	38,368	26,419	40,800	55,543	803,668	98,565	18,480
1873	6,402,170	501,648	2,143,975	201,513	73,244	26,752	46,834	70,269	1,043,071	104,377	13,613
1874	6,874,372	512,195	5,876,817	486,159	50,337	20,007	23,788	47,922	1,073,530	70,417	12,757
1875	6,745,817	504,619	5,726,156	468,717	64,189	37,561	28,807	68,644	954,961	84,129	26,026
1876	6,114,541	441,252	3,886,748	286,205	60,595	20,743	25,210	156,136	1,062,687	79,153	11,182
1877	6,497,136	407,604	2,808,228	224,181	57,278	24,763	26,672	57,880	786,365	53,383	14,233
1878	7,202,895	398,013	3,657,611	312,824	87,258	56,898	34,867	118,793	1,201,574	60,950	27,719
1879	13,134,877	732,746	3,528,669	318,517	47,831	54,781	43,742	75,055	996,089	58,500	21,124
1880	10,506,533	568,839	3,523,873	292,009	106,406	87,313	49,627	80,369	1,257,731	53,466	25,133
1881	14,121,636	743,370	3,030,749	250,345	193,639	111,542	145,397	95,230	2,582,346	48,207	45,953
1882			3,886,748	318,517	296,132	155,099	226,125	98,303	4,239,712	85,327	65,517
1883			3,523,873	292,009	185,329	100,428	303,783	119,491	3,772,287	86,788	65,102
1884			3,030,749	250,345	236,325	46,198	139,604	191,918	2,402,024	77,273	53,442
1885			2,298,445	187,356	114,421	39,826	48,342	187,479	1,208,979	48,751	28,849
1886			2,273,447	175,756	90,427	72,872	9,631	128,118	904,554	53,558	30,049
1887			1,837,595	141,052	119,605		1,968	175,834	1,363,378	40,826	33,208
1888			1,975,139	148,559	144,533		10,495	254,380	1,946,948	36,723	48,421

a Included in "All other cotton manufactures."

TABLES. 279

No. 1.—IMPORTS INTO AND EXPORTS FROM, THE UNITED STATES FROM AND TO MEXICO, ETC.—Continued.

MEXICO, 1860-1888—Continued.

EXPORTS OF DOMESTIC MERCHANDISE.

YEAR ENDING June 30,—	Oils: Mineral, refined.	PROVISIONS, COMPRISING MEAT AND DAIRY PRODUCTS.					Quicksilver.	Sugar and molasses.	Tobacco, and manufactures of.	Wood, and manufactures of.	Other merchandise.	Total exports of domestic merchandise.	Total exports of foreign merchandise.	Total exports of merchandise.
		Bacon and hams.		Lard.		All other.								
		Pounds.	Dollars.	Pounds.	Dollars.	Dollars.	Dollars.	Dollars.	Dollars.	Dollars.	Dollars.	Dollars.	Dollars.	Dollars.
1860		60,551	7,709	956,106	103,120	107,060	103,128	21,359	9,527	84,372	433,924	3,309,379	2,015,334	5,324,713
1861		37,502	4,885	117,487	17,344	15,875	197,765	11,391	9,526	55,405	303,733	1,559,062	651,364	2,210,426
1862	15,901	69,170	6,453	656,851	56,692	20,795	436,231	5,723	22,790	78,900	352,516	1,840,720	340,454	2,181,174
1863	15,901	487,992	49,440	1,357,512	150,279	76,066	572,436	13,922	302,234	326,014	1,571,195	7,441,579	1,579,045	9,020,624
1864	26,657	321,760	40,781	2,825,411	340,683	16,024	302,222	53,275	270,972	541,885	2,057,301	7,765,133	1,505,464	9,270,597
1865	26,657	294,721	50,750	2,334,693	453,797	142,116	207,090	36,364	436,420	872,314	4,078,852	13,809,972	2,539,867	16,350,839
1866	97,687	120,333	28,264	889,408	212,236	72,238	182,120	34,593	26,663	211,876	1,383,963	3,704,599	871,619	4,573,218
1867	60,887	93,418	18,402	893,794	137,262	78,743	379,238	53,699	32,763	137,319	928,871	4,823,614	572,182	5,395,796
1868	92,000	98,499	16,710	981,178	134,619	32,962	335,729	32,847	27,354	179,130	927,348	5,045,420	1,392,919	6,411,339
1869	64,657	86,113	12,658	630,541	108,798	20,494	328,117	44,025	91,301	141,477	815,681	3,835,699	1,047,408	4,883,107
1870	157,034	95,852	17,555	734,683	124,107	41,583	225,301	26,254	87,690	151,231	680,986	4,544,745	1,314,955	5,859,700
1871	90,073	124,770	30,010	764,704	93,708	33,356	325,980	13,355	129,567	144,272	820,315	5,044,033	2,568,080	7,612,113
1872	172,230	216,001	31,686	1,079,754	121,082	71,316	177,316	33,268	71,239	178,636	730,402	3,420,658	2,122,931	5,543,589
1873	143,149	277,536	33,918	809,445	83,081	46,362	263,370	158,572	140,730	156,055	862,093	3,941,019	2,323,882	6,264,901
1874	164,160	269,862	28,052	364,646	36,628	32,067	405,048	127,613	91,218	251,051	700,289	4,016,148	1,930,691	5,946,839
1875	108,368	110,799	14,909	388,420	52,243	29,438	471,808	50,328	100,499	253,249	787,431	3,872,004	1,865,278	5,737,282
1876	171,348	128,953	19,338	311,862	41,762	40,994	365,097	38,142	109,546	226,816	640,801	4,700,978	1,499,594	6,200,572
1877	221,394	64,360	9,091	550,718	65,491	29,536	352,606	58,485	147,347	161,013	577,004	4,503,802	1,389,692	5,893,494
1878	173,438	141,505	16,565	1,255,063	137,119	30,135	290,249	75,704	122,844	252,055	771,730	5,811,429	1,649,275	7,460,704
1879	132,438	75,643	9,378	1,204,422	102,052	42,869	344,006	38,800	160,516	240,289	782,486	5,400,380	1,351,864	6,752,244
1880	155,328	90,496	11,312	1,508,525	126,319	61,530	377,823	41,673	152,791	274,532	887,156	6,065,974	1,800,519	7,866,493
1881	173,155	169,312	19,765	1,313,086	132,597	65,750	462,159	63,750	135,174	514,201	1,359,218	9,198,077	1,973,161	11,171,238
1882	226,115	214,523	30,013	1,183,647	145,293	102,022	316,714	71,552	142,671	1,426,411	2,540,478	13,324,505	2,158,077	15,482,582
1883	240,404	243,583	37,955	1,392,134	163,797	104,537	304,572	73,298	141,185	1,385,420	2,559,436	14,370,992	2,216,628	16,587,620
1884	210,378	179,198	26,532	1,726,520	184,043	86,728	196,259	75,246	140,897	965,714	2,003,022	11,089,603	1,614,689	12,704,292
1885	237,278	163,362	21,318	2,232,130	197,367	79,077	166,912	103,937	147,109	317,457	1,280,304	7,370,599	970,185	8,340,784
1886	185,821	146,071	18,072	2,858,313	209,522	93,334	192,111	72,621	181,434	310,506	1,177,100	6,856,077	881,546	7,737,623
1887	268,286	129,037	17,056	2,295,093	174,341	107,578	220,167	50,069	145,475	748,763	1,433,567	7,267,129	692,428	7,959,557
1888	175,537	270,557	37,023	1,825,244	148,751	204,451	256,357	65,729	102,382	1,280,126	2,228,383	9,212,188	655,584	9,867,772

No. 1.—IMPORTS INTO, AND EXPORTS FROM, THE UNITED STATES FROM AND TO MEXICO, ETC.—Continued.

CENTRAL AMERICAN STATES, 1869-1888.

IMPORTS OF MERCHANDISE.

YEAR ENDING JUNE 30—	Cocoa, or cacao, crude, and leaves and shells of.	Chemicals, drugs, dyes and medicines	Coffee.		Fruits of all kinds, including nuts. a	Hides and skins, other than furs.	India rubber and gutta-percha, crude.	Sugar, brown.		Other merchandise.	Total imports of merchandise.
	Dollars.	Dollars.	Pounds.	Dollars.	Dollars.	Dollars.	Dollars.	Pounds.	Dollars.	Dollars.	Dollars.
1869	b22,026	36,215	4,022,492	403,125	8,084	63,389	32,460	2,776,536	110,963	54,452	730,714
1870	b2,267	58,090	3,508,248	386,507	2,599	51,658	76,337	2,621,762	120,936	30,171	734,565
1871	b4,364	43,360	8,630,177	1,002,643	10,709	169,558	58,475	2,321,503	127,775	64,042	1,481,016
1872	b16,299	59,752	9,508,964	1,182,053	5,605	71,229	73,357	2,249,403	99,994	81,722	1,599,011
1873	14,051	19,789	11,225,484	1,600,459	44,359	64,492	39,854	3,223,700	123,773	68,191	1,974,968
1874	47,656	20,714	12,512,041	2,442,119	8,887	60,395	60,606	2,700,104	89,552	125,164	2,855,093
1875	11,916	14,291	11,932,157	1,885,631	38,499	75,307	132,287	4,046,997	131,415	145,805	2,435,151
1876	33,886	21,391	6,884,264	1,169,203	66,403	53,329	119,819	438,087	12,612	90,942	1,597,515
1877	19,335	6,478	13,446,587	2,289,562	75,801	43,716	74,616	2,222,995	82,836	96,328	2,678,672
1878	23,415	43,510	13,868,955	2,473,178	27,643	97,713	131,170	2,345,759	114,434	57,933	2,968,996
1879	37,594	42,641	11,463,136	1,699,231	45,335	80,959	106,073	3,640,174	155,108	83,748	2,251,589
1880	44,953	53,811	19,254,218	2,567,786	90,110	107,002	257,891	1,351,826	68,997	122,889	3,313,469
1881	46,163	101,151	15,858,327	1,939,958	89,722	249,231	467,370	1,786,996	71,886	144,306	3,159,786
1882	29,567	166,020	22,449,112	2,512,230	100,698	600,947	1,027,015	3,211,658	148,708	50,213	4,735,398
1883	7,362	226,218	24,715,028	2,475,942	120,672	597,448	1,376,490	2,724,333	120,489	196,694	5,121,315
1884	909	176,921	31,827,573	3,288,521	508,336	556,571	1,373,051	4,291,350	183,254	73,664	6,161,227
1885	6,508	137,878	36,811,072	3,833,372	721,556	599,818	799,089	6,987,514	254,094	140,700	6,409,015
1886	2,623	151,946	29,867,739	3,091,810	768,745	549,341	843,707	12,268,837	441,876	65,365	5,915,413
1887	540	102,214	32,734,302	4,269,967	1,034,332	570,311	1,104,890	10,340,119	434,983	60,424	7,637,651
1888	9,210	111,415	30,986,831	4,567,165	1,079,427	454,080	1,092,465	7,697,075	262,513	47,103	7,623,378

a Except such fruits and nuts as are free of duty, included under "Other merchandise," from 1869 to 1883, inclusive.
b Including manufactures of, other than chocolate.

No. 1.—IMPORTS INTO, AND EXPORTS FROM, THE UNITED STATES FROM AND TO MEXICO, ETC.—Continued.

CENTRAL AMERICAN STATES, 1869-1888—Continued.

EXPORTS OF DOMESTIC MERCHANDISE.

YEAR ENDING JUNE 30—	BREADSTUFFS.		All other.	Chemicals, drugs, dyes and medicines.	Cotton, manufactures of.	Iron and steel, and manufactures of.	Leather, and manufactures of.	Malt liquors.		Oils: Mineral, refined.	
	Wheat flour.										
	Barrels.	Dollars.	Dollars.	Dollars.	Dollars.	Dollars.	Dollars.	Gallons.	Dollars.	Gallons.	Dollars.
1869	34,485	205,275	8,207	6,111	11,268	38,238	17,246	....	....	4,916	1,890
1870	18,235	95,583	9,450	3,321	1,876	13,795	7,447	326	120	5,367	2,242
1871	33,611	214,414	13,674	9,157	12,007	51,337	16,160	1,841	836	20,228	7,455
1872	48,702	329,213	23,735	13,218	14,196	128,438	26,687	2,455	1,311	25,354	8,979
1873	42,329	270,000	25,097	15,221	17,772	146,225	34,039	4,067	2,456	22,063	7,123
1874	49,072	328,105	31,247	6,255	13,451	81,867	21,069	1,708	970	21,318	5,862
1875	64,137	344,823	15,717	12,606	19,749	42,519	16,913	1,778	1,303	41,349	10,990
1876	57,125	349,639	21,199	15,030	27,758	126,542	19,825	3,140	1,645	56,140	12,682
1877	51,811	334,175	12,455	19,958	41,561	75,847	26,779	2,121	1,201	45,483	15,313
1878	73,949	473,685	21,130	18,398	92,184	105,828	21,807	6,306	4,594	97,391	20,664
1879	81,315	435,652	75,551	25,349	45,717	91,070	18,067	18,147	13,317	115,477	17,593
1880	102,791	602,977	170,296	40,312	78,468	211,609	32,851	21,240	16,862	131,240	17,876
1881	96,532	509,127	62,510	30,267	71,777	188,847	28,506	36,246	27,553	194,572	28,890
1882	84,416	468,450	64,999	40,095	101,614	244,781	25,957	28,991	19,384	279,069	41,980
1883	94,587	531,054	119,596	39,581	124,264	306,317	37,756	33,727	23,243	169,533	27,123
1884	104,141	555,874	83,241	146,097	312,347	614,705	61,780	78,445	64,522	409,487	60,431
1885	94,904	449,156	63,548	138,875	268,847	564,851	43,428	74,264	58,645	328,868	52,136
1886	114,593	514,176	52,126	124,591	287,514	447,834	44,186	103,001	57,071	356,065	59,626
1887	122,782	538,195	83,519	162,806	377,612	479,961	45,795	118,343	68,648	494,196	64,995
1888	153,049	653,830	167,488	217,135	446,800	879,020	59,829	134,911	82,227	526,117	69,961

No. 1.—IMPORTS INTO, AND EXPORTS FROM, THE UNITED STATES FROM AND TO MEXICO, ETC.—Continued.

CENTRAL AMERICAN STATES, 1869–1888—Continued.

EXPORTS OF DOMESTIC MERCHANDISE.

YEAR ENDING JUNE 30—	Provisions, comprising meat and dairy products.	Sugar and molasses.	Wines.		Wood, and manufactures of.	Other merchandise.	Total exports of domestic merchandise.	Total exports of foreign merchandise.	Total exports of merchandise.
			Gallons.	Dollars.					
	Dollars.	Dollars.			Dollars.	Dollars.	Dollars.	Dollars.	Dollars.
1869	47,085	564	5,605	6,510	33,079	60,682	428,645	16,484	445,129
1870	19,342	3,095	4,974	5,920	9,571	26,780	199,132	33,346	232,478
1871	42,858	6,294	9,791	12,624	30,416	91,085	501,616	20,206	521,822
1872	70,870	5,663	7,453	7,393	70,034	175,967	880,965	56,060	937,025
1873	95,033	10,780	9,982	9,997	101,615	166,906	899,570	62,240	961,810
1874	63,354	12,540	7,285	7,740	84,571	127,768	787,956	41,904	828,860
1875	57,295	21,370	10,761	11,026	57,680	125,669	734,374	49,858	784,232
1876	90,435	19,414	29,084	15,603	62,388	135,005	891,988	37,853	929,841
1877	59,062	16,058	10,888	11,769	51,550	244,345	913,307	47,423	960,730
1878	76,032	14,282	11,767	12,571	76,559	268,248	1,205,180	49,577	1,254,757
1879	73,243	7,920	14,692	16,609	88,545	295,508	1,110,603	45,173	1,155,776
1880	124,613	20,907	26,999	27,979	13,070	264,305	1,729,215	55,640	1,784,855
1881	132,405	19,443	18,793	19,015	130,688	283,237	1,541,229	84,509	1,625,738
1882	130,471	26,833	16,450	17,252	119,839	283,140	1,586,558	57,455	1,644,013
1883	135,648	28,939	18,337	20,020	155,980	390,060	1,936,813	66,654	2,003,467
1884	187,072	41,435	18,133	19,930	200,270	717,004	3,064,798	113,055	3,177,853
1885	145,942	24,100	24,477	22,468	139,156	698,319	2,667,943	94,588	2,762,531
1886	136,476	24,313	40,615	33,951	102,327	578,435	2,442,171	70,571	2,512,742
1887	159,548	26,291	54,393	46,570	163,890	656,915	2,861,126	74,321	2,935,447
1888	265,873	54,136			205,160	986,545	4,131,574	134,012	4,265,586

No. 1.—IMPORTS INTO, AND EXPORTS FROM, THE UNITED STATES FROM AND TO MEXICO, ETC.—Continued.

BRITISH HONDURAS, 1879-1888.

IMPORTS OF MERCHANDISE.

YEAR ENDING JUNE 30—	India rubber and gutta-percha, crude		Coffee.		Chemicals, drugs, dyes and medicines.	Hides and skins other than furs.	Fruits of all kinds, including nuts. a	Sugar, brown.		Other merchandise.	Total imports of merchandise.
	Pounds.	Dollars.	Pounds.	Dollars.	Dollars.	Dollars.	Dollars.	Pounds.	Dollars.	Dollars.	Dollars.
1879	161,241	51,586	19,326	3,528	35,248	5,154	3,760	1,036,561	39,210	20,604	159,090
1880	249,184	122,728	479,749	67,740	53,395	21,037	18,044	2,821,793	105,797	64,668	453,319
1881	150,747	74,657	728,476	98,349	58,279	24,230	29,396	2,514,939	107,869	50,430	443,120
1882	161,288	80,316	829,604	118,323	35,788	18,815	60,202	2,867,905	124,435	51,590	489,469
1883	94,625	52,186	1,544,753	216,916	45,737	21,755	63,097	1,720,686	79,887	60,451	531,839
1884	33,232	16,579	148,439	21,964	18,034	5,888	80,469	2,339,024	89,854	30,003	262,791
1885	79,060	35,010	15,496	2,064	7,591	6,629	101,951	1,722,773	50,717	14,398	218,360
1886	120,307	51,851	167,199	20,686	17,146	7,809	121,389	1,358,977	40,968	10,571	270,363
1887	45,563	26,057	115	19	4,247	2,910	233,333	979,711	26,202	10,515	303,283
1888	38,157	19,254	28,909	3,306	532	1,968	132,186	928,873	23,761	2,688	183,635

a Except such fruits and nuts as are free of duty which are included under "Other merchandise," from 1879 to 1883, inclusive.

No. 1.—IMPORTS INTO, AND EXPORTS FROM, THE UNITED STATES FROM AND TO MEXICO, ETC.—Continued.

BRITISH HONDURAS, 1879–1888—Continued.

YEAR ENDING JUNE 30—	Bread-stuffs.	Cotton, manufactures of.	Fish.	Iron and steel, and manufactures of.	Leather, and manufactures of.	Provisions, comprising meat and dairy products.	Tobacco, and manufactures of.	Vegetables.	Wood, and manufactures of.	Other merchandise.	Total exports of domestic merchandise.	Total exports of foreign merchandise.	Total exports of merchandise.
	Dollars.	Dollars.	Dollars.	Dollars.	Dollars.	Dollars.	Dollars.	Dollars.	Dollars.	Dollars.	Dollars.	Dollars.	Dollars.
1879	72,396	42,521	7,013	11,675	25,297	47,478	9,822	1,714	23,990	51,856	293,762	4,960	298,722
1880	91,902	66,703	8,174	22,180	21,698	67,484	10,734	2,331	26,283	52,673	370,252	35,430	405,682
1881	93,892	77,790	15,116	25,826	27,484	88,863	9,366	3,665	41,307	87,993	471,302	14,657	485,959
1882	103,292	88,568	12,460	33,923	27,552	89,951	12,932	4,797	51,941	73,465	498,881	9,432	508,313
1883	123,424	52,396	11,875	31,237	24,240	109,597	12,470	7,451	38,096	76,029	487,535	16,882	504,417
1884	94,036	45,575	11,505	17,016	24,746	99,528	10,911	7,041	37,750	66,638	414,746	16,338	431,084
1885	71,552	35,519	11,501	11,216	22,463	98,471	9,014	8,264	31,689	60,041	359,730	10,023	369,753
1886	75,597	58,679	9,280	11,096	18,823	82,564	9,993	8,574	26,444	63,568	364,528	15,121	379,649
1887	78,741	27,883	8,549	13,773	16,260	96,205	10,602	8,008	26,712	62,777	349,510	5,422	354,932
1888	58,496	33,344	9,384	10,850	15,388	99,210	5,901	6,879	18,430	64,663	321,525	4,969	326,494

TABLES.   285

No. 1.—IMPORTS INTO, AND EXPORTS from, the UNITED STATES FROM AND TO MEXICO, ETC.—Continued.

THE WEST INDIES.

CUBA, 1870–1888.

IMPORTS OF MERCHANDISE.

YEAR ENDING JUNE 30—	SUGAR AND MOLASSES.					LEAF TOBACCO AND CIGARS.				Fruits and nuts.	Hides and skins.	Wood, unmanufactured.	Other merchandise.	Total imports of merchandise.
	Sugar, brown.		Molasses.	Melada.		Tobacco, leaf.		Cigars.						
	Pounds.	Dollars.	Gallons.	Dollars.	Pounds.	Dollars.	Pounds.	Dollars.	Pounds.	Dollars.	Dollars.	Dollars.	Dollars.	Dollars.	Dollars.
1870	801,613,343	38,086,448	45,084,152	9,696,783	35,828,771	1,247,249	5,820,452	2,355,020	491,096	1,578,725	334,887	36,097	61,133	362,416	53,777,108
1871	759,291,655	40,397,973	33,117,858	7,006,217	86,620,921	3,280,630	7,815,071	3,314,421	270,410	2,523,704	44,494	16,733	54,017	493,256	57,534,925
1872	877,015,222	49,872,935	32,106,440	7,184,306	48,313,285	1,946,086	9,193,148	4,255,247	859,692	2,808,431	502,542	777	46,217	647,874	67,264,415
1873	939,880,932	54,061,372	34,164,235	7,420,660	108,190,180	4,567,703	10,597,605	6,436,659	953,187	3,308,653	431,749	17,877	39,053	774,699	77,077,725
1874	1,223,632,524	62,981,973	37,671,279	8,380,988	104,504,725	4,361,233	9,265,775	5,415,373	866,958	3,079,443	116,376	35,362	61,775	995,624	85,428,797
1875	1,090,650,433	45,844,152	36,467,907	8,012,831	95,679,120	3,114,352	6,261,856	3,510,359	841,154	3,037,488	481,384	18,572	19,408	529,171	64,587,167
1876	1,108,413,671	41,039,046	29,717,526	5,737,321	79,382,325	2,496,479	7,209,218	3,041,102	634,542	2,333,137	394,628	28,600	4,192	424,361	56,088,866
1877	926,163,842	52,702,160	21,012,392	5,392,975	39,191,602	1,645,299	7,319,106	3,640,521	517,537	1,963,339	182,663	65,783	4,077	316,668	65,908,395
1878	914,711,165	44,702,311	18,452,691	4,265,196	31,441,778	1,119,975	7,769,955	4,020,981	634,864	2,439,425	266,646	5,195	5,009	277,174	56,134,332
1879	1,275,836,966	50,732,600	29,941,203	4,349,122	49,436,292	1,404,771	6,101,593	3,288,596	597,310	2,237,104	224,011	46,505	42,263	327,594	61,649,056
1880	1,087,330,787	49,594,840	28,626,577	6,435,786	35,009,654	1,139,517	9,299,637	4,742,701	615,277	2,340,890	236,539	74,026	242,256	667,443	65,423,918
1881	1,056,913,678	51,282,815	21,283,055	4,609,102	11,015,301	342,089	6,895,505	3,596,511	559,827	2,170,891	288,936	21,062	233,764	458,237	70,459,657
1882	1,107,578,529	53,297,787	28,308,320	7,132,024	10,175,794	339,458	10,377,360	5,415,141	735,583	2,936,548	413,234	15,550	162,162	538,712	65,184,534
1883	1,139,794,337	50,827,729	24,391,926	4,991,619	3,638,699	105,182	10,917,635	5,012,178	781,219	3,069,075	545,807	43,891	419,722	559,534	57,396,793
1884	1,191,233,954	43,650,449	25,388,734	3,498,902	(a)	(a)	11,703,393	5,238,234	862,042	3,144,101	803,058	89,815	509,291	417,747	57,396,793
1885	1,115,045,360	30,442,097	23,660,978	2,726,710	(a)	(a)	9,754,099	3,939,500	876,203	3,045,891	1,007,312	142,162	544,574	466,777	51,110,780
1886	1,210,503,201	37,297,411	33,155,574	4,411,148	(a)	(a)	10,883,666	4,074,299	965,495	3,182,453	1,004,019	159,657	569,391	421,492	49,515,434
1887	1,394,716,310	35,396,982	30,059,310	3,827,970	(a)	(a)	11,830,898	4,372,944	1,086,829	3,263,437	1,274,730	264,401	385,341	679,629	63,149,056
1888	1,209,170,332	34,545,116	28,137,227	4,135,228	(a)	(a)	11,504,749	4,627,705	1,106,265	3,291,537	1,462,574	185,452	383,491	797,984	49,319,087

a Included with sugar.

No. 1.—IMPORTS INTO, AND EXPORTS FROM, THE UNITED STATES FROM AND TO MEXICO, ETC.—Continued.

CUBA, 1872-1888—Continued.

EXPORTS OF DOMESTIC MERCHANDISE.

YEAR ENDING JUNE 30—	Animals.	Breadstuffs.	Chemicals, drugs, dyes and medicines.	Coal.	Cotton, manufactures of.	Fish.	Iron and steel, and manufactures of.	OILS, MINERAL.		Paper and manufactures of.
								Crude.	Refined.	
	Dollars.	Dollars.	Dollars.	Dollars.	Dollars.	Dollars.	Dollars.	Dollars.	Dollars.	Dollars.
1872	366,052	1,515,196	153,458	179,469	77,130	194,056	1,490,220	53,493	424,105	220,932
1873	479,982	1,207,753	204,740	261,214	57,973	160,734	1,966,277	156,243	349,407	242,349
1874	655,267	2,412,253	145,639	427,049	62,918	196,833	1,928,572	131,291	327,842	146,509
1875	618,095	1,294,610	175,418	282,098	44,573	161,375	1,992,514	141,859	223,672	179,248
1876	577,194	1,320,419	158,529	201,724	60,126	218,436	1,365,060	90,067	341,764	148,852
1877	623,990	1,251,570	179,053	251,556	272,257	222,429	1,177,845	73,659	527,757	218,409
1878	871,721	744,670	143,736	277,704	74,940	284,965	1,625,855	158,533	233,320	162,842
1879	826,045	1,431,349	290,542	376,702	62,850	287,098	1,774,246	201,770	100,928	147,606
1880	822,607	1,187,153	399,260	245,323	90,693	283,317	1,396,288	152,868	97,938	153,639
1881	665,253	823,431	164,877	372,563	160,027	303,282	1,184,512	132,709	113,112	213,477
1882	580,592	1,026,653	295,410	409,970	91,995	199,790	1,679,677	191,906	223,248	223,814
1883	411,260	1,947,667	199,600	451,925	95,531	254,993	2,323,541	238,731	78,148	192,030
1884	166,943	1,024,198	178,422	372,977	67,833	210,246	2,156,476	288,587	74,569	91,765
1885	88,311	1,077,619	161,580	385,932	206,869	107,010	837,342	223,302	90,680	170,274
1886	30,417	1,162,425	198,829	409,158	341,999	79,926	1,378,823	335,397	95,651	236,545
1887	15,052	1,235,538	197,632	373,886	234,668	91,084	1,516,529	260,965	154,618	191,943
1888	8,778	1,387,752	194,876	460,584	112,221	76,802	1,257,423	299,513	138,965	166,404

No. 1.—IMPORTS INTO, AND EXPORTS FROM, THE UNITED STATES FROM AND TO MEXICO, ETC.—Continued.

CUBA, 1872–1888—Continued.

YEAR ENDING JUNE 30—	EXPORTS OF DOMESTIC MERCHANDISE.					Total exports of domestic merchandise.	Total exports of foreign merchandise.	Total exports of merchandise.
	Provisions, comprising meat and dairy products.	Tobacco, and manufactures of.	Vegetables.	Wood, and manufactures of.	Other merchandise.			
	Dollars.	Dollars.	Dollars.	Dollars.	Dollars.	Dollars.	Dollars.	Dollars.
1872	2,826,671	91,091	384,374	3,416,736	1,567,848	12,960,831	889,796	13,850,627
1873	3,155,398	83,777	360,211	4,138,152	2,183,557	15,117,767	1,280,110	16,397,877
1874	3,238,180	90,952	349,691	4,386,028	1,188,692	15,677,716	1,426,902	17,104,623
1875	3,108,012	80,751	419,211	4,416,245	1,318,275	14,185,956	1,166,481	15,352,437
1876	2,927,701	60,436	317,621	3,177,622	1,114,752	12,080,393	768,107	12,848,470
1877	3,539,848	75,640	426,428	2,601,043	1,207,519	12,709,003	662,575	13,371,578
1878	2,958,965	44,911	435,130	2,396,459	954,562	11,365,013	624,250	11,989,263
1879	2,600,878	75,226	407,331	2,745,679	891,441	12,201,691	529,364	12,731,055
1880	2,498,857	52,207	386,852	2,588,998	758,624	10,924,633	301,066	11,225,699
1881	3,249,619	136,787	361,536	2,215,833	902,358	10,999,276	365,309	11,364,585
1882	2,325,116	79,393	323,914	2,907,331	1,303,324	11,775,073	359,751	12,134,824
1883	3,303,696	58,562	318,856	3,213,960	1,489,318	14,507,918	535,785	15,103,703
1884	2,360,698	49,566	432,148	2,044,472	1,144,040	10,562,880	347,873	10,910,753
1885	2,279,724	51,945	317,170	1,846,958	874,489	8,719,195	286,965	9,006,160
1886	2,148,299	68,020	407,272	1,866,198	1,322,100	10,020,879	388,291	10,409,170
1887	2,499,979	59,351	394,790	1,604,159	1,309,696	10,138,930	407,481	10,546,411
1888	2,648,910	35,410	390,323	1,320,536	1,235,027	9,724,124	329,436	10,053,560

No. 1.—IMPORTS INTO, AND EXPORTS FROM, THE UNITED STATES FROM AND TO MEXICO, ETC.—Continued.

BRITISH WEST INDIES,a 1869–1888.

IMPORTS OF MERCHANDISE.

YEAR ENDING JUNE 30—	Chemicals, drugs, dyes, and medicines.	Cocoa, or cacao, crude, and leaves and shells of.	Coffee.	Fruits, of all kinds, including nuts. b	Sugar, brown.	Molasses.	Salt.	Spices.	Other merchandise.	Total imports of merchandise.
	Dollars.	Dollars.	Dollars.	Dollars.	Dollars.	Dollars.	Dollars.	Dollars.	Dollars.	Dollars.
1869	479,652	42,410	166,367	213,243	3,697,519	1,170,576	166,837	168,785	566,531	6,551,920
1870	779,675	89,058	137,078	268,804	3,664,709	807,553	167,195	23,421	574,536	6,453,529
1871	273,645	87,224	330,315	311,233	4,969,097	666,870	125,513	64,937	524,735	7,293,569
1872	317,297	130,352	383,924	390,145	6,733,618	773,037	145,783	56,562	634,412	9,465,130
1873	505,789	109,211	131,993	301,191	927,308	387,866	168,495	89,924	1,021,392	3,643,169
1874	150,736	62,050	646,145	122,560	799,616	542,555	137,505	76,635	1,105,201	3,634,003
1875	311,926	85,311	528,517	329,931	1,434,445	568,321	124,658	77,216	772,308	4,533,113
1876	554,804	101,676	143,676	264,044	844,144	592,554	117,792	57,718	686,402	3,302,810
1877	278,775	36,832	600,789	325,843	3,086,357	1,088,079	151,884	91,753	637,156	6,224,368
1878	263,890	130,996	364,579	391,834	2,875,648	802,401	109,448	103,555	605,357	5,647,708
1879	382,652	97,631	235,369	416,492	1,184,933	406,110	79,522	77,116	680,170	3,559,995
1880	312,962	225,195	211,813	541,866	2,450,810	633,629	50,116	197,643	857,968	5,482,002
1881	171,437	187,655	194,039	471,035	3,377,390	678,304	96,103	114,577	1,003,456	6,294,046
1882	190,124	281,523	286,865	925,131	2,002,845	559,335	91,080	133,253	1,283,231	6,644,387
1883	153,250	198,884	428,203	856,188	4,936,290	520,830	112,665	100,253	1,429,549	8,736,112
1884	111,085	381,201	385,184	1,383,795	5,900,079	265,055	98,828	254,215	1,112,174	9,791,616
1885	143,940	512,398	318,114	1,210,033	6,896,699	150,245	90,756	107,710	933,486	10,363,381
1886	215,599	476,126	234,514	1,342,863	6,028,328	166,384	116,655	147,778	1,128,463	9,853,680
1887	245,863	459,125	492,586	1,349,423	7,512,368	211,113	84,586	102,668	1,112,047	11,569,779
1888	430,822	591,739	953,593	1,766,118	6,936,995	211,628	104,537	90,283	1,463,225	12,550,940

a Including British Honduras, from 1873 to 1878, inclusive.
b Except such fruits and nuts as are free of duty, included in "Other merchandise," from 1869 to 1883, inclusive.
c Including manufactures of cocoa, except chocolate.

No. 1.—IMPORTS INTO, AND EXPORTS FROM, THE UNITED STATES FROM AND TO MEXICO, ETC.—Continued.

BRITISH WEST INDIES, a 1869-1888—Continued.

EXPORTS OF DOMESTIC MERCHANDISE.

YEAR ENDING JUNE 30—	Animals.	BREADSTUFFS.				Cotton, manufactures of.	Fish.	Iron and steel, and manufactures of.	Oils: Mineral, refined.
		Corn meal.		Wheat flour.	All other.				
		Barrels.	Dollars.	Barrels.	Dollars.	Dollars.	Dollars.	Dollars.	Dollars.	Dollars.
1869	370,776	115,586	610,133	334,875	2,664,627	703,024	77,270	29,453	101,264	199,606
1870	383,405	86,785	410,041	419,456	2,599,879	668,456	64,698	54,298	110,210	208,714
1871	471,486	96,356	448,763	400,938	2,720,953	782,052	31,646	74,894	105,007	185,301
1872	446,122	108,529	434,369	421,963	2,993,516	799,117	89,132	68,114	76,867	183,932
1873	278,309	129,694	488,516	353,253	2,701,378	681,219	51,379	36,370	148,160	261,932
1874	270,238	117,752	478,341	343,052	2,456,953	674,723	41,978	28,382	102,530	237,876
1875	474,604	92,433	432,816	382,329	2,300,885	670,268	60,313	43,915	111,882	196,461
1876	373,604	126,132	492,585	444,155	2,065,101	760,091	139,555	58,700	113,613	156,165
1877	434,292	92,533	316,519	314,053	2,323,674	603,517	170,710	87,701	86,358	221,905
1878	399,962	117,855	385,961	340,372	2,152,480	673,614	202,981	95,443	105,839	176,326
1879	429,129	108,127	312,187	361,411	1,799,891	573,271	175,285	60,966	105,798	197,341
1880	358,721	96,568	302,910	333,950	2,062,225	659,401	131,734	65,593	125,748	107,257
1881	339,535	163,448	529,035	446,922	2,563,776	733,558	108,129	58,860	148,466	210,041
1882	297,338	94,844	357,655	361,630	2,390,158	680,977	87,539	85,426	145,526	134,247
1883	247,532	80,336	323,678	374,038	2,100,852	616,537	95,796	167,114	151,576	165,857
1884	348,675	81,072	278,713	408,117	2,105,233	558,446	117,809	150,069	167,399	156,009
1885	169,616	89,541	298,817	414,782	1,865,216	557,507	116,114	131,702	137,009	163,080
1886	182,690	108,266	333,413	443,583	2,030,491	574,126	161,672	94,491	147,770	165,664
1887	220,456	77,766	217,087	399,196	2,702,990	595,463	152,672	64,175	134,675	163,674
1888	297,396	76,846	233,906	452,893	1,939,989	542,889	160,642	62,404	115,755	206,291

a Including British Honduras from 1873 to 1878, inclusive.

No. 1.—IMPORTS INTO, AND EXPORTS FROM, THE UNITED STATES FROM AND TO MEXICO, ETC.—Continued.

BRITISH WEST INDIES,[a] 1869-1888—Continued.

EXPORTS OF DOMESTIC MERCHANDISE.

YEAR ENDING JUNE 30—	Oil-cake.	Provisions, comprising meat and dairy products.	Tobacco and manufactures of.	Vegetables.	Wood and manufactures of	Other merchandise.	Total exports of domestic merchandise.	Total exports of foreign merchandise.	Total exports of merchandise.
	Dollars.	Dollars.	Dollars.	Dollars.	Dollars.	Dollars.	Dollars.	Dollars.	Dollars.
1869	211,573	1,720,130	261,578	66,443	913,004	1,083,357	9,102,228	101,760	9,203,988
1870	142,671	1,689,977	256,855	80,540	609,647	777,923	8,087,284	98,954	8,186,238
1871	159,042	1,966,737	310,731	60,119	708,482	779,519	8,804,926	95,448	8,900,374
1872	154,487	1,488,957	276,530	72,050	755,540	776,160	8,614,923	137,629	8,752,552
1873	116,371	1,152,970	224,012	49,833	569,766	697,608	7,457,823	205,054	7,663,477
1874	78,494	1,351,818	231,927	47,587	700,261	766,792	7,467,897	168,861	7,636,758
1875	112,817	1,498,629	276,761	49,015	725,564	629,738	7,583,668	171,497	7,755,165
1876	133,900	1,535,209	277,866	48,776	738,418	703,359	8,196,842	223,693	8,420,535
1877	90,033	1,626,438	229,690	37,390	743,587	754,184	7,519,908	185,557	7,705,465
1878	170,908	1,335,066	247,864	43,554	696,211	766,580	7,392,679	213,722	7,606,401
1879	133,362	1,181,703	159,689	32,676	657,187	666,706	6,485,391	217,045	6,702,436
1880	122,514	1,288,655	159,026	43,643	599,447	823,004	6,849,878	217,870	7,067,748
1881	186,210	1,548,616	186,727	30,030	667,086	825,487	8,138,565	257,579	8,396,144
1882	184,963	1,562,382	170,860	26,671	778,411	922,140	7,824,293	217,073	8,041,366
1883	182,151	1,665,615	213,707	23,677	921,336	1,366,200	8,241,622	260,531	8,502,153
1884	205,672	1,524,352	206,719	73,101	857,456	1,803,591	8,553,244	296,070	8,849,314
1885	153,059	1,443,761	214,967	86,160	656,011	970,680	6,963,219	247,660	7,210,879
1886	160,815	1,288,942	188,564	102,154	621,409	1,661,498	7,113,699	208,427	7,322,126
1887	130,451	1,296,102	174,959	110,336	627,749	964,191	6,405,030	182,174	6,647,204
1888	139,701	1,603,818	199,381	122,467	753,000	1,072,379	7,450,018	161,515	7,611,533

[a] Including British Honduras from 1873 to 1878, inclusive.

TABLES. 201

No. 1.—IMPORTS INTO, AND EXPORTS FROM, THE UNITED STATES FROM AND TO MEXICO, ETC.—Continued.

PORTO RICO, 1869–1888.

YEAR ENDING JUNE 30—	IMPORTS OF MERCHANDISE.								EXPORTS OF DOMESTIC MERCHANDISE.		
	Coffee.		Fruits of all kinds, including nuts.a	Sugar, brown.		Molasses.		Other merchandise.	Total imports of merchandise.	BREADSTUFFS.		All other.
	Pounds.	Dollars.	Dollars.	Pounds.	Dollars.	Gallons.	Dollars.	Dollars.	Dollars.	Wheat flour.		
										Barrels.	Dollars.	Dollars.
1869	371,681	28,641	25,817	111,419,703	5,823,339	4,946,066	1,475,551	54,302	7,407,650	77,309	681,272	150,693
1870	5,716	745	15,617	130,706,182	6,681,072	7,119,928	2,046,172	39,643	8,183,249	67,803	449,351	95,580
1871	230,190	27,399	76,311	149,219,683	7,109,592	7,359,583	2,195,100	40,043	9,452,445	65,824	469,835	78,666
1872	2,021,891	319,558	46,530	167,109,647	8,697,590	7,807,535	2,207,834	56,251	11,327,766	65,706	502,218	92,929
1873	2,257,254	394,371	42,213	122,637,116	5,734,356	6,160,454	1,719,049	89,042	7,079,031	41,497	351,370	100,681
1874	6,433,044	1,372,960	7,304	98,761,576	3,857,558	5,276,173	1,584,134	62,763	6,884,719	46,233	358,632	82,208
1875	1,107,336	210,569	34,238	110,022,610	4,597,341	6,013,947	1,962,110	199,424	6,913,682	60,097	368,698	55,389
1876	724,248	138,952	26,437	70,155,045	2,610,418	4,782,937	1,302,856	35,131	4,173,794	46,510	303,953	80,998
1877	311,446	60,183	23,040	62,733,886	3,182,734	3,495,400	1,100,862	38,933	4,405,752	42,655	299,403	93,344
1878	105,856	13,083	18,626	73,924,186	3,344,135	4,656,967	1,396,744	28,229	4,800,817	20,396	132,073	75,149
1879	120,309	19,701	18,679	84,704,473	3,120,960	5,952,010	1,159,869	65,745	4,384,654	47,434	249,252	86,051
1880	2,937,083	502,090	28,447	83,873,661	3,592,477	4,798,715	1,342,269	67,603	5,443,886	56,520	351,728	176,321
1881	3,465,572	482,574	25,079	50,271,347	2,128,162	3,419,023	1,166,011	58,373	3,860,199	46,261	271,574	83,873
1882	2,187,716	248,006	6,666	78,768,975	3,392,855	5,426,704	2,010,280	59,067	5,716,874	40,038	277,846	72,234
1883	80,286	5,451	17,961	83,940,670	3,559,343	4,448,321	1,841,406	53,332	5,477,493	75,327	427,959	67,093
1884	217,827	20,467	19,451	138,382,724	5,162,287	6,375,088	1,654,782	53,409	6,890,456	76,017	410,324	47,135
1885	4,864,188	603,564	30,347	159,799,898	4,200,888	6,039,923	1,213,709	55,755	6,104,263	78,534	364,372	29,893
1886	2,929,175	356,106	40,270	93,002,688	3,244,023	3,945,952	881,187	72,958	4,594,544	96,833	470,463	39,080
1887	81,292	11,590	53,671	131,443,622	3,343,747	5,313,611	1,213,102	39,580	4,661,690	108,503	508,133	35,771
1888	1,329,659	224,374	60,793	115,653,809	2,997,713	4,995,306	1,685,554	44,049	4,412,483	134,549	608,352	31,838

a Except such fruits and nuts as are free of duty, included in "Other merchandise," from 1869 to 1883, inclusive.

292   DELMAR'S MERCANTILE MANUAL AND BUSINESS GUIDE.

No. 1.—IMPORTS INTO, AND EXPORTS FROM, THE UNITED STATES FROM AND TO MEXICO, ETC.—Continued.

PORTO RICO, 1869-1888—Continued.

EXPORTS OF DOMESTIC MERCHANDISE.

YEAR ENDING JUNE 30—	Candles	Chemicals, drugs, dyes and medicines.	Fish.	Iron and steel, and manufactures of.	Oils: Mineral, refined.	Paper, and manufactures of.	Provisions, comprising meat and dairy products.	Vegetables.	Wood, and manufactures of.	Other merchandise.	Total exports of domestic merchandise.	Total exports of foreign merchandise.	Total exports of merchandise.
	Dollars.	Dollars.	Dollars.	Dollars.	Dollars.	Dollars.	Dollars.	Dollars.	Dollars.	Dollars.	Dollars.	Dollars.	Dollars.
1869	77,678	15,812	39,628	53,008	40,115	......	472,783	27,650	645,211	138,689	2,333,539	106,632	2,440,171
1870	78,192	24,208	41,230	53,082	80,438	21,735	481,528	29,183	685,482	190,396	2,220,705	80,006	2,300,711
1871	68,892	22,883	121,860	80,170	54,758	23,229	516,689	26,685	900,407	147,801	2,511,305	86,334	2,597,639
1872	59,815	26,530	83,031	116,738	63,630	40,682	501,932	28,765	694,077	196,535	2,406,252	136,907	2,543,159
1873	65,650	24,378	17,973	103,493	61,614	21,147	593,829	18,349	499,307	145,542	1,913,333	88,857	2,002,190
1874	65,273	15,796	30,374	95,092	60,237	26,577	538,682	22,668	443,448	118,073	1,857,060	149,329	2,006,389
1875	43,137	29,657	18,277	110,481	46,639	32,359	621,021	21,469	598,462	168,049	2,113,638	97,563	2,211,201
1876	45,154	21,443	41,283	68,385	42,611	25,483	610,111	10,059	357,430	143,252	1,750,162	65,794	1,815,906
1877	47,810	35,317	40,471	91,017	65,097	35,004	681,712	22,301	357,707	210,122	1,980,265	109,320	2,089,585
1878	40,546	23,109	22,107	67,989	49,294	34,212	526,338	11,960	344,430	175,824	1,504,431	49,358	1,553,789
1879	55,001	39,691	18,046	161,312	34,764	39,223	437,879	16,426	398,572	234,666	1,771,483	39,191	1,810,674
1880	44,889	46,143	8,570	128,031	35,496	33,810	554,110	13,923	384,301	191,962	1,969,284	47,289	2,016,573
1881	36,756	27,101	2,773	110,289	37,252	65,316	592,515	7,274	318,710	159,299	1,712,732	50,980	1,763,712
1882	47,930	27,375	3,595	84,028	65,118	54,703	636,602	5,590	383,081	179,212	1,838,214	24,367	1,862,581
1883	40,735	46,123	13,223	126,643	37,684	45,030	603,416	2,370	433,661	214,062	2,116,499	48,209	2,164,708
1884	40,305	53,592	21,524	115,071	59,052	36,419	621,774	9,751	549,856	223,806	2,188,609	36,006	2,224,615
1885	47,822	35,460	14,760	48,069	59,176	23,702	501,425	17,260	282,490	116,948	1,533,177	36,028	1,641,225
1886	26,526	46,280	8,890	43,297	55,993	46,234	481,241	25,898	285,260	138,767	1,676,929	33,640	1,710,569
1887	24,296	43,625	4,311	50,666	63,674	25,618	482,023	17,547	287,171	103,806	1,707,241	31,251	1,738,492
1888	18,824	46,845	4,932	75,539	74,462	38,566	537,751	15,999	293,071	174,179	1,920,358	49,260	1,969,618

TABLES. 293

No. 1.—IMPORTS INTO, AND EXPORTS FROM, THE UNITED STATES FROM AND TO MEXICO, ETC.—Continued.

HAYTI,a 1869-1888.

YEAR ENDING JUNE 30—	Chemicals, drugs, dyes and medicines.	Cocoa, or cacao, crude, and leaves and shells of		Coffee.		Cotton, unmanufactured.		Hides and skins, other than fur skins.	Sugar, brown.	Other merchandise.	Total imports of merchandise.	EXPORTS OF DOMESTIC MERCHANDISE.		
												BREADSTUFFS.		Other.
												Wheat flour.		
			Dollars.	Pounds.	Dollars.	Pounds.	Dollars.	Dollars.	Dollars.	Dollars.	Dollars.	Barrels.	Dollars.	Dollars.
1869	164,882	81,354		3,114,151	255,385	849,298	141,268	20,459	42,307	83,873	714,528	38,412	325,287	9,199
1870	307,260	620,779		2,437,355	243,946	767,499	131,055	32,442	62,436	126,909	1,924,777	64,165	377,765	28,551
1871	371,301	69,955		3,283,355	287,462	275,198	35,943	38,037	85,723	179,061	1,007,482	67,677	492,986	12,749
1872	386,626	618,638		3,874,781	468,864	625,084	101,391	9,274	37,467	56,351	1,078,611	55,863	425,682	10,665
1873	329,539	43,590		6,187,560	993,189	2,039,550	310,321	1,599	16,765	44,800	1,049,598	82,164	607,039	19,088
1874	310,592	23,385		4,752,330	868,700	725,224	102,524	3,953	2,336	26,113	1,367,593	141,466	1,058,251	44,710
1875	444,443	5,474		9,545,410	1,584,484	235,270	28,129	4,695	13,518	61,244	2,142,047	178,470	1,092,958	27,580
1876	645,993	8,128		11,837,508	2,070,618	190,189	21,026	4,674	37,024	41,295	2,829,358	161,987	1,105,620	46,391
1877	610,415	30,261		12,269,344	2,097,406			7,219	11,969	22,140	2,779,410	109,652	752,330	42,774
1878	822,822	17,249		12,813,113	1,891,297	488,225	45,493	2,183	20,510	27,599	2,827,603	166,283	674,053	45,060
1879	674,978	72,232		16,660,030	1,946,706	646,888	59,848	7,156	873	28,683	2,790,476	121,493	628,414	40,834
1880	1,109,486	188,093		12,659,285	2,026,544	549,015	52,917	16,467	7,319	38,360	4,339,186	85,356	526,487	35,891
1881	1,008,762	142,879		31,908,074	3,352,971	411,130	44,250	29,131	8,937	43,339	4,717,256	174,932	1,029,357	45,922
1882	1,168,109	141,124		22,527,950	2,106,874	253,329	25,108	41,417	2,618	52,687	3,537,937	91,664	626,880	34,322
1883	1,216,452	155,433		17,944,600	1,384,915	218,952	23,397	71,527	42,846	78,945	2,971,515	96,203	547,770	20,563
1884	771,144	122,053		16,285,183	1,292,491	495,569	53,765	71,249	35,619	42,852	2,389,173	82,882	408,208	12,381
1885	832,838	113,179		19,034,988	1,390,731	180,393	22,862	66,379	30,623	14,824	2,471,436	88,600	448,703	13,808
1886	1,134,240	195,437		16,023,221	1,115,145	439,242	51,827	61,147	7,567	38,629	2,603,992	97,976	485,156	17,732
1887	863,320	79,904		5,745,198	709,976	32,963	3,649	67,849	1,928	25,911	1,752,537	82,137	374,893	13,113
1888	1,049,586	63,415		14,896,487	1,711,529	94,741	9,475	55,524	15,104	14,187	2,918,320	134,695	615,435	19,694

a Including San Domingo prior to 1872.   b Including manufactures of cocoa, other than chocolate, prior to 1873.

No. 1.—IMPORTS INTO, AND EXPORTS FROM, THE UNITED STATES FROM AND TO MEXICO, ETC.—Continued.

HAYTI,a 1869–1888—Continued.

EXPORTS OF DOMESTIC MERCHANDISE.

YEAR ENDING JUNE 30—	Cotton, manufactures of.	Fish.	Iron and steel, and manufactures of.	Oils: Mineral, refined.	Provisions, comprising meat and dairy products.	Soap, other than toilet.	Tobacco, and manufactures of.	Wood, and manufactures of.	Other merchandise.	Total exports of domestic merchandise.	Total exports of foreign merchandise.	Total exports of merchandise.
	Dollars.	Dollars.	Dollars.	Dollars.	Dollars.	Dollars.	Dollars.	Dollars.	Dollars.	Dollars.	Dollars.	Dollars.
1869	54,722	187,186	60,177	10,576	314,657	110,480	44,280	62,291	114,627	1,320,482	129,462	1,449,944
1870	352,914	305,942	62,955	23,692	620,177	218,492	105,085	112,682	362,964	2,571,519	183,700	2,755,219
1871	126,729	292,720	60,511	21,388	636,281	212,013	79,617	197,050	266,396	2,398,440	172,989	2,571,429
1872	118,429	304,744	52,850	14,121	795,590	262,128	87,928	144,387	180,684	2,487,210	204,373	2,691,583
1873	121,126	402,972	47,254	22,569	158,556	300,720	148,384	190,564	230,485	3,308,757	346,704	3,655,461
1874	232,379	537,738	54,895	23,359	1,203,891	292,456	119,715	241,331	283,036	4,089,764	151,425	4,241,189
1875	188,576	704,060	169,297	27,223	1,384,773	307,898	163,405	261,866	310,676	4,638,312	94,720	4,733,032
1876	203,512	745,222	121,491	26,638	1,416,902	287,658	166,483	284,377	281,591	4,685,875	105,998	4,791,873
1877	188,257	629,800	50,143	38,703	1,169,296	299,328	163,316	233,870	246,753	3,814,566	64,664	3,879,230
1878	305,814	790,592	102,258	81,191	1,188,918	268,526	192,430	205,452	249,529	4,105,823	61,038	4,166,861
1879	295,162	504,345	36,354	40,247	929,237	252,547	88,188	159,270	174,129	3,148,757	61,318	3,210,075
1880	450,756	564,639	74,593	30,694	1,031,102	267,084	92,755	226,435	290,714	3,591,150	60,368	3,651,518
1881	394,097	611,337	73,355	47,270	1,319,827	224,544	101,774	285,433	241,415	4,372,321	116,307	4,488,628
1882	273,701	440,390	57,496	30,265	999,889	222,289	85,881	183,860	235,956	3,495,931	49,673	3,545,604
1883	370,368	453,048	128,847	36,244	897,854	241,007	86,882	155,718	224,437	3,162,738	60,363	3,223,101
1884	461,677	357,307	98,679	21,268	729,182	224,231	71,494	132,728	222,995	2,735,150	34,959	2,770,109
1885	430,198	437,886	152,442	24,782	869,187	196,357	102,169	255,289	286,178	3,227,059	80,248	3,307,347
1886	454,094	409,211	60,044	25,250	752,430	231,039	83,526	198,095	246,570	2,963,147	104,573	3,067,720
1887	565,403	403,106	42,718	28,830	854,535	228,345	92,911	169,681	282,783	3,059,318	170,810	3,230,128
1888	368,949	579,178	67,193	31,912	1,265,121	214,342	99,041	229,911	334,877	4,322,653	294,472	4,617,125

a Including San Domingo prior to 1872.

No. 1.—IMPORTS INTO, AND EXPORTS FROM, THE UNITED STATES FROM AND TO MEXICO, ETC.—Continued.

SAN DOMINGO, 1874-1888.

IMPORTS OF MERCHANDISE.

YEAR ENDING JUNE 30—	Chemicals, drugs, dyes and medicines.	Coffee.		Hides and skins, other than fur skins.	Sugar, brown.		Molasses.	Wool, un-manu-factured.	Other merchan-dise.	Total imports of merchan-dise.
	Dollars.	Pounds.	Dollars.	Dollars.	Pounds.	Dollars.	Dollars.	Dollars.	Dollars.	Dollars.
1874	64,259	31,864	6,357	17,676	2,662,693	103,818	2,115	61,723	26,240	282,188
1875	49,279	13,713	2,186	10,003	4,183,230	153,183	2,357	37,873	37,506	292,357
1876	105,857	42,932	7,848	2,140	4,677,279	172,449	2,680	37,875	37,825	366,674
1877	84,578	189,712	32,958	19,977	5,621,227	234,205	9,061	47,054	91,333	519,166
1878	45,293	....	....	28,507	5,269,857	218,537	4,422	74,886	14,590	386,235
1879	27,202	94,040	14,265	29,591	7,922,211	291,886	20,374	38,372	13,043	434,733
1880	32,055	150,709	24,073	55,707	10,180,946	424,581	52,247	36,827	35,003	660,493
1881	32,730	237,366	26,734	66,288	15,037,883	601,274	67,776	59,998	69,981	924,781
1882	72,910	13,266	1,634	43,203	16,417,338	691,287	28,768	45,472	24,846	908,060
1883	26,096	674	60	48,700	27,281,049	1,149,577	86,720	77,006	29,360	1,417,519
1884	3,107	....	....	27,294	32,009,573	1,292,965	38,248	42,991	35,248	1,439,853
1885	5,437	44,387	3,891	56,932	42,523,746	1,332,684	160,34	16,688	29,753	1,461,419
1886	48,737	155,255	13,929	105,377	39,018,824	1,334,305	39,231	84,327	30,225	1,656,131
1887	15,792	....	....	84,612	42,054,795	1,180,901	....	77,215	21,606	1,380,126
1888	34,988	133,530	25,412	72,492	44,793,992	1,248,544	1,462	55,927	20,567	1,459,392

No. 1.—IMPORTS INTO, AND EXPORTS FROM, THE UNITED STATES FROM AND TO MEXICO, ETC.—Continued.

SAN DOMINGO, 1874-1888—Continued.

EXPORTS OF DOMESTIC MERCHANDISE.

YEAR ENDING JUNE 30—	BREADSTUFFS.		Cotton, manufactures of.	Fish.	Iron and steel, and manufactures of.	Oils: Mineral, refined.	Provisions, comprising meat and dairy products	Soap, other than toilet.	Sugar, refined.	Wood and manufactures of.	Other merchandise.	Total exports of domestic merchandise.	Total exports of foreign merchandise.	Total exports of merchandise.
	Wheat flour.	Other.												
	Barrels.	Dollars.	Dollars.	Dollars.	Dollars.	Dollars.	Dollars.	Dollars.	Dollars.	Dollars.	Dollars.	Dollars.	Dollars.	Dollars.
1874	18,782	156,814	4,289	24,972	34,560	14,248	16,271	81,823	63,988	10,790	32,399	58,706	498,860	49,976	548,836
1875	15,997	107,587	4,526	34,402	43,815	43,220	12,893	68,322	45,777	9,021	42,561	67,241	479,425	28,652	508,077
1876	24,286	178,232	5,973	53,349	62,853	54,258	19,387	96,855	64,340	17,196	38,155	80,762	674,360	40,554	714,914
1877	25,620	200,472	7,865	97,197	42,898	38,092	22,245	68,769	52,646	20,027	28,612	64,822	644,324	42,920	687,244
1878	16,531	120,098	9,333	130,060	36,696	72,280	15,041	66,827	40,346	14,856	30,789	87,895	624,221	27,884	652,105
1879	18,700	107,842	11,665	180,582	40,785	65,751	12,711	78,364	42,817	16,031	41,204	130,966	728,738	28,477	757,215
1880	21,364	139,472	16,577	165,205	46,045	221,151	19,632	103,121	28,546	16,313	64,805	118,634	939,501	23,453	962,954
1881	20,793	132,085	11,868	158,271	32,166	166,261	12,180	83,615	17,638	18,521	88,993	95,962	757,590	30,300	787,890
1882	18,432	135,013	12,962	196,963	42,647	138,889	19,993	120,986	11,531	30,190	62,160	130,815	904,149	9,855	914,004
1883	25,020	155,763	18,686	210,528	49,734	310,199	18,370	104,236	19,593	22,004	103,138	166,609	1,179,200	22,674	1,201,874
1884	30,641	177,414	15,873	149,210	45,582	378,824	24,657	118,884	9,035	24,171	123,056	191,263	1,257,969	36,201	1,294,170
1885	29,014	148,069	12,748	161,703	51,199	121,783	24,313	133,874	7,778	12,926	119,332	168,703	962,428	24,273	986,701
1886	37,021	193,543	10,532	225,694	59,418	87,077	26,207	143,113	3,332	22,845	85,426	160,098	1,017,285	26,645	1,043,930
1887	29,649	143,689	9,241	262,433	47,996	78,636	35,312	112,613	1,665	14,352	102,193	206,284	1,014,414	18,451	1,022,865
1888	28,295	135,285	8,348	118,496	45,096	86,719	22,788	114,954	53	18,603	76,593	166,525	792,560	25,147	817,707

TABLES. 297

No. 1.—IMPORTS INTO, AND EXPORTS FROM, THE UNITED STATES FROM AND TO MEXICO, ETC.—Continued.

FRENCH WEST INDIES,a 1875-1888.

YEAR ENDING JUNE 30—	Imports of Merchandise.							Exports Domestic Merchandise.			
	Cocoa, or cacao, crude, and leaves and shells of.	Sugar, brown.		Molasses.		Other merchandise.	Total imports of merchandise.	Animals.	Breadstuffs.		All other.
									Wheat flour.		
	Dollars.	Pounds.	Dollars.	Gallons.	Dollars.	Dollars.	Dollars.	Dollars.	Barrels.	Dollars.	Dollars.
1875	5,629	49,851,925	1,983,565	121,123	30,840	15,405	2,035,439	65,953	60,173	360,723	83,700
1876	4,034	49,687,265	1,751,478	184,110	46,277	55,889	1,857,668	62,082	80,662	523,474	110,165
1877	3,339	48,210,096	2,274,819	120,628	30,870	13,625	2,322,653	51,948	65,155	447,129	107,183
1878	11,068	65,828,322	2,807,827	156,812	41,040	16,968	2,576,903	106,138	74,339	462,770	131,879
1879	......	70,551,547	2,554,736	255,042	52,416	11,149	2,618,301	122,620	80,150	419,607	89,620
1880	76	70,023,988	2,692,183	49,048	10,833	13,912	2,717,004	170,559	94,531	576,989	161,424
1881	......	59,964,077	2,429,837	77,554	16,461	18,279	2,464,577	96,990	94,741	540,275	145,156
1882	95	59,952,340	2,385,578	128,437	32,788	6,294	2,424,755	94,390	82,608	560,118	128,716
1883	217	74,910,338	2,875,801	46,340	12,569	7,270	2,895,857	121,851	91,976	531,618	154,005
1884	......	88,509,811	3,117,175	1,584	284	18,943	3,136,402	137,729	85,297	462,482	128,057
1885	5,623	45,724,233	1,104,240	26,288	5,258	32,394	1,147,515	22,874	101,589	478,412	117,143
1886	388	20,056,931	449,164	10,662	1,511	33,288	534,351	22,198	98,022	483,488	99,411
1887	6,145	17,588,332	363,418	30,614	9,741	22,321	406,625	53,552	89,657	411,322	86,317
1888	......	5,706,337	109,359	......	......	7,031	116,890	118,425	94,696	425,655	115,867

a Including French Guiana from 1874 to 1878, inclusive.

No. 1.—IMPORTS INTO, AND EXPORTS FROM, THE UNITED STATES FROM AND TO MEXICO, ETC.—Continued.

FRENCH WEST INDIES,a 1875-1888—Continued.

EXPORTS OF DOMESTIC MERCHANDISE.

YEAR ENDING JUNE 30—	Coal.	Fish.	Oils, Mineral, refined.	Provisions, comprising meat and dairy products.	Tobacco, leaf.		Wood, and manufactures of.	Other merchandise.	Total exports of domestic merchandise.	Total exports of foreign merchandise.	Total exports of merchandise.
					Pounds.	Dollars.					
	Dollars.	Dollars.	Dollars.	Dollars.		Dollars.	Dollars.	Dollars.	Dollars.	Dollars.	Dollars.
1875	14,350	70,372	25,401	207,495	472,376	63,342	217,649	59,191	1,167,276	15,284	1,182,560
1876	....	110,416	34,191	279,196	700,781	100,127	203,177	64,200	1,486,925	12,926	1,499,851
1877	13,159	110,055	33,470	211,619	823,448	109,318	225,978	58,215	1,368,074	39,504	1,407,578
1878	2,709	102,712	39,942	235,741	1,011,712	102,464	246,822	138,703	1,569,880	20,785	1,590,665
1879	15,807	118,430	24,783	219,383	574,171	47,425	305,930	102,276	1,465,881	15,884	1,481,765
1880	11,406	60,525	23,348	286,001	954,846	71,287	311,972	126,461	1,799,972	28,424	1,828,396
1881	7,977	27,231	31,532	253,312	153,960	38,666	269,454	110,055	1,520,651	34,970	1,555,621
1882	28,379	24,176	31,224	224,406	375,570	39,861	300,858	124,265	1,556,393	16,390	1,572,783
1883	....	36,330	25,825	261,394	729,377	84,496	401,680	166,133	1,783,332	30,223	1,813,555
1884	250	80,445	26,834	288,743	698,854	72,873	457,680	130,091	1,790,584	29,534	1,820,118
1885	4,675	18,063	35,971	237,023	683,380	76,743	289,996	113,201	1,394,101	24,872	1,418,973
1886	6,730	22,440	38,217	249,838	734,981	72,566	315,846	115,049	1,426,683	11,902	1,438,585
1887	23,917	7,641	32,822	258,866	738,939	64,780	283,607	111,490	1,334,314	18,434	1,352,778
1888	43,358	12,783	32,047	350,313	529,543	44,667	352,552	79,661	1,574,728	29,099	1,603,827

a Including French Guiana from 1875 to 1878, inclusive.

TABLES. 209

No. 1.—IMPORTS INTO, AND EXPORTS FROM, THE UNITED STATES FROM AND TO MEXICO, ETC.—Continued.

DANISH WEST INDIES, 1871–1888.

YEAR ENDING JUNE 30—	IMPORTS OF MERCHANDISE.						EXPORTS OF DOMESTIC MERCHANDISE.				
	Hides and skins other than fur skins.	Sugar, brown.		Molasses.		Wines, spirits and cordials.	Other merchandise.	Total imports of merchandise.	BREADSTUFFS.		All other
									Corn meal.		Wheat flour.	
	Dollars.	Pounds.	Dollars.	Gallons.	Dollars.	Dollars.	Dollars.	Dollars.	Barrels.	Dollars.	Barrels.	Dollars.	Dollars.
1871	6,836	6,849,895	323,867	620,264	193,061	64,015	82,404	670,183	28,768	136,775	38,369	268,073	36,216
1872	249	8,281,146	421,990	940,659	269,499	27,423	37,301	756,462	27,097	106,640	32,379	254,954	34,226
1873	302	3,718,138	198,408	332,850	95,316	69,986	80,707	444,719	30,661	118,490	34,061	280,364	48,735
1874	1,519	1,665,584	70,858	234,486	72,904	31,603	50,753	227,637	36,360	156,484	35,657	273,635	67,239
1875	12,656	5,513,349	216,634	638,400	187,379	55,638	43,341	515,648	25,825	121,488	34,088	279,886	48,647
1876	50,488	4,119,354	150,248	393,357	114,588	32,310	19,357	363,991	27,311	114,369	39,677	247,206	42,007
1877	......	3,555,716	162,359	294,222	84,243	26,250	14,638	284,480	29,411	102,049	33,788	228,205	41,170
1878	1,266	3,877,559	186,635	293,733	80,344	14,263	53,033	335,541	28,845	94,207	26,699	173,399	36,575
1879	107,125	4,899,559	186,054	551,244	107,879	13,286	28,483	442,827	24,617	73,240	34,548	174,846	32,230
1880	31,784	6,333,387	249,959	355,635	56,657	23,301	99,796	461,497	28,845	71,287	30,794	194,336	35,100
1881	6,438	4,974,528	213,630	285,692	66,127	17,056	56,649	359,900	22,427	78,046	32,614	185,870	46,943
1882	516	6,179,080	279,149	390,719	104,331	29,037	125,991	539,024	23,160	92,469	25,600	173,440	32,895
1883	851	5,679,119	231,098	325,397	92,779	28,681	30,594	384,093	22,621	81,245	30,397	171,159	35,804
1884	721	6,946,086	249,673	289,380	70,365	27,441	39,623	387,863	29,016	70,068	28,273	152,544	20,942
1885	3,285	10,948,008	250,862	238,514	40,692	16,643	24,820	336,393	20,268	67,588	30,312	139,632	18,064
1886	553	6,552,405	188,858	119,949	16,202	17,107	22,901	245,921	19,702	64,756	29,154	143,804	16,065
1887	523	15,043,972	385,930	262,231	34,166	25,571	54,485	500,675	19,340	56,370	30,818	136,600	19,438
1888	2,111	11,103,826	295,312	156,317	19,581	20,187	62,029	399,220	19,115	62,317	30,276	132,047	14,970

No. 1.—IMPORTS INTO, AND EXPORTS FROM, THE UNITED STATES FROM AND TO MEXICO, ETC.—Continued.

DANISH WEST INDIES, 1871-1888.

EXPORTS OF DOMESTIC MERCHANDISE.

YEAR ENDING JUNE 30—	Coal.	Cotton, manufactures of.	Fish.	Iron and steel, and manufactures of.	Provisions, comprising meat and dairy products.	Tobacco, and manufactures of.	Wool, and manufactures of.	Other merchandise.	Total exports of domestic merchandise.	Total exports of foreign merchandise.	Total exports of merchandise.
	Dollars.	Dollars.	Dollars.	Dollars.	Dollars.	Dollars.	Dollars.	Dollars.	Dollars.	Dollars.	Dollars.
1871	536	14,341	18,577	16,065	112,289	24,822	119,658	153,830	901,182	13,993	915,175
1872	16,511	13,458	21,509	59,198	118,024	15,740	112,030	159,162	911,452	36,866	948,318
1873	123,291	12,755	11,485	65,587	115,224	18,572	90,110	131,513	1,022,126	33,145	1,055,271
1874	42,885	9,100	8,742	14,808	142,979	17,412	54,217	118,077	905,629	20,721	926,350
1875	23,185	12,266	5,175	19,521	133,014	16,562	93,369	106,883	759,976	9,026	769,002
1876	19,723	10,857	4,794	22,148	120,626	47,359	48,519	92,641	767,309	13,498	780,807
1877	15,399	27,741	5,817	19,751	116,771	16,567	53,755	114,469	741,664	8,592	750,256
1878	40,893	52,019	18,414	13,014	106,170	25,255	63,583	115,267	738,696	7,613	746,309
1879	39,836	139,653	5,092	29,095	104,826	19,079	114,246	154,604	886,857	15,737	902,594
1880	15,384	32,322	5,658	17,070	113,142	19,727	59,398	125,636	689,104	8,691	697,795
1881	35,687	18,656	8,506	24,985	114,587	15,116	67,334	125,398	721,128	12,563	733,691
1882	34,700	22,435	11,656	26,297	108,547	11,479	74,769	127,904	716,591	12,137	728,728
1883	8,801	21,969	7,315	34,951	103,475	14,718	80,124	135,004	694,565	7,561	702,126
1884	3,584	13,709	6,828	23,374	86,036	22,160	59,277	120,775	578,997	11,043	590,040
1885	25,627	15,039	7,450	9,577	95,042	16,559	55,024	121,451	571,103	15,056	586,159
1886	23,122	22,800	7,101	11,052	72,278	20,316	52,846	156,282	587,572	12,611	600,183
1887	51,281	21,253	10,950	18,703	87,958	22,823	51,577	127,891	604,844	8,782	613,626
1888	72,438	15,458	10,284	13,299	92,758	12,857	44,943	131,139	603,140	8,999	612,139

a Includes foreign exports to Denmark.

TABLES. 301

No. 1.—IMPORTS INTO, AND EXPORTS FROM, THE UNITED STATES FROM AND TO MEXICO, ETC.—Continued.

DUTCH WEST INDIES,a 1869-1888.

YEAR ENDING JUNE 30—	IMPORTS OF MERCHANDISE.										EXPORTS OF DOMESTIC MERCHANDISE.		
	Chemicals, drugs, dyes and medicines.	Cocoa, or cacao, crude, and leaves and shells of.b	Coffee.	Guano.	Hides and skins, other than fur skins.	Salt.	Sugar, brown.	Molasses	Other merchandise.	Total imports of merchandise.	BREADSTUFFS.		All other
											Wheat flour.		
											Barrels.	Dollars.	Dollars.
1869	Dollars. 104,330	Dollars. 644,717	Dollars. 37,840	Dollars.	Dollars. 237,724	Dollars. 39,163	Dollars. 352,555	Dollars. 73,636	Dollars. 62,699	Dollars. 952,664	23,795	202,042	91,446
1870	44,756	616,555	1,161	......	212,770	35,011	204,442	50,934	106,687	672,336	38,983	246,936	145,356
1871	26,390	638,044	16,771	......	147,681	20,556	453,874	7,713	399,304	1,020,339	34,907	240,448	35,739
1872	105,986	642,766	20,470	......	390,935	29,303	290,255	12,905	171,891	1,064,501	32,612	250,996	59,679
1873	71,982	112,904	115,476	......	440,227	34,429	244,519	33,648	129,809	1,182,991	32,584	280,539	97,340
1874	44,065	62,554	468,355	......	569,726	54,812	182,099	48,315	150,819	1,580,736	35,445	275,391	128,807
1875	44,978	118,740	597,907	......	336,665	48,819	152,159	58,309	129,540	1,486,577	33,257	210,051	83,568
1876	51,387	129,859	154,439	......	171,863	47,071	185,553	24,507	46,047	671,726	33,169	217,278	108,092
1877	25,869	151,448	4,407	......	93,778	30,373	303,376	48,014	32,469	690,691	31,960	232,203	130,066
1878	34,408	86,638	6,896	......	172,681	45,178	200,978	35,397	45,758	624,934	24,527	165,764	135,509
1879	33,944	......	87,197	......	453,075	36,461	6,387	3,281	27,057	647,402	25,356	134,009	103,922
1880	43,865	968	169,318	45,059	893,368	15,154	138,247	390	49,268	1,355,517	33,591	216,552	97,480
1881	54,582	40,025	1,480,005	147,283	755,856	34,132	12,970	2,186	58,337	2,594,376	39,016	176,269	221,557
1882	48,495	21,371	432,699	109,981	791,675	20,041	72,424	......	85,447	1,582,133	25,823	176,594	195,687
1883	47,598	226	98,287	23,157	592,404	55,910	772	3,739	59,965	882,058	21,955	124,365	137,418
1884	40,727	13,450	123,257	13,452	376,909	41,490	297	384	37,626	647,802	24,237	131,911	164,445
1885	35,642	868	33,892	20,247	240,415	39,272	1,799	......	14,593	386,668	25,063	126,200	172,138
1886	37,921	65,917	34,560	27,940	224,611	29,595	7,358	1,086	24,759	453,747	24,668	119,569	128,237
1887	36,417	11,588	33,036	17,057	91,557	19,755	......	......	45,648	256,695	20,489	95,460	75,603
1888	27,066	6,118	176,164	14,171	96,014	19,237	1,637	......	50,064	388,534	23,086	104,003	75,025

a Including Dutch Guiana from 1869 to 1878, inclusive. b Including manufactures of cocoa, except chocolate.

No. 1.—IMPORTS INTO, AND EXPORTS FROM, THE UNITED STATES FROM AND TO MEXICO, ETC.—Continued.

DUTCH WEST INDIES, a 1869-1888.

EXPORTS OF DOMESTIC MERCHANDISE.

YEAR ENDING JUNE 30—	Cotton, manufactures of.	Fish.	Oils: Mineral, refined.	Provisions, comprising meat and dairy products.	Tobacco, and manufactures of.	Vegetables.	Wood, and manufactures of.	Other merchandise.	Total exports of domestic merchandise.	Total exports of foreign merchandise.	Total exports of merchandise.
	Dollars.	Dollars.	Dollars.	Dollars.	Dollars.	Dollars.	Dollars.	Dollars.	Dollars.	Dollars.	Dollars.
1869	18,483	96,331	16,437	239,044	34,044	5,734	37,262	158,786	899,609	29,595	929,204
1870	20,314	95,700	16,518	194,117	45,299	7,926	56,792	106,307	937,265	33,672	970,937
1871	30,278	70,141	20,764	195,276	51,983	7,172	44,901	127,418	824,120	25,788	849,908
1872	20,579	58,103	23,077	154,358	59,781	5,767	35,817	99,187	767,344	24,946	792,290
1873	22,438	54,853	29,087	203,071	57,163	6,497	80,248	123,616	954,852	43,359	998,211
1874	12,328	58,276	25,089	209,574	78,955	6,789	65,117	118,675	979,001	21,386	1,000,387
1875	19,576	78,662	17,810	203,698	50,732	5,804	50,259	98,264	818,424	20,843	839,267
1876	14,499	84,326	24,195	223,887	61,432	5,099	38,501	80,237	857,546	15,450	872,996
1877	37,256	93,166	38,054	239,506	46,648	7,199	53,566	88,718	966,322	18,308	984,630
1878	23,657	42,990	19,972	134,906	34,812	6,180	49,166	72,833	685,789	3,588	689,377
1879	47,855	6,942	12,982	77,342	66,120	2,372	42,608	128,019	622,171	7,955	630,126
1880	58,956	11,102	13,171	110,264	51,911	5,572	53,802	212,158	837,288	11,253	848,541
1881	59,610	12,024	17,749	126,278	61,891	8,748	43,012	194,337	921,475	18,943	940,418
1882	49,598	10,197	11,196	98,552	22,613	10,175	42,031	126,661	743,304	10,077	753,381
1883	41,258	9,742	11,432	83,195	46,646	8,258	35,242	82,164	579,690	9,922	589,612
1884	49,821	8,231	11,202	79,768	55,961	13,342	27,127	96,222	580,115	3,843	553,958
1885	54,578	8,266	10,224	70,057	32,412	20,638	31,997	127,403	653,853	12,989	666,842
1886	54,524	8,659	10,973	63,606	43,781	17,109	27,689	95,812	570,159	4,392	574,551
1887	96,725	9,946	10,917	60,164	21,990	13,848	39,476	112,171	536,300	3,505	539,805
1888	70,380	10,733	12,209	70,827	64,565	16,077	43,371	113,866	581,055	2,538	583,593

a Including Dutch Guiana from 1869 to 1878, inclusive.

TABLES. 303

No. 1.—IMPORTS INTO, AND EXPORTS FROM, THE UNITED STATES FROM AND TO MEXICO, ETC.—Continued.

UNITED STATES OF COLOMBIA, 1869-1888.

IMPORTS OF MERCHANDISE.

YEAR ENDING JUNE 30—	Chemicals, drugs, dyes and medicines.	Cocoa, or cacao, crude, and leaves and shells of.	Coffee.	Hides and skins, other than fur skins.	India rubber and gutta percha, crude.	Fruits of all kinds, including nuts.a	Sugar, brown.	Other merchandise.	Total imports of merchandise.
	Dollars.	Dollars.	Dollars.	Dollars.	Dollars.	Dollars.	Dollars.	Dollars.	Dollars.
1869	1,058,848	b207,294	178,600	460,057	534,648	17,872	966	2,226,169	4,684,454
1870	1,084,851	b179,608	130,124	583,805	631,998	38,024	2,377	1,857,936	4,568,723
1871	1,300,064	b156,796	334,144	733,238	1,443,339	89,944	12,077	1,809,850	5,570,052
1872	1,771,630	b170,480	498,696	818,179	2,042,359	131,161	6,388	692,479	6,131,372
1873	1,336,741	186,330	642,376	851,872	2,698,139	70,635	2,246	360,001	6,146,840
1874	1,452,360	93,778	1,168,673	1,127,372	1,978,450	22,971	480	1,519,673	7,363,757
1875	1,147,336	50,717	950,976	1,333,689	1,450,562	105,246	1,092	7,154,445	12,284,063
1876	1,323,817	84,273	673,380	1,118,333	1,253,243	95,470	4,098	481,639	5,034,273
1877	732,045	129,481	918,063	1,033,079	1,570,511	112,386	71,338	426,423	5,023,326
1878	1,472,213	116,972	1,022,216	1,401,347	1,006,521	136,151	66,737	625,886	5,848,043
1879	1,519,123	205,027	1,354,938	1,293,353	1,047,266	142,175	14,225	754,239	6,330,946
1880	1,327,295	375,031	2,018,471	1,775,206	1,909,851	156,184	46,909	833,025	8,441,972
1881	503,620	132,406	1,200,358	1,512,293	1,893,744	188,200	42,370	518,899	5,991,890
1882	1,103,200	220,221	857,612	1,321,816	767,426	315,261	6,391	369,543	4,961,470
1883	678,945	91,672	1,245,434	1,414,683	1,046,603	261,975	14,947	415,196	5,171,455
1884	300,263	14,902	887,519	1,285,322	853,545	276,966	20,243	253,143	3,891,843
1885	162,315	27,770	482,539	793,710	360,116	294,887	1,151	219,589	2,342,077
1886	79,233	98,775	659,501	1,230,048	341,981	307,205	1,493	290,685	3,008,921
1887	95,104	75,838	1,437,177	1,355,770	420,929	360,653	99	205,383	3,350,953
1888	87,793	45,676	1,749,862	1,293,158	388,691	402,685	123,047	302,346	4,393,258

a Except such fruits and nuts as are free of duty, included in "Other merchandise," from 1869 to 1883, inclusive.
b Including manufactures of cocoa, other than chocolate, prior to 1873.

304   DELMAR'S MERCANTILE MANUAL AND BUSINESS GUIDE.

No. 1.—IMPORTS INTO, AND EXPORTS FROM, THE UNITED STATES FROM AND TO MEXICO, ETC.—Continued.

UNITED STATES OF COLOMBIA, 1869-1888—Continued.

EXPORTS OF DOMESTIC MERCHANDISE.

YEAR END- ING JUNE 30—	Books, maps, engrav- ings, and other printed matter.	BREADSTUFFS.		Carriages, railroad and horse cars.	Chemicals, drugs, dyes, and medicines.	Coal.	Cotton, manu- factures of.	Fish.	Glass and glass- ware.	IRON AND STEEL, AND MANUFACTURES OF.		Leather, and man- ufactures of.	Oils: Mineral, refined.	Paper and sta- tionery.
		Wheat flour.	Other.							Sewing machines, and parts of.	All other.			
	Dollars.	Dollars.	Dollars.	Dollars.	Dollars.	Dollars.	Dollars.	Dollars.	Dollars.	Dollars.	Dollars.	Dollars.	Dollars.	Dollars.
1869	58,826	138,772	25,633	10,937	171,959	182,018	605,498	11,335	17,096	832,282	20,180	50,366	22,346	......
1870	18,161	175,071	54,192	5,081	254,630	22,364	300,663	27,596	7,547	1,231,304	16,567	15,947	34,862	24,093
1871	18,347	196,146	18,218	7,344	402,091	157,755	266,068	20,780	6,691	831,335	55,623	10,206	62,474	8,067
1872	7,770	243,182	17,245	12,794	279,646	168,229	89,267	27,495	46,371	973,055	137,135	10,003	48,874	22,973
1873	22,901	302,253	41,339	14,654	413,755	143,628	38,225	41,339	82,588	1,265,090	209,201	14,557	52,505	27,609
1874	77,809	317,373	54,746	20,473	257,787	124,443	50,473	33,152	61,532	1,160,453	174,289	15,662	47,715	43,324
1875	53,409	202,691	46,993	26,325	274,287	120,094	104,859	49,202	42,450	758,469	115,734	19,450	38,595	73,229
1876	43,727	282,529	39,154	36,712	279,000	104,292	103,347	27,528	25,839	688,661	90,227	11,254	53,873	70,450
1877	32,374	174,587	20,385	15,318	266,231	35,210	466,109	31,578	48,558	942,431	80,734	24,914	44,138	49,573
1878	29,568	220,175	26,521	63,631	362,365	66,073	545,017	23,585	79,509	952,231	93,800	28,698	80,847	71,361
1879	46,797	179,720	42,340	20,562	290,841	48,980	664,267	35,550	46,502	1,124,619	203,879	40,642	29,559	136,449
1880	40,885	224,561	68,365	25,850	311,733	61,107	586,692	32,632	30,620	1,322,596	115,152	60,634	55,213	185,683
1881	38,752	223,368	193,996	57,896	289,649	27,902	858,138	24,152	38,680	1,930,983	158,105	73,723	64,502	147,322
1882	40,104	372,099	257,287	104,557	301,411	41,914	627,383	46,681	45,855	1,155,827	128,415	87,100	35,816	123,115
1883	49,144	306,740	107,432	280,342	333,213	55,336	549,433	89,307	41,077	1,497,138	130,857	111,998	43,222	140,434
1884	31,779	364,142	113,592	294,615	199,299	30,025	387,562	135,275	34,321	1,225,102	83,841	122,510	65,059	60,668
1885	26,579	294,806	106,791	165,677	134,915	18,818	269,515	188,344	29,094	685,335	41,453	140,662	52,436	84,818
1886	48,942	310,567	97,749	200,319	206,886	79,802	339,620	187,999	34,227	55,619	736,457	143,752	56,129	87,570
1887	62,431	353,171	107,468	116,101	184,008	97,790	443,112	201,202	40,700	41,503	1,056,946	154,023	56,609	83,654
1888	41,575	342,982	97,816	37,454	169,913	154,194	376,529	170,845	39,356	47,101	663,391	103,094	91,217	88,569

No. 1.—IMPORTS INTO, AND EXPORTS FROM, THE UNITED STATES FROM AND TO MEXICO, ETC.—Continued.

UNITED STATES OF COLOMBIA, 1869–1888—Continued.

EXPORTS OF DOMESTIC MERCHANDISE.

YEAR ENDING JUNE 30—	Provisions, comprising meat and dairy products.	Soap, perfumed and other.	Sugar, refined.	Tobacco, and manufactures of.	Vegetables.	Wood, and manufactures of.	Other merchandise.	Total exports of domestic merchandise.	Total exports of foreign merchandise.	Total exports of merchandise.
	Dollars.	Dollars.	Dollars.	Dollars.	Dollars.	Dollars.	Dollars.	Dollars.	Dollars.	Dollars.
1869	631,299	64,581	78,285	140,034	25,666	190,504	775,984	4,054,501	178,451	4,232,952
1870	702,186	115,710	94,490	260,550	26,981	102,640	488,761	3,979,396	178,759	4,158,155
1871	636,214	139,688	106,661	237,916	57,190	85,361	512,062	3,836,837	227,712	4,064,549
1872	902,823	75,279	148,600	128,018	23,233	180,406	715,487	4,259,398	181,501	4,440,899
1873	809,505	109,009	136,148	166,226	28,965	226,406	900,900	5,106,703	267,070	5,373,773
1874	965,681	112,754	174,870	219,886	33,946	212,924	886,524	5,043,146	223,654	5,266,800
1875	1,110,443	110,931	108,866	86,829	32,288	197,053	631,621	4,206,618	226,349	4,432,967
1876	828,448	139,393	118,063	128,306	21,679	147,958	645,770	3,887,210	164,804	4,052,014
1877	641,095	121,595	75,836	117,028	10,324	143,755	600,769	3,942,742	78,167	4,020,909
1878	680,619	113,397	126,633	112,334	14,572	164,632	515,130	4,371,198	124,124	4,495,322
1879	720,866	76,292	114,807	103,503	21,921	153,322	1,197,541	5,199,648	328,366	5,528,014
1880	559,118	75,999	105,696	74,714	23,467	165,682	1,093,687	5,228,836	108,478	5,337,314
1881	575,700	81,501	126,174	91,945	28,583	212,507	937,788	5,179,366	203,772	5,383,138
1882	1,039,551	64,761	176,115	97,269	35,513	529,296	920,847	6,230,916	177,430	6,408,346
1883	992,717	80,126	199,311	111,699	35,309	470,212	1,094,140	6,719,787	149,184	6,868,971
1884	397,533	94,531	215,646	100,051	54,791	887,072	1,050,060	6,174,574	207,247	6,381,821
1885	654,231	89,766	173,280	99,674	92,420	1,022,831	1,005,967	5,397,412	185,957	5,583,369
1886	540,867	105,319	229,323	143,611	109,569	627,453	943,048	5,294,798	185,659	5,480,457
1887	592,942	104,603	226,498	146,668	109,345	694,117	1,071,074	5,973,965	140,976	6,114,941
1888	607,474	94,105	227,324	120,913	109,200	457,519	882,688	4,923,259	100,621	5,023,880

No. 1.—IMPORTS INTO, AND EXPORTS FROM, THE UNITED STATES FROM AND TO MEXICO, ETC.—Continued.

GOLD AND SILVER COIN AND BULLION, 1869-1888—Continued.

WEST INDIES.

YEAR ENDING JUNE 30—	HAYTI.a		SAN DOMINGO.b		BRITISH WEST INDIES.c		FRENCH WEST INDIES.d		DUTCH WEST INDIES.e	
	Imports.	Exports.	Imports.	Exports.	Imports.	Exports.	Imports.	Exports.	Imports.	Exports.
	Dollars.	Dollars.	Dollars.	Dollars.	Dollars.	Dollars.	Dollars.	Dollars.	Dollars.	Dollars.
1869	15,104	28,956			130,471	40,116			46,435	26,442
1870	54,875	46,114			119,026	93,389			59,637	
1871	47,831	393,577			51,519	79,626			43,835	18,500
1872	2,180	250,278	4,815	47,820	85,217	44,514			3,063	21,911
1873	91,899	798,033	109,078	145,749	159,132	38,163			6,379	
1874	201,759	175,922	81,637	15,793	111,103	292,682			74,224	32,344
1875	65,126	232,500	48,829		109,778	3,550	1,827		32,661	31,090
1876	246,841	46,849	38,689	21,499	116,581	200		26,000	25,446	16,000
1877	524,299	36,770	41,543	17,937	206,483	44,628	1,067	77,572	44,831	21,000
1878	773,708	67,213	188,918	10,175	185,115	19,284	4,156		34,613	
1879	787,348	52,567	222,776	46,100	247,055	76,769		14,500	46,476	21,687
1880	789,088	922,756	217,171	153,666	446,825	87,623	2,752		29,605	14,900
1881	467,983	101,281	131,555	14,700	453,237	28,737	2,041		116,187	
1882	968,294	49,000	71,298	45,469	494,397	146,704		135,000	106,399	41,818
1883	258,954	52,474	70,611	56,335	262,087	46,204	1,900		43,418	32,250
1884	160,028	138,538	46,607	168,439	393,247	58,051		8,925	186,989	30,795
1885	226,510	16,287	66,384	168,788	618,374	45,102		5,694	280,746	2,086
1886	292,977	56,698	23,751	125,298	873,743	1,400		21,437	254,289	45,348
1887	209,728	404,161	27,045	239,184	712,902	7,453			142,610	40,356
1888	74,173	1,141,074	18,889	209,230	305,035	28,228		24,474	90,283	19,166

a Including San Domingo from 1869 to 1871, inclusive.
b Included with Hayti from 1869 to 1871, inclusive.
c Including British Honduras from 1873 to 1878, inclusive.
d Including French Guiana prior to 1879.
e Including Dutch Guiana from 1873 to 1878, inclusive.

TABLES. 307

No. 1.—IMPORTS INTO AND EXPORTS FROM, THE UNITED STATES FROM AND TO MEXICO, ETC.—Continued.

GOLD AND SILVER COIN AND BULLION, 1869-1888—Continued.

YEAR ENDING JUNE 30—	WEST INDIES.		UNITED STATES OF COLOMBIA.		SOUTH AMERICA.					
	DANISH WEST INDIES.				VENEZUELA.		GUIANA.		BRAZIL.	
	Imports.	Exports.	Imports.	Exports.	Imports.	Exports.	Imports.	Exports.	Imports.	Exports.
	Dollars.	Dollars.	Dollars.	Dollars.	Dollars.	Dollars.	Dollars.	Dollars.	Dollars.	Dollars.
1869	50,597	78,586	607,252	847,390	83,644	347,029	....	....	202,475	....
1870	122,378	150,951	497,467	603,465	119,997	457,785	....	....	14,740	43,523
1871	400	166,111	866,724	355,530	73,538	671,441	....	....	9,433	75,421
1872	11,705	191,302	458,077	235,860	19,055	1,336,079	....	....	11,865	73,141
1873	20,539	137,478	262,124	241,913	35,616	1,510,404	....	....	17,652	2,200
1874	69,942	209,500	385,676	92,544	62,346	598,564	....	....	22,668	3,664
1875	63,208	160,000	658,242	66,332	462,649	560,600	....	....	5,183	3,000
1876	29,621	38,000	463,373	59,232	358,926	610,584	....	....	6,792	1,000
1877	....	1,500	431,667	93,490	428,758	312,773	....	....	....	1,000
1878	476,870	....	656,656	197,107	134,131	235,730	....	....	3,663	....
1879	399,591	7,200	856,167	243,449	394,683	78,768	a2,698	b2,900	10,197	....
1880	248,623	21,658	598,683	155,780	253,270	110,000	a7,969	....	10,881	....
1881	158,202	....	523,140	231,241	292,467	322,500	a10,616	....	872	....
1882	28,125	....	429,813	290,540	442,058	186,200	a16,436	....	....	800
1883	29,501	1,255	374,558	475,384	53,201	318,480	a34,767	b100	499	6,250
1884	81,763	16,995	349,453	864,631	81,090	525,598	a31,344	....	300	8,525
1885	93,137	....	966,956	825,072	147,590	81,400	a60,571	....	3,666	5,275
1886	70,707	....	933,642	942,277	481,505	934,045	a8,596	....	16,392	9,821
1887	81,609	....	820,350	1,043,294	183,731	2,933,496	a6,457	....	2,415	....
1888	29,019	48,238	1,134,097	791,085	170,525	804,384	a13,594	....	29,100	16,357

a Dutch Guiana. b British Guiana.

No. 1.—IMPORTS INTO, AND EXPORTS FROM, THE UNITED STATES FROM AND TO MEXICO, ETC.—Continued.

GOLD AND SILVER COIN AND BULLION, 1869-1888—Continued.

SOUTH AMERICA.

YEAR ENDING JUNE 30—	URUGUAY.		ARGENTINE REPUBLIC.		CHILI.		PERU.		ALL OTHER COUNTRIES IN SOUTH AMERICA.	
	Imports.	Exports.	Imports.	Exports.	Imports.	Exports.	Imports.	Exports.	Imports.	Exports.
	Dollars.	Dollars.	Dollars.	Dollars.	Dollars.	Dollars.	Dollars.	Dollars.	Dollars.	Dollars.
1869			67,271	75,047						
1870				9,571				1,819,018		
1871				80,743				1,200,000		
1872								4,500,000		
1873							7,522	1,549,099		
1874						154,936	20,090	707,035		52,352
1875										146,963
1876						200	53,360			
1877	2,433		250		9,348	100	14,930	175,200	4,603	
1878	6,326		1,351				65,950	5,134		
1879			1,000	889			546,705			
1880							512,698			
1881							96,927	275		
1882					500		21,355	12,166	25,960	1,200
1883					8,155		4,800	50,000	3,291	59,316
1884					723	25,000			500	9,725
1885	50,000						9,840	14,960		
1886							30,844	11,300		750
1887			3,213				9,543	102,598		15,000
1888			3,910					25,500	500	20,000

No. 3.—STATEMENT SHOWING THE VALUES OF IMPORTS OF MERCHANDISE INTO, AND OF DOMESTIC MERCHANDISE EXPORTED FROM, THE UNITED STATES DURING THE YEAR ENDING JUNE 30, 1888, TO THE SPANISH WEST INDIES, MEXICO, THE CENTRAL AMERICAN STATES, THE UNITED STATES OF COLOMBIA, VENEZUELA, BRAZIL, URUGUAY, THE ARGENTINE REPUBLIC, CHILI AND PERU, RESPECTIVELY, COMPARED WITH LIKE IMPORTS AND EXPORTS FROM AND TO THE SAME COUNTRIES, INTO AND FROM THE UNITED KINGDOM DURING THE CALENDAR YEAR 1887, AND INTO AND FROM FRANCE, GERMANY AND SPAIN DURING THE CALENDAR YEAR 1886.

SPANISH WEST INDIES.

ARTICLES.	IMPORTS.				
	Into the United States.	Into the United Kingdom.	Into France.	Into Germany. a	Into Spain.
	Dollars.	Dollars.	Dollars.	Dollars.	Dollars.
Asphaltum or bitumen, crude.........	31,284	....	219,633	....	....
Chemicals, drugs and dyes.............	20,444	....	....	151,368	....
Cocoa, crude........................	8,484	....	704,847	....	284,998
Coffee..............................	224,913	3,650	1,004,675	16,898	611,237
Copper, and manufactures of.........	3,265	....	....	....	19,601
Fruits, including nuts...............	1,523,367	....	....	....	74,934
Hides and skins.....................	193,188	....	8,141	....	132,064
Honey..............................	(b)	....	....	....	31,890
Jewelry.............................	157	....	....	....	....
Leather, and manufactures of........	1,832	....	....	....	....
Spirits, distilled....................	19,065	20,031	5,109	....	459,130
Sponges............................	38,533	....	499,829	....	....
Sugar and molasses:					
Sugar.............................	37,542,829	532,979	....	15,232	5,353,528
Molasses..........................	5,220,782	....	....	....	....
Tobacco, and manufactures of:					
Leaf..............................	4,607,705	....	42,775	16,660	1,433,353
Manufactures of..................	3,334,013	190,358	696,862	113,526	1,056,721
Wood, and manufactures of..........	404,660	85,091	123,862	211,582	43,531
All other articles...................	557,049	184,571	59,072	192,066	143,233
Total...............................	53,731,570	1,016,680	3,364,805	717,332	9,644,320

a Imports from total West Indies.   *b* Not specified.

MEXICO.

Chemicals, drugs and dyes............	1,268,554	418,036	90,418	4,284	24,256
Coffee...............................	2,111,130	1,796	329,626	17,612	18,602
Copper ore.........................	10,929	....	....	....	....
Flax, hemp, jute, and other vegetable substances........................	5,239,432	277,751	176,276	12,614	23,144
Hides and skins.....................	1,562,008	....	....	8,806	57,146
Honey..............................	(a)	....	....	....	....
Silver ore...........................	4,803,667	251,180	55,948	b 1,471,554	....
Sugar...............................	14,653	99,559	....	....	....
Tobacco, and manufactures of:					
Leaf..............................	7,278	....	37,474	476	....
Manufactures of..................	13,029	275,965	81,488	1,190	....
Wood, and manufactures of..........	539,007	812,812	676,871	262,752	....
All other articles...................	1,760,202	169,734	91,962	9,044	17,404
Total...............................	17,329,889	2,306,833	1,540,063	c 1,788,332	140,552

    a Not specified.
    b Classified as "Ores of precious metals."
    c Includes the imports into Germany from Central America.

No. 3.—IMPORTS AND EXPORTS OF DOMESTIC MERCHANDISE, ETC.—Cont'd.

CENTRAL AMERICAN STATES.

ARTICLES.	IMPORTS.				
	Into the United States.	Into the United Kingdom.	Into France.	Into Germany.	Into Spain.
	Dollars.	Dollars.	Dollars.	Dollars.	Dollars.
Chemicals, drugs and dyes.............	111,415	....	164,827	....	....
Cocoa.................................	9,210	1,067,331	2,641	....	....
Coffee................................	4,567,165	5,172,325	327,133	....	....
Cotton, raw...........................	21	....	....	....	....
Fancy goods: Feathers, ornamental....	427	....	3,587	....	....
Hides and skins.......................	454,080	....	....	....	....
Sugar, brown..........................	262,513	39,818	....	....	....
Wood, and manufactures of............	19,899	111,365	658,748	....	....
All other articles.....................	2,198,648	135,994	30,210	....	5,700
Total.............................	7,623,378	6,526,833	a1,187,146	b	5,700

a Imports from Costa Rica, Guatemala, and Honduras.
b The imports into Germany from Central America are included with the imports into Germany from Mexico.

UNITED STATES OF COLOMBIA.

Breadstuffs: Wheat.....................	....	133,809	....	....	....
Chemicals, drugs and dyes.............	87,793	118,913	500,970	....	....
Cocoa.................................	45,676	8,001	1,281,878	....	30,397
Coffee................................	1,749,862	363,664	2,406,259	....	....
Cotton, raw...........................	101	40,363	92,679	....	....
Fruits, including nuts.................	402,685	....	114,386	....	....
Hides and skins.......................	1,293,158	56,524	158,752	....	....
India rubber and gutta-percha.........	388,691	72,136	99,592	....	....
Silver ore.............................	3,592	89,694	....	....	....
Tobacco, leaf.........................	587	31,949	....	....	....
All other articles.....................	421,113	379,447	246,209	....	6,394
Total.............................	4,393,258	1,294,500	4,900,742	a	36,791

a The imports into Germany from the United States of Colombia are not separately stated.

VENEZUELA.

Chemicals, drugs and dyes.............	27,850	127,862	32,509	....	....
Cocoa.................................	100,689	22,089	1,398,201	....	852,011
Coffee................................	8,863,599	10,497	4,370,979	....	....
Copper ore............................	....	383,432	....	....	....
Cotton, raw...........................	....	....	2,697	....	....
Hides and skins.......................	907,235	....	....	....	....
Wood, and manufactures of............	31,655	....	124,239	....	....
All other articles.....................	120,222	28,328	17,895	....	11,775
Total.............................	10,051,250	572,208	5,946,520	a	863,786

a The imports into Germany from Venezuela are not separately stated.

BRAZIL.

Bones, hoofs, horns, etc..............	a	174,683	91,289	....	....
Breadstuffs...........................	14	10,317	28,387	11,424	....
Chemicals, drugs and dyes............	55,908	50,105	....	6,188	....
Cocoa................................	297,853	242,050	2,097,344	....	....
Coffee...............................	33,460,595	5,335,606	15,778,248	635,698	6,147
Cotton, raw..........................	....	7,516,875	138,575	....	16,359
Fancy goods..........................	1,472	....	20,835	....	....
Flax, hemp, jute, and other vegetable substances...........................	....	....	....	74,256	....
Fruits, including nuts	318,823	332,518	22,572	....	....
Hair.................................	146,617	11,689	32,459	11,424	....
Hides and skins......................	1,659,286	861,916	2,602,903	46,886	31,461
India rubber and gutta-percha........	10,811,952	7,811,292	710,063	....	....

a Not specified.

No. 3.—IMPORTS AND EXPORTS OF DOMESTIC MERCHANDISE, ETC.—Cont'd.

SPANISH WEST INDIES.

ARTICLES.	EXPORTS.				
	From the United States.	From the United Kingdom.	From France.	From Germany.a	From Spain.
Breadstuffs:	Dollars.	Dollars.	Dollars.	Dollars.	Dollars.
Wheat flour	1,846,419	....	....	....	1,486,236
All other	181,523	....	....	952	....
Chemicals, drugs, dyes and medicines	241,721	67,205	39,278	4,998	236,276
Coal	467,323	224,774	....	....	....
Copper, and manufactures of	13,270	32,425	....	5,712	....
Cotton, manufactures of	135,554	2,653,507	43,771	69,972	1,970,964
Earthen, stone, and china ware	3,483	114,830	15,795	44,744	52,554
Fancy articles	64,131	....	64,573	29,988	414,883
Fertilizers	9,006	....	54,040	....	....
Fish	81,734	....	19,644	....	30,208
Flax, hemp, and jute, manufactures of	241,564	1,577,155	....	9,282	574,551
Fruits	23,128	....	....	....	388,131
Glass and glassware	66,857	41,813	....	9,990	24,076
Iron and steel, and manufactures of	1,332,962	1,525,599	36,395	139,230	225,384
Jewelry, and manufactures of gold and silver	16,307	....	5,984	....	....
Leather, and manufactures of	190,807	....	362,805	24,038	2,418,741
Malt liquors	17,062	137,581	....	....	....
Paints, and painters' colors	23,541	64,340	....	....	....
Paper and stationery	219,826	....	99,572	3,794	249,004
Provisions, comprising meat and dairy products	3,186,661	....	96,260	....	704,084
Rice	113	....	....	....	65,470
Silk, manufactures of	230	....	54,000	2,856	41,913
Soaps	2,507	....	....	3,094	884,747
Spirits, distilled	1,077	....	....	....	910,455
Umbrellas and parasols	10	....	....	....	57,774
Vegetables, including pickles, etc	406,322	....	....	....	487,239
Watches	1,294	....	....	....	....
Wearing apparel	(b)	60,676	70,556	3,094	....
Wine	331	....	83,707	....	3,523,640
Wood, and manufactures of	1,613,607	....	21,039	6,664	....
Wool, manufactures of	2,388	178,566	99,703	34,034	102,517
All other articles	1,253,714	394,547	264,369	24,276	715,965
Total	11,644,482	7,073,078	1,441,591	451,724	15,664,812

a Exports to total West Indies.   b Not specified.

MEXICO. b

Agricultural implements	25,365	....	....	....	....
Animals	427,296	....	....	....	....
Breadstuffs	345,048	....	....	....	....
Candles	21,544	....	17,137	....	....
Chemicals, drugs, dyes, and medicines	264,987	128,588	225,677	160,650	47,284
Coal	149,635	105,905	318,067	....	....
Cotton, manufactures of	1,036,462	2,574,802	....	185,102	....
Earthen, china, and glass ware	87,478	....	106,250	17,850	....
Fancy articles	32,576	....	422,241	138,754	21,822
Fish	33,918	....	....	....	....
Flax, hemp, and jute, manufactures of	50,179	437,216	....	31,416	....
Gunpowder and other explosives	264,875	....	....	....	....
India rubber and gutta-percha, manufactures of	41,413	133,410	....	4,284	....
Instruments and apparatus for scientific purposes	67,970	....	....	41,888	....

b Exports from the United States to Mexico are defective, embracing only exports in vessels.

No. 3.—IMPORTS AND EXPORTS OF DOMESTIC MERCHANDISE, ETC.—Cont'd.

MEXICO—Continued.

ARTICLES.	EXPORTS.				
	From the United States.	From the United Kingdom.	From France.	From Germany.	From Spain.
	Dollars.	*Dollars.*	*Dollars.*	*Dollars.*	*Dollars.*
Iron and steel, and manufactures of....	1,946,948	1,050,804	149,382	57,596	79,566
Jewelry, and manufactures of gold and silver.................................			316,990		
Leather, and manufactures of...........	85,144		359,918	53,788	
Malt liquors...........................	144,774				
Musical instruments....................	23,945				
Oils—					
Mineral, refined.....................	175,537				
All other............................	147,756			714	
Paper and stationery...................	123,226		229,040	6,188	a268,501
Provisions, comprising meat and dairy products...............................	390,425		64		91,843
Quicksilver............................	256,357				41,814
Silk, manufactures of...................	2,658	17,232	62,607	16,660	
Spirits, distilled.......................	19,648		93,082		63,953
Sugar, refined.........................	58,123				
Tobacco, leaf..........................	92,581				
Watches...............................	4,887		5,589		
Wearing apparel........................	(*b*)	32,391	430,091	17,136	
Wine...................................	32,255		473,040		317,024
Wood, and manufactures of..............	1,280,126			6,188	
Wool, manufactures of..................	39,543	577,615	758,426	159,222	
All other articles.......................	1,569,509	327,350	489,649	62,594	112,003
Total...............................	9,242,188	5,385,313	4,457,250	*c*960,330	1,043,810

a Includes books. *b* Not specified. *c* Includes the exports from Germany to Central America.

CENTRAL AMERICAN STATES.

Breadstuffs.............................	$21,318				
Candles................................	14,061	28,707	1,809		
Cotton, manufactures of.................	446,800	3,103,285	2,442		
Chemicals, drugs, dyes and medicines...	217,135	35,311	5,830		
Earthen, china and glassware............	33,114	17,826	15,415		
Fancy articles..........................	40,287				
Flax, hemp and jute, manufactures of...	48,131	131,517			
Fish....................................	15,570		733		
Fruit...................................	21,324		1,139		
Gunpowder and other explosives.........	100,748				
Iron and steel, and manufactures of.....	879,020	676,906	4,102		
Jewelry, and manufactures of gold and silver...................................	8,416				
Leather, and manufactures of............	59,829	24,391	5,875		
Oils: Vegetable........................	9,414				
Paper and stationery....................	54,611		a13,854		
Provisions, comprising meat and dairy products...............................	265,873				
Silk, manufactures of...................	3,107	37,112			
Soap...................................	19,865	14,594			
Spirits, distilled.......................	29,758		11,561		
Sugar, refined.........................	39,451				
Wearing apparel........................	(*b*)	106,270	7,856		
Wine...................................	46,570		30,408		22,057
Wood, and manufactures of..............	205,160		1,702		
Wool, manufactures of..................	18,035	204,203	18,484		
All other articles.......................	733,977	328,280	70,972		14,565
Total...............................	4,131,574	4,708,402	191,912	(*c*)	32,662

a Includes books and engravings. *b* Not specified. *c* The exports from Germany to Central America are included with the exports from Germany to Mexico.

No. 3.—IMPORTS AND EXPORTS OF DOMESTIC MERCHANDISE, ETC.—Cont'd.

UNITED STATES OF COLOMBIA.

ARTICLES.	EXPORTS.				
	From the United States.	From the United Kingdom.	From France.	From Germany.	From Spain.
Breadstuffs	440,798				
Carriages, horse-cars and cars for steam railroads	37,454		41,670		
Candles	7,830	45,258			
Chemicals, drugs, dyes and medicines	169,913	52,140	237,547		
Coal	154,194	104,537			
Cotton, manufactures of	376,529	3,166,992	464,120		9,799
Earthen, china and glassware	44,616	22,780	78,568		
Fancy articles	42,492		757,788		
Fish	170,845		109,104		
Flax, hemp and jute, manufactures of	102,392	381,154			
Gunpowder and other explosives	47,874		124,498		
India rubber and gutta-percha, manufactures of	27,254	31,569			
Iron and steel, manufactures of	710,492	553,686	329,895		105,842
Jewelry, and manufactures of gold and silver	12,986		57,671		
Leather, and manufactures of	103,094	94,770	1,399,765		10,638
Malt liquors	50,872	44,903			
Oils: Vegetable	14,326		67,480		
Paints and painters' colors	24,889	33,832			
Paper and stationery	88,569		163,519		a28,994
Provisions, comprising meat and dairy products	607,474				12,415
Silk, manufactures of	694	22,167	23,839		10,524
Soap	94,105				
Spirits, distilled	32,111		78,965		11,277
Sugar, refined	227,324				
Tobacco, and manufactures of	120,913				
Wearing apparel	(b)	388,322	1,115,982		
Wine	8,917		762,116		159,782
Vegetables, including pickles, etc	109,200	26,595			
Wood, and manufactures of	457,519		79,152		
Wool, manufactures of	15,252	284,257	673,646		
All other articles	622,331	420,559	539,366		55,624
Total	4,923,259	5,673,521	7,104,691	(c)	404,895

a Includes books.
b Not specified.
c The exports from Germany to the United States of Colombia are not separately stated.

Mexican Tariff

AND

CUSTOM-HOUSE LAWS.

MONEY, WEIGHTS AND MEASURES OF MEXICO.

The Money, Weights and Measures of Mexico are as follows:
The money consists of gold and silver.
The gold coins are $20 and $10 pieces, and are worth in U. S. gold about $19.65 and and $15.65, respectively.
The silver consists of dollars, halves, quarters, dimes and half-dimes.
The silver dollar is worth about 86c. U. S. money.

WEIGHTS AND MEASURES.

The *Arroba* { For Wine.....................=3½ Imperial Gallons.
              { For Oil......................=2¾ Imperial Gallons.
The Square "Vara"............................=1.09 Vara=1 Yard.
The Fanega...................................=1½ Imperial Bushels.

METRIC SYSTEM.

The following are the approximate values:
1 Metre..................................is equal to 3 feet 3-10ths of an Inch.
1 Decimetre..............................=4 Inches.
5 Metres.................................=1 Rod.
1 Kilometre..............................=5 Furlongs.
1 Square Metre...........................=10⅞ Square Feet.
1 Hectare................................=2½ Acres.
1 Cubic Metre............................=¼ Cord.
1 Litre..................................=1 Quart.
1 Hectolitre.............................=2¾ Bushels.
1 Gramme.................................=15½ Grains.
1 Kilogramme.............................=2 1-5 Pounds.

MARITIME AND FRONTIER CUSTOM HOUSES OF MEXICO.

PORTS OF ENTRY.

GULF OF MEXICO.

Matamoros, Tampico, Túxpam, Vera Cruz, Coatzacoalcos, Frontera, Isla de Carmen, Campeche and Progreso.

PACIFIC OCEAN.

Soconusco, Tonalá, Salina Cruz, Puerto Angel, Acapulco, Manzanillo, San Blas, Mazatlan, Altata, Guayamas, La Paz, Cabo de San Lucas, Bahia de la Magdalena and Todos Santos.

NORTHERN FRONTIER.

Tijuana, Quitovaquita, Nogales, Sásabe, Palominas, Ascencion, Paso del Norte, Presidio del Norte, Piedras Negras, Laredo de Tamaulipas, Guerrero, Mier and Camargo.

SOUTHERN FRONTIER.

Zapaluta.

PORTS FOR THE COASTING TRADE.

GULF OF MEXICO.

Soto la Marina (*Tampico); Tecoluta, Nautla, Alvarado, Tlacotalpam, Santecomapam (Vera Cruz); Tonalá (Coatzacoalcos); Tenosique (Frontera); La Aguada, Villa de Palizada (Isla de Carmen); Champoton (Campeche); Celestum, Isla de Mujeres, Isla de Cozumel (Progreso).

PACIFIC OCEAN.

Tecoanapa, Zihuatanejo (Acapulco); Chamela (Manzanillo); Maria Madre (San Blas); Topolobampo, Perihuete, Teacapam (Mazatlan); Agiabampo (Guayamas); Mulegé San José del Cabo (La Paz); Isla de Guadalupe (Todos Santos).

CUSTOM HOUSE SECTIONS.

NORTHERN FRONTIER.

Las Vacas. Pacuache (Piedras Negras); Reynosa (Matamoros).

* The name in parentheses refers to the maritime or frontier custom house on which the place named, preceding it, depends.

GENERAL ORDINANCE

FOR

MARITIME AND FRONTIER CUSTOM HOUSES.

CHAPTER I.

General Rules for the Commerce of the Republic.

SECTION I.

GENERAL TRAFFIC.

ART. 1. The ports and the maritime and the frontier custom houses of the United Mexican States are open to the commerce of all the nations of the world and their recognized possessions.

ART. 2. The importation, exportation, re-exportation and transit of goods will be subject to the conditions contained in this law, in the custom house regulations and treaties now in force. To which the importers, exporters, consignees, captains, supercargoes, crews and others, charged with conducting and keeping the goods, as well as the vessels, cars and other means of transportation, will be subject, and that relating to the payment of the duties and fines imposed for their violation, from the moment they enter the territory or the waters of the nation.

ART. 3. The importation of foreign goods of any kind into the Republic is not prohibited. The importation of war materials may temporarily be prohibited by the Executive of the Union, and regulated by the War Department at their introduction into the country.

ART. 4. The importers of foreign goods can determine the designation of the goods in the Republic, the transit through the national territory, the deposit, or the re-exportation. The carrier of goods can transfer them from one vessel to another in the waters of the Republic. All these operations are subject to the laws now in force.

ART. 5. When any nation is at war with the United Mexican States, the privileges granted in the former articles will be suspended in respect to that nation.

Special decrees from the Executive will declare and regulate the manner of making this interdiction.

ART. 6. The refusal to obey the Federal Government wherever there may be a maritime or frontier custom house, or the occupation of the place by rebellious forces, will cause the place to be closed to legal traffic, and thereafter no federal office will authorize the dispatch of merchandise for the place mentioned by this order, nor receive any coming from such place, until its submission to the federal power. The goods on the way to this closed custom house will be received at any custom house in accordance with the provisions of this law. Any persons violating the same shall be punished as are contrabands under this law, but such punishment shall not render them less liable to the other punishments provided for in such cases.

ART. 7. I. Foreign goods imported into the Republic in foreign vessels shall pay the rates, assigned in the tariff of this ordinance, or in their stead those fixed on them according to the rules established by this law.

II. Foreign merchandise imported in national steam or sailing vessels shall enjoy the difference in the import duties, according to the law of December 12, 1883, provided they have complied with the requirements there indicated.

III. Of all the import duties there shall be delivered monthly to the Municipal Government of the ports or places where the custom houses may be situated, one and one-quarter per cent. granted by this law to the said corporations.

ART. 8. No change in the rates of this tariff or in the system of applying them to the goods which have no rate mentioned, can go into operation until after the time be fixed by the law which may establish them. The same will be observed in respect to all changes which increase the obligations or fines established.

ART. 9. On the subject of importation, exportation, re-exportation, and transit, the Federal Executive power will have, besides its constitutional powers, those detailed in the present law.

ART. 10. The Treasury Department is the only one legally authorized to transmit to the Federal custom houses the orders for the exemption of duties, as well as all classes of dispositions relating to this law.

SECTION II.

POWERS AND OBLIGATIONS OF THE EXECUTIVE OF THE UNION.

ART. 11. The powers conferred upon the Federal Executive, on the subject of importation, are the following:

I. To declare free from the payment of duties all kinds of merchandise which come expressly for the public use of the Federation, and of the several departments, provided that any of them order the goods from some functionary or Federal employé abroad, and that he shall be the direct shipper.

II. To make also the declaration of the exemption of duties, when a citizen commissioned by the Executive makes the purchase abroad, and in this case the goods should come consigned to the Executive, or some of the departments. Contracting with persons or corporations for the free entry of foreign goods, even when they are intended for the direct use of the Federation, is prohibited.

III. To declare exempt from the payment of duties armaments and materials of war for the States, provided the Governors solicit the exemption from the Federal Executive and in accord with the Legislatures of the States which they represent.

IV. To authorize in exceptional cases, and when extraordinary circumstances demand it, that the importation of the goods may be made at different custom houses from those to which the goods were intended.

V. To establish by means of decrees for general observance, which the Executive cannot change, fixed rates which the goods imported and not included in the tariff must pay, and that the rates shall be imposed to correspond with those on goods rated.

These rates will be the results of the operation made in accordance with the provisions of the articles of this law relating to the subject.

VI. To decide, in case of controversy and disagreement of experts, in accordance with the requirements of this law.

VII. To define the articles of this tariff by means of explanations, definitions and all that may be thought necessary for the easy comprehension of the rules that may be established, so that the meaning given to the law will be the same in all the offices where duties are collected; besides taking into consideration that the rates fixed in this tariff will not be modified.

The decisions which the Executive may give will be published by means of a decree, without which requisite they will not be considered legal.

VIII. The index or vocabulary annexed to the tariff, which embraces the names of the different kinds of merchandise, with the numbers by which they are found, will be modified by the Executive when in the course of the fiscal year there are modifications made which make it necessary, and they will be published by means of decrees, placing in the vocabulary all the names of the merchandise which may have been added in the previous year.

IX. To prohibit temporarily the importation or transit of war materials when, under the circumstances, it may be deemed necessary. Special decrees will declare and abolish this prohibition.

CHAPTER II.

Loading of Vessels in Foreign Ports.

SECTION I.

RULES TO WHICH FOREIGN SHIPMENTS WILL BE SUBJECT AND THE DUTIES WHICH THEY ARE TO PAY AT MEXICAN PORTS.

ART. 12. Vessels of all kinds and nationalities in ballast or loaded with merchandise, coming to the United Mexican States, should be cleared for some of those ports which the Federal Executive has ready for the commerce of the high seas.

ART. 13. Steam or sailing vessels, national or foreign, can carry passengers, mail and cargo, for one or more ports of the Republic, and for foreign ports, or for these only, as long as the cargo is entered according to this law at Mexican ports.

ART. 14. Vessels in ballast coming from a foreign port, and which come with the object of fishing or diving on the Mexican coast, or with the purpose of receiving and taking passengers and mail, or loading live-stock, wood, or any other national product, will go to ports open for the traffic of the high seas, that from some of them they may clear for their destination.

ART. 15. When a vessel in ballast requests permission to go and load national products at a port where there is no custom house established, the collector may grant permission, provided it complies with the requisites expressed in Article 276 of this law.

ART. 16. Foreign and national vessels can come freely to the ports of the Republic to winter, to get water, replenish stores or repair injuries, without being obliged to pay tonnage or any other duty, with the exception of pilotage, which foreign and national vessels shall pay only when they solicit the services of the pilot; being subject to all the provisions of this law.

ART. 17. National or foreign merchant vessels, steam or sailing, are subject to the payment of pilotage, which will be collected by the Captain of the Port, in accordance with the orders promulgated by the Department of War and Navy, which may be in force at the time of entering. They shall also be subject to the payment of light-house taxes when these exist. Said tax shall be as follows:

I. For steamers loaded with merchandise $100 on arriving, and the same on leaving.

II. For sailing vessels loaded with merchandise $25 on arriving, and the same on leaving.

III. Foreign vessels which, sent out with ballast, arrive directly at some port of the Republic in order to load national products shall pay, on leaving, a light-house tax of $100 for steamers, and $25 for sailing vessels.

IV. Vessels which carry merchandise consigned to one or more ports of the Republic shall pay the light-house tax but once; having done this on their entrance into the first port where such a tax is collectable, the same shall not again be levied at any of the other ports which may be touched for the purpose of unloading the rest of the cargo; a proper certificate proving the payment of said tax shall be furnished, and the custom house receiving the tax shall officially notify the other ports at which said vessels propose to stop of said payment.

ART. 18. Foreign vessels bringing merchandise from abroad, with the exception of coal, will pay but once, at the first port which they may touch, the tonnage duty which may exist, at the rate of $1.50 for the tons measured, determining the number of tons according to the respective regulations of the War and Navy Departments.

ART. 19. Foreign vessels which come from abroad destined to ports of the Republic, and conducting merchandise and coal, will only pay tonnage dues on the number of tons occupied by the merchandise. In order that the tonnage dues, which vessels referred to in this and the previous article must pay, may not be charged them again at other national ports, to which they may go with any object whatever, the captains will obtain from the custom house which collected the duty a certificate to prove the payment of said duty.

ART. 20. The following are exempt from tonnage dues:

I. Vessels referred to in articles 14 and 16 of this chapter.
II. Steamships.
III. Foreign sailing vessels which arrive at the ports of the Republic bringing coal only.
IV. National vessels.
V. Foreign men-of-war.

ART. 21. National or foreign vessels after having discharged the merchandise which they brought and having paid the corresponding duties are considered as vessels in ballast, according to Articles 14 and 15, and can engage, under the same regulations, in the same operations, but the foreign vessels will be subject to the pilot dues, and the national vessels only when they apply for a pilot.

ART. 22. National and foreign merchant vessels, from the moment they enter the waters of the Republic, are subject to the vigilance, examination and visits which the Mexican Federal custom houses may deem necessary to exercise over them.

SECTION II.

DUTIES OF CAPTAINS ABROAD.

ART. 23. The captain of every vessel intending to sail to a Mexican port with merchandise is obliged to form a general manifest of the merchandise, according to form No. 1, found at the end of this law, with others cited in it. The general manifest mentioned must contain:

I. The name of the Mexican port to which the vessel is bound, the name of the captain, the class, nationality, and name of the vessel, the number of tons burden expressed in figures and writing, and the name of the consignee of the vessel.

II. Marks, counter-marks, and numbers of the packages, quantity of packages, their class and their corresponding gross weights (expressing the quantity in figures and writing), kind of merchandise, name of remitters or shippers of each lot, and their respective consignees, and the total number of packages expressed also in figures and writing.

III. The name of the port where the merchandise was loaded, the date, and signature of the captain, together with a certificate by him according to form No. 1.

ART. 24. The captains of vessels consigned *to order* will be considered as consignees of them if they do not designate any person resident at the port who may act as such within twenty-four hours after the entering of the vessel in port. Within the same time captains can name a consignee resident at the port for the merchandise that they have brought *to order* . If this is not done, the custom house will proceed as in the case where no consignee is mentioned, according to Article 44 of this law.

ART. 25. Should interlineations, erasures or corrections appear on the manifests, a fine shall be imposed which shall not be less than $10 nor more than $50. The following cases shall form the only exceptions:

I. When they have been altered by the interested parties, with explanatory notes placed at the end of the documents before obtaining the certificate mentioned in Article 61.

II. When, notwithstanding the corrections, the several copies of the same document are found to agree.

III. When the interlinings, erasures, etc., are or fall on matter of no importance in the liquidation of the duties.

ART. 26. The captains will present for their certification to the Mexican consul, consular or commercial agent residing at the port where the vessel loads, four copies of the general manifest of the merchandise which they carry to any port of the Republic, leaving three copies of this document at the Consulate or Agency, and receiving from the Mexican functionary the other copy with its respective certification and corresponding receipt.

This copy and receipt captains will bring with them for the purpose mentioned in Article 70, Fraction II.

ART. 27. Should there not be, at the port where the cargo is loaded, any Mexican official authorized to certify a general manifest, the captains shall prepare three copies of this document, two of which they shall deposit in the postoffice of the place, duly certified or especially recommended to the postmaster, and addressed respectively, the one to the Secretary of the Treasury in Mexico, and the other to the Collector of the Custom House of the port of destination; they shall receive therefor the receipt prescribed by Fraction II, of Article 6 of the Postal Union, and this, annexed to the third copy, they shall present at the Mexican custom house where the vessel may unload.

ART. 28. In case the vessel carries freight for two or more ports of the Republic, the captains will form the corresponding manifests for each port in accordance with the formalities mentioned in the previous articles.

ART. 29. The captain is obliged to deliver to the representatives of the custom house as soon as these come to visit the vessel before anchoring:

I. The general manifest of the merchandise which he has for the port he proposes to enter, with the respective consular receipts or the postal receipts, and certification referred to in Articles 26 and 27.

II. A statement of the packages of samples which he brings in his care (Model No. 2).

III. A list of the passengers, if he has any (Model No. 3).

IV. A minute declaration of the stores left, and other articles which he may have on board for the service of the ship (Model No. 4).

ART. 30. I. Should the manifest and consular receipt be entirely wanting, the following fines shall be imposed: When the vessels are loaded with merchandise, the fines shall be not less than $25, nor more than $500. When they carry simply ballast, it shall vary from $5 to $100, at the discretion of the collector.

II. The absence of the postal receipt mentioned in Article 27 shall be punished in the same manner as though there were no manifests whatever, unless, at the time of presenting said manifest, there is found in the custom house of the place to which the vessel is destined a corresponding copy of the same.

III. The failure to deliver the manifest and consular or postal receipts to the custom-house official, immediately upon the boarding of the vessel for the purpose of searching the same, shall be punished by a fine of from $5 to $25.

IV. The failure to present any of the other documents mentioned in fractions II, III and IV of the preceding article, shall be punished by a fine of from $1 to $10.

V. All the fines which for the foregoing reasons may be imposed by the custom houses remain subject to the approval of the Secretary of the Treasury.

ART. 31. When the captains comply with the presentation of the general manifest and the consular or postal receipts with the respective certification, and the custom house has not, as yet, received its corresponding copy, the collectors will insist on seeing the log-book of the ship, the bills of lading and any other documents that may be needed to compare the date of sailing of the ship with the custom house documents. If the documents agree as to dates, there will be copies made of the manifest presented so as to be able to proceed with the discharge of the cargo, and notice shall be given to the Treasury Department so that the cause of the delay may be inquired into by the consulate.

ART. 32. If there should be a difference between the dates of the sailing of the vessel and the mentioned documents, and it is not sufficiently proven that the unforeseen events had been the cause of the difference, the collectors will proceed to investigate what had taken place during the passage, making the passengers (when there are any), and the crew of the ship, declare what took place during the trip, giving immediate notice of what transpired to the Treasury Department for its knowledge and resolution.

The irregularities mentioned in this article will not impede the discharge of the cargo nor the sailing of the vessel, if it should be solicited; provided, always, that the captain or his representatives give a bond to the satisfaction of the collector, and promising to comply with the decision of the Government.

ART. 33. When the captains do not present the copy which they should bring; and those of the custom house and Treasury Department have been received, the collector will furnish the captain, at his expense, an exact copy of that in his possession, which copy, signed by the captain, will take the place of the one which should have been presented on entering the port.

ART. 34. The formalities expressed in the previous articles are obligatory on the captains even when their vessels come in ballast to the ports of the Republic; but, in case they conduct merchandise to a foreign port, the captains ought to comply with the provisions of the following article:

ART. 35. The captains of vessels carrying merchandise for national and foreign ports shall, during their stay, deposit in the custom house of each Mexican port, at which they stop, the respective manifests of the other cargoes which they may have aboard.

ART. 36. The documents which the captains of the vessels should present according to this law shall be written in Spanish or in the language of the nation to which the ship belongs.

ART. 37. The manifests dated before the sailing of the vessel carrying merchandise will be considered null by the collectors, who will proceed, in consequence, the same way as if these documents were missing.

ART. 38. The captains will take care that packages containing samples for Mexican ports are mentioned in a separate document from the general cargo which they carry.

ART. 39. It is the duty of captains to preserve in good condition the seals which the custom house officers may place on the hatchways and bulkheads; the breaking of these seals, except when the same shall be proved to have been done without any one being to blame, shall be punished with a fine not exceeding $200: this fine shall, however, be no bar to such other punishments as may be provided for the acts which may have been committed.

ART. 40. It is the duty of captains to show their log books, the bills of lading and all other documents which the collectors may require for the purpose of overcoming the difficulties; and to treat with due respect the officers which the custom house sends on board to watch what takes place on the ship, and consider them as first-class passengers.

ART. 41. During the discharge of a vessel, the captain shall form a ticket of the packages discharged and loaded on the launch, giving the details mentioned in Model No. 5. This ticket shall be duly numbered and shall be delivered to the man in charge of the launch which carries the cargo.

ART. 42. In the absence of a captain, the persons who legally represent him are responsible and have the same obligations as mentioned in this chapter.

SECTION III.

OBLIGATIONS OF SHIPPERS OR TRANSMITTERS.

ART. 43. The shippers or remitters of merchandise to any port of the Republic are obliged to form invoices of the goods which they send, even when these are intended for the public service of the Federation, or of the States, or when it refers to those articles which this law exempts from duty; the shippers or remitters should make one separate invoice for each one of their consignees, forming them in triplicate or quadruplicate, as the case may be determined by this law; they must be in accord with Model No. 6, and shall contain the following:

I. The class, nationality and name of the vessel, the name of the captain, of the consignee, of the goods, and of the port to which the vessel is bound.

II. The marks, countermarks and numbers of the packages.

III. The number (expressed in figures and letters) of bales, boxes, barrels, or other kinds of packages in which the cargo is contained, together with their respective gross weights, which shall also be expressed in figures and letters.

IV. The net or legal weight (also expressed in figures and letters) of the merchandise which is to pay duty according to said weights.

V. The numbers (also expressed in figures and letters) of the pieces, pairs or thousands of such goods as are taxed by the piece, pair or thousand.

VI. The length and breadth (in figures and letters) of the goods which are taxed according to the measurement.

VII. The length, breadth and weight of the square metre of woolen cloth according to the quality of each lot.

VIII. The name, kind and class of merchandise mentioned in the manifest according to the nomenclature of the tariff or vocabulary, if they are mentioned therein; even more in detail when such mention is not made.

IX. The nation where the goods are produced, their corresponding values and the sum total of the packages.

X. Name of the place where the invoice is made, the corresponding date, the signature of the shipper or remitter affirming to the truth of what he declares, and that he proceeds with fidelity and good faith.

XI. To the end that shippers may intelligently form their invoices, they must take into consideration, in declaring the goods, the dispositions established by this tariff for the payment of the import duties.

ART. 44. When the shippers or remitters omit to express on the consular invoices the consignee or consignees of their merchandise, or when they are consigned *to order*, and when the captains of vessels do not make use of the facilities afforded them in Article 24 of this law, the collector of the port will be considered as consignee, and will discharge said duty according to the following rules:

I. The collector of the port will name a person in whom he has entire confidence, who will act as provisional consignee of the merchandise, without a consignee, or *to order*. He will see that the general rules of this ordinance are complied with, and in the meantime he will wait for the consignee to present himself, until the time for the sale of the goods.

II. The owners of the goods consigned *to order*, or who have not mentioned a consignee, should present themselves to the collector within twenty-four hours from the moment in which the vessel entered port, to prove their indentity, and exhibit the corresponding documents, and manifesting, by written declaration, that they accept the consignment of the goods. The said time having expired, the above declaration will not be accepted, and the collector shall proceed to name a consignee.

III. If the owners or consignees reside away from the port, they can make it known to the custom house by telegraph, and present themselves to verify their indentity and right within fifteen days, counting from the day after the custom house has taken charge of the ship bringing the goods, in order to follow the custom house proceedings from the point at which they are left by the provisional consignee previously appointed before the discharge was ordered.

IV. In all cases where the name of the consignee does not appear on the manifest of the ship, or is consigned *to order*, or when the consignee named or the collector of the port has taken charge of the consignment, the discharge of the ship will be made, and the goods shall not be stored without a previous examination of them to prove their agreement with the consular invoice of the custom house; should the custom house not have received said invoice, the description of the goods shall be reduced to writing, as provided in the next section.

V. The examination spoken of in the previous fraction will be made by the officer appointed by the collector, who will witness this examination, and, besides the collector, or the officer appointed in his stead, the provisional consignee, and the captain of the vessel which brought them, should he desire it, making a declaration in triplicate, which they will sign, as to the result of the examination. Immediately after they will proceed to close and tie the packages with wire, and seal them with leaden seals in such a way that they cannot be opened without destroying the seals, and they will store them separate from other goods in store.

VI. All expense incurred by the examination, sealing, unloading, transit, etc., will be for account of the consignees or owners of the goods, should these have to be sold in accordance with the provisions of this law.

ART. 45. Shippers of goods may unite into a single package a number of bales, boxes, bags, bundles, or other kind of packages containing the same kind of stuffs, provided that in the consular invoice the number of said packages be set forth. Should the latter be wanting, and should the error not be corrected within the time allowed the consignees by Art. 109 of this law, double duties shall be charged upon the goods contained in the packages not appearing on the manifest.

The following are excepted:

I. Merchandise naturally bulky and generally tied together, as iron bars, metal plates or sheets, shingles for roofs, shooks or other similar goods.

II. Boxes containing petroleum or coal oil, olive oil, and other like goods which generally come in large cans.

III. Pieces of dry goods in bales or boxes. bottles, vessels and flasks containing alimental substances, drugs, perfumery, etc., and in general small packages, bags, boxes, or any class of packages under one cover.

ART. 46. On the consular invoices, the gross and net weight of packages of merchandise containing different kinds of goods, or differently packed, shall be separately expressed. Neither shall bundles containing dry goods, nor cotton, linen, woolen or silk stuffs, be united into a single lot, if the difference in weight between some of them exceeds ten (10) kilogrammes.

Unless the consignees claim the benefit of the exemption of Article 109, the violation of the present article shall be punished by the imposition of double duties upon such goods as may be contained in the package or packages improperly declared in the manifest.

ART. 47. Neither shall the average width of dry goods paying duty by the square metre be used, if the difference between the same exceed five centimetres.

The violation of this provision shall be punished by the imposition of double duties upon that portion which is improperly declared; provided, always, that the interested party shall not correct the same within the time allowed by Article 109.

ART. 48. Interlineations, erasures, corrections or amendments shall not be allowed in the consular invoices subject to a fine of from $5 to $50 for each violation of this order.

These mistakes will only be tolerated in the following cases:

I. When they have been corrected by the interested parties, with notes explaining them, which will be placed at the end of the document before obtaining the certification treated of in Articles 61 and 62.

II. When, notwithstanding the corrections, the different copies of the same document are found to agree.

III. When said interlineations, erasures, etc., affect matters which in nowise relate to or may be used in fixing the amount of the duties.

ART. 49. The shippers of merchandise, when they remit in one package several kinds of goods paying different duties, besides declaring in the consular invoice the gross weight, will also declare the exact net weight of each of the articles which the package contains, to the end that the distribution will be proportional between the tare of the merchandise contained in the packages. Should any one or more of these requirements be lacking, there shall be charged upon the weight of the whole package the duty corresponding to the article paying the highest tax, unless the consignee in due time correct his declaration.

ART. 50. The remitters of packages containing samples will not need the consular certificate on their invoice. It will be sufficient to express on them whether they have value or not, the class of the goods, the gross weight of the packages, their marks and numbers, and the name of the consignee. (See Model No. 7.)

In case said samples, so sent, belong to that class which by this law are made subject to the payment of import duties, if the consignee fail to declare in the invoice the class, quality, and other details descriptive of said goods, the same shall be considered as wanting on the invoice, and shall be subject to the payment of double duties.

ART. 51. The shippers of goods will present, before the sailing of the vessel, four copies of each invoice to the consul, consular or commercial agent of Mexico resident at the port from which the goods are shipped, or from the port where the vessel loads, leaving three copies at the consulate, and receiving the other from the consul with its certification and corresponding receipt. This copy of the consular invoice and its receipt should be sent to the consignee of the merchandise, that he may be able to comply with the requisites of this law at the Mexican port.

ART. 52. The impossibility of having the consular invoice certified at the place from which the goods are sent, on account of there not being a Mexican consul at that place, will be substituted by the certification by said officer at that port where the goods are shipped, and in case there should be no Mexican consul or commercial agent at either of the places named, the custom house will proceed as provided in the following article.

ART. 53. In places where there are no Mexican consuls or commercial agents the shippers will form their consular invoices in triplicate, and in other respects in accord with the previous rules, sending them the same day by registered letter, or recommended by the postoffice of the place (fraction II, of Article 6, of the Postal Union) one to the Treasury Department, and the other to the custom house at the port or ports to which the goods are sent.

The sender will take care to exact from the postmaster the corresponding receipt, which he will send the consignee at the port where the goods are remitted, that he may present it, with the other copy of the invoice, when he asks for the dispatch of the goods.

ART. 54. The omission of the consular invoice, which the consignee of the goods should present, together with the receipt attached to it by means of the seal of the consulate, will be punished by the imposition of double duties upon the goods imported.

ART. 55. If the consignee should present his consular invoice, with the receipt attached, and the custom house has not received its copy, there will be a copy of it made by the custom house to place on file; but if he does not have it to present, and the custom house should have its copy, the omission shall be supplied by the consignee obtaining a true and exact copy of the one found at the custom house, subscribing the same with his signature and placing thereon a stamp of the value of fifty cents for each page of the ordinary size, which shall be canceled by the custom house when the corresponding presentation and certification of the document is made. These cases shall all be reported to the Treasury Department.

Art. 56. When goods come from a place where there is no Mexican consul or consular agent, and the vessel conveying the goods also comes from a port where there is no Mexican representative, the presentation of the postal receipts is indispensable, and it can only be overlooked when the custom house and the Treasury Department have received their corresponding copies. In case the invoice presented to the consignee of the goods be not in accord (either by reason of addition or subtraction) with those in possession of the custom house and Treasury Department, there shall be imposed a fine of double duties upon such articles in respect to which said differences exist in said invoices.

Art. 57. In case of the omission either of the custom house invoice, or of that of the interested party, or of the Treasury Department, the custom house will proceed in same manner as with the consular invoices.

Art. 58. The custom house invoices should be written in Spanish, or they can be made out in any other known language when the shippers are totally ignorant of the official language of the country.

Art. 59. Any mistake committed on the consular invoices will be punished by the collectors with the penalties established by the articles relating to them.

Art. 60. The consignee of ships will be responsible, according to law, for the mistakes made by the shippers or remitters of merchandise.

SECTION IV.

DUTIES OF MEXICAN CONSULS IN FOREIGN COUNTRIES.

Art. 61. The duties of consuls or consular agents of the Republic in foreign countries in matters relating to the observance of this law are as follows:

I. To receive the four copies of the manifest for their certification before the sailing of the vessel, and not after; to examine if the total number of packages is correct, and if all the copies agree, if they have properly explained at the end of any corrections, interlining or erasures, or if the signatures are alike.

II. To certify each of the four copies directly under the last line written, declaring that they have been received, the name of the captain who signs the manifest the number of packages on the manifest, the number of pages the manifest consists of, the date of presentation, that it has the seal of the consulate, and if it has any notes, and in what number, date and signature, at the end. (Model No. 8.)

III. One of said four copies of the manifest shall be returned to the interested party with a receipt attached thereto, made out in the form indicated by model No. 1, and which is made a part of this law. Said receipt should contain the serial number corresponding to said manifest, the date of its delivery and the seal of the consulate.

IV. The Mexican consuls and consular agents are obliged to show this law to any person asking for it, and to give the captains and shippers all the data and information possible regarding the laws of the country and the requisites exacted by the nation in its international commerce.

V. The consuls are authorized to use stamps, with blank spaces to be filled in writing, as long as they inform the Treasury Department of it, and send an impression of the stamp they have adopted.

ART. 62. The obligations mentioned in the previous articles respecting the manifests of vessels which the captains present to the consuls to certify are applicable to the invoices which the remitters or shippers present to him.

ART. 63. The three manifests and invoices which, in compliance with this law, the captains and shippers should leave with the consuls, they will dispose of as follows:

I. They will form two collections, subdivided in groups, including in each one the manifest and the invoice corresponding to the same vessel and to the merchandise intended for the same port. These groups of manifests and invoices should be sent registered, through the postoffice of the place and by the vessel to which the documents refer, provided this be a steamer, to the Treasury Department and to the collector or collectors of the custom houses of the ports for which the vessel carries merchandise. If the vessel carrying the merchandise is not a steamer, they will avail themselves of the first direct mail to make the remission of the documents.

II. With the third copy of the manifest and the third lot of invoices they shall form two dispatches, in which those documents shall separately appear in the same order as is followed in the stub books.

ART. 64. The consuls are strictly prohibited, under the responsibilities and penalties mentioned in Article 381, from certifying manifests or invoices after the sailing from the port of the vessel or merchandise to which those documents refer.

ART. 65. The consuls are also strictly prohibited from giving copies of manifests or invoices which they have certified, under the penalties included in the article previously mentioned.

The only certificate which a consul can give is that which certifies that the manifests and invoices were duly presented, or that the corresponding receipts had been given, or any other act registered in the consulate; these they can give at all times to the interested parties, stating the number of the manifest, invoice or receipt to which the certificate may refer.

ART. 66. For the fulfillment of Fraction II, of Article 61, and for other similar uses, the consuls will have a special stamp, which will say, "*Consulate of the United Mexican States at* ———."

ART. 67. The consuls will charge for the certification of the documents which the captains and shippers of goods may present them the following rates: *

I. For certifying a manifest referring to a vessel carrying merchandise to the Republic, $10.

II. For certifying a manifest referring to a vessel going in ballast, $4.

III. For certifying each set of custom house invoices, $4.

IV. For any certificate which they may give to the captains or shippers, $2.

V. When the certificates referred to in the previous fraction are required in duplicate, triplicate, etc., they will charge for each extra copy $1.

The amounts collected by the consuls or consular agents for certificates of all kinds should be paid at the time of certification, in the current coin of the country in which said consuls or consular agents reside — reference being had to the accompanying table, at the end hereof, which fixes the value of the various foreign moneys as compared with the Mexican dollar, which is the monetary unit of our Republic.

ART. 68. The consuls should place exactly the same certification on each of the four copies of the manifest or invoice, without charging more than the rates mentioned in the previous article.

ART. 69. The Mexican consuls are also obliged:

I. To inquire into all the circumstances of importance respecting the mercantile expeditions directed to ports of the Republic, especially those proceeding from the place where they reside.

II. To send to the Treasury Department a monthly statement of the number of vessels cleared for Mexican ports, with the number of manifests and invoices corresponding to each vessel, as is set forth in Model No. 9.

III. To send also a notice of the number of vessels arriving at the port where they reside from Mexican ports, together with all the details set forth in Model No. 10, and such others as he may deem of interest.

IV. Lastly, to send to the Treasury Department, on the first days of the month, the notices mentioned in fractions II and III of this article, and duplicate notices of the prices current of the merchandise at the place where they reside.

A copy of the current prices should be dispatched to the collectors of custom houses whenever there are documents to be sent.

CHAPTER III.

Duties of Captains of Foreign Vessels and Their Consignees at Mexican Custom Houses.

SECTION I.

ARRIVAL AND DISCHARGE OF VESSELS COMING FROM FOREIGN PORTS.

ART. 70. The duties of the Mexican Federal custom house at ports open to traffic of the high seas, respecting vessels, will begin from the moment these enter the ports, and immediately after the visits of the health officer and captain of the port, made in compliance with the Naval Ordinance. The custom houses mentioned will observe the following rules on the arrival of the vessels:

I. As soon as the ship nears the anchoring place and the doctor of the board of health and the captain of the port make their visits, the employés of the custom house will go to the ship and remain near by until the representative of the above-mentioned board declares the ship free. Having received this information, the captain of the port and the employés of the custom house whom the collector has selected will board the ship under a commander or any person acting as such.

II. The commander of the said custom house officers, or the person acting for him, shall collect from the captain of the vessels the documents enumerated in Article 29 of this ordinance, for which shall be executed the corresponding receipt (Model No. 14). This done, whenever the same may be considered practicable and advisable, he should at once order the hatchways and bulkheads to be closed and sealed; which having been done, he shall thereupon retire with his aids, unless unforeseen circumstances require that, for greater security and vigilance, said employés remain on board, in which case the captain of the vessel, at the request of the commander, shall consent to their remaining on board, and shall show them all the attention which Article 40 prescribes.

III. Immediately upon returning ashore, the commander of the custom house officials, or the person who has been acting for him, shall proceed to make a detailed report of all that may have occurred during the said visit, delivering the said report personally to the collector, together with the documents received from the captain of the vessel of (Model No. 12.)

IV. The documents required by this law having been delivered to the custom house, and being found in accordance with it, the discharge of the cargo will be permitted as soon as it is requested, according to the provisions of this chapter. If any document is missed, or any of the requisites have not been complied with, the collector will request the captain of the vessel, or its consignee, to appear at the office, for the purpose of informing him of the mistake or mistakes found, and the legal means by which they can be remedied or lessened, and the fines which this law imposes, proceeding in this matter according to the rules established by it.

V. If the vessel, during the voyage, should meet with accidents which caused diminution of the cargo expressed in the documents, as the throwing overboard or sale on account of having to put into any port, the captain will inform the boarding officer as soon as he visits the ship. The officer will immediately take copy from the log-book of these facts, which he will certify, requesting the passengers and crew, or, in their stead, three or five persons, to present themselves before the collector as soon as possible, to enable him to make the corresponding investigation.

In case it shall be necessary to sell the cargo at a port where the vessel has been obliged to put in, the captain will deliver to the custom house a certificate from the authorities of the port where the sale took place, making affidavit to that effect, and have it certified by the Mexican consul at that port, if there is one residing in it.

The directors will make a record of the investigation which he makes, examining separately the captain and each one of the passengers and crew designated. If, in his judgment, he thinks that, by the testimony and investigation, the accidents which took place were accounted, he will so declare it, informing the Treasury Department of his decision, and will proceed to discharge the vessel, without charging duties for the merchandise sold or thrown overboard; but, in case the collector thinks that the course taken by the captain is not proved to his satisfaction, judging by the documents or from any other cause, he will send all the information he has in the case to the District Court, for it to know and decide the case, placing, at the same time, the captain of the vessel at its disposition.

VI. In the cases mentioned in the two previous fractions, the collector of the custom house will allow the discharge of the cargo, provided the captain will give bond to assure the fiscal interests. In the same way the collector can allow the sailing of the vessel after the custom house officials have made their last visit, provided the case has not been submitted to the District Court, in which case he will not give the said permission without first receiving it from the said court.

VII. The collector shall remit to the auditor's office the document delivered by the captains, giving thereby a commencement of the proceedings contemplated by this law. The auditor's office shall enter in a book, to be provided for the purpose, all the details indicated in Model No. 13.

In case one book is not sufficient, owing to the increase of work at the custom house, there shall be two books kept, and the numeration shall be divided, giving one the even and the other the odd numbers.

Art. 71. The regular discharge of the vessels arriving at the ports will be made according to the following rules:

I. The captain or consignee of the vessel whose discharge is asked will petition the collector, according to the form indicated by Model No. 15, accompanying two copies of the general manifest in Spanish, and two copies, also in Spanish, of the samples on board.

Even when the copies mentioned in this fraction do not accompany the request, the collector should allow the immediate discharge of the packages containing inflammable materials, and, if he should think it convenient, he will allow, under the same circumstances, the discharge of the samples and goods which the vessel carries, but in this case the consignee will give bonds to procure the said copies in the time which the collector may think prudent, *which should never pass beyond the time actually necessary,* that the discharge of the vessel may not be retarded.

II. The collector, having received said copies, shall remit the same to the auditor for the purpose of having them compared with the original manifest and papers; if they appear to be in accord, he shall so certify over his signature, placing on each copy the number corresponding in proper order of the vessel.

The copies presented with corrections of *any kind* will be returned and replaced by new ones. Those found correct will be passed by the auditor to the collector, so that, at the time of giving his consent for the discharge of the vessel, he may order that they be sent to the commander of the guards and the warden of the warehouses, for the purposes indicated in the following fractions:

III. Immediately after the commander of the guards receives the permit referred to in the previous fraction, he will appoint, with the approval of the collector, one or more inspectors, as they may be needed, to go on board the vessel to be discharged, in union with the commander or the officer appointed in his stead, to open the hatches, to begin or continue the discharge; the inspector or inspectors will remain on board during the hours of the day required to perform said operation, and will certify, if correct, the tickets made and signed by the captains, of the goods sent ashore in the launches. (Model No. 6.)

If there should be any difference, they will so express it on the tickets. Having finished or suspended the discharge of the vessel, they will again seal the hatches, and return ashore with the officer who went on board to place the seals. In case the hatches cannot be sealed, or it is suspected that there are packages concealed outside of the hatches, or on account of any other circumstances, the collectors will order that one or more inspectors remain on board the ship until the discharge is completed, or until such a time as he deems proper, that they may guard against the landing of merchandise without the knowledge of the custom house.

IV. The tickets mentioned in the previous article will be numbered in order from one up, and with special numeration for each vessel. These tickets will be given the man in charge of the launch which carries the merchandise ashore, who will deliver them to the custom house officer in waiting at the wharf.

V. The officer commissioned, and the inspector or inspectors placed on the wharf to receive the merchandise, will compare them with the tickets, and, finding them arranged in quantities, marks and numbers, the first inspector will declare that they are in "accord," and will sign the ticket, and one of the others will declare, by signing the ticket, that "all has been complied with;" but in case it should not be correct, they will so declare it on the ticket, and inform the commander of the guards, who will immediately proceed to investigate the reasons why the ticket is not correct, and will inform the collector of the result of his investigation, that he may proceed as ordered for such cases.

VI. It shall be the duty of the commission, composed of one or more inspectors as circumstances may require, to inspect the marks, countermarks and the number of packages of unloaded merchandise, having present the copies of the general manifest and of the account of samples remitted by the collector to the commander. Said commission shall separate, and order to have placed apart according to consignees, such packages as contain inflammable substances, such as are declared to contain samples, and all such as the consignee may have obtained permission to keep out of the storehouses, as prescribed in the next article.

This commission has also the power to detain, for the time it deems necessary, before its dispatch or before all suspected packages are sent to the stores, those packages the importation of which this law prohibits, or for having greater weight than is declared, or on account of their not being on the manifest, or on account of any other circumstance requiring a thorough examination.

These proceedings having been terminated, said commission shall note at the foot of the copy of the manifest all matters worthy of mention, making a résumé of the packages containing inflammable substances, of those containing samples, of those which have not been sent to the store and of those which have been placed in the same.

ART. 72. When it would not be convenient for the interested parties to have the goods sent to the custom house stores on account of their quality, weight or bulk, the collector can permit their dispatch on the wharf, attending to it personally or by means of a commissioner, in union with an appraiser and commander of inspectors; but in no case will this be allowed with linen, cotton, wool, silk, fancy goods and other kinds of merchandise requiring a scrupulous and thorough examination.

ART. 73. When in the same shipment there are found packages having the same marks or numbers upon them, the said third commission of inspectors shall note the same on the copy of the manifest, notifying the collector immediately of the fact, to the end that he may take such steps as he may deem proper.

ART. 74. All inflammable or explosive materials which by themselves or by their contact with others, and those which are liable to corrode, whose detention in the stores might cause a fire or other damages, should always be kept out of the stores, and under the immediate vigilance of the collector, and in a place selected for that purpose by him.

The consignees of this class of merchandise, from the moment that the unloading of the vessel is solicited, are bound to present to the collector a declaration respecting them, setting forth the marks, countermarks and number of packages containing the same. (Model No. 15.) The consignee neglecting to comply with this provision shall be punished by a fine not less than fifty nor more than five hundred dollars.

ART. 75. The packages of samples mentioned in the corresponding statement may be unloaded immediately upon the first inspection of the vessel, and the collectors shall forthwith authorize the discharge of the same, if the parties interested should so desire. In regard to the packages of samples which come declared in the manifests, these shall, for the purposes of unloading and discharge, be considered in the same manner as any other merchandise.

ART. 76. When the inspectors on board, or on shore, or when the warden of the stores find any packages broken, with signs of having been opened, or with any other suspicious marks, they will immediately notify the collector, either verbally or by writing, who will order the package examined on the spot, in the presence of an appraiser, whom he will select, and of the interested party, and taking, without loss of time, the necessary steps to discover the fraud, if there should be any, and to cover the interests of the Treasury and the interested party.

If the interested party and the custom house should be satisfied with the contents of the package or packages opened, they will be closed so as to dispatch them in their turn.

ART. 77. When the captain of a vessel does not present his manifest according to article 29, the third commission of the guards at the discharge of the vessel will take the weight, numbers, marks, countermarks and classes of the packages, so that by this means the auditor may proceed to form the manifest.

For the compliance of the provisions of this article, the collector, on giving the permit for the discharge of the vessel, will state, by a note, that the vessel is without its general manifest.

ART. 78. The commander of inspectors is obliged to go on board of the vessel when they discharge, whenever it is necessary, to open, close and seal the hatches, watch and arrange the fiscal service.

The seals with which the above mentioned operations are made will be in charge of the collector, who will order them to be delivered to the commander whenever he needs them.

ART. 79. Having finished the discharge of the vessel, the commander of inspectors, with one or two persons of his staff, will go on board to make a thorough examination of the vessel, to see that all the merchandise that the vessel had for the custom house has really been discharged, and, in case there should be other merchandise on the ship which was not manifested, the custom house shall proceed in the same manner as with cases of contraband.

Of this examination he shall immediately advise the collector, reporting to him the result, and annexing the documents which were used in the discharge of the vessel (Model No. 16).

ART. 80. The discharge of the vessels will be made in order of entering, and in accordance with their respective dates, and the discharge will be made as soon as possible, and without interruption; the mail steamers, and all those which have fixed dates for sailing, will have the preference.

The collectors will have the right to allow or suspend the discharge of a ship whenever they think it necessary.

ART. 81. The discharge of vessels will not be made except by daylight, and never on days considered by law as holidays.

The collectors will so arrange the discharge of the vessels that by nightfall all packages taken from a ship will be in the places assigned them.

ART. 82. The collectors are empowered to order and concede, on special occasions, the discharge of a vessel by night and on holidays, whenever they think it indispensable, or when they are obliged to do so on account of some unforeseen event. Whenever these discharges are allowed at the request of the consignees of the ships, they will accompany the request with a petition of a majority of the consignees of the goods.

ART. 83. It is the duty of the commander of the guards to watch, in all cases, the discharge of the ship, with the officers of his staff, the route which the goods take until they are deposited at their proper place according to the rules previously established.

ART. 84. In places where peculiar circumstances oblige vessels to anchor outside of the bar, or at a long distance from the ports, the commander of the guards will leave on board, on visiting the ship, one or two inspectors as guards to watch it, the discharge being made according to the rules previously established.

ART. 85. In ports where a bar exists, and where the shallowness of the water will not permit the entrance of vessels without unloading part of the cargo, the custom house will observe the following rules:

I. As soon as a vessel is sighted coming toward the port, the commander of the guards will go to the bar, accompanied by two officers, so that as soon as the vessel anchors they may proceed to visit it. If the ship should not be able to cross the bar, the custom house officers will remain near by until she can do so with safety; but if the bar can be crossed without unloading part of the cargo, the commander will make his visit at the entrance of the channel, and proceed to discharge the vessel according to the rules established in this chapter.

II. When it is found impossible for a vessel to cross the bar without unloading part of the cargo so as to enter the port, the captain will ask permission to do so from the collector. The collector, being assured of the necessity of this operation, will permit it to be made, according to the rules mentioned in article 71 for the regular discharge of vessels, and only a sufficient part of the cargo will be discharged as will permit the vessel to reach the port with safety.

The commander of the guards, or the person acting in his stead, will witness the unloading of the cargo, closing and sealing the hatches in his presence as often as they are opened.

III. In cases when it would not be advisable to delay the unloading of part of the cargo without endangering the ship and the cargo, the discharge will be made at once, giving notice immediately to the collector that he may issue such orders as the urgency of the case may require, and, as well in these cases as in the ordinary ones, the captain of the vessel and the consignee shall subject themselves to the provisions relating to the arrival and discharge of vessels. In the same manner shall the merchandise taken from the vessels remain under the inspection of the employés of the custom house, and be subject to the formalities of discharge and storage.

ART. 86. The custody and vigilance of the ships anchored in the ports, or near them, especially when the ships are discharging, will be intrusted to the shore wardens and the water patrol.

The rounds, whenever the weather permits, should be made by day and night when it is necessary to watch vessels anchored at a distance from the ports.

ART. 87. The employés who will perform the duties of the collector, auditor, commander of the guards, and the man in charge of the custom house stores, will assume these responsibilities.

SECTION II.

DUTIES OF CONSIGNEES OF SHIPS AND MERCHANDISE.

ART. 88. The persons designated as consignees on the manifests of ships will be considered as such for vessels arriving at Mexican ports, or the persons whom the captain may name on his arrival at the port, and within the twenty-four hours allowed by this law. (See Art. 24.)

The choice of consignee made by the captains, within the time allowed by this law, will be delivered in writing and in duplicate to the collector of the Federal custom house. (See Model No. 17.)

ART. 89. Persons mentioned on the manifest of a ship as consignees of merchandise, will be regarded as such. It will, however, be considered as proof to the contrary should the consular invoice mention another person, and when that person presents the invoice which the remitter received from the consul.

In cases where the person named on the manifest, or consular invoice, as consignee is not known at the port, or the shipment comes *to order*, the custom house will permit the person presenting the consular invoice, duly certified, to act as consignee, and in that case will require the person presenting the invoice to declare, at the end of each copy of the invoice he presents, and that which the custom house has, that he takes charge of the merchandise mentioned in said invoice, and will be subject to the provisions of this law.

ART. 90. The consignees of the ships will be the only persons the custom house shall recognize as the legitimate representative of the captains, furnishing them the documents of the ship whenever it may be necessary, granting them whatever they ask in accordance with this law, and informing them of the fines which captains incur when they cannot appear when summoned.

The consignees of ships should sign all documents and copies of them in the name of the captains, being responsible by law for the mistakes made by their constituents, provided they cannot prove satisfactory their inculpableness.

ART. 91. The consignees of merchandise are the only persons whom the Federal custom houses, the Government, or any other authority, will permit to discuss subjects relating to custom house operations.

ART. 92. The duties on merchandise correspond directly to the Treasury, as well as the fines and pecuniary penalties incurred by their consignees, without their being able in any case to allege any law against this obligation.

ART. 93. Every act agreed to or signed by the consignees of vessels and merchandise will be final in its effect, as this law does not empower any authority to make any alterations in any act authorized or signed by them.

ART. 94. The collectors of the custom house will take care, under their responsibility, not to admit in any of the custom house operations any other person or signature except that of the consignee of the merchandise, unless the mentioned consignee gives the right to some other person, or at least gives him power, as attorney, to attend to all his custom house affairs, and in these cases the consignee will abide by all that his attorney may do, sign and approve, as long as he does not revoke the authority which he had conceded him, and make it known at the custom house.

SECTION III.

RENOUNCEMENT OF CONSIGNMENT.

ART. 95. The consignees of vessels have the right to renounce their consignments within forty-eight hours, counting from the moment the correspondence of the ship has been received on shore, and before asking the discharge of the vessel. The renouncement will be presented to the collector written, in duplicate, and expressing some cause. In case they do not renounce the consignment in the time indicated, or after having asked the discharge, the custom house will consider then as consignees, and will not admit the renouncement.

ART. 96. When the consignees of a ship have renounced the consignment in time, the custom house will notify the captain, so that he may, within a certain time allowed by the collector, name another consignee.

ART. 97. In case the captain does not name a consignee in the time allowed him, the collector will name one, who will take charge of all the work done, without being responsible for any mistakes committed before he took charge of the consignment, and for which the captains of vessels will be responsible, and they will not be allowed to sail from the port until they have paid all duties, fines and expenses which they may have incurred.

ART. 98. The consignees of merchandise have also the right to renounce their consignments, in the same time of forty-eight hours, counted from the moment the correspondence of the ship has been brought ashore. The renouncement will be made before the collector, in writing, accompanying the renouncement with the consular invoices and the postal receipts, if they have them.

ART. 99. When it is proved that the owner of the goods is a Mexican citizen, the collector will appoint a consignee chosen from the merchants of the port.

ART. 100. If no one accepts the consignment, and the goods are of such a kind as cannot be kept without loss or damage, the collector will immediately order them to be sold at public auction, according to the provisions in Chapter XVI, before they are dispatched.

ART. 101. When the goods are not of such a kind as in the case mentioned in the previous article, they will be deposited in the custom house stores, or the place selected for that purpose by the collector, for the time allowed by this law; the collector will make known what has occurred, both in this case as well as in the previous article, to the consul or functionary who certified the documents, and will order it published by the press, that it may in this way reach the interested parties.

The time fixed by law having expired, without any one appearing to claim said merchandise, so deposited, the custom house shall proceed to dispose of the same at public sale, reference being had to the provisions of Chapter XVI.

ART. 102. In cases where the consignee renouncing the consignment is only a commission merchant, and the custom house has positive information that the owner of the goods resides in the country, he will be the one recognized by the custom house for all the operations which this law requires, and he can, if he does not reside at the port, name a consignee to represent him at the custom house through which the importation is made, precisely according to the terms of this law.

ART. 103. When the collector of the custom house knows the shipper of the goods whose consignment is refused to be a foreigner, he will officially inform the consul or consular agent representing the nation of the shipper, in order that he may signify his intention whether he will receive the consignment or not within the term of three days. If he does not accept it, or should allow the time mentioned to pass without accepting it, the custom house will proceed in the same way as if the shipper were a Mexican. The collectors will proceed in the same way as provided in these articles when they do not know the nationality of the shipper, or when, in case it is known, there is no consul, vice-consul or consular agent representing the nation of the shipper at the port.

ART. 104. Consignees of goods, when they do not renounce a consignment within the time allowed by Article 98, will be considered as such by the collectors.

ART. 105. The term having expired during which it is permitted the consignees to renounce, and these having neglected to present, according to the provisions of Articles 123 and 124, their respective petitions asking for the dispatch of the merchandise, the collectors will proceed as mentioned in Articles 100 to 104 inclusive, but charging the person appearing as consignee the total amount of expenses and duties paid for the goods, and the fines which they may have incurred, excepting when the party interested shall conclusively prove that he has had no knowledge of the consignment.

SECTION IV.

RULES FOR THE ADDITION AND RECTIFICATIONS OF THE MANIFESTS AND CONSULAR INVOICES.

ART. 106. The consignees of vessels have the power to add to or rectify their manifests and statements of samples within forty-eight hours, counted from the time when the custom house officers made their visit to the ship bringing the goods. This time will be limited to two hours after the whole of the cargo of the ship has been landed on shore, when the discharge is made before the forty-eight hours have passed, for which purpose the time will be mentioned on the ticket when the discharge is completed.

ART. 107. The additions and rectifications spoken of in the previous article will be certified by the collectors, according to the following dispositions:

I. The increase will be admitted by the collectors, without imposing fines, providing it is proposed to add to or rectify the manifests in some part which will not increase or diminish the number of packages indicated by the manifest.

II. These shall also be exempt from fine. The addition or omission of packages is included when they have been mixed up with those of other shipments in the transfers, or in the loading or unloading of vessels, if such a case can be completely proved to the satisfaction of the collectors. In case there should not be sufficient proof, the Government alone, previously informed by the collectors, shall or shall not admit the increase, the packages in the meantime being detained by the custom house.

III. When, at the time of discharging, there appear more packages than are mentioned in the manifest, which, however, are covered by their respective consular invoices, the collectors shall permit these to be added, imposing upon the captain a fine of from one to twenty-five dollars for each of said additional packages.

IV. When packages in excess of the proper number do not come under the provisions of the two preceding sections, the captains shall pay a fine of from five to fifty dollars for each package not included in the manifest, and, in addition thereto, the duties to be paid upon the merchandise in said packages contained shall be doubled. Except as provided in Section II, the corrections in the manifest of one or more packages shall be permitted only in case the consignee of the goods prove by the certificate of the proper consul, placed at the foot of the invoices, that such and such packages appearing in the manifest of the vessel were not shipped, but, in such a case the party interested shall not be permitted to renounce the consignment of the remaining goods covered by said invoices.

ART. 108. In cases of jetson, sale on account of having been forced to enter a port, or on account of other superior force, the same can be rectified on the manifest; but they shall proceed as provided in this law in such circumstances.

ART. 109. The consignee of goods have the right to increase or rectify their consular invoices within ninety-six hours, counted from the moment the custom house admits the ship bringing the goods. The time is limited to the moment the consignee presents the application for the discharge, if he makes it, as the law requires, before the ninety-six hours.

ART. 110. Consignees of merchandise have the further privilege of examining the class or quality of the goods before presenting the corrections, subject, however, to the following conditions:

I. They will present an application in triplicate to the collector of the custom house, indicating the class of package or packages which they wish examined, their marks, countermarks, numbers, name of the ship bringing them, the reason for making the application, the fact that they have been consigned to them, and presenting for examination the consular invoice.

II. The examination shall extend no further than to one of those containing the doubtful goods.

III. For this examination the collectors shall appoint an appraiser to witness it, in connection with the warden of the warehouses, if the goods have been stored, or of a commander of the guards, if the examination is made before their storage, the consignee of the goods, the collector or a person representing him. These employés shall only witness the examination, and in no case, or for any reason, shall they give their opinion, even when consulted by the interested parties.

IV. The examination being made, the packages shall be carefully closed and tied with wire, on the ends of which there shall be a seal of lead placed in the presence of the interested party, to avoid the stealing or changing of the goods.

V. All expenses incurred by the examination shall be for account of the interested parties, and the workmen employed in the examination should be those in whom the collector has entire confidence.

ART. 111. The additions and corrections made by the consignees of merchandise on their consular invoices shall be admitted without the imposition of a fine by the collector, in all cases when the following data is not involved:

1. When the amount of merchandise declared in the invoices is diminished, the import duties suffering a diminution at the same time, the liquidation shall be made on the basis fixed by the consular invoice.

II. When the amount of merchandise declared in the invoices is augmented, increasing thereby the import duties, the goods thus corrected shall pay an additional duty of ten per centum.

III. Should the length, width, weight, number of pieces or thousands be wanting when the goods pay duty according to such data, the duty to be charged upon the same, when a correction has been made, shall be increased by fifteen per centum.

IV. When the kind or nature of the goods declared in the invoices is entirely changed, the corrected articles shall be charged additional duties to the extent of twenty per centum.

V. When the name, kind or class of the goods does not appear, or when the manifests are vague and ambiguous, as for instance, *Merchandise, Goods, Cottons, Linens, Wools, Silks, Parisian Articles, Groceries, Fancy Goods, Drugs, Cloths*, etc., the duties on the corrected goods shall be liquidated, adding thereto twenty-five per centum.

VI. When in the consular invoices the declaration of any merchandise is entirely omitted, it may nevertheless be added, the duties being increased fifty per centum.

VII. The correction mentioned in the preceding section having been admitted, if it should appear that the goods to which reference has been had come hidden so that they might pass without being noticed at the time of discharging, said corrections shall be null and void, and the goods referred to shall be subject to the payment of double duties.

ART. 112. Consignees of goods who do not take advantage of the privileges granted to them by Section I, of the preceding article, shall be fined no less than one dollar, nor more than twenty-five, for each error appearing in the invoices.

ART. 113. The term fixed by Art. 109 having expired, if the consignees of the goods have not corrected or made proper additions to their invoices in the manner referred to by Sections II, III, IV, V and VI of Art. 111, there shall be imposed upon the merchandise improperly declared the fine of double duties.

ART. 114. The additions made by the consignees of ships, as well as those of merchandise, shall be made in writing, quadruplicate, without abbreviations, defects, corrections or erasures; they shall be written in a plain hand, that there may be no doubts, and shall have horizontal lines from the end of each paragraph written on the margin. In case they do not have all the points mentioned, the custom house shall not receive them, but request that they be made over again, with the corresponding corrections.

ART. 115. The collector or, in his stead, the auditor shall personally receive the additions, having the date and hour of their presentation placed on them immediately, and in the presence of the persons presenting them, when he shall sign each leaf of the copy. The collectors, in accord with the auditors, shall make, on the same day of their presentation, and before the closing of the office, the corresponding classification of the admission or rejection, having previously compared the four copies, and making the interested parties compare them as well, when they do not agree, and keeping always, as original, the copy which has the corresponding stamp, which shall be of twenty-five cents.

ART. 116. The act of presenting the dispatch papers shall entirely close the time for making additions; consequently, when the merchant should present his petition, the additions shall be classified immediately, if he has done so, and before the comparison of the application for dispatch.

ART. 117. The consignee cannot modify in any way the elucidation or addition which he has made, except in case an error has been committed in the addition, evident without doubt, in which case he can correct it within the time allowed by this law for additions, and the Treasury Department shall decide as it thinks convenient.

ART. 118. The consignees of merchandise can, when they are not satisfied with the classifications which the collectors may make of their additions or elucidations, apply to the Treasury Department, that it may decide as it thinks best, provided it is done immediately, with the understanding that if the consignees do not present to the collector their protest within the twenty-four hours after its making, they shall be considered as satisfied.

ART. 119. In case the collectors reserve the classification of the additions or elucidations for the Treasury Department, they shall consult it immediately, and they cannot order the dispatch of the merchandise except when, calculating the maximum of the duties and fines that may result from the decision of the government, the consignees shall agree to make the corresponding payment without losing their rights to the return of the excess. These requisites shall be required to order the dispatch of the goods, in case the consignees apply to the Treasury Department on account of inconformity in the classification of their additions.

ART. 120. The four copies of the additions, duly compared and certified as provided by this law, shall be distributed as follows: The collector shall immediately deliver the copy with the stamps, another without stamps, to the auditor's office, to be compared with the petition for dispatch and with the account remitted to the general treasury, and the copy of which is retained at the custom house; another copy will be sent, certified, through the postoffice the same day, and by the first mail, to the Treasury Department, and the fourth copy shall be kept for the purpose of reference with the corresponding applications for dispatch.

CHAPTER IV.

Dispatch of Foreign Goods, Analogy, Decision of Experts, Samples, Passengers' Baggage and Damage of Merchandise.

SECTION 1.

DISPATCH OF FOREIGN MERCHANDISE.

ART. 121. The dispatch of samples and foreign merchandise for consumption shall be made according to the dispositions in the present chapter.

ART. 122. The consignees shall present in triplicate a petition for the dispatch of their samples, which they can do as soon as these are brought on shore, subject to all the provisions contained in Section IV of this chapter.

ART. 123. The consignees of foreign merchandise, in the case mentioned in Article 72, are obliged to present their applications for the dispatch of the merchandise the moment the ship bringing them begins to discharge; the collectors are authorized to store the goods and collect the storage from the interested parties imposed by Article 303, when the said applications are not presented before the conclusion of the discharge of the ship that brought the merchandise.

ART. 124. The consignees of foreign merchandise, not referred to in the previous article, are obliged to present to the collectors the application for dispatch of their merchandise precisely within the fifteen days after or before the discharge of the ship bringing them, as otherwise storage shall be charged them according to the rate specified in Article 303, and, if necessary, the collector shall proceed as the case may require, according to the provisions of Fractions I and II of Article 443 of this law.

ART. 125. These applications by which the merchandise shall be delivered to the consignees shall be presented in quadruplicate, all of which shall be alike without abbreviations, mistakes, corrections or erasures; should be written in a plain hand that there may be no doubts, each horizontal line to be written from the end of the last paragraph to the termination of the line, in such a way as to leave no space for later corrections. Each permit shall have sufficient space on the margin for the use of the custom house. In cases where they do not contain all that is required the custom house should not accept them, but should see that they are replaced by others having the requisite degree of clearness.

The consignee shall see that his application sets forth whether the delivery of the goods shall be made subject to the giving of a bond properly executed and to the satisfaction of the collector, or whether the duties shall be paid down in cash, before the delivery of the goods. (See Model No. 18.)

ART. 126. The applications shall have the stamps required by law, excepting that of the paper used by the custom house.

ART. 127. The applications for discharge shall contain the same information exacted for consular invoices (Art. 43 and its fractions.)

ART. 128. The consignees shall present with their applications the consular invoices duly certified according to the articles for the formation of consular invoices contained in this law, and besides, an account in duplicate, signed by them, containing the number of the packages, their marks and countermarks and the total number of packages mentioned in their applications. (Model No. 19.)

ART. 129. The consignees of foreign merchandise are obliged to make separate applications for the packages they wish dispatched outside the warehouse, according to the facilities conceded them by Article 72.

ART. 130. The collectors having received the applications for discharge shall pass them to the auditor's office, to be there compared with the manifest and invoices, corrected by the additions or corrections which the consignee may have made. If the application differs in any part from the corrected consular invoices, the auditor's office shall be careful to mention it in the column for observations. (Model 18.) In the corresponding place it shall mention the mistakes which the invoice contains, in case this latter has not been corrected or added to.

ART. 131. The auditor's office, having found the four copies of the application to be alike, and according to the manifest and consular invoices, shall certify them according to the following rules:

I. To place on each copy the number in order corresponding to the application and seal of the auditor's office, and recording in a book, which it shall have for that purpose, the number of the application, the register of the vessel, the name of the consignee, name of the ship, its class, nationality and the date of entering.

The numeration of the petitions shall be consecutive, beginning each year with the first document dispatched in the month of July.

In case one book shall not be sufficient, owing to the great amount of work at the custom house, there shall be two books, dividing the numbers into even and odd.

II. When an application is composed of several leaves the employé making the comparison shall arrange them in pages, placing on each one of the corresponding number his signature and the seal of the office.

III. Each copy of the application shall also have the signature of the employé that made the comparison, giving it its corresponding number, the number of pages it consists of, and if any of the documents required were missing the auditor shall declare them correct, if so, and manifesting whether or not the duties are secured by bond, or if the payment of the duties is to be made before the delivery of the goods.

The deposition mentioned in Article 132 should be signed by the employé who made the comparison with the application, declaring it to be correct, and the auditor's Vo Bo (=O. K.) "all right," with the seal of the office.

ART. 132. The documents for dispatch having been certified by the auditor's office, according to the form indicated, they shall be passed to the collector, who shall say at the end, "Allow the dispatch with the intervention of Appraiser C——"

Three of the applications should be sent with the corresponding deposition to the appraiser designated, and the other copy of the application be kept for the purpose of being sent to the Treasury Department. The separate copies of the applications to be sent to the Treasury Department shall be sent by the collectors through the postoffices, certified, *the same day that they have been certified by the auditor's office.*

ART. 133. Before the appraisers begin the examination of the goods they shall inform the collector that he may give them whatever special instructions he may have, and they should not commence the dispatch without his consent and without the presence of the interested parties or their legal representatives. (See Art. 94.)

ART. 134. Merchandise in the warehouses of the custom house shall not be delivered by the warehousemen until they receive from the appraiser who made the dispatch, the deposition referred to in Art. 128, giving notice to the appraiser when the goods have been delivered, and to get from the consignee of the goods the corresponding receipt at the end of the deposition when the appraiser has ordered the delivery. The operations mentioned in this article serve as vouchers to the warehousemen, and other employés of the custom house charged with the delivery of the goods.

When goods are dispatched outside of the warehouses, the deposition mentioned shall be given the employé watching the goods remaining outside, that he may perform the same operations as the warehousemen, and the aforesaid deposition shall have the "correct" of the appraiser of dispatch to permit the removal of packages from the place where the dispatch is made, and the signature of the party receiving it.

These operations shall serve those to whom they correspond, to prove that the packages that were not stored were received by the interested parties.

ART. 135. The examinations made by the appraisers shall be in accordance with the following rules:

I. They shall compare with the application, as a preliminary examination, the quality, class, weight of the packages, their marks and outside appearances, and particularly if the provisions of Articles 45 and 46 of this law have been complied with.

The examination of the gross weight shall be made whenever the goods are quoted by gross weight, and besides in cases in which, even when these circumstances do not exist, the appraiser deems it convenient.

II. They shall examine the net weights of the merchandise which pays the net weight, the number of pieces of goods quoted by the piece, pair, length, width, etc., attending particularly to the classification, when any of these items make a difference in the rates.

III. To rectify or add to the applications for dispatch, annotating and making clear on them all items incorrectly or ambiguously manifested, expressing also the packages examined and the date when the dispatch was made.

When goods have not been declared they shall be examined together, every package containing them being opened, so that the appraiser may give in the application all information required to justify the quotations and make practicable the adjudication of the duties.

The corrections or additions made by the appraisers shall be written in ink on the principal copy of the three remitted to him by the custom house, and immediately after each examination, writing the date of dispatch immediately after. (See Art. 143.)

ART. 136. The number of packages that the appraiser shall order to be opened for inspection, even when the subjects of examination are free goods, or are among those enumerated in Article 11, Fractions I, II and III, shall be at least ten per cent. of each lot specified in the application.

If the employés have a suspicion that there is intention to defraud, they can extend the examination to the other packages, with the permission of the collector, and even all the packages embraced in the application.

ART. 137. As the appraiser finishes the examination of the merchandise which he is dispatching, he shall have the packages which have been examined marked by the employé named by the collector for that purpose.

ART. 138. If, for any reason, it is not possible to examine at once all the packages mentioned in an application, the appraiser shall order the packages examined to be delivered to the interested parties, stating on the margin of the application, opposite the corresponding lot, the number of packages which have been delivered; and he shall make a declaration, which he shall sign, giving the date on which the packages were delivered, and the reason for the suspension of the dispatch.

ART. 139. The appraisers are empowered to divide, with the consent of the collector, a dispatch of merchandise into several lots, when so required by the nature of the examination they are making, or the quantity of the packages embraced in one application, or for any other important reason which required the division indicated.

ART. 140. The wardens of the warehouses, and other employés acting in that capacity, are obliged to receive from the collectors and appraisers the merchandise which they indicate at the time of the dispatch, annotating the corresponding relations, and receiving from the interested parties their approval in writing when goods are re-stored after having been brought out for dispatch.

ART. 141. The examination of the merchandise must be done publicly, and all persons who wish can be present.

ART. 142. Any difference of opinion that may occur in the examination between the appraiser and the interested party shall be decided immediately by the collector, or the person acting in his stead.

ART. 143. The dispatch having been made of all the goods on one application, the appraiser who made it shall proceed, when he has time, to place on the three copies of the application the notes and corresponding rates, making an extract of the principal copy, if he thinks it convenient, in the book which each appraiser shall have for that purpose.

This extract or copy, as well as the three copies aforesaid, shall be dated and signed by the appraiser, who shall declare them to be "in accord," if so, in the corresponding space for observations, so that said copy shall be exactly like the original.

The operations treated in this article should be concluded within three days following the dispatch of the goods, and, once terminated, the appraisers are obliged to deliver to the collectors the applications annotated, with the quotation of the goods, and already copied in his book, or to present in their stead a justifiable excuse for not presenting them.

ART. 144. All notes relating to ratifications, doubts, etc., which the appraiser may note on the applications, they shall make a separate report of in triplicate, which they shall send to the collectors together with the respective applications. In said reports, and signed by the interested parties, they shall signify their conformity with those observations or give the reasons why they are not satisfied.

ART. 145. Of the three copies of the applications delivered by the appraisers to the collectors, two shall be sent to the auditor's office that the operations of adjudication and collection of duties may be proceeded with, the third copy being reserved for that provided in Article 120 relating to the fourth copy.

ART. 146. Respecting the reports mentioned in Article 144 the collectors shall proceed, within the seventy-two hours after receiving them, according to the rules specified in rules XIV and XV of this law.

ART. 147. Only at the time, and in consequence of the dispatch of the goods on which they are giving rates or are examining, shall the collectors, or the persons acting in their stead, as well as the appraisers, be allowed to express their official opinion about the class, quality or any other particular relating to the packages which they are examining. Outside of this case, all the employés of the custom house are prohibited from giving their opinion to the interested parties about any circumstance that takes place.

ART. 148. The collectors, or the persons commissioned by them, have a right to witness the dispatch of merchandise made by the appraisers, and to make them comply with the provisions which may concern them.

ART. 149. The collectors, or the persons who may represent them, should have before them, when they witness the examination of merchandise, one of the copies of the application for dispatch, making the observations which they may deem convenient. The collectors can have re-examined some or all of the packages that have been examined, and order the examination, as soon as the appraiser finishes, of those packages which he did not think necessary to examine. This right of the collectors shall be exercised before the interested party and the appraiser making the dispatch for some cause existing before the classification and delivery of the goods.

ART. 150. The appraisers shall not give their consent for the delivery of the goods to the interested parties, not even under their personal responsibility, if the application for dispatch does not have at the end the note assuming the payment of the duties on the goods; and, in case this has been paid before their delivery, they shall only give the order for delivery when the consignee presents the receipt of the cashier declaring that he has received the amount of the duties authorized by the collector and auditor.

ART. 151. Merchandise not included in the nomenclature of the present tariff, or in the annexed vocabulary, will pay the rate assigned those which they resemble, subject to the provisions of the following chapter.

ART. 152. The appraiser to make the adjudication of the duties caused by the merchandise, shall do so in accordance with the following rules:

I. In order to fix the duties on goods quoted by gross weight, the weight of woolen, clay, glass or other kind of box or wrapping in which the same are contained shall be included; but the weight of these latter shall not be included when the goods are quoted by net weight or measure.

II. Packings not mentioned in the previous fractions are subject to the payment of the duties assigned to them, according to its class and material, when the payments of the duties is by net weight or measure.

In cases where the merchandise pays by gross weight the greatest duty shall be applied between that assigned the packing and the merchandise, even when this latter is free.

III. The inside coverings of goods and articles of cotton, linen, wool and silk shall be exempt from the payment of duties, provided they do not exceed ten square metres and that in the tariff their class is quoted up to 13 cents per square metre. When its texture has a high rate assigned, or if it exceeds the ten square metres, they shall pay duty as provided by the law without even discounting the ten metres that this fraction allows.

IV. Any difference in excess in the length, width, weight or number of things between that declared and that examined, even when it is insignificant, they shall inform the collectors in writing that these may proceed as the law determines.

SECTION II.

DISPATCH OF GOODS BY ANALOGY.

ART. 153. The assimilation or establishment of rates by analogy shall be made use of whenever there is merchandise not considered in this tariff or in the annexed vocabulary, and in this case the custom house shall fix the rate according to that ordered in Article 154 to 161 inclusive, and the Executive, through the Treasury Department, shall establish the final rate, observing the provisions herein mentioned.

ART. 154. The assimilation shall be made according to the following rules:

I. The appraiser who finds merchandise not quoted in the tariff, shall proceed to give it a rate by analogy, taking into consideration especially the material, the use, the properties, and other circumstances which show its similarity or analogy to some of the goods quoted in the tariff, hearing the opinion and observation of the consignee of the merchandise, and immediately informing the collector, that he may examine the case.

II. The collector will examine the merchandise in question, and if he is of the opinion that it is a case of assimilation, and if he agrees with the appraiser and importer, the merchandise shall be dispatched, applying to it the similar rates corresponding to it.

III. If the interested party should not be satisfied with the assimilation made by the appraiser, the collector shall consult other appraisers, and in places where there are but one, that of the auditor, and if he thinks convenient he can consult with one or two experts on such material, either merchants or any other persons of the place, afterwards giving his opinion, without being obliged to follow that of the majority; but he must always bear in mind the allegations made by the appraiser making the dispatch and the importer.

IV. In cases requiring it, the collector can take twenty-four hours to decide to which fraction of the tariff the merchandise in question corresponds. It being decided which is the fraction of the tariff corresponding to the goods in question, he shall notify the consignee of the merchandise and the appraiser making the dispatch, and if one of them is not satisfied, he shall inform them of their obligation to select an expert to decide according to Article 159, making known in this act all the incidents that may occur; and of all the steps taken in cases of assimilation there shall be a record made, in which shall be stated the opinions and propositions of those who have taken part in the classification, and in these cases the custom house cannot deliver the merchandise, not even when the consignee offers to pay the duties, until the Treasury Department decides which rate the merchandise shall pay.

V. In all cases of assimilation there shall be a record made in triplicate, stating the opinions of those taking part in it.

VI. Even when there have been goods of one kind dispatched in a custom house by assimilation, he shall not be relieved from proceedings in other cases of the importation of the same kind of goods in the proper manner established for determining the similarity, but giving as a rate the same one agreed on the first case of assimilation of the same kind of goods. The proceedings shall be continued until the government, by virtue of its powers, declares by decree the final rate agreed upon.

ART. 155. From the merchandise quoted by assimilation the appraiser shall take three samples, so as to send one of them to the Treasury Department, and the other two to be kept at the custom house in charge of the empleyó designated for that purpose by the collector.

The samples shall remain packed and sealed in the presence of the interested party, who shall place on them his private seal and signature.

The custom house shall send to the Treasury Department one of the samples, with a special communication, a copy of the corresponding record, and any further information needed to form an exact judgment of the merchandise.

ART. 156. In case the sample sent to the Treasury Department is lost, the custom house shall send another with duplicate communication and copy of the corresponding documents.

ART. 157. When, owing to the cost, the size, or other circumstances of the goods in question, it is not possible or easy to separate the samples previously treated of, it shall be so stated in the communication, and the collector shall order a minute description of it to be sent with the decree, even drawings, if it is considered indispensable, that a proper judgment of the merchandise may be made.

ART. 158. When the consignee of goods assimilated, from which there can be no samples taken, asks that it be remitted to the capital of the Republic, he can be entirely relieved from furnishing the samples, provided always that the remission is made for his account and exclusive risk, and by the custom house, which shall keep sufficient information to know the class and quality of the goods quoted.

For the provisions of this article the collector shall order that at the time of the dispatch of the merchandise the packages containing all or part of the goods assimilated to be sent to the Treasury Department be closed, arranged, and sealed, and in this state placed in the warehouses until they are sent to the said department.

ART. 159. It is the duty of the consignees of goods quoted by assimilation, in case they are not satisfied with the decision of the collector, to name an expert at the capital, subject to the provisions of Art. 163 of this chapter, who may represent them at the Treasury Department, to illustrate the case when the rate is to be placed on the goods by analogy.

The appointments, to be of use, should be mentioned on the records of the proceedings made on the assimilation, or they should be presented in writing to the collectors within the twenty-four hours conceded by Art. 154, Fraction IV, that within the following twenty-four hours the documents relating to the doubts or controversy may be remitted to the Treasury Department.

The appointments made after the expiration of the time shall not be accepted by the collectors.

ART. 160. Samples of commercial value which have served for the purpose of classifying and quoting the class or quality of doubtful or disputed merchandise shall be kept at the custom house, and shall be delivered to the interested parties, or to the persons whom these may authorize to receive them, as soon as the Treasury Department has settled the doubt or question of which they served.

The documents and samples which the custom houses send to the Treasury Department, referring to the assimilation of goods, doubts and controversies occurring in the examinations, should be sent registered through the postoffice of the place, and when it is impossible to do so they shall send the samples by the safest way.

These samples of value not claimed by their owners during the six months following the decision of the Treasury Department shall be considered as abandoned merchandise, and the custom houses shall proceed in consequence to sell them, according to the rules established in Art. 443, Fraction IV, of this law. In case the Treasury Department or the custom house, with its approval, thinks necessary to keep the samples that have a commercial value, they can do so by paying the interested party their value.

ART. 161. The employé of the custom house who has charge of the samples treated of in the previous article, shall keep a record of them, in which shall be stated the date they were received from the appraiser, the name and description of the object, its value, and all the information required by Model 20.

ART. 162. Every year, before the month of July, the Treasury Department shall request the municipality of the City of Mexico to furnish a list of one hundred persons to be selected from the merchants, brokers, agriculturists, artizans, professors of arts and sciences, artists and mechanics resident at the capital, capable of being experts in their respective branches; and the Treasury Department shall print and circulate this list sufficiently, so that by the 1st of July there shall be in each maritime custom house through which foreign goods are legally imported, copies of it, which shall contain, besides the names of the persons designated as experts, their professions or occupations, and their residences.

The Secretary of the Treasury shall signify the number of persons of each occupation or profession which the municipality is to appoint, and who shall serve for the term of one year with the privilege of being re-elected.

ART. 163. Only one person mentioned on this list can serve as legal expert on the case of assimilation treated on in this chapter, as well as the judgment of experts mentioned in the following, and the employés of the custom house as well as the consignees of goods are at liberty to select from this list the experts they may desire.

Every three months the municipality shall of their own accord, or at the request of the Treasury Department, replace with others, on the previously mentioned list, those persons who, by resignation, death, or prolonged absence from the city are unable to serve as experts.

ART. 164. As soon as the Treasury Department receives the docket relating to the assimilation mentioned in the previous article it shall give it in charge of one of the expert appraisers connected with the department, that he may proceed to study it along with experts designated by the respective custom house and by the consignee of the merchandise in question.

ART. 165. In the report which these experts make to the Treasury Department they shall give all their opinions, whether they agree or not, with their reasons for the same.

The experts shall present their report within five days, and the Secretary of the Treasury is the only person who can extend the time, whenever it is necessary for some good reason.

ART. 166. The Secretary of the Treasury shall definitely decide the rate corresponding to the goods, whether his opinion be in conformity with that of the experts or contrary thereto; but if the opinion of the secretary does not agree with that of the experts, or if the opinions of the experts disagree, the department shall have a consultation with the other experts assigned as appraisers, and even with other competent persons who shall have only an informal vote.

ART. 167. The Secretary of the Treasury can, in no case, establish a new rate, but shall assimilate the merchandise to some other item of tariff without increasing or diminishing the existing rate.

ART. 168. The Secretary of the Treasury can declare that the case treated is not one of assimilation, as the goods are quoted in the item of the tariff which especially mentions it. In this case the decision of the department governs all subsequent cases that may occur, without causing any innovation respecting the adjustment of the duties made by assimilation in the custom house in accordance with the corresponding provisions of this law.

ART. 169. The Treasury Department shall decide, as soon as possible, all the doubts on comparison with the corresponding decrees of fixed rates, and when it gives its decision the dispatch of the merchandise shall not be suspended, proceeding always in accordance with the provisions of this chapter.

SECTION III.

JUDGMENT OF EXPERTS.

ART. 170. In the doubts and controversies which may arise over the dispatch of the merchandise, between the appraiser and consignee as to the class of some merchandise which is included in the tariff, the collector shall be called, if he is not present to proceed immediately according to the proceedings herein expressed:

I. The collector shall try to get the consignee and the appraiser to agree, if he thinks the opinion of the latter is just; otherwise he shall order him to make the dispatch in accordance with the opinion of the consignee, without disregarding that expressed in the following item.

II. In case the consignee is not in accord with the opinion of the appraiser, confirmed by the collector, or that the appraiser insists upon his opinion contrary to that of the collector and consignee, there shall be samples of the merchandise taken in the same manner as provided for the assimilation of goods in Articles 155 to 160 inclusive, complying exactly with what is expressed in them.

III. In case the consignee of the goods at the port and the appraiser making the dispatch disagree, there shall be a record of the proceedings made, in triplicate, in which shall be expressed the opinions and propositions of the appraiser and consignee, as well as the decision of the collector. The collector shall notify the consignee of his obligation to name three experts at the capital, according to Articles 162 and 163. The appraiser making the dispatch shall also be notified.

IV. Of the experts named, the seconds and thirds shall act successively and respectively in the cases of absence, sickness, impediment, or excuse of the first or of the seconds.

In case that the three experts named by the appraiser or by the consignee do not accept the appointment, due notice shall be given to the custom house, that it may notify the interested parties so that they may name other experts.

V. As soon as the docket relating to the controversy between the consignee and the appraiser of the custom house is made up, and has been submitted to the Treasury Department for approval, the two experts aforesaid shall, before proceeding to exercise their functions as said experts, unite in naming a third expert who shall act as referee, and in that capacity decide all cases. If they, the aforesaid experts, do not agree upon the said appointment of a third expert, then the Treasury Department shall appoint. At all events a third person shall be appointed before proceeding with the case.

VI. In all cases in dispute, the expert appraiser, as representative of the Treasury Department, can give, if so requested by the experts named by the appraiser of the custom house and the consignee, an opinion respecting the class and quality of the merchandise in question, but he cannot take part in the discussion on the subject, if not requested.

VII. If the experts named by the appraiser and the consignee, after having examined the docket and the samples shown them, agree upon a decision, it shall be regarded as final, and the department shall inform the interested parties. If, on the contrary, the experts differ, their opinions shall be passed, together with the docket and the samples, to the referee, so that in view of what has taken place he may give his decision, which shall be the final resolution of the case.

VIII. If, from the examination made by the experts of the merchandise in question, it shall appear that there was no reason for such proceedings, and that it is a case similar to those mentioned in Article 378 of this Ordinance, the Treasury Department shall instruct the respective custom house to immediately inform the consignee of the result of the investigation, and he shall apply the fines according to Article 388, and besides he shall make him pay the expenses of the experts who took part in the investigation.

From the decision given by the experts in accord, or by the referee, there can be no further appeal. These decisions shall be published in the " *Diario Oficial*," (*Official Organ.*)

IX. The experts appointed and the acting referee shall receive compensation for their work, which shall be paid, in all cases, by the Government, except when the final decision of the experts may be contrary to the consignee of the merchandise, when he will pay all the expenses which may have been incurred.

In cases where the opinion of the appraiter is found to be indiscreet or capricious, the Government shall be reimbursed for the expenses incurred, making the Treasury Department collect them from the appraiser, and, if the collector approves the capricious opinion of the appraiser, the expenses shall be charged to both of them, besides the penalty or fine which the Treasury Department may impose on them.

X. The decision made by experts, according to the previous rules, shall only serve to determine the case treated of, without being considered as precedents for subsequent cases.

SECTION IV.

SAMPLES.

ART. 171. All small parts of merchandise, or the whole of the merchandise intended to be introduced, shall be considered as samples, and the permits for such shall be granted for their unloading and dispatch, even when they have a commercial value, if they come under the conditions provided for them. (Art. 71, fraction 1, paragraph 2.)

ART. 172. Several objects of one class shall not be considered as samples when they come together, and in such a manner as to show that they are intended for sale or presents.

ART. 173. The samples shall pay the same import duty as the merchandise which they represent, and they shall be charged according to the corresponding fixed rates.

ART. 174. When cases of samples of fancy goods or hardware arrive containing articles subject to different rates, and the weight of each class cannot be determined, the whole shall pay according to the highest rate corresponding to the articles contained in the sample case.

ART. 175. Samples of linens, textures and other goods coming in small lots, either separate or on paste-boards, and which are readily seen to have no commercial value, but that they are for the purpose of describing the class of the merchandise, shall be admitted as samples without value and free of duty.

ART. 176. When remnants of pieces of more than twenty centimeters in length or width, or handkerchiefs or extra-sized handkerchiefs, shirts, or any other entire object come as samples, they shall pay the corresponding duties, or they shall be branded so as to lose their commercial value and still retain their condition as samples.

ART. 177. If an importer has an interest in preserving for re-exportation the samples in question, they shall be admitted without the payment of duties, provided the custom house can identify them at their re-exportation, and, in such a case, the collector shall require a bond for double the duties to which the goods may be liable, fixing a time up to six months within which the samples shall be re-exported. If, during the time granted, the interested party desires to pay the corresponding duties, he shall pay the same as if they had been paid at the time of entering; but, if the samples are not re-exported within the time mentioned, or the duties paid on them, the bond shall become liable for double the duties.

SECTION V.

PASSENGERS AND THEIR BAGGAGE.

ART. 178. Passengers are obliged to present their baggage to the employé of the custom house charged with their examination, and if they bring any goods which are liable to duty they shall inform the officer in writing, giving all necessary details, so that he can fix the rate of duty on them.

ART. 179. I. The baggage of a passenger, for which duty should not be charged, includes his clothing, if it is not excessive in quantity, and the qualification is left for the discretion of the collector, according to the means of the passenger.

II. The articles which passengers have upon them, or for their use, such as watches, chains, buttons, canes, etc., one or two braces of fire-arms, equipments, and up to 100 charges, are allowed duty free.

III. If the passengers are professors or artizans they can bring books, instruments or tools most essential or indispensable in the exercise of their profession or calling.

IV. Besides the exemption referred to in the previous fraction the collector can allow each adult passenger the free introduction of ninety-nine cigars, forty packages of cigarettes, and one-half kilogramme of snuff or chewing tobacco.

ART. 180. If the passengers are artists or any opera company, dramatic, comedy, circus, etc., besides the exceptions conceded in general in the previous articles, it is permitted them to introduce free of duty their properties and scenic adornments, under the condition that they shall be re-exported within a year, and under the following conditions:

I. The manager or representative of the company shall present to the custom house a detailed declaration of the dresses, ornaments, etc., which they may bring, and also expressing in the declaration the special marks or signs which each article may have.

II. The custom house shall proceed to examine and appraise the properties according to the tariff of this Ordinance, exacting from the representative a bond for the total amount of the duties on the properties.

III. In case the manager of the company declares that the exportation of the properties shall take place by another custom house, the collector will inform the custom house selected by the manager for the export, and remit to it immediately a certified copy of the entry, so that the merchandise may be compared on their exportation.

IV. If the exportation of the merchandise is made by the same custom house where they were entered, there shall be a close examination made of the objects, and if found correct, permission shall be given for their exportation, and returning to the representative of the company the bond previously given. If the exportation is made by another custom house, the dispatch of the goods shall be made as indicated, and the custom house shall give the representative a certificate in which shall be stated that the goods have been exported; and it will advise the custom house at which the entry was made of the result of the examination and at the same time remit to it a copy of the goods exported, so that the representative of the company or his agent may have the bond cancelled.

V. Any object wanting according to the inventory shall pay the corresponding duties.

VI. When the collector of the custom house notices among the goods imported objects not included in the above concessions, he shall proceed to form an invoice and charge the corresponding duties, and he can, in cases where the goods show wear, reduce the duties, according to the condition in which the goods may be.

ART. 181. All goods which, in the judgment of the collectors, have not been in use, and are included in the tariff, are subject to the payment of duty, even when they are brought by passengers with their baggage, and also to the provisions of this law, if they are intended to be sold.

ART. 182. When passengers bring with them furniture, or any part of their household goods which show that they have been in use, the collectors are authorized to reduce the duty on them, taking into consideration their state or condition.

ART. 183. Small articles intended for gifts or for personal use brought with the baggage by passengers shall be exempt from making a consular invoice, if, on their arrival on the national territory, they make the verbal manifestation of the articles which they bring, but always before examination of their baggage, and the collector can, in case it is solicited by a passenger, grant him twenty-four hours for the presentation of the statement, provided, always, the goods are deposited to the satisfaction of the collectors in the place where they may select.

ART. 184. When a passenger declares that there is some package in her baggage which she does not think proper for male employés to examine, it shall be examined by a female appointed by the collector. This person shall be properly paid by the treasury, and shall enjoy the benefit of such smuggled goods which she may discover.

ART. 185. The examination of the persons of the passengers, and especially the females, shall only be made in exceptional cases, and by a person of the same sex, when there is a specified complaint, or when owing to some good cause it is suspected that fraud is intended, and in no case shall the examination of a person proceed without the collector being informed thereof.

ART. 186. The packages belonging to passengers should correspond in numbers, marks and countermarks to those mentioned in the statement presented by the captains of vessels or the conductors of railroad trains; if not they shall be considered as irregular, and the collectors shall immediately proceed to make the necessary investigation.

ART. 187. The employés of the custom house shall be careful to inform passengers that they are not to pay for the examination of their baggage, excepting the payment of the duties on the goods or the sealing, in case they request it as authorized by this law.

ART. 188. The examination of the baggage shall be made in a commodious and safe place gradually, and each passenger respectively, without distinction and in his turn. Notwithstanding this the collectors shall hurry the examination as much as possible, so as not to detain passengers any longer than is necessary.

ART. 189. When passengers coming from abroad go to the capital of the Republic, or any other interior place where there are counterguards or federal customs offices, they shall be allowed to have their baggage examined at those places instead of at port of arrival, as long as the railroad companies, stage lines, or the passengers themselves give bonds, to the satisfaction of the collector, that in case said baggage may be dutiable the duties shall be paid at the place of examination.

ART. 190. Similar concessions can be made, provided the transportation of the baggage is made by some special company called express, which in all cases must be solvent to the satisfaction of the collector.

ART. 191. In cases mentioned in the previous article, the importation of merchandise can only be allowed without examination after the passenger has made the manifestation in accordance with Article 178 of this chapter, or the person conducting the baggage, when the passenger is not present. This being done, the packages will be bound with wire and sealed with lead in such a manner that they cannot be opened before their examination; and the conductors are held responsible under bond, and the penalties of the law, if the said seals are found destroyed or opened.

Art. 192. When railroad companies, conductors of trains, or express companies, charged with conducting the baggage, receive the same from the passengers who may not accompany said baggage, they shall ask them for the keys and all information necessary for complying with the provisions contained in the previous article. If, for some reason, this notice is not presented, the baggage shall be deposited in some place in the custom house, and the time having expired in which goods can be dispatched, they shall be considered abandoned, and the custom house officials shall proceed as directed in such cases.

Art. 193. All inferior employés engaged in the dispatch of baggage are forbidden and strictly prohibited reading the private papers of the passengers, professional diplomas or titles of property, books and accounts either private or of any commercial or industrial firm or society; and superior officers are cautioned not to tolerate or permit such violations. The examination of such things shall be limited to indispensable cases, when it is necessary to ascertain that there are no dutiable goods among them.

Art. 194. The collectors of customs shall be careful to see that the employés under them treat with all politeness and decency the passengers who arrive in the Republic; to inform them, before examining their baggage, of the custom house rules with which they are to comply, and not allow any inferior employé to make the examinations except under the orders of a superior. In cases where a passenger has to pay duties on the goods which he brings, an appraiser shall fix the rates to be paid thereon, having previously applied for their dispatch according to this law. The federal employés shall also see that passengers do not commit the offense of inattention to, or disrespect for, the country in which they are, or the Government represented by said employés, and they can send the passenger committing the offense to the local authority, that he may be punished according to law.

Art. 195. The examination of the baggage shall be made without disarranging the same, and when passengers desire to make the examination themselves it shall be allowed, provided the employés are satisfied that there are no other articles in the baggage except those shown by the passengers.

Art. 196. The baggage brought by foreign ministers accredited to this Government are exempt from examination and duties according to the laws relating to them.

Art. 197. The collectors are authorized to allow the landing of the baggage at the same time with the passengers, if the captain has delivered the statement of their baggage, and they can also dispatch them at extra hours, provided the passengers have to continue their trip and the packages are not numerous, or contain goods which require a long and minute examination. In general the collectors shall favor the passengers with all possible concessions, provided no harm is done to the fiscal interests.

Art. 198. When passengers bring with their bagggge trunks having double bottoms or any other secret apartments with evident intention of defrauding the Government, when they are known to be smugglers, and when they make frequent trips, or there are other circumstances attendant upon their arrival in port, the collectors have the right to limit the privileges granted in this chapter, and they shall inform the Treasury Department of what they have ordered, and of the reasons which they have had for doing so, without suspending the order.

Art. 199. The mail, mail agents, civil and military employés, on entering the country, are subject to the same rules as other passengers. The federal employés of the custom house can examine the rooms assigned to mail agents, at the same time respecting every letter, mail bag or box containing mail matter that may be duly closed and sealed. The mail bags can also be examined by an employé appointed for that purpose by the collectors. This examination can only be made inside the postoffice, in presence of the postmaster or the person representing him, according to the provisions of the Postal Ordinance, and without opening or in any way injuring any package containing mail matter.

Art. 200. The custom house collectors shall have this chapter printed in English, French, German and Italian separately, the same, respectively, being an exact translation of the Spanish, that they may serve as notice to passengers coming to the country.

ART. 201. The collectors shall also have these notices posted in public places, especially in the place where the examination of the baggage is made.

These notices shall also be distributed on board steamers which make regular trips to the country, as well as on railroad trains or express conducting the baggage, so that the passengers, if possible, may have them before they arrive in national territory.

SECTION VI.

DAMAGE TO MERCHANDISE.

ART. 202. Damage will be considered reduction in value which merchandise imported by sea may suffer on account of storms or other unforeseen events at sea, such as wreckage or other similar events caused during the voyage of the vessel, that is to say, from the port of departure to the port of destination, and in such cases merchandise will have a reduction in duties in proportion to their depreciation.

ART. 203. Accidents which may occur to merchandise during the discharge and transportation of them in ports where, on account of particular circumstances, vessels are obliged to anchor outside the bar, or at great distances from it, shall also be considered as damage.

ART. 204. Merchandise damaged by any other way shall not enjoy any reduction in duties. Merchandise not injured by contact with water shall not enjoy the above privilege, such as metals in bulk, materials, packings or accessories, even when these may have suffered leaving the merchandise in good condition.

ART. 205. To prove any damage caused by bad weather during the voyage, the captain is obliged to present within twenty-four hours after the arrival of the vessel in port, to the collector of the custom house, a statement of the causes of the accident; which shall also be strengthened by an examination of the log-book.

ART. 206. The damage to the merchandise being justified, the custom house shall proceed to examine the merchandise, separating that part in good condition from the damaged.

ART. 207. When the collectors deem that the said merchandise is in a condition calculated to imperil the public health, and the consignee is in accord with this opinion, it shall be destroyed by custom house employés, in a place designated for that purpose. If it is doubtful that the merchandise may be injurious to the public health, or if the consignee is not willing to abandon it for destruction, the collector shall inform the municipal government, or the board of health, where there is one, to decide the case, then the merchandise shall be destroyed without further appeal.

ART. 208. In cases of salvage, damage on account of bad weather, jetson, or forced arrival at a port by stress of weather, and when the captains ask for the sale of the merchandise which they may have for foreign ports, the collectors shall refer such cases to the judge of the district, so that he may proceed and decide as is deemed best according to the laws, the custom house remaining charged with the collection of the import duties, of the storage of the part of the cargo saved, and of the auctions, sales, and discharge of the goods.

ART. 209. For cases of partial damages conceded by this law, the reduction to be made of the duties shall be qualified in the following manner: The appraisers shall name an expert for the custom house and the consignee of the merchandise shall do likewise; both experts, before giving their opinions, shall name a third, as referee, to decide in cases of disagreement as to the damage. If they fail to agree upon a person to serve as referee. the collector of the custom house shall name one, and the decision given shall be final, even in cases that the two experts agree in the classification, as well as when the third expert is obliged to give a separate opinion owing to the non-agreement of the first two in the entire matter.

Art. 210. Whenever merchandise is declared damaged, there shall be a record made of the proceedings so as to verify the reduction of the duties. There shall be four copies of this document made, and signed by all who took in the qualification, and with the Vo. Bo. (O. K. or correct) of the collector.

Of this document a copy shall be sent to the Treasury Department, to be attached to the corresponding dispatch papers, and the other three copies shall be attached to the respective applications.

CHAPTER V.

Adjudication and Payment of Import Duties.

Art. 211. The operations of the appraisers being completed, they shall deliver to the collectors, or to the persons whom they may appoint, three copies of the application for dispatch, duly certified as ordered. The collector, or some employé in his confidence, shall see if the three copies are rated alike and have no alterations or modifications made before their presentation. Two of the copies shall be delivered to the auditor's office for the adjudication and collection of duties, as indicated in the following articles, and the third shall be kept to form a docket of the dispatches made by the appraisers, and for the purpose of comparison in the event of doubts arising, based on the contents of the other copies.

Art. 212. The auditor shall keep a book in which shall be written the entry and departure of the documents which the auditor's office may have, the number, in order corresponding with each document, of the manifests belonging to the ship bringing the merchandise, and the name of the consignee of the merchandise; and these books shall have corresponding columns to annotate, at the proper time, the number of the bill ready for payment, the date, and amount of the duties paid. (Model No. 21.)

Art. 213. Immediately after the two corresponding entries have been made in the aforesaid book the two copies of the application shall be passed to the bureau of adjudication. This bureau shall be careful, in making the calculation of the duties, to examine if the rates are correct; and if the applications do not have any irregularities which are inconsistent with the provisions of this law, or other circumstances which indicate or justify suspicion of fraud, they shall give immediate notice to the auditor that he may inform the collector. On making the calculations of the duties the employés of the bureau making the same shall be careful to have them examined by others, and each shall sign the calculation that he made, either of the adjudication, the duties or the revision.

Art. 214. The copies having been returned to the collector, he shall pass them to the bureau in charge of the revising and the applying of the duties, which shall:

I. Revise and compare all the copies of the applications to see that the rates have been justly arranged, if the calculation of the duties is correct, and is the same on the two copies.

II. To state, at the end of each application, the arrangement of the duties according to that determined by the law, and entering in a book which the custom houses are to have for that purpose, authorized by the Treasury Department, all the details required by said book. This book shall be arranged according to Model No. 22, and each application shall have placed the seal of the respective desk and also the signature of the employé who made the revision and the arrangement of the duties; any observation which this employé has to make about the operations contained in the application shall be made to the auditor, who shall immediately inform the collector, who shall, if he considers the omission or error of any importance, order that the remarks be made in writing, so as to proceed as the law requires.

ART. 215. The same bureau shall make out a bill for payment by the responsible consignees, which shall contain the exact copy of the said liquidation, and it shall pass with the respective application to the auditor, who shall put his "*correct*" upon it, if found to be so, and he shall pass it to the collector for his signature, and it shall then be remitted to the consignee that he may pay within the time indicated.

ART. 216. If the interested party, on receiving the liquidation made by the custom house, makes some observation about it, these shall be taken into consideration by the collector and auditor, so that together they shall approve or not of the same. In case the application of the claimant is just, the difference shall be expressed in the corresponding column of liquidation, without changing in any way the first amount, neither reducing nor increasing the sums caused by said operation.

ART. 217. If the interested party is satisfied with the bill made out by the custom house, he shall pay it, obtaining from the cashier the corresponding receipt, which he shall take from a stub-book kept for this purpose, and stating on the stub, as well as on the receipt, the details marked according to Model No. 23. This receipt shall have the signature of the cashier, the "*correct*" of the auditor, and the Vo Bo (O. K., all right) of the collector, with its corresponding signatures.

ART. 218. The duties once paid, they shall not be returned under any condition, except in cases of miscalculation, and in this case, as well as in any other, the order must be given by the Treasury Department, and the collector shall officially inform said office of the petition and the reasons given for requesting the return of the duties.

ART. 219. Merchandise which after being examined result short in length, width, weight, quality, etc., than that declared in the applications, shall pay as declared.

ART. 220. The copy of the liquidation mentioned in Article 215, with the agreement of the debtor, shall be considered as sufficient voucher for the entry in the cash of *duties from importations.*

ART. 221. The debtor, on receiving his receipt for the payment made, should claim the certificate mentioned in Art. 358, so that at the proper time they can be changed for the custom house revenue stamps which may correspond with them.

ART. 222. The employés charged with making the liquidation, as well as the cashiers, shall be sure to note the items relating to the pecuniary fines imposed by this law, and entirely separate from the import duties.

ART. 223. In the importation of merchandise referred to in Fractions I, II and III of Art. 11, the custom house shall liquidate the duties to which the goods may be subject as if it treated of a particular importation, debiting and crediting in the books of the office for "*Public Treasury*" the total sum of each one of them, and comparing the items with the original orders from the Treasury Department and the General Treasury of the Federation.

CHAPTER VI.

Other Maritime Operations in the Maritime Custom House.

SECTION I.

ARRIVAL, UNLOADING AND DISCHARGING OF THE VESSEL, IN CONSEQUENCE OF FORCED ARRIVAL IN THE PORT BY STRESS OF WEATHER OR OTHER ACCIDENTS, AND THE RE-SHIPMENT OF THE MERCHANDISE.

Art. 224. Any ship which may arrive at any port of the Republic to repair injuries, get water, replenish stores, or on account of accident, shall be visited, examined and placed under vigilance in the same way as if it had arrived directly to load goods. To this end the chief of the guards, or the person commissioned by the collector to visit said ship on entering, shall obtain the reason of said arrival by means of the written declarations of the passengers, or, if there should be none, then of the crew, and the respective entries of the log-book, closing and sealing the hatches of said ship and obtaining the documents with which the said ship comes, to be given in charge of the collector, who shall preserve them in the same way that he received them, and, in view of the circumstances, disposing of the case as he thinks best so as to avoid any fraudulent act being committed.

Art. 225. If it should be necessary for the ship which arrived to discharge its cargo the captain shall petition the collector in writing, and shall place on the paper used the revenue stamps required by law for the discharge on the importation of foreign merchandise, giving the name of the ship, number of tons burden, port sailed from, port of destination, and the numbers and marks of the packages, boxes, barrels, etc., composing the cargo. The collector shall authorize the discharge, passing this permit to the auditor, who, having had a certified copy of it made, shall deliver the original to the commander of inspectors, who shall see that the rules established by this law are fully complied with. Of all that takes place in such a case the collector shall duly inform the Treasury Department.

Art. 226. The discharge having been completed, the goods deposited in the warehouses, the anchorage visit having been complied with, and the respective annotations made, the commander of inspectors shall return to the collector the application used for those operations, which, with the statement of stores, passengers and baggage, and the tickets with which the discharge was made, shall be deposited in the safe of the custom house.

Art. 227. In case it is not necessary to discharge the merchandise brought by the ship, the injuries having been repaired, water and stores having been taken, or the cause for having put into port having been remedied, the captain shall ask permission in writing to sail, using the same amount of revenue stamps used on applications for exportation of goods. The collector shall grant the permit for the vessel to sail, and shall return through the commander of inspectors to the captain the documents which he had in the safe, and said commander of inspectors shall continue the vigilance over the ship until it leaves the port.

Art. 228. In case the vessel was obliged to discharge the merchandise, and when the captain gives notice of his having completed the repairs, and desires to continue his voyage, he shall make a written application, with revenue stamps attached as in the case mentioned in the previous article, for the re-loading of the merchandise which may have been deposited in the warehouses, but he shall not be required to repeat the contents aforesaid in that of the discharge; and the collector shall permit it, ordering the original application to be delivered to the commander of inspectors who served the permit for the discharge, and the warehousemen shall deliver the copy certified by the auditor's office, mentioned in Article 225, so that he may be able to make the delivery of the goods, exacting from the interested party a receipt for the same.

Art. 229. The merchandise having been taken from the warehouses for the purpose of re-shipping it, an inspector shall be commissioned to make a ticket for each of the launches taking it aboard of the ship. Another inspector stationed on board the ship shall deliver to the captain, with the ticket sent by the man in charge of the launch, the merchandise which he brought, and shall receive a receipt from the captain for the entire cargo when it has been re-shipped. He will return to the custom house all the tickets, to be annexed to the corresponding docket, which shall constitute a voucher.

Art. 230. The reloading of the vessel having been completed the commander of inspectors shall go on board of the ship to make his last visit, returning to the captain the documents which had been deposited in the custom house during his stay in port, and at the same time keep a strict watch of the ship until it is out of the port.

Art. 231. All the documents used in the discharge and reloading, with the annotations required to be made by the respective employés, shall be annexed to the dockets formed, and the collectors shall be careful to inform the Treasury Department at their earliest convenience.

Art. 232. If the damage to the vessel is of such a nature as to prevent her continuing to the port of destination, and if the captain should desire to make the discharge of the cargo, of the merchandise and the payment of the duties, he shall solicit permission to do so, using the revenue stamps used for the applications for discharge. The collector shall allow it, after comparing the documents deposited with him, and the said application, the subsequent operations being made as in general cases.

Art. 233. In cases where a vessel puts into port which intended to go to another Mexican port, the rules mentioned in the previous articles shall be complied with, according to the circumstances of the case, and, when the vessel has been reloaded, a special communication shall be sent to the collector of the custom house of the port to which the vessel is bound, minutely informing him of what took place, accompanying all the documents which may have been deposited, which shall be delivered to the captain in a sealed envelope, so that he may proceed to his destination.

Art. 234. When a vessel going from one foreign port to another is lost on the coasts of the Republic, the nearest custom house shall proceed immediately, after it is informed, to send to the place of the accident a section of the guards with the commander of the inspectors, or the person acting in his stead, in connection with an employé named by the collector to represent him.

Art. 235. The employé, in view of the circumstances, shall take the precautions necessary for saving all the merchandise that is possible, and have it brought to the port, receiving from the captains all the documents relating to the cargo, in case it has been saved.

Art. 236. The collector, with the knowledge of the consul of the nation to which the vessel belonged, shall take such measures as are in his power to insure the goods either in the warehouses of the custom house or at the place which may be determined for that purpose.

SECTION II.

TRANSFERRING OF THE MERCHANDISE.

Art. 237. Foreign merchandise shall be allowed to be transferred at Mexican ports in the following cases:

I. When a vessel arriving from a foreign port brings a cargo with its corresponding documents expressly for the purpose of transferring it to some vessel at a Mexican port, the collectors shall permit the transfer, except in special cases when, for some good reasons, it is advisable to inform the Government through the Treasury Department.

II. When a vessel brings a cargo to a certain port, and the consignee of said cargo asks that it be transferred to some Mexican port open to the traffic of the high seas, as a convenience to them, the Government only can make the concession through the Treasury Department, in which case the collector of the respective custom house shall address the said department by telegraph if necessary, informing it of the desires of the consignees, and stating whether, in his opinion, it would be a convenience or not.

III. When, on account of forced entry into a port, or other cause, a vessel cannot continue its trip to the port for which its merchandise is consigned, either Mexican or foreign, the captain or consignee shall ask the transfer, the collector shall, in such case, follow the respective maritime laws in force, and shall also assist in all the operations of the transfer, loading or unloading of the merchandise.

IV. When, on account of smuggling or fraud, the ship has to delay its course, or cannot continue it, and it has merchandise for another port with its respective documents duly certified, the collectors in such case shall order the discharge of the cargo, or its transfer, on their responsibility, or with previous permission from the judicial authority, if the case has been referred to it.

V. When a captain or consignee asks for permission to transfer part of the stores from another ship necessary for himself without paying duties, the collector shall allow it, if there are no serious objections to granting such a request.

VI. When the passengers of a ship have to be transferred to another, so as to continue their trip, their baggage shall also be transferred.

Art. 238. On transferring passengers their baggage shall not be examined, except when the class or form of the packages make it necessary, or when, for other good reasons, it is suspected that they contain merchandise and not baggage, and in such cases they can be examined, permission having been previously obtained from the collectors.

Art. 239. In all transfers the provisions of Art. 71 contained in Fractions I, II, III, IV and V shall be followed, with the difference that the operations usually made on shore by the inspectors shall be performed on board of the ship receiving the merchandise.

SECTION III.

COASTING TRADE.

Art. 240. For the purpose of the law the coasting trade shall be constituted as follows: The transportation of national or nationalized goods or merchandise from one port to another of the United Mexican States, and the transportation of national merchandise from any place on the coast to a national port open either for coasting trade or commerce of the high seas.

Art. 241. Only national vessels carry on the coasting trade, except in the following cases, when it may be carried on by foreign vessels:

I. Transportation of baggage belonging to passengers from one national port to another.

II. In cases where the Government is assured that at the port from which merchandise is shipped for another Mexican port there are no national vessels which can carry on the coasting trade, and it is deemed expedient to authorize foreign vessels to do it; and in such cases the concession of the Government shall only be for a specified time, and as long as there are no national vessels which can carry on the coasting trade, and it is deemed expedient to authorize foreign vessels to do it, and in such cases the concession of the Government shall only be for a specified time, and as long as there are no national vessels which can do it.

Art. 242. The loading of a national vessel shall be done as follows:

I. The shipper shall present to the collector an application to open the register of the ship, annexing the certificate of the captain of the port certifying that the vessel is national, and is in condition to go to sea.

This certificate may be omitted when the captain of the port has previously given the custom house notice of the national vessels which have complied with the aforesaid requirements.

II. The collector, having given permission for a ship to open her register, the commander of the guards shall be informed, so as to allow the shipment of the goods which merchants may present with their dockets duly certified from the custom house.

Art. 243. The maritime custom house shall only give for foreign goods the documents which they require for the coasting trade, with the same formalities and requirements necessary for importation; but, in such cases, the interested parties shall present their applications in quadruplicate, using, on one of the copies, the stamps required by law.

Art. 244. National goods conveyed for coasting trade do not require any other documents, except a notice in triplicate of its class, number, weight and value; and one of the copies should have the corresponding revenue stamps. In case the State or the municipality where the port of sailing is situated exacts some shipment of national goods, the custom house has no right to exact it, nor to detain, on this account, the dispatch of the shipment.

Art. 245. For the loading of the cargo the collector of the custom house shall say, under his signature on each document, "*permit the shipment;*" the commander of inspectors shall say, "*passed,*" and, after the comparison of these documents with the package to be shipped has been made by the commissioner at the wharf and the guards, the first shall say "correct," and the second shall cancel the custom house revenue stamps, as indicated in Art. 296, with the words "*complied with.*" These requirements having been complied with the packages may be sent on board.

Art. 246. The loading of the vessel having been completed, and all the documents which served that purpose having been examined by the maritime custom house, there shall be made out with them the register, according to Model No. 24, found at the end of this law, and, having been certified and sealed, it shall be addressed to the collector of the custom house of the port to which the vessel is bound, and stamping on the back of the envelope, with sealing-wax on the junctures, the seal of the office, they shall be delivered to the captain.

Art. 247. This document shall be the one that shall describe the goods, so that they may be legally admitted at port for which they are intended; and, in default, even when the documents have been presented, if the goods imported do not have the documents accompanying them, shall incur the fines specified.

Art. 248. The copy of the register of the sailing of the vessel engaged in the coasting trade, which should remain on file at the custom house, shall consist of the original application of the captain in which he requested the opening of the register, a set of duplicate documents given by the office, and a set of copies of the respective documents of the national goods cleared by other offices, which two copies should be delivered by the interested party, according to the requirements of this law on presenting the originals.

Art. 249. Another copy shall be made of said registers with a copy of the original application of the captain, another set of duplicate documents given by the maritime custom house, and a triplicate copy of the other documents for the purpose of remitting them to the Treasury Department on the first opportunity.

Art. 250. Only on account of stress of weather shall vessels engaged in the coastwise trade be allowed to enter a port other than that to which it was bound, and in such cases, if the vessel puts into some port on the coasts of the Republic, the captain shall obtain from any civil authority at the place a certificate as to the cause of its detention. If the vessel should have put into some foreign port, the certificate shall be given by the Mexican consul at said port, or if there should be no Mexican consul, the collector of the port or some other local authority. The captain that does not comply with this requisite shall be placed in charge of the district judge to investigate the case and to apply the penalty imposed by this ordinance.

Art. 251. When a vessel engaged in the coasting trade arrives at a port, the requirements provided for foreign vessels shall be complied with, exacting from it the sealed envelope containing the register, which should be immediately given up and passed to the collector of the custom house. The collector, as soon as he receives it, shall, with the auditor or with the officer acting for him, open it, so that both can see if the vessel was cleared by the custom house at the port from which it came in accordance with all the requirements.

Art. 252. The discharge shall be made immediately, for which the captain or consignee of the vessel shall present an application with the necessary stamps, according to law, giving the name of the vessel, captain, port from which it came, and the contents of the cargo it carries, specifying the documents which refer to them, their numbers, shippers and consignees; the auditor's office shall compare this application with the documents contained in the register, and, finding it correct, the same steps shall be taken for the discharge and examination of the merchandise as are designated for foreign vessels, and exacting from the consignees of the goods one copy of the application, with the stamps required by the internal revenue law for the dispatch of merchandise.

Art. 253. When, upon examination, there are found undescribed articles or excesses in the foreign goods, the custom house shall proceed according to the provisions of the law in such cases; and the same course shall be pursued if, upon examination, it is found that the goods were received by the vessel on the high seas, on the coast, or in some foreign port; taking into consideration the facts, the documents which refer to and describe all the nationalized goods destined for the coasting trade shall have the special custom house revenue stamps attached, as described in Article 359 of this law.

Art. 254. The examination and dispatch of the merchandise having been made, that destined for the port shall be delivered to its consignees. That unloaded at intermediate ports shall be left at the maritime or coastwise custom house in whose warehouse the goods shall be deposited, and shall remain until they are released by their owners or continue to their destination, to which they shall go with the same documents granted by the custom house at the port from which they came, and on which the collector of the custom house shall annotate that they proceed to their destination. If the extraction of the packages is made fifteen days after their arrival in port, the custom house shall charge storage on the goods according to Art. 303.

Art. 255. When it is desired to import or transport to another port foreign goods, nationalized in some one of the ports competent for the commerce of the high-seas, and that, according to the documents by which they were introduced, they appear to have been intended finally for the port at which they were unloaded, the interested parties shall request from the maritime and coastwise trade custom house a document, at the end of which the collector of the custom house shall make a note, authorizing it with his signature and the seal of his office, expressing that the goods mentioned correspond to documents numbers so-and-so, of such a date, of the custom house at ————, and on which the corresponding revenue stamps have been canceled.

Art. 256. With the original certificate given by the custom house at which the vessel cleared, the register and the permit for discharge, also the original, shall be made out, the entry registers numbered in order according to years, which shall be kept on file at the maritime custom house. From this register there shall be a literal copy made at the auditor's office, which shall be sent to the Treasury Department at the first opportunity.

Art. 257. At coastwise trade custom houses, where there is only a collector, he shall perform the duties which in this law are assigned the auditor and commander of inspectors. When there is an auditor or inspector, each one shall perform the duties assigned him, and they shall alternate in common accord for the performance of the duties assigned the guards.

Art. 258. The coastwise trade custom houses, dependent on the maritime ones open to the traffic of the high seas, shall remit to the Treasury Department directly all documents and the monthly statements corresponding to them.

Art. 259. The certificate setting forth the employés of the coastwise trade custom houses shall be made out by the collector of maritime custom houses on which they depend, being their immediate chief, and he shall remit them to the Treasury Department at the first opportunity.

Art. 260. The coastwise trade custom houses shall remit annually, through the maritime custom houses on which they depend, the books and papers corresponding to each fiscal year.

SECTION IV.

EXPORTATION IN GENERAL.

Art. 261. All national products, goods and manufactures shall be free from export duty, with the exception of those specially mentioned and provided for in the law.

Art. 262. The exportation of Mexican antiquities is strictly prohibited.

Art. 263. Captains of vessels who intend to load national products or manufactures for foreign ports shall present to the collector an application signed by himself, giving the name of the ship, the number of tons measurement, and its destination.

Art. 264. The collector shall state on the said application "*permit and open the register,*" and, in accord with the commander of the guards, shall name one or two inspectors to remain on board while the vessel loads.

Art. 265. Each shipper or remitter shall present to the collector an application for shipment in quadruplicate, in sheets of common size, and placing on one of the copies the stamps required by law. These applications shall state the name of the ship, of the captain, and of the port of destination, marks, numbers, number of packages and their class, statement of the products or goods that they contain and their value.

Art. 266. The copies of the application for shipment having been compared with each other, and numbered in order, the auditor shall place " *correct* " on each copy having the revenue stamps. The collector shall designate an appraiser to verify the dispatch, adding "*permit the shipment,*" and with the document thus certified the interested party may proceed to ship the goods, the commander of inspectors placing on the document the word "*passed.*" The appraisers who take part shall say "*dispatched,*" and the warehouseman assisting in the operation shall say " *complied.*"

Art. 267. The commander of inspectors shall receive all the applications, and, the loading being completed, he shall make a visit to the ship to see that the goods shipped are those described in the applications and none others. Immediately after he shall pass the aforesaid documents to the collector, and from them there shall be an extract made of the register, which shall consist of a set of the applications authorized by the auditor's office, and, having been closed, sealed, and signed by the collector, it shall be delivered to the captain along with a certificate signed by the collector and the auditor, presented in the terms required by Model No. 25.

Art. 268. Of all the original applications for shipment numbered in order there shall be a statement made, in case the goods shipped did not pay duties, and a general adjudication shall be made if otherwise, so that at first sight the amount of the register may be ascertained, which shall also be numbered in order by years, and shall consist of the application of the captain with its corresponding stamps, a copy of the certificate given him, and the aforesaid application for shipment. Said register shall be sent as voucher with the account.

Art. 269. With another copy of the application of the captain, copies of the certificate delivered him, and of the statement of adjudication or not, as the case may be, and one copy of the application for shipment, there shall be made another copy of the aforesaid register, which shall be remitted to the Treasury Department.

Art. 270. With similar copies to those referred to in the previous article, and another set of the applications for shipment, there shall be made the aforesaid register to be kept on file at the custom house.

Art. 271. When a vessel desires to leave in ballast for foreign ports, the captain shall present a simple application requesting the permission and dispatch from the custom house. In the application he shall state the name of the ship, its nationality, tonnage and destination. The collector shall give permission in these terms, "*permit it, previously complying with the visit and other formalities of the law,*" giving it in charge of the commander of inspectors, who shall go on board of the vessel with a sufficient number of guards, and after making a scrupulous search to make sure the vessel does not carry any merchandise, he shall leave, and render a report of his visit, returning the application to the collector, based upon which a certificate shall be made according to Model No. 26, which shall be delivered to the captain, so that he may be able to go to sea. The same requirements shall be observed in respect to vessels that come with the intention of diving and fishing on the Mexican coast, provided they comply with the laws and regulations.

Art. 272. When the commander of inspectors finds on board the ship one or more packages not described on the application for shipment, he shall have them taken out and deposited in the warehouses, giving circumstantial information to the collector for the proper investigation and other proceedings.

Art. 273. When the exportation is solicited of goods that have paid duties on their importation, besides having complied with the requirements provided for in the previous articles, the auditor's office shall state "these goods have paid the import duties," without which the guard shall not permit their shipment. In such cases, the duties once paid, as aforesaid, shall not be returned.

Art. 274. Articles which, according to the tariff, may be temporarily admitted without the payment of duties, shall be re-exported only by the same port through which they were introduced, and having been previously proved to be those so admitted.

Art. 275. National goods which, on their export, the shippers request to have particularly examined, shall be examined, permission having been first obtained from the custom house, and the goods being found in the condition prescribed by Section VI of this chapter.

Art. 276. National or foreign vessels, after they shall have unloaded at the port or ports to which they may have been destined, if they ask permission to load goods at any port on the coast where no branch custom house exists to inspect said loading, said permission shall be granted them, provided the place they propose to touch at be within the jurisdiction of the respective custom house, reference being had to the following provisions:

I. The captain, supercargo or consignee shall request from the collector the proper permit. In this request they shall use revenue stamps to the value of fifty cents.

II. Permission having been given, the custom house shall proceed to certify the application for opening the register, which should be presented by the captain, using on said document stamps according to law, and complying with the same requirements mentioned in Art. 271 of this chapter. On giving the certificate mentioned in this chapter the place to which the vessel is bound, and its object in going there, shall be stated.

III. The custom house which dispatches the ship shall give immediate notice to the custom house or custom house section nearest the place to which the vessel goes, that it may take part in all the operations that may be made there, watching it until its departure, so that there may be no abuse of this concession, and dispatching it definitely. The section that takes part in these operations shall give an account of all that transpired to the custom house from which it received the number and class of packages that had been shipped and their contents, with their value and weight or measurement, respectively.

IV. The custom house which clears the ship shall inform the Treasury Department what took place at the proper time.

Art. 277. When the collector has good reasons to believe that there is any intention of defrauding or cheating the Government he shall name a body of employés, giving them the necessary instructions that they may go and witness the shipment of the goods. This concession shall only have force when the captain shall agree under bond to keep on board of his ship the employés, and return them to the port of their residence when the loading of the ship has been finished.

The chief of the body named shall give an account of the result to the collector to whom he is responsible, and, if the law has been complied with, he shall grant the dispatch of the vessel for its destination whenever it is solicited, or he shall detain it, proceeding as he is directed, and giving immediate notice by telegraph to the Treasury Department of what has occurred that it may act accordingly.

SECTION V.

EXPORT AND RE-IMPORTATION OF NATIONAL PRODUCTS.

Art. 278. National products that may be sent in national or foreign vessels, to ports of the United States, to make use of the railroads or other means of transportation afforded in that country to cross its territory, destined to some maritime or frontier custom house of the Republic, may be re-imported free of all duties, subject to the following rules:

I. The interested parties shall present to the proper custom house three copies of a petition, without stamps, according to Model No. 27.

II. The collector, after the comparison of the documents has been made, shall name an appraiser to revise the cargo in the presence of the commander of the guards. These shall take samples of the merchandise and shall make three statements of them, of which two shall be delivered to the collector and the other shall be kept by the first-mentioned employé. Of the samples taken, the collector shall send by mail a set of them to the custom house through which the goods shall be re-imported, and the duplicate set shall be kept by the employés referred to in Art. 155, Chapter IV, for the purpose therein indicated. The collector of the clearance custom house shall remit to that through which the goods shall enter a copy of the invoice to the merchandise exported, stating on the dispatch by which he makes the remission such reservations and recommendations as he may think necessary.

The custom house authorizing these permits shall require of the shipper a bond for double the amount of the import duties which may have been charged upon the goods, in case these latter are foreign nationalized goods; and in case they are national goods, he shall require a bond simply for the duties charged upon the import of an article similar to that which it is proposed to re-import.

III. The bond having been executed, the collector shall sign the "*permit*" ordering the packages to be marked and sealed, after which the commander of the guards shall say and sign "*complied with*" on the same document, and the packages shall be placed on board the ship or the railroad car under the vigilance of one of the guards.

IV. The maritime or frontier custom house through which the merchandise enters the country shall verify the dispatch of them, provided the interested parties have presented the application for their dispatch, giving notice to the custom house from which they came of their arrival, so that the bond which was executed may be canceled.

V. In case the goods thus exported are consumed while passing through American territory, or in case the re-importation of said goods into the country is made impossible by circumstances which cannot be controlled, the parties intended should procure from the Mexican consul, or, in his absence, from any official residing at the place where the consumption or other act took place, a certificate setting forth what has occurred. This certificate shall have the effect of canceling the bond filed in the custom house from which the goods were sent.

Art. 279. The time for the bonds referred to in this chapter shall be two months, which shall not be prolonged, and, if these are passed and the interested party does not present any of the documents referred to in the section of the preceding article, the collector who made the dispatch shall proceed to make effective the bond that was given.

SECTION VI.

RE-IMPORTATION OF NATIONAL MERCHANDISE FROM FOREIGN COUNTRIES.

Art. 280. The re-importation, free of duties, of national goods coming from foreign ports, shall be permitted only when said goods are not of those which by this law are excepted and when the consignees have observed the following conditions:

I. All national goods not referred to in the next section, and whose origin may be determined by inherent marks placed upon them by the clearance custom houses at the time of their exportation, shall be admitted on their return free of duty pending proper authority from the Treasury Department.

II. Goods whose origin cannot be determined owing to their resemblance to foreign products are excepted from the benefits of this law.

III. When the consignees of export goods desire to avail themselves of the privileges granted by Section I, they shall apply to the collector of the respective custom house for an order to have the goods examined and marked, so that in the exportation permit may appear the fact of the marking of the same.

IV. The authority referred to in Section I shall not be granted by the Treasury Department until after the party interested shall have authoritatively proved, by a certificate issued from the clearance custom house, the date of the exportating of said goods.

V. Goods referred to in Section I which may have remained in foreign ports for one year shall be considered as of foreign origin, and consequently not entitled to be re-imported free of duty.

VI. In case the custom house is in doubt as to the origin of an article re-imported as national, proceedings in relation thereto shall be suspended until an expert's opinion decides the controversy. For this purpose the collector shall bring the matter to the notice of the Treasury Department, setting forth the grounds upon which he founds his doubts as to the origin of the goods, and remitting at the same time a sample of the same in order to have the case determined.

VII. If such expert examination shall prove the goods to be of foreign origin, the same shall be forfeited, and the consignee shall be placed at the disposal of the corresponding District Court, so that, according to the provisions of this law, there may be imposed upon him the penalties prescribed for contrabandists.

CHAPTER VII.

Re-Exportation of Foreign Merchandise.

Art. 281. The re-exportation of foreign merchandise without the payment of the fiscal duties shall only be permitted on goods that may be deposited in the Government warehouses established by the maritime and frontier custom houses of the Republic, in which case the re-exportation shall be subject to the following rules:

I. Merchandise, which on its introduction into the country is deposited in the warehouses, can be re-exported within the six months allowed by Art. 302, which this law concedes with this object, without their paying any charges except storage, according to Article 303 of Chapter XI.

II. The re-exportation of merchandise can be made of either part or of all the packages mentioned on the consular invoices.

III. The re-exportation of merchandise, on applying to the proper custom house for the corresponding permit, shall present in quadruplicate a document in accordance with Model No. 28.

IV. The document shall be passed by the collector to the auditor's office, and being there compared with the originals which served for the importation of the goods, the collector shall state under his signature whether they agree, and shall give the order to the warehouseman to deliver the package or packages therein mentioned. (See Model No. 29.)

V. The collector, on receiving from the auditor's office the documents duly compared, shall name the appraiser who is to make the examination of the goods, and he shall proceed to make it according to the rules established in Chapter IV, Section I, of this law.

VI. If, in the examination made by the appraiser, there results a difference in quality or quantity of any of the merchandise, he shall give immediate notice in writing to the collector, to the end that he may impose a fine, on the packages on which there is a difference, of double the import duties to which they would be ordinarily liable.

VII. In case merchandise is fined and the re-exporter refuses to pay the fine of double the duties imposed by the custom house, the collector shall order the said goods to be restored, without allowing any further operations to be made in regard to them, until the judge to whom the case is referred gives his decision.

Art. 282. The owner or consignees of the merchandise to be re-exported shall make, before the collector of the custom house, a bond equivalent to the total amount of duties that according to the tariff of this ordinance the goods should pay. This bond, which shall assure the Government that the merchandise is carried to the place of destination, shall have a term corresponding to the time it takes the goods to reach their destination, taking into consideration the means of transportation.

Art. 283. During the time fixed by the bond, the interested parties shall present a certificate signed by the collector of the custom house, or the highest authority, if there should be no collector in the place to which the goods were destined, in which should be stated that the ——————— of merchandise covered by document number ——————— of the custom house ——————— of the Mexican Republic reached its final destination. This certificate shall serve to cancel the bond given.

Art. 284. If, at the expiration of the stipulated time, the interested party does not present to the collector of the custom house from which the re-exportation of the goods was made, the certificate referred to in the previous article, the collector shall proceed to make effective the aforesaid bond without further recourse on the part of the interested party.

Art. 285. In regard to merchandise which, to be exported, has to cross some part of the country, the conductors shall, on reaching the last custom house of exit, deliver to the collector of it the goods with their corresponding documents, so that when the regular examination is made he shall sign the "*pass*" so as to enable them to continue to their destination.

Art. 286. If the examination which the custom house makes of the goods there results in a difference between them and the document which refers to them, they shall be fined according to the case mentioned in the present law.

Art. 287. In all re-exportation of merchandise, the custom house shall give notice of the arrival and departure of the goods to the office at the place to which they proceed as well as to the Treasury Department.

Art. 288. When, upon the examination made of the merchandise, it appears that the articles were those destined to be re-exported, the signer of the bond, as well as the owner or shipper to whom the custom house gave permission, shall be considered as the principal author of the irregularity, and shall be subject to the fines imposed in such cases.

Art. 289. The custom houses, on giving permission for the re-exportation of merchandise, shall remit to the Treasury Department, certified, one of the copies of the document that the interested parties present. In the same way they shall send, on the very day that it is received, an authorized copy of the certificate which proves the departure of the goods for their destination.

Art. 290. Notwithstanding that ordered in the present chapter, the custom houses, on giving permission for the re-exportation of merchandise, shall adjust their proceedings according to the provisions of this law.

CHAPTER VIII.

Internation of Foreign Merchandise Coming from Ports Open to Traffic of the High Seas.

Art. 291. Foreign merchandise which has paid import duties according to the tariff of this law, can be internated to other ports of the Republic, subject to the following provisions:

I. For the internation of foreign goods the shipper shall present to the custom house a duplicate application according to Model No. 30, one of which shall have attached thereto the stamp or stamps as provided by the stamp law. The duplicate does not need stamps.

II. To the original application, or the one having the stamps, the shipper shall place on an equal amount in special custom house stamps, these latter being for the value of the total amount of import duties which may be charged upon the goods which it is proposed to take into the interior.

III. The auditor's office, on receiving the application, shall raise all the rates and amounts that caused the import duties, and, being in accord with the value of the special custom house stamps attached to the document, shall proceed to cancel them with a perforated seal which shall be provided for such cases, numbering it in order, and fixing, immediately after, the time deemed long enough for the arrival of the merchandise at its destination, taking into consideration the means by which it has been transported.

IV. The collector shall authorize the "*sailing permit,*" and the inspector and the guard house through which the goods pass, besides placing the "*complied with,*" shall make a note of it in the proper book. Said application shall cover the goods until they reach their final destination.

Art. 292. The internation documents shall be valid only for the time allowed by the custom house from which they are cleared, but in case some unforeseen event or other circumstance prevents the merchandise from reaching its destination at the time allowed, the interested parties, so as not to incur a fine, shall prove, to the employé who examines the merchandise, what caused the delay.

Art. 293. The special custom house revenue stamps being the proof that the goods were legally imported, it is provided that all foreign merchandise transported, and the document relating to it, which have not all the requisites mentioned in this chapter, shall be taken where it may be found and subjected to the payment of double the duties, without the interested parties having any other recourse.

Art. 294. When the goods thus forwarded have for their destination some port or point on the coast, the custom house or branch custom house there established shall be the one to examine and dispatch the same.

Art. 295. If the examination made of said goods should show that there had been changes, either in quantity or quality, there shall be imposed upon the part which may have been changed, according to the provision of this law, double import duties, in addition to which the party interested shall produce the special custom house stamps corresponding to the duties in relation to which the fraud was attempted. The stamps shall be placed upon the corresponding document, and shall be cancelled by the officer discovering the irregularity.

In the other mistakes or omissions which may be discovered on the application to forward into the interior foreign merchandise, the proceeding shall be as may be determined by the Treasury Department.

CHAPTER IX.

Internation for the Dispatch of Foreign Merchandise at Some Place in the Interior of the Republic.

Art. 296. Only in exceptional cases shall the Treasury Department allow the internation of foreign merchandise for dispatch at some place in the interior of the Republic joined by some railroad line established, and in such cases the shippers shall comply with the following provisions:

I. For all internation of merchandise authorized in a competent manner to be dispatched at some place in the interior, the interested parties shall present an application in duplicate in which shall be given a minute description of the goods.

II. The collector on receiving the document shall grant the permit, passing it to the auditor's office to be compared with the consular invoices, declare their conformity and proceed to obtain payment of the respective duties.

III. The payment being made, according to the provisions of this ordinance, the interested party, unless excused by the Treasury Department, shall give a bond for double the duties payable on the merchandise to be internated.

IV. The auditor's office shall state on the document whether or not the payment of the duties according to that prescribed in the previous fraction have been assured, giving the corresponding ticket to the warehouseman to deliver the package or packages to be internated.

V. With the proper permit annotated on the *"pass"* of the commander of the guards, shall be made, under the vigilance of the same, the shipment of the packages in the cars or platform cars, which he shall close with the special seals and padlocks which the Government has for that purpose at each custom house. He shall then deliver to the employé named by the collector to take charge of the train until it reaches its destination, the regular permit and consular invoices received on the importation of the merchandise.

VI. The employé in charge of the train shall not allow on the cars or platform cars on which the goods are conveyed any packages other than described in the custom house papers.

Under no consideration, except in unavoidable circumstances, shall the cars or vehicles which convey the merchandise be opened during their transit, and, if they should be opened, the employé in charge of the train, as well as the conductor, shall prove to the judge of the district the cause which obliged him to do so, by means of the authorities of the place where the act was committed, if this place should happen to be inhabited, or by all the employés of the same train, if the act is committed in an uninhabited place.

VIII. When the goods reach their destination, the chief of the federal office, before ordering the opening of the cars or platform cars which contain the merchandise, shall examine the seals and padlocks placed on each one of them; and, being satisfied that they are intact, shall order the discharge, carefully seeing that the number of packages unloaded are in accord with the descriptions in the documents which refer to them.

If the examination made of the seals and padlocks placed upon the cars and wagons should show that these have been opened during the journey and goods extracted therefrom, the conductor of the train, as also the custom house officer who accompanied the same as guard, shall be sent before the District Court for the purpose of having the matter investigated. In case the conductor be found guilty, in addition to imposing upon him the penalties by this law prescribed for contrabandists, the company owning the train shall be compelled to pay a fine up to five hundred dollars at the discretion of the Treasury Department. In regard to the custom house officer, anything appearing against him shall be punished as prescribed in Section I of Article 384.

IX. The discharge being completed, the chief of the office shall give to the employés in charge of the train a receipt for the documents which he shall have delivered, so that on his return to the custom house from which he came he can exchange it for the document which he signed previous to his departure from that place.

Art. 297. For the examination and dispatch of merchandise, the officers who receive it should be subject to the provisions of the present ordinance, informing the custom house from which the goods came of the result so that it may cancel the bond given by the shipper of the merchandise.

Art. 298. The custom houses, on allowing the internation of the merchandise to be dispatched at some place in the interior of the country, shall send to the Treasury Department a certified copy of the document presented by the shipper. The same shall be done by the custom houses to which the goods are consigned, as soon as they have been dispatched.

CHAPTER X.

International Transit of Foreign Goods Through the Territory of the Republic.

Art. 299. The international transit of foreign goods through the territory of the Republic shall be allowed, under the following conditions:

I. All merchandise to be transported through the territory of the Republic shall make its entry at the places previously mentioned by the Government for such purposes.

II. Merchandise in transit shall be accompanied by the corresponding manifest and consular invoices, with the certification of the respective consul in the form and terms mentioned in the articles of this law relating to it, and the employés of the port or frontier custom houses through which the entry is made shall exercise, respecting them, the same formalities as ordered by this law for goods destined for consumption in the Republic.

III. For the delivery and dispatch of goods in transit, whatever may be their quality or kind, there shall be presented to the custom house the regular application in quadruplicate, according to Model No. 31, in which the parties interested shall request that, before the custom house proceed to an examination of the goods, their documents be corrected or added to as provided by Section IV, Chapter III, of this law.

IV. The goods having been properly examined, the collector shall order that each bundle be bound with wire and sealed with lead seals at the extremities of the same, and that the auditor's office proceed to fix the import duties, in order that he may charge as transit duties two per centum upon the total amount of said duties.

This duty shall be the only one to be charged by the public treasury on said goods, these latter being free from all other duty, even from such as may be charged by the various municipalities, no matter through what municipality the goods may be carried.

V. Foreign coffee which may be transported through the country shall not pay any duties whatsoever, provided the distance traveled through the national territory be not greater than thirty leagues.

VI. Parties bringing in goods intended for transportation as aforesaid shall have the right of applying to the collector of the port either of entry or of clearance to sell or consume part or the whole of their goods, provided they accompany said application with the consular invoice which they should have in their possession, and provided also they pay the import duties chargeable on said goods.

VII. If their application is for leave to use the whole of their goods, the custom house shall treat the consular documents in the same manner as though the case were the usual one of importation; but where only a portion of the goods is used, there shall be noted on the documents which are used to protect the balance of the goods during their transit, the number of packages which have been dispatched.

VIII. The importers of merchandise in transit shall give a bond for the satisfaction of the collector of the respective custom houses, for the payment of the total amount of the import duties corresponding to said goods. This bond shall be canceled the moment that the interested parties present the certificate given by the custom house through which the merchandise passes out of the country, and in which shall be stated that it has been dispatched in conformity with the document referring to it.

IX. When application is made at the port of clearance for permission to use or consume a part of the goods intended for transit, the custom house shall require of the parties interested a proper bond conditioned for the payment of such import duties as may be chargeable upon the goods to be exported, which said bond shall be made effective in case the parties fail to present within four months (a term not to be prolonged) a certificate subscribed by the Mexican consul, or, in his absence, by any other official of the place to which said goods were destined.

X. Merchandise in transit, to be transported from the point of entry to that through which it passes out of the national territory, shall be conducted safely by some railroad established in the country, and the collector, on granting the permits asked, shall immediately order that one of the employés of his office shall take charge of the train by which the goods are to be conveyed, as well as the documents referring to them, until their delivery at the custom house to which they are consigned.

Only in the case provided for by Section V of this article shall it be permitted to transport the goods in any kind of conveyance.

XI. When, during the transit of merchandise, it is necessary to transfer it, it shall be so stated on the manifest, indicating the place or places at which these operations shall be made, which must be at some place where there is a Federal office established.

XII. The collector of the custom house which authorizes the transit shall previously advise by telegraph and official documents the offices at which the transfers are to be made.

XIII. When the merchandise reaches the place at which it is to be transferred, the employé aforesaid in Fraction X of this article shall present to the chief of the office the documents referring to it, who shall examine the seals and padlocks placed on the cars, and finding them intact, shall order them opened, naming one of his own employés to examine in his presence whether the marks, countermarks and numbers of the packages correspond to those expressed in the custom house documents.

XIV. If they are found to agree, it shall be so stated at the foot of the document by the employé making the examination, and under his signature; and the chief of the office shall give permission to re-ship the merchandise, closing and sealing the cars or platform cars in which they are to be transported, and returning to the employé in charge of the train the documents, with the order to continue to their destination.

XV. When the merchandise in transit reaches the place through which it is to pass out, the collector of the custom house, along with the commander of inspectors, shall again examine the seals and padlocks of the cars or platform cars in which it is deposited; and finding them in good condition, shall give a certificate to that effect to the employé in charge of the train.

In case said seals or padlocks appear to have been tampered with, the custom house shall proceed as provided in Section VIII, of Article 296.

XVI. At the port or frontier custom house through which the merchandise passes out, it shall again be examined by the collector, appraiser and commander of inspectors, comparing it with the documents which should have been attached to the regular application, and being found in accord the certificate mentioned in Fraction V, of this article, shall be given.

XVII. If, from the examination made by the custom house through which the merchandise in transit is introduced, there are found differences between it and the documents coming from the place from which it was shipped, or if, on dispatching it at the custom house through which it passes out, there are found differences between it and the documents given for its transit, it shall be fined as provided by this ordinance, and the merchandise shall be considered as common importation, subject to the rates imposed by this tariff and not on the proportional part that it pays for its transit.

XVIII. Of all the proceedings observed by the custom houses at the ports of entry or of clearance, with regard to goods intended for international transit, immediate notice shall be given to the Treasury Department, accompanying therewith the documents provided by this law.

CHAPTER XI.

Warehouses for the Deposit of Foreign Merchandise.

Art. 300. The Government shall establish, when it deems it convenient, warehouses for the deposit of merchandise in connection with the maritime and frontier custom houses.

Art. 301. These warehouses shall be the property of the Federation or owned by private individuals, subject to the exclusive custody and vigilance of the custom houses where they may be established.

Art. 302. Merchandise left in the warehouses may remain in them for six months, after which time it must be withdrawn by its owners or consignees within fifteen days after it passed, and if its withdrawal has not been made, the custom house shall proceed to sell it at public auction, charging the custom house duties, storage and other expenses which it may have incurred. The balance left from the sale shall be left on deposit in the same office at the disposal of the owner or consignee, for such term as the law may provide.

Art. 303. Merchandise imported shall pay a storage duty as follows: For the first two months, one cent per day for each hundred kilogrammes or fraction thereof; for the two second months, two cents, and for the rest three cents. This time shall be counted from the moment the term mentioned in this ordinance for the immediate dispatch of merchandise has expired.

Art. 304. Merchandise which, by its nature, may suffer by decomposition during the six months mentioned for storage, shall not be admitted in the warehouses for any longer than the time necessary for its dispatch. The introduction into the warehouses of any packages which contain any kind of inflammable, explosive or corrosive materials, is also prohibited under the penalty mentioned in Art. 74.

Art. 305. The warehouses should be near the offices to which they belong without their being connected with any dwelling, and apart from factories or workshops in which fire is used. Their construction shall be such as to prevent damages, larceny or any other loss.

Art. 306. The goods stored shall be so arranged as to easily allow the taking out of any packages whenever their owners may request it.

Art. 307. The entry and withdrawal of the merchandise from the warehouse shall be made according to the rules established for each of these cases by this law.

Art. 308. The record of the entry and withdrawal of merchandise deposited, even when it belongs to private individuals, shall be taken by a warehouse guard of the Government with the same formalities as the warehousemen.

Art. 309. The auditor's office of the custom house shall control the books of the warehouses, in which shall be stated the dates of entry of the goods, withdrawal, storage paid, name of owner or consignee, where from, and lastly the destination. These entries shall be in complete harmony with those kept by the custom house and at the warehouses.

Art. 310. The deposit warehouses shall be opened and closed at the same hour as the custom house; its doors shall have four keys, to be in charge of the collector, auditor, guard to the warehouses, and the proprietor of the warehouses when these belong to private individuals.

Art. 311. The collector and the auditor of the custom house shall go alternately to the warehouse whenever their occupation shall permit it, and, if they are not able to do so, shall name an employé in their entire confidence to act in their stead.

CHAPTER XII.

General Traffic of Foreign Merchandise through the Zona Libre (Free State).

SECTION I.

OF THE FREE BELT.

Art. 312. The Zona Libre shall continue and be extended on the frontier of the Republic from Matamoros to Tijuana, and the States of Tamaulipas, Coahuila, Chihuahua, Sonora and the Territory of Lower California, in a longitudinal sense, and the width of which shall be twenty kilometers from the border line to the interior.

The concession of the Zona Libre provides that the goods imported through it shall enjoy in their dispatch and traffic all the prerogatives established by this chapter.

Art. 313. I. To enjoy the benefits of the Zona Libre, it is required that the importation be made by or through some point where there are established frontier custom houses of entry, and that the provisions for such cases be complied with.

II. No freight train can enter through the Mexican frontier except between the hours of five in the morning and five in the afternoon from the 15th of April to the 15th of September, and between seven in the morning and four in the afternoon from the 16th of September to the 14th of April.

III. Passenger trains shall be allowed to enter until ten o'clock at night, the car or platform cars containing the baggage being left over night in charge of the custom house, to be examined on the following day at the hour appointed for that purpose. Passengers shall be allowed to take with them the small packages of baggage that they may bring in their hands.

IV. In case of necessity a train can be allowed to pass during hours of the day and night other than those mentioned, but it must have express orders from the Executive of the Union sent through the Treasury Department.

Art. 314. All the provisions contained in this law respecting the ports open by the Republic to the traffic of the high seas shall be in force in frontier custom houses, so far as practicable, with the exceptions mentioned in this chapter.

SECTION II.

IMPORTATION OF FOREIGN MERCHANDISE INTO THE ZONA LIBRE (FREE BELT.)

Art. 315. Foreign merchandise shall not be introduced into the Zona Libre except through the frontier custom houses of entry.

And the shippers of goods destined for said territory shall observe in their importations the following rules:

I. All goods imported by any of the various railroads which join the United States and the National territory, shall come protected by the number of consular invoices and manifests mentioned in Articles 23 and 43 of Sections II and III, of Chapter II, of this law; and said documents shall contain the requisites prescribed by Models Nos. 32 and 33.

II. The conductor of a freight train, on reaching the custom house through which he must enter the Mexican territory, shall present to the guard house a general manifest of all the merchandise contained in the cars, platform cars, or any other class of vehicle composing the train, so that said employé may immediately transmit the same to the collector, accompanied by the report which it is his duty to make, giving the hour of arrival of the train, and noting any other circumstances which he may deem proper to include in his report.

III. The omission to deliver the consular manifest immediately upon the arrival of the train shall be punished by a fine of from twenty-five to fifty dollars, at the discretion of the collectors, and subject to the approval of the Treasury Department.

IV. In case, upon examining the cargo, it appears that there are more packages than there should be, and the conductor has failed to manifest the same to the collector of the port of entry immediately upon his arrival, the company shall be fined from five to fifty dollars for each package, and, in addition thereto, there shall be charged double duties upon the goods contained in said packages.

When, upon the arrival of the train, the conductor gives notice that he brings a greater number of packages than appear on the general manifest, by reason of his having received the same during the trip with their respective consular invoices, the custom house shall permit these to be added on to the general manifest, without imposing any penalty whatever.

VI. The unloading and discharge of goods imported by rail shall be effected immediately upon the presentation by the consignees of their respective applications, and the custom house, on receiving the same, shall proceed with its work as prescribed by Section I, of Chapter IV, of this law, subjecting itself, in the matter of charging duties, to the provisions of Section VIII of the following article.

VII. Consignees of goods imported by rail have the privilege of adding to or correcting the consular invoices at any time before the expiration of twenty-four hours, counted from the moment of the arrival of the train, provided said additions or corrections are made in accordance with the provisions of Section IV of Chapter III of this law.

VIII. In all cases of importation of goods by rail, the custom houses at the port of entry shall observe the provisions of this law relating to the custom houses at seaports.

Art. 316. When the importation of goods into the Free Belt is effected by other means of transportation than those contemplated in Section I of the preceding article, and when the said goods come from the cities, towns or villages of the United States situated on the frontier of our Republic, the following rules will be observed:

I. Every importation shall be made upon postal applications, which the importer shall present in triplicate to the collector of the corresponding custom house, stamping only one of said copies with stamp of the value of twenty-five cents on each leaf of paper of the common size; said applications shall contain all the requisites set forth in Model No. 34.

II. The collector shall place at the foot of the stamped copy the words, "*Let this be passed to the auditor's office for examination and for the comparison of the three copies,*" adding thereto his approval, if such it has: in case his approval be not had, the permit shall be revoked, and the party interested shall be ordered to replace the application.

III. The said applications having been compared, the auditor shall place, either upon the original permit or upon the stamped copy, the number corresponding to the same, and which shall be taken from a stub-book which the custom house shall receive for that purpose, authorized by the Treasury Department; he shall also place upon the stub, which should remain in said book, all the details thereon specified, after which he shall pass the same to the collector so that he may write thereon over his signature, "*permit the importation.*"

IV. These permits having been procured, the parties interested should present them to the consul or Mexican consular agent residing in the foreign town or city from which said goods come, in order to have the same certified, in the following form: "The present permit, presented in —— sheets of paper, contains —— packages." The date, signature of the consul or consular agent and the seal of the consulate.

V. The parties interested shall leave the "*duplicate*" of the application with the consul or consular agent, keeping for themselves the third copy, the principal or original being used to protect the goods on their entrance into Mexican territory.

VI. The cargo and the permit shall be presented at the corresponding custom house outpost so that the guard in charge of the same may compare the marks, countermarks and number of packages, marking the permit after copying it, and placing thereon the following: "Complied with and noted on page —— of the corresponding book." Date, signature of the guard and seal of the outpost. This done, said employé shall remit the permit with the cargo to the storehouses of the custom house, in order that it may there be examined and passed, at the same time officially notifying the collector of the differences, if such exist, or making such observations as he may deem proper in the matter; the goods should be accompanied from the custom house outpost by another guard.

VII. The goods having arrived at the custom house, the collector shall proceed to name an inspector to examine and dispatch the same; this shall be done by said employé in accordance with the provisions of Chapter IV, Section 1, of this law.

VIII. The examination and dispatch of said goods having been accomplished, the auditor's office shall calculate the total amount of duties in accordance with the tariff annexed to the ordinances, charging the parties interested, to be payable immediately, three per centum upon the quota of importation, which shall be divided as follows: 1.25 per centum to the municipality, and 1.75 per centum to the public treasury.

Art. 317. In order to avoid the necessity, on the part of the shipper, of presenting consular manifests and invoices for each importation which they may make, in fulfillment of what is by this law prescribed, they shall have the privilege at the end of each month of writing, in one manifest and one consular invoice, their several partial permits; said documents shall be issued subject to the terms prescribed by Articles 23 and 43 of this law, and in the forms given in Models Nos. 32 and 33, setting forth the numbers of the partial permits.

Art. 318. The shippers or brokers shall present to the consul or Mexican consular agents four copies of the manifest and invoices, for examination, to have the same compared with the partial permits, and to have them properly certified in the terms prescribed by Section I of Article 64. Consular charges, such as are specified in Article 67, shall be paid for said certification; a copy of each one of the partial permits mentioned in the manifest shall be forwarded to the Treasury Department, together with the third copy of the manifest and invoices.

Art. 319. The shippers and consignees of goods shall have the privilege, which by Section IV of Chapter III is granted to captains and consignees, to correct and make additions to their partial permits already issued and referred to in Section I of Article 316, provided this be done with in twenty-four hours after the issuing of said permit subjecting themselves to the penalties of this law.

Art. 320. The partial permits treated of in Section I of Art. 316 shall become void and of no effect on and after the third day from the date thereof, in case the goods for which they were issued have not been brought in; nevertheless the parties interested shall present them to the consul or Mexican consular agent, so that he may take note of the same, and in order that he may return to the collector of the Mexican custom house with the corresponding annotations the stamped copy which should have served to protect the goods on their entry. The custom house which issued said permits shall cancel the applications by means of a note, and shall include them in the general monthly account.

Art. 321. The frontier custom houses shall specify the places at which goods to be imported into the national territory are to be brought in.

Art. 322. All mistakes made by the importers on the documents, as well as in cases of fraud or irregularity, shall be punished as provided by this law.

SECTION III.

INTERNATION OF FOREIGN MERCHANDISE IN THE ZONA LIBRE (FREE BELT).

Art. 323. The internation of merchandise coming from frontier custom houses of entry in the Zona Libre shall be made according to the following rules:

I. The shipper shall present to the proper custom house an application in quadruplicate according to Model No. 30, using on one of the copies the revenue stamps required by the internal revenue law.

II. The collector having received those documents, he shall appoint thereon the inspector who is to make the examination and who is to dispatch the goods; the auditor's office shall note, in a special book, the number corresponding to the document, the name of the shipper, the number of packages, details in regard to the goods, place of destination and the inspector appointed to dispatch them.

III. This having been done, the application shall be delivered to the inspector for the purpose of enabling him to proceed with the examination and dispatch of said goods, with the same formalities observed at the time of their importation; the shippers, for this purpose, should present said goods at the storehouses of the custom house.

IV. The goods having been dispatched, the auditor's office shall proceed to a liquidation of the duties; these shall be payable forthwith by the shipper, the three per cent. which was paid at their importation according to the provisions of Article 316, Section VIII of this Chapter, being first deducted; there shall then be delivered to said shipper the document specified in Article 358, for the total amount of the duties chargeable on said goods, without any deduction of the amount paid at the time of importation, so that the interested party can proceed to place on it the special custom house stamps as expressed in Fraction II of Art. 291.

V. The auditor's office shall cancel, in the manner provided by Section III of Article 291, the stamps placed upon the application, and, fixing thereon the words "import duties paid," shall pass it to the collector, so that under his signature he may say, "*permit the internation.*"

VI. The same document shall be presented to the commander of the guards, who shall place on it the "*pass to its destination,*" sending it with an inspector to the guardhouse or railroad station through which the merchandise should pass or be shipped, so that the employé appointed by the collector, after comparing the cargo with the document, shall note in the corresponding book the number of the document, name of the shipper, number of packages, their marks, countermarks, general class of merchandise, amount of duties, consignee and destination; he shall in addition thereto mark said document "*complied with,*" dating and signing the same.

VII. If, from the examination made by the guard at the custom house outposts, or at the railroad station, it results that the packages are in accord with the document, they shall be delivered to the interested party; but if, on the contrary, it is found that there are more packages, or any other difference, the employé shall immediately inform the collector in writing, retaining the merchandise so as to proceed as the law may require.

Art. 324. After the goods destined for the interior have been examined and dispatched, the shippers of said goods may request the custom houses of the port of entry that the packages composing the cargo be bound with wires, to be sealed at their extremities by lead seals, in order to avoid having the same re-examined before leaving the last place within the jurisdiction of the Federal custom house police, or until their arrival at the capital of the Republic.

Art. 325. The custom house shall grant this request only in case the goods are carried into the interior by some of the lines of railroad, charging the shippers therefor two cents for each bundle which may be wired and sealed.

Art. 326. When the goods sent into the interior have the capital of the Republic for their destination, or some other place where there is permanently established a branch of the Federal custom house police, they shall be examined at that place; but if the goods are destined for other points it shall be the duty of the last section of the Federal custom house police by whom said goods are passed, to make the examination, collecting the seals and wires placed upon the packages, and giving account of the result to the respective commander of the Zona.

Art. 327. Of the four copies of the application for internation which the interested party should present according to the first fraction of Article 323, the one with the stamps shall serve to cover the merchandise to be internated, another shall serve as voucher for the ingress of the principal account, another shall justify the copy of the same which remains on file, and the last shall be sent to the Treasury Department by the first mail following the day when the documents are given.

SECTION IV.

TRANSFER OF FOREIGN GOODS FROM ONE FRONTIER CUSTOM HOUSE OF ENTRY TO ANOTHER IN THE ZONA LIBRE (FREE BELT.)

Art. 328. The transfer of foreign merchandise free of duties from one frontier custom house to another, or those established in the Zona Libre, shall be made according to the provisions herein expressed.

I. The shippers shall present four copies of an application in the same terms as ordered for internation, and the same steps shall be taken excepting as to the payment of duties, and also excepting the declarations to be made by the collector and the auditor, which latter shall be as follows: "Free of duties by reason of their being for consumption within the Zone," signed by the auditor, "*permit transportation*," with the signature of the collector and the seal of the custom house; the route by which the goods are to go being marked on the documents, this being always within the Free Belt.

II. The persons in whose favor the permit for transfer is granted shall present, within the time mentioned in the same permit, a certificate, subscribed by the collector and the auditor of the place to which the merchandise was sent, stating that they reached their destination, and were in accordance with the documents which covered them.

III. To enable the custom house from which the goods were sent to present the document mentioned in the previous fraction, the auditor shall exact in all cases a bond to the satisfaction of the collector for the total amount of the duties payable upon the merchandise according to the tariff of this law.

IV. The time mentioned having expired, and the shipper not having presented the certificate which proves the arrival of the goods at their destination, the custom house shall proceed to make effective the bond given, without the interested party being able to appeal.

V. The documents for the transportation of merchandise cannot be given except for one place, and with the intermediate places, and final destination shall be expressed on the same.

VI. The custom houses granting these documents shall immediately notify the office to which the goods are consigned, as well as those established on the route, to the end that they may order the route watched over which the goods are to pass over.

VII. The custom houses or branches of the place to which said goods are directed shall make the examination and dispatch of the goods, observing the same formalities as at the time of their importation, and giving notice of the result thereof to the custom house from which the same came.

Art. 329. For the commerce and transfer of merchandise made by the Rio Grande, there shall be observed, besides the requisites mentioned, those indicated in Chapter VI, Section III of this law, which treats of the coasting trade.

Art. 330. The merchandise transported from one frontier custom house of entry to another, as well as the cars, mules or any other means of conveyance, shall suffer the punishment assigned by the law whenever they violate the following:

I. When found outside of the route marked in the custom house document which covers the shipment.

II. When the documents do not contain all the requisites indicated by law.

III. Going without the custom house document referring to the shipment.

IV. For conveying a shipment with fraudulent documents.

Art. 331. All other cases of fraud or irregularity in the transfer of merchandise shall be punished with the penalties indicated by this ordinance.

Art. 332. The custom house granting the permit for the transfer of merchandise, as well as that which receives it, shall remit by first mail to the Treasury Department a certified copy of this document.

SECTION V.

CONSUMPTION OF MERCHANDISE AT PLACES OF THE ZONA LIBRE IN WHICH ENTRY FRONTIER CUSTOM HOUSES OR CUSTOM HOUSE SECTIONS ARE NOT ESTABLISHED.

Art. 333. The dispatch of foreign merchandise proceeding from entry custom houses or custom house sections, intended for consumption in the towns or ranches situated in the Zona Libre, shall be subject to the following:

I. That the inhabitants of the towns or ranches may be able to get from the places where there are custom houses or custom house sections of entry the goods for consumption up to twenty-five dollars, these shall present themselves and the goods to the custom house or custom house section to which they correspond to obtain the proper permit.

II. In each of the entry custom houses or custom house sections the collectors or chiefs of the bureaus shall designate an employé to write the applications for consumption for the inhabitants that are entitled to them and who cannot write them themselves, making them in duplicate, and without receiving pay. One of the copies shall bear a twenty-five cent revenue stamp.

III. The collector or chief of the custom house section shall commission an employé to take account of the permits, and enter them in a book for that purpose, authorized therefor by the highest political authority of the place, and in which shall be entered the date, corresponding number, name of the interested party, value of the goods, and name of the town or ranch for which they are intended. This employé shall cancel the stamps placed on the aforesaid permits.

IV. The permit having been numbered by the employé referred to in the previous fraction, the interested party shall present it to the collector or chief of the section, that he may declare and sign "*permit their delivery free of duties,*" and the commander or inspector acting in his stead shall declare "*pass to its destination.*" After the goods have been examined by the appraiser or employé designated by the collector or chief of the section, and if he is satisfied that the value does not exceed twenty-five dollars, he shall note "*conformable,*" and sign it.

V. The inspectors of the respective guard houses shall take account of the aforesaid permits, and shall state on them "*complied with this day, and recorded on page ——— of the book kept for this purpose,*" adding the seal of the guard house and the signature of the inspector.

Art. 334. The entry custom house, as well as the custom house sections, shall ask every six months from the municipal authorities a certified copy of the census of the inhabitants of the towns or ranches of their respective jurisdictions, so that they may watch the employés who write the permits, that they may not give them to other persons, nor duplicate them to one person at one time, so as to guard against the abuse of frequent repetitions.

Art. 335. All merchandise which requires the corresponding pass, or which has not complied with the necessary requisites, when it reaches the guard houses or leaves the towns shall be subject to the penalties indicated by Article 372. Merchandise which, although it has the proper pass, goes beyond its point of destination, shall also be subject to the same fines.

Art. 336. The collectors or chiefs of custom house sections shall grant to the owners of the village or ranches situated in the Zona Libre general permits for the free use of their cars and carriages within the belt; said permits shall have stamps to the value of twenty-five cents, which the interested party shall cancel on the proper application, and shall give a bond to the satisfaction of the collectors or chiefs of the section, who shall exact the payment of the import duty if the said vehicles pass out of the Zona Libre.

Said permits shall be good for one year, and the parties interested must renew the same on penalty of forfeiting their security by reason of not complying with this requisite.

SECTION VIII.

PASSENGERS AND THEIR BAGGAGE AT FRONTIER CUSTOM HOUSES OF ENTRY IN THE ZONA LIBRE.

Art. 337. On the arrival of a passenger train on the Mexican frontier, the chief of the section of guards placed at the railroad station shall order that one or more inspectors board the cars and examine the packages which the passengers carry in their hands, placing on those examined and which do not contain dutiable goods, a ticket saying: "*Dispatched by the guards of the custom house at—————.*" Packages containing dutiable goods shall be conducted, under the vigilance of the employés making the examination, to the place where the baggage is examined.

Art. 338. No package shall be taken from the train while the examination of the baggage is being made.

Art. 339. All baggage in the car, or platform car which conveys it, shall be unloaded at the place assigned for that purpose by the railroad.

Art. 340. The unloading of the baggage shall be made in the presence of one of the inspectors appointed by the collector, who shall be obliged to examine the car or platform car which contained the baggage, after it is unloaded, to make sure that all the packages are taken to the place where their examination is to be made.

Art. 341. The passengers shall open their packages, or give their keys, so that the appraiser appointed by the collector can make the examination along with the commander of inspectors.

Art. 342. If, in the baggage examined, there are found articles which should pay duty, the passenger shall immediately make a declaration in writing, according to Model No. 35. The custom house shall have these declarations printed, so that they can be given to the passenger when necessary.

Art. 343. In case the owner of the goods refuses to pay the duty on them, they shall be sent to the custom house, where they shall be kept thirty days, and if, during that time, they are not claimed, they shall be sold at public auction, and from the amount obtained from their sale be deducted the import duties, storage, and other expenses, and the balance shall be on deposit to be delivered to the owner of the goods.

Art. 344. As the baggage is examined, the inspector commissioned by the custom house shall place on each of the packages a ticket saying: "*Examined at the custom house of*—————," and the inspector guarding the gate through which these goods are to pass shall permit the withdrawal or shipment of the package or packages dispatched.

Art. 345. If, on the termination of the examination of the baggage, there remains one or more packages whose examination has not been asked, the appraiser shall order them sent, under the vigilance of one of the inspectors on duty at the railway station, to the custom house.

Art. 346. The collector of the custom house, on receiving the package or packages sent by the appraiser, shall order that before they are deposited in the warehouse they shall be bound with wires and lead seals fixed on their extreme ends.

Art. 347. If, after the baggage of a passenger remains unclaimed for six months in the warehouse of the custom house, the packages shall be opened and the goods examined, and the collector shall order them sold at public auction, the proceeds of the sale shall be declared "*Profit of the National Treasury.*"

Art. 348. When the owner of the baggage refuses to open it for examination, and there are found in it dutiable articles which were not declared, it shall be considered as a case of contraband, and subject to the penalties established by this law.

Art. 349. If, in the baggage, there is found some package of merchandise whose value is more than one hundred dollars, its owner shall bring it duly covered by its proper custom house invoices, so that the custom house may proceed as indicated in cases of importation.

Art. 350. The inhabitants and transit persons of the American frontier shall be allowed to pass a horse and carriage without the payment of custom house duties, provided the person bringing it intends to return the same day or the next with the same horse and carriage.

Art. 351. Inhabitants of the Zona Libre temporarily passing into the American territory are allowed to pass an altered horse and carriage the exportation requisites shall not be exacted from them, nor shall they be charged custom duties for said horse and carriage on their return to the Zona Libre.

Art. 352. The owners of cars and carriages that, for a certain time, pass from the American side into the Zona Libre, shall obtain from the collector of the custom houses the respective permit, giving a bond for the payment of the import duties, so that in case the cars and carriages are not promptly returned to their destination within the time granted, the duties shall be collected on them. Said time shall not exceed six months in any case.

Art. 353. It shall be stated on the permits granted by the custom houses that the cars and carriages allowed to enter temporarily shall not pass beyond the limits of the Zona Libre, and in case of abuse the bond given shall be declared forfeited.

Art. 354. The inhabitants of the Zona Libre are also allowed by the collectors of the custom houses temporary permits to pass with their cars and carriages into the American territory, and if they are returned to the place from which they started within the time specified, the interested parties shall return to the custom house granting the permit the corresponding export documents that it may cancel the bond which they gave.

Art. 355. It is the duty of every person taking passage, at places on the frontier for the interior of the Republic, on board of any railroad train to present his baggage for examination the same as passengers coming from abroad.

Art. 356. Besides that disposed in the previous articles, Section V of Chapter IV of this law shall also be observed.

CHAPTER XIII.

Custom House Stamps.

Art. 357. There shall be established for all foreign merchandise for internal use certain special stamps, which shall be called "*Custom House Stamps.*" These shall contain the marks of the corresponding fiscal year, the name of the point to which the goods are destined and that of the place from which the importation is made. The use of these stamps is intended solely for the time specified in this law. The value of these special custom house stamps shall be as follows:

Of	$1,000 00
Of	500 00
Of	100 00
Of	25 00
Of	10 00
Of	5 00
Of	1 00
Of	0 25
Of	0 10
Of	0 05
Of	0 01

Art. 358. The custom house shall give to the importer, on payment of the duties according to the tariff of this ordinance, a receipt for the entire sum, which, on being presented to the collector, or the clerk in charge of the stamp office, residing at the place where the goods are imported, shall be charged for an equal amount in custom house stamps. For this operation the interested party shall pay to the collector from whom he receives the stamps 2 per cent. cash on the total amount of the stamps.

Art. 359. These stamps, which shall correspond in value with the total amount of duty on the importation, shall be placed on the documents covering the merchandise when its internation is applied for.

Art. 360. On receiving the application for internation, the custom houses shall cancel with the seal of the office the stamps which are placed on the documents covering the merchandise as aforesaid, and shall compare the value of the stamps with the amount of duty on the importation.

Art. 361. The stamps received by the importers of merchandise shall not be serviceable after the year in which they are issued and the one following, but stamps to any amount remaining unused after the period named shall be deemed valueless.

Art. 362. Any importer of merchandise who shall use any stamp or stamps discarded as aforesaid according to this law, shall incur the penalty of paying an amount equal to double the duties chargeable upon said merchandise as declared on the documents.

Art. 363. The documents covering merchandise which passes, in transit, through the territory of the Republic, as well as that which is taken out of the frontier custom houses of entry for consumption in the Zona Libre, shall not require the special custom house stamps.

Art. 364. Special custom house stamps shall not be used on the documents which cover merchandise transferred from one custom house to another in the Zona Libre, but, upon their arrival at the point of destination, a part or all of them are to be internated; the custom house shall give the interested party, in order to comply with the law, as provided in these cases, the proofs of the payment of the total amount of duties chargeable upon the merchandise that is to be internated, without discounting, in this case, the 3 per cent. which, according to this law, should have been paid at the custom house from whence the goods came.

Art. 365. The collectors or persons in charge of the stamp offices shall change, for the accommodation of importers of merchandise, the special stamps of the custom house which they may have on hand and desire to sub-divide for use.

This change shall always be made when the stamps presented have not become worthless by reason of the term mentioned in Article 361, of this chapter, having expired; the change shall be made into stamps of the same fiscal year which is marked upon those presented.

If the stamps presented are torn, stained or defaced in such a manner that they cannot be again used, the change shall not be made.

Art. 366. The custom house documents which, according to this ordinance, require stamps, shall be subject to that provided in the stamp law for its respective tariff.

CHAPTER XIV.

Infractions of the Law, and the Penalties.

SECTION I.

INFRACTIONS OF THIS LAW.

Art. 367. The infraction of this law, in cases of importation or exportation of merchandise, are divided into crimes, violations and faults.

Art. 368. Crimes are:
I. Contraband.
II. Fraud committed in connivance with one or more of the public employés.

Art. 369. Violations are:
I. Fraud without connivance with the employés, or falsifying in quality, quantity or in both, the merchandise which, manifested legally, would pay a higher duty.
II. Omission, or inexactness respecting the requisites indicated by this law for the operations relative to the collection of the import and export duties which are essential to said collection.

Art. 370. Faults are:
I. The omission, or inexactness in the statement of requisites such as are not essential for the collection of the exchequer.
II. What has been said has reference to private individuals.

In the case of public employés of the treasury, crimes are: bribery, peculation and collusion; violations are: omissions in the fulfillment of their duty, causing or which may cause losses to the treasury; and faults are: such omissions as do not involve such losses.

Art. 371. Contraband is the offense committed by importing or exporting merchandise which is subject to the payment of the fiscal duties, and without the knowledge or intervention of the proper public employés, whether done clandestinely or by violence.

Art. 372. It is also considered contraband to import goods that are not subject to the payment of duties, without giving the proper information to the custom house. War materials are contraband in the period during which their transportation is prohibited by the Federal Executive; goods proceeding from a nation that is at war with the United States of Mexico; the landing of goods through parts or places in rebellion against the Government; the omission in the general manifest of one or more packages of the cargo of a vessel, when not added to the manifest in time to conform with the provisions of this law, and the importation of counterfeit money of whatever coinage.

Art. 373. The internation of merchandise without the documents certifying to their having been legally imported, and upon which the payment of the fiscal duties has been made, and that imported with false or fraudulent documents, shall also be considered contraband.

Art. 374. Fraud consists in attempting to elude, all or part, the payment of the fiscal duties on importation or exportation, concealing the right quantity or quality of the merchandise, or making it appear to be such as exempt from duty, or rating it in less quantities on the face of the custom house dispatch.

Art. 375. Employés of the treasury commit the crime of bribery, whatever may be their positions, who conspire with those paying duties of importation or exportation, to elude, in all or in part, the payment of said duties; and those parties who conspire with the employés for the same purpose also commit the said crime of bribery.

Art. 376. Employés of the public treasury commit the crime of peculation who divert from their object the funds or values of whatever class belonging to the Federation, and which they have received on account of their positions as employés.

Art. 377. Employés of the treasury commit the crime of collusion who, in the exercise of these functions, fraudulently exact of those persons owing fiscal duties a greater amount than the legitimate duties, whether committed by themselves or other persons, and which consist in the illegal exaction of moneys, values, services or any other thing whatsoever.

Art. 378. The violations are those made either by omission or commission, or by omitting not to duly comply with one or more of the provisions contained in Articles 39, 45, 46, 47, 54, 56, 74, and Sections III and IV of Article 107, and Sections II, III, IV, V, VI and VII of Article 3 of this law.

Art. 379. It shall be considered a fault always not to obey, for any reason whatever, any of the precepts contained in Arts. 25, 30, 48 and 112.

Art. 380. These faults shall be punished only by fines, as set forth in the following section. They are only punishable when they are proven to have been consummated, and the penalties shall be inflicted by the administrative authorities. Violations are punished by pecuniary penalties, administratively or judicially, according to the selection made by the interested parties in conformity with what is provided in Art. 385. Crimes are determined on investigation made by the judicial authority, and the administrative authority shall previously secure the payment of the fiscal duties. Guilty parties shall be punished by the personal and pecuniary penalties that are hereafter provided, and shall remain subject to the rules of the common Penal Code.

Art. 381. The violations and faults of consuls and consular agents of the Republic in foreign countries shall be punished by the Secretary of State, that official having been previously officially informed by the Secretary of the Treasury as to said violations and faults.

SECTION II.

PENALTIES.

Art. 382. The penalties for the crimes, violations and faults described in the last section are the following:

I. Forfeiture in favor of the treasury, as an indemnification for damages and injuries, of the vessels, cars, beasts of burden, arms, and whatever else may have been used in the perpetration of the crime.

II. To be forfeited in favor of the treasury, as an indemnification for damages and injuries, the goods in the importation or exportation of which there has been discovered fraud or an intent to defraud.

III. Payment of duties.
IV. Fines.
V. Ordinary imprisonment.
VI. Suspension of employment and salary.

VII. Deprivation of employment, charge or commission.
VIII. Disqualification to obtain certain employments or charges.
IX. Disqualification from all classes of employment, charges, commissions or honors.

Art. 383. Persons guilty of contraband, who in committing the same shall have used violence, shall suffer imprisonment for not less than six months nor more than five years; and this penalty shall be imposed on the owners, conductors, captains or agents under any other title who import or export goods, employing force to evade the payment of the fiscal duties.

If the importation, exportation or internation is done clandestinely, without the knowledge of the employés to whom should be paid the fiscal duties, or by the use of false or fraudulent documents, then the guilty parties shall be punished with imprisonment for not less than six months nor to exceed two years.

The accomplices and receivers connected with said contraband transactions shall suffer one-half of the penalty visited upon the principal delinquents, and one and all deprived of whatever employment or commission they have, besides being disqualified for obtaining employment, charge, commission or honors.

In every case of contraband all the merchandise affected thereby shall be forfeited to the Government as a means of indemnification for damages and loss.

Art. 384. In case of fraud committed or attempted by collusion with the employés, the following penalties shall be imposed:

I. The responsible employés will be punished with not less than six months nor more than five years imprisonment, with loss of employment, and disqualification for any other commission, employment, charge or honor under the Government.

II. Persons who have been parties to the defrauding of the Government, but who have no official standing or connection, shall be punished with not less than three months nor more than four years imprisonment, besides the payment of double duties on the merchandise affected, and with a fine of not less than two hundred dollars nor more than three thousand dollars.

Art. 385. The crime of bribery on the part of the employé shall be punished with not less than six months nor more than four years imprisonment, a fine equal to double the amount of the bribe, the loss of employment, and disqualification for any other under the Government.

The individual who bribes, or offers to bribe an employé or public functionary, besides incurring the penalty of Art. 384, Fraction II of this law, shall suffer half the penalty therein stated.

Art. 386. The peculator shall be punished with not less than one nor more than five years imprisonment, and a fine of double the amount taken, besides the loss of employment and disqualification for any other under the Government.

Art. 387. The crime of collusion shall be punished by the exaction of a fine in favor of the treasury of double the amount illegally received, and the loss of employment.

Art. 388. The violation consisting in defrauding the Government of the duties without collusion with the employés shall be punished with the penalty of double the duties of importation, solely on merchandise affected either in quality or quantity, or in both cases.

When an invoice has received any addition or additions, and in the dispatch the class, quality, length, width, weight, etc., of the merchandise rectified are increased, or exchanged for others, the consignee shall pay, besides the amount set forth in the correction as indicated by the articles covered by this law, double importation duties on the goods attempted to be introduced fraudulently.

Art. 389. The violations consisting of the omission or inexactness of the necessary data for the adjustment of the fiscal duties shall be punished with the corrections expressed in Articles 39, 45, 46, 47, 54, 56, 74, and Sections III and IV of Article 107, and Sections II, III, IV, V, VI and VII, of Article 111 of this law.

Art. 390. The faults shall be punished by the fines in the proportions expressed in Articles 25, 30, 48 and 112.

Art. 391. Whenever any infraction of this law is made in connection with the perpetration of other crimes known to the common law, the judges of the district shall punish the offenders in conformity with the Federal law, observing the cumulative rules.

CHAPTER XV.

Judgments.

SECTION I.

GENERAL DISPOSITIONS RELATING TO JUDGMENTS.

Art. 392. The administrative power to decide that an infraction of the law has been committed, relating either to importation or exportation, belongs exclusively to the collectors of the maritime and frontier custom houses and to the Treasury Department, except when a definite decision has already been given by the judicial authority as required by this law. The collectors are authorized to make the corrections in accordance with which punishment for omissions is to be determined, subject to revision by the Treasury Department in the event of appeal by interested parties.

The infractions shall be punished by the administrative authority, provided the interested party has not expressed his intention to appeal from the judicial order to make the declaration mentioned in Art. 395.

Art. 393. It is the duty of the collectors and auditors of the custom houses, and of the attorneys of the courts of the district and of the Circuit Courts, each in its own jurisdiction, and in the order of its passage, to carry the judicial representation of the treasury as far as possible so as to collect all the fiscal duties, as well as to accuse and prosecute the authors, accomplices and concealers of the infractions of this law. All the functionaries shall act in accordance with the instructions received from the Treasury Department. They may, however, make observations to said department if they entertain opinions contrary to said instructions; but if they are renewed, then they shall follow them with the exception of that provided for in Art. 395.

Art. 394. The violations of the fiscal duties guaranteed by this law can be prosecuted in two ways: the one, merely civil, shall proceed to make effective the collection of the fiscal duties belonging to the treasury and the pecuniary penalties which the law in each case provides; and the other, of the penal order, shall impose the sentences which may have been pronounced.

Art. 395. In every case of infraction of this law the administrative authority, before there shall have been any judicial proceedings in the case, shall institute a brief proceeding, in which, after assigning the cause of and the declaration of what constitutes a fault, violation or crime, shall also dictate the official disposition as to the manner of assuring the fiscal duties and the pecuniary penalties which are provided for in this law. It shall immediately make known the submission or opposition of the responsible parties; and in view of one or the other, and of the provisions of this law, shall order the docket filed, if the interested party submits to the punishment imposed on him, or they shall remit it to the Secretary of the Treasury, if it is so desired. In a case of violation in the second case, that is to say, where he does not submit, the defendant shall have the right to appeal against the decision of the collector, either to the district court or to the Treasury Department, with the understanding that if no appeal be taken within eight days from the moment of giving notice, the defendant shall be considered as consenting, and the sentence shall be enforced, it being the duty of the collector to transmit a copy of the proceedings to the District Court, when he shall be requested thereto.

Proceedings relating to the commission of a crime shall be sent immediately to the proper District Court.

Art. 396. In the judicial proceedings the civil and penal judgments shall be followed separately. In the first case the plaintiff shall make the claim against the declaration made by the administrative authority, whatever may be the amount demanded. To this declaration there shall be no entry given if it is not accredited with the certificate of the proper collection office where the fiscal duties are secured, and also the pecuniary penalties that have been imposed.

The penal judgment shall be followed by a separate course of the process opened on account of the claim mentioned in the foregoing article, until the imposition of the corresponding penalties which the judges officially make.

Art. 397. The accused party can appeal before the Secretary of the Treasury, in the form of Art. 39, or in any other form, against the decisions of the collectors of maritime and frontier custom houses; but on that account, only, the claims submitted to the courts shall not be admitted, and the right of recourse to them shall be denied.

Art. 398. The administrative decisions given in the cases of assimilation, and in those of the appraisers, with the observance of the rules established in this law, are there claimable, nor can they be subjects of the civil judgments of which the following section treats.

Art. 399. In these same cases the penal judgment only will take effect when, in the prosecution of them, there is discovered some of the crimes that are expressed in this law; but without this they will suspend the civil operation of the judgment of the appraisers, or of assimilation.

SECTION II.

CIVIL JUDGMENTS.

Art. 400. The proceedings of the judgments which arise from the claims made against the administrative decision shall be oral, provided they relate to amounts that do not exceed one thousand dollars; exceeding that amount the judgment shall be written.

Art. 401. In verbal judgments the following provisions shall be observed.

I. The suit against the administrative opinion shall only be granted, if it is commenced within eight days after it is made known to the interested party.

II. The promoter and the collector of the custom house together, or the persons acting in their stead, and the fiscal promoter shall proceed as follows: The first shall make the demand, which the second shall answer under the direction of the last, and there can be replies or questions and answers. After these are given, the several parties shall plead for their sides, respectively, and the judge shall pronounce sentence. If proofs are required there shall be a time stated, not to exceed ten days, during which all the proofs can be presented according to law; but the testimony shall be given in public and shall be received in the presence of the two parties, who can without limitation question the witnesses, of all of which a minute record shall be made.

III. The time having expired, a term of court shall be held, at the latest within three days, at which the judge shall hear the arguments of the parties, and render an immediate decision according to law.

IV. This decision shall not admit of appeal; but the judge shall always send the papers in the case to the Circuit Court, so that the latter may examine whether the judge might be held accountable in any way, and be punished officially by the same.

V. If the claimant instituting the action does not appear at the term held for the hearing of the case, or he fails to continue the same for one entire month, the judge shall release the officer at the request of his representative.

Art. 402. In summary proceedings the following procedure shall be followed:

A. The demand shall only be taken cognizance of when pressed within eight days after the administrative decision which he complains against has been made known to the interested party.

B. The demand being formulated by the claimant, a copy thereof shall be given, together with the corroboration set forth in Art. 396, for three days, to the administrative officer who made the disposition which gave rise to the complaint.

C. The transfer being made, or in want thereof the claimant acknowledging default, the case shall be open to proof, if any of the parties desire it, for a period not to exceed fifteen days.

D. The time having expired, publication of the proofs shall be made at the request of either of the parties, fixing a date within three days for the hearing of the argument, which must be verbal. The citation for the hearing shall have the same effect as a citation for rendering judgment.

The decision shall be made within twenty-four hours after the session for the hearing of the argument, whether the same has been held or not, and shall only be appealable so far as reinstatement can be had.

E. The appeal shall be made within three days, which shall extend, for the treasury officer, from the date when his representative has been notified, unless he, at the trial, declares that he desires instructions from the office of the Secretary of the Treasury, in which case the judge shall allow him a given time, according to distance, never to exceed forty days. The time shall extend, for the other party, from the date wherein he has been notified.

The representative of the treasury, in every case, shall send a copy of the judgment at first instance to the office of the Secretary of the Treasury.

F. If appeal is made, the judge, allowing it openly, shall send the papers in the case to the Circuit Court within forty-eight hours at the least, a reasonable time being given to the person having suit with the treasury officer to appear in this appeal court, whether he be appellant or not.

The treasury officer need not present himself to perfect the appeal; and to continue the same the Circuit Court, when the papers in the case have been received, shall cite his district attorney.

G. The appeal in this second court shall be had, issuing the citations for the hearing of the case, unless one of the parties move for evidence within twenty-four hours after the notification of the arrival of the papers in the case has been made, setting forth the steps which shall be taken.

H. The time given for presenting the evidence shall not exceed one-half of that fixed at first instance, and no other evidence shall be admitted therein in this second court than such as is in conformity with the law.

I. The judgment of this second court may result in issuing an execution, if it confirm or revoke the judgment at first instance, and from this judgment no relief can be had except that of holding the judge accountable therefor.

A certified copy of the writ of execution shall be sent to the office of the Secretary of the Treasury.

J. The treasury officer, at the request of his representative, shall be released by the proper judge or court, at any state of the proceedings, whenever the complaint against the dispositions of such administrative office shall cease for one whole month to press the case.

Art. 403. In the proceedings treated of in this section the judges shall not be made accountable.

Art. 404. The experts appointed by the representatives of the treasury officer cannot be objected to, being public employés.

Art. 405. No other employés than those which this law intrusts with the representation of the treasury shall be held to be parties, nor shall they be participants in the distribution of the pecuniary fines.

Art. 406. The pleadings shall not be taken out of the courts and tribunals, and in the transfers made from one court to the other only copies of the papers shall be delivered, the originals being shown when the copies are presented.

Art. 407. In all cases not provided for, the proceeding proper thereto shall be had in accordance with the laws of procedure in force in the Federal tribunals for another class of cases.

SECTION III.

OF PENAL PROCEEDINGS.

Art. 408. All public employés of the Treasury Department in the maritime and frontier custom houses are bound to investigate all offenses committed in said department, make the same known to the judicial authorities, and aid in collecting evidence thereof, and to ascertain who are the offenders, accomplices and concealers, giving account of what they shall do, in due course, to the Secretary of the Treasury.

Art. 409. Every person having knowledge that one of the offenses whereof this law treats has been committed, is being committed, or is about to be committed, is bound to make the same known to the proper judge, or to any of the treasury employés in the locality, without being bound thereby to continue in the proceedings. This obligation does not extend to such as have knowledge of the offense by virtue of privileged communications, nor to the consort, nor to the relatives of the guilty persons.

Art. 410. The authorities who are competent to take cognizance of the offenses of which this law treats are the district judges of the locality where the same are committed; and wherever there may be two judges, the one holding session by turn will be competent. The common law judges shall take the first steps in the proceedings in aid of the Federal justice, wherever there may not be any district judge.

Art. 411. The penal proceedings shall commence by a notice given to the proper judge by the administrative officer, or by direct disclosure made to the same, in accordance with Article 409, by any person, whether he be a public employé or not, or on petition of the district attorney, who in every case is the only one that can formulate the accusation and be considered a party in the proceedings.

Art. 412. When the judge has cognizance of an offense, he shall proceed to take all steps tending to prove the fact or omission constituting the same, causing the letter of description and the inventory of the property which may have relation thereto to be drawn up, detaining all persons that could testify, and holding safe all objects wherein the treasury might have some right, or which may serve to ascertain the truth.

Art. 413. With the same end in view, the judge shall take the necessary steps, examine the experts, who in the absence of others may be the same custom house employés, and shall omit nothing that may tend to prove the existence of the *corpus delicti*.

Art. 414. The judge himself shall then immediately examine whoever may appear as offenders, accomplices or concealers of the offense, within forty-eight hours after their arrest, the examination of the same concluding in making known to them the notice of the proceeding, and advising them to name a person or persons to defend them.

Art. 415. When these steps have been taken, witnesses examined, comparisons made, persons confronted, and other proper measures taken, the judge, if he find an illicit act proved which deserves punishment, and that there is sufficient evidence to justify the opinion that the persons detained as offenders, accomplices or abettors are guilty, shall declare them to be formally under arrest, and thenceforth the proceedings shall be public.

Art. 416. The other steps, until the inquiry is perfected, shall be taken in the shortest time possible, so that the same may be completed, at the latest, within one month; and, when this has been concluded, the papers in the case shall be delivered to the district attorney, with whom they shall remain for three days, so that he may demand what may be proper in the case.

Art. 417. The district attorney has power:

I. To formulate his accusation against the accused, if he find sufficient law and facts to sustain the same, but he shall specify carefully such cases.

II. To ask for a suspension, in case he does not find in the papers the existence of the offense, and guilt of the person or persons accused sufficiently proved.

III. To move for the taking of new steps in the case.

Art. 418. In this last case, the judge shall order the proceedings desired to be had, after which the papers in the case shall again be given to the district attorney, for the purposes set forth in the last article.

Art. 419. In the second case, the judge, after issuing citation, shall order the stay or suspension, if he finds the same in accordance with the law. Otherwise he shall return the papers to the district attorney, who shall draw up the accusation.

Art. 420. In the first of the cases specified in Art. 417, the papers in the proceedings shall be for three days at the disposal of the counsel for the accused, and, when his answer is received, a day shall be set apart from the three days following for the hearing of arguments, on which date the counsel of the accused and the representative of the treasury shall orally set forth their legal rights. A citation issued for such hearing shall be as effective as a citation for judgment.

Art. 421. From the time when the order of imprisonment is made to the time when the citation for the hearing of arguments is issued, the accused or their counsel may offer all evidence proper in law.

Art. 422. A decision shall be rendered within forty-eight hours after the term for the hearing of the arguments has been held, whether the parties have appeared or not.

Art. 423. This judgment shall be appealable in both respects. The orders of formal arrest and other dispositions made in the case shall only be appealable in so far as restoration of rights can be had.

Art. 424. If the appeal is allowed in both respects, the case shall be sent first to the Circuit Court; if it be only intended for the purpose of restoring rights, there shall only be sent to said court certified copies of such portions of the case as the parties may deem proper and which the judge may deem necessary for such revision.

Art. 425. When the papers in the case, or certified copies thereof, have been received, the judge of the circuit shall set apart a day for the hearing, wherein the district attorney and the counsel for the accused shall state the case, the appellant opening the same.

Art. 426. The parties in this second court can only offer evidence when they are cited for the hearing of the case, and they must then set forth the nature and object of such evidence, but testimony in regard to facts which were subject-matter for the examination of witnesses at first instance, shall not be admissible. The court shall clearly admit or reject the evidence in the former case, fixing the period, not to exceed five days, to receive the same, issuing thereafter a new citation for the hearing.

Art. 427. The citation issued for the hearing shall also be for judgment, and this shall be entered the day after the one fixed for the hearing, whether the parties have appeared to state their case or not.

Art. 428. The judgment of this second court shall be enforced by execution, whether it confirms or reverses the one rendered at first instance; but the papers in the case shall be sent to the Supreme Court of Justice, for the purposes of the law.

Art. 429. The judges cannot be objected to in these proceedings.

Art. 430. Whenever it shall become necessary to imprison a public employé who has charge of and cares for the interests of the treasury on his own responsibility, the judge shall always see that the money and other securities which said employé cares for, by reason of his office, be previously delivered to the proper person, but this shall not prevent the securing of the person of said employé meanwhile.

Art. 431. All subjects not modified by this section, the judges and courts shall be governed in the determination of the cases treated of therein by the procedure followed in other cases relative to offenses in the Federal courts.

SECTION IV.

DISPOSITION TO BE MADE OF THE FINES IMPOSED FOR VIOLATIONS OF THIS LAW.

Art. 432. Every person seizing foreign goods that may have been imported or brought inland by smuggling, or shall give notice of any fraudulent transaction of the same nature intended to be perpetrated, shall be entitled to receive the share therein fixed by this law, after deducting the proper duties due to the public treasury, and the two per cent. allowed to the hospitals, whenever by such notice it may result that in pursuance of this ordinance the final forfeiture of the merchandise or the payment of a fine is decreed.

In these cases, after making the reductions specified in the present article, the part which shall be paid to the informer and to the seizer shall be as follows: to the seizer, twenty-five per cent., to the informer twenty-five per cent.; in case there is no informer, the part which would otherwise belong to him shall go to those who make the seizure, though they be employés.

Art. 433. The amount of fines imposed upon the faults committed in violation of Articles 25, 30, 48 and 112 of this law shall be paid into the public treasury, under the designation of "Profits."

Art. 434. In other cases than those specified in the preceding article, the fines which may be collected by reason of infractions of the provisions of this law shall be divided among the custom house employés in the following proportions:

I. In the case of Article 432, the amount due to the informer and the seizer having been deducted, the balance of fifty per cent. shall be distributed as follows: eighteen per cent. to the collector of the custom house, twelve per cent. to the auditor, ten per cent. to the commander of the guards, and ten per cent. to pay the expenses of the seizure and as fees to the inferior employés of the custom houses and outposts.

II. In case of seizures made by the inspector at the time of dispatch, thirty-five per cent. shall go to the collector of the custom house, thirty-five per cent. to the inspector, ten per cent. to the auditor, ten per cent. to the commander of the guards, and ten per cent. to pay the expenses of the seizure, and as fees to the inferior employés of the custom houses and outposts.

III. In the seizures made by comparing the manifests and the invoices, as well as for additions and rectifications, other than those specified in Article 112, the amount of fines imposed shall be distributed in the following proportions: thirty-five per cent. to the collector, thirty-five per cent. to the auditor, twenty per cent. to the employés who may have been engaged in comparing said documents, and ten per cent. to pay the expenses of the seizure and as fees to the inferior employés of the custom houses and outposts.

IV. Whenever the seizure is made by a custom house police cutter, the crew shall receive twenty-five per cent., the commandant ten per cent., the officers ten per cent., the informer, if there should be any, twenty per cent., the collector fifteen per cent., the auditor ten per cent., and the commander of the guards ten per cent.

In case there is no informer, his part shall be distributed among the crew.

V. In all other cases of confiscations or fines, the divisions of the sums realized shall be divided, when there are no informers or seizers, as follows: to the collector thirty per cent., to the auditor thirty per cent., to the commander of the guards twenty per cent., and the balance of twenty per cent. to defray the expenses of seizure and as fees to the inferior employés of the custom houses and outposts.

In case there be an informer, the division shall be made as provided in Article 432 and in Section I of this article.

VI. Whenever the fines or confiscations are determined by judicial proceedings, the district attorneys shall receive fifty-five per cent. of the share assigned to the auditors.

VII. The share of the product arising from fines or confiscations, which is assigned to the collectors, auditors, inspectors, commanders of the guards and other custom house employés, shall be exclusively for the benefit of those who are actually employed at the time of the seizure.

VIII. The share assigned to the district attorneys shall be divided among persons who, filling said offices, have actually taken part in the proceedings.

IX. The rights of the seizers of foreign or national merchandise to the share awarded to them by this law is perfected the moment that the seizure is made.

Art. 435. In cases of smuggling discovered by the Federal employés, or by private parties, on the coasts, roads and towns, when there are neither maritime, frontier nor coastwise custom houses, nor custom house branch offices, even in cases where some of said offices intervene, the product of fines, etc., determined by the sentence either of the collector or of the court, shall be divided as follows:

I. Fifty per cent. of the proceeds of the sale of the confiscated goods, and of the beasts, carts or other vehicles which carried the same, shall be paid to the Federal treasury in compensation for the duties of importation, and from this share the two per cent. shall be paid to the hospitals, and the other expenses incurred satisfied.

II. Of the remaining fifty per cent. there shall be distributed without any reduction, among the participants, twenty per cent. to the informer, twenty per cent. to the seizer and ten per cent. to the employés of the office of the Federal treasury which may have received the goods to institute the proper proceedings, the distribution being made in the proportion of five per cent. to the chief of the office, two and a half per cent. to the cashier or the one discharging his duties, and two and a half per cent. to the employé making the examination of the seized merchandise.

III. The share alloted to the seizers shall be divided in equal proportions among all those making the seizure, without any distinction; and if there are no informers, the share that would have been alloted to them shall be divided among the seizers.

Art. 436. The distribution to the participants in all cases of confiscations and fines shall not be made until the corresponding office has received the approval of the Treasury Department, the product arising from said fines remaining in the meantime in the safe of the office itself, and the confiscated goods remaining stored in the warehouses.

Art. 437. The portion set apart to defray the expenses of seizure, and as fees to the inferior employés of the custom house, shall be allowed to accumulate and be deposited in treasuries of the respective offices until the end of the fiscal year, when the collectors shall make distribution of the same among the employés of the custom house and of the guards. The distribution shall be calculated in proportion to the various salaries paid.

Art. 438. All expenses which may be incurred in the seizure of goods shall be paid out of the funds set apart for that purpose; but when the judicial proceedings which may be instituted result favorably to the treasury, these expenses shall be repaid out of the products arising therefrom.

Art. 439. From every confiscation or fine two per cent. of the net residue shall be deducted, which shall be applied to the support of the hospital wherever the same may be situated; and in case there may not be any in the port, that amount shall be appropriated to the promotion of public instruction in the locality.

Art. 440. In case where the proceeds of the sale of any confiscated merchandise is not sufficient to cover the duties of importation fixed by the tariff, the net amount realized shall be entered to the account of duties of importation, stating in the entry to be made in the day-book the source whence said sum was obtained.

Art. 441. When the officers, who according to law must examine the accounts of the custom house of the Federation, observe that one or several of the mistakes contained in the custom house documents have not been noted by the respective employés, they shall immediately notify the Treasury Department, so that, in view of the facts which may appear, it may determine whether or not a fine should be imposed.

Art. 442. All fines approved by the Treasury Department shall be made effective in accordance with the provisions of the present law; and authority is hereby granted to the said department, at its discretion, to order distribution to be made among the employés who examined said accounts of the fines which may be imposed, in such proportions as it may deem proper, or, on the other hand, to order said sums to be paid into the account of "Profits of the Public Treasury."

CHAPTER XVI.

Sale of Merchandise at Public Auction.

Art. 443. The maritime and frontier custom houses are authorized to dispose at public sale of goods which have been seized as contraband, and of those which may have been abandoned by their owners or for which there is no consignee; but in holding such sales, the following rules shall be observed:

I. Goods which, on account of their perishable condition, cannot remain stored during the six months as prescribed by Art. 302, shall be disposed of at public sale one month (or sooner should this be necessary) after seizure or abandonment by their owners or consignees.

II. When the goods are not such as are described in the preceding section, they shall be disposed of at public sale fifteen days after the expiration of the term fixed by Article 302, or after judgment pronounced, in case the same are smuggled goods.

III. In all cases in which the custom house shall proceed with the sale of merchandise at public auction, the collectors or persons appointed by them shall attend to such auction sales, and the district attorneys or their representatives shall be present thereat. A memorandum of the steps taken at such auction sales shall be drawn up, and signed by all the employés present, and by the purchaser or purchasers of the merchandise.

IV. In the auction sales of merchandise abandoned for want of a consignee, the custom houses shall at once proceed to satisfy the duties and expenses which they have occasioned, and the balance of the product of such sale, if any there be, shall be kept deposited in the treasury of the said custom house for the space of one year, within which period, by publication in the newspapers, the owner of the goods shall be cited to appear, either personally or by attorney, to receive the amount deposited.

If said period has elapsed and no one has presented himself to claim the surplus, the collector of the custom house shall order that the same be paid to the treasury as "Profits of the Public Treasury."

V. The sale of goods shall be effected by brokers under the supervision of the custom house collectors or of the persons by them appointed; without this requisite nothing can be done.

The collectors, or the persons by them appointed, shall be present at the sale and make a note of each one of the articles sold, so that, the sale having terminated, the liquidation of duties may be proceeded with. This shall be done by computing the amount realized on the sale of each article with its value as declared in the consular invoices, or if this does not exist, with the highest quoted market price, and the percentage of difference between the value and the sale of the article shall be the proportion to be taken for the reduction of the duties.

CHAPTER XVII.

Special Instruction for the Custom Houses of the Republic.

Art. 444. The collectors and employés of the custom houses and wardens shall treat all persons having business in their offices with due consideration, without occasioning more delays than such as are indispensable for the fulfillment of the provisions of this ordinance.

Art. 445. It is left to the good judgment of the collectors to decide whether the quantity of food left over, and the effects for the economical service of a vessel, manifested by their captains or pursers in accordance with Art. 29 of this law, are excessive for the return trip to be undertaken by the vessel or not; and for this purpose its general nature, number of crew, whether it carries passengers or not, and the time which the trip may last, must be taken into consideration.

Art. 446. In case that the quantity of food or effects for the economic use of the vessel, left over, be more than what it may require, the collectors shall order that the proper duties be liquidated and paid for such excess.

Art. 447. When the amount of food or effects for the domestic use of the vessel, left over, be excessive, the custom houses shall impose on the captain or consignee of the vessel the penalty of double duties of importation on merchandise adjudged as excess.

Art. 448. If, from the amount of food allowed by the collectors, it shall suit the captains to sell a portion thereof in port, they shall be permitted to land the same, on paying the importation duties imposed by the tariff.

Art. 449. Merchandise which from its nature cannot be classified as included in Article 445, shall incur the penalty imposed on merchandise coming without consular invoices.

Art. 450. All former tariff laws are abolished, as well as all explanatory orders given up to the date when this ordinance goes into effect.

ALPHABETICAL INDEX

For the Application of the Mexican Tariff.

A.

	Rate of Duty, per Kilogram.
Acetates of copper and lead, alum and iron	08
Acetates, not specified	15
Acids, liquid or gaseous, not specified	20
Acids, in crystals or powder, not specified	1 10
Acids, acetic, nitric, oxalic and pyrolignic	Free
Acids, sulphuric, chloro-hydric and phenic acid	05
Aconitine and its salts	15 00
Accoutrements of all classes, with or without adornments which are not gold or silver	2 00
Accordeons. (See musical instruments.)	
Aconite and its salts	15 00
Addice or chip-axe	10
Adzes for agricultural purposes	Free
Agate. (See manufactures.)	
Alabaster in bulk or slabs, polished on one side up to 40 centimeters in a square	01
Alabaster of more than 40 centimeters in a square	
Alabaster in slabs of all dimensions polished on both sides	20
Alarms with wooden cases	05
Alarms, with metal cases not gold or silver	15
Albumen	10
Albums of all kinds, with or without photographs	1 10
Alcohol	70
Alcoholates	75
Alizarine, natural or artificial	10
Alkali	01
Alkaloid, not specified	15 00
Almonds, sweet or bitter, without shells	25
Almonds, with shell	12
Alpaca, wool, according to the weight of square meter. (See woolen textures.)	
Alpargatas, shoes known by that name, per pair	15
Alum	15
Ambergris	16 00
Amethyst. (See precious stones).	
Ammonia, liquid	01
Ammonia, gum	20
Anchors, with or without chains, for ships	Free
Animals live, excepting castrated horses	Free
Animals prepared for natural history cabinets	01
Anis	15
Aniset in vessels of glass. (See liquors).	
Antimony, metal	30
Anvils	05
Anvils of all sizes for tinsmiths	10
Apparatus, hydroterapic of all kinds	20
Apparatus for medical and surgical uses, not specified	1 00
Apparatus, all kinds not specified, for industrial, agricultural, mining purposes, arts and sciences, and their separate parts and pieces when they come with them	Free
Apparatus for extinguishing fire with extra charge of liquid	Free
Apomorfine	15 00
Arack (rum) in vessels of glass or wood. (See Rum).	

	Rate of Duty, Per Kilogram.
Arches of wood for holding awnings on cars.	06
Arms, fire, breech or muzzle-loading, all kinds and their extra parts.	1 25
Arms, fire, not repeating or breech-holding, all kinds and their extra parts.	82
Arsenic, metallic.	30
Arsenic, red or yellow.	10
Arsenic, white.	Free
Articles, not mentioned, of cotton cloth, all textures without embroideries.	1 60
Articles, not mentioned, of cotton cloth of all textures, embroidered with other material not gold or silver.	2 25
Articles, not mentioned, of linen cloth, all textures, without embroidery.	1 80
Articles, not mentioned, of linen cloth of all textures, embroidered with other material not gold or silver.	2 50
Articles, not mentioned, of woolen cloth, all textures without embroideries.	25
Articles, not mentioned, of woolen cloth, all textures, embroidered with other material not gold or silver.	3 50
Articles of woolen yarn, not specified.	2 20
Articles of silk, not specified.	16 00
Articles of silk mixed with cotton, linen or wool, with or without embroideries of the same material, not specified.	9 00
Articles, etc., with trimmings of bugles, beads of glass or metal, not fine, not specified.	8 00
Articles of silk with bugles, beads of glass or metal which is not fine, not specified.	12 00
Asbestos in powder.	Free
Asbestos in sheets or in any other form, and even when it contains rubber, provided it comes with machinery.	10
Asbestos with woolen, felt, cotton or cardboard.	10
Asphalt.	04
Atlases.	01
Atropine and its salts.	15 00
Axes and hatchets, with and without handles.	10
Axeltrees, iron and steel, for carriages.	10
Axletree box for carriages.	10
Azarine.	10

B.

Babbit metal in bars.	10
Bags or sacks of all other materials. (See the part to which the cloths correspond)	No price
Bags or sacks, ordinary, of jute, *pita*, hemp, and other similar fibers, for the exportation of fruit.	Free
Bags, traveling, of all classes and sizes, according to material composed of	No price
Bags for hunting, of all classes and sizes.	50
Bags, ordinary, made of cloths and with wood slats.	30
Bags of straw paper, *estracilla* or wrapping paper, without addresses or advertisements	10
Bags of straw paper, *estracilla* or wrapping paper, with printed addresses.	20
Baize of wool, (See woolen cloths).	
Balconies of iron not weighing over 20 kilograms.	20
Balconies of iron weighing more than 20 kilograms.	10
Ball molds of iron.	20
Ball molds of brass or copper.	30
Balls, billiard, of ivory.	4 00
Balsams, natural or in liquid.	1 10
Balsams, compounded.	1 65
Bands of linen, embroidered.	2 50
Bands of wool, or wool and cotton, embroidered.	3 50
Bands of cotton of all kinds of textures, without embroideries.	1 60
Bands of cotton, embroidered with cotton or wool.	2 25
Bands of cotton, embroidered with silk.	2 25
Bands, wool, all textures, without embroidery.	25
Bands of wool with embroidery of same material.	3 50
Bands of wool with silk embroidery.	3 50
Bands of silk and cotton, or of silk and wool, or of silk, wool and cotton embroidered with any material not of gold or silver.	9 00
Bands of silk, plain or embroidered.	16 00
Bands of cotton, knit, with wool fringe.	1 75
Bands of leather, when coming separate from machinery.	50
Bands of leather coming with machinery.	Free
Bands of rubber not coming with machinery.	10
Bands of rubber coming with machinery.	Free
Bands made of several sheets of cotton canvas tarred for machinery.	10
Bark for dyeing purposes. (See dye-wood).	
Bark, medicinal.	20
Barley, not pearl.	5

ALPHABETICAL INDEX.

	Rate of Duty, Per Kilogram.
Barley, pearl	20
Barometers of all kinds	01
Barrels of wood, empty, for exporting national products	Free
Barrel for guns or fire arms	82
Bass viols. (See musical instruments.)	
Batiste of linen. (See linen cloths.)	
Beads polished glass that are or are not cut or ground	20
Beads, covered with crape	1 25
Beads of common metal	30
Beads of gold or platinum. (See jewelry.)	
Beams, iron, for roofs	01
Beans	05
Beberine. (See alkaloids.)	
Bedsteads of iron, all kinds	20
Bedsteads of brass, all kinds	30
Bedsteads of ordinary wood	15
Bedsteads of fine woods, veneered or solid	25
Bed-wood for carriages. (See hubs and posts for carriages.)	
Beer in bottles	20
Beer in barrels	10
Bells, small, jingling, of iron, all kinds	20
Bells of brass, all kinds	30
Bells of all kinds of metal	30
Bells, electric, all kinds	30
Bells of metal for calling	30
Bellows for forge	10
Bellows, hand, for chimneys	30
Belts of all kinds with buckles not of gold or silver	50
Belts of all kinds for medicine and surgery	1 00
Belts of silk or other material not containing silk, with or without buckles not of gold or silver	2 00
Benzine of all kinds	10
Bicarbonate of ammonia	01
Bicarbonate of potash	05
Bicarbonate of soda	05
Billiard tables without including the cloth	30
Birds, live	Free
Birds, stuffed	01
Bird cages, according to material composed of.	
Biscuits, medical	75
Bismuth, metallic	1 50
Bits, iron, for animals	20
Bits	10
Bitters	30
Blackening, liquid or in paste, for shoes or harness	20
Blade, for sword, separate	45
Blankets or covers of linen for horses	1 80
Blankets of woolen cloth for horses	25
Blankets, cotton, plain or stamped	1 60
Blankets, plain woolen, without stamping	1 80
Blanks, for invoice, drafts, etc. (See documents, printed.)	
Blinds, Persian wood	30
Blotting sand	Free
Bluing of all kinds	1 35
Boards, wood, for building	Free
Boards, chess or checker, according to material.	
Bolts, iron, all classes	20
Bolts, brass, all classes	30
Bones. (See articles made of.)	
Bone, calcined	Free
Books or portfolios of slate	50
Books, blank, ruled, ordinary binding	95
Books bound in velvet, shell, ivory, tortoise-shell, gutta-percha, wood, composition, paste or metal, not gold or silver	1 20
Books, printed or manuscripts, bound, Dutch binding or leather binding	03
Books, printed or manuscripts, rustic	Free
Boots and half boots of leather, per pair	1 50
Boots of calf skin or patent leather, per pair	2 50
Boot-hooks, according to material.	
Bosoms, cotton, not embroidered, for shirts	1 60
Bosoms, cotton, embroidered, for shirts	2 25
Bosoms, linen, plain or embroidered, for shirts	6 00

	Rate of Duty, Per Kilogram.
Bottles, filled with liquid to extinguish fires...	Free
Bottles, clay..	15
Bottles of common glass for liquors, wines, beer and rum....................................	03
Bottles of crystal or glass...	20
Bottles or syphons, glass, for holding seltzer water..	20
Bottle-holder, iron, all classes..	20
Bottle-holder, copper or brass...	30
Bottle-holder, metal, gilt or plated..	1 30
Bottle-holder, pewter or white metal..	40
Bottle-holder, wooden...	30
Bottle-holder, pasteboard...	45
Bottle-holder, metal nickeled..	70
Bottle-holder, plaque..	1 25
Boxes of tin, all kinds..	20
Box-wood..	01
Bracelets, fur. (See manufactures of fur.)	
Bracelets of gold, silver or platina. (See jewelry.)	
Bracelets of ordinary metal, not gilt or plated..	30
Bracelets, metal, gilt or plated..	1 30
Bracelets, wooden..	30
Bracelets, metal, nickeled...	70
Bracelets of gutta-percha, celluloid, horn or whalebone....................................	30
Bracelets, jet or tortoise shell...	1 30
Brackets, according to class. (See furniture.)	
Bran, wheat or oat...	11
Braziers of iron, all kinds, not exceeding 20 kilograms in weight........................	20
Braziers whose weight exceeds 20 kilograms..	10
Brass, in sheets or rolls..	15
Brass, in bars...	30
Bread, wheat...	15
Breastpins of glass or crystal, all kinds..	20
Breastpins of delft or porcelain, all kinds...	15
Breastpins of metal, not gilded or plated, with or without false stones..............	30
Breastpins of metal, gilded or plated, with or without false stones....................	1 30
Breastpins of gold, silver or platinum. (See jewelry.)	
Breastpins, zinc, all classes...	07
Breastpins of gutta-percha, celluloid, whalebone, horn or bone.........................	30
Breastpins of jet, tortoise shell, shell or ivory..	1 30
Bricks, fire...	Free
Bricks, not fire proof, per 1,000..	1 80
Bricks for cleaning metal...	06
Bridles of leather, all kinds..	60
Bridles of all kinds for animals...	20
Brilliants. (See precious stones.)	
Bristles for shoemakers...	10
Brocatel, according to material.	
Brooms, heather of all classes and sizes..	15
Brushes of nickeled metal..	70
Brushes of gilded or plated metal...	1 30
Brushes of all kinds, mounted in wood...	30
Brushes of all kinds, mounted in bone, horn, whalebone, rubber or celluloid...	30
Brushes of all kinds, mounted in ivory, shell or tortoise shell............................	1 30
Braids, cotton, linen or hemp...	2 50
Braids, cotton, with elastics, up to 4 centimeters in width.................................	1 60
Braids, woolen...	3 20
Braids, wool, with elastics, up to 4 centimeters in width...................................	2 10
Braids, silk..	16 00
Braids, silk, mixed with cotton, linen or wool...	9 00
Braids, silk, with cotton wool or linen, with glass or imitation beads or fringes.	8 00
Braids, silk, with glass or metal beads or fringes..	12 00
Braids, silk, with cotton or wool, with elastics, up to 4 centimeters in width....	4 70
Braids, silk, with elastics, up to 4 centimeters in width......................................	7 00
Braids, hair, loose, for forming chignons or other ornaments for the head. (See cut hair.)	
Braids, imitation hair, loose, for forming chignons or other ornaments for the hair, not silk.	3 00
Braids, imitation hair, loose, for forming chignons or other ornaments for the head, made of silk...	7 00
Collections, mineralogical, geological or of natural history...............................	01
Gum-lac..	10
Brushes of all kinds...	20
Buckles, iron or steel...	05
Buckles of iron, brass or bronze...	30
Buckles of metal, silver plated...	1 30

ALPHABETICAL INDEX. 403

	Rate of Duty, Per Kilogram.
Buckles of metal, nickeled	70
Buckles of plaque	1 25
Buckles, iron, silk covered	90
Buckles of iron or brass, leather covered	25
Buckles of gold or silver with or without precious stones. (See jewelry.)	
Bungs of wood	06
Burines	10
Burners, iron, of all classes, for lamps	20
Burners, of brass or copper, all classes, for lamps	30
Busts of marble or alabaster, or gypsum or stucco, of less than natural dimensions	20
Busts of marble or alabaster, of natural size or greater dimensions	10
Busts of gypsum or stucco of natural size or greater dimensions	10
Busts of less than natural size	15
Busts of iron, of less than natural size	20
Busts of iron, of natural size or greater dimensions	10
Busts of brass, bronze or metal composition of less than natural size	30
Busts of brass, bronze or metal composition of natural size or greater dimensions	10
Busts of zinc, of less than natural size	07
Busts of zinc, of natural size or greater dimensions	10
Buckets of iron, all kinds	20
Buckets of tin, all kinds	20
Buckets of zinc, all kinds	10
Buckets of wood, all kinds	10
Bustles of cotton and silk, or wool and silk	3 80
Bustles of cotton, linen or wool	1 90
Butter	25
Buttons of iron or steel of all kinds	20
Buttons of metal without gilding or plating	30
Buttons of gilded or plated metal	1 30
Buttons of plaque or German silver	1 25
Buttons of wood	30
Buttons of silk, or silk and wool, covered or woven	90
Buttons covered or woven with cloth that does not contain silk	30
Buttons of paste or pressed paper	45
Buttons of crystal or glass, all kinds	20
Buttons of china or porcelain, all kinds	15
Buttons of bone, horn, whalebone or gutta-percha	30
Buttons of ivory, shell, tortoise shell or jet	1 30
Buttons of gold, silver, or platinum with or without pearls or precious stones. (See jewelry.)	
Buttons of nickel-plated metal	15

C.

Cable wire	Free
Cable of aloe or hemp, measuring from three centimeters of diameter or 94.2 milimeters of circumference	Free
Cable of aloe, hemp or other vegetable fibers, measuring less than three centimeters in diameter	13
Cacholet, pieces of	10
Cadmia, metallic	1 50
Cages, according to material.	
Calf skins. (See prepared skins.)	
Cambric. (See linen textures.)	
Camphor	50
Canary seed	5
Candles, stearine	15
Candles, tallow, pressed	15
Candles, common, tallow	15
Candles of all classes, not specified	60
Candlesticks, glass or crystal, all classes	20
Candlesticks, earthenware or porcelain, all classes	15
Candlesticks, iron, all classes	20
Candlesticks of tin, all classes	20
Candlesticks of brass or ordinary metal, neither gilt nor silver-plated	30
Candlesticks of metal, gilded, silver plated	1 30
Candlesticks of plaque	1 25
Candlesticks of pewter or white metal	40
Candlesticks of metal, nickeled	70
Candlesticks or night lamps, with or without frames	65
Canes, with handles not of gold or silver	95
Canes, with handles of gold and silver	3 60
Cantharides	2 00

	Rate of Duty, Per Kilogram.
Cantins of tin, lined with any other material	30
Canvass of flax or hemp	22
Canvass of duck or cotton	17
Canvass for embroidering of cotton	65
Canvass of linen or hemp	65
Capers, pickled	25
Capers, in brine	06
Caps, for fire arms	45
Caps, silk, knitted, mixed with cotton, linen or wool	7 00
Caps, silk and cotton, or silk and wool, all kinds	9 00
Caps, silk knitted	16 00
Caps, silk fabric, all classes	16 00
Caps, wool knitted	20
Caps, linen knitted	2 00
Caps, of cotton, knit	1 75
Caps, linen, knitted, for children. (See ready-made cotton clothing.)	
Capsicum, natural, in oil or in powder	25
Capsules, for bottles	20
Capsules, medicinal	1 25
Capsules, empty of gelatine	80
Capsules, explosive, with dynamite	Free
Caraway seed	10
Carob-tare. (See tare or fruit of Carob tree.)	
Carbonate of ammonia	01
Card receivers, according to material.	
Cardboard, phosphoric. (See phosphorous.)	
Cardboard of all thicknesses, beaten or unbeaten	20
Cardboard, Bristol or albuminated, and for making playcards	48
Cardboard, or *cartulina*, for making cards	45
Carpets of hemp or tow, of plain, crossed or figured texture, square meter	25
Carpets of hemp, shaggy cut	07
Carpets of coarse fibre, plain or crossed texture or beaten wool, square meter	75
Carpets of wool, Brussels, uncut, square meter	1 10
Carpets, Brussels or velvet, smooth, square meter	1 60
Carpets, wool, corded, square meter	90
Carpets of beaten wool, or not beaten, not trimmed or bordered	25
Carpets of beaten wool, or not beaten, bordered or trimmed, not of gold or silver	3 50
Carpets of silk	16 00
Carpenters' work bench	01
Carriages, weighing up to 100 kilograms	60
Carriages, weighing more than 100 and up to 250 kilograms	55
Carriages, weighing more than 250 and up to 500 kilograms	50
Carriages, weighing more than 500 and up to 750 kilograms	45
Carriages, weighing more than 750 and up to 1,000 kilograms	40
Carriages, weighing more than 1,000 kilograms	35
Carriages, small, for children	30
Cars, wagons or carts	06
Cars, for railroads	Free
Cartridges, loaded or unloaded, for firearms	50
Cases of crystal with nickeled metal	70
Cases of crystal with common metal	1 30
Cases of crystal with gilded metal, plated or nickeled	1 30
Cases of metal without gilding or plating	30
Cases of metal, nickel plated	1 30
Cases of music	45
Cases, gilded or plated metal	1 30
Cases, plaque	1 25
Cases of pewter or white metal	40
Cases of gold, silver, or platinum. (See jewelry.)	
Cases of common wood for packing, when they are to be used for the exportation of domestic products	Free
Cases with chemical reactives	3 30
Cases, straw or reed	45
Cases, tortoise-shell, ivory or shell	1 30
Cases of paper or cardboard, with or without ornaments, of common metal	45
Cases, etc., with ornaments of gilded or plated metal	1 30
Cases, etc., with nickeled metal ornaments	70
Cases of all materials, covered with cloth or skins of all kinds, with or without ornaments not gold or silver	50
Cases of all materials with ornaments or accessories of gold or platinum	3 60
Cases, fancy, with or without ornaments and trimming not gold or silver	1 10
Cashmere of wool, according to weight of square meter. (See woolen fabrics.)	

ALPHABETICAL INDEX. 405

	Rate of Duty. Per Kilogram.
Castors, metal, not gilded or silver plated, with or without cruets	30
Castors, not of silver, gilded or plated, with or without cruets	1 30
Castors of nickel plated metal, with or without cruets	70
Castors, plaque, with or without cruets	1 25
Castors, pewter or white metal, with or without cruets	40
Castors, wood, with or without cruets	30
Castoreums	4 00
Castor beans	Free
Catechu	10
Caucho. (See articles made of gutta-percha.)	
Caviar	12
Cement, Roman	Free
Cerate, medicinal	1 30
Ceresine	
Chains of iron, whose links have a diameter up to number 5 of the Birmingham measure	10
Chains of iron, whose links have a diameter of more than number 5 of the Birmingham measure	20
Chains of other metals. (See under the metal made of.)	
Chairs, iron. (See iron furniture.)	
Chairs, brass. (See brass furniture.)	
Chairs, wooden. (See wood furniture.)	
Chalk	10
Chamois, all kinds. (See skins.)	
Chandeliers of crystal with metal not gilded or plated	30
Chandeliers of metal not plated or nickeled	30
Chandeliers of crystal with gilded or plated metal	1 30
Chandeliers of crystal with nickeled metal	70
Chandeliers of metal gilded or plated	1 30
Chandeliers of metal, nickeled	70
Charts, geographical, topographical	01
Checkers of ivory or shell	1 30
Checkers of cardboard	45
Checkers of wood	30
Checkers of bone	30
Cheese, all classes	15
Chemical products, not specified	75
Chessmen of iron	10
Chessmen of wood	30
Chessmen of bone	30
Chessmen of ivory or shell	1 30
Chests of iron, all kinds, weighing up to 20 kilograms	05
Chests exceeding 20 kilograms in weight	10
Chick-peas	05
Chimneys of iron, all kinds, whose weight does not exceed 20 kilograms	10
Chimneys of iron, all kinds, whose weight exceeds 20 kilograms	10
Chintz. (See cotton, printed fabrics.)	
Chips, ivory or shell	1 30
Chips, pasteboard	45
Chips, wood	30
Chips, brass	30
Chips, bone	30
Chisels	10
Chloral, hydrate	1 50
Chlohydrate of ammonia	01
Chlorate of potash or soda	08
Chloride of ammonia	01
Chloride of gold	25 00
Chloride of platinum	25 00
Chloride of lime	Free.
Chloroform	1 50
Chocolate of all kinds	55
Chromos of all kinds, with or without frames, not lined or covered with cloth or wool	65
Chromos with frames covered with cloth or wool	65
Cianide of potassium, common	08
Cider, in barrels. (See beer in barrels.)	
Cider, in bottles. (See beer in bottles.)	
Citherns. (See musical instruments.)	
Cigars. (See tobacco.)	
Cigar-cases, tin, all classes	20
Cigar-cases of common metal without gilding or plating	30
Cigar-cases of gilded or plated metal	1 30
Cigar-cases of plaque	1 25

	Rate of Duty, Per Kilogram.
Cigar-cases of pewter or white metal.................................	40
Cigar-cases of wood...	30
Cigar-cases of cardboard..	45
Cigar-cases, leather..	60
Cigar-cases, horn, rubber or gutta-percha............................	30
Cigar-cases of straw or reed...	45
Cigar-cases, shell, ivory or tortoise shell.............................	1 30
Cigar-cases of gold or silver. (See jewelry.)	
Cigar-cases of metal, nickeled.......................................	70
Cigars or cigarettes, medicinal.......................................	75
Cigars, not medicinal. (See cigars made of tobacco.)	
Cigarrette holders, according to material.	
Cinnamon...	1 00
Clasps of iron wire, all kinds..	20
Clasps of brass wire, all kinds.......................................	30
Clasps of shell..	1 30
Clarinets. (See musical instruments.)	
Cloaks of rubber. (See rubber clothing.)	
Cloaks of skins. (See articles made of skins.)	
Cloaks of woolen yarn...	20
Cloaks, woolen. (See woolen ready-made clothing.)	
Clocks for mantel or wall, which are not specified nor being of gold or silver.............	1 25
Clocks for towers and public edifices.................................	Free
Clocks for table or wall, with wood cases............................	45
Cloth, woolen, according to weight of square meter. (See woolen fabrics.)	
Clothing, baby, according to material made of. (See ready-made clothing.)	
Clothing of cotton goods, cut in pieces for dresses, not specified......	1 70
Clothing, ready-made, and its parts, when they come sewed, of cotton cloth of all kinds and sizes, not specified...	2 50
Clothing, ready-made, and its separate parts, when these come sewed, of linen, all kinds, not specified..	3 00
Clothing of linen goods, cut in pieces for dresses, not specified	1 90
Clothing, ready-made, and its parts, when these come sewed, of woolen goods of all kinds, not specified..	5 50
Clothing, woolen goods, cut in pieces for dresses, of all kinds, not specified.............	4 00
Clothing, ready-made, and in parts, when they come sewed, of silk goods of any kind, not specified..	18 00
Clothing, ready-made, and its separate parts, when they come sewed, of silk goods mixed with cotton, linen or wool, of all kinds, not specified.....................	12 00
Clove...	65
Coaches, according to weight. (See carriages.)	
Coaches for railroads, all systems....................................	Free
Coal, all kinds..	Free
Coats of woolen textures. (See ready-made clothes.)	
Coats of rubber. (See rubber in pieces for dressing.)	
Cobalt, metallic...	1 50
Cocoa of all kinds..	16
Codfish, dried or smoked..	12
Coderine..	15 00
Coffee of all kinds..	10
Coffee with condensed milk...	10
Coffee for medicinal purposes..	10
Coffee roasters..	20
Collars of cotton cloth, embroidered.................................	2 25
Collars of cotton cloth, plain...	1 60
Collars of linen cloth, not embroidered...............................	1 80
Collars of cotton lace, with or without silk ornaments................	6 00
Collars of linen cloth, embroidered...................................	2 50
Collars of linen lace, with or without silk ornaments.................	9 00
Collars of woolen lace, with or without silk ornaments...............	8 00
Collars of silk, point or blonde, with or without ornaments...........	16 00
Collars of silk, point or blonde lace, with mixture of cotton, wool or linen, with or without silk ornaments...	9 00
Collars of silk, point or blonde lace, with mixture of cotton, wool or linen, glass or false metal beads..	8 00
Collars, with silk, point or blonde lace, with glass or metal beads.....	12 00
Collars of fur. (See manufactures of fur).	
Collodion, and its formulas..	1 00
Colors, crude or prepared...	10
Columns, iron, up to 20 kilos..	20
Columns, iron, more than 20 kilos...................................	10
Combs, wood...	30

ALPHABETICAL INDEX.

	Rate of Duty, Per Kilogram.
Combs, bamboo, all classes...	30
Combs, curved combs and fine combs, of iron, all classes....................	20
Combs, curved combs and fine combs, of tortoise shell, shell or ivory.......	1 30
Combs, curved combs and fine combs, of horn, bone, gutta-percha or celluloid.	30
Composition of silicious sand and impure and viscous substances, for cleaning boilers......	Free
Compasses, with or without cases...	01
Confections and sweetmeats...	1 00
Copper mills...	Free
Copper, pig or pieces..	10
Copper sheets..	15
Copper beaten in leaves, gilded or plated....................................	45
Coral, fine, wrought or unwrought..	3 00
Cord of silk...	16 00
Cord of silk, with mixture of cotton, linen or wool, with glass or false metal beads.........	8 00
Cord of silk, with mixture of cotton, linen or wool..........................	9 00
Cord of silk, with glass or metal beads......................................	12 00
Cord of hemp, covered with silk..	6 00
Cord of hemp, covered with silk and cotton or wool and silk..................	2 80
Cord of silk, with mixture of cotton or wool, with gum elastic...............	4 70
Cord of silk, with gum elastic...	7 00
Cord, wool, or wool and cotton with gum elastic..............................	2 10
Cord, wool, with or without glass, or false metal beads......................	3 20
Cord, cotton or hemp, covered with wool......................................	2 50
Cord, cotton, with gum elastic...	1 60
Cord, cotton, linen or hemp, with or without glass or false metal beads......	2 50
Cork, in plates or in bulk...	Free
Cordage. (See rigging.)	
Corks, with metal trimmings, nickeled..	70
Corks or stoppers for bottles..	20
Corks, with metal trimmings, gilt or plated..................................	1 30
Corks, with metal trimmings, not gilt or plated..............................	30
Corkscrews, according to material.	
Corn...	01
Corn or millet, ears of..	03
Cornets. (See musical instruments.)	
Corsets of cotton, linen or wool, of all kinds and sizes, with or without small ornaments of silk..	1 90
Corsets of silk, mixture of cotton, linen or wool, of all sizes..............	3 80
Cosmetics for the hair. (See perfumery.)	
Cosmetics for billiard cues..	30
Cots of iron...	20
Cots of brass..	30
Cots of wood...	15
Cotense, a coarse brown linen wrapper. (See linen or hemp fabrics.)	
Cotton powder..	Free
Cotton waste...	02
Cotton unginned..	03
Cotton ginned..	08
Cotton carded..	20
Cotton wadding...	20
Cotton fabrics, unbleached or white, plain textures, measuring up to 30 threads of warp and woof, in a square of half centimeter per side, square meter..................	09
Cotton goods, unbleached or white, of all kinds of plain textures, exceeding 30 threads to a square of half centimeter per side, square meter............................	11
Cotton waste...	02
Cotton waste for bearings of railroad cars...................................	02
Cotton waste of all colors...	90
Counterpanes of cotton, not embroidered......................................	1 60
Counterpanes of cotton, embroidered..	2 25
Counterpanes of woolen, not embroidered......................................	25
Counterpanes of woolen, embroidered..	3 50
Counterpanes of silk, all classes..	16 00
Counterpanes of silk and cotton, or silk and wool, of all kinds..............	9 00
Counterpanes of cotton, quilted..	50
Counterpanes of silk and cotton, or silk and wool, or silk and linen, quilted.	5 23
Coupés, according to weight. (See carriages.)	
Covers of canvas, with or without iron or wooden frame, for carriages or for cars.........	20
Coverlets of silk and cotton or silk and wool, quilted.......................	5 23
Coverlets of cotton, quilted...	50
Coverlets or counterpanes of cotton without embroidery.......................	1 60
Coverlets or counterpanes with embroidery....................................	2 25
Coverlets or counterpanes of wool without embroidery.........................	25

408   DELMAR'S MERCANTILE MANUAL AND BUSINESS GUIDE.

	Rate of Duty, Per Kilogram.
Coverlets or counterpanes of wool with embroidery............................	3 50
Coverlets or counterpanes of silk with or without garnitures......................	16 00
Coverlets or counterpanes of silk and cotton or wool and silk, with or without garnitures..	9 00
Covers, oil cloth for umbrellas..	80
Covers, felt for hats...	2 20
Crabs of iron for coach poles..	20
Crabs, preserved..	25
Crabs in brine..	12
Crackers, all kinds...	15
Cranes...	Free
Cravats of fur. (See articles made of fur.)	
Cravats of cotton cloth, not embroidered...................................	1 60
Cravats of cotton cloth, embroidered......................................	2 25
Cravats of cotton lace, all kinds..	6 00
Cravats of linen, not embroidered..	1 80
Cravats of linen, embroidered...	2 50
Cravats of linen lace, all kinds...	9 00
Cravats of wool, not embroidered..	25
Cravats of wool, embroidered...	3 50
Cravats of worsted, all kinds..	2 20
Cravats, point or woolen lace, all kinds....................................	8 00
Cravats of silk goods, with or without frames and springs......................	16 00
Cravats, silk, point or blonde lace, all kinds................................	16 00
Cravats of silk and cotton, with or without frames and springs.................	9 00
Cravats of silk and cotton, or silk and wool, point or blonde lace, with or without ornament of same material..	9 00
Cravats of silk and cotton, or silk and wool, point or blonde lace, with glass or false metal beads...	9 00
Cravats of silk, point or blonde lace, with glass or false metal beads............	12 00
Cream of bismuth...	75
Cream of tartar...	10
Creosote...	1 00
Crinoline. (See cotton glossed fabrics.)	
Crockery in pieces of all forms and sizes, with mountings or settings of metal, nickeled......	70
Crockery in pieces of all forms and sizes, with mountings of metal, gilt or plated..........	1 30
Crockery in pieces of all forms and sizes, with mountings or settings of metal, not gilt or plated..	30
Crockery in pieces of all forms and sizes...................................	15
Crosses of gold or silver. (See jewelry.)	
Crosses of crystal or glass...	20
Crosses of ordinary metal, not gilded or silver-plated........................	30
Crosses, gilded or silver-plated...	1 30
Crosses of wood...	30
Crosses of rubber or gutta-percha..	30
Crosses of shell, ivory, tortoise-shell or jet..................................	1 30
Crowns of artificial flowers. (See artificial flowers.)	
Crowns, rosaries of glass...	20
Crowns, porcelain flowers..	15
Crowns of metal, not gilded or silver plated................................	30
Crowns of metal, gilded or silver plated...................................	1 30
Crowns, funeral, of natural flowers.......................................	45
Crucibles...	Free
Crutches, according to the material made of.	
Crystal, plain. (See plain glass.)	
Crystal, manufactured in pieces, with mountings or settings of ordinary metal...........	30
Crystal, manufactured in pieces, with mountings or settings of gilt or silver-plated metals..	1 30
Crystal, manufactured in pieces, with mountings or settings of nickel-plated metal.........	70
Crystal, wrought in pieces, of all forms...................................	20
Crystal, cut imitating precious stones....................................	1 30
Crystals for chandeliers, without metal...................................	20
Cubebine. (See alkaloids)	
Cuffs, silk, point lace or blonde, with or without trimmings...................	16 00
Cuffs, cotton, plain...	1 60
Cuffs, cotton, embroidered...	2 50
Cuffs, cotton, point or lace, with or without trimmings......................	6 00
Cuffs, fur. (See manufactures of fur.)	
Cuffs, linen, plain..	1 80
Cuffs, linen, embroidered..	2 50
Cuffs, linen, point or lace with or without trimmings.......................	9 00
Cuffs, wool knit, wristlets..	2 20
Cuffs, point or wool lace, with or without trimmings........................	8 00

ALPHABETICAL INDEX. 409

	Rate of Duty, Per Kilogram.
Cuffs of point lace or blonde, of silk and cotton, or linen and silk, or wool and silk, with or without trimmings..	9 00
Cuffs, point lace or blonde, of silk and cotton, silk and linen or silk and wool, with or without bugles of glass or false metal..	8 00
Cuffs of point lace or blonde, of silk, with bugles of glass or metal........................	12 00
Cumin seed..	05
Cupping glasses..	20
Curtains of cotton muslin, plain, embroidered or open work, square meter.................	20
Curtains of cotton lace, all kinds..	6 00
Curtains of linen lace..	9 00
Curtains of woolen lace...	8 00
Curtains of silk lace..	16 00
Curtains transparent, painted in oil or water color...	35
Curtains of woolen and silk or cotton and silk lace.......................................	9 00
Curtains of woolen goods, embroidered...	3 50
Curtains of woolen goods, not embroidered...	25
Curtain cord of wool, with or without glass beads...	25
Cushions, not containing silk...	50
Cushions of silk or cloth containing silk...	5 23
Cymbals, a musical instrument. (See musical instruments).	

D.

Damask, woolen, according to weight of one square meter. (See woolen goods).	
Demijons, all sizes..	03
Delphine. (See alkaloids).	
Dentrifices. (See perfumery).	
Designs or models of machinery, monuments and ships.....................................	01
Dextrine...	10
Diamonds (precious stones)..	Free
Diamonds mounted, for cutting glass..	10
Dice, pasteboard..	45
Dice, ivory or shell...	1 30
Dice, wood..	30
Dice, brass..	30
Dice, iron...	05
Dice, bone..	30
Digitaline...	15 00
Diligences...	10
Dominoes, according to material composed of.	
Doors, wooden...	30
Drawers of cotton cloth...	1 80
Drawers of cotton net..	1 75
Drawers, linen net..	2 00
Drawers, linen..	2 45
Drawers of flannel..	2 10
Drawers of woolen knitting..	2 20
Drawers of silk knitting...	16 00
Drawers of silk and cotton, or of silk and woolen knitting................................	7 00
Dress patterns of cotton cloth, with or without ornaments of cotton.......................	1 20
Dress of linen, with or without ornaments of same material................................	1 50
Dress of woolen goods, with or without ornaments of the same materials and silk ribbons..	2 50
Dress of woolen goods, with fringes and embroideries of silk, and with or without ornaments of silk, or silk and cotton, or silk and wool.................................	3 80
Dress of silk goods, with and without ornaments of all materials...........................	16 00
Dress of silk with mixtures of cotton, linen or wool with or without embroideries or ornaments of the same material...	9 00
Drill, cotton. (See cotton goods).	
Drill, linen. (See linen goods).	
Drop-glasses of glass or crystal without metal trimmings.................................	20
Drugs, medicinal, not specified..	75
Dynamite...	Free

E.

Earth of Tripoli..	Free
Earrings of crystal or glass..	20
Earrings of porcelain..	15
Earrings of common metal, without gilding or plating, with or without mock stones........	30
Earrings of metal, gilded or plated, with or without mock stones..........................	1 30
Earrings of wood..	30

	Rate of Duty, Per Kilogram.
Earrings of jet, tortoise shell, shell or ivory..	1 30
Earrings of bone, horn, whalebone, gutta-percha or celluloid.........................	30
Earrings of gold or platinum, with or without pearls or precious stones. (See jewelry of gold.)	
Earrings of silver or silver and gold, with or without pearls or precious stones. (See jewelry of silver.)	
Edgings of lace, according to material. (See fringe.)	
Eggs, fresh, hen and fish...	Free
Elastics, up to 4 centimeters in width. (See braid with gum elastic.)	
Elastics of cotton and rubber, of more than 4 centimeters in width.................	60
Elastics of linen or hemp and rubber, of more than 4 centimeters in widthd........	70
Elastics of wool and rubber, of more than 4 centimeters in width...................	80
Elastics of silk, cotton or rubber, with buttons and ring of common metal..........	1 10
Elastics of silk and rubber, or of silk and rubber with cotton, linen or hemp, of more than 4 centimeters wide..	1 10
Elaterine...	15 00
Elixers for the toilet. (See perfumery.)	
Elixers for medicinal use...	1 00
Emeralds. (See precious stones.)	
Emery, in powder or grain...	Free
Engravings on paper, with or without frames, not covered with cloth or leather....	65
Engravings on paper, with frames, covered with cloth or leather.....................	65
Engines, steam...	Free
Envelopes, paper, linen-lined, for letters...	45
Enamel, in sheets or loose..	95
Essences, for the toilet. (See perfumery.)	
Essences of sarsaparilla...	30
Ether of all substances..	20
Extract of all substances for medicinal use..	3 00
Extract of Campeche dye wood..	05
Extract of beef...	25
Extract of coffee..	25
Extracts, aromatic, for the toilet. (See perfumery.)	
Explosives for giant powder..	Free
Eye-glasses mounted in gold. (See jewelry of gold.)	
Eye-glasses mounted in silver. (See jewelry of silver.)	
Eyelet machines, according to material composed of..............................	
Eyelets of white or yellow metal, all classes...	30
Eyelets, iron, of all classes...	20

F.

Facinators or nubias of cotton, knit...	1 75
Facinators of linen, knit..	2 00
Facinators of woolen, knit...	2 20
Facinators with lace and ornaments. (See corresponding fractions.)	
Facinators of cotton cloth. (See cotton ready-made clothing.)	
Fans, common, of straw, pasteboard or cloth, without ribs.........................	20
Fans, common, with ribs of wood, horn or bone.....................................	95
Fans with ribs of ivory, shell or tortoise shell, with or without ornaments........	2 50
Faucets, iron...	20
Faucets, copper, brass or bronze...	30
Faucets, metal, gilt or silver-plated..	1 30
Faucets, nickel-plated..	70
Faucets, zinc...	07
Faucets, plaque...	1 25
Faucets, pewter or white metal..	40
Faucets, wood...	30
Fish, fresh, preserved on ice...	Free
Fish, canned..	25
Fish, dry, smoked, salted, pickeled or soused...	12
Fish in oil...	15
Fish-hooks of all kinds and sizes..	20
Flags of marble, worked on one face, more than 40 centimeters square.........	20
Flags of marble, all sizes, worked on both faces.....................................	20
Flags of alabaster, worked on one face only, of more than 40 centimeters square	20
Flags of slate, worked on both faces..	20
Flags of alabaster, all sizes, worked on both faces..................................	20
Flags of stone, of all classes and dimensions, for floors............................	01
Flags of marble, worked on one face, up to 40 centimeters square, for floors..	01
Flags of alabaster, worked on one face only, up to 40 centimeters square, for floors..........	01
Flags of slate, worked on one face only..	01
Flagolets. (See musical instruments.)	

ALPHABETICAL INDEX. 411

	Rate of Duty, Per Kilogram.
Flannel, woolen, according to class and weight, of one square meter. (See woolen fabrics.)	
Flasks of earth	15
Flasks, crystal or glass	20
Flasks, crockery or porcelain	15
Flasks of metal or glass, covered with leather, reed or gutta-percha	30
Flax, crude or matted	08
Fleams, instrument for bleeding cattle, according to material.	
Flints and chips of flint	05
Flock-wool	02
Flour, wheat	01
Flour of other grains	11
Flour, mixed or nourishing, of all other substances	10
Flowers, medicinal	20
Flowers, artificial, not silk, metal, porcelain or crystal	3 00
Flowers, artificial, of silk or silk mixed with any other material	7 00
Flutes. (See musical instruments.)	
Flutings of cotton muslin, with or without cotton lace and small silk trimmings	4 30
Flutings of wool muslin	5 50
Fluting, woolen, with and without glass and false metal beads	3 20
Fluting of silk	16 00
Fluting of silk and cotton or silk and wool, or silk, cotton and wool	9 00
Fluting of silk and cotton, or silk and wool, with glass or false metal beads	8 00
Fluting of silk with glass or metal beads	12 00
Fodder	Free
Foils for fencing, with common hilt, not gilded or silver plated, with or without scabbard or ferrules	25
Foils with hilt, scabbard or ferrules gilded or plated	1 00
Foils with or without hilts	50
Forges	Free
Forms, blank of all kinds	65
Forms of iron, all classes	20
Forms of brass	30
Forms of plated or gilded metal	1 30
Forms of white metal or pewter	40
Forms of plaque	1 25
Forms with wooden handles	30
Forms with handles of shell or ivory	1 30
Forms with handles of horn, bone, whalebone or gutta-percha	30
Forms with handles of gold or silver. (See jewelry.)	70
Forms, nickeled metal	70
Feathers and down for pillows, mattresses and cushions	50
Feather dusters	32
Felloes, of wood, for carriages	06
Feathers, for ornaments, not silk	3 00
Feathers, for ornaments, of silk	7 00
Fecula of all materials	10
Ferrules for canes, according to the material composed of.	
Ferrules for billiard cues	50
Ferrules of metal for tailors and shoemakers, of all kinds	30
Felts of woolen in pieces, when the square meter weight, 350 grammes and upward	25
Felts of wool in round pieces for machinery	06
Felts for hat frames	
Felts of tarred woolen for machinery	10
Felts of cow hair for lining boilers	10
Felts, woolen, according to class and weight of square meter. (See woolen goods.)	
Fichu, worsted	2 20
Fichu, woolen embroidered with silk	5 50
Fichu, woolen with or without wool ornaments	3 50
Fichu of silk	16 00
Fichu, silk and cotton or silk and wool, with or without silk embroidery	9 00
Fichu, silk and cotton or silk and wool, with glass or false metal beads	8 00
Fichu, silk, with glass or metal band	12 00
Figles. (See musical instruments.)	
Figures or forms of wax for sideboards or dressers	50
Files (tools)	10
Filings of small pieces of iron	01
Fire-crackers or fire-works	68
Fire, English, a sort of fire-works	75
Fire clay	Free
Fountain, iron, marble or stone	10
Frames for umbrellas, shades or parasols	65

	Rate of Duty, Per Kilogram.
Frames, wood, gilt or not gilt..	45
Frames, cardboard or wood, covered with cloth or any kind of skins, of all classes, with or without adornments not gold or silver..	1 30
Frames of cotton canvas for ladies' hats..	25
Fringes of cotton or linen...	2 50
Fringes, woolen, with or without glass or false metal beads.........................	3 20
Fringes of silk...	16 00
Fringes of silk, mixed with cotton, linen or wool..................................	9 00
Fringes of silk and cotton or wool and silk, or silk and linen, with glass or metal beads, except gold and silver...	8 00
Fringes of silk with glass or metal beads...	12 00
Front part of a four-wheel carriage...	60
Fruits in vinegar...	25
Fruits, dried...	10
Fruits in syrup...	50
Fruits in their juice..	50
Fruits in brandy, wine or liquor..	50
Fruits, medicinal...	20
Fruits, fresh...	01
Fruits in brine...	06
Funnels of crystal or glass..	20
Funnels of tin..	20
Funnels of gutta-percha...	30
Fur goods..	3 00
Furniture, iron, all kinds, with or without marble slabs or mirrors..................	20
Furniture, brass, all classes, with or without marble slabs or mirrors................	30
Furniture, wood, ordinary willow, twisted wood, painted or varnished, with or without marble or mirrors...	15
Furniture, fine, wood, veneered or solid, covered with leather or cloth containing no silk, with or without marble or mirrors..	25
Furniture inlaid with shell, tortoise-shell, ivory or metal, covered with silk or cloth containing silk, with or without marble or mirrors......................................	36
Furniture, ordinary, with common cloth...	15
Fuscinas. (See colors in powder or ready mixed).	
Fuse for mines...	Free

G.

Galloon, cotton, with or without beads or false metal.............................	2 50
Galloon, linen, with or without beads or false metal..............................	2 50
Galloon, cotton and wool, with cotton and silk....................................	3 20
Galloon, wool, with or without beads or false metal...............................	3 20
Galloon of silk...	16 00
Galloon of silk, mixed with cotton, linen or wool..................................	9 00
Galloon, silk and cotton, or silk and wool, or silk and linen, with glass or false metal beads..	8 00
Galloon of silk with glass or false metal beads.....................................	12 00
Galloon, plated metal, up to 15 centimeters in width...............................	2 50
Galloon, yellow metal, not plated, up to 15 centimeters in width....................	1 50
Galloon, gold plated, pure or bound..	15 40
Galloon, silver, pure or bound...	13 20
Games, such as lottery, chess, dominoes, checkers and others, with or without the boards, according to the materials composed of	
Garnets (precious stones)...	Free
Garters, cotton, with or without trimmings and adornments.......................	3 70
Garters, hemp or linen, with or without trimmings and adornments................	90
Garters, wool, with or without trimmings and adornments........................	1 30
Garters, silk, all classes..	16 00
Garters, silk, mixed with cotton, linen or wool, all classes.........................	9 00
Gasoline..	10
Gauze, according to material.	
Gin, glass or wooden jars. (See rum.)	
Ginger ale, bottled. (See bottled ale.)	
Glass holders. (See bottle holders.)	
Glass, plate, quicksilvered or plated for mirrors. (See looking glasses.)	
Glass, fluted...	25
Glass, in sheets..	25
Glasses, prepared for photography...	25
Glasses, for eye-glasses and watches..	45
Glass, worked in pieces of all classes and sizes, without trimmings. (See crystal.)	
Gloss for shoes and harness...	20
Gloves of cotton or line, not lined...	3 70
Gloves of cotton or line, lined...	1 90

	Rate of Duty, Per Kilogram.
Gloves, woolen, without lining..	4 50
Gloves, silk..	16 00
Gloves, fencing, each..	30
Gloves, skin, with or without embroidery, and not lined........................	4 50
Gloves, skin, with or without embroidery, and lined............................	2 75
Glove-stretcher of wood..	30
Glove-stretcher of gutta-percha...	30
Glove-stretcher of ivory...	1 30
Glycerine, perfumed. (See perfumery.)	
Glycerine, without perfume...	Free
Go-carts, for children to learn to walk. (See elastics.)	
Gold, beaten, in leaves..	15 00
Gold jewelry, or objects of all kinds, with pearls and precious stones, hectogram..........	5 00
Gold jewelry, or objects of all kinds, without pearls or precious stones, hectogram.	4 00
Gold, in mass or powdered...	Free
Gold, legal money...	Free
Gold, *volador falso*...	45
Granules, medicinal..	65
Gridirons, iron, all classes...	20
Gridiron of brass, copper, or ordinary metal, not plated or gilt....................	30
Guns, repeating and breech-loading..	1 25
Guns, not repeating or breech-loading...	82
Guns, air...	70
Gum arabic, lac, tragacanth..	10
Gum, not specified...	20
Gutta-percha (manufactured)..	30
Glue, lip...	30
Glue, for carpenters' use...	10
Grindstones...	04
Gimp, according to material. (See fringes.)	
Garlic, fresh..	03
Globes for electric lights, with or without non-conductors, provided these are attached to the globes..	Free
Grenetine...	10
Greases, animal, not specified...	07
Greases for machines or carriages..	07
Gum-resin..	20
Gelatine, nourish..	25
Gelatine for industrial purposes...	10
Gutters of iron..	Free
Gauges...	10
Graphite...	08
Guards for candlesticks..	30
Grenades, hand, with liquid for extinguishing fires...............................	Free

H.

Hackles of iron, not applicable to agricultural implements.	20
Hair goods, not silk, for head...	10 00
Hair-nets of cotton..	3 20
Hair-nets of silk...	16 00
Hair-nets of silk and cotton...	9 00
Hair-nets of silk and cotton, with beads of glass or common metal.................	8 00
Hair-nets of silk, with beads or glass..	12 00
Hair-nets of silk, cotton and rubber or silk and rubber...........................	4 40
Hair-nets of human hair...	10 00
Hair goods silk, for the head..	16 00
Hair, beaver..	3 00
Hair, human, manufactured or not,...	10 00
Hair vicuna, rabbit hair or other like...	1 60
Handkerchiefs, linen, open worked embroidered, or with trimmings of linen lace, each.....	40
Handkerchiefs, cotton embroidered or with trimmings of cotton lace, "	18
Handkerchiefs, linen, not embroidered, according to class of web. (See linen fabrics).	
Handkerchiefs, wool, of all class of webs, with trimmings, squares or embroideries of silk, and with or without fringe of any material...............................	5 50
Handkerchiefs, silk, with mixture of cotton or wool, of all classes..................	5 50
Handkerchiefs, silk, all classes..	9 00
Handkerchiefs, cotton, without embroidery, according to class of web. (See cotton fabrics.)	
Handkerchiefs of silk and cotton. (See handkerchiefs of silk and cotton.)	
Handkerchiefs, silk. (Silk handkerchiefs.)	
Hand saws..	10
Handles of iron..	20

	Rate of Duty, Per Kilogram.
Handles of brass	30
Handles, wooden, for tools	10
Handles for canes, according to material.	
Hangings, crystal, without metal, for lamps	20
Hangings, crystal, with metal, for lamps	30
Hammers	10
Hammers, sledge, of iron	05
Hammocks netted, canvas, cord or jute. (See cordage.)	
Hams, smoked or salted	25
Harmonicas of all kinds. (See musical instruments.)	
Harness for carriages	1 50
Hat linings of any material for inside of hats	2 00
Hats of all classes not specified, with trimmings and with or without adornments, of whatever material, each	1 00
Hat boxes, leather	60
Hat boxes, pasteboard	45
Hats of feather grass bark, with or without trimmings, for children, each	20
Hats unfinished and without trimmings, each	50
Hat boxes, wooden	30
Hay	Free
Hazel-nuts	10
Herbs, medicinal	20
Hearths, iron, of all kinds, weighing more than 20 kilos	10
Hearths of iron of all kinds, weighing up to 20 kilos	20
Heels, shoe, leather or covered with leather	60
Heels, shoe, wooden	30
Hemp in the crude state	07
Hides, not tanned	10
Hides, tanned and varnished	1 55
Hilts for sword, of nickeled metal	70
Hilts for sword, of metal, silver-plated or gilt	1 30
Hilts for sword, of ordinary metal, neither gilt nor silver-plated	30
Hilts for sword, iron and steel	20
Hinges of iron, all kinds	20
Hinges of brass, all kinds	30
Homœopathic globules or pellets	65
Hooks, iron, all kinds	20
Hooks, brass, all kinds	30
Hooks, iron, for coach poles	20
Hoops of iron with rivets, for making packages	Free
Hoops of wood, for barrels	Free
Hematoxiline. (See alkaloids).	
Hones, whetstone, for sharpening edge-tools	05
Horns, deer, scraped	30
Hops	Free
Horses, not altered	Free
Horses, altered (each)	40 00
Horseshoes, iron	20
Houses, complete, of wood and iron, portable	Free
Hyposulphite of soda	Free
Hydroterapic baths of all kinds	20
Hubs, wood, for carriages	06

I.

Injection, any substances and author	50
Ice	01
Ivory billiard balls	4 00
Ivory in bulk or sheets	20
Ivory, manufactures of	1 30
Iron, manufactures of, of all kinds, not specified, weighing up to 20 kilos	20
Iron, manufactures of, of all kinds, not specified, weighing more than 20 kilos	10
Iron, made into rails for railroad	Free
Iron, pig	01
Iron in bulk	05
Iron, corrugated or in tiles for roofing	04
Iron in sheets, beaten, cast and wrought	10
Instruments for mechanics. (See tools for mechanics).	
Instruments, musical, all kinds and form	45
Instruments, scientific	01
Ink, printing	Free
Ink, writing, in ordinary packages	25

ALPHABETICAL INDEX. 415

	Rate of Duty, Per Kilogram.
Ink, indelible, for marking clothes...	25
Inkstands, according to material.	
Iodine of all substances..	2 00
Iodine of potassium...	1 00
Iodine, pure..	1 50
Iodoforme..	8 00
Iron in sheets, for the contruction of pianos................................	20
Iron, flat, for laundresses, tailors or hatters...............................	10

J.

Jackets, sleeveless, of rubber, lined with any material......................	1 10
Jacket, morning, according to material. (See ready-made clothing.)	
Jackets knitted of cotton..	1 10
Jackets knitted of wool...	1 40
Jacks, iron...	10
Jars, alabaster, marble or plaster...	20
Jars, plaster of Paris or earthen..	15
Jars, glass or crystal...	20
Jars, crockery or porcelain..	15
Jars, leather...	60
Jet manufactured into articles...	1 30
Jellies, medicinal...	20
Jewelry, gold or platinum, with pearls or precious stones, hectogram.........	5 00
Jewelry, gold or platinum, without pearls or precious stones, hectogram......	4 00
Jewelry, silver or silver and gold, with pearls and precious stones, hectogram	3 50
Jewelry, silver or silver and gold, without pearls or precious stones, hectogram	2 50
Jewelry, sets of glass on crystal with common metal..........................	1 20
Jewelry, sets of crockery or porcelain with common metal.....................	1 30
Jewelry, sets of common metal without gilding or silver-plating, with or without mock stones or pearls...	1 30
Jewelry of gilded or plated metal with or without mock stones or pearls.....	1 30
Jewelry of wood...	30
Jewelry of bone, horn, whalebone, gutta-percha or celluloid..................	30
Jewelry of jet, tortoise-shell, shells or ivory..............................	1 30
Juice of aloe tree...	30

K.

Keys, for watches, according to material composed of.	
Keys, iron, loose, for plates, locks or padlocks and for coaches.............	20
Keys, copper, brass or bronze, loose, for plates, locks or padlocks..........	30
Keys, iron, for barrels and other uses.......................................	20
Keys, brass or copper, for coaches...	30
Keys, metal, gilt or plated, for barrels or other uses......................	1 30
Keys, metal, nickeled, for barrels or other uses.............................	70
Keys, zinc, for barrels or other uses..	07
Keys, pewter or white metal, for coaches.....................................	40
Key-rings, iron or steel..	20
Keys, pewter or white metal, for barrels or other uses......................	40
Keys, brass, copper or bronze, for barrels or other uses.....................	30
Key-holes of iron or steel..	20
Key-holes of brass..	30
Key-holes, plated or gilded metal..	1 30
Key-holes, nickled-plated metal..	70
Key-holes, wood...	30
Key-holes, bone or gutta-percha..	30
Key-holes, ivory or shell..	1 30
Kirsch, according to packing. (See rum.)	
Knives and forks of iron...	20
Knives with gilded or silver-plated metal handles............................	1 30
Knives with wood handles..	30
Knives with shell or ivory handles...	1 30
Knives with horn, bone, whalebone or gutta-percha handles....................	30
Knives with nickeled plate handles...	70
Knives or pen knives, with iron handles......................................	30
Knives or pen knives with ordinary metal handles.............................	30
Knives with metal handles gilt or plated.....................................	1 30
Knives, metal, nickeled...	70
Knobs of brass, with or without screws.......................................	30
Knobs of wood, with or without screws..	30

	Rate of Duty, Per Kilogram.
Knobs of plaque, with or without screws	1 25
Knobs of iron, with or without screws	20
Knobs of crockery or porcelain, without screws	15
Knobs of metal, plated or gilt	1 30
Knobs of glass or crystal, without screws	20
Knobs of glass, crystal, crockery or porcelain, with screws	20
Knobs of metal, nickeled	70
Knit goods, cotton, not specified	1 75
Knit goods, linen, not specified	2 00
Knit goods, wool, not specified	2 20
Knit goods, silk, not specified	16 00
Knit goods, of silk and cotton, or silk and wool, or silk and linen, not specified	7 00

L.

Lac. (See colors in powder or prepared.)	
Lace, woolens	8 00
Lace, cotton	6 00
Lace, linen	9 00
Lace, silk	16 00
Lace, silk and cotton, or silk and linen or silk and wool	9 00
Lace, silk and cotton, or silk and linen or silk and wool, with beads of glass or common metal	8 00
Lace of silk with glass or metal beads	12 00
Lace, blonde, of silk	16 00
Lace, of silk and cotton, or silk and wool	9 00
Lace of silk and cotton, or of silk, wool and cotton, with bugles of false metal	8 00
Lace of silk with false metal bugles	12 00
Lamps, crystal or glass, without metal	20
Lamps, crockery or porcelain, without metal	15
Lamps, crystal, glass or porcelain, with metal, not gilded or plated	30
Lamps of metal only, not gilded or plated	30
Lamps of crystal, glass, crockery or porcelain, with gilt or plated metal	1 30
Lamps of crystal, glass, crockery or porcelain, with nickeled metal	70
Lamps of metal, gilt or plated	1 30
Lamps of metal, nickeled	70
Landaus, according to weight. (See carriages.)	
Lanterns, all classes	30
Lantern, glass, for light-houses	20
Lard	20
Lard, cocoa	16
Latches, according to material composed of.	
Lavender	06
Lawns, cotton, white or colored. (See cotton goods).	
Lead pencils, points for	65
Lead, crude, pig or in sheets, or granulated for assaying	07
Leather, morocco. (See calf skins).	
Leather for billiard cues	50
Leaves of medicinal plants	20
Leaves, artificial, for flowers	1 70
Leggings, for fencing, each	30
Lenses, ordinary magnifying, of glass, Nos. 1, 2 and 3	30
Lenses, not mounted in gold or silver	1 25
Letters, cast, for printing	Free
Lime, hydraulic	Free
Lime, common	Free
Linen, waste, hemp or tow	14
Linings of cotton, sewed or in patterns, for umbrellas or parasols	1 60
Lining of any material, for hats	2 00
Linings of silk, sewed or cut, for umbrellas, shades or parasols	16 00
Linings of silk, mixed with cotton, wool or linen, for umbrellas, shades or parasols	5 50
Linings, woolen, sewed and in patterns, for umbrellas, shades or parasols	25
Linings of linen, sewed or unsewed, for umbrellas and parasols	1 80
Links, iron or steel	20
Liniments, of all substances	75
Liquid, amber	45
Liquor stands, according to material composed of.	
Liquors in vessels of glass or wood	25
Litharge	15
Lithographs, with frames covered with cloth or fur	1 30
Lithographs, with or without frames that are not covered with cloth or fur	65
Lobsters, pickled	25
Lobsters, canned	12

ALPHABETICAL INDEX. 417

	Rate of Duty, Per Kilogram.
Locks of iron or steel, all kinds...	20
Locks of brass, copper or bronze, all kinds......................................	30
Locomotives..	Free
Lirones of iron...	10
Labels..	65
Leggings, of other materials, except leather. (See ready-made clothing).	
Leggings of leather..	60
Lycopodium..	33
Lentils..	05
Lye, concentrated..	Free
Laudanum..	75

M.

Maccaroni. (See nutritious paste.)	
Machetes, ordinary, without scabbard, for agriculture..........................	Free
Machines, sewing...	05
Machines, agricultural, industrial, mining and art, except those specified.......	Free
Madapolan, cotton. (See cotton fabrics.)	
Magnesia, calcined...	15
Maizena. (See fecula.)	
Mallets, iron..	25
Maltine...	1 00
Manikins, according to the dominant material.	
Manna...	75
Mantillas, silk lace..	16 00
Manufactures of iron or steel of all kinds, not specified......................	20
Manufactures of iron or steel, not specified whose weight exceeds 20 kilograms.	10
Manufactures of brass, copper or bronze, all classes, not specified............	30
Manufactures of nickel-plated metal...	70
Manufactures of brass, copper, bronze or any other common metal, gilded or plated	1 30
Manufactures of zinc, all classes, not specified...............................	07
Manufactures of plaque...	1 25
Manufactures of pewter or white metal...	40
Manufactures of tin, not specified..	20
Manufactures of wood, not specified...	30
Manufactures of paper or cardboard..	45
Manufactures of leather, not specified..	60
Manufactures of bone, horn, whalebone, gutta-percha or celluloid...............	30
Manufactures of straw or reed, not specified..................................	1 30
Manufactures of amber, jet, agate, tortoise shell, ivory or shell..............	1 30
Manufactures of reed, paper, cardboard or any other analogous material with cloth or skin of all kinds, and with or without ornaments of metal not silver, gold or platinum......	1 30
Manufactures of all kinds of material, with ornaments or accessories of gold or platinum	3 60
Manufactures for artificial flowers, not specified.............................	1 70
Manufactures of alabaster, marble or stucco, not specified.....................	20
Manufactures of gypsum or clay, not specified.................................	15
Maps..	01
Marble manufactured, with mountings of metal, gilt or plated...................	1 30
Marble in flags, of all dimensions, worked on both faces.......................	20
Marble manufactured, without mountings or settings, of any material............	20
Marble manufactured, with mountings or settings of metal, not plated or gilt...	30
Marble dust...	01
Marble in bulk or slabs, for floors, worked on one face, up to 40 centimeters square.	01
Marble in slabs, worked on one face, more than 40 centimeters square...........	20
Marble manufactured, with mountings or settings of metal, nickeled.............	70
Marrasquino. (See liquors.)	
Masks of wire, each..	45
Masks for fencing, each..	45
Masks, all kinds, not specified, each...	25
Mastic or putty..	10
Masts for ships..	Free
Matches of wood or any other material...	1 25
Match boxes of metal, not gilt or silver-plated................................	30
Match boxes of tin, japanned or enameled......................................	20
Match boxes, metal, gilded or silver-plated...................................	1 30
Match boxes of pewter or white metal..	40
Match boxes of plaque or German silver..	1 25
Match boxes of wood..	30
Match boxes of cardboard...	45
Match boxes of leather...	60
Match boxes of horn, rubber or gutta-percha...................................	30

	Rate of Duty, Per Kilogram.
Match boxes of gold or silver. (See jewelry.)	
Match boxes of metal, nickeled.	70
Match boxes of shell, tortoise shell or ivory	1 30
Mats from China	20
Mats of hemp, cocoa or tow	20
Mattresses or cushions, not of silk	50
Mattresses or cushions of silk, or cloth containing silk	5 23
Measures, of length and capacity, of all classes and materials	30
Meats, smoked or salted	25
Meats, preserved	25
Meats, extracts of	1 00
Meats, fresh, of beef, pork or fish	Free
Medals, metal, not gilt or plated	30
Medals, metal, gilt or plated	1 30
Medals, gold or silver. (See jewelry.)	
Medallions, according to material composed of.	
Medicine chests with filled or empty bottles	45
Merino wool, according to weight of a square meter. (See wool fabrics.)	
Mercury	Free
Metals and metaloids, and specified for medical uses	1 50
Metals, gold, silver or platina, in mass or powder	Free
Metal, leaf, gilded or plated	2 20
Metal, white or yellow, in leaves, not gilded or plated	1 20
Mills, hand, for all uses	15
Milk, condensed	25
Minerals, gold, silver, platina or copper	Free
Mining lead	07
Mirrors, with or without frames, of more than 30 centimeters on one of its sides	45
Mirrors, with or without frames, up to 30 centimeters on one side	25
Mixtures for gilding	18
Molasses or honey	08
Monetaries	01
Money, legal, gold or silver, of all countries	Free
Monuments	10
Morocco. (See skins.)	
Morphine and its salts	15 00
Mortar of marble or porphyry	20
Mortar of porcelain	20
Mortar of crystal	20
Mortar of iron	20
Mortar of brass, copper or composition	20
Mosaics of wood, for pavements	30
Mosaics of stone, for pavements	Free
Moulds, for the arts	01
Moldings, wood. (See frames.)	
Muffs, fur. (See manufactures of fur.)	
Music, bound a la Holandesa, or in leather	03
Music cases. (See cases.)	
Music, printed, in sheets	Free
Musk	10 00
Muslin, wool, according to weight of one square meter. (See wool fabrics.)	
Muslin, cotton. (See cotton fabrics.)	
Muslin, book. (See cotton fabrics.)	
Mustard seed	20
Mustard in powder or prepared in sauce	25

N.

Nails, iron	10
Nails, brass or copper	30
Nails, zinc	07
Napkins, cotton. (See cotton goods.)	
Napkins, linen. (See linen goods.)	
Napthaline	1 30
Naptha, purified	10
Naptha, crude	01
Necklace, of ordinary metal, not gilded or silver-plated	30
Necklaces, metal, gilded or silver-plated	1 30
Necklaces, metal, nickeled	70
Necklaces of leather	60
Necklaces, silver or gold. (See jewelry.)	
Needle work of cotton, in pieces or strips	2 25

ALPHABETICAL INDEX. 419

	Rate of Duty, Per Kilogram.
Needle work of linen, in pieces or strips.	2 50
Needle work of wool, in pieces or strips.	3 50
Needle work of silk, in pieces or strips.	16 00
Needle cases of tin.	20
Needle-cases of common metal, not gilded or plated.	30
Needle-cases of gilded or plated metal.	1 30
Needle-cases, plaque.	1 25
Needle-cases of wood.	30
Needle-cases of cardboard.	45
Needle-cases of bone, horn or gutta-percha.	30
Needle-cases of ivory, shell or tortoise shell.	1 30
Needle-cases of gold or silver. (See jewelry.)	
Needles up to five centimeters.	95
Needles of more than five centimeters in length.	35
Nets, according to materials. (See fringes.)	
Nicotine.	15 00
Nippers or pliers of iron or steel.	20
Nipples of rubber.	30
Nipple or bust covers of rubber.	30
Nitrate of silver.	8 00
Nitrate of ammonia.	01
Nuts for bolts, brass or copper.	30
Nuts for bolts of iron, of all classes.	10
Nut crackers, according to material composed of.	
Nursing bottles, crystal, without metal mountings.	20
Nursing bottles, crystal, with ordinary metal mountings.	30

O.

Oars for small boats.	Free
Oats, in the grain.	01
Oats, pulverized.	11
Objects of paper or pasteboard, ornamented with gilt or plated metal.	1 30
Objects of paper or pasteboard, with or without metal ornaments, not gilt or plated.	45
Objects commenced or finished on canvas.	1 00
Objects of natural history, for museums and cabinets.	01
Oil, olive, in vessels of glass.	15
Oil, olive, in jugs or tin cans.	15
Oil, fish or cod liver.	10
Oil, linseed.	25
Oil, fixed, not specified.	50
Oil, volatile or essential.	2 50
Oil, smelling, for the hair.	95
Oil, mineral, purified.	10
Oils, mineral, not purified.	10
Oils, essential, such as orange blossoms, geranium, nutmeg, mustard, *patchouli*, and rose.	5 00
Oil-cloths, all kinds, for tables and floors.	30
Oil-cloth in sheets, when united to machinery.	Free.
Oil-cloth in sheets, not united to machinery.	10
Oil-cloth in sheets, on cloths.	10
Oil-cloth in strips, for billiard outfits, and threaded oil-cloth.	48
Oil-cloth in shoes, in any form.	48
Oil-cloth for dress goods, in any form.	1 60
Oil-cloth prepared for dentists' use.	2 00
Olives, prepared or in oil.	10
Olives in brine.	06
Omnibus, all classes.	10
Onions, fresh.	03
Orchil.	05
Organs, hand, with handles. (See musical instruments.)	
Ornaments of iron, cast or stamped.	20
Ornaments of copper, brass or common metal without gilding or plating, stamped or cast.	30
Ornaments for the head, not of silk.	3 00
Ornaments for the head, of silk.	7 00
Ornaments of straw.	45
Ornaments of metal, gilded or plated.	1 30
Ornaments of metal, nickeled.	70
Ornaments of plaque or German silver.	1 25
Ornaments of pewter or white metal.	40
Ornaments of human hair.	10 00
Ornaments sacerdotal, of silk, mixed with wool or cotton, with or without metal and galloon borders not gold or silver.	4 75

	Rate of Duty, Per Kilogram.
Ornaments sacerdotal, of silk, mixed with wool or cotton, with or without metal and galloon borders of silver or silver gilt..	8 50
Ornaments sacerdotal, of silk, with or without metal and galloon borders of silver or silver gilt...	16 00
Opiates for the teeth. (See perfumery.)	
Opium...	2 30
Opodeldoc...	75
Ovens, iron, of all kinds, weighing up to 20 kilos...................................	10
Ovens, iron, all kinds, weighing more than 20 kilos.................................	10
Oysters, salted or pickled...	12
Oxalate of zinc...	15
Oxide of lead..	03
Oxides, of all substances, not specified..	75
Ochre, red...	15
Oleine...	07
Ointments, medicinal, of all substances and proprietary.............................	75

P.

Padlocks of iron, all kinds..	20
Padlocks of brass, all kinds...	30
Pails of wood..	10
Pails of leather..	60
Pails of zinc, of all kinds...	07
Pails of copper or brass, of all kinds..	30
Pails of iron, of all kinds...	20
Paintings on linen, crystal, metal, paper or cardboard, with or without frames covered with cloth or skin...	65
Paintings on linen, crystal, metal, paper or cardboard, with frames covered with cloth or skin..	1 30
Paint boxes, all kinds..	25
Paints (colors) crude or prepared...	10
Palladium, metallic..	1 50
Pancretina...	75
Papaverine. (See alkaloids.)	
Paper, painted to adorn or decorate glasses...	10
Paper, sand..	06
Paper, straw and wrapping...	08
Paper, blotting, all colors..	10
Paper, filtering..	10
Paper, not glued, and that half glued, of all classes.................................	10
Paper, straw or blotting, with printed notices or addresses...........................	10
Paper, cigarette, all classes...	32
Paper, letter or account, of all classes, ruled or unruled..............................	32
Paper, superfine, medium, ruled and unruled..	32
Paper, engraved or lithographed, for wrapping of cards..............................	65
Paper, water-marked, Bristol, albuminated or of porcelain...........................	48
Paper, impermeable or waterproof...	07
Paper, linen-backed, pitched or tarred..	07
Paper, wall, all classes...	20
Paper, marbled, lustrous and colored, for binders...................................	20
Paper, to color chinaware..	20
Paper, silk or Chinese, white or in colors..	20
Paper, gilt or silvered on one surface..	20
Paper, all classes not specified...	20
Paper, absorbing, for medicines..	75
Paper clippings, for the manufacture of paper.......................................	Free
Parafine, in cakes..	14
Parafine, manufactured..	60
Parasols, according to material. (See umbrellas.)	
Pastes, alimentary..	08
Paste, mineral, for razor strops...	45
Paste for cleaning metal..	45
Pastes and lozenges, medicinal...	20
Pastes for the toilet. (See perfumery.)	
Pearls..	Free
Pearls, imitation...	1 25
Pea, Spanish (Arvejones)..	05
Pegs, wooden, for shoes..	10
Pencils, all classes..	10
Pencil cases, not gold or silver..	65
Pencil cases, gold or silver. (See jewelry.)	

ALPHABETICAL INDEX.   421

	Rate of Duty, Per Kilogram.
Pencil brushes. (See brushes.)	
Penholders, not gold or silver.	30
Penholders, gold or silver. (See jewelry.)	
Penknives, with metal handles, not gold or silver-plated.	1 30
Penknives, with metal handles, nickel-plated.	70
Penknives, with handles of bone, horn, whalebone or gutta-percha	30
Penknives, with handles of wood.	30
Penknives, with handles of ivory, shell or tortoise shell	1 30
Pens of metal not gold or silver.	95
Pens of gold or silver. (See jewelry.)	
Pepper.	25
Pepsin.	3 00
Percale, cotton. (See cotton fabrics.)	
Perfumery, articles of.	95
Permanganate of potash.	Free
Petroleum, crude.	01
Petroleum, refined.	10
Pewter, manufactures of.	40
Phaetons, according to weight. (See carriages.)	
Phosphorus, white or red.	75
Photographs with or without frames not lined with cloth or leather...	65
Photographs with frames lined with cloth or leather.	65
Piano keys.	45
Pianos, all classes. (See musical instruments.)	
Piano works. See musical instruments.)	
Pick-axes for agriculture.	Free
Pickles.	25
Pieces loose for sewing machines. (See sewing machines.)	
Pieces loose for engines, or agricultural apparatus, etc.	Free
Pieces loose for fire arms. (See fire arms.)	
Pieces loose for springs, according to material.	
Pills, medicinal.	65
Pillows of all class of material not of silk.	50
Pillows of silk or of goods mixed with silk.	5 23
Pillow cases, cotton, not embroidered.	1 60
Pillow cases, cotton, embroidered.	2 25
Pillow cases, linen, embroidered.	2 50
Pillow cases, linen, not embroidered.	1 80
Pincers, according to material composed of.	
Pins, common, of iron or steel, all kinds.	20
Pins, common, of brass, all kinds.	30
Pipes, drain, for mines.	Free
Pipes, smoking, according to materials composed of.	
Pipes, wood, empty.	Free
Pipes of iron.	Free
Pipes of copper, brass or bronze.	30
Pipes, iron, covered with brass or copper.	30
Pipes, lead.	Free
Pipes of rubber or gutta-percha.	10
Pique, cotton. (See cotton fabrics.)	
Pistols, self-cocking or repeating.	1 25
Pistols, not self-cocking or repeating.	82
Pistols, air.	70
Pitch.	04
Pivots or pins of iron.	20
Pivots of brass or copper.	30
Plaids, cotton. (See articles not denominated, of cotton without embroidery.)	
Plaids, wool. (See articles not denominated, of wool without embroidery.)	
Plants, living.	Free
Plasters, of all substances, for medicinal uses.	75
Plastron, for fencing, each.	30
Plates of brass, copper or bronze, of all kinds.	30
Plates of iron or steel, of all kinds.	20
Platforms, for railroads.	Free
Platinum, in paste or powder.	Free
Plaque, in manufactures.	1 25
Plaque, in plates.	20
Playing cards, all classes.	1 05
Planes.	10
Plombago.	08
Plowshares.	Free
Plush, according to materials.	

	Rate of Duty, Per Kilogram.
Pocket-books of gilt metal or plated	1 30
Pocket-books, plaque	1 25
Pocket-books, leather	60
Pocket-books, ivory, tortoise-shell or shell	1 30
Pocket-books, gold or silver. (See jewelry).	
Pocket-books, metal, nickeled	70
Poison for preparing hides	Free
Pomade, pots, small, according to material composed of	
Pomades, medicinal, of all substances	75
Pomades for the toilet. (See perfumery).	
Ponchos of wool	25
Ponchos of silk and wool, or of silk and cotton	9 00
Porcelain, worked in pieces, of all forms	15
Porcelain, worked in pieces, of all forms, with mountings of trimmings of ordinary metal	30
Porcelain, worked in pieces, of all forms, with mountings or settings of metal, gilt or plated	1 30
Porcelain, worked in pieces, of all forms, with mountings or settings of metal, nickeled	70
Potash, chlorate of	08
Potash, carbonate of	05
Potash, bi-carbonate of	05
Potash, caustic	08
Potash, nitrate of	Free
Potash, prussiate of	08
Potassium, pure (metallic)	1 50
Potatoes	03
Pouches for hunters, all classes and sizes	50
Pouches of all kinds, for oxygen, with or without keys	30
Powder, tooth. (See perfumery.)	
Powder for the complexion. (See perfumery).	
Powder puffs. (See perfumery).	
Powders, medinical, of all substances	33
Powders for bronzing	1 30
Powder, glass	06
Powder, mining	Free
Powder, excepting that specified for mines	1 00
Powder flasks, according to materials composed of.	
Powder of iste	10
Presses of iron, of all classes, for copying letters, not exceeding 20 kilograms in weight	20
Presses of iron, of all classes, for copying letters, exceeding 20 kilograms in weight	10
Presses, printing and lithographing	Free
Printed advertisements, without frames	01
Printed matter, with pictures, lithographs or engravings, on paper or card-board, without frames	20
Printed advertisements, of all classes, with frames, according to the material of the frames	
Printed advertisements on wrapping or manila paper for wrapping purposes	10
Printed periodicals	Free
Prints. (See cotton fabrics stamped).	
Prism or crystal pieces for chandeliers and lamps	20
Proprietary medicinal preparations not otherwise specified	75
Proprietary or "patent" medicinal preparations, according to nature of compound. (See medicinal compounds of ingredients similar to any "patent medicine" in question.)	
Pulleys, iron	20
Pulleys, brass	30
Pulleys, wood	30
Pulp for making paper	Free
Pumice stone, stone-pumice, whole or powdered	Free
Pumps of all kinds	Free
Punches	10
Purses for keeping money, according to material.	
Pyrolignites of iron and of lead	08

Q.

Quills for writing	50
Quinine, and salts of	1 00

R.

Rabbet planes	10
Rags, for manufacturing paper	Free
Railings, iron, for balconies and windows, that weigh up to 20 kilograms	20
Railings, iron, for balconies and windows, that weigh more than 20 kilograms	10

ALPHABETICAL INDEX.   423

	Rate of Duty, Per Kilogram.
Rakes, of iron, for agriculture...	Free
Rasps...	10
Rat-traps, iron wire, all classes...	20
Razor strops, for razors...	45
Razors and penknives, wood handles...	30
Razors and penknives, with handles of horn, bone, whalebone or gutta-percha............	30
Razors or penknives, with handles of ivory, shell or tortoise shell.........................	1 30
Red ochre..	10
Reeds, for clocks, according to material.	
Reed, for furniture...	20
Refrigerators...	15
Reins, of all materials..	60
Reels, according to their component parts.	
Reps, wool, according to weight of one square meter. (See woolen fabrics.)	
Resin, of all classes, not specified. (See gums.)	
Ribbons, of cotton and wool, with woof of cotton and silk...............................	3 20
Ribbons, of wool, or wool and cotton with gum elastics, up to 4 centimeters in width.....	2 10
Ribbons, cotton, linen or hemp, with or without glass or false metal beads...............	2 50
Ribbons, cotton, with gum elastics, up to 4 centimeters in width........................	1 60
Ribbons, woolen, with or without glass or false metal beads.............................	3 20
Ribbons, silk..	16 00
Ribbons, silk, mixed with cotton, linen or wool...	9 00
Ribbons, silk, mixed with cotton, linen or hemp, with or without glass or false metal beads.	8 00
Ribbons, silk, with glass or metal beads...	12 00
Ribbons, silk and cotton, or silk and wool, with gum elastics, up to 4 centimeters in width..	4 70
Ribbons, silk, with gum elastic, up to 4 centimeters in width...........................	1 10
Ribbons, of all materials, for surgical purposes...	1 00
Rice...	5
Rigging and cordage...	13
Rings, of common metal, not gilded or plated, with or without mock pearls or stones.....	30
Rings, of metal, gilded or plated, with or without mock pearls or stones.................	1 30
Rings, of gold or platinum, with pearls or precious stones, hectogram...................	5 00
Rings, of gold or platinum, without pearls or precious stones, hectogram................	4 00
Rings, of silver, or of silver and gold, with pearls or precious stones, hectogram..........	3 50
Rings of silver or of silver and gold, without pearls or precious stones, hectogram........	2 50
Rings or staples, iron or steel, with or without screws, of all kinds.......................	20
Rings of brass, all kinds..	30
Rings of rubber..	30
Rivets, heads of brass, for carriages...	30
Rivets of iron, for carriages...	20
Rivets, brass or copper..	30
Rivets, iron..	10
Rods, small, of pewter or white metal...	40
Rods, small, of brass or copper, nickeled..	70
Rods, small, of brass or copper, gilt or plated...	1 30
Rods, small, of copper or brass, covered with cotton, linen, wool or silk................	40
Rods, small, of iron, covered with cotton cloth...	15
Roots, medicinal...	20
Rosaries, according to material composed of.	
Rowels of iron...	20
Rowels of brass..	30
Rubber, for erasing and liquid gum for desks..	30
Rugs, according to materials. (See carpets.)	
Rum, of all kinds, in glass vessels...	50
Rum, of all kinds, in wooden vessels..	40
Runners of iron..	20
Runners of brass...	30

S.

Sabres. (See side arms.)	
Saché bags. (See perfumery.)	
Saddles, with or without ornaments, that are not gold or silver..........................	2 00
Saddles, without gold or silver ornaments...	2 00
Saddles, with gold or silver ornaments..	3 60
Saffron, dried or in oil...	4 00
Safes of iron, for money, all kinds, whose weight does not exceed 20 kilograms...........	20
Safes exceeding 20 kilograms...	10
Safes for meats, etc., of brass or copper wire cloth......................................	30
Safes for meats, etc., of iron wire cloth...	20
Sago. (See fecula.)	
Salmon, salted or pickled...	12

	Rate of Duty, Per Kilogram.
Salmon, preserved.	25
Salts, not specified, for medicines.	15
Salts, ammoniacals.	01
Saltpetre or nitrate of potash or of soda.	Free
Salicine.	1 00
Salts of alkaloids, not specified. (See alkaloids.)	
Salts of quinine. (See quinine.)	
Salt, common or table.	03
Sand paper or sand cloth.	06
Santonine.	75
Sarsaparilla, essence of.	30
Sardines, in oil, tomatoes or butter.	15
Sardines, dried, smoked, salted or seasoned.	12
Satin, silk.	16 00
Satinet, of wool, according to the weight of one square meter. (See woolen fabrics.)	
Satchels, traveling, all kinds and sizes, according to material.	
Sausages.	25
Sauces, compounded, prepared or in powder.	25
Saws.	10
Saws, mechanical.	Free
Scarfs, cotton, striped or stamped.	1 60
Scarfs, wool, striped or stamped, without sleeves, borders not worked.	25
Scarfs, wool, imitation of Saltillo, square meter.	8 00
Scarfs, wool with sleeves and worked borders.	25
Scarfs of wool and silk, imitation of Saltillo.	13 40
Scarfs of cotton, all textures, without embroidery.	1 60
Scarfs of cotton, all textures, with embroideries.	2 25
Scarfs of wool, all textures, without embroideries.	25
Scarfs of wool, all textures, with embroideries.	3 50
Scarfs of woolen yarn.	2 20
Scarfs of silk.	16 00
Scarfs of silk and cotton, of wool and silk, of cotton, wool or silk.	9 00
Scapularies, with wool ribbons.	25
Scapularies, with cotton ribbons.	1 60
Scrapers and rubbers for slate pencils.	08
Scales of iron, all kinds, whose weight does not exceed 20 kilograms.	20
Scales of iron, all kinds, whose weight exceeds 20 kilograms.	10
Scales of copper or brass, all classes.	30
Scales of iron of all kinds.	20
Scales of tin of all kinds.	20
Scales of brass or copper.	30
Scaphanders.	Free
Scissors, wrought, up to 14 centimeters.	95
Scissors, wrought, more than 14 centimeters.	30
Scissors, cast.	20
Screw-bolts, for blacksmiths.	10
Screws, iron, of all classes and sizes, with or without nuts.	10
Srews, brass or copper, with or without nuts.	30
Screwdrivers.	10
Scythes for agriculture.	Free
Seals, for stamping, according to material composed of.	
Seals, for impressions, according to material.	
Seals or charms, for watches, according to material composed of.	
Sealing wax.	95
Seeds, medicinal.	20
Seeds for horticulture.	Free
Seeds, nutritious.	05
Seltzer aperient.	15
Shawls, silk, mixed with cotton, linen or wool, of more than 38 and up to 64 threads in web and woof in a square of half centimeter.	23 50
Shawls, silk, mixed with cotton, wool or linen, or more than 26 and up to 38 threads in web and woof in a square of half centimeter.	13 75
Shawls, silk, mixed with cotton, wool or linen, that have up to 26 threads in web and woof in a square of half centimeter.	9 40
Shawls, silk, more than 38 and up to 64 threads of web and woof in a square of half centimeter.	34 10
Shawls, silk, of more than 26 and up to 38 threads in web and woof in a square of half centimeter.	22 00
Shawls, silk, that have up to 26 threads of web and woof in a square of half centimeter.	16 50
Shawls, linen, of more than 38 and up to 64 threads of web and woof in a square of half centimeter, square meter.	6 15
Shawls, linen, of more than 26 and up to 38 threads of web and woof in a square of half centimeter, square meter.	2 90

ALPHABETICAL INDEX. 425

	Rate of Duty, Per Kilogram.
Shawls, wool, that have up to 26 threads in web and woof in a square of half centimeter, square meter	2 20
Shawls, wool, of more than 26 and up to 38 threads in web and woof in a square of half centimeter, square meter	1 45
Shawls, cotton, of more than 26 and up to 38 threads of web and woof in a square of half centimeter, square meter	2 20
Shawls, linen, that have up to 26 threads of web and woof in a square of half centimeter, square meter	1 95
Shawls, cotton, of more than 38 and up to 64 threads of web and woof in a square of half centimeter, square meter	4 90
Shawls, cotton, that have up to 26 threads of web and woof in a square of half centimeter, square meter	1 20
Shawls, cotton, with or without fringe or borders of cotton or wool	1 80
Shawls, with or without borders of wool or cotton, and fringe of silk and wool or silk and cotton	2 50
Shawls of linen point	9 00
Shawls of wool point	8 00
Shawls, wool, with or without borders of wool and with or without fringe of wool, or of wool and silk, or of silk and cotton	3 50
Shawls, wool, with borders of silk and fringe of any material	5 50
Shawls, silk, all classes	16 00
Shawls, silk, with mixture of cotton, linen or wool of all classes, with bugles, glass or false metal beads	8 00
Shawls of cotton net	6 00
Shawls, silk, with mixture of cotton, linen or wool of all classes with or without borders and fringes of same materials	9 00
Shawls, silk, of all classes, with bugles, glass or metal beads	12 00
Sheets of plaque or German silver	20
Sheets, cotton, without embroidery	1 50
Sheets, cotton, embroidered	2 25
Sheets, linen, without embroidery	1 80
Sheets, linen, embroidered	2 50
Sheets of brass or brass and iron for the construction of pianos	30
Sheets of zinc	20
Sheets of lead	07
Sheets of tin	20
Sheets, tin, up to 40 centimeters in length by 30 wide	Free
Sheets, tin, more than 40 centimeters in length	07
Sheets, tin, stamped or japanned	07
Sheets of brass, copper or composition	15
Sheets of iron or steel	10
Shell. (See manufactures of).	
Shell fish, dried, smoked, salted or pickled	12
Shell fish, canned	25
Sheep-skins, dressed. (See skins, prepared).	
Shirts of cotton, white or colored, all sizes	1 30
Shirts of cotton, with linen trimmings	2 00
Shirts, over or under	2 10
Shirts or chemises of cotton cloth, plain or embroidered, for ladies and girls	3 00
Shirts or chemises, linen, plain, all sizes and colors	3 80
Shirts or chemises, linen, embroidered, for ladies and girls	7 00
Shovels, iron, for agriculture	Free
Shoes of worsted	2 20
Shoes, low, skins or cloth, not silk, with or without trimmings or rubber, per pair	90
Shoes, low, of silk, with or without trimmings or rubber, per pair	1 25
Shoes, not low, of silk, with or without ornaments, per pair	1 25
Shoes, rubber. (See rubber in all styles.)	
Shoes, low, of silk, with or without ornaments, per pair	80
Shoes, not low, of leather or other goods, not silk, per pair	90
Shoes, low, of leather or goods not silk, with or without ornaments, per pair	45
Shot pouches, according to material composed of.	
Shot	07
Sickles	Free
Sieve of bristles or leather	20
Sieve of wire, copper or brass	30
Sieve, iron, wire or steel	20
Sieves of iron wire	20
Sieves of brass wire	30
Sieves of bristles or leather	20
Silk, hair, sewing or floss, of all classes and colors	8 00
Silk, raw or crude	2 00
Silver, in bars or in powder	Free

	Rate of Duty, Per Kilogram.
Silver, in legal money	Free
Silver, worked in all kinds of objects. (See silver jewelry.)	
Silver, German, in plates	20
Silver, leaf, plated or gilded	10 00
Sinapisms, medicinal	75
Skins, all classes, undressed	10 00
Skins, prepared. (See calf skins.)	
Skins, manufactures of	2 20
Skirts of wool, unmade, plain	25
Skirts of wool, unmade, embroidered	3 50
Skirts of linen, unmade, embroidered	2 50
Skirts of linen, unmade, plain	1 80
Skirts of cotton, unmade, plain	1 60
Skirts of cotton, unmade, embroidered	2 25
Slates, small, and its imitations	10
Slates, in slabs, worked on both sides	20
Slates, or its imitations, with or without frames, for drawing or other uses	10
Slates for roofs	Free
Slates, in slabs, worked on one side only	01
Sledge hammers of iron	05
Sledge hammers of iron or steel	05
Sleepers of iron or wood, for railroads	Free
Slicing bars	20
Slippers, made of all materials, not containing silk or metal, per pair	40
Slippers, cut, of silk	16 00
Slippers, patterns, worked in silk	16 00
Slippers, cut, of all materials that do not contain silk or metal	75
Slippers, pattern, of leather or any other goods but silk	75
Slippers, cut, not containing silk	75
Slippers, pattern, made of leather or cloth, not silk, with or without trimmings	3 30
Slippers, made, not containing silk, per pair	40
Slippers, cut, of silk	16 00
Slippers, in patterns, of silk, with or without metal	16 00
Slippers, made of any material, not of silk or metal, per pair	40
Slippers, in patterns, of all materials which do not contain silk or metal	75
Snuff trays, according to material composed of.	
Snuff. (See tobacco in powder.)	
Snuffers, iron or steel	20
Snuffers of pewter or white metal	40
Snuffers, brass	30
Snuffers of gilt or silver-plated metal	1 30
Snuffers of plaque	1 25
Snuffers of nickeled metal	70
Soap, fine, for the toilet, scented or not scented	1 25
Soap, ordinary, not scented	18
Soap, medicinal, such as phenic acid, camphorated, tar, arnica, chloride of mercury, ox-gall, cocoa butter, sulphurous, sulpho-alkaline and cocoa-nut	30
Soda caustic	Free
Soda, baking	15
Solder, copper, bronze or brass	10
Spaces for printing	Free
Spangles, yellow metal, not gilt	1 20
Spangles, silver or silver gilt	10 00
Spangles, metal, gilt or plated	2 50
Spades for agriculture	Free
Sperm, refined	60
Sperm, in cake	40
Speaking tubes of common metal, without gilding or plating	30
Spheres or globes, celestial or terrestrial	01
Spirits of wine. (See alcohol.)	
Spoons, all sizes, of horn, rubber or gutta-percha	30
Spoons, gold or silver. (See jewelry.)	
Spoons, all sizes, of white metal or pewter	40
Spoons, all sizes, of plaque or German silver	1 25
Spoons, all sizes, of gilded or silver-plated metal	1 30
Spoons, all sizes, of brass	30
Spoons, all sizes, of tinned iron	20
Spokes of wood for carriages	06
Sponge, fine	1 50
Sponge, common	30
Springs, iron or steel, of all classes	20
Springs, iron or steel, for carriages	10

ALPHABETICAL INDEX.

	Rate of Duty, Per Kilogram.
Spreads, bed, of cotton..	1 60
Spreads, bed, wool..	25
Spurs of metal not gilded or plated..	30
Spurs of metal, gilded or plated...	1 30
Spurs of gold or silver. (See jewelry.)	
Spurs of metal, nickeled..	70
Squeezers, iron...	01
Squeezers, iron, of all kinds..	01
Squeezers, wood..	30
Spy-glasses, known as opera glasses, with or without cases................	1 25
Spy-glasses, trimmed with any material not gold or silver..................	30
Spy-glasses, without glasses, known as Nos. 6 and 8........................	30
Spunk. (See matches.)	
Statues, zinc, less than natural size......................................	07
Statues, zinc, natural size or greater dimensions..........................	10
Statues, brass, bronze or composition, less than natural size..............	30
Statues, brass, bronze or composition, natural size or greater dimensions..	10
Statues and stone busts, less than natural size............................	15
Statues of iron, natural size, of greater dimensions.......................	10
Statues, iron, less than natural size......................................	20
Statues and stone busts, natural size or greater dimensions................	10
Statues, of marble, alabaster or stucco, less than natural size............	20
Statue, gypsum or earth, natural size or greater dimensions................	10
Statue, gypsum or earth, less than natural size............................	15
Statues of marble, alabaster or stucco, of natural size or of greater dimensionsc	10
Staves of barrels..	Free
Starch...	08
Stage coaches..	20
Staples of iron, when imported with the bail-wire, for fencing.............	Free
Staples of iron, not imported with the wire...............................	20
Stereoscopes, all kinds...	65
Stearine, refined...	15
Stearine, in cakes..	14
Stencil marking plates, according to material composed of.	
Stencils of tin, for marking..	20
Stencils of brass, etc..	30
Steel, in bars, cylindrical or octagonal, for mines........................	Free
Steel-yards, iron, of all classes, that weigh more than 20 kilograms.......	10
Steel-yards, iron, of all classes, that weigh up to 20 kilograms...........	20
Steel, sharpeners of, with or without handles..............................	10
Steel, in bulk..	05
Steel, in bars, cylindrical or octagonal, for mines........................	Free
Stirrups, wood or of wood and iron..	30
Stirrups, iron, all kinds...	20
Stoves, iron, weighing more than 20 kilos.................................	10
Stoves, iron, of all kinds, weighing no more than 20 kilos.................	20
Stones, imitation, of crystal...	1 30
Stones, fine, or precious...	Free
Stones, lithographic..	Free
Stone, in slabs...	01
Stone, mineral..	Free
Stones, grind...	04
Stockings, cotton, with or without silk ornaments..........................	1 75
Stockings, linen..	2 00
Stockings, wool...	2 20
Stockings, silk...	16 00
Stockings, silk and cotton, or silk and wool...............................	7 00
Stockings, elastic, for varix..	1 00
Storax-gum, in liquid or solid form.......................................	75
Strings, all classes and materials, for musical instruments................	45
Straw, manufactures of, not specified.....................................	45
Straw covering, for bottles...	03
Straw, for hats...	45
Strainers of iron wire..	20
Strainers of brass or copper wire...	30
Strainers of bristles or leather..	20
Sub-nitrate of bismuth..	75
Succory...	10
Sugar, common, refined..	15
Sugar, rock-candy...	35
Sugar, in powder, prepared with lemon.....................................	35
Sulphate of copper..	Free

	Rate of Duty, Per Kilogram.
Sulphate of quinine. (See quinine.)	
Sulphates, not specified............	15
Sulfo-oleine............	07
Sulphur............	01
Sun shades, according to class. (See umbrellas.)	
Suspensories, of all materials............	1 00
Suspenders, cotton, with or without trimmings............	3 70
Suspenders, linen or hemp, with or without trimmings............	90
Suspenders, woolen, with or without trimmings............	1 30
Suspenders, silk, with or without trimmings............	16 00
Suspenders, silk, mixed with cotton or wool, with or without trimmings............	9 00
Sweetmeats, of all kinds, not specified............	25
Swords, according to class. (See arms).	
Syphons of tin, covered with any material............	30
Syphons of glass, with or without settings of metal, of all classes............	20
Syringes, according to material.	
Syrups, all classes, for medicinal uses............	50
Syrups, not medicinal............	1 00

T.

Table cloths, linen. (See linen fabrics).	
Table covers, cotton. (See cotton fabrics).	
Tacks, copper or brass............	30
Tacks, iron............	10
Tacks, zinc............	07
Taffeta, gummed............	75
Tallow, all classes............	07
Tapioca. (See fecula).	
Tar............	04
Tares (the fruit of the Carob tree)............	05
Tartar, crude............	08
Tassels of cotton............	70
Tassels of wool............	1 30
Tassels of silk and wool or silk and cotton............	2 80
Tea, all classes............	50
Tease of wire............	01
Tease, vegetable............	Free
Teeth, artificial, of all materials............	3 00
Telescopes for the sciences............	01
Tents, field, of all classes............	20
Textures of silk, mixed with cotton, linen or wool, stamped, marbled or striped, with figures or ornaments in imitation of Rebozos. (See shawls or Rebozos of silk mixed with cotton, linen or wool).	
Textures of silk, stamped, marbled or striped, with figures or ornaments in imitation of Rebozos. (See shawls or Rebozos of silk).	
Textures of cotton, stamped, marbled or striped, with figures or ornaments in imitation of Rebozos. (See shawls or Rebozos of cotton).	
Textures of linen, stamped, marbled or striped, with figures or ornaments in imitation of Rebozos. (See shawls or Rebozos of linen).	
Textures of wool, stamped, marbled or striped, with figures or ornaments in imitation of Rebozos. (See shawls or Rebozos of wool).	
Textures of gilded or plated metal on paper for the manufacture of artificial flowers. (See articles for artificial flowers.)	
Thimbles of bone, rubber or gutta-percha............	30
Thimbles, gold or silver. (See jewelry).	
Thimbles of ivory or shell............	1 30
Thimbles, iron or steel............	20
Thimbles of metal, gilt or silver-plated............	1 30
Thimbles of ordinary metal, not gilt or silver-plated............	30
Thread, counters, not of gold or silver............	30
Thread, cotton, carded, for long shawls............	1 60
Thread of cotton, of all kinds............	1 60
Thread of cotton, crochet............	1 60
Thread, crude, hemp or colored, fine or common, including half-twisted in balls and skeins..	13
Thread of linen, carded for long shawls............	2 00
Thread, linen or hemp, white or colored, in spools............	2 00
Thread, woolen............	1 90
Thread, woolen, mixed with silk or false metal............	3 00
Thread, silver-plated or gilded............	10 00
Thread of metal, plated or gilded............	2 50
Thread, white or yellow metal, not plated or gilded............	1 20

ALPHABETICAL INDEX.

	Rate of Duty, Per Kilogram.
Thread, twilled silk	8 00
Threshers	Free
Ticking, cotton, square meter	17
Ticking, linen, square meter	22
Tiles	7 25
Tiles, clay, of all classes	Free
Tiles of stone, square, known as *Baldosas*, for flooring	1 00
Tilmas of cotton, striped or stamped	1 60
Tincal	15
Tinctures for dyeing the hair. (See perfumery.)	
Tinctures, medicinal	75
Tin, in sheets, up to 40 centimeters long by 30 wide, not stamped or painted	Free
Tin, in sheets, more than 40 centimeters long by 30 wide, and stamped or painted, of all sizes	07
Tin, manufactured into all kinds of articles, not specified	20
Tin in plates, sheets and other articles, not specified	20
Tinsel	95
Tobacco, plug or chewing	68
Tobacco, sifted	1 10
Tobacco, leaf, not Virginia	1 37
Tobacco, Virginia leaf	18
Tobacco, powder or snuff	2 75
Tobacco, worked into cigarettes	1 37
Tobacco, worked into cigars	5 40
Tobacco, cut, for pipes	1 37
Tongs, iron, for chimneys	20
Tooth brushes of all classes, not gold or silver	30
Tools, mechanics'	10
Tortoise shell. (See articles made of it.)	
Towels of cotton. (See cotton fabrics.)	
Towels of linen. (See linen fabrics.)	
Tow or oakum, tarred or pitched	04
Tow (hemp packing)	14
Toys of glass or crystal	20
Toys of china or porcelain	15
Toys of all classes, not specified	45
Transparencies. (See curtains painted in oil or opaque colors.)	
Trays of iron enameled or japanned	20
Trays of brass or copper	30
Trays of gilded or plated metal	1 30
Trays of nickeled metal	70
Trays of plaque	1 25
Trays of pewter	40
Trays of wood	30
Trays of paper or cardboard	45
Trays of German silver	40
Tricopherous	15
Tri-sulphate of Seine	Free
Trombones. (See musical instruments.)	
Trout, preserved	25
Trout, salted or pickled	12
Truffles, preserved	25
Trunks of leather or covered with leather	60
Trunks of wood	30
Trunks not specified, according to material.	
Trumpets. (See musical instruments).	
Trusses of all kinds	1 00
Tubes, crystal or glass	20
Tubs of tinned iron	20
Tubs of tin	20
Tubs of brass	30
Tubs of zinc	07
Tubs, wooden, wash	30
Types of wood, and other appliances for lithographing	Free
Types for printing	Free
Turpentine	10
Tunny-fish in preserves	25
Tunny-fish salted, in brine, smoked or dried	12
Turbines of all classes	Free
Turning pins, iron, for pianos	20
Tufts of silk, or silk and cotton, or silk and wool, with metal adornments, not gold or silver	5 00

Rate of Duty, Per Kilogram.

U.

Umbrellas, cotton, each	60
Umbrellas, linen, each	85
Umbrellas, wool, each	1 00
Umbrellas, silk, or of silk mixed with cotton, linen or wool, all classes, each	1 75
Undershirts for ladies, cotton knitting	1 75
Undershirts for ladies, linen knitting	2 00
Undershirts for ladies, woolen knitting	2 20
Undershirts for ladies, silk and cotton or silk and woolen knitting	7 00
Undershirts for ladies, silk knitting	16 00

V.

Vaccine virus	Free
Valerianates of substances not specified	6 00
Valises, leather or covered with it	60
Valises, cardboard, covered with cloths	45
Valises, wood, covered with straw	45
Varnishes of all kinds	18
Vaseline, scented or not scented	25
Vases of gold or silver. (See jewelry of gold or silver.)	
Vases of other materials. (See respective class of goods.)	
Vegetables, fresh	01
Vegetables preserved, pickled or dry	25
Veils, cotton lace	6 00
Veils, linen lace	9 00
Veils, woolen laces	8 00
Veils, silk point or lace	16 00
Veils, silk and cotton silk, or wool and silk	9 00
Veils, silk and cotton or wool with beads of imitation metal	8 00
Veils, silk point or lace, with bead or metal trimmings	12 00
Vests of cotton knitting, all sizes	1 10
Vests of woolen knitting, all sizes	1 70
Vests, woolen, knitted, for ladies and girls	1 40
Vests of other material. (See ready-made clothing.)	
Velvet, according to class and material.	
Velocipedes	20
Veneering of fine wood and for pianos	02
Veratrine	15 00
Vermicelli. (See alimental pastes.)	
Vessels or jars of crockery or porcelain	15
Vessels or jars of crystal or glass	20
Vignettes for printing	Free
Violins. (See musical instruments.)	
Vinegar in wood	06
Vinegar in glass	11
Visors, leather	30

W.

Wads, pasteboard, for fire-arms	45
Wafers, all classes	75
Wagons	Free
Wash-basins, metal, gilt or plated	1 30
Wash-basins, iron, all classes	20
Wash-basins, crockery or porcelain	15
Wash-basins, crystal or glass	20
Wash-basins, copper, brass or composition, all classes	30
Wash-basins, metal, nickeled	70
Wash-basins, gold or silver. (See jewelry.)	
Wash-basins, zinc, all classes	07
Wash-basins, plaque	1 25
Wash-basins, tin, all classes	20
Wash-basins, leather	60
Wash-basins, pewter or white metal	40
Washing machines, wood	10
Watches of gold for pocket, with or without precious stones, and with repeaters, each	14 00
Watches, etc., nor repeaters, each	6 75
Watches of other metals, not specified, each	50
Watch works, without cases, repeater or other combination, each	1 30

ALPHABETICAL INDEX.

	Rate of Duty, Per Kilogram.
Watch works, without cases, with repeaters or other combination, each	5 00
Watches, silver, not repeaters, each	1 30
Watches, silver, repeaters, each	5 00
Watches, gold, with or without (precious stones), not being repeaters, each	6 75
Watches, gold, with or without (precious stones), also being repeaters	14 00
Water for plating, gilding or taking off stains	75
Water, aromatic, mixed, distilled or spirituous, for the toilet or medical purposes	50
Water, mineral, natural or artificial	10
Water closets, according to materials.	
Wax, shoe	50
Wax, white, yellow or virgin	50
Weights, iron, for scales and steel-yards	20
Weights, brass, for scales and steel-yards	30
Whalebone, polished or unpolished	30
Wheat	05
Wheelbarrow of one or two wheels	01
Wheels, for carts	15
Wheels, for carriages	60
Whips, without gold or silver butts	65
Whips, with gold or silver butts	3 60
Whisky, according to packages. (See aguardientes.)	
Whiting, Spanish	Free
White lead	10
Wicks, cotton, for lamps	30
Wicks of wool, felt, for locomotive reflectors	30
Wick, cotton	16
Windows, wooden	30
Wine, red or white, of all classes, in vessels of glass	20
Wines, medicinal	25
Wine, red and white, of all classes in the wood	12
Wild marjoram	20
Wire of brass or copper, in articles not specified	30
Wire of white metal, from number 20 up, of the Birmingham measure	1 00
Wire of white metal, up to number 19, etc	40
Wire of brass or copper, covered and prepared for the electric light, provided the wire is up to number 5 of the Birmingham measure	Free
Wire of brass or copper, lined with cotton, silk or other material	40
Wire, silver, with or without gilding	10 00
Wire, iron or steel, in articles of all kinds	20
Wire, iron or steel, for carding, from number 26 up	01
Wire, iron or steel, galvanized or ungalvanized	10
Wire, iron, with hooks and nails for fastening them to fences	Free
Wire, iron or steel, lined with cotton cloth	20
Wire, iron, prepared for making artificial flowers	10
Wire, iron, with clasps	Free
Wire, brass or copper	30
Wire of gilded or plate metal	2 50
Wire, brass or copper, articles made of yellow metal, not gilded	1 20
Wire, telegraph	Free
Wire-cloth of iron wire, for fences	20
Wood, worked in sets, for boxes	Free
Wood, fine, sawed in logs, beams, boards or planks	02
Woods, dye, in sticks or powder	05
Wood, ordinary for building	Free
Wood, worked roughly, for cart-poles or shafts	06
Wood, sawed in sheets	30
Wood, cuttings of, to fill furniture	Free
Wool, in fleece	13
Wool, carded	20
Woolen waste, of all kinds and colors	1 90
Worsted, of wool, with or without common metal	1 90
Worsted, of wool and silk, with or without common metal	3 00
Worm-wood, in bottles or barrels. (See rum).	

Z.

Zinc, in sheets	07
Zinc, in bars	07
Zinc, manufactured, in all classes, not specified	20

SUPPLEMENT TO
Mexican Tariff
AND
CUSTOM-HOUSE LAWS.

SUPPLEMENT TO MEXICAN TARIFF AND CUSTOM-HOUSE LAWS.

DEPARTMENT OF THE TREASURY AND PUBLIC CREDIT.

SECTION FIRST.

The President of the Republic of Mexico has been pleased to issue the following decree:

Porfirio Diaz, Constitutional President of the Republic of Mexico, to the inhabitants of the same, greeting:

That in accordance with the power vested in the Executive of the Union by the law of April 26, 1886, I have deemed proper to decree that from and after the first day of July next the General Ordinance for the Maritime, Frontier and Coastwise Trade Custom Houses and Custom House Sections, with its tariff and vocabulary annexed, which was decreed on January 25, 1885, be modified as follows·

OFFICIAL MEXICAN TARIFF CHANGES.

DEPARTMENT OF THE TREASURY AND PUBLIC CREDIT.

SECTION I. CIRCULAR.

The same circumstances existing at present which were considered when the circular of February 19, 1886, was issued, relative to permits for internation through the custom houses established within the Free Zone, of certain objects such as carriages, horses and their harnesses, for the period of six months, without the payment of the corresponding duties, the President of the Republic has been pleased to order said custom houses to continue issuing the above-mentioned permits for the period indicated and under the conditions established in the circular referred to, viz: that said objects shall be returned to the Zone within the specified time in each permit, otherwise duty shall be charged them; for which purpose a bond shall have been previously given to the satisfaction of the collector of the custom house.

I communicate it to you for the purpose herein stated.
Liberty in the Constitution.
MEXICO, July 5, 1887.
By order of the Secretary,

J. A. GAMBOA,
Chief Official.

TREASURY DEPARTMENT.

SECTION FIRST.

The President of the Republic has been pleased to address me the following decree:

Porfirio Diaz, Constitutional President of the United Mexican States, to the inhabitants of the same, greeting:

That in accordance with the power vested in the Executive by the law of December 11, 1884, in force at present, I decree the following:

Art. 1. The warehouses established in the custom house at Santiago Tialtelolco of this capital (Mexico City) shall be considered as deposit warehouses.

Art. 2. Merchants can deposit in them all classes of merchandise, either national or nationalized, for the space of one year, the introduction into them of any packages containing inflammable, corrosive or explosive materials being prohibited and subject to the fines imposed by the custom house ordinance. Merchandise of a perishable character shall be admitted into the warehouses for a period not longer than is required for their dispatch.

Art. 3. The international revenue office of Mexico shall be responsible for the value of merchandise as it was received, except in case of superior force.

Art. 4. Merchandise deposited in the warehouses of the custom house of Mexico can be taken from them whenever the merchant may desire. If the merchandise is to be used or consumed in the federal district, they shall pay the duties established by law for these causes, but they shall be allowed to go free to any other place of the Republic provided the regulations are complied with.

Art. 5. At the expiration of the year the owner or consignee shall withdraw the merchandise from the warehouses within eight days, which, if not done, the internal revenue collectors shall proceed to sell them at public auction, from the proceeds of which the storage and other charges shall be deducted.

The balance left from the sale shall be kept by the office in deposit, to be claimed by the owner or consignee.

Art. 6. National merchandise shall pay the following rates of storage:

Five cents per month for a package weighing 100 kilos for the first quarter.

Seven cents per month for a package weighing 100 kilos for the second quarter.

Twenty-five cents per month for a package weighing 100 kilos for the third quarter.

Fifty cents per month for a package weighing 100 kilos for the fourth quarter.

Art. 7. Nationalized goods shall pay double the rate of storage paid by national goods.

Art. 8. The warehouses shall open and close at the same hour as the office. Its doors shall have three keys, one of which shall be kept by the administrator, another by the collector, and the third by the chief of the warehouse.

Art. 9. The internal revenue office shall form a series of regulations, in which the manner of collecting, entering and delivery of merchandise shall be stated. These regulations shall have to be approved by the Secretary of the Treasury, and can not be altered without his permission being previously obtained.

Art. 10. While the internal revenue office of the City of Mexico is reformed, there shall be established a warehouse department with the following officers:

One chief of the warehouse with a salary of $2,000.20. Four assistants with a salary of ($1,200.85). $4,803.40.

Art. 11. The chief of the warehouse as well as the assistants shall give bonds for double the amount of their salaries.

In filling these offices preference shall be given to the present employés of the revenue offices, of the federal district which are found in excess.

Given at the National Palace of Mexico, the fourteenth day of September, eighteen hundred and eighty-six.

PORFIRIO DIAZ.

To the Secretary of the Treasury and Public Credit, C. Manuel Dublan.

I communicate it to you for compliance therewith.

Liberty in the Constitution.

Mexico, September 14, 1887.

DUBLAN.

TREASURY DEPARTMENT.

SECTION FIRST. CIRCULAR.

This department having been informed that some copies of the official edition of the present "General Ordinance for the Marine and Frontier Custom Houses" still contain several errors, which have not been corrected either in the list of corrections at the end of said book, or in the circular relating to "Corrections of the Tariff," issued by this office on the 3d of April last; the President of the Republic, wishing to avoid all difficulties which may arise in the declaration of foreign merchandise imported, has been pleased to order that the following corrections be made:

TARIFF.

Fraction 327. Gives net weight; should say, gross weight, kilogram.

EXPLANATORY.

Vests of woolen knit for ladies and girls, fraction 86; should say, fraction 81.

Gelatine for industrial uses, fraction 463; should be, fraction 171.

Grenetine, fraction 463; should be, fraction 171.

Mosaics of stone for pavements, "free;" should be, fraction 205.

Oxide of lead, fraction 493; should be, fraction 482.

Perfumery (articles of), fraction 559; should say, "*perfumery*" (articles of, not specified), fraction 559.

I communicate the above to you for compliance with the same.

Liberty in the Constitution.

Mexico, September 21, 1887.

DUBLAN.

TREASURY DEPARTMENT.

SECTION FIRST—CIRCULAR.

The President of the Republic hereby orders that all the copies containing additions to invoices presented to custom houses for classification, by consignees of vessels of merchandise, shall have stated upon them by the collectors whether there are fines or not imposed upon them at the time of classification.

I transmit it to you for your compliance therewith.

Liberty in the Constitution.

Mexico, October 6, 1887.

By order of the Secretary.

J. A. GAMBOA,
Chief Official.

TREASURY DEPARTMENT—MEXICO.

SECTION FIRST.

The President of the Republic has been pleased to address me the following decree:

Porfirio Diaz, Constitutional President of the United Mexican States, to the inhabitants of the same, be it known:

That in virtue of the power vested in the Executive of the Union, by Fraction I of the only article of the Estimated Income Law of the 28th of April last, to modify, during the year in which said law is to be in force, the General Ordinance for the Maritime and Frontier Custom Houses issued March 1, 1887, I hereby decree the following:

Only Article. Fraction I, of Article 107 of the Custom House Ordinance is reformed as follows:

I. The collectors of custom houses shall admit the additions and rectifications made to manifests, provided they refer to *points* which neither increase nor diminish the number of packages declared on the manifest; but when the interested parties do not avail themselves of their right to add or rectify their manifests, and there exist infractions of the law, they shall be fined from one to twenty-five dollars.

It is also ordered that this law be printed, published, circulated and duly complied with.

Given at the National Palace of Mexico, the twentieth day of October, eighteen hundred and eighty-seven.

PORFIRIO DIAZ.

To the Secretary of the Treasury and Public Credit, Manuel Dublan.
I communicate it to you for compliance therewith.
Liberty in the Constitution.
Mexico, October 20, 1887.

DUBLAN.

TREASURY DEPARTMENT, MEXICO.

SECTION THIRD. CIRCULAR.

The following dispatch has been sent to the Collector of Customs at Paso del Norte:

" The President of the Republic, in view of the doubts expressed by that custom house as to whether the decree of this department of September 15th, ultimo, modifies Article 432 of the General Custom House Ordinance at present in force, in that part relating to the collection of the federal tax on all confiscated goods and fines imposed upon them, desires me to say that he is of the opinion that as the tariff does not expressly mention this point, its prescriptions, therefore, do not suffer any modification, and that the federal tax was imposed while the revenue laws of 1874 and 1876 were in force; that the law of September 15, 1880, in Fraction XIX of Article 17, excepted the fines and confiscations authorized by the Maritime and Frontier Custom House Ordinance from taxation, and as that of the 31st of March last does not contain that exception, it is proper that the tax shall be collected according to the terms expressed in Article 31; that is to say, it shall be included in the total, a fifth of which is to be paid in stamps."

The above is in reply to your telegram of the 27th inst. and I communicate to you for compliance therewith.
Liberty in the Constitution.
Mexico, October 27, 1887.
By order of the Secretary.

J. A. GAMBOA,
Chief Official.

TREASURY DEPARTMENT, MEXICO.

SECTION FIRST.

The President of the Republic has been pleased to address me the following decree:

Porfirio Diaz, Constitutional President of the United Mexican States, to the inhabitants thereof, greeting:

That the Congress of the Union has been pleased to decree the following:
The Congress of the United Mexican States decrees:
"Only Article. That the export duty imposed on construction and cabinet woods by Fraction V of the only article of the Budget Law, for the present fiscal year, shall be computed by the number of tons burden of the vessel, notwithstanding the number of tons of wood exported by said vessel, provided no other merchandise is shipped by the same vessel at the port of clearance. Whenever a vessel loaded with construction and cabinet woods carries other merchandise, the wood shall pay at the rate of two dollars for every ton of it on the vessel.
A. Castillo, President of the House of Deputies; Marino Martinez de Castro, President of the Senate; A. Riba y Echeverria, Secretary of the House of Representatives; Pedro Sanchez Castro, Secretary of the Senate."
I therefore order this decree to be executed, published, circulated, and duly complied with.
Given at the National Palace of Mexico, on the sixth day of December, 1887.

PORFIRIO DIAZ.

To the Secretary of the Treasury, Manuel Dublan.
I communicate it to you for your information and compliance therewith.
Mexico, December 6, 1887.

DUBLAN.

TREASURY DEPARTMENT, MEXICO.

SECTION FIRST.

The President of the Republic has been pleased to address me the following decree:

Porfirio Diaz, Constitutional President of the United Mexican States, to the inhabitants of the same, be it known:

That in accordance with the power vested in the Executive of the Union by Fraction I of the only article of the Income Budget Law of April 28, of the present year, I have deemed proper to decree the following:

Art. 1. Section First of the "Rules for the Application of the Tariff of the General Ordinance for the Maritime and Frontier Custom Houses" is hereby increased with the following articles:

Section I. Merchandise free of duty.

1. Bank notes or Mexican currency.
2. Barrels or pipes of iron, empty.
3. Books, copy, writing, for primary institutions.
4. Pipes or tubes of iron, galvanized.
5. Posts, cross-pieces, clamp-nails, stakes, insulators for telegraph and telephones, provided it is proved to the satisfaction of the custom house collectors that they are to be used for such purposes.

Art. 2. The second section of the "Rules for the Application of the Tariff" is modified by the following articles:

XXV. White handkerchiefs of cotton or linen textures, which have in only one of their corners a small embroidery of cotton, linen, wool or silk, will be considered as not embroidered.

XXVI. Handkerchiefs of plain texture of cotton or linen which have a woven trimming, not embroidered or open-work, will be considered as of plain texture.

Art. 3. The 23d fraction of the tariff is modified as follows:

23. Cotton thread of all classes and colors on spools, up to 275 meters, per each 100 spools, $1.00.

Cotton thread of all classes and colors on spools, including cotton crochet thread, from 276 to 458 meters, each 100 spools, $2.00.

Cotton thread in balls, in skeins and ironed, for rebozos, kilogram legal, $1.20.

Art. 4. This law shall take effect March 1, 1888.

I hereby order that it be printed, published, circulated and duly complied with. Given at the National Palace of Mexico the 28th of December, 1887.

PORFIRIO DIAZ.

To the Secretary of the Treasury and Public Credit.
I communicate it to you for your compliance.
Liberty in the Constitution.
Mexico, December 28, 1887.

DUBLAN.

TREASURY DEPARTMENT. MEXICO.

SECTION FIRST.

The President of the Republic has been pleased to address me the following decree:

Porfirio Diaz, Constitutional President of the United Mexican States, to the inhabitants of the same, be it known:

That in virtue of the power vested in the Executive of the Union by Fraction V, Article II, Section II, Chapter I, of the "General Ordinance for the Maritime and Frontier Custom Houses," issued March 1st of the present year, and in view of the fact that several custom houses have quoted merchandise not classified in the vocabulary of the tariff, by analogy, according to the rules established in Section II, Chapter IV of the same law, I decree the following:

Only Article. The vocabulary of the tariff is hereby increased, with the following assimilations:

A.

Animal hair for stuffing cushions.
Animal hair threads.
Awning of canvas for ships, with or without eyelet holes, thimbles and bolt ropes.

B.

Bands of wool, with cotton embroidery.
Bands of cotton knit with wool fringe, not embroidered.
Bands of cotton knit with wool fringe, with cotton or wool embroidery.
Bands of hemp texture, mixed with wool and hair for machinery, when coming separate from it.
Bands of animal hair texture for machinery, when coming separate from it.
Bags, ready made, common, of hemp, cotton or any other material not specified in Fraction 30, Section 1st, of the provisions for the application of the tariff (according to kind of texture).
Brown paper with colored selvage.
Bodies of common wood, not painted, for carriages.

C.

Canvas sails for vessels.
Carpets of hemp and cow hair.
Curtains of hemp, cotton and wool.

E.

Earthen demijohns for manufactures of chemical products.
Engraved paper not specified.

F.

Felt blankets for saddles.
Felt of cow hair, when separate from the machinery.
Fenoline or oil for the preservation of woods
Flags of wool texture with its ropes.
Fruit juice.

G.

Grated cocoanut, mixed with sugar.

H.

Hair-cloth mixed with cotton, linen or hemp.
Hemp cord, covered with wool.

I.

Iron, mullers.

L.

Leads for curling the hair.
Leads for making seals for closing railway cars.
Lead nuts not threaded.
Linen drawing (tracing linen).

M.

Meat, or its likes.
Molasses extracted from fecula or sorghum.
Mouth-pieces, automatic, for carriages.

O.

Oil, cotton-seed, purified.
Oil, cotton-seed, not purified.
Oil, lubricating, vegetable, not purified.
Oriental tonic.

P.

Paper thread.

R.

Rubber umbrellas.
Rubber on cloth for stamps.

S.

Seaweed.
Slates for chimney ornaments.
Slippers of leather, embroidered with silk, with or without common metal.
Steel springs covered with cotton.
Steel articles covered with silk and cotton.
Steel articles covered with cotton.
Sticks for matches.

T.

Tanks or common wood deposits, rough, for liquids, with the iron bands for setting made up.
Tannin.

W.

Wagons, light, called "road wagons."
Wastes of wool, from the weaving manufactures of said material.
Whiffletrees of wood and iron for carts.
I therefore order this decree to be printed, published, circulated and duly complied with.
Given at the National Palace of Mexico, December 31, 1887.

PORFIRIO DIAZ.

To the Secretary of the Treasury, Manuel Dublan.
I communicate it to you for your compliance therewith.
Liberty in the Constitution.
Mexico, December 31, 1887.

DUBLAN.

WIRE.

WIRE—Insulated copper wire, with any matter for electric light, provided importers show conclusively at the custom house the indicated purpose. (Decree May 16, 1888.) Free.

COTTON THREAD CALLED "CROCHET."

COTTON THREAD CALLED "CROCHET."— According to a circular issued on January 12, 1888, by the Secretary of the Treasury, cotton thread called crochet, imported in spools, shall be dutiable in conformity with the following disposition:

On petition made by Messrs. JULIO ALBERT & Co., Sucs., requesting that the Secretary of the Treasury determine whether the cotton thread called crochet in 275 meter spools shall be considered within the provision of Fraction 23, referred to in Article 3, of the decree of the 28th of December last, an agreement was arrived at, which is to be construed as a general resolution, directing that in case the importation of the thread is made in spools containing less than 275 meters, whatever its measure may be, spools of 276 meters shall be formed, and a fixed rate of $2 per 100 spools be imposed.

For the character of the fiber (see Textures.)

MACHINERY — FREE.

MACHINERY.—The circular issued by the Secretary of the Treasury on January 21, 1888, reads as follows:

"Some doubts having been raised as to the application of Article 46, Section 1, and of 240, Section 3, of the tariff in force; and, whereas, the machines intended by the tariff to be free of duties are those imported for factories and large establishments, that is to say, those which require a powerful water, steam or electric motor, etc., the President of the Republic has decided that machinery of this kind only is comprised in paragraph 46, Section 1, of the tariff now in force:

And whereas, machinery in connection with all branches is daily improving, it would be impossible to designate in advance, and in detail, the machinery or apparatus which is not comprised in paragraph 46, Section 1. But, as a general rule, the machines and apparatus that can be moved by a single person come within the heading of sewing, writing, breaking and grinding machines for grain, paints and cutting, and others already quoted;

Now, therefore, those apparatuses and small machines for various purposes of industry which, as before stated, can be moved by one person, that are not comprised in the tariff, shall be classified by assimilation, subject to the governing rules as they appear in detail in the regulations of custom.

The preceding rules establish a clear distinction among the articles contained in this fraction; but it must be avoided that under protest of the franchise abuses be committed, to which end it is indispensable that the examination be strictly made by looking carefully into all packages, as they are presented for withdrawal, so as to get the conviction that they correspond with each other, and that the whole constitutes one machine, or conjunct of machines, which is what is properly called machinery; bearing in mind the exceptions to the franchise."

SULPHATE OF IRON.

SULPHATE OF IRON.—Sulphate of iron, circular of July 2, 1887. Free.

HARBOR IMPROVEMENT TAX.

The following decree has been issued by the President of the Republic:

Porfirio Dias, Constitutional President of the United Mexican States, to its inhabitants, greeting:

In exercise of the power conferred on the Executive by the law of December 11, 1884, existing by that of April 26 of the present year, and in conformity with that of the 28th of May, 1881, I am pleased to decree the following:

Article 1. To meet the expenses of improvements at the ports, which works have already been begun at Vera Cruz, there will be collected, from the 1st of February next (1889), an additional duty of 2 per cent. on importation duties collectible at all the maritime and frontier custom houses.

Art. 2. This additional duty is destined exclusively to the object for which it has been created, it being the duty of the custom houses to keep a separate account of it, and to hold it subject to the order of the General Treasury of the Federation.

Art. 3. The General Treasury of the Federation will keep a special account of this duty, and will invest its product according to the orders received from the Ministry of Finance.

TREASURY DEPARTMENT, MEXICO.

Section First.

The President has been pleased to approve this day the following resolutions:

" The Collector of the Frontier Custom House at Laredo, Tamaulipas, by his communication No. 1930, dated December 29th, last, consulting as to the meaning of the decree of November 30th in reference to the Free Zone, providing for an additional duty of 2 per cent. on the import duties from the 1st of February next; inquiry if the payment of such additional duty is to be exacted at the time the goods are imported in the Free Zone, or whenever the introduction is effected. The section informs: That the object of the Free Zone being to give those inhabitants all possible advantages, with a view to stimulate the development and advancement of trade in that important part of the northern frontier; the addition of 2 per cent. set forth by said decree, over the 3 per cent. now paid, would be an excessive overcharge, taking also into consideration that, thus far, the consumption throughout the whole Zone is unimportant, and it would not affect the interest of the National Treasury to a great extent to dispense with the said addition of 2 per cent.

Now, therefore, this Section has the honor to suggest, save your respectable opinion to the contrary, that the Collector of the Frontier Custom House at Laredo, Tamaulipas, be informed, in reply to his communication above mentioned, that the additional duty of 2 per cent., to be imposed from the first of February, proximo, shall be exacted at the time of the introduction, and not when the importation in the Free Zone is made; and as the same doubt may arise in the other frontier custom houses, that this resolution may be communicated to them for their guidance, in order to avoid tardy consultation or irregularity in the transaction of business."

All of which I beg to communicate to you for your knowledge.

Liberty in the Constitution.

Mexico, January 11, 1889.

By order of the Secretary.

J. A. GAMBOA,
First Officer.

To the Collector of the Frontier Custom House at———

Section First.

MERCHANDISE FREE OF DUTY.

1. Merchandise described as follows, admitted free of duty:
   1. [5] Acids, sulphuric, chloro-hydric, and phenic acid.
   2. [6] Anchors with and without chains for vessels.
   3. [7] Animals of all classes living, except altered horses.
   4. [8] Apparatus for extinguishing fires, with six charges of liquid.
   5. [13] Arsenic, white.
   6. [14] Asbestos in powder.
   7. [30] Bags, common, of all materials.
   8. [17] Barrels and pipes (casks) when empty.

9. [42] Books and music, printed and not bound.
10. [21] Boxes, common, of wood, nailed together or in pieces.
11. [39] Bricks of refractory earth.
12. [19] Cable of aloe or hemp, measuring from three centimeters of diameter or 94 2-10 milimeters of circumference.
13. [62] Caustic soda.
14. [28] Chloride, bisulphide, or trisulphide of lime.
15. [11] Clay, sand and blotting-sand.
16. [59] Clocks for towers and public buildings.
17. [27] Coaches and railway cars.
18. [24] Coal of all kinds.
19. [29] Cork, in bulk or in sheets.
20. [31] Crucibles of all materials and sizes.
21. [38] Eggs.
22. [33] Emery in powder or in grain.
23. [45] Engines, steam, locomotives, and other things necessary for building railways.
24. [40] Fire wood.
25. [51] Fish. fresh.
26. [49] Fodder, dry.
27. [35] Glycerine, odorless.
28. [48] Gold, silver and platinum in bullion or in dust.
29. [43] Hops.
30. [25] Houses of wood and iron, complete.
31. [36] Hyposulphite of soda.
32. [34] Iron and steel rails for railways.
33. [12] Iron with hooks for making packages.
34. [3] Iron hoops with rivets for the same objects.
35. [23] Iron or lead tubing of all dimensions.
36. [26] Knives, matchets, scythes, sickles, rakes, shovels, pick-axes, spades, hoes and mattocks of iron or steel for agriculture.
37. [41] Letters, plates, spaces, vignettes, type and other necessary articles for printing.
38. [22] Lime, common, hydraulic lime or Roman cement.
39. [43] Machinery and apparatus of all kinds not specified, for manufacturing, agriculture, mining, the arts and sciences, and their separate parts whenever these cannot be used separately.
40. [10] Masts for vessels.
41. [47] Money, legal, of gold or silver.
42. [60] Oars for boats.
43. [53] Ores.
44. [50] Periodicals and catalogues printed.
45. [56] Plants, living, and seeds for horticulture.
46. [9] Plows and plowshares.
47. [68] Poisons used in preparing skins.
48. [57] Powder, wicks, fuse and explosive compounds for mines.
49. [54] Pumice stone.
50. [15] Quicksilver.
51. [67] Rags, paper clippings and pulp of all kinds for paper making.
52. [66] Refractory earth.
53. [61] Saltpeter, whether nitrate of potash or soda.
54. [55] Slate for roofing, from 2 to 3 milimeters in thickness.
55. [18] Spanish white.

56. [16] Steel, bars of, round or octagonal, for mines.
57. [52] Stones, precious.
58. [64] Sulphate of ammonia.
59. [63] Sulphate of copper.
60. [65] Tiles, earthen, of all kinds.
61. [37] Tin in plates, up to 40 centimeters in length by 38 in breadth, not stamped or painted.
62. [44] Timber building.
63. [58] Vaccine.
64. [32] Vessels of all kinds when nationalized or sold.
65. [4] Wire, barbed, with staples for fencing.
66. [20] Wire cable of iron or steel, of all thicknesses.
67. [2] Wire, copper, insulated with any material, for electrical lighting, whenever the diameter of the wire, by itself, is up to No. 6 Birmingham measure, and the destination of wire is shown.
68. [1] Wire, telegraph and telephone, intended for said purpose.

SECTION II.

Application of Import Duties to Merchandise, According to that Provided in the Regulating Part of this Law.

II. All merchandise mentioned in the annexed vocabulary of the present ordinance, shall pay the rate stated in the fraction to which it corresponds in this tariff.

III. Cloth and articles of linen or hemp mixed with cotton in some proportion, shall pay the duty that corresponds to textures or articles of linen only.

IV. Textures of wool mixed with cotton, linen or hemp, in any proportion, shall pay the duty corresponding to the textures of wool according to the weight indicated in its proper fractions.

V. Articles of wool mixed with cotton, linen or hemp, shall pay the rate corresponding to articles made entirely of wool.

VI. The textures of cotton, linen or hemp, mixed with silk, and those of silk mixed with the aforesaid materials, shall pay duties as follows:

Warp.	Woof.	Materials to Dominate in the Payment of Duties.
Cotton, linen or wool.	Cotton, linen or wool mixed with silk.	Cotton, linen or wool.
Cotton, linen or wool mixed with silk.	Cotton, linen or wool.	Cotton, linen or wool.
Cotton, linen or wool mixed with silk.	Cotton, linen or wool mixed with silk.	Cotton, linen or wool.
Cotton, linen or wool.	Silk.	Equal parts.
Silk.	Cotton, linen or wool.	Equal parts.
Silk mixed with cotton, linen or wool.	Silk mixed with cotton, linen or wool.	Silk.
Silk mixed with cotton, linen or wool.	Silk.	Silk.
Silk.	Silk mixed with cotton or linen.	Silk.

VII. Those textures which are found mixed with the silk, cotton, linen or hemp shall be considered as such. Those goods mixed as aforesaid, found only on the edges, shall pay the duty corresponding to texture and articles of silk.

VIII. Cloth of plain texture shall include those in which the threads of the woof cross one by one the threads of the warp, taking one above and another under, repeating the same in a contrary direction, the lower ones being on top and the upper ones under. Those which have other combinations not mentioned, shall be considered of cloth of not plain texture.

IX. Textures of open work are those which have the threads cut at the warp and the woof to form the design, and not those in which the threads are missing or which are fixed in the warp or the woof, as these shall be considered worked cloth.

X. As dress patterns shall be considered those goods which come pinned, basted or tacked on cardboards, or on other materials serving the same purpose, and in such a way as to make it impossible, or at least not convenient to the importer, on account of the damage done to the goods, to undo them, and for that reason the separate parts composing the package cannot be divided and measured separately, such as ribbons, laces, buttons, etc., and in all such cases the rates charged on such goods shall be the same as for "dress patterns."

Should the cloth come wrapped in such a manner as to be easily weighed or measured, as the case may be most convenient, and if the lace or other ornaments come separate, each article shall pay the rate assigned to it in the tariff.

XI. As handkerchiefs will be considered those which do not exceed ninety centimeters on a side; those which exceed this measure shall be counted as shawls.

XII. Handkerchiefs which have but one letter or name embroidered in one of the corners shall be considered as not embroidered.

XIII. To determine the number of threads in a piece of cloth in a square of half centimeter, the threads of the warp and woof contained in a square centimeter shall be added, without taking into account the fractions which may result; if this sum is exactly divisible by two, the quotient shall be the number of threads which the cloth has in a square of half centimeter per side. In cases where a fraction results after dividing the sum by two, said fraction shall be considered as a whole thread and added to the result obtained by the division.

XIV. Merchandise mentioned in the tariff or vocabulary annexed to this ordinance with the words "of all classes," without placing after the exception of those not specified, shall pay the rate which they may have assigned in the corresponding fraction, even when they contain other material not gold, platinum or silver.

XV. Articles composed of two or more materials not detailed in the tariff or in the vocabulary, shall pay the rate corresponding to the material which pays the highest duty.

XVI. Merchandise of unknown materials shall pay the duties subject to that provided in Section II, Chapter 4, of the present law.

XVII. Jewelry made of gold, platinum or silver when they come in small cases, shall bring, declared separately, their weight and material of which they are made, so that the duty on them may be properly fixed.

XVIII. Crockery and porcelain, as well as crystal and glass, manufactured into pieces of all forms, painted or unpainted, gilded, plated or decorated with flowers, pictures or colored ornaments or reliefs made by hand or by mold, and that are not rated in this tariff, shall pay the duty provided in Fraction numbers 211 and 216 of this tariff. (Translation numbers 213 and 212).

XIX. Crockery and porcelain, as well as crystal and glass, manufactured into pieces of all forms, with mountings or inlaid work of any kind that are not expressly mentioned in this tariff, shall pay the rate stated in note No. XV of this section.

XX. All substances shall be considered as rum which, according to the centesimal alcoholmeter of Gay Lussac, weigh from 15 to 88 degrees or 12.06, and 35 degrees of Cartiers. Those exceeding this weight shall be considered as alcohol.

XXI. When medicinal drugs or chemical products bring on their interior packings a label or ticket different from the contents declared, the merchandise shall be charged the highest rate between it and the merchandise mentioned on the label or ticket.

XXII. Net weight shall be understood to be the intrinsic weight of the merchandise, as legal weight is that which includes, besides the net weight, that of the interior bottles, boxes, bobbins, wrappings, etc., in which they come, and the gross weight shall be the total weight of the package. When the merchandise rated at its legal weight should have any other wrapping but that which forms the package, the intrinsic weight of the merchandise shall be considered its legal weight.

XXIII. Pipes made of copper, brass, bronze, rubber, gutta-percha and iron covered with copper or brass, when they do not come with some machinery of which they form a part, shall pay the duty provided therefor by the tariff.

XXIV. Goods which can be made use of separately from the machinery or apparatus, as iron in bulk, rough iron hoops (in bars or rods), oils, textures of wool or other materials, leather, skins (tanned or untanned), even when imported with machinery, shall pay the duty which corresponds to them, according to the tariff in this ordinance.

TARIFF

AND

CUSTOM HOUSE REGULATIONS

OF THE

ISLAND OF CUBA.

1888.

(449)

CUSTOM HOUSE TARIFF

OF

THE ISLAND OF CUBA.

NOTICE.

To understand more easily the signs and marks printed in the text of this tariff, and which correspond respectively to the notes in the appendix, attention is called to the following explanations:

1st. A cipher is placed at the end of each corrected or changed portion of the tariff on importations, and corresponds to the same numeral in the margin of the note in the appendix which has reference to that portion.

2nd. When a single note in the appendix comprises reference to more than one portion of the tariff the cipher is repeated at the end of all such portions.

3rd. The letter in the table of free articles, which precedes the tariff on importations, corresponds to another note which will be found in the respective place of the appendix.

4th. At the head of all the notes of the appendix is printed the number of the portion or portions which they affect, the ordinal number of each note being likewise printed in the margin as above mentioned.

DISPOSITIONS FOR THE APPLICATION OF THE TARIFF.

ARTICLES FREE OF IMPORT DUTY, NO MATTER BY WHOM IMPORTED.

No. 1. Trees, live plants and seeds for nurseries and corn-fields, and collections of herbs scientifically prepared.

No. 2. Statues and oil paintings by celebrated artists.

No. 3. Printed matter, periodicals, geographical charts and books, the importation of which may be authorized.

No. 4. Mules, asses, horses, cattle, sheep and swine, imported to improve the breeds.

No. 5. Guano and every kind of natural and artificial manures.

No. 6. Birds and every kind of animals dissected, whether or not serviceable for public instruction.

No. 7. Cabinets of samples and collections of historical antiquities of all classes.

No. 8. Live fish. (451)

No. 9. Cabinets of ancient coins, and moneys the circulation of which may be authorized.
No. 10. Silver-bearing minerals in their primitive state or after being refined.
No. 11. Minerals in bulk applicable to the study of mineralogy.
No. 12. Samples of woven goods in clippings of a size sufficient to show the quality of the cloth.

ARTICLES FREE OF EXPORT DUTY.

All productions of the country not included in the tariff on exportations.

IMPORT TARIFF.

No. of portions.	ARTICLES.	DUTIES.			
		SPANISH PRODUCTIONS IN		FOREIGN PRODUCTIONS IN	
		Sp'nish vessels.	Foreign vessels.	Sp'nish vessels.	Foreign vessels.
	SECTION OF FOODS.				
1	Wines, oils and all spirituous liquors: Oil, olive and others for eating, including for the payment of duty the weight of the interior case, when classified, 100 kilograms..........	2 50	4 10	5 55	7 30
2	Liquors made from wine, simple or compound, with or without sugar, as those of Spain and the Canary Islands, anisado, liqueurs, mistelas and ratafias, in wood and in demijohns, 100 liters..........	1 60	3 70	4 65	5 90
3	In bottles or other cases not specified in the preceding, 100 liters..........	2 90	6 60	8 35	10 65
4	Gin,————, the liquors distilled from potatoes, barley, and like articles, in wood and in demijohns, 100 liters..........	3 20	7 40	9 30	11 80
5	In bottles, glass or earthen flasks, or in any other kind of case not specified in the preceding, 100 liters..........	4 80	11 10	13 95	17 70
6	Cognac brandy, rum and the like, in wood and in demijohns, 100 liters..........	3 95	9 10	11 50	14 65
7	The same in bottles, flasks or other cases not specified in the preceding, 100 liters..........	5 15	11 90	15 00	19 15
8	Beer and porter in wood (a) 100 liters..........	1 25	2 90	3 65	4 65
9	In bottles or earthen flasks (b) 100 liters..........	2 90	6 60	8 35	10 65
10	Vinegar, in wood and in demijohns, 100 liters..........	0 75	1 55	2 05	2 70
11	In bottles, 100 liters..........	2 90	6 60	8 35	10 65
12	White and red wines of inferior quality, and those of apples and pears, in wood or demijohns, (2) (a) (b), 100 liters..........	0 75	1 50	2 00	2 65
13	In bottles, (2) (a) (b), 100 liters..........	2 90	6 60	8 35	10 65
14	White and red of superior quality to those of the preceding portion, in wood or demijohns, (2) (a), 100 liters..........	2 90	6 60	8 35	10 65
15	In bottles, including bitters and other similar liquids, (2) (a) (c), 100 liters..........	8 35	19 15	24 15	30 85

(a) It is the practice of the custom houses to appraise lager beer by these portions. In respect to the capacity of the barrels of this liquid, it should be borne in mind that although the barrels in which it is generally imported, 51 centimeters high by 31 in diameter, has the measure of 31 to 32 liters, yet it only contains 29 of lager beer, it being necessary to leave empty the space for two liters for the expansion of the gases.

(b) It is ordered that in the declarations of beer in bottles, it shall be expressed, besides the liters of each barrel, the number of bottles that each may contain.

(a) It must be understood as inferior wines—in wood, all those whose value does not exceed 15 cents per weight of liter in the productive country; in bottles, those that do not exceed two

No. of portions.	ARTICLES.	TARIFF.			
		SPANISH PRODUCTIONS IN		FOREIGN PRODUCTIONS IN	
		Sp'nish vessels.	Foreign vessels.	Sp'nish vessels.	Foreign vessels.
	MEATS.				
16	Ordinary hog or black cattle meat, smoked, salted or prepared, such as hams and shoulders, Spanish and American, bacon, hogs' lard, ribs, salt, dry meat, with all the salt it contains, 100 kilograms...	2 35	4 70	6 25	8 35
17	Superior to those of the preceding portion, such as mutton, smoked tongues or buffalo tongues, family meat, Westphalia hams and others of northern Europe, 100 kilograms.....	5 20	12 00	15 10	19 30
18	Black cattle meat in pickle, including weight of pickles, 100 kilograms..	0 70	1 35	1 80	2 45
19	Hogs' meat in the same form as the preceding portion, 100 kilograms..	1 15	2 25	3 00	4 05
20	Hung beef, 100 kilograms..	0 80	1 55	2 10	2 80
21	Stuffed meats of all kinds, such as pork sausage, long sausages, sausages in lard and canned sausages, 100 kilograms......	5 20	11 90	15 00	19 15
22	Preserved for the extraction of air, or in lard, including duty of containing vessel, 100 kilograms..................................	8 70	20 00	25 20	32 15
22a	Fresh, 100 kilograms...	0 55	1 10	1 45	1 95
	SPICES.				
23	Aniseed, common seed, wild majoram, ground pepper, dried peppers, bay leaves, and other like spices, 100 kilograms.....	1 75	3 50	4 70	6 25
24	Saffron, dried or in oil, kilogram...............................	2 17	5 00	6 30	8 04
25	Ceylon cinnamon and nutmegs, kilogram......................	1 30	3 00	3 80	4 85
26	From other points, kilogram.....................................	0 8	0 20	0 25	0 32
27	Chinese cinnamon, cloves and pepper, kilogram...............	0 3	0 8	0 10	0 13
	FRUITS.				
28	Fruits, green or fresh, such as apples, peaches, melons, sapotillas, pears, grapes and olives, including the weight of containing vessel, when imported in glass flasks, 100 kilograms	0 85	2 00	2 50	3 20
29	Dried, with shells, such as almonds, hazel nuts, walnuts, chestnuts and those pressed, such as raisins, plums, figs, 100 kilograms..	1 30	3 00	3 80	4 85
30	Shelled, such as almonds and the finer classes of the preceding portion, when imported in glass jars or of other precious metal, dates, and other like, including for the duty and weight of the containing vessel, when of glass or of other precious metal, 100 kilograms....................................	3 25	7 50	9 45	12 05
31	Preserved in their juice, in alcohol, in syrup or in paste, stuffed olives, all kinds of jams, chocolate and sugar candy, including the containing vessel when of glass or tin, 100 kilograms..	2 75	6 35	8 00	10 20
31a	Puerto Rico sugar, 100 kilograms...............................	1 65	....	8 00	10 20
	FISHERY.				
32	Ordinary fish, smoked, dried, salt or in pickle, such as codfish, herring, horse-mackerel, skate-fish, salted, dried or smoked bream, Halifax and Newfoundland codfish, and dried sardines, not including the weight of the pickle, 100 kilograms	0 70	1 35	1 80	2 45
33	Of superior classes to those of the preceding portion, dried or in				

dollars and fifty cents for each case of 12 bottles, which circumstance must be credited with certified invoice, and sealed by the local authority of port of issue.

(b) The ordinary wines of national production are free of duty, coming direct or under national flag, according to Article 10 of the Royal decree of August 14, 1884.

(c) It is ordered that the French wine, called "Champagne," be appraised as per Portion 15.

Note.— For that which can be related to the preceding portions, see addenda No. 7 on breakage of containing vessel.

No. of portions	ARTICLES.	TARIFF.			
		SPANISH PRODUCTIONS IN		FOREIGN PRODUCTIONS IN	
		Sp'nish vessels.	Foreign vessels.	Sp'nish vessels.	Foreign vessels.
	pickle, such as anchovy, tunny-fish, salmon, breasts, dewlaps, tongues and fish-roes, codfish from Scotland, Sweden and Norway, stick fish and other fisheries of the north of Europe, and all kinds of shell fish alive or dried, including in duty, the weight of the pickle, and containing vessel if of glass, 100 kilograms...	1 05	2 15	2 85	3 80
34	Sardines preserved in cans, including in duty the weight of can, 100 kilograms...	4 30	9 90	12 50	15 95
35	Fish of other kinds, preserved in oil, pickle or in other form, fresh and preserved oysters, including in duty the weight of containing vessel, kilogram..	0 6	0 15	0 18	0 24
35a	Live (Royal decree March 13, 1882), 100 kilograms...........	0 6	0 15	0 18	0 24
	Note—It is ordered that for live fish imported under foreign flag a deduction of 5 per cent. will be made (in the gradual order, which will be determined by the law of commercial relations, being exempt of duty in the rest of the columns.)				
	GRAIN, SEEDS, GREASES, PRODUCTION OF GARDENS, VEGETABLES, FLOUR, ETC.				
36	Celery, garlic (*a*), onions, young onions, turnips, potatoes or sweet potatoes, beets, carrots, plantains, and other like vegetables, 100 kilograms..	0 40	0 80	1 05	1 40
37	Canary seed, white barley, wheat and other like grain, 100 kilograms	1 15	2 35	3 15	4 20
38	All kinds of shelled rice, 100 kilograms..........................	0 75	1 45	1 95	2 65
38a	Unshelled (Royal decree of October 28, 1878), 100 kilograms....	0 35	0 70	0 95	1 30
39	Oats, unshelled barley, common rye, corn, peanuts, pine nut, and other like grain, 100 kilograms..............................	0 40	0 80	1 05	1 40
40	Carácas cocoa, Soconusco, Barinas, Maracaibo, and similar, 100 kilograms..	0 40	0 80	15 10	19 30
41	Trinidad, Guayaquil, Marañon, and for its similars, 100 kilograms...	0 40	0 80	7 30	9 75
42	Coffee, 100 kilograms...	2 35	4 70	7 55	9 65
43	Cassava or nut-pan cake, 100 kilograms.........................	1 95	3 90	5 20	6 95
44	Biscuit, common or pilot (hard tack), 100 kilograms...........	1 15	2 35	3 15	4 20
45	Fine and soda biscuits, cream, lemon, and others in wooden barrels or cases, including the weight of containing vessel, when imported in valuable small trunks or cases (*y b*), 100 kilograms..	2 20	5 00	6 30	8 05
46	Chick-pea, lentils and French beans, kidney bean, and others for cooking, 100 kilograms...	0 70	1 35	1 80	2 45
47	Flour, common rye, corn and bran. 100 kilograms.............	0 40	0 80	1 05	1 40
48	Wheat, including the weight of containing vessel (*c*), 100 kilograms...	2 25	4 50	4 69	5 51

(*a*) As the garlic coming from Mexico do not come in string, but in bundles of 20 heads, and in baskets, they must not be allowed the tare taken off of those coming from Spain.

(*b*) When the interior package of the biscuits, or be it the immediate, is of tin plain without ornament, its weight will be included in the duty. (*c*) On the 20th of March, 1878, it was granted by the general management of the State that barrels of wheat flour be assessed by gross weight, at the rate of 100 kilograms each, unless a marked difference is noted and implies the purpose of fraud, in which case they will be weighed and assessed according to weight, not including in this agreement other packages, such as bags, which will be strictly adjusted by the resulting weight, and by Royal decree of 21st of June of the same year this measure was approved of.

The general management of State, in accordance with the consultations of Tariffs, resolved, on the 17th of August, 1878, in the expedient of Campos & Company, on account of the excess that resulted in the weight of 2,480 barrels of flour, that the 5 per cent. of excess on each 100 kilograms, ordered by the Board on each barrel, must be considered as produced by the difference that may exist in the packages, and, therefore, the assessment in this case must be made per 100 kilograms; but if it should exceed this 5 per cent., the duty will be imposed by the resulting weight, in the estimation that as a general rule the barrel is assessed per 100 kilograms in accordance with the Royal decree of June 21, 1878, and that it be able to proceed to the weight by changing said decree when at sight or by information the administration of the differences will justify the change.

No. of portions.	ARTICLES.	TARIFF.			
		SPANISH PRODUCTIONS IN		FOREIGN PRODUCTIONS IN	
		Sp'nish vessels.	Foreign vessels.	Sp'nish vessels.	Foreign vessels.
49	Garden seeds and vegetables pickled or in vinegar, including liquid and weight of vessel, 100 kilograms................	2 15	4 95	6 25	7 95
50	Preserved in their own juice or by extraction of air, mushrooms, prepared mustard for table use, and other like provisions, including in the duty the liquid in which they may be prepared and the weight of the vessel containing them, 100 kilograms......................................	4 35	10 00	12 60	16 10
51	Eggs of birds, 100 kilograms................................	2 35	4 70	6 25	8 35
52	Ice, 100 kilograms..	2 35	4 70	0 17	0 21
53	Lard of cream or butter, including in the duty for the weight of vessel when of glass or earthen ware, and the salt with which it is preserved, 100 kilograms............................	3 90	9 00	11 35	14 50
54	Hogs' lard (a), 100 kilograms...............................	2 75	5 50	7 30	9 75
55	Grass, dried grass or hay (b), 100 kilograms.................	0 25	0 60	0 80	1 00
56	Farinaceous paste for soups, corn starch, and all kinds of fæcula foods, 100 kilograms.......................................	1 60	3 15	4 20	5 60
57	Cheese, Spanish, Holland, Canary Isles and the like, 100 kilograms...	3 35	6 65	8 65	11 80
58	English, Swiss and the like, 100 kilograms..................	6 50	15 00	18 90	24 10
59	Of the United States and the like...........................	2 35	4 70	6 25	8 35
60	Salt, sea salt in grain (g), 100 kilograms..................	0 30	0 60	0 85	1 85
61	Ground or foam salt, including in the duty the weight of the vessel containing same when of earthenware or glass (g), 100 kilograms..	0 60	1 20	1 71	2 37
62	Condensed milk and other nutritive foods not mentioned, including in the duty the weight of containing vessel, kilogram..	0 05	0 12	0 15	0 20
63	Tea, kilogram..	0 21	0 50	0 63	0 80
	SECTION OF TIMBERS, ROUGH AND FINISHED.				
64	Pine wood, in boards, beams, etc., thousand superficial feet....	1 80	3 60	4 80	6 40
65	Poplar, thousand superficial feet...........................	2 70	5 40	7 20	9 60
66	Maple or oak and cedar, thousand superficial feet............	3 60	7 20	9 60	12 20
67	Hickory, thousand superficial feet..........................	4 50	9 00	12 00	16 00
68	Dye woods, such as campeachy wood, mulberry wood and Jamaica wood, 100 kilograms.................................	4 50	9 00	0 17	0 21
69	Groove and tongued, planed, hewed or prepared by some workmanship, or those that on account of similarity cannot be assessed by the preceding portions, will be assessed by the same with an additional 25 per cent.				
70	Hard, rough or with mountain labor, thousand superficial feet..	2 70	5 40	7 20	9 60
71	In hoops or twigs, for casks, over 220 centimeters long, with or without bark, thousand hoops.............................	1 95	3 87	5 16	6 88
72	For casks, up to 220 centimeters long, thousand hoops........	0 81	1 62	2 16	2 88
73	In staves for casks, hogsheads, etc., and loose for casks, thousand staves (c)...	2 92	5 85	7 80	10 40
	Note—The thickness of one inch must serve as a basis for estimating the superficial foot, as in mercantile transactions it is effected in this manner, and the official valuation answers this principle.				
74	Rough lumber for barrels, planed or grooved, including heads, thousand staves..	0 76	1 53	2 04	2 72
75	Cut out for casks, pipes, and barrels, including their respective heads, and excluding the hoops, one pair...................	0 09	0 19	0 26	0 35
76	In heads loose for casks, one pair..........................	0 01	0 03	0 04	0 06
77	In pieces for cases and half cases for sugar, one pair.......	0 03	0 07	0 15	0 22

(a) It is ordered that lard imported in cans be appraised also for its duty without including the containing vessel.

(b) It is practice that millet bush coming from the ear of this grain, that is imported for the manufacture of brooms, be assessed, on account of similarity, by this portion.

(c) It is ordered that staves must be computed at the rate of 33 to form a thousand.

No. of portions.	ARTICLES.	TARIFF.			
		SPANISH PRODUCTIONS IN		FOREIGN PRODUCTIONS IN	
		Sp'nish vessels.	Foreign vessels.	Sp'nish vessels.	Foreign vessels.
78	In casks, new or used, pipes and barrels of more than 30 liters capacity, and mounted cases, new or used, will be assessed by the preceding portions, with an additional 30 per cent. (*a*)				
79	In barrels, up to 30 liters capacity, in buckets, tubs, baths, trays, plates applicable to domestic uses; shoemakers' and hair dressers' lasts, carpenters' mallets, tool handles, rat traps without wirework, bungs, ship brushes, millet brooms, small implement boxes for druggists' use, spoons, chocolate mills and other like articles, kilogram...	02	04	06	08
80	Lumber in screws and presses for carpenters, wheelbarrows, with or without iron trimmings, type cases, pump boards, and orher like articles, kilogram.	0 01	0 03	0 04	0 05
81	In shoe brushes, models for casks and other like articles, kilogram	0 02	0 05	0 70	0 10
82	In very common hair and clothes brushes generally used by the army, in brushes and brooms for counters, bars, soot cleaners, including handles even if knocked down, horse brushes, blocks, pulleys blocks, and rigging blocks, and other like articles, kilogram.	0 04	0 09	0 12	0 16
83	In water levels, kilogram.	0 07	0 14	0 19	0 26
84	In clothes clamps, oars, looking glasses and broom handles, kilogram.	0 01	0 02	0 03	0 04
85	In finished pieces, and plain applicable to carriage and saddle making, such as felloes, hubs, poles, bars, lathe frames, saddle bows, horse hames, pistol cases, or in other like articles in which wood alone figures or with some portion of iron, covered or not with common cloth, (*b*) 100 kilograms	3 90	7 85	10 43	13 90
86	In shingles, 100 kilograms.	0 01	0 03	0 04	0 06
87	In match sticks, kilogram.	0 07	0 01	0 01	0 02
88	Fine prepared for covering furniture, valuation.	0 10%	0 23%	0 29%	0 37%
89	Various kinds in hydraulic pumps. (*c*). In small boats, the importation of should not demand a standard, and in other like articles not tariffed, valuation.	0 09½%	0 18½%	0 24½%	0 32%
90	In paint brushes not exceeding one kilogram of weight, per dozen, kilogram.				
91	In the same, when the weight per dozen exceeds one kilogram, kilogram.	0 18	0 36	0 48	0 64
92	In hair and clothes brushes fine and common, rulers, even if metal mounted, set squares and meter rulers, pencils and pen holders, tooth brushes, nail and jewelry brushes, combs and cards and other like articles, kilogram.	0 09	0 18	0 24	0 32
		0 31	0 63	0 84	1 12
93	In carpenters' pencils, kilogram.	0 04	0 09	0 12	0 16
94	In feather dusters, kilogram.	0 3	0 72	0 96	1 28
95	In keys for pianos and dressers, kilograms.	0 72	1 44	1 92	2 56

FURNITURE AND OTHER MANUFACTURES.

96	Common lumber, comprising in such, pine, silver tree, chestnut wood, beech wood, cherry, poplar, common maple, black poplar and the like, plain, painted or varnished, in furniture or other manufactures, even with some small sculpture, as, for instance, a single flower and rods for frames, painted or prepared for gilding, kilogram.	0 09	0 18	0 24	0 32
97	In chairs (each), weight of which does not exceed three and one-third kilograms, and in rocking chairs and large chairs (each) weight does not exceed six and one-third kilograms, kilogram.	0 03	0 05	0 07	0 10
	Note—The chairs—large chairs and rocking-chairs—weight of which is less than three and one-third and six and two-thirds kilograms will be assessed by portion 96.				

(*a*) As for instance, the new or used casks, that are assessed by portions 71, 75 and 78.
(*b*) It is practice in custom houses to assess wooden stirrups by this portion.
(*c*) It is ordered that pumps for wells and cisterns be assessed as per portion 231.

No. of portions.	ARTICLES.	DUTIES.			
		SPANISH PRODUCTIONS IN		FOREIGN PRODUCTIONS IN	
		Sp'nish vessels.	Foreign vessels.	Sp'nish vessels.	Foreign vessels.
98	Lumber, of superior quality to those of the preceding portion, such as oak, evergreen oak, hickory, mahogany, fine maple, pear tree and the like, kilogram....................	0 15	0 34	0 43	0 55
99	Of superior quality to those of the preceding portion, such as osewood and ebony, and of any quality, as long as it has gikling or ornament of any metal, kilogram................	0 20	0 46	0 58	0 74
100	Furniture and other manufactures, excepting chairs and stools (each), weight of which does not exceed two kilograms, will be assessed by the preceding portions, with an additional 50 %. Marble slabs, fastened to furniture, will be included in the weight of the furniture.				
101	With sculptures—that is, when the sculpture is limited to a single flower—they will be assessed by the preceding portions, with an additional 50 %. Loose marble slabs, plates, mirrors, dressers or washstands, even if they form part of the whole piece of furniture, will be assessed by the special portions assigned to them in this tariff.				
101a	Used furniture (a), valuation................	4%	6%	8%	10%
102	Mnufactured lumber in trunks or valises, of all sizes, covered with paper, zinc or raw leather (unscraped), with or without leather belts, kilogram............................	0 18	0 03	0 04	0 06
103	Said trunks or valises covered with cloth, morocco, leather, oil cloth or any other kind of like material as long as the weight of the lumber predominates, kilogram.................	0 03	0 07	0 09	0 12
	Sole leather and cardboard trunks only. (See mountings).				
	VEHICLES.				
104	Carriages, carts, landeaus and coupes, four-wheeled and four-seated, each.....................................	72 00	144 00	192 00	256 00
105	Half carts or victorias, and two-seated landeaus, with or without front folding seat, and complete four-wheeled omnibuses covered with wood, each.............................	54 00	108 00	144 00	192 00
106	High open carriages, surreys and others, two and four-wheeled, with or without leather tops, one and two-seated, included in the preceding portions, each.........................	22 50	45 00	60 00	80 00
107	The same carriages of the preceding portion, single and without leather top, known as road carts or buggies, not including fancy ones, in which figure those of osier box and other like, in which case will be assessed by the preceding portion, each.	11 25	22 50	30 00	40 00
108	Carriages and other carts for railroads (b), valuation...........	11 25	22 50	4%	6%
109	Loading trucks for beasts, valuation......................	9%	18%	24%	32%
110	Sundries for carriages, vehicles, such as wheels, outfits, boxes, etc., valuation.......................................	9%	18%	24%	32%
	SECTION OF ANIMALS.				
111	Ferocious animals, such as the elephant, lion and those not expressed in this tariff (c), valuation.....................	10%	23%	29%	37%
112	Small ones, such as monkeys, foxes, squirrels and badgers, each.	0 40	0 92	1 16	1 48

(a) In a Royal decree of June 5, 1879, it was approved in accordance with the general government of this Island of the 4th of April of the same year, ordering that for the assessment of used furniture the types of portion 23, be used, announcing that, to avoid frauds that could be committed in its introduction, the importer produce a detailed list of the furniture, accompanied by a certificate of the local authority from the point of issue, if coming from Spanish ports or Spanish Consuls abroad, stating that the furniture has been used and is property of the introducer.

In Royal decree of July 15, 1882, it was also ordered that furniture introduced in this Island by its owners, with the justification of having reported it before, be free of duty.

(b) See additional note No. 41.

(c) It is practice to appraise dogs by portion 111.

No. of portions	ARTICLES.	DUTIES.			
		SPANISH PRODUCTIONS IN		FOREIGN PRODUCTIONS IN	
		Sp'nish vessels.	Foreign vessels.	Sp'nish vessels.	Foreign vessels.
	BIRDS.				
113	Domestic birds, such as hens geese, pigeons, ducks, turkeys and other like, kilogram..................................	0 25	0 04	0 06	0 08
114	For amusement, such as macaws, parrots, pheasants and peacocks, each..	0 20	0 46	0 58	0 74
115	Of birds praised for their singing and beauty, such as canaries, robins, nightingales and other like, such as the magpipe, linnets, humming birds, etc., each..........................	0 10	0 23	0 29	0 37
	DONKEYS.				
116	Jack asses and female asses not imported to improve the breed, kilogram..	1 80	3 60	4 80	6 40
	BELONGING TO HORSES.				
117	Horses and mares of more than 63 inches (1,484 millimeters) height, not imported to improve the breed, kilogram......	25 00	57 50	72 50	92 50
118	Said horses up to 63 inches (1,484 millimeters), kilogram......	10 00	23 00	29 00	37 00
	BELONGING TO MULES.				
119	Mules over 58½ inches (1,261 millimeters) high, kilogram......	12 00	27 60	34 80	44 40
120	Said mules up to 58½ inches (1,261 millimeters), kilogram.....	3 82	7 55	10 20	13 60
	BELONGING TO CATTLE.				
121, 122	Bulls, heifers, cows, calves, kilogram........................	1 35	2 70	3 60	4 80
	LANIFEROUS.				
123	Lambs, goats and sheep, with or without foal, and male goats, kilogram..	0 36	0 72	0 96	1 28
	SWINE.				
124	Hogs or pigs of all kinds, 100 kilograms.......................	1 95	3 90	5 20	6 95
	OTHER ANIMALS.				
125	Leaches, valuation...	4%	6%	8%	10%
	SECTION OF CLAYS, STONES AND GLASS. (a)				
126	Clay manufactured in bricks and paving stones of common quality, 100 kilograms...	0 09	0 18	0 24	0 32
126a	Fire clay manufactured in bricks at the rate of 25 pesos per thousand, thousand...	10%	23%	29%	37%
126b	In paving flags at the rate of 50 pesos per thousand, thousand..	10%	23%	29%	37%
127	In fine tiles, or of screened clay, 100 kilograms...............	0 25	0 51	0 68	0 91
128	In enameled blue tiles and other like and in piping, 100 kilograms...	0 40	0 81	1 08	1 44
129	In roofing tiles, 100 kilograms................................	0 11	0 22	0 30	0 40
130	In German tiles or borders for terraces, kilogram..............	0 01	0 03	0 04	0 05
131	In pipes for smoking, for distribution on estates, cuspidors, bowls, flower-pots and urns, chambers, jars, kitchen utensils and other like articles, whether enameled or not, 100 kilograms.	0 60	1 15	1 55	2 10

(a) For that which it may bear relation in certain cases to the portions of this section.
(b) It is ordered that marble dusts be appraised by portion 138, whenever justified that their market value is equal to or less than that of gypsum or lime.

No. of portions.	ARTICLES.	DUTIES.			
		SPANISH PRODUCTIONS IN		FOREIGN PRODUCTIONS IN	
		Sp'nish vessels.	Foreign vessels.	Sp'nish vessels.	Sp'nish vessels.
132	Not enamelled, in toys, statues, pitchers, jars, large jars, decanters, bottles and water filters, 100 kilograms.............	1 95	3 90	5 20	6 95
133	Not enameled, or enameled in the same articles of the preceding portion, with trimmings, embossed or painted, kilogram.	0 05	0 12	0 15	0 20
	Finely enameled, in articles not mentioned in the preceding portion. (See flint-ware).				
134	Flint-ware in all forms not mentioned, 100 kilograms.........	1 15	2 35	3 15	4 20
135	White porcelain, 100 kilograms............................	2 60	6 00	7 55	9 65
136	Gilded porcelain or of superior qualities, such as china, japan and the like, kilogram..................................	0 10	0 25	0 31	0 40
137	In ornaments for dresser, fancy articles and in porcelain vases, kilogram...	0 15	0 34	0 43	0 55
	STONES.				
138	White stone for making molders' sand, fine sand and other like material, lime and gypsum of all kinds, grindstones, waterfilters, stones for grinding cocoa and corn, and those prepared for paving, such as those from the Canary Isles and other like granitic stones (a)100 kilograms........................	0 15	0 25	0 35	0 50
139	Small stones for setting and sharpening tools, 100 kilograms....	0 45	0 90	1 20	1 60
140	In slates framed, pumice stone, ground or not, and flint stones, 100 kilograms..	1 00	2 00	2 65	3 50
141	Marble, jasper or alabaster in flags for pavements and in cut slabs not polished, 100 kilograms.......................	0 30	0 70	0 85	1 10
142	In cut slabs and half polished, 100 kilograms.............	0 50	1 15	1 45	1 85
143	Manufactured in washstands, mortars, fountains and other articles without ornaments or sculptures, 100 kilograms....	1 15	2 60	3 25	4 13
144	Rough stones, for steps and articles of use of great weight in sculptures and ornamental objects (17), valuation........	10%	23%	29%	37%
144a	Precious stones, such as diamonds, topazes, emeralds, etc., loose or set, polished or not, valuation.................	5%	5%	5%	5%
	GLASSES.				
145	Common glass, dark, or natural green more or less dark, manufactured in bottles, demijohns, flasks and other like articles, 100 kilograms..	0 60	1 15	1 55	2 10
146	Glasses or crystals, flat, smooth or flowered, white or colored, up to 600 square inches each, 100 kilograms.................	1 30	3 00	3 80	4 85
147	Of over 600 to 1,000, 100 kilograms......................	1 75	4 00	5 05	6 45
148	Of more than 1,000 and upwards, 100 kilograms............	2 60	6 00	7 55	9 65
149	Plated or coated with mercury, without frames, will be assessed by the preceding portion with an additional 500%.				
150	Plated or coated with mercury, with frames, up to 1,000 square inches of surface, will pay duty by the portions 146, 147 and 148, with an additional 500%.				
151	Plated or coated with mercury, with frames over 1,000 square inches of surface, will pay duty by the portions 146, 147 and 148, with an additional 1,000%.				
152	Glass and crystal, white, colored or painted, ground, cast or cut, in bottles, glasses, cups, polished jars, sugar bowls, cake dishes, stand lamps, including in the duty the weight of the stand, and that of any other material forming part of the article, common lanterns and in other articles not expressed, that are alike, and the glass of Bohemia, 100 kilograms...	3 00	6 90	8 70	11 10
153	Common glass manufactured in retorts, globes, apothecaries' vessels, mortars and flasks applicable to druggists' uses, not				

(a) By agreement of the direction of estate on the 14th January, 1881, it was ordered that building and paving stones be assessed by this portion.

By another agreement of the same direction it was ordered that artificial stone be assessed by the same portion.

No. of portions.	ARTICLES.	DUTIES.			
		SPANISH PRODUCTIONS IN		FOREIGN PRODUCTIONS IN	
		Sp'nish vessels.	Foreign vessels.	Sp'nish vessels.	Foreign vessels.
154	polished; and manufactured crystal in lamp shades, globes, chimneys, suspended lamps, and chandeliers, fire lanterns, including in the duty for the weight of the material forming part of the article, and in other light articles by their weight or class, 100 kilograms....................	10 85	25 00	31 50	40 20
155	In ornaments for dressers and fancy articles, kilogram.......	0 25	0 57	0 72	0 92
156	Glasses for spectacles and watches, and that known as muslin, in all kinds of articles, kilogram.......................	1 08	2 50	3 15	4 02
	SECTION OF FURRIERY—LEATHERS OR HIDES.				
157	Hides or skins, precious or fancy, such as those of lion, tiger, leopard, bear, ermine, otter and other like, valuation......	10%	25%	29%	37%
158	Common and dried raw, belonging to donkeys, horses and cattle, 100 kilograms.....................................	2 35	4 70	6 25	8 35
159	Undried, 100 kilograms.......................................	0 80	1 55	2 10	2 80
160	Tanned (soles or belts) 100 kilograms........................	3 50	7 05	9 40	12 55
161	Varnished (sole or varnished leather) 100 kilograms..........	7 85	15 65	20 85	27 80
162	Sole or split leather, without crust and unvarnished, in pieces applicable to the industry, 100 kilograms................	6 75	13 50	18 00	24 00
163	Undressed hides or skins belonging to woolly cattle or goats, 100 kilograms..	5 85	11 75	15 65	20 85
	Note.—All those that retain all their thickness must be considered as skins or soles, as also the various layers and fleshy skins that the industry takes out of them, with exception of the exterior layer or be it the crust. Those that retain the scarf-skin (epidermis) will be considered as hides, whatever be their form or preparation, such as calfskin, buffalo, patent-leathers, or of other denomination, and will pay duty by the portion corresponding to these hides.				
164	Hides or tanned hides, such as sole leather, dressed sheep skin, and morocco leathers, 100 kilograms....................	9 80	19 55	26 10	34 80
165	Superior to those of the preceding portions, small goats and black and shiney calves	18 60	37 15	49 55	66 10
166	Varnished hides, such as buffalos and calves, and others not varnished, such as hog skin and those of chamois, 100 kilograms	29 25	58 50	78 00	104 00
	COVERING FOR THE FEET—SHOES.				
167	Sandals, open or closed, dozen pair.........................	0 16	0 32	0 43	0 57
168	Riding boots, and also for coachmen, polished or not, dozen pairs	5 40	10 80	14 40	19 20
169	All kinds of men's shoes with elastics for fastening, dozen pairs..	1 89	3 78	5 04	6 72
170	Of silk, or those the principal portion of which is silk, for women, dozen pairs......................................	2 82	6 48	8 17	10 43
171	Of other kinds for women, with ornaments, even if these are of silk, dozen pairs..	1 62	3 24	4 32	5 76
172	Without ornament, button or lace shoes dozen pairs..........	1 08	2 16		
173	Shoes or gaiters, pumps and slippers of all kinds for men and women, dozen pairs.....................................	0 67	1 35	2 88	3 84
				1 80	2 40
174	Shoes for boys, up to 23 centimeters (35 French points), and for girls up to 20 centimeters (30 French points), will pay duty according to quality, as per preceding portions, with a deduction of 50%. Rubber shoes. (See elastic rubber.)				
	HARNESSES AND OTHER MANUFACTURES.				
175	Harnesses, common or inferior, such as harnesses for loading wagons, and other articles of saddlery, such as saddle bows, and for harnesses, when they contain any part of hide or leather, buckets, pistol cases, trunks, valises, sachels, portmanteaus, hat boxes and carpet bags, oilcloth bags, sole leather or common hide bags, including in the duty the				

No. of portions.	ARTICLES.	DUTIES.			
		SPANISH PRODUCTIONS IN		FOREIGN PRODUCTIONS IN	
		Sp'nish vessels.	Foreign vessels.	Sp'nish vessels.	Foreign vessels.
	wood, cardboard or any other metal forming part of the article, kilogram...	0 07	0 14	0 19	0 25
176	Superior to those of the preceding portion, such as harnesses for carriages not for loading, ordinary saddles, even if with hog leather, morocco or velvet corduroy seats, half embroidered with some part of silk or silk floss, and its annexes, such as bits, stirrup and crupper straps, etc., halters, including the buckles, hoops and plates, if any, and belting for machinery, water hose and hat bands, kilogram...............................	0 15	0 30	0 40	0 53
177	Harness of superior quality of all kinds, such as saddles, the flaps of which or the whole are of hog or buffalo skin, with or without backstitching or embossments, with velvet seats, embroidered or not, and single harness for carriages their value not exceeding 80 escudos, or double harness not exceeding 160, belts and other annexes when cut, embroidered, stitched or ornamented, and all kinds of hunters' outfits, shoulder belts and buffalo bags, Russia leather and other like, excepting fancy handbags for ladies, which will pay duty by portion 233, kilogram...................................	0 24	0 55	0 70	0 89
178	Gloves, kid, kilogram.......................................	1 50	3 45	4 35	5 55
179	Doeskin, dressed buffalo or chamois skin gloves, kilogram......	0 60	1 38	1 67	2 22
	SECTION OF HABERDASHERY, SMALL ARTICLES, AND OTHERS NOT EXPRESSED IN THE OTHER SECTIONS.				
180	Glass beads, very small beads, pieces of rock crystal, frosted glass beads, puff paste, small wires and other like articles in strings or loose, kilogram..	0 75	0 17	0 21	0 27
	In ornaments of all kinds, see Haberdashery, small articles, etc., portion 233.				
181	Fans of all kinds, valuation....................................	10%	25%	29%	37%
182	Oils, vegetable, animal and mineral. (See provisions and drugs.) Starch, 10 kilograms..	1 75	4 00	5 05	6 45
	Tar, pitch, asphaltum, etc. (See drugs.)				
183	Jackets for ladies, dozen.......................................	1 00	2 30	2 90	3 70
184	For girls, dozen..	0 70	1 61	2 03	2 59
185	Rough whalebone, kilogram...................................	0 10	0 23	0 29	0 37
186	Cut and prepared for some industry, but not polished, kilogram..	0 15	0 34	0 43	0 55
187	Shined or polished for use in dresses, corsets, and other like objects, even with trimmings of other material, kilogram...	0 30	0 69	0 87	1 11
188	Spanish whalebone for mattrass makers, called vegetable hair, kilogram..	0 01	0 02	0 02	0 03
189	Varnish, common and medium, fine for furniture, 100 kilograms..	5 35	10 70	14 25	19 00
190	Fine for portraits, valuation....................................	10%	23%	29%	37%
191	All kinds of manufactured buffalo, kilogram...................	0 60	1 38	1 74	2 22
192	Pasteboard, raw and in paper called tissue, composed of straw, Spanish grass, hemp or cloth, 10 kilograms..................	0 70	1 35	1 80	2 45
193	Manufactured in hats and other like objects, and printed, lithographed or engraved for advertising sale establishments, as long as the importers are the owners of the establishments to which said advertisements refer, kilogram..................	0 45	0 09	0 12	0 16
194	In small pill boxes and other like uses, kilogram...............	0 09	0 18	0 24	0 32
195	In masks or dominos, kilogram...............................	0 20	0 46	0 58	4 74
196	In small boxes for ornamenting dressers, for sweetmeats and other uses, trimmed, painted or gilded, kilogram............	1 50	3 45	4 35	5 55
197	Wax manufactured in all forms, kilogram......................	0 15	0 34	0 43	0 55
198	In masks or dominos, kilogram	0 10	2 53	3 19	4 07
	Glue. (See drugs.)				
199	Shell of cognama, rough, kilogram.............................	0 20	0 46	0 58	0 74
200	Manufactured in all forms, even if with trimmings of other materials, kilogram..	0 55	1 26	1 59	2 03
201	Rough tortoise shell, kilogram..................................	1 10	2 53	3 19	4 07

No. of portions	ARTICLES.	DUTIES.			
		SPANISH PRODUCTIONS IN		FOREIGN PRODUCTIONS IN	
		Sp'nish vessels.	Foreign vessels.	Sp'nish vessels.	Foreign vessels.
202	Manufactured in all forms, even if with trimmings of other materials, kilogram............	3 80	8 74	11 02	14 06
203	Cork in boards, cakes and corks for bottles, and others, 100 kilograms............	1 55	3 15	4 20	5 55
204	Corsets, valuation............	10%	23%	29%	37%
205	Strings of guts for musical instruments, in ordinary or single classes, kilogram............	1 25	2 87	3 62	4 62
206	Classed as fine or double, called Roman, kilogram............	2 50	5 75	7 25	9 25
207	Of silk and metal, called bass strings, kilogram............	0 30	0 69	0 87	1 11
208	Oil skin, called silk oilcloth, in bolts, aprons, and in other forms, kilogram............	0 40	0 92	1 16	1 48
209	Common or oilcloth, used for covering tables and other like uses, kilogram............	0 68	0 13	0 18	0 24
210	Said cloth for covering floors, kilogram............	0 02	0 05	0 07	0 09
	Emery. (See drugs.)				
	Spanish grass. (See textile matters.)				
	Sperm and starine not manufactured. (See drugs.)				
211	Manufactured in candles, kilogram............	0 05	0 10	0 14	0 18
212	Flowers of paper, silk, cloth or other materials, loose and in bunches and garlands, kilogram............	1 00	2 30	2 90	3 70
213	Matches of all kinds, including those perfumed for cigars and the weight of the interior package, kilogram............	0 22	0 45	0 60	0 80
214	Bellows for blacksmiths' shop, kilogram............	0 01	0 02	0 03	0 04
215	Hand bellows, kilogram............	0 06	0 12	0 16	0 22
	Rubber, elastic or cautchouc. (See drugs.)				
216	Manufactured in sheets and belting, applicable to machinery, in hose and in other like articles, kilogram............	0 09	0 19	0 26	0 34
217	In shoes, leggins, seats, life preservers, in coats and other like articles, kilogram............	0 13	0 27	0 36	0 48
218	In waterproof, on cotton or linen cloth, kilogram............	0 30	0 69	0 87	1 11
219	On woolen cloth, kilogram............	0 45	1 03	1 30	1 66
220	On silk cloth, kilogram............	0 90	2 07	2 61	3 33
221	Elastic or cautchouc and gutta-percha, manufactured in combs with large wide teeth, or combs, pins and other headgear, tooth brushes, nail and jewelry, brushes, penknives, penholders, and other like articles, even if there is other metal composing the article, such as bone or other material, kilogram	0 50	1 15	1 45	1 85
222	In catheters, sounds, slates and strips for desk use, nail files, scales, syringes and other like articles, by their weight and mechanism, even if framed with some other material, kilogram............	0 80	1 84	2 32	2 96
	In articles of less weight such as rings, or fancy articles such as drop earrings, bracelets, etc., see Haberdashery, small articles, etc., portion 233.				
	Yarn and linen. (See textile matters.)				
223	Bone and norns, excepting that of the buffalo and manufactured ivory in buttons and small lasts of common quality, applicable to fittings, shoe horns, horse combs and equally common, of like weight, kilogram............	0 09	0 18	0 24	0 32
224	Polished and finished bone in buttons, lasts, combs with wide teeth or combs, tooth, nail and jewelry brushes, mouth pieces with or without cocks, and other like articles, by their weight and quality, even if there is other material or metal in their composition, kilogram............	0 35	0 80	1 01	1 29
225	Instruments, musical, such as cornets, baritones, bombards, trumpets, clarionets, bugles, musical horns, flutes, fifes, whistles, guitars, bandores, mandolines, viols, violins, and other like, by their weight, 100 kilograms............	0 50	1 15	1 45	1 85
226	Of larger size, such as violincellos, bass viols, war drums, double-beat drums, large drums, drums and kettle-drums, 100 kilograms............	0 20	0 46	0 58	0 74
227	Pianos, piano-fortes, and small upright pianos, one............	20 00	46 00	58 00	0 74
228	With heavy legs, one............	35 00	80 50	101 50	129 50

No. of portions.	ARTICLES.	DUTIES.			
		SPANISH PRODUCTIONS IN		FOREIGN PRODUCTIONS IN	
		Sp'nish vessels.	Foreign vessels.	Sp'nish vessels.	Foreign vessels.
229	Instruments, musical, not tariffed, as seraphs, hand-organs, music-boxes, large organs, and others, valuation.......... The boxes, cases or bags in which these instruments are placed for protection, will have their weight deducted from the above, but will pay duty as per their respective portions. The mouth-pieces, tunes and other extra pieces, excepting the strings, will pay duty as per portions of the instruments they belong to. The accordeons, up to one octave, imported for the amusement of children, will pay duty as haberdashery, small articles, etc., No. 233.	10%	23%	29%	37%
230	Soap, common, 100 kilograms................................ Jewelry. (See gold and silver in ornaments, jewels, watches and stones.) Games and toys. (See haberdashery, small articles, etc., portion 233.) Junk. (See textile materials.)	1 35	5 15	4 20	5 55
231	Steam engines of all kinds, hydraulic machines, electric and others used as motors, machine tools, mechanisms and apparatus for manufacturing purposes, no matter what materials they are made of (22) (a) valuation................	4%	6%	8%	10%
232	Ivory manufactured in billiard balls, large-toothed combs, combs, clothes brushes, hair brushes, tooth, nail and jewelry brushes, pen holders, paper cutters and other like articles, kilogram..	1 70	1 03	3 91	4 93
b233	Haberdashery, small articles, games and toys, and fancy articles in general, not rated in this tariff, valuation................... Osier (See textile matter.)	10%	23%	29%	37%
234	Mother-of-pearl, manufactured in buttons, for shirts, vests, coats and pants, kilogram..	0 45	1 03	1 30	1 66
235	In hair brushes, tooth, nail and jewelry brushes, buckles for belts, hair pins, pen holders, and paper cutters, and other like articles, even if they contain ornaments of some other common material), kilogram....................................	2 60	5 98	7 54	9 62
236	Wafers, of any farinaceous matter, gummy or glutinous, including the weight of the interior package, kilogram..........	0 40	92	1 16	1 48
237	Paper, writing, drawing or painting, for cigarettes, and all other kinds of pasteboards, 100 kilograms.....................	4 90	9 80	13 05	17 40
238	For copying letters, the one called onion peel, common tracing paper, china tracing paper, blotting paper, honey-comb paper, granite or dog-fish skin, or spotted, painted, fancy and other like, kilogram..	0 09	0 19	0 26	0 34
239	Vegetal for tracing for embroidering, and gilded or silver-coated of inferior quality, kilogram............................	0 21	0 50	0 63	0 80
240	Gilded or silver-coated, of fine quality, kilogram...............	0 87	2 00	2 52	3 21
241	White printing paper of inferior quality, such as used in newspapers, 100 kilograms..	1 15	2 35	3 15	4 20
242	Of superior quality, white and colored, whether superior or inferior, used also for wrapping, 100 kilograms..............	3 50	7 05	9 40	15 55
243	Called brown paper, inferior to half white paper, but superior to brown or wrapping paper, which is generally used in drugstores, 100 kilograms..	1 55	3 15	4 20	5 55
244	Wrapping paper such as the yellow one of the United States and the slate-colored one, of England, composed with tar (tar) (23), 100 kilograms..	1 10	2 15	2 85	3 80
245	Light wrapping paper, such as used for wrapping cigars, 100 kilo.	3 50	7 05	9 40	12 55
246	For covering walls and ceilings, not gilded or coated with plush, kilogram..	0 04	0 09	0 11	0 14

(a) It is ordered that steam gauges, pumps for wheels and cisterns, sewing machines, windmills, gasometers, and other corresponding accessories to this portion, shall pay a duty by the same.

(b) By this portion of valuation, merchandise not tariffed is made to pay duty, even when they are not of the branch of haberdashery, small articles, etc., as proved by the superior dispositions that order the duties of passage tickets to be imposed by said portion. Residue cotton-seed oil, etc., and other articles of the same nature.

No. of portions	ARTICLES.	DUTIES.			
		SPANISH PRODUCTIONS IN		FOREIGN PRODUCTIONS IN	
		Sp'nish vessels.	Foreign vessels.	Sp'nish vessels.	Foreign vessels.
247	Gilded, silver-coated or plush-coated, kilogram...............	0 08	0 18	0 23	0 29
248	Tin foil, lead foil, cloth and sand paper, kilogram............	0 02	0 03	0 05	0 07
249	Prepaper for any industry, but not printed or lithographed, such as comes in small books for cigarettes, lace paper for flowers and ornaments, such as those called stage decorations, those for lamp shades and envelopes and other forms, will pay duty as per the preceding portions, with an additional 50%.				
250	Printed or lithographed in newspapers, reading books, geographical maps and music will pay at the rate of the pastes, valuation	10%	23%	29%	37%
251	Printed, lithographed or engraved with one color only, in labels for cigars and cigarettes and in other forms, kilogram.....	0 05	0 11	0 14	0 18
252	Chromo lithographed or of several colors, kilogram............	0 10	0 23	0 29	0 37
253	Printed, lithographed or engraved with or without paints, in stamps or plates, kilogram :				
254	In form of blank-books or ruled, of all kinds and sizes, rustic or bound, with or without metal corners, will pay duty as per the preceding portion of paper to which they correspond, with an additional 50%, kilogram........................	0 06	0 14	0 18	0 23
256	Perfumery, liquid or solid, in oils, pomades and cosmetics, including the weight of the immediate package, kilogram....	0 14	0 33	0 42	0 53
257	Solid, in soaps that are wrapped up separately, including for the duty the weight of the wrapper, kilogram................	0 14	0 33	0 42	0 53
258	In soaps, without wrappers, or put up in lots of three or in greater number, and those of common quality, wrapped up separately, in only one paper, without any label or drawing, so as not to increase their value, kilogram................	0 45	0 10	0 13	0 16
259	Perfumery, in powders or pastes, for the teeth and in leaflets, and rouge for the cuticle, including the weight of the immediate package...	0 22	0 50	0 63	0 81
260	In rice powder, egg-shell and shells, and in other powders used as rouge, including the weight of the immediate package......	0 45	0 10	0 13	0 16
261	Paints of all kinds ground in oil, 100 kilograms.................	0 90	2 05	2 60	3 35
262	In powder, common, such as red ochre, ochre, Spanish white (chalk or carbonate of native lime), 100 kilograms...	0 25	0 60	0 80	1 00
263	Superior to those of the preceding portion, such as raw sienna, burnt sienna, Italian gray, zinc white (oxide of zinc) and ground white lead (carbonate of common lead) 100 kilograms	0 65	1 50	1 90	2 40
264	Superior, such as red-lead (minum) and lampblack, 100 kilograms	1 00	2 25	2 85	3 65
265	Superior, such as Chinese white (carbonate of fine lead) and sky blue (blue artificial ochre) 100 kilograms...........	0 25	0 60	0 80	1 00
266	Superior, such as Holland vermillion or English red, crown yellow (chromate of common lead) and oxide of copper, 100 kilograms...	2 85	6 50	8 20	10 45
267	Fine, of all kinds, such as blue, carmine, Chinese vermillion, indigo and others, valuation.............................	10%	23%	29%	37%
268	Gunpowder, and fuses for mines, in barrels and large flasks, (a) kilogram	0 03	0 06	0 08	0 11
	In cans and other small flasks (a) kilogram	0 05	0 13	0 16	0 20
270	Watches, of wood, iron, and common metals, or fine that are not of gold and silver, and gas meters and gauges, valuation....;	9%	18%	24%	32%
	Of gold and silver, will pay duty by the portions of gold and silver in jewels.				
	Tallow melted or in bricks. (See drugs).				
271	Manufactured in candles, 100 kilograms	2 35	4 70	6 25	8 35
272	Hats of common palm (plaited) such as used by the staffs of estates, dozen..	0 13	0 27	0 36	0 48

(a) It is ordered that for the importation of gunpowder, the offices be guided by the ruling of dispositions.

No. of portions	ARTICLES.	TARIFF.			
		SPANISH PRODUCTIONS IN		FOREIGN PRODUCTIONS IN	
		Sp'nish vessels.	Foreign vessels.	Sp'nish vessels.	Foreign vessels.
273	Straw of all kinds, trimmed or without linings, bands, ribbons, bindings or ornaments, up to four straws, counted with the thread counter in the square of 6 millimeters, dozen.......	0 54	1 08	1 44	1 92
274	Over four to six straws, dozen.............................	1 08	2 16	2 88	3 84
275	Over six and upward, dozen................................	3 24	6 48	8 64	11 52
276	Straw of all kinds, trimmed, with or without linings, ribbons and ornaments, will pay duty by the three preceding portions, with an additional 100%.				
277	Felt, very common donkey felt, oilcloth and leather, and other like, such as used by laborers, firemen and watchmen, dozen	0 24	1 08	1 44	1 92
278	Of other classes, called beaver, and those of silk, cloth or any other like, for men and women, dozen......................	2 43	4 86	6 48	8 64
	By Royal decree of October 27, 1878, it was ordered that this portion be modified in the sense that 50% be deducted for hats imported untrimmed, without linings, ribbons, bands or binding.				
279	Small hats and caps of velvet, corduroy, straw or cotton cloth, oilcloth or leather, dozen.............................	0 67	1 35	1 80	2 40
280	Silk or wool, dozen..	1 08	2 16	2 88	3 84
281	Tobacco, in paste called plug tobacco or early fig, kilogram.....	0 04	0 07	0 10	0 14
282	In snuff or in other preparations, the importation of which may be authorized, kilogram..................................	0 19	0 39	0 52	0 69
283	Blacking for shining, liquid or in paste, kilogram	0 16	0 03	0 04	0 05
283a	Ink, for writing, in earthenware jugs, including the weight of the immediate package, kilogram..........	0 08	0 01	0 02	0 02
283b	In glass vessels, including for the weight of the immediate package, kilogram..	0 01	0 02	0 03	0 04
284	For printing, kilogram.....................................	0 02	0 03	0 05	0 07
	SECTION OF METALS—STEEL.				
285	Steel, native, of cementation and cast, in bars and plates of all sizes, 100 kilograms...................................	1 55	3 15	4 20	5 55
286	In parts for watches, valuation.............................	4%	6%	8%	10%
287	In files, rasps and other like instruments, kilogram...........	0 04	0 09	0 12	0 16
	Note — The duties on steel are applied only to articles of pure steel determined in the preceding portions. Generally, utensils and instruments of iron charged with steel, and other doubtful ones are treated as iron.				
	COPPER, BRONZE, BRASS AND YELLOW METAL.				
288	Copper in sheets, 100 kilograms............................	4 10	8 20	10 95	14 60
289	In burnished plates for different uses, and in wires, bars, rivets and spikes, 100 kilograms...................................	4 90	9 80	13 05	17 40
290	In bolts, washers, bells, small bells, bedsteads, cots and cradles, chairs, tacks, water cocks, seives, hinges and other like articles, including precisely the part of iron or wood that must appear in the article, 100 kilograms......................	5 80	11 55	15 40	20 55
291	In clamp-rings, Morris bells, curtain chains, buttons for foremen, locks and padlocks, cuspidors, clothes-hooks, door-hooks, piping, pins for clothes, including the weight of the paper on which they are fastened, hooks and eyes for dresses and other like articles, even if they contain some part of iron (28), 100 kilograms..	0 18	0 36	0 48	0 64
292	In cruets, curb chains for bits, bushings, in pumps for bull-dog collars, all kinds of lamps, block pulleys, table springs, thimbles, even if they are some part of iron or steel, and other like articles, kilogram.....................................	0 18	0 36	0 48	0 64
	TIN.				
293	Tin in bricks, bars and sheet, for coating, 100 kilograms....... Manufactured in all forms. (See pewter.)	3 90	7 85	10 45	13 90

No. of portions.	ARTICLES.	TARIFF.			
		SPANISH PRODUCTIONS IN		FOREIGN PRODUCTIONS IN	
		Sp'nish vessels.	Foreign vessels.	Sp'nish vessels.	Foreign vessels.
	IRON.				
294	Iron, cast, in pigs, 100 kilometers...........................	0 09	0 19	0 26	0 34
295	Cast, in coal pots, pressing irons, pots and kettles, grates and small furnaces, furnace throats, piping and other like articles, 100 kilograms...	0 60	1 15	1 55	2 10
296	Cast or forged, tinned, enameled or galvanized, or without enamel or galvanize or tin, in kettles, coffee pots, pots, strainers, buckets, spoons and ladles, skimmers, boilers, urinals, steam kettles, jars, fish pans, frying pans, cake pans, roasters and other like articles, 100 kilograms............	1 55	3 15	4 20	5 55
297	Cast in hinges, balls, balconies, portable ranges, columns, water tanks, steps and other articles for buildings, stoves, sarcophagi, sofas and other like articles, 100 kilograms..........	0 80	1 55	2 10	2 80
298	Forged in the same articles pertaining to the preceding portion (*a*), 100 kilograms..	1 15	2 35	3 15	4 20
299	Cast and forged in nails, 100 kilograms.....................	1 10	2 25	3 00	4 00
300	In wires, anchors, heavy anchors, whims, rails, anvils, sledges and other like articles, 100 kilograms.....................	0 80	1 55	2 10	2 80
301	Letter copying presses, 100 kilograms........................	0 02	0 03	0 05	0 07
302	Forged in rods, stems, link chains, square rods, flanges, small plates, shafts, and in plates or sheets for the construction of tanks, clarifiers, roofs, floors, platforms and other like articles, 100 kilograms.........	0 50	1 00	1 30	1 75
303	In the same articles, galvanized, 100 kilograms...............	1 15	2 35	3 15	4 20
304	In plates, cut and prepared for sugar molds, 100 kilograms.....	0 20	0 25	35	45
305	In pad-locks, locks and door bolts, even if they have some part of yellow metal, 100 kilograms........................	2 75	5 50	7 30	9 75
306	Wrought and branched, that is to say, even if castiron enters into the manufacture; or without branching, in bits, nose bands, spurs and stirrups of common quality, not polished, even if coated with common metal, 100 kilograms....	5 85	11 75	15 65	20 85
307	In the same articles, polished, bronzed, gold and silver-plated, 100 kilograms............	19 55	45 00	56 75	72 40
308	In hooks, not applicable to railroads, trunk clamps, bolts, washers, rings with or without screw bolt, large chain fish hooks, harpoons, goad shoes, dead latches, locks, large hinges, horse-shoes, door bolts, bolts, pulleys, cross pieces of carriages, and in clamps, rings, stirrups, hooks, tongs, buckles, large buckles, springs, straps, carriage bolts, or harness-makers' bolts, and other like articles, 100 kilograms	1 15	2 35	3 15	4 20
309	In the same articles, bronzed, gilded or silver-plated, of common quality, 100 kilograms...................................	4 90	9 80	13 05	17 40
310	In the same articles, bronzed, gilded or silver-plated of fine quality, kilogram...	0 17	0 40	0 50	0 64
311	In chains up to ¼ inch thick, counted in the length of the link, kilogram...	0 01	0 05	0 47	0 06
312	Of over one-quarter inch thick, 100 kilograms................	1 00	1 95	2 60	3 45
313	In trays, money safes and in other articles not tariffed, valuation	10%	23%	29%	37%
314	In fishhooks, kilogram.......................................	9	19	26	35
315	In bedsteads, cots and cradles, even if ornamented with some other metal, including precisely the weight of the bars, 100 kilograms...	1 80	4 15	5 20	6 65
316	In the same, dipped in metal or imitation of yellow metal, will pay duty as per preceding portion, with an additional 100%				
317	In screens or cage rat-traps, including the wood used for forming the article, kilogram......................................	0 02	0 05	0 07	0 09
318	In dish covers and food preservers, kilogram................	0 07	0 17	0 22	0 28
319	In hand mills, with wooden box for grinding coffee and spices, kilogram...	0 03	0 07	0 07	0 12

(*a*) It is practice to appraise iron piping as per portion 298.

No. of portions	ARTICLES	TARIFF			
		SPANISH PRODUCTIONS IN		FOREIGN PRODUCTIONS IN	
		Sp'nish vessels.	Foreign vessels.	Sp'nish vessels.	Foreign vessels.
320	In stationary mills of all kinds, with or without fly-wheel, for grinding coffee and shelling corn, 100 kilograms...........	1 80	3 60	4 80	6 40
321	In wire netting. 100 kilograms..................................	1 75	3 50	4 70	6 52
322	In screws for hinges and wood, up to three inches in length, 100 kilograms...	2 75	5 50	7 30	9 75
	In the same, of more than three inches in length. (See portion 308.)				
323	In hair pins, with or without varnish, kilogram...............	0 18	0 03	0 04	0 06
324	In the same, with or without steel point, generally not varnished.				
325	In bagging, needles, brad-awls and shoemakers' awls, kilogram..	0 12	0 28	0 36	0 46
326	In brands, for shoemakers, kilogram..........................	0 08	0 19	0 24	0 31
327	In steel or iron numbers, kilogram............................	0 07	0 17	0 21	0 27
328	In all kinds of sailmakers' needles and sewing needles of German manufacture, kilogram...................................	0 25	0 57	0 72	0 92
329	In English sewing needles, kilogram	1 50	3 45	4 35	5 55
330	In steel pens, kilogram.......................................	0 62	1 43	1 81	2 31
	In small chains and other articles, coated with steel or polished, not stated. (See haberdashery, small articles, etc., portion 233.)				

TOOLS — IMPLEMENTS.

331	Tools, common tools, applicable to agriculture or other uses, such as plow-shares, picks, hoes, spades, rakes, coffee planters, scythes and paddle staffs (a), 100 kilograms...............	0 80	1 60	2 10	2 80
332	Of other kinds, such as cutlasses for trimming leaves, Belgian and German three-grooved blades, with or without cases, and the like, kilogram..	0 02	0 05	0 07	0 09
333	Of superior quality, or be it the cutlass for cutting cane (b), kilogram..	0 04	0 09	0 12	0 16
334	For general uses, such as axes, hatchets, adzes and bricklayers' trowels, kilogram..	0 04	0 08	0 10	0 14
335	Cutlasses, the application of which, although it may be adapted for trimming, serves for other uses, such as those of Collins and others, it being understood that in these must be included those of imitation (29), (c), kilogram...............	0 10	0 20	0 27	0 36
336	Tools, stone masons' hammers, carpenters' and shoemakers' pliers, stone cutters' edge hammers, shovels, iron-cutters, punches, coopers' punches, and other like articles, 100 kilograms...	2 10	4 25	5 65	7 50
337	Knives, carpenters', coopers' and tanners' planes, small planes, smooth planes, rabbet planes, molding planes, joint planes, and other like, including the wood that forms the article, kilograms...	0 03	0 06	0 08	0 11
338	In cutters, bits, chisels, compasses, sickles, pincers, screw-drivers, gouges, wrenches, dogs, tongs, squares, farriers' fleams, caulking tools, loose bits for planes, and other like tools of this sort, kilogram..	0 05	0 10	0 14	0 19
339	In knives, with or without forks, and carvers with horn, bone, whalebone, iron or wooden handles, 100 kilograms.........	6 75	13 50	18 00	24 00
340	In ivory handles, tortoise shell, mother of pearl or metal, plated with gold or silver, kilogram.................................	0 22	0 45	0 60	0 80
	In pocket knives and razors. (See haberdashery, small articles, etc., portion 233.)				

(a) See Note in No. 28, the Royal decree, which declares free of duty all such tools for exclusive use of agriculture, such as plowshares, hoes, rakes, narrow spades and weed cutters.

(b) See, in the addition note No. 38, the Royal order which declares free of duty the cutlasses for trimming and cutting cane.

(c) It is ordered that for the importation of long cutlasses at the same time as swords and other blank arms, the offices be guided by the ruling dispositions.—Gazette of January 15, 1879.

No. of portions	ARTICLES.	TARIFF.			
		SPANISH PRODUCTIONS IN		FOREIGN PRODUCTIONS IN	
		Sp'nish vessels.	Foreign vessels.	Sp'nish vessels.	Foreign vessels.
341	In twisted gimblets without handles or eyes, treenails without handles, and common gimblets not twisted, with wooden handles, kilogram...............................	0 04	0 09	0 12	0 16
342	In twisted gimblets with handles, brace bits, braces with or without bits, kilogram...............................	0 12	0 24	0 33	0 44
343	In framing saws, cross-cut saws and two-men saws, kilogram...	0 04	0 08	0 10	0 14
344	In all kinds of saws and circular saws, and gang saws for machines, kilogram...............................	0 08	0 17	0 22	0 30
345	In screw plates of all sizes, kilogram.......................	0 15	0 34	0 43	0 55
346	In cast iron shears of all sizes, and bench shears for tinsmiths, kilogram...............................	0 04	0 09	0 13	0 17
347	Wrought iron hand shears for same, kilogram...............	0 18	0 36	0 48	0 64
348	Of steel or polished iron in assorted sizes for sewing purposes, kilogram...............................	0 87	2 00	2 52	3 21
349	Of superior kind, for sewing purposes, kilogram.............	1 52	3 50	4 41	5 64
350	For tailors, gardeners, kilogram...............................	0 39	0 78	1 04	1 39
351	For trimming and other like, by their quality, kilogram........	0 11	0 22	0 30	0 40
352	Arms, blank and fire (a), valuation............................	10%	23%	29%	37%
353	Scales, valuation..	9%	18%	24%	32%
	TINNED IRON.				
354	Tin in plates or sheets, 100 kilograms......................	1 35	2 75	3 65	4 85
355	Manufactured in blank articles or painted, such as oil cans, oil cruets, washstands, sugarbowls, candlesticks, pots, coffeepots, chocolate pots, snuffers, funnels, cuspidors, cold meat baskets, jars, bath-room sets, pastry molds, pails, plates, reflectors, ladles, skimmers, and other like manufactures, 100 kilograms...............................	4 90	9 80	13 05	17 40
	GOLD.				
356	Gold in plates, jewels, watches with or without jewels, valuation,	5%	5%	5%	5%
	PEWTER.				
357	Pewter, manufactured in all forms, kilogram.................	0 08	0 16	0 21	0 28
358	Plaque, plantine, cristop, and other like compositions, in all forms, not tariffed, valuation...............................	10%	21%	29%	37%
	SILVER.				
359	Silver, in plates, jewels, watches with or without jewels, valuation...............................	5%	5%	5%	5%
	LEAD.				
360	Lead in pigs, sheet, balls, shot and piping, 100 kilograms.....	1 10	2 15	2 85	3 80
361	In toys, bottle caps and other like articles, kilogram..........	0 04	0 09	0 13	0 17
	ZINC AND CALAMINE.				
362	Zinc and calamine, in pigs, 100 kilograms....................	1 00	1 95	2 06	3 45
363	In sheets or plates, 100 kilograms...........................	1 25	2 55	3 40	4 55
364	In nails, 100 kilograms.....................................	1 95	3 90	5 20	6 95
365	In suspended or table lamps, painted or bronzed, and in printers' types, 100 kilograms...............................	8 55	17 10	22 80	30 40

(a) It is ordered that for the importation of blank fire-arms, the offices be guided by the ruling dispositions.—Gazette of January 15, 1879.

No. of portions.	ARTICLES.	DUTIES.			
		SPANISH PRODUCTIONS IN		FOREIGN PRODUCTIONS IN	
		Sp'nish vessels.	Foreign vessels.	Sp'nish vessels.	Sp'nish vessels.
	SECTION OF TEXTILE MATERIALS.				
1a	The counting of the threads must be effected in the chain of the knitting and in the square of 6 millimeters.				
2a	Doubts arising as to the square of the thread counter, whether or not it comprises a whole thread or more than those given as a limit, they shall always be favorably decided for the duty-payer.				
	HEMP AND SISAL HEMP.				
366	Sisal hemp and sisal hemp in strand, kilogram..............	0 08	0 01	0 02	0 02
367	Twisted in tackle, tarred or not, 100 kilograms.............	1 95	3 90	5 20	6 95
368	In ropes, 100 kilograms...................................	2 74	5 50	7 30	9 75
369	Hemp, knitted, in large sacks, or formed sacks, or in half-formed sacks, or in pieces for the same, 10 kilograms............	2 45	4 90	6 50	8 70
370	In hammocks, valuation....................................	10%	23%	29%	37%
	COTTON.				
371	Cotton in strands, 100 kilograms...........................	2 25	4 50	6 00	8 00
372	Twisted, in wicks, 100 kilograms...........................	2 95	5 85	7 08	10 45
373	In wicks, for cigar lighters, kilogram.......................	0 19	0 39	0 52	0 69
374	Prepared, in lining for tailors, kilogram....................	0 12	0 25	0 33	0 44
375	Twisted, in thread for sewing, in balls and strands, white and colored, and in bobbins, including in the duty the weight of the bobbin, or that of the tin or interior package, kilogram	0 13	0 27	0 36	0 48
376	Waste for machinists, 100 kilograms........................	2 75	3 50	7 30	9 75
377	In lace work, with wood interior, kilogram..................	0 24	0 49	0 66	0 88
378	With the interior of iron or metal, in strings and lacings, with metal points, applicable to shoestrings, kilogram..........	0 13	0 27	0 30	0 48
	SECTION OF TEXTURE.				
	FIRST GROUP.				
379	Plain and smooth fabric, white or unbleached, or dyed, such as Rouen, whitish calico, nankin, silesia, those wrapped up in uncarded cotton and other like fabrics, up to 10 threads, 100 kilograms..	5 65	11 25	15 00	20 00
379	From 11 to 16, 100 kilograms..............................	7 90	15 75	21 00	28 00
381	From 17 to 22, 100 kilograms..............................	0 22	0 51	0 65	0 83
	From 23 threads and upward. (See the Third Group.)				
	SECOND GROUP. (a)				
382	Plain and smooth fabrics, stamped, painted or striped, whose threads have been dyed before weaving, such as chintz, percale, figured gros de tour, prints ruled, striped, and the like, up to 12 threads, 100 kilograms...........................	9 75	19 50	26 00	34 65
383	From 13 to 16, 100 kilograms..............................	11 80	23 65	31 50	42 00
384	From 17 to 19, kilogram...................................	0 17	0 40	0 50	0 64
385	From 20 to 22, kilogram...................................	0 22	0 51	0 65	0 83
	From 23 threads and upward. (See the Third Group).				
	THIRD GROUP.				
386	Light fabrics, fair or common, whether solid or transparent, or fine fabrics even if they are not light, and all those that				

(a) (1a) The cotton cambric must be appraised by this group according to the portion which corresponds to it.

(2a) The poplin must also be appraised by this group in the same form.

No. of portions	ARTICLES.	DUTIES.			
		SPANISH PRODUCTIONS IN		FOREIGN PRODUCTIONS IN	
		Sp'nish vessels.	Foreign vessels.	Sp'nish vessels.	Foreign vessels.
387	contain 23 threads and upward, plain, smooth or loom made, white, stamped or dyed, such as muslin, jaconet and ——, and those called lining muslins up to 8 threads, 100 kilograms..........	12 00	28 00	35 00	43 00
388	From 9 to 12, 100 kilograms..................	20 55	48 00	60 00	73 70
389	From 15 to 16, 100 kilograms.................	34 30	80 00	100 00	122 85
390	From 17 to 22, kilogram......................	0 41	96 00	1 20	1 47
391	From 23 to 28, kilogram......................	0 51	1 20	1 50	1 84
392	From 29 to 34, kilogram......................	0 68	1 60	2 00	2 45
393	From 35 and upward, kilogram................	0 85	2 00	2 50	3 70
	The fabrics contained in the preceding group, embroidered by hand or loom, or with extra embroidery, will pay duty by their respective portions, with an additional 20%.				
394	The same fabrics, hand or loom, embroidered or trimmed with silk or wool, and braided wick for candles, valuation..	10%	23½%	29%	37½%
	FOURTH GROUP.				
395	Tulles, smooth, flowered or embroidered, white or colored, up to five threads, kilogram...................	0 34	0 72	1 00	1 27
	From six threads and upward, kilogram..................	1 03	2 38	3 00	3 82
	FIFTH GROUP.				
	FIRST SPECIES.				
397	Linen laces, kilogram........................	0 31	0 71	0 90	1 14
	SECOND SPECIES.				
398	Lighter laces or those not of linen, and the narrow lace edging, smooth, worked or embroidered, white or colored, kilogram	0 69	1 58	2 00	2 55
	THIRD SPECIES.				
399	Knittings in pieces, shawls or cloaks, ornaments for the head and in other forms, kilogram.............	0 38	0 79	1 00	1 27
	SIXTH GROUP.				
	FIRST SPECIES.				
400	Quilted fabrics and plain or worked piqué, white or colored, kilogram.......................	0 34	0 79	1 00	1 27
	SECOND SPECIES.				
401	Crossed or twilled fabrics, white, stamped or colored, of common quality, such as the duck canvas, light canvas, lamp-wicks and other like, (a) 100 kilograms................	7 50	15 00	20 00	26 65
	THIRD SPECIES.				
402	Fabrics of superior quality to those of the preceding portion, such as the drills and those wailed, flowered or damasked, such as the German table-cloth or crossed madapolam calico, (31) (b) 100 kilograms..............	13 15	26 25	35 00	46 65

(a) Canvas hose must be appraised by this portion.

(b) It is ordered that cotton cloths, blankets the weaving of which is crossed, loose damasked, not showing two sides, and one of the species known as German table-cloths be appraised by this portion.

No. of portions.	ARTICLES.	TARIFF.			
		SPANISH PRODUCTIONS IN		FOREIGN PRODUCTIONS IN	
		Sp'nish vessels.	Foreign vessels.	Sp'nish vessels.	Foreign vessels.
	SEVENTH GROUP.				
403	Stocking-stitch fabrics in undershirts, stockings and socks, drawers, caps and in other forms, 100 kilograms..........	48 75	97 50	130 00	175 35
	EIGHTH GROUP—CARDED TEXTURES, VELVETS, PLUSHES AND CARPETS.				
	FIRST SPECIES.				
404	Carded fabrics, such as the cloaks or blankets, whether raw or white or colored (32) (a), 100 kilograms	7 50	15 00	20 00	26 65
	SECOND SPECIES.				
405	Velvet fabrics, such as imitations, whether plain or worked, 100 kilograms..	0 20	0 47	0 60	0 76
	THIRD SPECIES.				
406	Velvet down fabrics shag clipped, or carpet weaving in pieces, shawls, cloaks and others, 100 kilograms...............	0 25	0 57	0 72	0 92
	FOURTH SPECIES.				
407	Velvet down fabrics unclipped or shag, in cloaks and towels, such as those called Turkish, 100 kilograms.............	0 15	0 35	0 45	0 57
	NINTH GROUP—RIBBONS.				
	FIRST SPECIES.				
408	Ribbons, Ferret silk, white or colored, kilogram.............	0 11	0 22	0 30	0 40
	SECOND SPECIES.				
409	Ribbons of other kinds, plain or worked, white or colored, applicable to the branch of hats and dress trimmings, even if of cotton velvet, called imitation, kilogram............	0 34	0 79	1 00	1 27
410	Ribbons of other kinds, such as shoemakers' tape, and those used as reins for horses, kilogram.............................	0 13	0 26	0 35	0 46
	TENTH GROUP—HANDKERCHIEFS.				
	FIRST SPECIES.				
	Handkerchiefs in pieces or loose, with or without fringe, but without any handwork, will pay duty by the preceding group.				
411	Handkerchiefs, purified a second time or with some hand work, will pay duty by the preceding portion, with an additional 20%.				
	THIRD SPECIES.				
	Handkerchiefs with hemmed edges or with lace, will pay duty in the following form:				
412	Up to 17 threads, kilogram................................	0 44	1 03	1 30	1 65
413	From 18 to 20, kilogram..................................	1 65	1 50	1 90	2 42
414	From 21 to 22, kilogram..................................	0 88	2 02	2 55	3 25
415	From 23 upward, kilogram................................	1 31	3 01	3 80	4 84

(a) Cloths and blankets with corresponding borders to this portion must be appraised by the same without the additional 20%.

No. of portions	ARTICLES.	TARIFF.			
		SPANISH PRODUCTIONS IN		FOREIGN PRODUCTIONS IN	
		Sp'nish vessels.	Foreign vessels.	Sp'nish vessels.	Foreign vessels.
	ELEVENTH GROUP—READY-MADE CLOTHES.				
416	Ready-made clothes in general, from fabrics of this section, with an additional 100%. The count of the threads in shirts must be effected in the bosom, collar and cuffs.				
417	Cotton shirts with linen bosoms, collars and cuffs, will pay duty as linen fabrics, with an additional 50%. The threads counted in the same form as indicated by the preceding portion, and as if they did not contain cotton.				
418	Cotton umbrellas and sunshades, dozen......................	0 45	0 90	1 20	1 60
	TWELFTH GROUP.				
419	Fabrics with elastic back (cotton elastic), kilogram...........	0 30	0 60	0 80	1 06
	HEMP AND FLAX.				
420	Strand oakum fabrics, even if tarred, 100 kilograms..........	0 95	1 85	2 50	3 35
421	In untarred tackle, 100 kilograms............................	2 35	4 70	6 25	8 35
422	In ropes, kilogram...	0 04	0 09	0 13	0 17
423	In bundle and bagging twine, kilogram......................	0 03	0 06	0 08	0 11
424	In hemp twine and in yarn raw or unwound, including shoemakers' yarn, kilogram..................................	0 06	0 13	0 13	0 24
425	In bleached or colored yarn, kilogram......................	0 10	0 19	0 26	0 35
426	In millinery, kilogram.......................................	0 30	0 69	0 87	1 11
	FABRICS—FIRST GROUP.				
427	Unbleached flax fabrics, dyed or half bleached, even if they have colored stripes, plain or crossed, such as coarse canvas, sackcloth and Scotch cloth and Russian cloth, brown linen, and all kinds of osnaburgs and girt strips up to five threads, (a), 100 kilograms..	1 90	3 75	5 00	6 65
428	Plain and smooth, raw or half bleached, even if with colored stripes, such as coarse canvas, sackcloth, Scotch cloth, sail cloth, Russian sheeting, Ghant linen, and all kinds of brown linen, Bamant linen, Irish linen, blue glazed cotton, and other like, and Dutch linen, even if dyed when unbleached, not lead color, from six to ten threads, 100 kilograms......	5 65	11 25	15 00	20 00
429	Like those mentioned in the preceding portion, excepting those half bleached from eleven to sixteen threads, 100 kilograms,	11 25	22 50	30 00	40 00
430	Seventeen threads, upward, with the same exception, kilogram, *Note.*—Half bleached fabrics, such as brown linen and the rest of this group, and other like, whatever be their commercial denomination, from eleven threads upward, will be considered as white, and will pay by their respective portions of the third group of linen weavings. *Another*—Bags made of fabrics, corresponding to this group, an additional charge of 10% for confection.	0 17	0 39	0 50	0 63
	SECOND GROUP.				
431	Unbleached fabrics or dyed unbleached, even if they have colored stripes, crossed or twilled, such as drills of all kinds, 100 kilograms...................................	11 25	22 50	30 00	40 00
	THIRD GROUP.				
432	Smooth and plain fabrics, striped or dyed, up to 9 threads, 100 kilograms	8 45	16 90	22 50	30 00

(a) Five-thread linen canvas must be appraised by this portion, it being understood that threads composed of more than one strand only constitute one, the weft counting the threads as they cross.

No. of portions.	ARTICLES.	TARIFF.			
		SPANISH PRODUCTIONS IN		FOREIGN PRODUCTIONS IN	
		Sp'nish vessels.	Foreign vessels.	Sp'nish vessels.	Foreign vessels.
433	From 10 to 12, 100 kilograms.............................	12 70	23 35	32 50	43 35
434	From 13 to 16, 100 kilograms......................	17 25	39 65	50 00	63 80
435	From 17 to 20, 100 kilograms................................	0 27	0 63	0 80	1 02
436	From 21 to 23, 100 kilograms.............................	0 34	0 79	1 00	1 27
437	From 24 to 27, 100 kilograms..............................	0 44	1 03	1 30	1 65
438	From 28 to 30, 100 kilograms...............................	0 69	1 58	2 00	2 55
439	From 31 upward, 100 kilograms............................	1 03	2 38	3 00	3 82

SECOND SPECIES.

Stamped fabrics will pay duty in the following form:

440 Light ones, such as French and English perforated prints and their like, will pay duty by the preceding portions, with an additional 60%.

441 The solid ones, or those not light, such as the English cloth, cutrés and the silecias, will pay by the same portions, with the additional charge of 20 %.

FOURTH GROUP.

442	Crossed, twilled, damasked or branched fabrics, white stamped, painted, dyed or striped, such as drills, German table-cloths, and those called jipijapa, and the like, in pieces, table-cloths, napkins and towels, 100 kilograms.......................	22 50	45 00	60 00	80 00

FIFTH GROUP.

Tape for shoe catches and saddle girts and others, whether plain, smooth or twilled, will pay by the preceding groups.

SIXTH GROUP.

443	Stocking-stitch fabrics in socks and stockings, gloves, undershirts, drawers, and other like manufactures, in common quality or with seams, kilo..............................	0 18	0 37	0 50	0 66
444	Fine or without seams, kilo................................	0 86	1 98	2 50	3 19

SEVENTH GROUP.

445	Tulles, laces, embroidery and all kinds of fabrics with embroidery, valuation.....................................	10%	25%	29%	37%

EIGHTH GROUP—HANDKERCHIEFS.

FIRST SPECIES.

446 Handkerchiefs without stitching will pay as fabrics of this section, with the additional charge of 20 %.

SECOND SPECIES.

447 Handkerchiefs with borders will pay as the same fabrics, with the additional charge of 50 %.

THIRD SPECIES.

448 Handkerchiefs with borders, even if formed in the loom, will pay duty by the fabrics of this section, with an additional charge of 100 %.

NINTH GROUP—READY-MADE CLOTHES.

449 Ready-made clothes in general, plain or loom bordered shirts, will pay duty as fabrics of this section, with an additional charge of 100 %.

The threads must be counted in the bosoms, collars and cuffs,

No. of portions.	ARTICLES.	TARIFF.			
		SPANISH PRODUCTIONS IN		FOREIGN PRODUCTIONS IN	
		Sp'nish vessels.	Foreign vessels.	Sp'nish vessels.	Foreign vessels.
	SECOND SPECIES.				
450	Shirt fronts, collars, cuffs and trimmings for shirts, and swaddling articles, and other like, will pay duty as fabrics of this section, with the additional charge of 250 %.				
451	Fabrics for ready-made clothes, with hand embroidery, valuation....................................	10%	25%	29%	37%
	BRISTLES, HORSE-HAIR AND HAIR.				
452	Bristles for shoemakers, kilogram...........................	0 65	1 50	1 90	2 42
453	Horse-hair, for filling or stuffing pillows, seats, etc., kilogram..	0 05	0 11	0 15	0 21
	HORSE-HAIR FABRICS.				
454	Horse-hair fabrics, smooth, crossed or twilled, for furniture covers, seives, etc., kilogram........................... In cigar cases, false hair, and chest covers, and other like articles. (See haberdashery, small articles, etc., portion 233.)	0 16	0 37	0 47	0 60
	WOOLENS.				
455	Wool in lumps, or waste wool from tanneries, applicable for use in saddleries, kilogram..................................	0 01	0 02	0 03	0 04
456	Twisted in worsted yarn or split wool, and in lace work, generally of wool only or with mixture of cotton, balls, buttons, tassels, cords, fringes, tapes, small ribbons, bands, serpentines, and other works of this class, with or without wooden frame work, kilogram..	0 32	0 75	0 94	1 20
457	With the interior or frame of iron or common metal, kilogram	0 15	0 34	0 43	0 55
458	With glass bead trimmings, kilogram........................	0 35	0 80	1 01	1 29
	FIRST GROUP — WEAVINGS.				
	FIRST SPECIES.				
459	Pure woolen fabrics, smooth, such as alpaca, orleans, muslin, very fine flannels and other like, up to 10 threads (36), kilogram..	0 25	0 57	0 72	0 92
460	From 11 to 16, kilogram......................................	0 45	1 03	1 30	1 66
461	From 17 to 20, kilogram.....................................	0 60	1 38	1 74	2 22
462	From 21 upwards, kilogram..................................	0 90	2 07	2 61	3 33
	Note—Nap cloths, called summer woolens, that, for their make, are similar to muslins, fine flannels, and others contained in this group, must pay duty by the——with the benefit of portion 612 when they contain cotton mixture.				
	SECOND SPECIES.				
463	Light fabrics or transparent, such as gauze or barege, kilogram	1 32	3 05	3 85	4 91
	SECOND GROUP.				
	FIRST SPECIES.				
464	Smooth, crossed or twilled fabrics, of wool only, such as merinos, whether single or double, cassimered or not, and other like, such as those called thin serges and Italian cloths, kilogram...	0 60	1 38	1 74	2 22
	SECOND SPECIES.				
465	The same fabrics with cotton mixtures, kilogram............	0 37	0 75	1 00	1 33

No. of partions.	ARTICLES.	DUTIES.			
		SPANISH PRODUCTIONS IN		FOREIGN PRODUCTIONS IN	
		Sp'nish vessels.	Foreign vessels.	Sp'nish vessels.	Foreign vessels.
	THIRD SPECIES.				
466	The same fabrics weft or with silk mixture, kilogram..........	0 90	2 07	2 61	3 33
	THIRD GROUP.				
	FIRST SPECIES.				
467	Smooth or crossed fabrics of wool only, with one or both sides rough, not put through pulling mill, such as baize, coating, blankets and cloaks of the same, whether carded or not, and sailors' caps, 100 kilograms..............................	10 00	23 00	29 00	37 00
	SECOND SPECIES.				
468	The same fabrics with cotton or hemp, linen flax chain, or formed from the waste wool from looms, 100 kilograms..... *Note* — The blankets or shawls with borders, corresponding to this group, must be appraised by the same with the additional 20%.	7 05	16 25	20 50	26 15
	FOURTH GROUP.				
469	Fabrics called spotted, such as felt composed of heterogeneous matters, the surface of which is of wool, for saddle clothes and stable blankets, 100 kilograms......................	4 30	9 90	12 50	16 95
	FIFTH GROUP—CLOTHS AND CASSIMERES.				
	FIRST SPECIES.				
470	Woolen cloths only, common double, known as pilot castor and other like, kilogram.................................	0 29	0 67	0 85	1 08
	SECOND SPECIES.				
471	The same cloths, with cotton chain, kilogram................	0 14	0 32	0 41	0 52
	THIRD SPECIES.				
472	Cloths, cassimeres and velvets of wool only, the kinds generally used for jewelry, known by the name of damask cloth, satin, cassimere and other like, kilogram......................	68 95	158 60	200 00	255 15
	FOURTH SPECIES.				
473	The same, with cotton chain, kilogram.....................	25 85	59 50	75 00	95 70
	SIXTH GROUP.				
	FIRST SPECIES.				
474	Smooth fabrics, crossed, twilled or damasked, of wool only, such as damask reps and other like, kilogram............	0 40	0 92	1 16	1 48
	SECOND SPECIES.				
475	The same fabrics, with cotton or worsted yarn chain, kilogram	0 30	0 69	0 87	1 11
	SEVENTH GROUP.				
	FIRST SPECIES.				
476	Fabrics of other kinds, such as Brussels, camlet and flannel, of wool only, kilogram.....	0 25	0 57	0 72	0 92

No. of portions.	ARTICLES.	DUTIES.			
		SPANISH PRODUCTIONS IN		FOREIGN PRODUCTIONS IN	
		Sp'nish vessels.	Foreign vessels.	Sp'nish vessels.	Foreign vessels.
	SECOND SPECIES.				
477	The same fabrics, with cotton or worsted yarn chain, kilogram....................	0 17	0 39	0 50	0 63
	Note.—Vests and waists of this group (479) must pay duty by the same without the additional charge for ready-made clothes, these accessories not being considered as tailors or modistes' work.				
	TENTH GROUP—CARPET WEAVINGS.				
	FIRST SPECIES.				
480	Coarse freize carpets, excluding the fringes, square meter	0 05	0 11	0 14	0 18
	SECOND SPECIES.				
481	Frizzled shag carpet, not cut, square meter..................	0 09	0 20	0 26	0 33
	THIRD SPECIES.				
482	Brussels, velvet carpet, square meter......................	0 14	0 32	0 40	0 51
	ELEVENTH GROUP—HANDKERCHIEFS.				
483	Cloaks or shawls for ladies, and handkerchiefs, will pay duty according to class by the preceding groups, with the additional charge of 30%.				
	TWELFTH GROUP—RIBBONS.				
	FIRST SPECIES.				
484	Woolen ribbons, or with cotton mixture, applicable to the branch of saddlery, for girts, reins and other like uses, kilogram..	0 14	0 29	0 39	0 52
	SECOND SPECIES.				
	Woolen ribbons with cotton mixture, for general uses, will pay duty according to class by the groups of fabrics of this section.				
	THIRTEENTH GROUP—READY-MADE CLOTHES.				
	FIRST SPECIES.				
485	Ready-made clothes from alpaca, orleans, merino and other cloths, with exception of broadcloth, cassimere and worsted, will pay by the portions of fabrics to which they correspond, with the additional charge of 100%.				
	SECOND SPECIES.				
486	Ready-made clothes from broadcloth, cassimere and worsted will pay duty by its respective portions, with the additional charge of 200%..................................				
	HAIR.				
487	Human hair in strands, kilogram..........................	2 42	5 15	6 50	8 29
488	Manufactured, valuation.................................	10%	23%	29%	37%
	Spanish grass, junk and osier:				
489	Osier in strands or prepared for caning chairs, 100 kilograms...	2 95	5 90	7 85	10 50

No. of portions.	ARTICLES.	DUTIES.			
		SPANISH PRODUCTIONS IN		FOREIGN PRODUCTIONS IN	
		Sp'nish vessels.	Foreign vessels.	Sp'nish vessels.	Foreign vessels.
	FABRICS—FIRST GROUP.				
	FIRST SPECIES.				
490	Spanish grass, junk and osier, woven in panniers, crates, mats and in other like articles, kilogram	0 01	0 02	0 03	0 04
	SECOND SPECIES.				
491	Steamed or unsteamed grass in mats and carpets, kilogram.....	0 02	0 04	0 06	0 08
	THIRD SPECIES.				
492	Grass, junk and osier in baskets and large baskets, baby carriages, chairs, rocking chairs, sofas, beds, cradles and other furniture, or like articles, by their weight, including the lumber forming part of the article, kilogram	0 04	0 09	0 02	0 16
	FOURTH SPECIES.				
493	Grass in tableware baskets, table mats, baskets and crates and other like articles, whose weight does not exceed ½ kilogram per unit (each) kilogram	0 25	0 57	0 72	0 92
	FIFTH SPECIES.				
494	Grass, in small baskets, sewing baskets, flower baskets and other like articles, trimmed with silk or any other material, whatever be their weight, kilogram........................	1 00	3 30	1 90	3 70
	VARIOUS STRAWS.				
	Various straws, including Panama plaited in hats (see Hats), in telescope baskets, cigar cases and fancy articles (see Haberdashery, small articles, etc., portion 233).				
	AGAVE.				
495	Agave, twisted into ropes, reins, bits for horses, carriage lines, and in other like articles, kilograms.....................	0 10	0 25	0 31	0 40
	FABRICS.				
496	Agave weavings, in all kinds of articles, valuation.............	10%	23%	29%	37%
	Note.—Agave bags, lined with paper, for bagging sugar, one meter long by 75 centimeters width, must be appraised at 25 cents for weight, and pay duty by this portion (496).				
	SILK AND SILK CLOTHS.				
497	Silk, twisted or loose, kilograms............................	1 20	2 76	3 48	4 44
497a	Silk in bobbins, valuation...................................	10%	23%	29%	37%
498	Silk, millinery, or with silk mixture, fringes, tapes, ribbons, bandas, braids and other manufactures of this class, with the interior (back) of cotton, wool, linen, rubber or wood, kilogram............	0 80	1 84	2 32	2 96
499	With the interior of iron or common metal, kilogram........ ...	0 25	0 57	0 72	0 92
500	With glass bead trimmings, kilogram........................	0 45	1 03	1 30	1 66
	FIRST GROUP — WEAVINGS.				
	FIRST SPECIES.				
501	Plain fabrics, twilled or smoothed, stamped or figured, of any color or denomination, such as light silk veil (Canton crape), satin, satinet, gros-grain, taffety, etc., kilogram............	2 39	5 50	6 93	8 84

No. of portions.	ARTICLES.	DUTIES.			
		SPANISH PRODUCTIONS IN		FOREIGN PRODUCTIONS IN	
		Sp'nish vessels.	Foreign vessels.	Sp'nish vessels.	Sp'nish vessels.
	SECOND SPECIES.				
502	Brocaded fabrics, or loom-embroidered, even so when embroidered with corded silk, cord or other trimmings, including damasks, kilogram............................	2 82	6 50	8 19	10 45
	SECOND GROUP.				
	FIRST SPECIES.				
503	Spun silk, silk floss fabrics, plain, plain twilled or smooth, stamped or figured in any denomination (38), kilogram ..... *Note*—All fabrics with all-silk face and cotton, linen or worsted weft, or *vice versa*, must be appraised by this portion.	1 12	2 59	3 26	4 16
	SECOND SPECIES.				
504	Said, brocaded or loom figured, even when with corded silk, twist or other trimmings, kilogram............................	1 89	4 35	5 48	6 99
	THIRD GROUP.				
	FIRST SPECIES.				
505	Light or transparent fabrics, even if they have fringes or designs, smoothed, taffetyed or in other forms, plain, embroidered or loom figured, kilogram........................	5 65	12 99	16 38	20 90
	SECOND SPECIES.				
506	Light or transparent floss fabrics, such as crepe and other like, kilogram..................................	3 00	6 90	8 75	11 10
	FOURTH GROUP.				
	FIRST SPECIES.				
507	Velvets and smooth drubbing, stamped, dyed, striped or figured, kilogram......................................	5 43	12 50	15 76	20 10
	SECOND SPECIES.				
508	Loom embroidered velvets, kilogram........................	7 27	16 72	21 08	26 90
	FIFTH GROUP.				
	FIRST SPECIES.				
509	Tulles, smooth, figured or in lace, kilogram..................	2 17	5 00	6 30	8 04
	SECOND SPECIES.				
510	Tulles, loom embroidered, kilogram	5 00	11 50	14 50	18 50
	SIXTH GROUP.				
	FIRST SPECIES.				
511	Lace, point, blonde, narrow blonde, plain, figured, open or loom embroidered, kilogram................................	8 69	20 00	25 20	32 17
	SECOND SPECIES.				
512	Lace, hand knitted, valuation.............................	10%	23%	29%	37%

No. of portions.	ARTICLES.	DUTIES.			
		SPANISH PRODUCTIONS IN		FOREIGN PRODUCTIONS IN	
		Sp'nish vessels.	Foreign vessels.	Sp'nish vessels.	Foreign vessels.
	SEVENTH GROUP.				
	FIRST SPECIES.				
513	Silk fabrics of any kind, plain, smooth, or loom embroidered, in undershirts, caps, socks, stockings and other like articles, by their weight, kilogram.............................	4 43	9 50	11 97	15 28
	SECOND SPECIES.				
514	Silk fabrics of any kind, in purses, gloves, mits and other like articles of their weight, kilogram......................	5 62	13 00	16 39	20 91
	EIGHTH GROUP.				
515	Fabrics, with rubber (base) backs. (Silk elastic), kilogram...	0 55	1 26	1 59	2 03
	NINTH GROUP.				
	FIRST SPECIES.				
516	Unbleached silk handkerchiefs, called Indian silk, kilogram.....	1 75	4 04	5 09	6 49
	SECOND SPECIES.				
517	Floss silk or crape silk handkerchiefs, kilogram...............	0 82	1 90	2 39	3 05
	TENTH GROUP.				
518	Handkerchiefs and neckties of superior quality to those of the preceding portion, or those of satin, taffety, gros, moiré serge, striped muslin, plain or loom embroidered, will pay duty by the portion of finished fabrics twilled, etc., or by those of lace, light fabrics, with the additional charge of 30%.				
	ELEVENTH GROUP.				
519	Shawls, cloaks and other like articles will pay duty by the same portions, without any additional charge. Hand embroidered, valuation.................................	10%	23%	29%	37%
	TWELFTH GROUP — RIBBONS.				
520	Ribbons, smooth, brocaded, loom figured, twilled, finished or embroidered, of any colors or denominations, of silk or with silk mixture, in every case that the silk exceeds 50%, valuation..	1 75	4 02	5 07	6 47
	THIRD SPECIES.				
522	Ribbons for girts, reins and carriage trimmings that do not correspond to the branch of millinery, brocaded or with silk mixture with wool, linen or cotton warp or of any other inferior material, valuation............................	0 34	0 79	1 00	1 27
	THIRTEENTH GROUP.				
523	Muslin mosquito nets, prepared with cords and rings or without, one...	0 30	0 69	0 87	1 11
	FOURTEENTH GROUP.				
	FIRST SPECIES.				
524	Silk umbrellas or mixed silk of over 418 millimeters, doz......	2 40	5 52	6 96	8 88
525	Silk parasols or mixed silk up to 418 millimeters, doz.........	3 60	8 28	10 44	13 32

No. of portions	ARTICLES.	DUTIES.			
		SPANISH PRODUCTIONS IN		FOREIGN PRODUCTIONS IN	
		Sp'nish vessels.	Foreign vessels.	Sp'nish vessels.	Foreign vessels.
	FIFTEENTH GROUP—READY-MADE CLOTHES.				
526	Shawls, capes, mantillas, and veils, mantelets, trimmings, bracelets, chemises, collars and all ready-made clothes, valuation..	10%	23%	29%	37%
	SECTION OF DRUGS.				
	GENERAL CHEMICAL PRODUCTS, PHARMACEUTICAL PRODUCTS AND SPECIAL MEDICINES.				
	FIRST GROUP — *Products of animal reign in their natural state, or improved, but without losing their primitive character of simple.*				
527	Musk, umber. civet, castoreous and other articles of small volume and consumption, even if their value is high, kilogram...	1 17	2 34	3 13	4 17
528	Spanish flies and cochineal, kilogram......................	0 11	0 23	0 31	0 41
529	Vegetable coal, 100 kilograms.............................	0 30	0 45	0 60	0 76
530	Glue, common or of inferior quality, kilogram..............	0 20	0 03	0 05	0 07
531	Pisces and for soup, kilogram.............................	0 10	0 25	0 31	0 40
532	Greases, liquid of fishes, such as those of whales, sardines, codfishes, refined or not, including the weight of the immediate package when it is of glass, 100 kilograms..................	1 95	3 90	5 20	6 95
533	Solid, such as whale, sperm, stearine, purified tallow and artificial and mineral wax, 100 kilograms......................	4 90	9 80	13 05	17 40
534	Tallow, raw and melted, 100 kilograms.....................	1 65	3 35	4 44	5 90
	SECOND GROUP — *Products of mineral reign in their natural state, or improved, but without losing their primitive character of simple.*				
535	Solid or liquid products, such as asphaltum, black glue or wax, and petroleum in their natural state, just as they come from the mines (a), 100 kilograms...........................	0 32	0 48	0 64	0 80
536	Purified, such as those called coal oil, kerosene, gasoline, benzine, parafine and oils and greases for painting or lubricating (b), kilogram..	0 01	0 03	0 04	0 06
537	Waters, mineral, natural and artificial, not including the package or vessel, 100 kilograms..................................	1 00	1 95	2 60	3 45
538	Mineral tar or pitch, 100 kilograms.........................	0 16	0 33	0 44	0 59
539	Mineral coal, 100 kilograms...............................	0 24	0 26	0 48	0 60
	Note— When mineral coal is imported in any kind of packages, the duty corresponding to these must be liquidated.				
540	Emery, kilogram..	0 08	0 06	0 02	0 02
	THIRD GROUP — *Vegetable products in their natural state, or improved, but without losing their primitive character of simple. Vegetables in plants, leaves, flowers, sprouts, roots, bark, grains, seeds, fruits, sticks and coal.*				
541	Plants, whole and sprouts, such as those of worm-wood, garden angelica, mugwort, henbane, bitter-sweet, common ceterah, fumitory, hipericon, and other like, whose values are alike, kilogram...	0 02	0 03	0 05	0 07

(a) Crude petroleum in its natural state, such as it comes from the mines, is of a dark green color, more or less dark, not very transparent and very inflammable at all temperatures; the refined being noted for its transparency and whiteness, and not inflammable, but at a high temperature of 100 degrees Fahrenheit. There is no intermediate class of greater or less labor between that one, which in itself is crude, and the refined, as the term refining cannot be applied to the operation of extracting from the mines or wells the first matter, but to any process that will change or improve its class by adding the materials that constitute it when crude or natural, such as the gases, mineral, coal and other impurities that cannot be separated but by the means of distillation commonly called refining.

(b) It is ordered that the duties of coal oil shall be made to include the package.

CUSTOMS AND TARIFF REGULATIONS OF CUBA. 481

No. of portions.	ARTICLES.	DUTIES.			
		SPANISH PRODUCTIONS IN		FOREIGN PRODUCTIONS IN	
		Sp'nish vessels.	Foreign vessels.	Sp'nish vessels.	Foreign vessels.
542	Such as those of sweet majoram, kilogram..................	0 04	0 09	0 13	0 17
543	Leaves, such as belladonna, stramonium, arnica, and others whose are alike, kilogram........................	0 01	0 03	0 04	0 07
544	Like those of aconite, agrimony, vervain, maidenshair, plantain, nettle, meliot, and other like whose values are alike, kilogram...	0 03	0 05	0 07	0 10
545	Like those of mint, myrtle, senna, and others whose values are alike, kilogram...	0 03	0 05	0 07	0 10
546	Flowers, like those of lavender, chamomile, knot-grass, elder, and others whose values are alike, kilogram..............	0 01	0 03	0 04	0 05
547	Like those of French lavender, rosemary, rose, poppy, mallows, marshmallow, linden, violet, and others whose values are alike, kilogram......................................	0 03	0 07	0 10	0 13
548	Roots, like those of marshmallow, burdock, fen-root, houndstongue, turmenic, gentian, iris, licorice, ink-makers' madder, valerian, and others whose values are alike, kilogram.....	0 01	0 03	0 04	0 05
549	Like those of aconite, mugwort, arnica, belladonna, calamus, colchicum, piony, pellitory, purze, tormentil, Veracruz, brambles, and others whose values are alike, kilogram.....	0 03	0 06	0 08	0 11
550	Like those of contrayerva, majoram, hellebore, arrowroot, Honduras, bramble, and others whose values are alike, kilogram...	0 04	0 09	0 13	0 17
551	Like those of jalap, milk-wort, thurbit, and others whose values are alike, kilogram..................................	0 08	0 17	0 23	0 31
552	Like those of ipecacuanha and rhubarb, kilogram...........	0 19	0 39	0 52	0 69
553	Barks, like those of sassafras, mezeseor, squill, cider, pomegranate, oak and others whose values are alike, kilogram......	0 02	0 03	0 05	0 07
554	Like those of angostura, elm, common Peruvian bark, Guiana bark and others whose values are alike, kilogram.........	0 03	0 07	0 10	0 13
555	Like those of calyx and loach, alkanet and others whose values are alike, kilogram	0 09	0 19	0 26	0 34
556	Grains, fruits and seeds, like those of linseed, mustard, fenngreek and others whose values are alike, kilogram..............	0 01	0 02	0 03	0 04
557	Like those of poppy, colchicum, coriander, fennel, white mustard, lavender, cotton, flea-wort and others whose values are alike, kilogram	0 02	0 04	0 05	0 07
558	Like those of starry anise, colocynth and others whose values are alike, kilogram	0 04	0 08	0 11	0 15
559	Like those of cardamonum, carthamus and others whose values are alike, kilogram	0 10	0 21	0 28	0 38
560	Logs, such as those of occidental, sandle wood and tamarisk, kilogram .... Like those called lignumvitæ, mulberry, baziletto and other dye woods. (See section of timbers).	0 01	0 03	0 04	0 05
561	Tan-barks and vegetable coal (charcoal) valuation............	4%	6%	8%	10%
	OILS, FIRM AND SCENTED — (PERFUMED.)				
562	Firm oils like those of raw and boiled linseed, those of palm, cotton, palma-christi, cocoanut, pea-nut and others whose values are alike, 100 kilos.........................	1 95	3 90	5 20	6 95
563	Of turpentine (spirits of turpentine), 100 kilos................	1 35	2 75	3 65	4 85
564	Of hazel-nut, sweet almonds, cocoa, and others whose values are alike, kilo...	0 05	0 10	0 13	0 18
565	Of nutmeg, crotontiglium and others whose values are alike, kilo. .	0 48	0 97	1 30	1 75
566	Scented and their like, for all applications, like those of roses, orange or lemon flowers, angelica, cardamonium sweet basil and others whose values are alike, kilo..............	5 43	12 50	15 76	20 10
567	Of bitter almonds, chamomile, cubeb, occidental sandal, laurel, cherry and others whose values are alike, kilo............	2 17	5 00	6 30	8 04
568	Of aniseed, bergamot, citron, orange, wormwood, cinnamon, cider, majoram and others whose values are alike, kilo......	0 43	1 00	1 26	1 60
569	Of sage, rosemary, thyme and others whose values are alike, kilo.	0 10	0 25	0 31	0 40
570	Camphor, crude and refined, kilo........................	0 07	0 17	0 22	0 28

No. of portions	ARTICLES.	DUTIES.			
		SPANISH PRODUCTIONS IN		FOREIGN PRODUCTIONS IN	
		Sp'nish vessels.	Foreign vessels.	Sp'nish vessels.	Sp'nish vessels.
	GUMS, RESINS AND GUM RESINS.				
571	Gums, like the arabic, tragacanth, senegal, manna, and others of equal value, kilogram.............................	0 04	0 09	0 13	0 17
572	Gum arabic, loose, kilogram................................	0 01	0 02	0 03	0 04
573	Tar and vegetable pitch, including, for the duty, the weight of the immediate package, 100 kilograms................	0 25	0 45	0 60	0 85
574	Pitch, red and black, and pine resin, including in the duty the weight of the immediate package, kilogram.........	0 35	0 70	0 90	1 20
575	Gum resins and solid resins, soft or liquid, not tariffed in other portions, like the turpentine of different places; Burgundy pitch, white pitch, damar gum, and others of equal value, kilogram...	0 01	0 02	0 03	0 04
576	Like the gum lac, gum copal, mangle tree gum, and others of equal value, kilogram................................	0 03	0 01	0 10	0 13
577	Those called balsams, like those of Peru, tolu, copabia, and others of equal value, kilogram......................	0 07	0 17	0 22	0 28
578	Like the asafetida, the officinal spurge, the common juniper, the incense, the myrrh, the mastic, the benzoin, the gum storax, chyme, dragon, and others of equal value or of rare importation, even if their values are greater, kilogram.......	0 05	0 12	0 15	0 20
579	Of opium (a), the scammony from all parts, the jalap resin, and others of greater or equal value, kilogram............	0 65	1 50	1 89	2 41
	FOURTH GROUP—*General chemical products.*				
	Note—The prodigious number of which this important group is formed demand, for the establishment of the possible, not the absolute equity, a number of subdivisions like those established, in which remain absorbed, by the similarity of their values, such products existing to-day and such as the scientific progress may continue to discover. And even if it should be noticed that in some groups are found articles whose values are greater than those of the corresponding group, their small importance as regards importation must be counted upon, and the danger the exchequer would be taking if they were assessed by their proper values.				
580	Acids, mineral acids of industrial application, like the arsenic, muriatic and the sulphuric of the market, 100 kilograms...	0 15	0 25	0 35	0 45
581	Like the nitric of the trade and pure, the pure sulphuric and muriatic and the electrum, 100 kilograms...............	1 75	4 00	5 05	6 45
582	Vegetables and mineral for all applications, such as the acetic, baracic, gallic, oxalic and others of equal value, kilogram...	0 03	0 07	0 08	0 11
583	Like the citric, tannic, tartaric and others of equal value, kilogram	0 07	0 17	0 22	0 28
584	For exclusive medicinal application, like the lactic, benzolic, hydrocianic, phosphoric and others of more value, but of rare importation, kilogram.............................	0 87	2 00	2 52	3 21
585	Other products, such as sulphur in powder and paste, caustic soda or soapmakers' lye for application to soap and match industry, 100 kilograms.................................	0 25	0 40	0 50	0 65
586	Bicarbonate of soda, the carbonates of soda, of potassium and lime, the sulphates of alum, of ammonia, of iron, of soda and magnesia, the sulphuret of antimony and other products of equal value...	0 65	1 50	1 90	2 40
587	Like ammonia, hyposulphate of soda, litharge, nitrate of potassium and soda, sulphate of zinc, the glucose and other products of equal value, kilogram..........................	0 01	0 02	0 03	0 04
588	Like the carbonates of magnesia, that of zinc and refined potassium, the hydrochlorate of ammonia, kaolin and other products of equal value, kilogram......................	0 02	0 05	0 06	0 08

(a) By decree of the General Government of 20th of July, 1863, reiterated June 9, 1877, and recorded again Jan. 21, 1882, it is ordered, that merchants that are not druggists must fulfill the formalities established, in order to take opium out of the custom houses.

		TARIFF.			
No. of portions.	ARTICLES.	SPANISH PRODUCTIONS IN		FOREIGN PRODUCTIONS IN	
		Sp'nish vessels.	Foreign vessels.	Sp'nish vessels.	Foreign vessels.
589	Other products, like borax, carbonate of ammonia, chloride of antimony, cream of tartar, bicarbonate of potassium, glycerine, nitrate of barytes, the yellow prussiate of iron and potassium, the red, and others of equal value, kilogram....	0 33	0 07	0 09	0 12
590	Like acitate of potassium, the carbonates and oxides of iron, soluble cream, the ethers of all kinds, the sulphite of carbon, the cyanide of potassium for the arts, and others of equal value, kilogram...........................	0 52	0 12	0 15	0 09
591	Chlorate of potassium, 100 kilograms.................	2 10	3 15	4 15	5 20
592	Like quicksilver, the chlorides and oxides of mercury, the chloroform, the creosote, the citrate of iron, iron reduced by hydrogen, and other products of equal value, kilogram..	0 09	0 22	0 28	0 36
593	Like phosphor, 100 kilograms.........................	4 35	6 50	8 70	10 85
594	Like bromo and the bromides, iod and the iodides, the carbonate and oxide of bismuth, the permanganate of potassium, the pure cyanide of potassium, and others of equal value, kilogram	0 54	1 25	1 57	2 01
595	Like quinine and its salts, the morphine salts, the alcaloids and their salts (the neuter principles), the salts of gold, of silver, of platinum, and of other rare and precious metals, and such chemical products, by their scarce use and reduced volume, even if of greater values, should be called to this portion, whatever be their application, kilogram...............	3 47	8 00	10 08	12 87

FIFTH GROUP—*Pharmaceutical products and special medicines.*

596	Pharmaceutical products that do not constitute those known as Patent Specifics or Secret Medicines, like the tinctures, the ointments, compounded oils, the medicinal vinegars, the sugared gum pastes, and those called pectoral, like those of jujube, etc., and the plasters, kilogram...................	0 04	0 10	0 12	0 16
597	The vegetable extracts, like those of opium, ipecacuanha, rhubarb, the ergotine and others of equal value, kilogram.....	1 30	3 00	3 78	4 82
598	Those of arnica, belladonna, stramonium, sarsaparilla, valerian, and others of equal value, kilogram......................	0 21	0 50	0 63	0 80
599	Those of colchicum, colocynth, Peruvian bark, cubebs, rattan, and others of equal value, kilogram...................	0 43	1 00	1 26	1 60
600	Those of braziletto, campeachy, licorice, and others of preparation and application to industry, of equal value, kilogram.......	0 02	0 06	0 07	0 09
601	Distilled waters, like those of orange flower, rose, valerian, and others of equal value, kilogram...........................	0 02	0 06	0 07	0 09
602	Preparations, patented or specific, of known or anonymous authors, in glass vessels, up to liters 0.125 capacity, like "Forget's" and "Delabarre's" syrup, Saville's liquors and pills, including the weight of the immediate package, kilogram.........	0 20	0 46	0 58	0 75
603	In glass vessels of more than liters 1.125 up to 0.250, like the "Guillé" elixir, and "Leras" phosphate, including the weight of the immediate packages, kilogram..............	0 13	0 31	0 39	0 50
604	In vessels of more than liters 0.250 up to 0.500, like "Albert's" bramble, "Dupont's" syrup, not including the weight of the packages, kilogram....	0 06	0 15	0 19	0 25
605	In vessels of more than liters 0.500, like "Laffecteur's" rob, "Bristol's" sarsaparilla, "Swain's" panacea, not including the weight of the packages, kilogram....................	0 03	0 07	0 09	0 12
606	Those contained in wooden, cardboard or heavy paper packages, like Brandreth's "Frank's" pills, "Nafé Regnault's" lozenges and their like, including the weight of the immediate packages, kilogram..	0 13	0 31	0 39	0 50
607	Those contained in tin and pewter packages, like seidletz and soda powders, "Guern's" opiate, "Albespeyer's" caustic and others, including the weight of the immediate package, kilogram........	0 05	0 12	0 15	0 20

Note—The natural products, drugs and chemical products that are generally imported in powders because that should be their

No. of portions	ARTICLES.	TARIFF.			
		SPANISH PRODUCTIONS IN		FOREIGN PRODUCTIONS IN	
		Sp'nish vessels.	Foreign vessels.	Sp'nish vessels.	Foreign vessels.
	natural state, or because it is practice to prepare them so directly or because the pulverization should be part of the whole preparation, or for other causes, as for instance, the tartaric acid, " Rochelle's " salts (tartar of potassium and soda), the minium litharge, white lead (carbonate of lead), zinc white (oxide of zinc), sub-nitrate of bismuth, carbonate of iron, red precipitate (oxide of mercury), rods of the same metal, calomel (proto chloride of mercury), rods of the same metal, arsenious acid, precipitated sulphur, carmines, emery, chromium, vermillion, bronzes, red corals, peroxide of manganese, venitian talc, verdigris and other like, will not undergo any extra charge.				
	Drugs whose pulverization constitute a special industry, will be subject to the 15 and 35 % additional charge on the duties consigned in their respective portions, as follows:				
608	Powders whose alteration does not exceed 25% will pay the 15% extra, such as those of rhubarb root, Florence ties, marshmallow, houndstongue and licorice, mustard and linseed, gum arabic, cinnamon bark, lignumvitæ, emitec tartar, gallnut, pepper of all kinds and other seed, nitrate of potassium sugar of milk, sulphide of antimony, cream of tartar, calcined bones, sal-ammoniac, chlorate of potash and other like products.				
609	Powders whose alteration exceeds 25%, like those of opium, tragacanth gum and gum resins in general, ipecacuanha root, jalap root, turbith root, sarsaparilla root, quill root, castorcums, flowers and leaves in general, sneezewort, paradise grains, nux vomica, Peruvian bark, Spanish fly, colocynth, treacle and other like.				

MIXED FABRICS.

	on fabrics, with mixture of hemp, flax or jute, will pay duty by the section of hemp, flax and jute.				
	Hemp fabrics, flax and jute, with cotton mixture, will pay duty by the section of hemp, flax and jute.				
	Cotton fabrics, with woolen mixture, will pay duty by the section of woolens.				
610	Cotton fabrics, with silk mixture up to one-fifth, will pay duty by their respective portions, with the additional charge of 140%.				
611	The same fabrics, with more than one-fifth part silk mixture up to two-fifths, will pay duty by the same portions of cotton, with the additional charge of 280%.				
	The same fabrics, with more than two-fifths silk mixture, will pay duty by the sections of silk.				
612	Woolen fabrics with cotton mixture, not tariffed in the section of woolens, will pay duty by the sections of pure woolen fabrics, with a reduction of 120%.				
613	Woolen fabrics with silk mixture, not tariffed in the section of woolens, and *vice versa*, will pay 50% as woolen fabrics, and 50% as silk fabrics.				
614	Articles exclusively applicable to the operation whose object is the industrial development of the genius, from the raking of the cane and grinding of the same up to the packing of the fruit and its extraction from the estate, will pay duty (see note No. 30). Estimation, ...	1%	1%	1%	1%

CUSTOMS TARIFF AND PORT REGULATIONS

OF THE

BRITISH WEST INDIA ISLANDS.

N. B.—Each island of the British West Indies has its own customs tariff and regulations, but they do not differ very materially, and the following schedule, which covers about all the principal articles which are usually imported from the United States, will be found to be very near the correct tariff for all the English West India Islands and the Colony of Demerara:

TARIFF.

ARTICLES.	DUTY.
Arrowroot, 100 lbs.	$0 24
Alewives, brl.	10
Beef, half brls., 100 lbs.	1 20
Bread, brown, 100 lbs.	12
Bread, Bordeaux, 100 lbs.	12
Bread, white, 100 lbs.	12
Bricks, fire, M.	72
Bricks, building, M.	72
Butter, Morlaix, 100 lbs.	1 80
Butter, American, 100 lbs.	1 80
Candles, tallow, 100 lbs.	2 00
Candles, stearine, 100 lbs.	2 00
Cattle.	Free
Cement, brl.	30
Cheese, American, 100 lbs.	1 80
Coal, steam, ton.	60
Cocoa, 100 lbs.	50
Coffee, 100 lbs	60
Corn, bag 112 lbs., 100 lbs.	12
Cornmeal, brl.	30
Crackers, packed, 100 lbs.	12
Fish, dry or salted, 112 lbs.	5
Flour, brl.	1 00
Hams, 100 lbs.	1 20
Hay.	Free
Herring, pickled, brl.	10
Herring in boxes, smoked, 112 lbs.	5
Hoops, wood, 1,200 lbs.	1 44
Horses, head.	9 60
Kerosene oil, cases 85°, gal.	5
Lard, 100 lbs.	1 00
Lumber, all kinds, M.	1 20
Mackerel, brl.	10
Malt liquor, wood, hhd.	4 50
Malt liquor, bottled, dozen quarts.	30
Manures.	Free
Matches, box, gross.	24
Mules, Kentucky, head.	7 20
Mules, South America, head.	4 80
Oats, bag 160 lbs., 100 lbs.	15
Oilmeal, 750 lbs., 100 lbs.	10
Onions.	Free
Peas, 100 lbs.	12
Pollard, 100 lbs.	15
Potatoes.	Free

	Duty.
Pork, all kinds, 100 lbs.	1 20
*Powder, blasting. (See below.)	
Rice, 100 lbs.	12
Salmon, brl.	12
Salt.	Free
Sheep.	Free
Shingles, M.	36
Shooks, sugar hhd., 1,200 lbs.	1 44
Soap, 100 lbs.	30
Staves, red oak, 1,200 lbs.	1 44
Sugar, refined, 100 lbs.	2 40
Tobacco, manufactured, 100 lbs.	36
Tobacco, leaf, 100 lbs.	24

*There is no duty now on gunpowder of any description; but there is a storage fee, payable in advance, of 6 cents per pound for the first year, and 4 cents per pound for every subsequent year, during which there is any remaining in the Government powder bulk.

IN ADDITION THE SUBJOINED OTHER ARTICLES PAY THE FOLLOWING SPECIFIC DUTIES—VIZ:

Asses, per head	$1 20
Bran, 100 lbs.	15
Cider and Perry, hhd.	4 50
Cider and Perry, in quart bottles, dozen.	30
Cigars, cheroots and cigarettes, lb.	1 20
Gin and rum, gal.	1 20
Horses, under 13½ hands, per head	2 40
Snuff, lb.	36
Spirits and cordials, except gin and rum, gal.	1 80
Tallow, 100 lbs.	48
Tea, lb.	6
Tobacco, in outer packages, manufactured leaf, lb.	48
Tobacco of less than 80 lbs net, manufactured leaf, lb.	36
Wine, sparkling, gal.	60
Wine, other kinds, gal.	22½

Note.—The duty on spirits is per proof gallon, wine measure, by Sykes' hydrometer, an additional duty being paid in proportion for every degree of strength above proof.

Kerosene oil is prohibited to be imported (under penalty of forfeiture) under a lesser test than 85° Abel.

ON ALL OTHER PRINCIPAL ARTICLES NOT MENTIONED ABOVE OR EXEMPTED IN THE FOLLOWING TABLE, AN AD-VALOREM DUTY OF 8 PER CENT. IS PAYABLE.

Asphalt; Bones and Horns; Printed Books, Forms and Papers; Bottles of Glass or Stoneware; Cassaripe; Cattle; Cocoanuts, Cotton Wool; Fresh Fruit and Vegetables; Fresh Meats and Fish; Fuel, Wood and Charcoal; Green Ginger; Hay and Straw; Ice; Lemon and Lime Juice; Lime, Building and Temper; Live and Dead Stock, not enumerated in Tariff of Duties; Logwood; Manure; Molasses; Oars and Sweeps; Salt; Soda and Mineral Waters; Spars; Sugar, raw or Muscovado, and Crystallized Vacuum Pan; Tar, Pitch and Resin.

Port Regulations and Miscellaneous Charges, Barbadoes.

LANDING AND SHIPPING CHARGES AND PORT CHARGES.

TONNAGE DUES—On sailing vessels and steamers not bringing a regular mail.
    24 cents registered ton if a full cargo is discharged.
    24 cents registered ton if a full cargo is loaded.
    48 cents registered ton if a full cargo is discharged and loaded here.
If the quantity of cargo discharged or loaded does not exceed one-fourth or one-half of vessel's capacity, the above dues are then only paid in such proportions; but if it exceed a fourth the dues are paid on a half, and if it exceed a half, on the whole registered tonnage. These dues are paid also on the deck loads of vessels, on the space occupied, according to measurement.

Steamers bringing *a regular mail* pay only 24 cents a ton, on every ton of cargo discharged or laden here.

CUSTOMS AND HARBOR MASTER'S FEES.

Customs bond	$3 00
Anchorage	2 00
Boarding officer	1 00
Harbor Master's clearance	3 00

HARBOR POLICE FEES.

Vessels not over 100 tons	4 00
Vessels over 100 and not over 200 tons	4 50
Vessels over 200 and not over 300 tons	5 00
Vessels over 300 tons	6 00

CAREENAGE DUES.

Groundage, per ton per day	0 01
Unloading and loading, per ton per day	0 02
Heaving down and careening, per ton per day	0 03

N. B.—Vessels only calling for orders, or trying the market, incur no fees beyond three dollars ($3).

COOPERAGE — On general cargoes of merchandise or breadstuffs, as per agreement; on molasses, 28 cents per puncheon.

LABOR — 80 to 100 cents per day. For hauling up lumber — White pine, etc., 10 cents, and pitch pine 20 cents per M. Weighing coal, 10 cents per ton.

PILOTAGE — None. The masters of vessels may, however, obtain advice from the crews of *licensed fare boats*, at a moderate cost.

BALLAST — Stone per ton, $1.20. Sand per ton, 80 cents.

WATER — Per 100 gallons, 72 cents.

WHARFAGE — None.

LIGHTERAGE.

On staves, M. pieces	$0 60
On shingles, loose, M	20
On shingles, in small bundles, M	5
On shingles, in 10 inch bundles, M	8
On shingles, in 12 inch bundles, M	15
On molasses, puncheon	16
On molasses, stowage packages, puncheon	10
On molasses, stowage packages, hhd	5
On molasses, stowage packages, brl	2½
On rum, puncheon	20
On sugar, hogshead	25
On sugar, tierce	18
On sugar, barrel	4
On breadstuffs, barrel	2½
On provisions, barrel	3½
On coals, ton	35
On merchandise, load of 15 tons	4 00

STEVEDORE'S CHARGES.

On sugar, hogshead	20
On sugar, tierce	12
On sugar, barrel	6
On molasses, puncheon	10
On molasses, hogshead	6
On molasses, barrel	4

Note — Vessels loading, in accordance with the custom of the port bear the expense of lighterage and stevedore's charges on both sugar and molasses, and in addition, hose-hire (three cents per puncheon) and half cooperage on molasses.

WHARFINGER'S CHARGES.

For receiving white pine, etc., M	$0 10
For receiving pitch pine, M	20
For receiving shingles in bundles, M	2½
For receiving shingles, loose, M	5
For receiving staves, M	12
For receiving coal, ton	10

BILLS OF HEALTH.

Harbor master	96
French consul	2 32
United States' consul	2 50
Netherland consul	1 00
Spanish consul { If under 200 tons	2 36
{ If over 200 tons	3 44
Venezuelan consul	2 50
Haytian consul	5 00

ADVICE TO MASTERS.

Note — The masters of vessels arriving for the purpose of "Trying the Market" or awaiting advices, would do well to bear in mind that the mid part of Carlisle Bay, in a northerly and southerly direction, between "Needham's Point Buoy" and the "Pelican Reef" — the latter distinguished by a large wooden Lazaretto — is of great depth, varying from 20 to 30 fathoms; by running well past this and to leeward of the shipping, in the lower part of the bay, good bottom will be found at 6 to 8 fathoms.

TONNAGE.

We beg to particularly remind ship-masters and owners that vessels calling here for orders or seeking freight, incur no expense beyond three dollars, or 12/6, for boarding officer and harbor police fees.

Miscellaneous Regulations and Charges — Trinidad and Demerara.

EXPORT TAX.

Upon sugar, hogshead	$1 08
Upon sugar, tierce	72
Upon sugar, barrel or bag	11
Upon molasses, puncheon	36
Upon molasses, tierce	18
Upon molasses, packages less than a tierce	11
Upon rum, puncheon	72
Upon cocoa, bag	30
Upon coffee, bag	30
Upon asphalt, crude, ton	48
Upon asphalt, refined epureé, ton	96

PORT CHARGES.

Lighterage loading sugar, 50 to 70 cents, hogshead.
Lighterage loading molasses, 30 to 40 cents, puncheon.
Stowage sugar, 22 cents, hogshead.
Stowage molasses, 10 cents, puncheon.
Discharging general cargo, 65 cents ship, registered ton.
Discharging loose coals, 60 cents ton, landed.
Discharging rice, 3 to 4 cents, bag.
Discharging flour and other breadstuffs, 3 cents barrel.
Ballast sand, 40 to 50 cents ton.
Ballast stone, $1 to $1.20 ton.
Water, puncheon, 24 cents at wharf, and $1 alongside.
Labor on board, $1.20 per diem.

TRADE ALLOWANCES, ETC.

Sales, as a rule, are made at three months.
Bank rate of discount, 6% per annum.
On white and pine spruce, 5% for splits.
No allowance on pitch pine.
No allowance on American white pine.
Staves, hoops and slates are sold per 1,000 pieces.
A charge of 36 cents per M. is made for wharfage on all lumber landed at San Fernando.

HARBOR DUES.

(Island currency, British silver.)

Harbor Master's visit fee	$1 00
Anchorage fee	2 00
The above payable by all vessels, whether coming to an entry or not.	
On entering, the following are charged in addition:	
Tonnage dues (inward and outward each way), ton	24
Colonial Secretary's fee, vessel	3 00
Harbor Master's fee	2 00

HARBOR POLICE DUES.

Vessels under 100 tons	2 00
Vessels over 100 tons, but not over 200 tons	2 50
Vessels over 200 tons, but not over 300 tons	3 00
Vessels over 300 tons	4 00

Vessels under 75 tons pay only twice per annum.
Vessels discharging or embarking only quarter or half cargo, pay tonnage dues accordingly.

LIGHTERAGE.

General cargoes, such as rice, oats, bricks, dry goods, fifteen ton boat load	4 00
Coals, ton	35
Salted meat, pickled fish, lard, candles, butter, cement, and such like articles, barrel	03
Flour, meal, corn bread, crackers, and such like articles, barrel	02½
Kerosene oil, wines, and other liquids, barrel	05
Oil meal, per puncheon—550 lbs at 10 cts, 750 lbs at 15 cts	
Shooks, bdle	02
Horses and mules, from two to twelve head	4 00
Cattle, from four to sixteen head	4 00
Fish, per quintal, box or drum	1½
Staves, per 1000 pieces	60
Shingles—small 15 cts, 10 in. 8 cts, 12 in. 15 cts, Wallaba 10 cts, loose 20 cts per M	
Firewood, per cord	50
Sugar, hogshead 25 cts, tierce 18 cts, barrel 4 cts	
Tobacco, per hogshead	30
Molasses, per puncheon	16
Dirt ballast, per ton	80
Stone ballast, per ton	1 20

WATER.

72 cents per 100 gallons, put alongside.

BILL OF HEALTH.

If required	60

CAREENAGE DUES.

Vessels under 60 tons, or vessels in distress, allowed only on enter, each day, ton	01
Whilst loading or unloading, each day, ton	02
Using careening pits, each day, ton	03

GOVERNMENT BONDING CHARGES, INCLUDING PORTERAGE.

Flour, meal, crackers, bread, etc., brl	05
Rice, 100 lbs	02½
Salted meat, pickled fish, brl	08
Butter, cheese, cocoa, coffee, 100 lbs	03
Malt liquors, hhd. of 60 galls	36
Malt liquors, bottled, dozen	02½
Spirits, wine, 60 galls	36
Spirits, wine, bottled, dozen	02½
Sugar, Muscovado, 100 lbs	04
Sugar, other kinds	02½
Tobacco, 100 lbs	08
Tobacco, manufactured, 100 lbs	05
Corn, peas and other grain, bushel	01½
Cement, brl	10
Candles, 100 lbs	04
Lard, 100 lbs	03½
Soap, 100 lbs	02½
Other goods, brl	05

GOODS ABSOLUTELY PROHIBITED TO BE IMPORTED.

RUM — Unless in casks or other vessels of no less capacity than eighty gallons, or in demijeans of no less capacity than two gallons each, or in cases containing each twelve glass or stone bottles, such glass or stone bottles containing altogether not less than one gallon and a half.

COCOA — Except cocoa the produce of and imported from Venezuela.

*SPIRITS — Not being perfumed or medicinal spirits, unless in ships of 30 tons burden at least, and in casks or other vessels capable of containing liquids, each of such cask or other vessel being of the size or contents of 20 gallons at the least, and duly reported, or in cases of not less than 12 glass or stone bottles capable of containing together not less than one gallon and a half in the whole, or in demijeans capable of containing each not less than two gallons and being really part of the cargo of the importing ship and duly reported.

TOBACCO — Except in packages containing not less than 50 pounds of net weight and in ships of not less than 10 tons burden.

CIGARS, CIGARILLOS OR CIGARETTES — Except in packages each containing not less than 20 pounds of net weight and in ships of not less than ten tons burden.

GUNJA, BANG, CANNIBAS INDICA, or any preparation or mixture thereof, except under the license of the Governor.

OPIUM — Unless in ships of at least one hundred tons burden and unless in packages each containing not less than 20 pounds net weight and forming part of the cargo of the importing ship and duly reported.

INFECTED CATTLE, SHEEP or other animals.

* For all wines in wood containing less than the following rates of proof spirit as verified by Sykes' hydrometer, viz :

22 degrees, the gallon... 0s. 8d
32 degrees, the gallon... 1s. 0d
42 degrees, the gallon... 2s. 6d

And for every degree of strength beyond the highest above specified, an additional duty of three pence per gallon.

Customs Tariff of French West India Islands of Martinique and Guadaloupe on Principal Articles Imported from the United States.

ARTICLES.	IMPORT DUTY.
	Dollars.
Beans, white, 100 kilos...	2 70
Beef, family, 100 kilos...	3 46
Beef, mess, 100 kilos..	3 46
Bread, Bordeaux, brl...	1 57
Beer, hectoliter...	4 55
Butter, French, firkin...	1 81
Butter, American, firkin...	1 81
Claret, Vin-de-Cote, hectoliter..	3 20
Corn, yellow, 100 kilos..	1 30
Cornmeal, 100 kilos..	3 40
Coals, loose, 100 kilos..	0 30
Flour, American extra, brl...	5 70
Flour, French kiln-dried, brl..	5 55
Fish, cod, large, 100 kilos..	4 20
Fish, cod, small, 100 kilos..	4 20
Haddock, 100 kilos...	4 20
Hams, American, 100 kilos..	3 81
Horses, American, S. and D., head..	41 00
Hoops, wood, 1,000 strands...	1 82
Herrings, split, 100 kilos...	2 95
Herrings, smoked, 100 kilos..	2 95
Lard, American, 100 kilos..	4 50
Leaf tobacco, 100 kilos..	50 20
Lumber, W. P., M...	7 05
Lumber, P. P., M...	10 29
Lumber, spruce, M..	7 05
Mules, American, head..	15 50
Mackerel, 100 kilos..	2 95
Oats, 100 kilos..	1 86
Oil, olive, basket...	64
Oil, kerosene, case..	3 90
Oil, cotton, 100 kilos...	45 25
Onions, 100 kilos..	1 30
Pork, mess, 100 kilos..	3 46

CUSTOMS TARIFF OF THE FRENCH INDIA ISLANDS. 491

ARTICLES.	IMPORT DUTY.
	Dollars.
Peas, B. E., 100 kilos	2 70
Peas, green, 100 kilos	2 70
Potatoes, 100 kilos	75
Rice, yellow, E. I., 100 kilos	1 30
Rice, white, table, 100 kilos	1 30
Shingles, cypress, M	1 57
Shingles, cedar, W. P., M	0 34
Shingles, Wallaba, M	1 14
Staves, W. C., culls, M	7 35
Shooks, second-hand, bundle	0 30
Vermouth, hectoliter	16 25

GENERAL INFORMATION.

INTERPRETER'S FEES.

Payable by all foreign vessels:

	Francs per vessel.
20 tons and under	10 "
21 to 40 tons	15 "
41 " 60 "	20 "
61 " 80 "	25 "
81 " 100 "	30 "
101 " 150 "	35 "
151 " 200 "	40 "
201 " 300 "	50 "

And 10 francs per 100 tons up to 700.

N. B.—Vessels trying the market may do so during three days, on payment of 12.35 francs in full.

PORT CHARGES.

	Francs per ton.
Water dues	0.15 "
Health "	6.00 "

	Francs per vessel.
Buoy dues	30.30 "
Light "	22.00 "
Permit and clearance	6.05 "
Pilotage, 30 tons and under	13.20 "
" 31 to 60 tons	19.80 "
" 61 " 100 "	47.30 "
" 101 " 150 "	71.50 "
" 151 " 200 "	90.20 "
" 201 " 250 "	110.00 "
" 251 " 300 "	129.80 "
" 301 " 350 "	148.50 "
" 351 tons and above	168.30 "

TRADE USAGE.

Fish is sold at three, four and five months. Provisions at four and five months. Lumber at four and five months; 5 per cent. allowed for splits; no allowance on pitch pine.

Exchange bank bills on Paris, 90 d., 3 per cent.; 60 d. s., 3.50 per cent.; 30 d. s., 4 per cent.

Lighterage, always payable by vessel, except under special agreement. Unloading, per lighter of 150 barrels, 25.00 francs. Loading sugar, per hogshead, 1.20 francs; per tierce, 90 centimes; per barrel, 35 centimes.

Current equivalents—$1, 5.25 francs; 50 kilos, 1 cwt.; 3.75 litres, 1 gallon.

www.ingramcontent.com/pod-product-compliance
Lightning Source LLC
Chambersburg PA
CBHW020831020526
44114CB00040B/534

9783447296342